STREISAND

STREISAND

The Intimate Biography

James Spada

LITTLE, BROWN AND COMPANY

A *Little, Brown* Book

First published in the United States in 1995 by Crown Publishers, Inc.,
a member of the Crown Publishing Group
First published in Great Britain in 1995 by Little, Brown and Company

Photo credits for text pages:
Title page: Osamu Honda/AP.
Parts 1 and 3: Richard Giammanco collection.
Parts 2 and 5: Chris Nickens collection.
Part 4: author's collection; Part 6: Bob Scott.
Epilogue: Arthur Pollock/*Boston Herald*.

Barbra Streisand's speech to Women in Film
on June 27, 1992 © 1992 Barbra Streisand

Barbra Streisand's speech at the APLA Commitment to Life Awards
on November 18, 1992 © 1992 Barbra Streisand

Barbra Streisand's speech to the John F. Kennedy School of Government at
Harvard University on February 3, 1995 © 1995 Barbra Streisand

A CIP catalogue record for this book is available from the British Library.

ISBN 0 316 87487 6

Designed by Lauren Dong

Typeset by Palimpsest Book Production Limited,
Polmont, Stirlingshire
Printed and bound in Great Britain by
Clays Ltd, St Ives plc.

Little, Brown and Company (UK)
Brettenham House
Lancaster Place
London WC2E 7EN

To

Laura Van Wormer

and

Glen Sookiazian

. . . very special friends

CONTENTS

PART 1

Mieskeit

'What a mieskeit!'

—*Barbra Streisand,*

reacting to a picture of herself at thirteen

MR AND MRS EMANUEL STREISAND
take much pleasure in announcing
the rather expected and hoped-for arrival of
BARBARA JOAN
(a cute little trick even if they must say so, weighing 7 lbs. 5 ozs. net)
at
5:04 A.M., Friday, April 24, 1942
After 10 days at her original residence,
The Jewish Hospital of Brooklyn,
she moved to 457 Schenectady Ave., Brooklyn, N.Y., where she is
living with her proud parents and her especially proud brother,
Sheldon Jay

Outside, the world was on the cusp of catastrophe. Five months earlier the United States had gone to war against Germany, Italy, and Japan, and American boys were being carried off to battle by the tens of thousands. Austria, from which Emanuel Streisand's father had emigrated in 1898, had been overrun by Hitler's Nazis in 1938, and its Jews, some of them Streisand family members who had stayed behind, were being systematically slaughtered in concentration camps. Russia, the homeland of Mrs Streisand's parents, had been under siege by the Nazis for months.

But inside their well-kept apartment on a quiet residential street in the East Flatbush section of Brooklyn, Manny and Diana Streisand lived a separate peace, and most was right with their insular world. Thirty-four when his daughter was born, Manny hadn't been called up for service because of his age, his fatherhood, and the fact that he had carved out an extraordinary career as a teacher of troubled young men. The firstborn son of a man who still barely spoke English, in 1941 he had been included in the Science Press directory *Leaders in Education*. He made a decent living as a teacher of truants and delinquents at the Brooklyn High School for Specialty Trades, and supplemented his $4,500 annual salary by tutoring at a yeshiva

in the late afternoon during the school year and at educational camps every
summer.

Manny Streisand worked hard – too hard, his wife often thought – but in
Thoreau's words, he loved turning the 'free meandering brook' of an errant
teenager's life into a 'straight cut ditch' of education, discipline, and prospects
for a future. And he was determined to give his wife, his seven-year-old
son, and his new baby girl the best possible life, one free from the terrible
hardships his own parents, Isaak and Anna Streisand, had endured over the
past half century.

ISAAK STREISAND STOOD on the train station platform at Lvov, surrounded
by his sisters and parents, covered in layers of sheepskin against the frigid
Baltic air. It was the first day of January 1898, and the strapping seventeen-
year-old was on the verge of a new life. He was leaving the harsh world of the
Jewish *shtetl* in the village of Brzezany in eastern Galicia, a principality under
the control of Austria-Hungary and bordered by Poland in the north-west,
Russia in the east, and Austria-Hungary in the south. He was going to
America, a land of seemingly endless opportunity: in the prior twenty years in
the United States a former newsboy from Ohio named Thomas Alva Edison
had become rich and famous by inventing, among many other things, the
light bulb, the phonograph, and the motion picture camera and projector.

The *konduktor* blew the train's shrill whistle to signal the *schnellzug*'s
departure, and a series of thick noises rumbled from the engine as it struggled
to start. Isaak picked up his three bulky bundles and said his final farewells.
His mother's stoicism dissolved into tears as she hugged her only son, whom
she would never see again. Mali Feldman Streisand and her husband, Kesriel,
had been born in Brzezany, and they would stay there. It was for the young
to seek a better world.

Conditions in Galicia demanded that Isaak leave. One of the most destitute
spots in eastern Europe, the country barely provided sustenance for its
people, most of them farmers with only primitive skills and no outlet outside
the village in which to sell what they produced. Villages consisted of two rows
of thatched huts along either side of a muddy dirt path; next to each hut lay
a great heap of manure, which every summer Isaak and his sisters kneaded
with earth to form bricks that were then baked hard in the sun and used the
following winter as fuel against the often thirty-below-zero cold.

The Streisands had two rooms, the 'hot room' and the 'cold room.' In
the first the entire family, which included Kesriel's parents, ate, slept, and
worked in a twelve-by-sixteen-foot space. The cramped quarters contained
just two pieces of furniture, a table and a narrow wooden bench, and the

pripitshik, a huge brick stove-fireplace in the middle of the room from which a seven-foot-long wooden shelf extended. The parents and grandparents slept on this shelf, the warmest spot in the hut, while the children slept on the wooden bench, which extended along the side and back walls. The manure that fueled the fire turned the indoor air caustic.

For Galicia's 10 percent Jewish minority, persecution and hopelessness joined poverty. Two years before Isaak Streisand left Brzezany, a series of nighttime rape-and-plunder raids against the people of the *shtetlach* by their Slavic neighbors had left the Jews terrorized, their spirit dashed. The plight of the Galician Jew became a worldwide cause célèbre, but not much help ever came, and thousands of Galicians were among the one-third of eastern Europe's Jewish population that emigrated to America between 1880 and 1930, a group that included over a dozen Streisands from Brzezany and its neighboring villages. Now Isaak was among them.

Kesriel Streisand helped his son onto the train, then stood and watched as the long black clattering hulk chugged slowly out of the depot. The rail journey lasted nearly a week as the *schnellzug* made its way northwest at barely fifteen miles an hour through Poland and Germany to the port city of Bremen. There, on Saturday, January 8, Isaak hauled his bags onto the S.S. *H.H. Meier*, a mid-sized ship of the North German Lloyd Company, along with three hundred and sixty other mostly Jewish émigrés who were pressed together into cramped steerage quarters.

The ship wended its way up the Weser River to the North Sea, then veered westward into the Atlantic for an arduous two-week crossing. Illness caused by damp and cold, poor sanitation, and spoiled food claimed several lives; the bodies were tossed overboard. By the time the ship approached Ellis Island, many of the huddled masses on board were weak and dispirited. But the sight of the Statue of Liberty renewed the hope that had propelled them westward.

Isaak was processed through Ellis Island on Friday, January 21. A doctor checked his health, and a German-speaking translator recorded his responses to the standard questions. Then, along with hundreds of others, he shuffled aboard one of the boats that ferried immigrants from Ellis Island to Manhattan around the clock. At a dock on the Lower East Side, he stepped off the gangplank to face an uncertain future.

OVER THE NEXT nine years, Isaak was assimilated into the teeming immigrant neighborhoods of Manhattan's Lower East Side. He worked as a common laborer, doing odd jobs for his German-speaking neighbors. He had little need to learn English, and he never spoke it more than haltingly. By 1905 his three sisters had come through Ellis Island as well.

Late in 1906 Rachel Streisand introduced her twenty-seven-year-old brother to a pretty, vivacious blue-eyed fifteen-year-old girl named Annie Kesten, who had come to America the year before from Galicia with her father, Max, her mother, the former Dreijzie (Daisy) Cohen, and her sister, Berthe. On May 1, 1907, Isaak and Annie were married in Manhattan by magistrate Elias Friedman.

The newlyweds settled into a small tenement apartment at 248 East Seventh Street at a rent of $15 a month. Almost exactly nine months later, on February 5, 1908, their first child, Emanuel, was born. At more or less regular two-year intervals afterward, Annie gave birth to Maurice (nicknamed Murray), Herman (Hy), and Philip. In 1916 a daughter, Daisy, named after Annie's mother, was born, but she died in infancy. In 1918 the Streisands' last child, Molly, was born.

Slowly, Isaak Streisand made his way up in the world. Molly Streisand, now Mrs Nat Parker and Isaak's only surviving child, recalled that her father 'used to carry a sewing machine around on his back' as he went from house to house doing odd tailoring jobs. 'He made I guess eleven dollars a week. He didn't have much, but we ate pretty good.'

Annie's cooking skills helped. She kept a kosher home, and Molly recalled that 'my mother was a marvelous cook, a great baker. She would make huge cheesecakes, and sponge cakes with a dozen eggs. She'd stay up all night when it came a holiday and she'd make five cakes and gefilte fish and pickled herring and cherries with plums and peaches, and matzo balls. Her matzo balls were perfect, they weren't hard – like some of them that you can bounce off the wall!'

The Streisand brood remained in the cramped Seventh Street apartment until 1919, when Annie fell and injured herself on the building's rickety and debris-strewn inside stairs. She sued the landlord, Henry R. Stern, for the $166 medical bill. On December 8 a judge ruled that Stern should pay the medical bill, but granted his request that the Streisands be ordered to vacate the premises by the end of the month.

That was fine with Isaac (who now spelled his name with a *c*) because he had decided to go into a new business. Using a nest egg he had struggled for years to save, he had found a store in Brooklyn that rented more reasonably than most in Manhattan. And so, on January 1, 1920, Isaac and Annie Streisand and their five children moved to Brooklyn, where Isaac set himself up as a fishmonger.

THEIR NEW HOME was an apartment building at 196–198 Stockton Street in the borough's Williamsburg section, a scant four blocks from the elevated train that ran along Broadway and over the Williamsburg Bridge into Manhattan. Stockton Street provided a more pleasant, leafier residential area than the Streisands had known in Manhattan, but within the building itself there seethed a similar microcosm of New York immigrant life. The children shared one of the two bedrooms, two boys to a bunk bed and Molly in a third. They shared clothes, toys, household duties.

Emanuel, as the oldest child and a boy, naturally would have been looked up to by his siblings, but by the age of twelve he had displayed special leadership qualities. He was good-looking, with intense, close-set hazel eyes and wavy brown hair, and his intelligence had set him apart in school, where he particularly excelled at English and history and was allowed to skip two grades. Good-natured and generous with his time, he read to Hy and Phil every day and helped them with their homework. He showed a talent for speaking, so much so that at Phil's bar mitzvah in 1927 he read the passages from the Torah and the Haftarah on his brother's behalf. 'Manny wasn't bashful,' Molly recalled. 'He was a good talker.'

He displayed a talent for athletics, too, and played handball and tennis during an era, his daughter would later proudly point out, 'when Jewish boys didn't do things like that.' Manny also baby-sat for his brothers and sisters most days after school while his mother and father worked in the fish store at 175 Sumner Avenue, about nine blocks from the apartment. 'My father would get up before three in the morning three times a week and take the train into Manhattan to the Fulton Fish Market,' Molly recalled. 'He would pick out only the best and the freshest fish. Then it would be delivered in these big heavy boxes, and my father had to lift them. He had to have three hernia operations.'

Manny helped out in the store on Thursdays, the busy day before the start of the Jewish Sabbath at sundown on Friday, by cleaning and chopping fish. As the younger boys grew older, they pitched in, too. Molly helped her mother scrub the floors and walls of the shop after closing. 'The store was spotless,' she said. 'My parents never went out. They never did anything but work.'

In September 1920 Manny, not yet thirteen, entered Boys High School on Marcy Avenue, fifteen blocks south of the apartment. During his four years at the school, he distinguished himself through his love of reading, his facility with English, and his talent for tutoring less accomplished students. Toward the end of his high school career he decided he wanted to be a teacher. In the fall of 1924, at sixteen and a half, he entered the College of the City of New York on a partial scholarship with a double major in English and education, traveling back and forth by subway to the school on 139th Street in Manhattan. He was the first Streisand to attend college, and his father fairly burst with pride. 'He's so smart he could be president!' Isaac boasted.

Molly believes that her brother got most of his intelligence from their mother. 'She was a very smart lady, smarter, really, than my father. She knew English fluently, and after her kids left the house she went back to school, not for any reason other than an interest in learning. She was interested in everything; she was ambitious.'

To help pay for the educational expenses not covered by his scholarship, Manny worked part time at the American Telephone and Telegraph Company. One summer he drove a Good Humor ice-cream truck in New Jersey; during another he worked as a lifeguard, and he spent a third hitchhiking through Canada and the northern United States, taking odd jobs for a few days at a time. 'He was an *adventurer*,' Barbra has boasted, and Molly agreed. 'He'd try anything, Manny. He wasn't afraid of anything.'

In June 1928 Manny received his bachelor of science degree in education and a Phi Beta Kappa key. That fall he was hired as an elementary school English teacher in Manhattan, and the following year he taught at a junior high school. At night he took courses toward his master's degree at CCNY, and over the next two summers he took additional courses at Cornell, Hunter, and Columbia. He received his master's degree in 1930, and that fall got a job at a vocational high school. He was paid very little as a novice teacher, and his education had been expensive, so he continued to live in his father's home, which was now an apartment above the fish store on Sumner Avenue.

Manny had every intention of pursuing his education until he earned his Ph.D., and he had begun work toward that goal. But he never received a doctorate because in 1928 his attentions were diverted by a petite, pretty blue-eyed nineteen-year-old named Diana Rosen. 'Manny had a lot of girlfriends,' Molly recalled. 'He started dating very young, and oh, were they crazy about him. They were very nice girls. But I guess there was something special about Dinah.'

SHE WAS BORN Ida Rosen on December 10, 1908, the third child of Louis Rosen, a thirty-year-old Russian immigrant, and his wife, the former Ida Friedland, also thirty and from Russia. Later she would adopt the name Diana, which evolved into the nickname Dinah. She and her three siblings lived in the family apartment at 1554 Pitkin Avenue in the East New York section of Brooklyn.

Louis Rosen worked as a tailor in a Manhattan shop and officiated part time as a cantor in his synagogue. 'My father was a very religious man,' Diana recalled. 'Very spiritual, a strong man. He would put on the prayer shawl and sing religious songs around the house. I believe the musicality in the family came from my father. I inherited it from him, and Barbra inherited it from me.

'I grew up the way Barbra grew up, hearing singing around me. My greatest pleasure in those days was listening to singers on our Victrola. I've always loved to sing, but my parents wouldn't have dreamed of letting me do it professionally. I remember when I was seventeen, I registered with my best girlfriend to sing in the Metropolitan Opera Chorus. But we attended rehearsal only once. I brought us home too late and worried our parents. So both of us girls gave it up and put it out of our minds.' Still, at parties Diana and her friend could always be found around a piano, singing with the other boys and girls. 'I was far too shy to sing alone before a crowd, but in a group I loved it.'

Although she was a good student, Diana gave no thought to higher education. Her goal – the same as that of most young women of her generation – was to meet a nice boy with a solid career ahead of him, get married, and give her parents grandchildren. In Emanuel Streisand – tall, dark, handsome, just turned twenty – she found him. 'It was love at first sight, oh, boy!' Diana recalled years later of her introduction to Manny at the home of one of her girlfriends early in 1928. They dated for a year, during which he dazzled her with love poems and courtly attentions and charmed her with his sense of fun. He was serious and ambitious, but he also had a silly side. 'My brother liked to put on skits at parties,' Molly recounted. 'He had a great sense of humor.'

A year after they met, a misunderstanding escalated into a nearly year-long separation. Neither could get past foolish pride long enough to telephone the other. 'If he likes me enough,' Diana proclaimed, 'he'll call me.' When he finally did, late in 1929, she was at a Saturday movie matinee and missed the call. Having decided to continue to play hard to get, she didn't call him back. But a few days later her fate was sealed when she ran into Manny at the El station. He was on his way to school. 'I was dumbfounded,' she said. 'If that wasn't an act of God, nothing else was.' Embarrassed, Manny apologized for not having called for so long, and explained that he had been busy with his master's degree studies. Amused by his discomfort, Diana forgave him, and their romance was rekindled.

ON A FINE spring day in 1930, Diana and Emanuel stood under the *chuppah*, the traditional satin Jewish wedding canopy, which was held aloft by his brothers Murray and Hy. In the crowded Sumner Avenue living room, as dozens of family members and friends watched and beamed,

Manny slipped a simple ring on Diana's finger and they became husband and wife.

Unable to afford a real honeymoon, the Streisands drove into Manhattan in his rickety tin lizzie for a show and a night at a nice hotel. On the way back into Brooklyn, a driver in front of them braked sharply and Manny was unable to stop in time. The cars collided. Manny's forehead slammed against the windshield, cracking the glass.

When Molly next saw her brother, she exclaimed, 'What happened to you?' Manny's head was bandaged, his eyes black-and-blue. 'He didn't say much about it, though. Dinah was hurt, too. Something happened to her leg.'

Within a few days Manny began to suffer dizzy spells and searing headaches. 'He took a lot of aspirins,' Molly recalled. 'But he was the type who never complained. I don't think my mother ever even knew about the accident.' Over time the headaches lessened, and although they never stopped, they were infrequent enough for a stoic sort of man like Manny to ignore.

Over the next thirteen years, Emanuel Streisand's life seemed blessed. He and Diana were happy in their marriage; she was a *folks mensch*, an uncomplicated, unpretentious woman who delighted in being Mrs Emanuel Streisand, keeping her home spotless and her husband well fed with good kosher food. The only thing missing was a baby, but Manny told his wife that the Great Depression, which had fallen across America after the stock market crash of 1929, made everything too uncertain for them to take on the financial burden of a baby. He promised her he would make as much money as possible so that within a few years they would be able to add to their family.

For the first two years of the marriage, Manny and Diana lived with his family over the fish store, but in 1932 he got an attractive offer to help organize the education department of the Elmira Reformatory, a penal institution for youthful offenders in western New York State. The pay was better than anything he'd been offered before, so he and Diana moved to Elmira and set up a household of their own.

The following year Manny was promoted to assistant superintendent, and in the summer of 1934 he felt secure enough to add a child to the family. Diana became pregnant in August, and on the following Mother's Day, May 12, 1935, Sheldon Jay Streisand was born in Elmira. Now Emanuel Streisand had a wife, a baby, and a teaching career. He seemed on top of the world, even though he couldn't seem to shake those headaches . . .

A few months after Sheldon's birth, a frantic Diana called Manny's mother in Brooklyn. Manny had had a seizure – he had fallen to the floor, his body had twitched and convulsed uncontrollably, he had lost consciousness. 'Please come, Anna, please come,' Diana pleaded. When Anna arrived, she stood with her daughter-in-law next to Manny's hospital bed as his doctor explained that he had had an epileptic fit brought on by the head injury five years earlier. Nothing could be done, the doctor said, and another attack might happen at any time. The seizures could be dangerous, he went on, and he outlined to both women the procedures for dealing with another one should it occur.

Now a frightening, unpredictable illness threatened the otherwise happy, strong, athletic Manny Streisand. And in that less enlightened era, his affliction was considered shameful, something to be hidden. Only his immediate family knew about it.

When Manny recovered, Diana pleaded with him to return to Brooklyn, where they could be closer to both their families in case he 'got sick' again. He agreed when he was able to secure a good-paying job – $2,500 a year – teaching social studies to truants and delinquents at the Brooklyn High School for Specialty Trades on the Flatbush Avenue extension at Concord Street, in the shadow of the Brooklyn Bridge. In July 1935 he moved his family to a roomy, high-ceilinged one-bedroom apartment in an attractive six-story building with a French château facade at 163 Ocean Avenue in Flatbush, directly across the street from Prospect Park.

Peter Greenleaf worked with Manny Streisand at the High School for Specialty Trades from the beginning of his tenure there, and he recalled his colleague as 'very nice and well liked' by all. 'We had some of the worst students in the country at that time. The principal used to send the teachers out into the street to pick up any boy who looked like he was under sixteen and drag him into the school. We prepared the boys for vocational careers. Manny and I taught academic subjects, which most of the students weren't very adept at. But Manny actually was able to teach the boys something.'

By 1942 Manny had written an instruction manual for teachers entitled *Individual Instruction in English* and had distinguished himself enough to be listed in *Leaders in Education*. His salary now was $4,500 a year, another colleague, Leonard Boyer, estimated, and he and Diana felt financially confident enough to have another baby. At the end of August, Diana found out she was nearly a month pregnant. She and Manny were thrilled, and both hoped for a girl.

In preparation for the baby's arrival, the Streisands moved ten blocks directly east to a two-bedroom apartment in a six-story brick building at 457 Schenectady Avenue. Still a nice building today, with its marble walls and intricately carved moldings in the lobby, it must have been quite an impressive place to live in 1941. And on April 24, 1942, the family rounded

out nicely with the addition of the healthy little girl her parents named
Barbara Joan.

NAMED AFTER HER grandmother Anna's sister – Barbara is the English
equivalent of the Yiddish Berthe – she was a bright-eyed baby with a ready
smile, so fascinated by everything around her that she rarely cried. Her
head was a little too big for her body, and its size seemed accentuated
by a complete lack of hair until she was two, but everyone agreed with
her parents' assessment of her on her birth announcement as 'a cute little
trick.' In fact, some friends even told Diana that Barbara had the makings
of the next Gerber baby food baby, but Diana found that notion unseemly.
At school, Manny lost few opportunities to brag about his new daughter and
show his colleagues pictures of her.

With the child came added expenses, and Manny took advantage of every
opportunity to earn extra money. Immediately after school he'd hurry to the
yeshiva at 656 Willoughby Avenue, where he taught remedial classes. The
year after Barbara's birth, he worked as a counselor and tutor at a youth
camp in upstate New York, a situation that kept money coming in during
summer recess.

The following summer Manny accepted an offer to be head counselor at
Camp Cascade in Highmount, New York, run by one of his fellow teachers
at Specialty Trades, Nathan Spiro. Diana, high-strung and a chronic worrier,
felt uneasy about spending the summer at Camp Cascade: 'I don't know,
something within me was nervous.' But she was an obedient wife, and during
the last week of June 1943 she, Manny, Sheldon, and baby Barbara arrived in
the Catskill Mountains.

Manny's job was rigorous. He led the kids on hikes, umpired softball
games, coached swim meets, taught tutorials, and supervised the entire
staff. In July his workload grew even heavier when several counselors
suddenly quit. At the end of most of his eighteen-hour days now, he felt
unaccustomedly tired.

On Wednesday, August 4, 1943, a suffocatingly hot day, Manny awoke
with a headache. By midmorning, after he had coached a swimming race,
the pain had grown so severe he felt sick to his stomach. He told Nathan
Spiro he would have to go back to his cottage and lie down for a while.
He went to his bedroom and asked Diana to wake him in an hour. When
she tried to, she couldn't rouse him. She ran out and found Spiro, who
called an ambulance. While she waited for medical help to come, Diana
paced back and forth at the foot of the bed, her uncomplaining infant in
her arms. Her husband's breathing was shallow, and terror bit at her gut.

'It's going to be all right,' she kept repeating to herself. 'It's going to be all right.'

Spiro's wife accompanied Diana to Fleischmanns Hospital, a small infirmary nearby, while his daughter baby-sat with Barbara. Before she left the camp, Diana had composed a telegram to Anna and Isaac that was delivered to the fish store that afternoon: 'Manny very ill. Come immediately.'

By the time Anna got to Fleischmanns Hospital, her son was dead. Shortly after Manny arrived at the hospital, he had suffered a seizure. A doctor had injected morphine into his neck to halt the convulsions, and within a few minutes Manny had stopped breathing. Whether the dosage was too high or he had had an adverse reaction to the drug isn't known, but at 2:45 P.M. Emanuel Streisand was pronounced dead of respiratory failure.

His wife sat stock still in the hospital waiting room, her mind uncomprehending. His mother maintained the presence of mind to make the arrangements. The Jewish religion required that Manny be buried within twenty-four hours, but he owned no cemetery plot. Anna called home, and a stunned Isaac quickly sought the help of friends at his temple, who arranged for Manny to be buried at Mount Hebron Cemetery in Queens after funeral services at the Kirchenbaum Funeral Parlor that began at 3 P.M. August 5.

At the burial, in accordance with custom, the mourners tore their lapels ('the rending of the garments') and intoned 'Blessed be the righteous Judge.' As her husband's body was lowered into the ground, Diana Streisand whispered to her eight-year-old son, 'Now you're the man of the family.' Immediately afterward, the seven-day mourning period began. Diana sat shivah at her parents' apartment; the Streisand family sat in their apartment above the fish store. Mirrors were covered with cloth so that all focus would remain on the deceased; conversation was limited to praises of the dead and expressions of condolence. Friends brought food, and twice a day a minyan of ten holy men came to the residences to hold services and lead the mourners in a recitation of the Kaddish, the mourners' prayer. After a week the mourners left the apartments for the first time and walked around the block to symbolically cast off their sorrow.

It wasn't that easy for Diana, or for Anna. Beth Streisand, the widow of Manny's brother Murray, remembered that period with lingering sadness. 'It was a terrible time. Dinah was just bewildered. Manny's mother took it so hard. She was very devoted to him, very close to him. I don't remember her carrying on with grief at the funeral, but after the shivah she wouldn't go out, she didn't do her shopping, she didn't want to do anything. She fell apart completely.'

Diana spent much of her time in the ensuing months crying in her bed, the emptiness next to her like a chasm that threatened to swallow her up.

Her mother and her sister helped with the children, but her situation was bleak. Manny's pension would be only a fraction of what he had been making, and the September rent on their apartment loomed ahead of her. The Streisands couldn't help out much, and neither could Diana's parents. Louis Rosen, never a well-to-do man, was sixty-five now and retired. All he could do was take his daughter and her children into his modest one-bedroom apartment in the Philip Arms, a four-story brick building at 365 Pulaski Street in Brooklyn's Bedford-Stuyvesant section.

Shattered, depressed, frightened, Diana Streisand sold her furniture, packed up her belongings, and moved back in with her parents. Her mind heavy with worry, she wondered whether she and her fatherless children would have any kind of future at all.

Two-and-a-half-year-old Barbara toddled into her grandparents' bedroom and climbed onto a chair next to a low mirrored dresser. Somehow she managed to clamber on top of it, and finally she sat staring at her reflection. She picked up a tube of lipstick and drew vivid red slashes across her cheeks and forehead. Then, using the edge of a blanket, she smeared the goo all over her face. When she leaned back to admire her handiwork, she came precariously close to falling off the dresser. Just at that moment Diana passed by the bedroom door, rushed in to grab her daughter, and saved Barbara from calamity.

As soon as the baby learned to crawl, she got into everything, her bright eyes aglow with delight and intrigue at each new discovery. One afternoon Diana watched as Barbara crawled over to a window, climbed up onto a chair, and stared longingly out at the street. Her heart ached when she realized that the baby was waiting for her father to come home.

Diana's father wasn't much of a substitute dad for his grandchildren. Overweight, his health in decline, Louis Rosen wanted little more at this stage of his life than peace and quiet. Now his household had more than doubled, and the apartment in the Philip Arms was too small for five people. Rosen and his wife slept in the one bedroom, Diana and Barbara slept in the living room, which had been converted into a bedroom, and Sheldon camped out on a cot in the dining room. Diana's bed took the place of the living-room couch, and Barbara grew up thinking that sofas were 'what rich people had.' Although World War II had ended in 1945 and America had begun its two-decade economic recovery from the Great Depression, circumstances had seen to it that the Rosen-Streisand family wouldn't share in America's new bounty.

Louis Rosen showed little patience with a prepubescent boy and a toddler in his home. As Sheldon recalled, 'There was no love in that house. I remember there was a huge table in the dining room, and Barbara and I would scuttle under it to avoid beatings.'

Absorbed in her grief, uncomfortable with displays of affection, their mother provided little nurture. 'Emotionally, my mother left me at the same time' as her father had, Barbra has said. 'She was in her own trauma.' Diana was soon absent physically as well when the financial strains on the Rosen household forced her to return to work for the first time since before her marriage. She got a job as a bookkeeper, and every morning for the first few months of her mother's employment Barbara would burst into tears when Diana walked out of the apartment: 'I was always terrified something would happen to her and I would be alone in the world.'

As often as Barbara was shuttled from one caretaker to another, she might as well have been an orphan. Her uncle Murray Streisand recalled that 'her mother was always leaving her with friends and relatives . . . [and] she felt deserted.' Grandmother Rosen did her best to care for Barbara and Sheldon while Diana worked, but the children proved a handful for the overweight, asthmatic woman, herself nearly seventy. In the fall of 1946, to ease the burden on her mother, Diana sent four-year-old Barbara to nursery school, and the following two summers she shipped both children to her sister's farm in Colchester, Connecticut.

If there was a positive aspect of life on Pulaski Street for Barbara, it was the music that surrounded her. There was neither a radio nor a Victrola, but Louis Rosen continued to sing the traditional religious songs at home every Sabbath and on holidays. 'He sang with the children,' Diana said. 'Of course, Barbara didn't understand the Hebrew words to the hymns, but the musicality of them reached her. I'd sing to her, too, but I'd sing the popular songs.'

In the fall of 1947 Barbara began grade school at the yeshiva on Willoughby Street where her father had once taught. She proved an excellent but troublesome student. 'I had very good marks,' Barbra recalled, 'but my conduct was always marked poor. I was so impatient. I'd sit there holding up my hand and when the teacher ignored me, I'd talk anyway. We'd study the Bible and I had questions: why, why, why? It didn't go over well.'

It was at the yeshiva that Barbara first encountered the cruelty of other children. She wasn't a pretty girl. Her body, thin and ungainly, often seemed to move in several directions at once. Her head was still too large for her small frame, and a lazy left eye constantly threatened to drift into her nose, which had begun to grow in disproportion to her face. She became the butt of jokes and tauntings – 'Big beak,' they called her, and 'Cross-eyes,' and 'Mieskeit,' a

Yiddish word for an ugly person. To block the pain, she adopted a haughty, defensive air that only spurred her tormentors on.

TOBEY WANDER BOROKOW, a warm, loving Austrian immigrant who lived on the first floor of the Philip Arms with her husband and their six-year-old son, Irving, took a liking to the odd little girl who lived two floors above when Barbara and Irving began to play together in the hall. Tobey called Barbara *bubeleh* – her little darling – and she was probably the first adult who ever showed the child sustained and unreserved affection.

'My mother was a very friendly, outgoing sort of person,' Irving Borokow recalled. 'She was very motherly to Barbara; she was probably in contact with her more than her own mother was. My mother became her mother, basically.' Another neighbor, Anna Lopatton, saw Tobey 'take Barbara in and hug her and call her pet names, and I never saw her mother or her grandparents do that.' When Tobey saw that Barbara had only a hot-water bottle to play with as a doll, she knit a sweater for it. 'It sounds awful,' Barbra has said, 'but when I'd fill it with water it was like this warm human being. It had much more life and feeling than an ordinary doll.'

Tobey offered to baby-sit for Barbara after she got home from school and before Diana returned from work. Tobey would knit sweaters or cook stuffed cabbage, blintzes, and noodle pudding while Barbara and Irving sat transfixed in front of the Borokows' seven-inch television screen. 'We used to watch Laurel and Hardy every day,' Barbra has said, 'on a tiny little television with a big magnifying glass attached to it so it would blow up the screen and the picture would seem bigger.' But when Irving's father, Abe, came home at five o'clock, it was time for the children to clear out. According to Irving, 'My father was just the opposite of my mother. He liked his privacy. He wasn't very sociable with the children.'

'Whenever he came home,' Barbra has said, 'Irving would say to me, "You have to go now." That really set me back years.' Once again, it seemed to Barbara, a father figure had rejected her. 'She always felt a yearning for her father,' Irving said. 'That was apparent even when we were kids.'

Barbara and Irving played house together, and she helped him run his lemonade stand on the sidewalk in front of the building. Before long, he developed a crush on her. He doesn't recall ever telling Barbara how he felt, nor does he think she returned his feelings 'because she always considered me like a brother.' But years later Barbra described him as 'my first boyfriend' and recalled that he had told her he 'liked' her. 'He hit me over the head with a [toy] gun once – I guess that was his way of showing affection.'

HER MOTHER FRETTED constantly over Barbara's lack of interest in food. According to Irving Borokow, 'a Jewish child had to be round, and Barbara was like a toothpick. So her mother constantly tried to feed her.' One concoction her mother made Barbara eat has stuck in Irving's mind. 'It was called a guggle muggle. It was like a shake with milk and chocolate and a raw egg. It was supposed to fatten her up.'

It didn't, and neither did her mother's virtual force-feedings. Diana became so frustrated with her daughter's finicky eating that she often propped her up in bed and spoon-fed her as though she were an infant. At those times Barbara lapped up both the food and the rare attention from her mother. 'When I wanted love from my mother,' Barbra has said, 'she gave me food.'

During the summers of Barbara's sixth and seventh years, 1948 and 1949, Dinah took another tack after a doctor told her that her daughter was anemic: she sent her away to 'health camps' in upstate New York. 'Those camps were the most horrible experiences of my life,' Barbra said. Once again her mother was sending her away, and this time to total strangers. 'I'd get there, they'd dump me in a bathtub . . . like I was a piece of dirt.' The counselors scrubbed her, washed her hair with lice-killer, and put her into the camp's drab uniform.

Homesick, missing the Borokows especially, Barbara cried miserably day after day, clutching the only link she had to her happiness with Irving and Tobey – 'my identity, my sense of self' – a maroon sweater with wooden buttons that Tobey had knitted for her. Inevitably, the other kids mocked her tears, and when they did, her haughtiness would kick in. She'd turn up her nose and sniff. 'I'm not crying,' she would tell them. 'I have a loose tear duct that just runs.'

When Barbara returned home at the end of August, she hadn't plumped up much. 'The food was so awful at this camp that was supposed to make me healthy that I used to throw it under the table just to get it off my plate.'

BARBRA HAS RECALLED that her desire to be an actress took form when she was about five, just around the time that she began to watch television every afternoon with Irving Borokow. She adored the flickery images dancing from that tiny set through the magnifying screen, loved the laughter and the emotion – the escape – provided by old Hollywood B movies, a staple of the afternoon television schedule in the late 1940s. But the respite they provided from her drab, love-starved family life lasted only the few hours a week she spent with the Borokows. To a little girl who felt ugly and unwanted, that wasn't enough. She would have to create her own fantasy world, and she did. As her mother put it, 'Once she saw television, that was the end of it. She wanted to become those people on the screen.'

She loved to sing – 'Barbara started to sing as early as she could talk,' Diana said – and the confines of the Philip Arms became her stage. 'I used to sing in the hallways on Pulaski Street. The building had great halls with these brass railings, and the ceilings were very high and there was this echo.' She would sit on the stairway steps inside the building and sing songs she'd heard on the radio. Some of the neighbors were annoyed, others delighted.

But Barbara soon got a taste of a real audience's approval. In the spring of 1949, having just turned seven, she made 'my first public singing appearance' in the yeshiva's PTA assembly program. 'She was awfully excited about it,' her mother recalled, 'and she practiced like a demon. But when the day came, she came down with a bad cold. I put her to bed and told her to forget about the PTA, but she got angry and wouldn't hear of it. She leaped out of bed, put on her new dress, which hung on her like a rag because she was so skinny, and went to the meeting. Cold or no cold, she sang. She always had that kind of determination. I had to put her back to bed when we got home, but she'd had her moment of glory and was satisfied.'

A photograph of the event shows, as Barbra put it, a 'weird-looking kid standing pigeon-toed and very skinny with bows in her hair.' But she looks pleased at the delighted applause being led by the school principal, Miss Weisselburg.

When Barbara ran off the stage, she asked breathlessly, 'Ma, what did you think?'

'Your arms are too thin,' Diana replied.

'I think I started to eat then,' Barbra recalled – but still not enough to suitably fill her out. That summer of 1949 her mother sent her to a Hebrew health camp, and Barbara hated it as much as she had the one before. But she would harbor a particularly bad memory of this one, for it was here that she first met her future stepfather, Louis Kind.

Diana was now forty, and she wanted to marry again before it was too late. Still pretty, pert, and pliant, if increasingly plump, she had had no trouble finding dates when she emerged from her prolonged period of mourning. Barbara hated every one of these men. One was a butcher, and she recalled seeing him kiss Diana. 'I thought he was killing her. Except that she was laughing.' Barbara would scream and cry whenever a suitor came to pick Diana up for an evening out, certain that her mother would never come back. Always, eventually, the men stopped coming around. Louis Kind continued.

Tall, good-looking, a sharp dresser, and sixteen years older than Diana, Kind was separated from his wife, Ida, and his three children. Born in 1893, he had come to America from Russia in 1898 with his Orthodox Jewish parents, a brother, and a sister. His father bought a pants factory on the Lower East Side of Manhattan, and Kind learned men's tailoring at a young age. He worked most of his life as a piece sewer in the garment industry, and later owned several rooming houses, first in Manhattan and then in Brooklyn, the rents from which provided his primary source of income.

He was all charm while he courted the widow Streisand. She recalled that 'he came with nice ideas and little gifts,' and he seemed well-nigh perfect as a suitor; with his Old World manners and background in the garment trade, he got along well with Diana's father. Most importantly, he told Diana he liked children. Indeed, his son, Merwyn, remembered his father as a man who was 'very gentle with children. Family was of primary importance to him. He wasn't nearly the disciplinarian my mother was.' When Diana told him she planned to visit Barbara at camp, Kind asked if he could come along. Diana was delighted.

Barbara wasn't. She knew that for this man to accompany her mother on a visit meant that things were serious between them, and the thought of her mother remarrying horrified her. No man could take the place of her father! She barely looked at Kind when her mother introduced him, and she remained sullen during the entire visit. When the couple rose to leave, Barbara became hysterical and screamed, 'You're not leaving here without me! I'm not staying here any longer!' Diana tried to soothe her, but finally she had no choice but to pack her daughter's things and bundle her into the car. On the trip back to Brooklyn, the three of them sat in grim, torpid silence. According to Barbra, Louis Kind 'hated me ever since. I must have been pretty obnoxious.'

Whenever Kind called for Diana at Pulaski Street, he recalled, 'I would wait for her in the living room, and then when she was ready to go out with me, I would take her arm and lead her to the door. Barbara, sensing that her life was to undergo some terrifying change, would hold on to her mother's skirts, pulling her back, fearful that this strange man was taking her mother away from her. "Don't go, Mommy, stay with me," she would plead.'

Kind tried to win Barbara over by bringing her a doll, the first real one she had ever had. 'It was the kind that peed in its pants,' she recollected. 'You had to feed it with a little bottle and then just watch it – go!' Perhaps portentously, Barbara played with the doll for only a short time before its head fell off.

Barbara's vague hopes that somehow Lou Kind would go away faded as he continued his courtship of her mother. But when Diana made clear that she wanted him to marry her, Kind resisted. He'd already had one failed marriage – his divorce had just recently become final – and he didn't relish taking on the responsibility of a wife and two youngsters at age fifty-six.

Even when Diana told him late in April of 1950 that she was expecting his baby, he wouldn't marry her, and she clearly faced a mortifying predicament. She kept her condition secret as long as she could, but when that was no longer possible, her worst fear came to pass: her deeply religious father demanded that she leave his house.

In June, with Louis Kind's refusal to marry her ringing in her ears, Diana moved herself and the children to a one-bedroom apartment at 3102 Newkirk Avenue, on the corner of Nostrand Avenue in Flatbush. The building was part of the Vanderveer Estates, a recently built complex of monolithic six-story cinder-block-and-steel structures in a middle-class neighborhood. The buildings had scant charm, but they were new and clean and the rents were affordable. Diana's apartment cost her $105 a month.

Barbara, frightened of change and devastated at having to leave the Borokows, awoke after the first night in the new apartment with a clicking in her ears. When she told her mother about the noise, Diana told her, 'Well, sleep on a hot-water bottle,' and never asked her about it again. 'From that day,' Barbra recalled, 'I led a whole secret life. Something was wrong with me – I had these clicks in my ears.'

The stress of her situation threatened to undo Diana. She dreaded the embarrassment of having a baby out of wedlock. Her job didn't pay very well, and she couldn't afford to furnish the apartment with anything but the barest necessities. She didn't have the money to send Barbara to yeshiva any longer, but Public School 89 was directly across the street from the new apartment, so Barbara could enroll there as a fourth grader in September. But what on earth would Diana do when the baby came in January and all *those* expenses began?

Finally, on Saturday, December 23, 1950, Louis Kind did the right thing and married Diana Streisand. They drove to New Jersey, where they were pronounced husband and wife by a justice of the peace. Two and a half weeks later, on January 9, 1951, their daughter Rosalind (later Roslyn) was born.

Now Barbara's unhappiness, her sense of alienation, worsened. There was a baby in the house to take up all of her mother's attention and absorb all of her stepfather's love. Kind doted on his infant daughter. According to his son Merwyn, 'he thought Rozzie was the beginning and the end of all baby girls. Perhaps because she was born when he was at a later age, he lavished all his attention on her. His feelings for her were *huge*. He thought she was the most beautiful, the brightest, the smartest baby in the world.' Still, he was quite happy to let his wife do all the parenting. According to Diana, 'He was a strange man who didn't know too much about children. He didn't know how to play with them.'

If Diana had imagined that marrying Louis Kind would improve her family's living conditions, she soon learned she'd been wrong. Kind professed not to have enough money for them to move to a larger apartment, and the sleeping arrangements settled pretty much the way they had on Pulaski Street, with Barbara on the living room couch and Sheldon on a cot in the dining room.

Louis Kind came to abhor Barbara. He found her braying, bratty, maddening, and unpleasant to look at. Years later she would bitterly recall that 'I don't think I had a conversation with this man. I don't think this man asked me how I was in the seven years we lived together.' That, as it turned out, was the least of it.

Maxine Eddleson, a neighbor Barbara's age who befriended her shortly after she moved to Newkirk Avenue, recalled that Lou Kind 'was very nasty to Barbara. She seemed to try so hard to please him. He was so loving, kind, and sweet to everyone else, but he was verbally abusive to Barbara. He would yell at her and say mean things to her and criticize her clothes in front of her friends.'

Despite Kind's mistreatment of her, and her resentment at what she saw as his usurpation of her real father's memory (she refused to change her last name to his), Barbara so desperately wanted to be seen as 'normal' that she pretended Kind was her real father. 'When I asked her why he had a different last name she replied, "Oh, he uses that name for business,"' Maxine recalled. 'She tried to hide that he was her stepfather. It wasn't until we were teenagers that she said anything about her real father.'

SHE FELT LIKE a victim. Why did her father have to die? 'I always felt there was a gaping hole somewhere,' she said, 'something missing.' She would lie awake at night and imagine that she was an alien from the planet Mars. She thought of herself as chosen, somehow special: 'I could feel people's minds. I could see the truth.'

She became totally self-absorbed. As her mother put it, 'Barbara was a very complex child. She always saw everything depending on how it affected her. She bottled up everything inside her. Perhaps if she could have voiced to me how she was feeling, things might have been easier, but she didn't.'

But whenever Barbara tried to do that, it seemed to her, Diana gave her short shrift, perhaps because by age nine Barbara had become something of a hypochondriac. When she read a booklet about cancer, she convinced herself that she had all the symptoms and had only six months to live. Another time she suddenly felt an enormous pressure on her chest and told her mother about it. Although Diana always admonished her to bundle up and be careful and eat properly, 'if anything ever happened to me, she'd say, "I told you so. Now you take care of it."'

Barbara took it upon herself to see a doctor about the sensation in her chest. It took her a week to muster up the courage to climb the steps to his office and ring the bell. Then she realized he didn't have office hours that day, and suddenly she felt the pressure dissipate. 'That was my first psychosomatic illness.' Throughout her life, Barbra's emotional stresses would invariably take a physical toll on her.

THE MARRIAGE OF Diana and Louis Kind, off on the wrong foot from the outset, soured quickly. Kind often stayed away from the apartment for days at a time, and when he got home, he and Diana fell into terrible rows. He verbally abused her, Sheldon, and Barbara. After Sheldon grew up and left the house, Kind more and more frequently physically abused Diana. Apartment 4G became a place of fear and loathing.

Two years after she had first heard the clicks in her ears, Barbara woke up after a night of shouting and violence with a high-pitched ringing inside her head. It was as though her soul were trying to block out all the unpleasantness, to hear nothing but white noise. This condition, known as tinnitus, can be brought on by one's emotions, and for Barbara it has never gone away. 'I never hear the silence,' she has said. 'There were periods in my life when I was very unhappy, and [the sound] would drive me nuts.' She never told anyone about it, but wore scarves wrapped around her head in a misguided attempt to purge the noise from her brain. 'The scarf only made the sound louder. I felt totally abnormal. I had this secret.'

Another secret in her secret life. But there was nothing hidden about her show business ambitions. If Louis Kind had added anything to Barbara's life, it was the television set he brought with him, and she parked herself in front of it whenever she could. The medium had advanced tremendously since the late 1940s. Now Barbara could watch Milton Berle, Jackie Gleason, Bob Hope, Perry Como, Lucille Ball, and especially Ed Sullivan, who presented the finest singers and comedians of the day, as well as veterans of vaudeville like the sublime Sophie Tucker and scenes from Broadway shows, the first Barbara had ever seen.

She loved it all, even the commercials. When she was alone in the apartment she'd stand in front of the bathroom mirror – the only one in the house – and imitate them. She'd brush her teeth while smiling dazzlingly or smoke a cigarette with utter sophistication. 'I smoked between the ages of ten and twelve,' she recalled. 'I'd go into the bathroom and blow the smoke out of the window. My mother smoked too, but she held her cigarette awkwardly and I'd say, "No, Ma, you have to hold it like *this!*" and show her how.'

She experimented with makeup, just as she had clumsily tried to do when she was two and a half, and usually made a mess in the process. 'I would make funny lipstick. My brother was an artist, so he had pencils – blue pencils – and there was this white medicine for your skin called zinc oxide, and my mother wore purple lipstick – you know, from the fifties. So I would make concoctions, mixtures, like a chemist, of purple lipstick and white cream and make fuchsia lips and blue eyes from my brother's paint kit. Then I'd do a smoking commercial. I was always trying to be an actress, I suppose.'

Sheldon Streisand remembered that 'she was always mischievous, experimental, and curious. I'll never forget the time she squeezed the paints out of my oil paint set. And I had saved up a dollar seventy-five for that set!' Sheldon was sixteen when Barbara was nine, and he considered his little sister a pain in the neck. 'I had to baby-sit for her, and then she was always tagging after me and my friends. But we had a lot of fun together too. One of our biggest kicks was watching TV while eating sliced raw onion on white bread that had been spread with chicken fat.'

Barbara could be painfully shy in one-on-one interactions at this age, but she appears not to have been inhibited when it came to performing. To her, that was the best way to express her feelings and to win the attention she craved. She would sit on the low stoop of her building and sing with the other kids, imitating Joni James's hit 'Have You Heard?' Louis Kind described the scene: 'I can see her now, singing songs she had heard on the radio in her little-girl voice, which even then was remarkably true and delivered with great feeling. The neighbors would stick their heads out of the window, clap loudly and yell, "More, Barbara, give us more!" She was only too happy to oblige. Then, as a final encore – double-jointed as she was – she would lie down on the pavement, take both of her feet, wrap them around her neck, and roll like a human ball!'

'BARBARA WAS EXTREMELY apprehensive about going to a public school,' Maxine Eddleson recalled. 'She was nervous about the kind of people she'd meet; her stomach got unsettled. She had been kind of cloistered at the yeshiva academy. And when she entered P.S. 89 in the fourth grade, I was her only friend for a while.' Barbara kept so much to herself that classmates mistook her shyness for a sense of superiority. 'I never liked Barbara,' one of her classmates, now Mrs Phyllis Zack, said. 'I thought she was a snob.' The school's principal, Mrs Dorothy Sultan, recalled that Barbara was 'a quiet child who liked to sing and did sing in assembly. I knew she had a sense of humor, but she never really displayed it – she didn't project herself. At the time I thought she was an average child, one who really didn't make her presence felt.'

But eventually Barbara began to make more friends, and her performing talents became well known throughout the school. Phyllis Zack recalled that Barbara 'wanted to be an actress even then, and she was good, too. I remember once some of the kids wanted to set up a surprise for a teacher they liked, so Barbara pretended to faint while she was in another room. The teacher ran to her side, and while he was out of the room the kids put this present on his desk. Barbara had him convinced all the time, too.'

After a few years at P.S. 89, Barbara met the personable dark-haired twins Marilyn and Carolyn Bernstein. 'We took it upon ourselves to befriend her,' Carolyn said. 'We had a lot of friends, and we kind of felt sorry for her because she always looked so alone. I don't think she was very secure about the way she looked. I remember her in the sixth grade with the white mantailored shirts that she used to wear, long-sleeved always, and a skirt and saddle shoes – conservative, like we all dressed in those days.'

Barbara and the twins became fast friends. Nearly every day after school she would go to their house, where they would gather around the piano and sing while Mrs Bernstein played. They'd eat snacks, then scramble onto the top bunk of the twins' bunk beds with a pile of movie magazines. They would cut out pictures of their favorite stars and tape them to the walls. Barbara always seemed reluctant to leave, and after a while it became clear to the twins that she didn't plan to return the favor and invite them over to her house. The girls didn't press the issue. 'When a young person doesn't welcome you to their home over and over again,' Carolyn reflected, 'you begin to think that they're not very happy there. It's an assumption that people made about Barbara.'

Barbara and the twins stayed fast friends, and before long they formed a singing group they called Bobbie and the Bernsteins. 'Barbara, of course, was Bobbie, and we were her backup girls,' Carolyn said. 'We'd sing the popular songs of the day around the gymnasium and the playground. It wasn't something that amounted to very much. Barbara had that voice even then. Of course, it became stronger, but she certainly had the same quality, absolutely.'

Carolyn recalled that Barbara often expressed an interest in becoming a singer at this time. 'She would talk to us about her dreams, and she always stressed singing. She was very intense about it.' According to William

Corride, another classmate, Barbara sang a little too much for some kids. 'Her voice wasn't so great at that time – it was immature. We used to tell her, "Barbara, please, don't sing anymore."'

BEGINNING WHEN SHE was around ten, Barbara constantly badgered Diana to let her take ballet and singing lessons, to let her audition for the movies, to let her perform in public. Mrs Kind was reluctant for two reasons. She didn't think her daughter had the looks to be a successful child performer. 'She was not a good-looking girl,' Diana has said. 'In show business at that time, there were very pretty girls around.' She also worried about the expense of lessons.

But Barbara wouldn't accept no as an answer. 'She was a demon as a little girl,' Diana said. 'I never could stop her from doing what she wanted to do, because she was always ready to jump into something and carry it out on her own.' When Diana relented and allowed Barbara to take ballet lessons at Miss Marsh's School, she worried constantly. 'She kept practicing, and I thought it might hurt her, because it's not very nice when you're on your toes.'

Barbara took ballet lessons for six months. 'She wanted everything [that went with the lessons],' Diana recalled. 'She had a high hat, a stick. I couldn't believe this kid!' But after six months Miss Marsh moved away, and Barbara's interest in ballet went with her. 'Was I happy!' Diana exclaimed.

Still, there was no holding Barbara back. When she was ten, the family spent two weeks in August at the Barbary Hotel in South Fallsburg, New York. The hotel had a casino and a twice-weekly talent show for youngsters. Barbara sang and danced in the shows, delighting once again in the audience's friendly applause.

When she was eleven she heard about singing auditions being held locally by the Metro-Goldwyn-Mayer Studio, which was looking for kiddie talent. Diana reluctantly agreed to let Barbara try out when she pointed out that if she was accepted she'd be put under contract and paid quite well.

On the way to the Steve Allen Studio for the audition Barbara, wearing a blue dress from Abraham & Straus with a white collar and cuffs, fantasized about how it would go. 'I thought I'd wear a beautiful gown and dance under a huge sparkling chandelier.' But when she arrived, her illusions evaporated. 'Instead, there was a microphone in a glass-enclosed cagelike cell and a man in a booth who said, "All right, kid, sing!" I sang "Have You Heard" behind a glass booth. You couldn't hear anything outside – they had to press a button to talk to you.' When she finished her song she was confident they would hire her. 'But they just said thank you, and that was that.' In fact, Barbara had impressed the talent scouts enough that they wanted her to join their training classes, but Diana nixed the idea. 'When they said "No pay," I said "No child."'

The following year, Barbara pleaded with her mother to let her audition for Star Time, a school for child performers on Brooklyn's Church Avenue. Graduates got a chance to appear with pay, on the television show of the same name, and Barbara was certain the training would turn her into a star. Diana, eyeing that potential income, agreed, and the school accepted Barbara. She first took general classes, then graduated to more advanced instruction. She adored every minute of it, but after four months Diana abruptly pulled her out of the school, saying only that she had decided it was too far away from home. To the devastated Barbara this was just another betrayal by a mother who didn't believe in her dreams.

What Diana didn't tell her daughter was that she could no longer afford to pay the tuition because Louis Kind's financial support of the family had become sporadic. During his increasingly long absences, which Diana explained to friends and family as 'business trips,' he was in fact AWOL from his marriage: Diana had no idea where he was. 'He had places to go where he enjoyed doing his own thing away from us,' she said with some delicacy.

Still, Barbara found ways to keep performing. During the summer of 1955, Diana took her and Roslyn for another vacation in upstate New York, this one a week at the Coronet Hotel in Glen Wild. Barbara, focused and competitive, won the Ping-Pong and rowing contests. She also won the talent contest, and afterward two different guests asked her if she would sing at weddings being held the following two weekends – and offered her a small fee to do so. After she exclaimed 'Yes!' she whispered to her mother, 'Y' see, Ma, I can make money at this!' At one of the weddings, a piano player from Brooklyn came up to Barbara and Diana and told them that Barbara had such a good voice she should cut a demo record. He told them about a studio where they could make an acetate recording for a few dollars, and he offered to be the accompanist.

Barbara bubbled over with excitement, and Diana murmured some vague acquiescence. Once again, however, Mrs Kind was preoccupied. Her week in the Catskills would soon be over. Then she would have to return to Brooklyn and face her husband.

3

The late-summer air lay still, hot and heavy as Barbara slept restlessly on the small living room sofa. It was three in the morning, and the light still shone under the closed door of her mother's bedroom: her stepfather hadn't come home yet. More and more often now Lou Kind stayed out until the early-morning hours, and Diana later charged in court that he frequently didn't come home for weeks at a time, leaving his family without a father and without income. Barbara dreaded what would happen when he walked through the door.

The court documents would paint a grim picture of life in apartment 4G. Whenever her husband finally returned home, Diana said, he would flaunt his associations with other women. He would savage her with obscene invective, threaten her, and assault her. Kind countercharged that Diana nagged him, lied about him, flew into unprovoked rages, threw things, and hit him. Their fights grew so loud that they disturbed the neighbors.

One can well imagine the impact all this had on the impressionable thirteen-year-old Barbara. 'I had a miserable relationship with my step-father,' she said. 'I was abused.' Kind treated Barbara nearly as badly as he did her mother. When she asked him for fifteen cents for an ice-cream cone as the bell of the Good Humor truck tinkled outside, he replied, 'No, you're not pretty enough.' Whenever he compared Roslyn to Barbara, he called them Beauty and the Beast. As he watched the Friday night fights on television, wearing only a T-shirt and shorts and swigging beer, Barbara was so afraid to obstruct his line of vision that she would crawl along the floor.

Trapped in this cramped, dreary apartment with a man she hated, Barbara blamed no one so much as her mother. 'I resented her terribly for letting it happen.' She retreated further and further into her fantasy world of glamour and fame, but reality proved inescapable. As she listened helplessly to the terrible rows between her mother and stepfather, thoughts of her real father would flood her mind, and she found herself gripped with anger at him. 'It was like "Why did you die and leave me?"' she said. '"What did I do wrong? Was I a bad girl or something? Or didn't you like me?"'

BARBARA'S FIRST DAY of high school – Monday, September 12, 1955 – afforded respite, but Erasmus Hall High School held terrors of its own. She didn't know what to expect when she boarded the Nostrand Avenue bus outside her building for the ride to the school at Flatbush and Church Avenues, dressed in gingham and lace to project a frilly femininity. When she got there the sheer size of the place overwhelmed her. At P.S. 89 Barbara had been part of a class of 136; at Erasmus the freshman class numbered over 1,300. The sprawling Erasmus Hall campus resembled a university more than a high school, and surely must have inspired awe and trepidation in its wide-eyed freshmen.

Still, the educational standards at Erasmus were top-flight, and from the start Barbara ranked among the school's academic elite. Her IQ, found to be 124, had made her a part of the Intellectually Gifted Opportunity (IG-OP) program at P.S. 89, and that automatically put her in honors classes in high school. During her first term she applied herself so diligently to her studies that her grade adviser described her as 'hard-driving.' She scored 92 in English, 90 in Modern History, 98 in Spanish, 90 in General Science, 96 in Elementary Algebra, and 95 in Freshman Chorus. Her 93.5 average put her in the top 3 percent of the class.

She might have become 'Miss Erasmus,' but she wasn't a joiner; most of her classmates thought of her as 'a loner, aloof.' One classmate, Diane Hirschfeld, recalled that after lunch 'everyone would stand around in groups and kind of chat until the bell rang for us to go back in, and Barbara was always standing off to one side, alone. The strongest memory I have of her is her standing and waiting by herself, holding her books.'

'I wouldn't know who to talk to,' Barbra has said. 'I was smart, but the smart kids wearing oxfords and glasses wouldn't look at me, and the dumb kids I wouldn't want to associate with. So I was a real outsider.' She made no effort to fit in. While most of the 'cool' kids rushed over to Garfield's Cafeteria across the street for lunch (twenty-five cents minimum), Barbara usually ate in the school lunchroom. While many students joined clubs and stayed after school for extracurricular activities, Barbara worked in Choy's Chinese restaurant.

Jimmy and Muriel Choy lived one flight up from Barbara, and the moment she first saw them in 1953, they seemed marvelously exotic to the inquisitive eleven-year-old, who asked unending questions about their Chinese heritage and their strange customs and culture. Before long, their warmth and openness had captivated her, and they became, just as the Borokows had been before them, a second family to her. 'I loved them,' Barbra said.

She baby-sat for the Choys' two daughters, five-year-old Debbie and two-year-old Pam, for thirty-five cents an hour. Barbara's maturity and reliability so impressed Jimmy and Muriel that the following year they asked her to help out on Sundays in their restaurant, Choy's Chinese on Nostrand Avenue across the street from their building, even though she was only twelve. Barbara had no trouble getting her mother's permission. Diana, faced with her husband's financial irresponsibility, figured the sixty-cents an hour Barbara would earn would come in handy.

'Barbara was anxious to learn Chinese words,' Jimmy Choy recalled, 'and she learned how to order in Chinese.' Everything about the culture fascinated her. She wore silk kimonos. She put her hair up into a bun and crisscrossed darning needles through it. She let her nails grow an inch long and painted them Dragon Lady red. She also came to love Chinese food, so much more delicious, so much more exciting than the bland kosher food her mother prepared. She thrilled to egg rolls and chow mein and moo shu pork, enjoying every chomp of that verboten meat as much as she had enjoyed yelling out 'Christmas!' at yeshiva. Ironically, though, the strongest gastronomic memory Barbra holds of Mrs Choy was that she made the best spaghetti sauce she ever tasted. It was probably Muriel Choy who turned Barbara into the voracious food addict that she would become: if Barbara had to accept food in place of love, it might as well be delicious.

Every day she grew closer to her surrogate parents, and as she entered puberty, it was Muriel Choy to whom Barbara went with questions about the facts of life. She couldn't even broach such things to her mother. 'In my family, sex was taboo,' she said. 'You don't screw anybody until you get married, you don't hold hands, you don't kiss, because you'll get a disease. It was all so awful.'

But Muriel Choy 'used to tell me about things. About love, and life, and sex.' One of the questions Barbara asked was whether, during intercourse, the man was always on top. 'Not necessarily,' Muriel replied.

'What!' Barbara yelped in amazement. But Mrs Choy would say no more.

She worked at Choy's Chinese for four years, and she continually spoke of her desire to be an actress. 'We all knew of her ambitions,' Muriel recalled. Coincidentally it was the Choys who put Barbara Streisand's image on celluloid for the first time. At a birthday party for one of his daughters in 1956, Jimmy Choy tried out his new 8mm movie camera. The film shows laughing kids in party hats, a birthday cake festooned with candles – and fourteen-year-old Barbara, dressed in a blue sweater with white fur trim and a dark skirt, her hair pulled back into a ponytail. Every time the camera turns her way; Barbara ducks her head and puts her hands in front of her face.

BARBARA STOOD NERVOUSLY in front of the music department chairman, Cosimo DePietto, and sang with all her heart. She was auditioning in the hope of winning a spot in the Erasmus Choral Club, the elite group of student singers that each year put on memorable Christmas and Easter concerts in the school's chapel. But Barbara wanted to win DePietto's approval for another reason as well. Like many of the girls at Erasmus, she had a crush on the dark, handsome Italian with the wavy salt-and-pepper hair. She dreamed of being taken under his personal tutelage; surely he would recognize her talent and help her become a world-class singer.

But when she finished her performance, DePietto seemed unimpressed. Tears burned in her eyes as she left the room, and a few days later he told her what she already knew: that she hadn't been accepted. DePietto's official reason was that she couldn't read music, but years later he recalled that 'I never knew her to have any particular or outstanding talent.'

As she would for the rest of her life when faced with rejection, Barbara dug in her heels and persisted. She auditioned again a few months later, with the same disappointing results. Then she came up with a plan. If she couldn't win DePietto over directly, she reasoned, maybe she could do it in a roundabout way. She reminded her mother of that Catskill pianist who had told them about the studio where she could make a record, and she begged Diana to take her there, using the argument that to cut a record would impress her music teacher and get her into the Choral Club.

Diana finally agreed, Barbra later said, 'because *she* wanted to be a singer.' Over Christmas recess, mother and daughter met their pianist friend at the Nola Recording Studio in Manhattan. Diana went first, singing 'One Kiss' and an operetta piece in the Jeanette MacDonald style she had loved as a girl. But Barbara was bothered by the fact that after Diana's first stanza, 'the pianist went off and played two minutes of his own thing' before she had a chance to finish the song, and the discs were only three minutes long.

As she got ready to record her songs, Barbara said to the man, 'Can you cut down on the part you do? I wanna sing the whole song.'

Barbara first sang 'Zing! Went the Strings of My Heart,' then 'You'll Never Know.' She had planned to perform the latter song exactly as written, but on the last few notes she found herself warbling, 'You'll never know if you don't know . . . oh . . . oh . . . now.'

She astonished herself. 'I wondered, Who was that? Where did that come from? It was like *The Exorcist*, you know? . . . I guess you could call that inspiration. It's a nice feeling when that happens. If you're in the moment, you're free to just let the music go through you and do what it wants.'

Now she was armed with a professionally recorded disc of her voice, and when she auditioned for Mr DePietto a third time she played it for him. Perhaps impressed by her enterprise, perhaps worn down, he accepted her into the Choral Club, but not exactly with open arms. A fellow student, Adele Lowinson, recalled that 'Barbara had to stand in the very back row where she would not be seen or missed.'

To Barbara's dismay, DePietto never allowed her to sing a solo. Another Choral Club member, Barry Tantleff, recalled that DePietto 'didn't seem to get along with Barbara very well. He much preferred a girl named Trudy Wallace. She was the one who sang all of the solos at our school functions. That may be why Barbara dropped out of Choral Club after the second year. Maybe she was frustrated because she wasn't being recognized.'

'I don't think Barbara ever considered me a rival,' said Trudy Wallace, who now occasionally serves as a cantor at a temple in Manhattan. 'We were friends. We'd walk to the bus every day after school, things like that. I think Barbara understood that Mr DePietto preferred me only because I had a light operatic voice. That was all there was to it.'

Barbara's friend from P.S. 89, Carolyn Bernstein, remembered watching her during Choral Club performances. 'There was always an expression on her face like she was dreaming that someday she would be alone, doing it all by herself.'

ON APRIL 22, 1956, as her daughter's fourteenth birthday present, Diana allowed Barbara to go into Manhattan with a friend, Anita Sussman, to see a Sunday matinee performance of *The Diary of Anne Frank*, the true story of a young Jewish girl's struggle to survive and become her own person in the midst of Nazi terrorism during World War II. Directed by Garson Kanin, the Broadway hit featured Susan Strasberg, the seventeen-year-old daughter of Actors Studio head Lee Strasberg, in the title role.

Barbara had wanted to see *My Fair Lady*, which had just opened to tremendous acclaim, but Diana thought the ticket prices too high. A matinee seat to *The Diary of Anne Frank*, in the last row of the balcony, cost just $1.89. Besides, Diana reasoned, this play was a serious work. It had won the Pulitzer Prize, and it represented an important piece of Jewish history.

The play left Barbara with deeply conflicted emotions. Although she was thrilled by the drama of the piece, she found the 'dreary setting' of the Frank family's attic hideaway depressing. Her own life was bleak enough; she would have much preferred the fantasy and glamour of a glittery, colorful musical. On the other hand, the similarities between Anne Frank and herself nearly overwhelmed her. 'We both loved the show,' Anita Sussman recalled. 'We cried when it was over. There were a lot of personal things in the play for Barbara.' Indeed, certain passages resonated for her. Had the author sat down expressly to write a play that would touch Barbara Streisand at fourteen, he could scarcely have come up with anything better than *The Diary of Anne Frank*.

Anne is thirteen when the play opens. She is a bright, precocious youngster fascinated by the world outside her family's suffocating hiding place. She dreams of living a glamorous life; she cuts movie star photos out of magazines and pins them to the wall next to her bed. She tells her father that he's the only person she loves. When he insists that she must love her mother as well, she replies, 'We have nothing in common. She doesn't understand me. Whenever I try to explain my views on life to her, she asks me if I'm constipated.'

Mrs Van Daan, whose family is hiding out with the Franks, admonishes Anne, 'Why do you have to show off all the time?' She adds that men don't like girls like Anne; they prefer 'domestic girls' who cook and sew. 'I'd cut my throat first!' Anne exclaims. 'I'd open my veins! I'm going to be remarkable . . . I'm going to be a famous dancer or singer . . . something wonderful!'

Barbara could have been watching herself on that stage, and she knew in her heart that she could have played Anne Frank at least as well as Susan Strasberg.

Back home, she fairly burst with excitement as she described the play to her mother. 'I could do that, Mama!' she exclaimed.

'Do what, dear?'

'Play that part – I could play Anne Frank. I *knew* what she was feeling!'

'Yes, dear.'

Barbara quieted down. Just as Mrs Frank hadn't understood Anne, Diana didn't seem to have a clue as to what was important to her. If she was going to make it, she'd have to make it entirely on her own. Barbara went over every detail of the play, mulled over each nuance of the young star's performance in her mind, as her resolve to become an actress hardened within her. 'I want to do so much,' Anne Frank had said near the end of her life. 'I want to go on living even after my death. Another birthday has gone by, so now I'm fifteen. Already I know what I want. I have a goal.'

A FEW DAYS later Barbara could barely believe her eyes when she saw a notice in the newspaper that the film director Otto Preminger was holding open auditions to select an unknown teenager to play Joan of Arc in his forthcoming film of George Bernard Shaw's play *Saint Joan*. There were parallels between Anne Frank and Joan, the seventeen-year-old French peasant girl who attempted to reclaim the French throne for its rightful heir, Charles VII, in 1429 by disguising herself as a man and leading the Dauphin's troops to a series of victories over the English. Both Anne and Joan were persecuted because of their religious beliefs, both were still teenagers when they were put to death by their enemies, and both had been elevated to sainthood – Anne's figurative, Joan's literal.

Oblivious to the fact that she was far too slight and skinny to be believable as someone who could lead men into battle, Barbara excitedly told her mother about the auditions, to be held the next Saturday at a hotel in Manhattan, and persuaded the skeptical Diana to take her. To prepare she read Shaw's play, checked biographies of Joan out of the library, and practiced day and night.

When mother and daughter arrived at the appointed time and place, both were shocked: hundreds of girls were milling about, hoping for a chance at movie stardom. A seeming eternity later Barbara read briefly for a panel of three Preminger assistants. Her reading was 'excellent,' one of them told her, and he added that she would hear from Mr Preminger's representatives within a few weeks if she had been chosen.

Day after day Barbara waited for the call that would tell her she had won the role. It never came. A few weeks later she read in Walter Winchell's gossip column that Preminger had chosen a conventionally pretty, fair-haired seventeen-year-old Iowa farm girl named Jean Seberg for the part. Heartbroken, Barbara moped around the house like a *farbissener* – a sullen, depressed person – for weeks.

Diana looked upon Seberg's selection as proof of her fear that Barbara was too much of a *mieskeit* ever to have the career she so craved. The MGM audition had been unsuccessful, and now this. She was afraid that Barbara would be continually rejected and that her spirit would surely be broken. It was now that Diana began actively to discourage Barbara's theatrical ambitions. Without hope of success, what kind of future would her daughter have? Constant disappointment? Failure? Financial insecurity? The thought made her heart heavy. Maybe Preminger's rejection would open Barbara's eyes to the truth. Maybe her daughter would come to her senses.

✦

BARBARA COMPLETED THE second half of her freshman year much as she had the first. She again had an excellent average (92.5), and her 98 average in Spanish won her an award for the highest freshman average in the language. She didn't participate in any extracurricular activities, although she did help collect money for the Choral Club's spring concert. Still, few of her classmates were willing to try to penetrate her insular, inner-directed world. She had some close friends – Susan Dwaorkowitz, Anita Sussman, Barbara Sankel – but it took a long time for her to make new ones. Her second term evaluation by her homeroom teacher neatly summed it up: Barbara, he noted, was 'self-centered.'

ON MAY 14, 1956, Louis Kind removed his belongings – including the television set – from apartment 4G, took a $20-per-week single room at the Saint George Hotel on Clark Street in Brooklyn, and never returned to the Vanderveer Estates. 'I thought it was my fault,' Barbra later said. 'And so did my mother.' The following September, Diana took Kind to court to win a legal separation and alimony payments, and accused him of abandonment and failure to support her or Roslyn. She was unable to work full-time while caring for Roslyn, she told the court, and she had so little money that the telephone had been disconnected. Oddly, Barbara's name appears nowhere in the lengthy court documents, although presumably Diana's need to support two underage children would have bolstered her case for alimony.

The legal papers reveal bitter domestic discord. Mrs Kind estimated that her problems with her husband had begun in January 1953 and continued thereafter 'throughout their married life.' Louis Kind, she charged, had 'engaged upon a general course of cruel and inhuman treatment' of her, 'consisting of many acts of persecution, abuse and neglect arising out of his unkind, harsh, unreasonable, capricious, inconsiderate, niggardly, nagging and vicious treatment.'

Further, Diana alleged, her husband stayed away from their home 'most of the day and night without proper excuse or purpose, either business or personal,' and returned home 'in the late hours of the night or the early hours of the morning,' leaving her 'at home alone, against her protests, and on some occasions staying away from the home . . . for weeks at a time.'

According to Diana, Kind associated 'openly with numerous women,' and his 'open and scandalous flaunting of his affairs with them' caused her great embarrassment. He used 'vile, obscene and scurrilous language,' and both threatened to and did physically assault her.

Kind denied all of Diana's allegations and threw a few of his own back at her. He accused her of 'constantly resorting to the use of vile and obscene language [and] nagging and embarrassing [him] both at home and in the presence of friends and relatives; failing to prepare meals for him when he returned from work and to provide for his welfare; flying into fits of rage without provocation and hurling objects at him and striking him on repeated occasions; and accusing [him] of consorting with other women, all of which accusations were malicious and untrue and known to [her] to be false when made.'

His absences, Kind explained, were caused by his need to work nights and weekends in order to meet Diana's 'ever increasing demands for money.' He concluded that he was unable to work because of illness and had only a small income from Social Security and rents from the rooming houses he owned. He was also responsible for $25 a week in child support from his previous marriage, he said, and could not afford to pay Diana alimony.

His health, Kind claimed, began to deteriorate in April 1956 when he 'became ill, suffered severe and rapid loss of weight, pain, dizziness, nausea and sleeplessness.' Justice Louis L. Friedman, after hearing the in-person testimony of both combatants in the stately oak-paneled Brooklyn Court House, granted Diana a decree of separation on May 2, 1957, and he was harsh in his assessment of Louis Kind. Barbara's stepfather, the judge believed, was 'a pathological liar. I think he testifies in any manner which he thinks will best fit his needs on the particular occasion, and that he would say anything if he felt that it would aid his cause.'

Friedman doubted Kind's claims of illness: 'I think a great deal of it was put on. I think he is a malingerer ... and I think [he] gave up his employment deliberately for the purpose of stopping his wife from getting any support. I think that [he] has other sources of income which are not disclosed, and apparently he is engaged in several different undertakings.' The judge ordered Kind to pay Diana $50 a week in alimony, but he also gave him the opportunity to be examined by a court-appointed doctor. When the doctor confirmed that Kind's health was indeed poor, Justice Friedman reduced the alimony award to $37 a week.

That wasn't very much, and once again Diana found herself a single mother struggling to make ends meet. Several of her neighbors were struck by just how careful she had to be with money now. Marvin Stein, a young man who worked in a produce store across the street, recalled that Mrs Kind 'used to come in with Barbara and her baby sister. Barbara was very thin, and the sister was very chubby. Barbara's mother was an *extremely* careful shopper. She would look at the prices, and if an item went up two or three cents she'd stay away from it. Sometimes she would stand there for what seemed like an eternity before deciding to buy one or two items. I can't tell you how cautious she was.'

Esther Waxman, who lived in the building adjacent to Diana's in the Vanderveer complex, recalled that 'Diana used to come into the laundry room in my building and try to sell undergarments – girdles and stockings and things like that – to supplement her income. She'd buy them at a wholesale house and try to resell them and make a little profit. I never bought anything from her, and I don't think many other people did either.'

Sometimes things got so bad that Diana told Barbara to go out into the lobby of their building and steal the bottles of milk left by the milkman outside their neighbors' doors.

IF LOUIS KIND'S permanent departure left Diana alone to struggle over a price increase of a few cents at the supermarket, at the same time it lifted a great weight from Barbara. No longer did she have to cower in fear as her stepfather hit her sobbing mother; no longer was he there to disparage her. Still, the financial problems hit Barbara hard too. The family had never had much money for anything but the barest necessities; now there was even less. Again they were left out of the country's economic boom that saw a television in nearly every home and a huge tail-finned car in many garages. 'I was so jealous of the rich Jewish girls in my school,' Barbra said, 'who always wore the latest clothes and had money to spend on whatever they wanted.'

With Diana working, Barbara would pick Roslyn up from school and baby-sit for her until her mother got home. She would rather have baby-sat for the Choys and made some money at it, but she loved caring for her baby sister. She had a strong maternal instinct, and the chubby, bubbly little girl who shared the living room sofa with her at night brought some real joy into her life. Barbara played with her, sang to her, tickled her back with her long red fingernails, and bribed her to stay quiet with coffee ice cream.

Whenever Barbara sang, Roslyn wanted to sing, too. Whenever Barbara danced, she wanted to dance. 'She taught me how to harmonize on "Row, Row, Row Your Boat,"' Roslyn recalled, 'and she taught me how to do the cha-cha, mambo, and lindy.' After she saw Barbara imitate a commercial in front of the bathroom mirror, she would race her into the bathroom every day and do a few of her own. But Roslyn found there was also something about *her* that fascinated Barbara: her face. 'She would take pictures of my profile. I was the fat but pretty one . . . Mama made me eat to compensate for Barbara's skinniness.'

With no father figure in her life, and with her mother out working, Barbara had far more freedom than most children her age. 'I didn't have any boundaries. I didn't have much discipline. We never ate together as a family; we never had time for a meal. I was a child of the streets. We played in the gutter, and when a car came, we moved out of the street. It was a tough childhood . . . I was kind of wild.' Once Diana ordered Barbara, stricken with chicken pox, to stay in bed. 'When she left, I just climbed out the window and went to play with my friends.' A younger neighbor, Cee Cee Cohen, recalled that Barbara's fire escape came in handy at other times, too. 'After school Barbara would have sock hops in her apartment. Kids would come over and listen to records and dance. They would time it so they'd be gone before Barbara's mother got home. But sometimes they had to scramble out the window and down the fire escape so she wouldn't catch them.'

THE FAMILY'S TIGHT finances left Barbara with few playthings. While the other kids in the neighborhood spent hours on their bicycles, Barbara had to use whatever she could for outdoor amusement. 'Someone gave me a pair of wooden shoes,' she recalled, 'and I schlepped all over East Flatbush in them. I ended up with blisters on the backs of my feet and bunions on my toes.'

Indoors, while her girlfriends served tea to their doll families, Barbara contented herself with games of her own devising. Several times a week she would go over to a friend's house after school to play 'Crack the Safe': Barbara would pick a number from the telephone book, dial it, and pretend she was the operator announcing a long-distance call. Then she would put on a different voice and say that she was calling from a radio program in Chicago.

'You have been selected to play "Crack the Safe"!' she'd proclaim. 'All you have to do is identify this tune, and you'll win one hundred dollars! But first, we have to break for a commercial.'

She would then affect a third voice to do an entire commercial for laundry detergent. Returning to the 'program,' her friend would place a record on the Victrola, and Barbara would give the 'contestant' thirty seconds to identify the song. 'Congratulations!' she'd chirp when the answer was correct. 'You're one hundred dollars richer!' She would then put her friend on the phone to get the address of the 'winner.' Finally the two conspirators, laughing merrily, would mail their unsuspecting victim one hundred dollars in Monopoly money.

On the weekends, with her mother home from work, Barbara had a less carefree time of it. Cee Cee Cohen felt that 'if there was any one person who could get to Barbara, it was her mother. Everything else could roll off her back. But Mrs Kind would embarrass Barbara in front of the other kids. She'd come down to where we were singing on the stoop and yell at her for not doing things around the house she was supposed to have done, that sort of thing. Barbara and her mother were always fighting with each other.'

For escape now, more and more, Barbara would go to the movies. Next door to Erasmus Hall there was a theater that usually played Italian films. 'I'd come out of school and go directly to this theater,' Barbra said. 'I never knew much about the films or who made them, and I didn't understand the language, but Italian films enchanted me. As a matter of fact, one of my most significant experiences was when I saw Eleonora Duse in an Italian film made in 1916. On every level it was extraordinary.'

She liked American movies too. On Saturday she'd attend matinees at the Loews' Kings Theater on Flatbush Avenue, a cavernous picture palace built in 1928 in a grand melange of Baroque, Art Deco, and Italianate styles dominated by a huge curving stairway with elaborate rococo banisters. 'I used to go there because they had the greatest ice cream,' Barbra said. 'They had these cones filled with ice cream that was *inside* the cone – there was nothing sticking out on top. Very unusual, I thought, and great. I didn't care what the movies were, it's just the ice cream was sensational.'

But the movies, whatever they were, usually enthralled her. That summer she saw *Guys and Dolls* and fell in love with Marlon Brando. 'I thought, What a *gorgeous* man!' On film, everything seemed perfect – even Damon Runyan's world of Broadway low-lifes. The clothes were colorful, the hairdos and makeup flawless, the streets pristine. 'Life was so beautiful in the movies,' she recalled. 'Handsome men, beautiful women falling in love, and music playing when they'd kiss.' She longed to be Jean Simmons and kiss Marlon Brando.

According to the manager of the theater, whenever Barbara left a movie starring Jerry Lewis, she would hang around the lobby and imitate the goofy, rubber-faced comedian to the delight of the other patrons.

The glittery movie worlds that entranced her so made her own life in that small apartment with no telephone and no room of her own seem all the worse. 'My mother used to hate it when I went to the movies, because I was always grouchy for a couple of days afterward. All I remember of those Saturday afternoons was walking out into the grim reality of a hot New York summer and not having enough money to [take the bus] back home.' She would approach a policeman, put on her most forlorn face, and ask, 'Could you tell me how I could walk to Nostrand and Newkirk?' The patrolman would invariably tell her to wait rather than embark on such a long trek on foot. When the bus came he would tell the driver to let her on for free and give her a transfer. 'It was really great,' Barbra recalled. 'I would save the ten cents!'

DURING THE SECOND half of her sophomore year, Barbara learned about the Malden Bridge Playhouse in Malden Bridge, New York. Its artistic director, John Hale, was on the lookout for young apprentices to spend the summer toiling in all aspects of the theater. Applicants had to be over seventeen and would be judged on the basis of a letter explaining their desire to be involved in summer stock. Those accepted would be charged $300 the season for room and board.

Lying about her age, Barbara wrote to Hale about her ambition to become an actress, about how much she wanted to learn everything she could about the theater. The letter persuaded Hale to meet with Barbara when he visited New York City. During the interview, her fervor – or perhaps it was her chutzpah – led him to take her on, and he told her to be in Malden Bridge as soon as school let out early in June.

Diana balked. Barbara was too young, she insisted, to go so far away by herself. She'd be gone too long. She'd never fit in with the company, all of whom would be older than she. Barbara, of course, wouldn't take no for an answer. She begged, she flew into a rage, she cried, and Diana realized that if she didn't let Barbara go, there would be no living with her that summer. But there was another problem: money. Diana didn't have $300, but she did have the modest legacy of $150 that Grandfather Rosen had left Barbara in his will. Diana had set that money aside for her daughter's college education. She told Barbara that in order to go to Malden Bridge, she would have to use the money earmarked for college. She strongly advised her not to do that.

Without a second thought, Barbara decided to let college be damned, and Diana resigned herself to the inevitable. 'As long as she'll be happier there and doing something she wants to do,' she sighed to a friend.

BARBARA ARRIVED AT Malden Bridge the second week of June 1957. Her first sight of the rustic wooden three-hundred-seat playhouse, a converted barn, thrilled her: this was where she would be *working* for the next three months! She settled happily into her living arrangements at the Lodge, a two-story barnlike building with rough-hewn wooden beams overhead, wooden tables and benches for meals, and a family of raccoons under the floor.

Upstairs, the six female apprentices slept in a dormlike bedroom that the boys referred to as the Cherry Orchard. One of the apprentices was Ingrid Meighan, and her memories of her first encounter with Barbara have remained fresh. 'I was in the bathroom, brushing my teeth. She walked over and without saying "Excuse me, can I get in here?" she shoved her elbow into me and pushed me aside. It was like, "Shove over, kid!" And that's the kind of person she was. I'm sorry to say that she was a little Brooklyn brat.'

Barbara rarely joined in with the other girls to talk about boys and family and personal problems. 'When she did open up,' Ingrid said, 'she had the attitude, "Me first! I'm gonna get where I'm going no matter what. And nobody's gonna get in my way."' Whenever dinner was served, especially spaghetti, Ingrid noticed that Barbara 'would always edge toward the front of the line in hopes that the food wouldn't give out before she was served. She wasn't a popular person. But she was very determined.'

The apprentices worked hard, but acted very little. 'We literally worked from eight in the morning until after the performance at night,' Ingrid recalled. The kids swept out the theater, scrubbed the toilets, hammered scenery, scrubbed flats, took tickets, and ushered the patrons to their seats. For every production, they'd tumble into an old De Soto hearse with questionable brakes and rattle across the countryside in search of cheap props. Dress rehearsals usually went until three in the morning, and after every performance the cast would hop around to a local nightspot to drink and eat sandwiches. 'We would get awfully punchy,' Ingrid said.

Emily Cobb, a leading lady in the regular company, recalled Barbara singing 'Tammy' late one night outside the dormitory while she scrubbed down a scenery flat. 'Finally I stuck my head out the window and screamed, "Barbara, will you *shut up!*"'

Barbara's fascination with the work of the lighting man led him to take her under his wing and teach her all he knew. Finally, toward the end of the summer, he allowed her to do the lighting for one of the plays; she made copious notes about cues and colors and coordination.

The only job Barbara groused about, Ingrid said, was scrubbing flats. 'It was a very messy job. You had to use a hose and wet down these flats laid across two sawhorses, then scrub them with a brush. All this horrible scummy paint would come off and you'd be into it up to your elbows. I remember Barbara going "Ecch!," throwing her hands up in the air and whining, "I'm not going to do this anymore!"'

BARBARA STAYED BEHIND the scenes for the first two plays that summer. She watched the experienced actors in the company and studied every nuance of their technique. Her eyes and ears missed no aspect of John Hale's direction. Finally, after three weeks of manual labor, she got her chance to act, in John Patrick's *Teahouse of the August Moon*. She had begged Hale to let her play the pivotal role of Sakini, the young male narrator of the piece, essayed the year before on screen by her idol Marlon Brando, but this time Barbara's chutzpah wasn't enough. Instead Hale gave her a small role as one of the Japanese children, and she turned out to be an audience pleaser when she

led a goat across the stage to delighted laughter and applause. The bit
warranted a mention in the local newspaper's review of the show – her
first critical notice. After the final curtain, Barbara cleaned up the goat's
droppings with a dustpan and broom.

The playhouse's next production, *The Desk Set*, presented July 16 through
21, gave Barbara her first meaty role: Elsa, a man-crazy secretary. She gave it
her all, recalling every flirtatious move she had ever seen any woman make,
in or out of the movies. 'Can't you just see me at fifteen,' she later said with
a laugh, 'coming on the stage, sitting down on a desk, swinging my leg and
playing sexy?' A local reviewer thought she pulled it off quite well. 'Barbara
Streisand,' he wrote, 'turns in a fine performance as the office vamp. *Down
boys!*' The *Chatham Courier* critic called her 'a fine young comedienne' and
added, 'We hope [Mr Hale] gives this young lady more of an opportunity
in future productions.'

He didn't, but Barbara's delight carried her through the following five
weeks even though she didn't have another speaking part in the next four
productions. So immersed had she become in her greasepaint heaven that she
never thought to write her mother. 'I had to contact the director,' Diana said,
'to find out how she was.' When Barbara finally did write early in August,
she gave her mother the alarming news that the playhouse cook had left in
a huff because he hadn't been paid. Diana was certain her daughter was near
starvation. 'Can you imagine how I felt hearing such news, when what she
needed most was good food and rest to go on with her studies in the fall?'

Perhaps it was Mrs Kind who spilled the beans about Barbara's age during
one of her phone calls to John Hale. 'John was very upset,' Ingrid Meighan
recalled. 'He got very nervous because the work was so hard and the hours
so long that the playhouse had to be in violation of child labor laws!'

DURING THE LAST week of the season, John Hale made good on a promise
to the apprentices and gave them a matinee production all their own,
Picnic, William Inge's Pulitzer Prize-winning romantic drama set in a small
Kansas town. Stanley Beck, a good-looking, muscular twenty-four-year-old
member of the regular company, directed the show, to be performed
outdoors. Earlier Ingrid had noticed that Beck seemed to have taken
a shine to Barbara. 'There was definitely something there. He used
to stare at her a lot. But at that point she was just too young, you
know?' (Three years later, when Barbara was of age, Beck would make
his move.) Beck gave Barbara the choice part of the teenage tomboy
Millie Owens, who wants to be more like her beautiful older sister. Ingrid
Meighan, five years older than Barbara, played her mother. 'Barbara was

quite good,' Ingrid felt. 'She wore a baseball cap and chewed gum and whined a lot.'

The production proved 'a disaster,' according to Ingrid. 'John Hale had pretty much lost control of the playhouse by then, and our evening audiences were dwindling. At the three matinees we did over the last weekend, we had maybe twenty, thirty people in the audience.' Before the last performance on Sunday, Ingrid recalled, a black Cadillac drove up alongside the stage. A tall, balding man got out and slipped into a back row seat. 'About halfway through the performance, somebody whispered offstage, "William Inge is here!" We were all flabbergasted,' Ingrid said. 'He didn't stay very long. I'm sure he sat there and said to himself, "Oh, dear."'

On the last day of the season, the company threw a farewell party. Barbara partook liberally of the punch, which was spiked. Emily Cobb recalled what ensued: 'Barbara started looking a little green, so she excused herself and said she was going to lie down. I was concerned about her, so I followed her to the dormitory. When I got there she had vomited all over the floor and she lay on the bed, moaning. I got a mop and started cleaning up. She struggled to an upright position and protested, "Emily, no, you can't be cleaning up after me. You're a leading lady and I'm just an apprentice!"'

THE NEXT DAY Barbara took a bus back to Brooklyn, and the most stimulating, exciting summer of her life so far drew to a close. 'I had such a *wonderful* time!' she burbled to her mother. 'Well, she finally got home,' Diana later said, 'and I thought she was cured of her acting ideas. But no way.'

When she got back to school the second week of September, the halls of Erasmus seemed bleaker than ever. Barbara had tasted real theater, had bathed in the glow of a paying audience's applause. A theater critic had implied she was *sexy!* She felt she *had* to continue what she'd started at Malden Bridge. There could be no turning back. Despite the demands of school, she auditioned for the role of Ethel Merman's daughter in *Happy Hunting*, a musical based on the marriage of Grace Kelly and Prince Rainier of Monaco. She didn't get the part.

A few weeks later she read about a year-round apprenticeship program at the Cherry Lane Theater in Greenwich Village. Without her mother's knowledge, she took the subway into Manhattan the next Saturday to audition, and she was accepted. This time Diana argued that Barbara couldn't possibly work at a theater in Manhattan several nights after school and on weekends and still keep up her grade average, but Barbara assured her mother that she would – 'If I don't get good grades, I'll quit.' Once again Diana relented and, rather remarkably, allowed her fifteen-year-old daughter, barely a high school junior, to join the bohemian world of the off-Broadway theater.

Barbara could not have anticipated the impact her sojourn at the Cherry Lane Theater would have on her life. There she would meet an acting mentor who would influence her life and career for years to come. She would develop a maturity far beyond her years. And with the help of a handsome twenty-three-year-old fellow acting student, she would experience the joys of sexual awakening.

4

The people who surrounded Barbara in Manhattan that fall of 1957 were actors to the core. They sat in Greenwich Village coffee shops quoting Shakespeare and arguing about Jean Genet. They wore black sweatshirts and berets and trench coats; they drank espresso and smoked Gitanes. They'd analyze the films of Fellini and Bergman and vow never to sell out to Hollywood. They were bohemian and liberal and free-spirited, sexually unconstrained and intellectually exuberant. And fifteen-year-old Barbara Streisand hungrily soaked up every ounce of their ambience and intelligence and creative ardor like the culturally starved sponge that she was.

THINGS DIDN'T BEGIN all that promisingly for Barbara at the Cherry Lane Theater, however. Three evenings a week after school, and on weekends, she traipsed to the Village by subway to help out with their production of Sean O'Casey's *Purple Dust*, which had been running for months. Mostly she swept floors and scurried out to pick up food for the cast and 'stayed on book,' holding the script offstage and throwing lines to anyone who forgot them. During lulls she did her homework. 'I called myself the assistant stage manager,' she said. An overstatement to be sure, but she was thrilled nonetheless just to work in a real off-Broadway theater, even without a chance to act. Noel Behn, the manager of the theater, later remembered Barbara only as 'a dirty little girl who was always running around humming.'

Anita Miller, the wife of the acting coach Allan Miller, played Avril in the show, and while Barbara has said she understudied Avril, Anita recalled that the production didn't have understudies. Still, as the weeks wore on,

Anita grew fascinated by this singular teenager. 'She was stagestruck and lifestruck,' Anita recalled. 'She had a voracious mind. She wanted to know what everything was, what everything meant. She was like someone who had been starved.'

More than she knew, Anita was right about Barbara. She was hungry for knowledge, for encouragement, for acceptance, and she latched on to Anita, who listened to her and answered her questions and came to strongly believe in her talent. Before long, Anita urged her husband to take this extraordinary girl into his acting classes. 'I don't want to talk to her,' he replied. 'I'm not going to talk to a fifteen-year-old about being in the theater. It's too hard. She's too young.'

Allan Miller preferred not to work with young people because, as he explained it, 'most teenagers are in such a state of flux about their own identities that to try to get them into emotional areas where they can truly express themselves is very difficult. But Anita kept bringing her name up to me.'

Barbara soon asked Anita to be her partner in a scene she wanted to do for an audition at the Actors Studio. Anita and Allan were both members of Lee Strasberg's cadre of Method actors, and Anita reminded Barbara that the minimum age for admission was eighteen. Barbara said she only wanted to 'practice for the real thing,' but she probably planned to lie about her age again.

Barbara chose a scene from N. Richard Nash's *The Young and Fair*, a drama set in a private girls' junior college, in which a troubled student tries to persuade a teacher to sanction the vigilante group she has created to catch a dormitory burglar. Why the material appealed to Barbara is clear: at one point her character says, 'Once I was an ugly little kid – afraid of everything – always scared! When my parents were divorced, I lived alone . . . I'd be alone at school and I'd be alone at home.' Anita found Barbara's reading of the scene 'fantastic' and thought it revealed 'tremendous talent.' Still, Barbara wasn't welcomed into the Actors Studio. 'I couldn't understand why they didn't accept her,' Anita said, 'unless they found out she was too young.'

Anita persisted with her husband, who remained implacable. Finally she invited Barbara to dinner at their apartment on Fifty-fourth Street near Sixth Avenue. Barbara chattered nonstop throughout the meal, asking Miller an avalanche of questions. At first he looked aghast at this 'creature' and thought, Oh, my God, if this was my kid I'd get her some good clothes to wear and cut down on her crazy eccentricities. He considered her 'a misbegotten, misshapen, skinny little nudnik' – a nuisance.

And yet as the evening progressed, Miller found himself agreeing with Anita's assessment of this girl as 'valuable and dazzling and interesting':

'There was no question that she had something special. She had an insatiable desire to know everything that anyone around her could impart, from acting to world politics to raising a kid. I had never been around a teenager who was so willing to expose herself as ignorant, to admit she didn't know something. She'd keep saying, "Can I ask you something?" It was not simpleminded openness and hunger. She was intellectually keen and very alive. I found myself wanting to convey to her everything I knew, make her feel loved and wanted. She was so hungry for nurturing – emotional as well as intellectual and spiritual.'

After dinner Anita announced that she and Barbara had a surprise for Allan, and they performed the scene from *The Young and Fair*. Barbara's reading, Miller thought, 'was the worst I think I've ever seen in my life. I couldn't believe that anyone could be so ignorant of acting technique that her arms and body would contort and do things that had nothing to do with the emotional life she was trying to project. The vocal patterns were equally disconnected. Nothing linked together.' Still Barbara impressed Miller. 'She was trying to achieve something but didn't have the tools to do it. I was dumbstruck by the ferocity of this young woman. I found myself wanting to help her.'

EARLY IN 1958 Miller took the delighted Barbara into his workshop, a part of the Theater Studio of New York on West Forty-eighth Street, in exchange for baby-sitting with his two sons (Barbara called this a 'scholarship'). The other students included Elaine Sobel, an Audrey Hepburn type with a sensitive spirit and a fluency in Yiddish; Bob Venier, an Alain Delon look-alike who had acted opposite Marilyn Monroe at the Actors Studio; Simon Gribben, a nineteen-year-old who was not really sure he wanted to be an actor; Davey Marlin Jones, an aspiring director; and Roy Scott, a short, handsome twenty-three-year-old in the Brad Davis mold who originally wanted to be a priest.

'We all loved Roy,' Elaine Sobel recalled. 'He was absolutely *gorgeous!*' Scott immediately felt attracted to and protective toward Barbara, who seemed to him 'very sweet, sensitive and shy. She was afraid of everything, and easily hurt. She was very plain, but I found her wondrous in her own way, with her big, beautiful eyes, her bone structure. There was sweetness and beauty inside her. She reminded me almost of a doe, a fawn.'

For months Barbara merely watched as the other actors performed scenes. 'She was very afraid,' Roy Scott felt. 'And very shy – too shy, really.' Occasionally she asked a question, but mostly she learned by watching.

'I learned what not to do,' she has said. 'Not learned deliberately, but subconsciously it seeped into my head.'

When she finally began to do scenes, Miller wouldn't allow her to speak during any of them. 'What I discovered very quickly with Barbara was that all the intellectual concepts about acting in the world would not help her act. So I began working with her purely physically. She had to make only sounds in her exercises, no words. I wanted her to make a connection between what was happening to her viscerally, without words interfering.'

One of her exercises required her to be a chocolate chip cookie baking in an oven, and she stunned her classmates with her expressiveness. As she was put in the oven, she let her body go limp and motionless. Then, as the heat built around her, she jumped to jerky life. She huffed and wheezed as the dough expanded and steam puffed out. Then she began to wilt and finally fell limp again as the cookie took its final baked shape. 'She was impressive,' Roy Scott said. 'We were Method actors, so we learned to have everything come from within.'

Barbara pestered Miller for months to let her do a speaking role, and finally he was pleased enough with her progress that he suggested a scene from Tennessee Williams's *The Rose Tattoo*, in which a young girl tries to get her sailor boyfriend to make love to her. Because her mother has made him promise that he won't sleep with her, he tries to deflect her advances. Barbara read the play and called Miller the next day. 'Hey, listen!' she said. 'I can't do *that* scene.'

'Why not?'

'Well, *you know*.'

'She meant she was a virgin,' Miller said. 'She didn't have any experience to base her performance on. I told her, "Listen, I want you to find some way of behaving in this scene without it having anything to do with sex," and I hung up.'

Barbara rehearsed the scene with a boy from class for about a week, but the night they performed it she shocked him by doing it totally differently. 'At one point he stood up,' she said, 'and I stood on his feet; one time I jumped on his back; one time I pretended I was blind, and while I was talking I was touching his face. It was this awkward sexuality.' Barbara had planned none of this. 'I didn't know what I would do next. I was as interested as the people watching.'

When the scene was over, Barbara's partner stood crimson-faced with embarrassment while the rest of the class cheered. 'It was a great scene,' Miller felt. 'She looked like a girl in the most extreme heat who didn't have the faintest idea how to behave toward a boy, which is exactly what the material called for.' Miller asked her to explain what she had been trying to do. She mumbled something, and he asked her to speak up. 'Louder, come on, say it.'

'I tried to touch every part of his body with every part of my body, without ever touching the same part twice.'

'And she did, too,' Miller recalled. 'She used the spaces between her fingers, her armpits, her neck, her eyelids, her feet. It was quite startling, believe me.'

According to Elaine Sobel, this intensity and unpredictability made the other students nervous about doing scenes with Barbara. 'People didn't like to work with her in class. Especially the guys. They were intimidated by her. She was relentless in her desire to learn. She would focus so completely that it was like "All of you can just float away."'

Before long, the girl who had performed the worst audition Miller had ever seen had become his star pupil – and his surrogate daughter. 'She started meeting me after class and going home with me on the bus. I literally began coaching her every day.' She began to sleep over at the Millers' whenever she baby-sat for them, rather than take the subway back to Brooklyn; she immersed herself in their impressive collection of books on theater, art, culture. 'She liked the way we lived,' Allan Miller said.

None of this sat well with Diana, Miller recalled. 'Her mother would call me on the phone and scream at me. She'd say, "You're ruining my daughter's life. You have no right to do this! She's only sixteen years old!" At one point she accused me of putting Barbara into white slavery! She was really something, the mother.'

'Her mother disapproved of everything Barbara did, especially the theater or any of the arts,' Anita said. 'Sometimes I would give Barbara clothes I was no longer wearing because she didn't have the money to buy her own. Her mother threw them out. I guess she was jealous of the role we were playing in Barbara's life.'

IF MRS KIND only *knew*. Barbara bunking with the Millers was the least of it. For with the help of Roy Scott, a lack of sexual experience was no longer a hindrance to Barbara's range as an actress. As Simon Gribben related it, 'Barbara was just one of the girls on tap for Roy. She was just someone he did, so to speak. I mean, she was much more hung up on him than he was on her.'

Scott holds far more romantic memories. 'We had very, very deep feelings for each other. I was probably the first man she ever loved. I gave her her first kiss. Everything was just exquisite.' Sexually, Scott found Barbara unadventuresome but 'inquisitive.' He thought of her as 'a beautiful, budding rose. She was growing up, dawning, learning to be a woman.'

How thrilling it must have been for Barbara, convinced she was unappealing, unsure that any man would ever desire her, to have the best-looking man in her acting class become her lover. 'She thought she was ugly, with her nose and all,' Scott recollected. 'I would tell her no, that she was a very pretty and attractive girl.'

Now Barbara would spend many of her nights at Scott's tiny eight-dollar-a-week apartment in the Park Savoy, a residence hotel for performers on Fifty-eighth Street. 'We would talk until all hours of the night,' Scott recalled. 'We would talk about acting, singing. We'd talk about life, what it was all about. She was very much into politics and very much caring about the children of the world and the people of the world. Everything affected her.'

Barbara began to go to the New York Public Library's main branch at Fifty Avenue and Forty-second Street and listen to old recordings of popular music. 'She'd say, "Roy, I listen to all these great singers for hours and try to learn their techniques." She'd listen to the jazz singers: Ella Fitzgerald, Billie Holiday – all of them. I don't think Barbara cared really whether she was an actress or a singer. She just wanted to be in show business.'

SOMEHOW, BARBARA'S MOTHER found out about her romance with Roy Scott. She badgered Barbara to end it, but she refused. Diana accosted Davey Marlin Jones outside Miller's class one day and pleaded with him to intercede and persuade Roy to stop seeing Barbara. Jones ignored the request. Then Diana took a new approach.

One evening, as Roy and Barbara practiced a scene from a play, Roy's mother and aunt paid him a surprise visit. 'It turned into a beautiful evening,' Roy recalled. 'They cooked us a great dinner, and we sat around for three or four hours talking and singing and having a hell of a good time.'

Then the phone rang, and Roy's mother answered it. Diana, nearly hysterical, demanded that Barbara come home immediately and yelled, 'I don't want her with that man!' Mrs Scott explained who she was and that they were in the middle of an innocent evening. 'I don't care!' Diana shrieked. 'My daughter's too young to be involved with your son! Put her on the phone!'

'Your mother wants to talk to you, Barb,' Mrs Scott gently informed her.

When Barbara came back into the dining room, she was crying profusely. 'I've got to go,' she told Scott.

'I walked her to the subway and she was just inconsolable about everything,' he recalled. 'She said, "Your mother doesn't like me. My mother doesn't want me to be with you. What am I going to do?" It was a mess, just dreadful. I did my best to calm her down. Her mother tried to control her too much, to protect her too much. And yes, it hurt our relationship.'

DESPITE THE WORLDLINESS Barbara had attained in the sophisticated milieu of the New York theater set, back in Brooklyn she remained a high school student. But by the end of her junior year, there had been such a marked change in her that her classmates barely recognized her. Cynthia Roth recalled that just about every day now Barbara wore 'a black sweater and a black skirt, black stockings, black shoes, and a black leather bag. It was enough to be scary to some young people!'

'She *was* strange,' Mike Lubell thought. 'She wore odd-colored nail polish and lipstick – like purple, things that girls at that time simply didn't wear. And when I say purple, it ran toward a shade of hot pink. It drew people's attention to her.'

Barbara had purposely set herself apart. 'I dressed the way I did to show everybody that I didn't care what they thought of me. I didn't know then that I really did. I always felt alone, a person apart from others.' Her closest friend at school now was Susan Dwaorkowitz, perhaps the only girl at Erasmus who was odder than Barbara. Susan 'used to wear pasty white makeup,' Barbra recalled. 'Pasty-face, I used to call her . . . She used to wear spaghetti shoes and black stockings, and had a black pixie haircut. So we gravitated toward each other. We were both pretty weird. But I liked the way we dressed. I thought everybody else looked terrible!'

It was around this time that Barbara set Erasmus abuzz with her choice of a boyfriend. A classmate, Ron Girsch, recalled that 'she was going out with a black guy and was one of the first girls to do so, and I thought that fit her. His name was Teddy, and they used to walk around together hand in hand. That was pretty shocking in those days, believe me.'

Many of Barbara's classmates considered her arrogant. 'My memories of Barbara are not pleasant,' Henya Novick said. 'She was inaccessible, disinterested in us and in school. She had one goal – to make it – and this she pursued with a frenzy. She was constantly reading *Variety* and going to auditions. She was a cold, aloof individual, not the stuff that friendships are made from.'

Other students, like Roberta Johnson, understood Barbara. 'She really wasn't a teenager. She had her mind on something else. I don't think she was arrogant or felt superior. She was simply occupied with something other than the usual teenage concerns.'

Barbara took only one acting class at Erasmus, an Honors English course called Radio Dramatics during the spring semester of her junior year. 'Whenever she got up,' Harry Myers recalled, 'no matter what she did, whether she was going for a funny shtick or something serious, we would all sit there spellbound. We always looked forward to her readings.'

Jane Soifer's strongest recollection of Barbara in the class is of her performance as the nurse in *Romeo and Juliet*. 'It was a comedy monologue, and she was *fabulous*. She was so good, this feeling washed over me: *Wow*, this girl's really talented. She could *do* something with this.'

Barbara also played the terrorized wife in a scene from *Dial M for Murder*, a role made famous on the screen by Grace Kelly. According to Roberta Johnson, her performance was 'astonishing. I was so impressed with how well she communicated the woman's fear.' Her Radio Dramatics teacher, Mrs Thrall, noted on Barbara's permanent record that she evinced 'real dramatic talent' and was a 'fine, cooperative person,' although she needed 'frequent encouragement.'

Still, 'silly student productions' did little to fulfill Barbara. She couldn't wait to get back into the heady theatrical world she had known with Allan Miller. Toward the end of her junior year she made it clear to her grade adviser, Mrs Cameron, that she had no intention of going on to college. The woman called Barbara and her mother to her office for a meeting. 'Your child has *got* to go to college,' she told Mrs Kind. 'She has a ninety-one average. It would be such a waste.'

When her mother agreed, Barbara stood up without a word and walked out of the room. By now, Mrs Kind knew better than to press Barbara, and on March 18, she wrote to Mrs Cameron granting her permission for Barbara to double up on her subjects so that she could graduate six months early. This, Mrs Kind wrote, would free Barbara up so that she could attain 'further [acting] experience in the city.'

THAT SUMMER OF 1958, Allan and Anita Miller asked Barbara to accompany them to Charlotte Harmon's Clinton Playhouse in Clinton, Connecticut, so that she could baby-sit for them. Although Barbara later claimed on her résumé that she was part of the company, both Allan and Anita insist she came along only to take care of their sons and did no work of any kind at the theater.

But while she was there she befriended another aspiring young actor, the handsome twenty-year-old Warren Beatty, who had been cast in major roles in most of the productions and stood poised on the verge of Broadway and television stardom. Occasionally Warren would join her while she baby-sat; they'd eat spaghetti and laugh and talk about the theater. 'She seemed to be a person of strong moral convictions,' he said. 'One of her convictions seemed to be that with the recent loss of my virginity, I might be experiencing too much of a good thing.'

Beatty also found her 'critical, encouraging . . . she had energy, she was funny, she was uninhibited by convention or tradition, she was sexy, she was honest.'

Beatty's remark about Barbara's saying he was having 'too much of a good thing' sexually might indicate that she rejected a pass from him. If she did, it wasn't because she didn't find him devastatingly attractive. Thirteen years would pass, however, before she and Warren did anything about their mutual attraction.

SHORTLY BEFORE CHRISTMAS, as Barbara prepared for her final exams and graduation from Erasmus, she answered a casting ad in *Show Business* for a new play to be presented quite far off Broadway in an attic space called the Garret Theater. She got the role – her first 'real' acting assignment.

Joan Rivers, then Joan Molinsky, was also in the cast, and she wrote about the experience at length in her 1986 autobiography *Enter Talking*. The play, she said, was called *Seawood* and was written by Armand de Beauchamp, a pretentious, flamboyant man who boasted that its 1954 Chicago production had launched the careers of Ralph Meeker and Geraldine Page. The characters had no names, but were called things like Man from the Sea and Lorna of the Dunes. After the few people who had turned up for the audition were cast except for her, Joan went on, there remained just one unfilled role – the one originally played by Ralph Meeker. Thinking on her feet, Joan piped up, 'Why couldn't we make Man in Black into Woman in Black? She could be a lesbian.' The author loved the idea, Joan wrote, and as the Woman in Black, she went on to play 'a big love scene where I told Barbara I loved her very much and she rejected me and I had a knife in my hand and tried to kill her and then myself.'

All this made for entertaining reading, but almost none of it is true. In fact the play was entitled *Driftwood* and was written by Maurice Tei Dunn. Geraldine Page had starred in a Chicago production in 1954, but while Ralph Meeker had tried out, he had lost the co-starring role to Edward Fielding Nicholls.

More important, according to Dunn, 'There was no lesbianism in my play. I can't imagine where Joan got that. In those days it would have been suicide in the theater. Barbara and Joan never had a single exchange together. They were never even onstage at the same time. That picture of them together in Joan's book was posed during rehearsals.'

The script of *Driftwood* bears Dunn out. The story revolved around Gregg Williams, an ex-con-turned-beachcomber along the shores of Lake Michigan in northern Indiana in 1924. Gregg is in love with Anne Carey, who has escaped from the clutches of a Chicago millionaire by pretending to be dead and now lives as Diana of the Dunes. A free spirit, she swims in the nude and, in the words of another character – the outraged Miss Blake, an uptight property owner who wants to run Diana out of the community – 'goes in for pagan dancing in the light of the full moon.'

Joan played Miss Blake, and she did brandish a knife – but at Diana, not at Barbara's character, Lorna. Lorna's a tough cookie, a hard-bitten thirty-five-year-old who hangs out at Bob White's saloon. As one unsophisticated character puts it, 'She make men bad.' Lorna has had a mysterious prior relationship with Gregg Williams, who may or may not now be involved in a series of truck hijackings along the interstate. In the course of the play's three acts, Miss Blake tries to stab Diana (but not herself as well); Gregg shoots dead Chuck, a luckless visitor he thinks is a stool pigeon; and Diana stabs Gregg to death.

There are oblique references to an enigmatic Woman in Black who helped Gregg make a second escape from prison, where he had been sent for shooting Chuck, and ominous whispers about the Chief, said to be the mastermind behind the hijackings.

Driftwood, as Maurice Tei Dunn freely admits, won't stand among the great plays, but it must have been fun to watch Barbara Streisand, at sixteen, play a character like Lorna. She had only one short scene in the first act, none in the second, and she didn't reappear until the last ten minutes of the play. But during those ten minutes the audience learns that Lorna is the key to everything when she reveals that she is not only the Woman in Black but also the Chief!

'Yer forgettin' yer in a tough spot,' Lorna hisses at Gregg. 'I wouldn't give a nickel for yer chances if they was to pick you up now and take you back to the Pen.' A few moments later, speaking of Diana, she says, 'You and I were pretty thick until she came along. You pulled a boner in that Chuck business. You shoulda used yer head and not let your feelings get mixed up in it . . . I'm gettin' fed up with yer takin' her part. I'm the one that got you outta jail. She'd let you rot there . . . Such dam' fools – if you'da listened to me you wouldn't have been sent up at all. You and yer moon-struck Diana!'

Dunn didn't consider it at all inappropriate to cast the teenage Barbara Streisand as Lorna. 'There was something, shall we say, sinister about Barbara, mysterious. Even at that age she seemed a lot older than she was. She seemed to have a history, a past.' He felt that Barbara's performances were 'credible and occasionally remarkable. She was *acting*. Joan was effective, although she really was just being herself. Barbara was more professional than Joan, and she was only a schoolgirl! I saw Barbara and Joan work on scenes together and they looked like friends, but I wonder if Barbara didn't think Joan was a nuisance.'

What Dunn called the Garret Theater was in fact the rickety unheated attic of his fifth-floor walk-up railroad flat on Forty-ninth Street in the shadow of the Third Avenue El. According to him, when rehearsals began on January 2, Barbara 'confiscated the star dressing room,' a closet with a sink and a large mirror, by always arriving before everyone else. 'She doted on herself in there and mouthed out her lines. Sometimes she stood in the doorway and shouted her lines out to me or someone else, and they'd answer. She carried her own makeup kit around with her, and always came in carrying a big bag of books because she was studying for her finals.'

Directed by a seventeen-year-old, Jim McDowall, *Driftwood* opened on Thursday, January 15, on a one-step-up platform stage that faced forty seats, most of which Dunn had purchased from a defunct shoe store. Admission was $1.50, but the box-office receipts barely covered expenses and didn't allow for pay to the actors. Nor was there a crew, paid or unpaid. Barbara offered to work the curtain during her extended periods offstage, but Dunn did that himself and told her, 'An actress is an actress, and you don't have to do anything here except worry about what you're doing onstage.'

Although the play didn't garner a single review, it remained open for six weeks, primarily on the strength of ticket sales to the cast's family and friends. Barbara's mother attended one performance, but her reaction remains unrecorded. Dunn's main reason for closing the show was that his attic became a fire hazard when audience members started putting their cigarettes out in the cracks in the wooden floor. 'When I shut down the show it was a terrible blow to the cast. Barbara just packed her stuff and walked away and never came back. She took it hard.'

DURING THE RUN of *Driftwood*, Barbara graduated from Erasmus Hall, receiving her diploma along with 136 others in a ceremony on January 26, 1959. She was three months shy of her seventeenth birthday. She was the fourth best student in the graduating class, with a final three-and-a-half-year grade-point average of 91.016.

Finally she was free. Within weeks of her graduation she moved to Manhattan, her mother's protests ringing in her ears along with her tinnitus. She and Susan Dwaorkowitz rented a tiny walk-up at 339 West Forty-eighth Street, next door to Allan Miller's workshop, for $80 a month, and Barbara could barely contain her excitement as she prepared to look for work as an actress. She was sure she'd get a part straightaway, but if it took a little longer than she expected, she had a few hundred dollars she had saved over the years from her pay at Choy's Chinese. The nest egg, which she put into her first savings account, at the Seaman's Bank, would provide her with the luxury of free time to make the rounds of auditions.

She typed up a résumé that listed her height at five feet five, her weight at 110 pounds, and her type as either ingenue or character ingenue. She listed her schooling with Allan Miller, her summer stock work at Malden Bridge, and *Driftwood*. She fibbed that she had played Ellie May in *Tobacco Road* at the Clinton Playhouse and lied again that she has been the assistant stage manager at the Cherry Lane and had understudied Avril in *Purple Dust*. Then she set out on her rounds – after stuffing socks into her bra and toilet paper along her hips to give the illusion of a more voluptuous figure.

She found the auditioning process numbing, dehumanizing, mortifying. She would trudge through the cold, dirty streets of Manhattan, climb stairs to dinky little offices, and mill around with dozens of other would-be actors just to read for the walk-on part of a beatnik. The casting people would take one look at her and ask if she had done anything else professionally. 'No,' she'd reply.

'Well, we have to see your work before we can hire you.'

'Why do you have to see my work?' she recalled asking them. 'It's a walk-on. I don't even have to say anything!'

'We have to see some work.'

'How are you going to see my work if you don't give me a chance to *do* the work?' But it was useless to argue. Over and over again she went through this charade, and whether she realized it at the time or not, the work prerequisite was just an excuse. Most casting directors didn't let her read because they didn't like her looks. Even when she auditioned for a walk-on role as a beatnik for a television show, dressed in her trench coat and black tights, she was passed over. 'I just had to look the part, and I looked the part but they said, "We have to see your work."'

When she went to an audition for a summer stock job with the New London Players in New Hampshire that April, she was allowed to read, but after she left, one of the owners turned to the others and said, 'She's very talented, but God, she's so ugly. What are we gonna do with her?' She wasn't hired. Sometimes darker prejudices came into play against Barbara as well. Years after she became a star, someone sent one of her résumés back to her. A casting agent had scribbled across it, 'Talented. Who needs another Jewish broad?'

Barbara was devastated by the rejections. 'I cried in every office,' she said. 'I was humiliated – people looked at me like I was crazy. I could only bring myself to go to auditions twice a week.' Sometimes her tears hardened into anger. 'Screw you!' she would yell at her startled judges. 'I ain't coming back and asking you for no work!'

She 'made terrible enemies' this way, but she didn't care. 'My pride as a person was more important to me. I thought I'd rather be a hat designer than ask people for a job.' She stopped making rounds, but when her money began to run out, she needed some kind of work. Finally she was hired as a clerk for the Michael Press, a printing company on West Forty-fifth Street. She filed papers, made coffee, answered the phones. This was precisely the kind of job her mother had always said she should get, and of course Barbara hated every moment of it. Still, her meager salary paid the bills, and Diana would have been proud of her daughter's responsible attitude toward money. Every payday she would cash her check, put some of the money into her savings account, then divvy up the rest into envelopes marked 'phone,' 'rent,' 'laundry,' 'food,' and finally 'miscellaneous.'

Nonetheless certain that on her own Barbara was headed for disaster, Diana called her every day on her JUdson-6 exchange to 'see how you're doing,' and once or twice a week she'd come by the apartment unannounced, laden with bowls of chicken soup, chopped liver, and matzoh balls. These visits were far too frequent for Barbara's taste, but her pleas to her mother to leave her alone went unheeded.

Barbara's job at the Michael Press didn't last long. Her lack of interest in her work, her insubordination, and her constant humming, which annoyed her boss no end, got her fired within nine months. She applied for unemployment benefits and collected a weekly check of $32.50. It was barely enough to survive, and when she and Susan Dwaorkowitz had a 'clash of personalities,' Susan moved back to Brooklyn and left Barbara in dire need of a roommate. She posted a notice on the Actors' Equity office bulletin board, and another aspiring actress, Marilyn Fried, answered the summons. 'We decided we could get along,' Marilyn said, 'and I moved in. Each of us was getting unemployment. It barely covered the rent and our fees for acting classes.' Once a week Marilyn made a trip home to stock up on food from her mother's refrigerator, and Barbara soon followed suit, figuring that would keep Diana from showing up at her door when she least expected it.

Diana used this admission of need from Barbara as further proof that she would never make it as an actress, that she should move back home and get a typing job in Brooklyn. Instead, buoyed up by Allan Miller's belief in her and by her classmates' positive reaction to her scenes and exercises, Barbara invited her mother to attend a class and watch her do a scene that she felt particularly confident about. She was sure it would change Diana's mind about her acting ambitions.

Diana came, Barbara did the scene, and Marilyn Fried thought it went extremely well. 'Barbara was very proud of it,' she recalled. But afterward Mrs Kind said nothing as she climbed the stairs to Barbara's apartment. Once they got inside, Barbara sat on the edge of her bed, and Diana began a tirade that shocked Marilyn and totally deflated Barbara. 'Her mother said Barbara should find another outlet for whatever she had to offer because she did not have the ability to be an actress,' Marilyn recollected. 'I was heartbroken. And yet Barbara never felt any anger or hostility about it. After that embarrassing session, one night Barbara and I sat together wondering what we would like most to do if we ever made it as actresses, and she said, "First of all, I want to buy my mother a mink coat."'

Such a possibility grew less likely than ever after Barbara lost her unemployment benefits when her caseworker checked up on her and found out that she hadn't looked for a job similar to the one she had lost, as required, but had tried out for acting work instead. But then disaster was averted when an audition finally worked out for Barbara. She was hired for another summer of stock, this one at the Cecilwood Theater in Fishkill, New York. She received $30.00 a week plus room and board, and between June 30 and September 7 she worked on ten plays. The only production in which she had anything substantial to do was *Separate Tables*, but as always, she loved all of it. For Barbara now, the theater was home.

And her actor friends were family. They often congregated at Roy Scott's place. He would whip up macaroni topped with ketchup and uncork cheap red wine, and everyone would philosophize about art and life and love and sex. As Simon Gribben recollected, 'Sex was on the menu, and people would kind of sleep with whomever they slept with. Barbara was usually there, and Roy told me that his thing with Barbara had cooled off and that she kind of liked me – that it was there for me if I wanted it. At these parties she would give me the eye and I'd go over and say hello to her, but I'd look at her nose and think, I can't do it.

'One time I brought a friend of mine to one of Roy's parties. I could have gone to bed with Barbara that night, but I was really interested in this little blonde who was another one of Roy's girls. So I went off with her, and my friend went to bed with Barbara. So the next morning my friend and Barbara and I went out for breakfast at a coffee shop across the street from Carnegie Hall. After Barbara left us, I asked him what had happened, and he said nothing, that they had just lain there.'

MOST OF THE time now she immersed herself in acting. Allan Miller arranged for her to study on scholarship with three other teachers – Eli Rill, Herbert Berghof, and Curt Conway. Barbara didn't know Miller had interceded on her behalf, and because she feared her new teachers would think her disloyal to Miller, she used an alias she had found in the telephone book: Angelina Scarangella.

What struck Eli Rill most about Barbara was that she didn't want to be funny. 'She would perform scenes, and the students would laugh because she had a comical way of speaking and using her hands,' Rill recalled. 'She hated it. She'd say to me, "If you're such a good teacher, make it so that they'll stop laughing." I told her they were laughing *with* her. But she wanted to be a *serious* actress.'

To help herself become a tragic muse, Barbara read Greek plays and biographies of actresses like Sarah Bernhardt and Eleonora Duse. She worked on innumerable scenes for her four classes. She did some radio work for WNEW, and occasionally she appeared in special projects in front of an audience on the stage of the Theater Studio, condensed versions of famous plays prepared by Allan.

One of the students at the Theater Studio was Dustin Hoffman, and his memories of Barbara in one of the projects have remained vivid. 'I remember this funny-looking girl on the stage sitting cross-legged . . . she had a very small part, she didn't have many lines. But, boy, by some magic wave of her wand she was making everybody look at her.'

Barbara's intensity seared into Hoffman's memory as well. 'Did you ever see those pictures of a mother bird with the worm and there's a bunch of baby birds with their mouths open?' he asked. 'Somehow there's one that's straining more than any other to get that worm from their mother. That would be Barbara.'

SHE HUNGERED, BOTH literally and figuratively. Food was love, she had learned from her mother, and she couldn't afford much of it. She seemed to have an unending appetite; she would raid friends' refrigerators, pick pieces of food off her companions' dinner plates, go back for seconds and thirds and fourths if she could. Everyone who knew her marveled: how could she eat so much and stay so thin? What she was too proud to admit was that in most cases the meal they saw her devour provided the only food she'd eaten all day.

Even more than food she craved excitement, novelty, recognition, an outlet for artistic expression. In a way, she was like the country she lived in. After nearly a decade of complacency under a benign elderly Republican president, Dwight Eisenhower, the United States stood on the verge of an extraordinary new decade. Within the next two years, America would elect its youngest president, the handsome, glamorous, visionary John F. Kennedy;

it would put a man in space and make giant – if often violently opposed – steps to end racial segregation.

Barbara was not yet eighteen as the fifties came to an end, and her single-mindedness about her career left her with little concern for what was going on in the outside world. For while America was moving toward exciting new frontiers, so was Barbara Joan Streisand.

B arbara sat on the living room floor of her apartment early in 1960, singing along to the guitar strums of a friend from acting class, Carl Esser. As her roommate, Marilyn Fried, prepared for bed in the next room she heard 'this remarkable voice' waft in from what she assumed was the radio. Who is that marvelous singer? she wondered. She peeked into the living room to investigate.

The radio wasn't on. Marilyn looked at Barbara and asked, 'Who was that singing?' Her eyes widened in surprise at the answer. 'Your voice is wonderful!' she blurted. 'Why aren't you singing?'

'I don't know . . . I don't think I'm that good,' Barbara said.

'Out came the sensitivity, the insecurity, the shyness,' Marilyn recalled to the author René Jordan in 1974. When she and Carl both begged to differ, Barbara got caught up in their excitement and pulled the demo record she had made at thirteen out of a closet and played it for them. Marilyn loved it and told Barbara she reminded her of Fanny Brice.

'Who's Fanny Brice?' Barbara asked.

'Barbara didn't think the record sounded very good,' Marilyn recalled. 'She could not believe she could sing. It was amazing.'

But the next day, unusually cheerful, Barbara flitted around the apartment singing. 'Do I sound okay?' she wanted to know.

'You sound great,' Marilyn replied.

'Should I go for a singing audition?'

'Absolutely.'

'But I'm an actress, not a singer.'

'If it gets you a job, who cares? You're broke!'

Barbara remained unsure. Standing up and singing seemed like so much silliness to her, compared to playing Medea or Juliet. And she later admitted that she wasn't immune to the Victorian notion that singers were floozies. No, she couldn't bring herself to do it. Instead she got a job as an usher at the Lunt-Fontanne Theater on West Forty-sixth Street, home of the Richard Rodgers-Oscar Hammerstein phenomenon *The Sound of Music*, starring Mary Martin. As she led people to their seats Barbara would turn her face away from them so that 'when I became a star nobody would remember I'd been an usher.'

Night after night she stood in the back of the theater and watched. She memorized every line and all of the songs. She studied Mary Martin's every move, learning from – and sometimes faulting – one of America's great musical comedy stars. She came to realize that acting in a musical could be artistically valid too. Now, just as she had when she saw *The Diary of Anne Frank*, Barbara told herself, I could do that.

Within a few weeks she heard that Eddie Blum, the show's casting director, would soon hold auditions for the choruses of several touring companies of *The Sound of Music*. She rushed home that night and put her résumé together with one of the photographs the students at a photography school had taken of her; the pictures had been given to her in exchange for the modeling. 'The results were awful,' she said, 'but I didn't have any money for pictures, and they were all I had.' The photo Barbara sent Blum showed her wearing a Japanese kimono, long dangling earrings, and a hairpiece bun on top of her head. She looked about forty years old.

She got no response from Blum until several months later. 'He told me he hadn't called earlier because of the terrible picture. He couldn't imagine what kind of actress would submit such a thing. Finally he decided to call me in "to see what this creep is like."'

Accompanied by Blum's pianist Peter Daniels, who would become her accompanist and friend, Barbara sang the popular radio hit 'Allegheny Moon,' and when she finished, Blum asked her if she could sing something else. She sang 'My Favorite Things' and 'Do-Re-Mi,' which she had memorized by watching the show every night. Blum then asked if she wanted to have lunch with him, and while they ate, he asked about her background and her dreams for her future. Her responses so captivated him that their conversation stretched through dinner and beyond. As Marilyn Fried recalled it, 'He spent the whole day talking to her. He was fascinated by her talent and her intelligence. Around ten-thirty that night he brought Barbara back to our apartment and gave her a lot of encouragement.'

She was all wrong for *The Sound of Music*, of course, so despite how much she had impressed Blum, he couldn't hire her. 'But for heaven's sake use that voice!' he told her. 'Get yourself a job singing in a nightclub or something.' Barbara fairly floated on air for the next few days, incredulous that someone as savvy as Eddie Blum had thought so highly of her talent. But she wasn't thrilled about his suggestion that she sing in clubs. She still feared that singing was a trifle, not *important* like drama. But just in case another musical should need an actress-singer, she added 'Voice' to her résumé under 'Training.'

In one of the more fortuitous twists of show business fate, it was during her next foray into legitimate acting that Barbara met a young man who finally persuaded her to sing for a living.

SHE FIRST SAW Barry Dennen on the stage of the Jan Hus Theater on East Seventy-fourth Street late in April while she and a raggle-taggle group of young performers who called themselves the Actors' Co-Op ('A Nonprofit Group') bustled around rehearsing their first and last show, a production of Karel and Josef Čapek's *The Insect Comedy*, billed as 'a parable of the human condition.' Barbara had been cast in three roles in the three-act play with prologue and epilogue: Apatura Clythia, one of the two main butterflies in Act I; the messenger in Act III; and the second moth in the epilogue.

Dennen, a twenty-two-year-old UCLA graduate from a wealthy Los Angeles family, played a cricket and a snail. Handsome in a gaunt, somber way, obsessive in his love for every aspect of show business, he would set his alarm clock for 3:00 A.M. in order to tape-record the soundtracks of old Mae West or Bette Davis movies from television. The shelves in his apartment on Ninth Street in Greenwich Village groaned under thousands of vintage records he had collected since childhood. He had all the greats: Ruth Etting, Al Jolson, Helen Kane, Lee Wiley, Ethel Waters, Edith Piaf, Fanny Brice, Fred Astaire, Mabel Mercer, Helen Morgan.

That he was also wonderfully pretentious, as 'men of the theatuh' can be, is suggested by the fact that he billed himself as Barré Dennen in the show's program. This was all guaranteed to attract and fascinate the impressionable Barbara, and Dennen returned the compliment. He considered the production they were in 'slapped together, unspeakable, tacky, awful,' but he found Barbara's performance 'hysterically funny' as she chased after a boy butterfly crying, 'Oh, you great, strong, handsome thing!' while her diaphanous pink wings fluttered and her wire antennae flopped wildly atop her head.

The Insect Comedy lasted only three days, Sunday through Tuesday, May 8, 9, and 10. On Monday morning the New York *World Telegram and Sun* critic, Frank Aston, gave the show a good-natured pan, pointing out that 'no one in it claimed to be anything like a pro.' He also gave Barbara her first Manhattan newspaper notice when he listed her as one of the residents of 'Butterflyland, where the girls assail men but get nowhere because everyone dies too soon.'

The cast reassembled a few weeks later to do an audio version of the play for Radio Free Europe. The show had closed, but Barbara and Barry's friendship had just begun. They started to date, first talking for hours in the nearby Pam Pam coffee shop, then watching late-show movies in his small, eclectically furnished eleventh-floor apartment stuffed with feathers and fans, Tiffany-style lamps, and candles. Soon the two were virtually inseparable. 'We went everywhere together,' he recalled. 'She was very young, endearing, and exceptionally serious about becoming a great actress.' Just as she had Allan Miller before him, Barbara asked Barry endless questions about acting and music and literature and art. He loved that she hung on his every word; she loved that she had met another man from whom she could learn.

Dennen owned a top-of-the-line Ampex stereo tape recorder with two microphones, so it followed naturally that when a prospective agent asked Barbara for a tape of her singing, she asked Barry to make it. She arrived at his apartment with Carl Esser in tow as an accompanist, and as Barry recalled it in 1974, 'We spent the afternoon taping, and the moment I heard the first playback I went insane – I knew here was something special, a voice the microphone loved.' And Dennen could tell that Barbara, although completely untrained, had an inherent musicality, the same instincts that had led her to improvise on 'You'll Never Know' when she was thirteen. Excited, Barry joined those who had advised Barbara to become a singer. She gave him her standard reply: 'I'm an *ehktress.*'

'Look,' he countered, 'you can continue your acting classes and still do this. You'll get seen, and you'll make money.' Then he stressed that singing was a form of acting, that songs – especially the classic ballads – could be treated as three-act plays. He told her that a singer could create a character just as vibrant as any actress could in a play. Barbara's eyes narrowed as she absorbed this argument. Later she said Barry had made her see that 'Singing could be like acting, except I played all the parts myself!'

Barry caught the waver in her skepticism and threw down a gauntlet: a bar directly across the street from his apartment had a weekly talent contest on Monday nights, and he challenged her to enter it. She studied him. He said he would help her learn some new songs. She twisted her mouth. When he added that the winner would receive fifty dollars, a week's engagement at the club, and free dinners, he saw the first real spark of interest flicker across Barbara's face. 'Mmm,' she murmured.

ON A HOT Monday morning a few weeks later Barbara, skeptical and scared, walked into the Lion, the dark, slightly seedy neighborhood watering hole on the ground floor of a brownstone at 62 West Ninth Street. Hopefuls for the talent show had to audition for the club's manager, Burke McHugh, on the morning of the contest, and the best four were invited back for the competition. McHugh was used to dealing with some very questionable characters at these cattle calls, and when he saw Barbara he muttered to his pianist, 'Oh, boy, here comes a winner.'

With her hair unwashed and uncombed, dressed in jeans and a sweatshirt, she looked, McHugh told the author Randall Reiss in 1992, like 'a kid off the street who hadn't been home to change her clothes.' He asked her if she had come to audition. Self-protectively, she feigned ignorance. 'Audition for what?' McHugh explained about the talent contest, and Barbara said, 'Well, I've never sung in public before, but I'll give it a try.'

She told him her name was Barbara Strinberg, and then she sang the haunting Harold Arlen-Truman Capote ballad 'A Sleepin' Bee' for him. McHugh and his piano player, a young man named Patty, felt goose bumps rise on their arms. When she finished, McHugh exclaimed, 'Oh, my God, Barbara, that was really magnificent!' He told her to come back for the contest and asked how to spell Strinberg.

Now that she had been accepted, there was no reason to hide her identity, but she didn't want to admit she'd lied. 'I've gotta change the name. I can't stand it . . . It sounds too Jewish.' According to McHugh, at that moment 'Footsteps in the Sand' blared from a radio in the next room. 'Sand,' Barbara said. 'I like that, that's a good last syllable. I'll call myself Barbara Streisand!'

When she came back at eight that evening, Barbara looked around the dark, smoky room and wondered, Where are all the women? Barry had neglected to tell her that the Lion was a predominantly gay bar. With her liberal leanings, Barbara had no problem with homosexuals; she had first encountered gay men during her summer at Malden Bridge and in her acting classes. But she had never seen them behave so openly before, and she watched them with fascination as she waited for the contest to begin.

They were arguably the toughest audience Barbara could have faced. Like Barry Dennen, most of them were immersed in show business history. They adored Judy Garland and Ethel Merman; they would trek miles to catch a performance by Mabel Mercer or Julie Wilson or Hildegarde; they bought the original cast album of every Broadway musical. For a young girl singer to excite these men, she'd have to be awfully good.

The Lion's talent night was popular for contradictory reasons. On the one hand, one never knew when a truly funny comic or a really fine singer would step up to the mike and make the evening special. On the other, there was always the delicious chance that some poor deluded soul would rock the room with unintended hilarity through sheer ineptitude. Burke McHugh preferred to have several different styles of singer and a comedian on the bill, and this night was no exception. Barbara's competitors were a comedian, a light opera singer, and Dawn Hampton, the niece of Lionel Hampton, a 'jazz belter' who 'sang like there was no tomorrow,' McHugh recalled.

Last on the bill, Barbara stepped timorously onto the parquet 'stage' next to Patty's piano, the lusty applause for Dawn Hampton ringing in her ears. She took what looked like a briefcase from under her arm, put it on top of the piano, opened it, pulled out her sheet music, and gave it to Patty. 'Tonight,' she said softly, 'I am going to sing "A Sleepin' Bee."'

If she heard the titters, she didn't let on. By now most of the audience suspected McHugh was having fun again. They looked at this gawky, skinny girl with her distractingly large nose and crooked teeth and eyes that seemed to watch each other, and they didn't know whether to laugh or groan. Her getup hardly helped. On top of her head she had bobby-pinned a Dynel hair-piece that looked, in the words of a friend, 'like a cheese Danish.' From under it her real hair fell stringily to her shoulders. She wore a short purple sheath and a jacket festooned with purple ostrich feathers, which the thrift shop clerk told her had once belonged to a countess. With feathers wisping around her shoulders and the audience ready to pounce, Barbara stood stock still under the spotlight, closed her eyes, and dramatically drew back her head as Patty tinkled out her introduction. Someone in the audience muttered 'Oh, boy.'

Then this eccentric, clearly misguided creature, her head still back, her eyes still closed, opened her mouth and sang 'A Sleepin' Bee,' and the voice that emerged from her grabbed the men's breath away. The titters and the talking stopped. She began that languid ballad of young love softly, her voice youthful but clear as a bell, her high notes enthrallingly pure. Then she gathered steam, took on more force as her voice built to 'Broadway belter' proportions. Finally she began a breathtaking swoop up the scale, leaping a full octave in one word, 'love,' and her first song in front of a paying audience came to an end.

For a few moments the seventy or so men sat in stunned silence. Then they burst into wild applause and cheers, shouting 'More! More!' as Barbara laughed nervously and looked around the room. She glanced at Burke McHugh and mouthed, 'Should I do another one?' He nodded, and she went back to her briefcase for another chart, pulling out 'When Sunny Gets Blue.' Again the voice was mesmerizing, and again that was only part of the magic spell she wove. She didn't sing these songs in the la-di-da style of so many pop vocalists, she seemed to have *lived* them, seemed to be making up the lyrics on the spot from her own experience. This jaded audience knew immediately that they had just seen someone very special, a girl with a beautiful voice who could bring drama and shading and vibrancy to a lyric.

The 'applause meter' gave Barbara the contest by a wide margin, and Burke McHugh told her to come back on Saturday night.

She and Barry ran over to the Pam Pam coffee shop on Sixth Avenue, Barbara floating on air, suffused with the approval she had just won. Barry let her fly awhile, then began to criticize her performance, pointing out areas where she could have given more or where she should have pulled back. 'Yeah, yeah,' Barbara replied, her eyes narrowing. 'You're right, you're right.'

Saturday night, on a bill with three other performers, she sang the same two songs plus 'Lullaby of Birdland' and again wowed the audience, many of whom had come expressly to see her after hearing the buzz about her Monday night performance. The following Monday she defended her title, adding 'Why Try to Change Me Now?' and 'Long Ago and Far Away' to her brief set. The gay comedian Michael Greer, who then called himself Mal James, was one of the contestants that night. The falsetto singer Tiny Tim was another.

'I had already heard rumblings about this strange girl with a lot of talent,' Greer recalled, 'so I knew she'd be tough competition. She looked like she had dressed herself from a garage sale. As I remember she wore a tiny high-heeled shoe in her hair because she liked the rhinestones in it. She sang something totally off-the-wall like "Happy Birthday" and it was a mind blower. When I heard her sing I thought, My God, who is she? The voice was so beautiful it captivated everyone there.'

Barbara won again – Greer came in second – and on the following three Mondays as well. By now word of 'this strange, incredible girl' had spread throughout New York's hippest audiences, and lines of people trailed down Ninth Street to Sixth Avenue on Monday and Saturday nights. During the second week Barbara told Burke McHugh she wanted three pictures of herself, not just one, on the signboard outside the club. And she wanted to change the spelling of her name. 'Back to Strinberg?' McHugh asked.

'No,' Barbara replied. 'I wanna take an *a* out of "Barbara." Who needs it? The name's pronounced Bar-bra. So that's how I want you to spell it: B-a-r-b-r-a.'

Boy, this one really is a nut, McHugh thought. But he did as he was asked, and Barbra Streisand was born. It was her answer to all those agents who had advised her to change her name to Barbara Sands because Streisand was too ethnic or too hard to pronounce. This way, she had changed her name and she hadn't. What she *had* done was become, among all the thousands and thousands of Barbaras in the world, the one and only Barbra.

✴

AFTER A MONTH of weekends and Mondays at the Lion, Barbra was forced to retire from the competition as an undefeated champion when Burke McHugh and his partner, Ernie Sgroi Jr., told her they wanted to give somebody else a chance. Without the fifty dollars a week and free meals she had grown used to, Barbra faced dire financial straits again, and she asked McHugh if there was something else she could do at the club. He said he needed a replacement coat-check girl for a couple of weeks, but she wouldn't want to do that, would she? 'Sure I would,' she replied. 'Why not?'

Every night she arrived at the club at eight o'clock, sloppily dressed, went into the coat room, closed the door, and reopened it a few moments later wearing a flashy cocktail dress. After a week of this, one of the regulars, a costume designer who called himself Peaches, noticed that she never cleaned the dress. 'Hey, Barbra,' he teased her, 'don't you think you should send that dress to the dry cleaners? It's gonna start to walk on its own pretty soon.' As he and his friends giggled, Barbra snapped back, 'Go ahead and laugh. When I'm a big star on Broadway, you'll still be just a bunch of drunken cackling hens!'

Broadway was pretty far off, but another nightclub engagement was not. Ernie Sgroi told Barbra that his father owned the nearby Bon Soir, a larger, classier, more mainstream joint on Eighth Street, and he had persuaded Ernie Senior to let her audition for his club. An engagement at the Bon Soir meant more money than she'd been paid at the Lion, more prestige, and a more influential audience.

It also meant that Barbra would have to come up with some new material, and quickly. She worked excitedly with Barry over the next few weeks, sitting on the floor of his living room listening to dozens of hours of tapes of the great singers who had gone before her. Dennen hammered home his idea that Barbra should approach each lyric as an acting exercise. 'I would work with her phrase by phrase,' he said, 'trying this, trying that, shaping gestures, timing, the kind of effect Barbra and I wanted.' He played only the musical crème de la crème for her, zeroing in on songs that best showcased her voice.

Barbra had never learned to read music, just as she had never taken a singing lesson. But she needed to listen to a song only once or twice to master it. She would hear a stylized vocal, imitate it, then give it her own special twist and make it her own. Barry knew he was in the presence of one of that mysterious, singular breed – a musical natural.

Perhaps Barry Dennen's greatest contribution to Barbra Streisand's musical vocabulary was his concept of reviving 'unusual, forgotten, or outrageous' material rather than regurgitating the old chestnuts that were a staple of every nightclub act. Barbra was all for it. 'The Bon Soir was a sophisticated little nightclub,' she said. 'That annoys me, anything that's supposed to be posh and sophisticated, you know. So I wanted to do something that was completely wrong!' Barbra told Barry she'd like to do 'a nursery rhyme or something,' and he suggested she sing the unlikely 'Who's Afraid of the Big, Bad Wolf?' in order to surprise, delight – maybe even shock? – the blasé New York audiences. Barbara soaked up this sensibility, one that would serve her well as her career took off.

Barbra needed new clothes for her Bon Soir act, too, so she asked Terry Leong, a friend of Marilyn Fried's who had designed for Seventh Avenue's garment district, to help her put together some outfits. He and Barbra scoured the thrift shops, picking up a pure silk beaded vest for five dollars, a pair of shoes for three dollars, or a hat for two dollars. Barbra would spend hours rummaging around in a dusty Ninth Avenue thrift shop to find the perfect dress to go with a vest she'd discovered on Second Avenue, then traipse back to Third Avenue on a quest for the right bag.

'She was so enthusiastic,' Leong recalled. 'We found beautiful things, like a 1920s leopard coat. We found bodices from 1900 and skirts to go with them. She loved to find things she could wear in her hair, like jewels and bows and ribbons.' Leong also made dresses from scratch for Barbra, using material she'd found. 'We devised the designs together,' he said. 'We bought these beautiful lace doilies, and I made an Empire dress around one of them, using it across her back. I found a pale green chiffon material, and I made a full-skirted dress with it, with a Chinese top and a Mandarin collar.

'She liked styles that were very fluid – things that moved with her,' Leong went on. 'She was very graceful and she moved well. She had a wonderful body to costume – thin, trim, long, lean. She experimented with a lot of different clothes, and it was exciting to watch the transformations that would come over her as she switched from one look to another.' Barbra's enthusiasm about all this caused Leong endless fitting problems. 'She wouldn't stop moving. She was just all over the place and jumping up and down. Very difficult to do a hem.'

As though by some cosmic design, the malleable Galatea that was Barbra Streisand met yet another Pygmalion when Bob Schulenberg, an artist and designer friend of Barry Dennen's from UCLA, moved to New York in July of 1960, in the midst of Barbra's preparations for her Bon Soir audition. He will never forget his first sight of her, running toward him, yelling 'Barry! Barry!' as he and Dennen left Barry's apartment late one night.

'She was carrying two shopping bags in each hand, overflowing with feather boas and sequined fabric,' Schulenberg recalled. 'And she had *everything* on.

She had on a new cherry-red velvet skirt that stopped about an inch above her knees, which was very unusual in 1960. She had on chocolate-brown nylon stockings and gold lamé and red satin strap 1927 shoes. Her top was a gold, silver, and cherry-red brocade with big square-cut Elizabethan sleeves. She had on two Venetian glass beaded necklaces, six glass bracelets, and drop earrings made of glass. She looked like a weird *Vogue* illustration from the twenties. I was *fascinated.*'

What Barbra hadn't done so well, Schulenberg thought, was her face. She had attempted the style of eye makeup popular at the time, an extended eyelash line to make the eyes seem larger, but Bob felt 'she really didn't know what she was doing. She had very little color on her skin and bright red lipstick. She had these wispy little bangs that fell down over her forehead to hide a bit of teenage skin. It just wasn't a good look, and I could tell she wanted to be glamorous by what she was wearing.'

Schulenberg found himself analyzing this odd creature as he sat across from her and Barry at the Pam Pam coffee shop that first night. He didn't think she was very good-looking, but he saw something in her. She had brilliant blue eyes, a long, sleek neck, and a face that from certain angles seemed to acquire a surprisingly classic beauty. 'Barbra was like undeveloped territory. I was looking at her and abstractly thinking, Well, she's got no structure in her cheeks, but that we can paint in. Somehow I thought she could be made to look like one of those Richard Avedon fashion models.'

Schulenberg burned to make Barbra over, but he hesitated to suggest that she needed it. 'When you see a young woman who wants to look a certain way, and you know how she could look, but she's doing it all wrong, you have to broach the subject nicely. You can't just say, "You look like shit!"'

But Schulenberg got his chance to 'play with Barbra's look' the day they were scheduled to see Barry play a messenger in Shakespeare's *Henry V* in Central Park. Bob suggested they surprise Dennen. 'Let's make you up like a *Vogue* model – like Audrey Hepburn or somebody. Wouldn't that be fun?' Barbra was all for it – 'She was willing to do anything' – and the two of them spent an hour and a half on the transformation while Barbra chomped on rye bread and herring and mumbled questions with her mouth full: 'Why are you doing that? How did you make it look that way?'

Schulenberg applied false eyelashes, in an era when no one wore them on the street. He contoured her cheeks with deep flesh-colored greasepaint. He extended her eyes with liner that made her look 'like Marlene Dietrich in *Morocco.*' He dusted her face with white translucent powder. He pulled her hair back and used her 'cheese Danish' hairpiece *under* her own hair to give it height.

Barbra finished off her makeover with black leotards under black slacks, black ballet slippers, a black leotard top, and a black cardigan sweater. 'Now, this is a 120-degree night in New York City,' Schulenberg said with a laugh. 'We had to use a lot of powder to keep her looking as cool as a cucumber. And she just looked sensational, like Martha Graham. People's heads turned when she walked by. They were wondering, Who *is* she? Barbra *loved* it.'

Once this striking twosome got to Central Park, however, they discovered they were so late that Barry's house seats had been sold. They went back to Dennen's place on the subway, and when he got home he was livid. 'How could you miss my performance?' he demanded.

'But, Barry,' Bob pleaded, 'doesn't Barbra look *great?*'

ON SUNDAY AFTERNOON, August 7, Barbra bounced down the thirty-one steps into the cavernous darkness that was the Bon Soir Club at 40 West Eighth Street and auditioned for Ernie Sgroi Sr.; his partner, Phil Pagano; and his emcee, Jimmy Daniels. She had brought Barry, Bob Schulenberg, and Burke McHugh with her, and after her two numbers McHugh murmured, 'It looks good,' and left. But Sgroi and his colleagues weren't sure. Yes, she had a wonderful voice, but she *looked* so strange. Yes, she'd been a hit at the Lion, but how would their mainstream audience react to her? There was only one way to find out. Sgroi told her to come back that night and do her songs again in front of the regular customers. If they liked her, he would give her a two-week booking.

That night Jimmy Daniels introduced her as 'a little extra surprise, a young singer who's been causing quite a stir over at the Lion.' She stepped onto the small stage and realized that she still had chewing gum in her mouth. She took it out and stuck it on the microphone. The audience laughed and wondered, Who's this kook? But when she began to sing 'A Sleepin' Bee,' Sgroi and Pagano looked around the room and noticed that everyone had stopped laughing. Then they noticed that everyone had stopped drinking, and by the time she came to the end of the song the waiters had stopped serving. Barbra had mesmerized the entire room.

When she completed the song, her head down, her eyes closed, her arms limp at her sides, the audience remained silent for what seemed an eternity. Then the patrons burst into applause and cheers. Before the clamor stopped, Barbra launched into 'Who's Afraid of the Big, Bad Wolf?' She flailed her arms, she let out whoops, she giggled, she seemed to become a totally different person. When she ended the song with 'Who's afraid of the big, big, big, big, big, bad, *wooo-oooo-oooo-lf!*' the audience rose to its feet with cheering, laughing, stomping delight.

When she stepped down off the small stage, that night's headliner, the comedian Larry Storch, looked at her and said, 'Kid, you're gonna be a star.'

Ernie Sgroi pulled her into his office and said, 'You start September ninth. Two weeks. Two shows a night. One hundred twenty-five dollars a week.'

'Just like in the movies!' Barbra later exclaimed.

She had one month to prepare for her first major nightclub engagement, but first she had to go back up to the Cecilwood Theater in Fishkill, where she had been asked to fill in for an indisposed actress and play Hortense, the French maid in *The Boy Friend* for two weeks. She was a hit in the show, cavorting on stage in her maid's outfit complete with ankle-strap high heels, fish-net stockings, frilly apron, and a huge hair bow.

While she twirled an enormous feather duster on stage in Fishkill, the first newspaper article about Barbra appeared in the August 21, 1960, edition of *Flatbush Life*, accompanied by the exotic, 'terrible' photograph she had sent to Eddie Blum. Under the headline 'Flatbush Actress Heads for Stardom,' the piece began, 'Barbra Streisand, who as a child was determined to become a dramatic actress, now finds herself in the rather enviable position of being considered for her singing ability as well.' After recounting her summer stock appearances, *The Insect Comedy*, and her audition for Blum, the article described her success at the Lion and concluded, 'Word of her splendid reception got around to the sharp ears of Bon Soir personnel, and she was given an audition . . . again Miss Streisand knocked 'em dead, and she was signed for a two-week shot, beginning September 9.'

ON THAT SULTRY Friday night, Barbra appeared third on a bill with the comic pantomimists Tony and Eddie and comedienne Phyllis Diller. Diller vividly recalled the moment, as she patted on her makeup and prepared to go on, that she first heard Barbra Streisand sing: 'On her third note, every hair on my body stood up! I am basically a musician, and when I heard that voice – and that heart – I knew this is a *star!*' Diller took Barbra under her wing, gently suggesting that she wear more traditional clothes while performing.

'She told me my taste was awful,' Barbra recalled. 'She bought me two woolen dresses. But she doesn't know that I brought 'em back, got the money for them, and made myself some outfits out of upholstery material.'

Traditional dress or no, night after night the Bon Soir audiences thrilled to Barbra Streisand. She had added two numbers to her repertoire: 'Who Can I Turn to Now?' and the 1920s Helen Kane number 'I Want to Be Bad.' Her two-week engagement stretched to four, then six, then eight, then ten as the word about this 'wild girl with an incredible voice' spread far beyond Greenwich Village and New York's gay community. As Michael

Greer remembered it, 'The buzz was on about her. It just kept increasing. I vividly remember everything she did. She giggled and waved her arms. We just couldn't keep our eyes off her. Man, everything she said or did we went "*Oh!*" It was like she was an angel. She was spellbinding.'

At the Bon Soir Barbra discovered that she liked making her audiences laugh. She used the chewing-gum-on-the-microphone gambit at every performance, and she increasingly told jokes and kibbitzed between songs. Her audiences loved it, and Barbra realized that humor helped her put on a good show.

Every night Barry Dennen brought his Ampex recorder to the club to tape her set. Afterward he and Barbra would sit up until three or four in the morning and listen to her breathing, analyze her phrasing, study how much emotion she had put into the lyric. Barry made suggestions, gave her examples of how other singers did the same things. Barbra sponged up every bit of it, and every night her act got a little better.

By now Barbra had fallen in love with Barry and had moved into his apartment. The serious turn their relationship took surprised Bob Schulenberg. 'One night I went over to their place,' he said, 'and they were on the floor, and Barbra was resting her head on Barry's lap, and it was very romantic. They had that kind of glow that says that two people have just been intimate. They started talking about getting married. I said, "Are you serious?" And they said. "Yeah, we're going to get married." It was sort of a sacred, hallowed moment. It was very *intense*. Barbra was enthralled with Barry. He has a brilliant mind. He was the first man who would ever trade jokes from Mae West or Groucho Marx movies with her and in the next moment enlighten her on art, theater, music. His influence on Barbra was tremendous. And he was thrilled with his creation.'

So too were the most hard-bitten critics. One of Barbra's first reviews appeared in the New York *World Telegram and Sun* on September 16, and Perry Rebell's comments were typical: 'The Bon Soir has swung into the new nightclub season with the find of the year. She is Barbra Streisand, a Brooklynite whose voice and poise belie her scant eighteen years. Vocally, there's range and power; stylewise, there appears to be a natural gift for musical comedy, but she handles with aplomb the most meaningful of ballads.'

The day before, she had received her first New York column mention, from Dorothy Kilgallen: 'The pros are talking about a rising new star on the local scene – eighteen-year-old Barbra Streisand, currently at the Bon Soir. She's never had a singing lesson in her life, doesn't know how to walk, dress, or take a bow, but she projects well enough to bring the house down.'

Shortly after this item appeared, Barbra did have a singing lesson. Her mother had come to see her act, and Mrs Kind thought the seventy-year-old white lace combing jacket Barbra wore looked like a nightgown. She also told her daughter that while her voice was good, it was a little thin, and she suggested she take lessons to build it up. This was the first time Mrs Kind had urged Barbra to do something that could further her show business ambitions, and she took the advice.

When she stepped into the voice coach's small studio with its one piano, a middle-aged woman with her hair pulled up into a severe bun greeted her and asked if she had something prepared. She did – 'A Sleepin' Bee' – and she handed the sheet music to the piano player. The teacher waited for her to begin.

'When a bee lies sleeping in the palm of your hand—'

The woman rapped her pointer on the edge of a nearby table. Startled, Barbra stopped cold. 'No. No. No. Your pronunciation is all wrong. The vowels must be *shorter*. It's "When a *beh* lies sleeping."'

'But, but—' Barbra stammered.

'It is beh . . . beh . . . *beh!*' the coach insisted.

'But the word is "bee"!' Barbra protested. 'Whoever heard anyone say "beh"?'

The teacher was losing her patience. 'Singing is not the same as talking, my dear.'

Barbra swallowed hard, finished the song her way, and walked out. She never took another voice lesson. 'I knew that singing had to be an extension of speaking. I felt, I'm an actress and I have to make the song real, you know? So that was the end of my singing lessons. It just felt all wrong.'

THE BON SOIR gig brought Barbra her first manager, Ted Rozar, and her first agent, Irvin Arthur. After seeing her two nights before her engagement was to end on November 20, the twenty-two-year-old Rozar went to her tiny dressing room, told her he was 'the only gentile manager in the business,' exclaimed 'I love you!' and asked if she had representation. The following Wednesday she signed a three-year contract with Rozar that gave him 10 percent of her salary if she earned less than $350 a week and 20 percent if she earned more, with an additional 5 percent to anyone who assisted him with out-of-town negotiations.

Barbra's success at the Bon Soir should have assured her a rash of bookings, but much to his chagrin Rozar could not get anyone else to hire her. He sent her picture and tapes to agents, Broadway producers, the bigger clubs in Manhattan, and local television shows, but Barbra was just too unlike the vast majority of successful vocalists of the late fifties and early sixties. Agent after agent told Rozar, 'Well, yes, she's got a nice voice, but her fingers are too long, she uses her hands too much, her nose is too big, her hairstyle, her clothes . . .' There were a million excuses.

Clearly, Barbra was ahead of her time. She would anticipate the free-wheeling fashions of the sixties; she would bring jazz elements into popular singing; she would change many people's attitudes about what constituted female beauty. And she was in the vanguard of the women's movement, taking responsibility for her own career and standing up firmly for what she believed before most performers did so. But along the way she had to struggle for everything she got. For every agent or club owner who loved her there were two dozen who didn't get her at all.

Finally, after every other agent in New York had turned her down, Rozar persuaded Irvin Arthur of Associated Booking Corporation to take Streisand on. Associated Booking at the time handled only personal appearances, and at first Arthur had no more luck than Rozar in landing Barbra a job. As the weeks wore on toward the end of 1960, Barbra, hurting for money, called Arthur every night at eleven-thirty to see if he had anything for her. The answer was always no. She went back to odd jobs, waiting on tables for a few weeks, clerking at a law firm for a few months. Now that she had tasted some measure of success, working in an office galled her.

That New Year's Eve, Barbra had no date because Barry Dennen was out of town. She called a girlfriend, and the two of them hopped on the Staten Island Ferry. Her friend knew of a club called the Townhouse on the island, and they headed there. When they arrived, Barbra asked to speak to the owner, Joe Darconte. According to Darconte, 'She told me her name was Angelina Scarangella and she was from Naples. She said she was a singing star over in Italy and she'd get up and sing if I paid her fifty dollars.

'I looked at her and said, "Yeah, right. You're a Jew from Brooklyn!" Then I asked if she really could sing, because it so happened I was short an act that night. So I told her, "Sure, get up there and show me what you can do."

'She sang about four songs, and of course she was great, but I had a problem. The girl she had come in with was black. This was a time when there was a lot of racial tension, and I could feel rumblings among the crowd. So I got Barbra's attention in the middle of the fourth song and made a cutting gesture across my throat – eight bars and off!

'She didn't think I was gonna pay her, but I gave her the fifty dollars and the two of them took off.'

6

The taxi carrying Barbra and Bob Schulenberg barreled toward Pennsylvania Station. It was February 19, 1961, and she was late to catch the Empire State Express train that would take her out of the North-east for the first time. Irvin Arthur had gotten her a booking, sight unseen and mostly on his own reputation, at the Back Room at the elegant Caucus Club restaurant-nightclub in Detroit. She'd been a nervous wreck, one moment exhilarated by the prospect of repeating her Bon Soir triumph, the next moment terrified of being alone in a strange city so far from home.

Suddenly, with only minutes to spare, she told Schulenberg they'd have to stop at a drugstore. 'Barbra, we can't stop, you'll miss the train,' Bob protested. 'What could you possibly have to get now?'

'Do you think they have toothpaste in Detroit?' she asked.

Thirty hours later, and just four hours before she was to begin her performance, Barbra showed up at the office of Ross Chapman, the booking agent for the club. 'She had a big stack of dog-eared music under her arm,' Chapman recalled, 'and she looked – weird is the best word. Her hair needed combing, and her clothes I can't describe.'

Chapman asked Barbra how old she was. 'I'll be nineteen in April,' she replied. Chapman flinched. Under Michigan law, performers in cabarets had to be twenty-one. 'You'll have to lie about your age,' Chapman told her. Then he asked her to step into a side room and go over her material with Matt Michaels, the Back Room's pianist. About ten minutes later Michaels returned, his face ashen. 'My God, Ross,' he whispered. 'That broad only knows *four songs!*'

'I don't think I've ever met a girl who looked more unqualified to be a singer in an intimate room,' Michaels recalled. 'All she needed was a broomstick. She told us she'd worked eleven weeks at the Bon Soir in New York. I didn't believe it. When we asked her what she'd done with only four songs, she said she'd done the same songs every show.' Ross Chapman reminded Barbra that she had four sets to do every night, and told her she'd need at least eleven songs. 'How are you going to learn all those songs by nine tonight?' he asked.

'I'm a fast learner,' Barbra replied.

Over the next three hours Michaels taught her seven tunes. 'Because she didn't read music, I'd simply play the songs over and over . . . and she'd learn 'em. So she knew the songs, but it took another two or three weeks for her to put her own stamp on them.'

Barbra checked into her room at the Henrose Hotel, changed for the show, and turned up at the Caucus Club a few minutes before she was due to perform. Sam Gruber, the co-owner of the club with his brother Les, looked at her in horror. 'She showed up for that first show wearing a turtleneck sweater and black pants. We had to send her home to put on a dress.' When she began her performance, Ross Chapman was certain he had made a big mistake. 'She had no poise whatever,' he recalled. 'She sat on a bar stool to sing, with her legs spread out like a cello player.' But of course she had that voice, and by the end of the evening Barbra had won over the audience.

She was habitually late for her shows; her usual excuse was that she couldn't get a cab, even though her hotel was two blocks from the club. One night she scrambled in so late she had no time to change, so she sang in snow boots and a monkey fur coat. She told her audiences that she was born in Turkey and had taken belly dancing lessons. After her shows, whenever anyone offered to buy her a drink, she'd say she preferred to have a pastrami and Swiss cheese sandwich. She flirted shamelessly with an obviously married man, the handsome, six-foot-three-inch Stan Rosenberg. One night she joined Max Fisher, a wealthy steel magnate, at his table, and during the course of the conversation she asked him, 'Why don't you give me ten thousand dollars to help my career?' Fisher just laughed.

As kooky and offhand as Barbra could seem, Matt Michaels was impressed by her capacity for work. 'She worked harder than any girl I've ever met. People would comment on the innate grace of her hands. A lot of it was instinct, but I saw her work in front of a mirror four and five hours a day perfecting her gestures.' Despite her dedication, Michaels doubted Barbra would go very far 'because of her attitude, her belligerence. If she didn't like the way the audience was listening, she'd walk out. One time, when people were too noisy for her, she told them, "Goddammit, shut up!"'

The process of working with Barbra on her material often angered Michaels. 'She'd always want to change things after we'd set them. She was never satisfied. I worked with her three or four hours a day three or four times a week for six weeks. And she would insist on her way, whether it was right or wrong. She didn't really know very much, but she had opinions like she did. She was tough to get along with.'

And yet, Michaels discovered, she had a thin skin when confronted. 'There was a bass player who used to come in and play for us once in a while if he happened to be in town, just for kicks. One night he came in and she was late, and he chewed her out. He said, "You know, I'm comin' in to play for nothing, and the least you can do is be on time." Well, Barbra started to *cry*. She was tough in many ways, but very sensitive, too.'

AT THE END of her first week in Detroit, Barbra made her radio singing debut on a local program, *The Jack Harris Show*. She giggled nervously throughout the broadcast and later said she thought she'd made 'a first class fool of myself.' Four days later she appeared on another local radio show, *Guest House*, hosted by Bud Guest. She didn't sing, but she did tell Guest that her dress was 'a little sofa number' she had made from the upholstery off a couch her mother had discarded. When Guest misspelled her name Strysand, she told him she liked it that way.

Betty Paysner was the publicist for the Caucus Club, and she recalled that Barbra 'talked about changing her name. She wanted to spell it Strysand.' For a time, in fact, she did spell it that way; when she made her network television debut soon thereafter, *TV Guide* listed her as Barbra Strysand.

As often happens in show business, Barbra had to go all the way to Detroit before she got booked on her first television show in New York. Ted Rozar had persuaded Orson Bean, who had seen Barbra at the Bon Soir, to book her on the late-night Jack Paar program while Bean was doing a one-week stint as substitute host. Barbra didn't have the money to fly back east, so Les Gruber, eager for the publicity the TV appearance would give his club, took up a collection among the regular customers in order to send her off.

The Paar show was the premier late night showcase at the time. Broadcast nationwide, it was quite an auspicious place to make one's television debut – which Barbra did on Wednesday night, April 5, 1961. Wearing a simple black cocktail dress and appearing as thin as a sylph even with the illusion of extra weight television cameras create, Barbra sang 'A Sleepin' Bee' and 'When the Sun Comes Out,' then she joined Phyllis Diller, Gore Vidal, Albert Dekker, and Hugh Downs on the panel. 'This is so *exciting*,' she gushed, her arms flailing, her eyes sweeping across the studio. 'I just can't tell you. All these people and cameras and lights – and people! Oh!'

She then plugged both the Caucus Club and the Grubers' other place, the London Chop House ('I was so delighted,' said Les Gruber, 'that when she came back I gave her a big kiss and a hundred dollars'), and added that she had been 'clothed by the Robinson Furniture Company in Detroit. I'm the original Castro Convertible – movable parts!'

SAM AND LES Gruber had extended Barbra's gig at the Caucus Club from two weeks to eight and increased her salary to $200 a week, and during her sojourn in Detroit she had made friends. Neil Wolfe, the pianist in the Caucus Club's front room, took her horseback riding and golfing. Arno Hirsch, a critic for the *Detroit Times*, helped her get her first driver's license, from the state of Michigan. Doris Gershenson also took Barbra under her wing. 'She would come to our house quite often. She was the biggest eater I ever saw. One time we were baking cookies. She ran in and ate the whole batch before they were cool from the oven.'

Barbra cadged cookies and stuffed herself whenever food was offered her because she still had very little money to buy food of her own. Her hotel room rent, commissions, and personal expenses used up most of her salary every week. One day Fred Sweet, the manager of the Telenews Theater, looked out his window and saw Barbra, whom he recognized from the Caucus Club, standing along Woodward Street thumbing a ride. He went downstairs, and she told him she didn't have cab fare to get to the Art Institute. 'Why don't you take the bus?'

'I don't have enough money to take a bus either,' Barbra replied. Sweet gave her a few dollars, and when he told the story to Ross Chapman, he added, 'Ross, she looked like she needed a bath.'

BARBRA COMPLETED HER Caucus Club engagement on April 15; two days later she opened at the Crystal Palace in St Louis, where she shared the bill with a comedy team called the Smothers Brothers. 'They became her surrogate family on the road,' Bob Schulenberg recalled, and before long Barbra and Tommy, the silly one, began a brief romance. According to Jay Landesman, owner of the Crystal Palace, 'Barbra lost her cherry to Tommy Smothers, of all people.' (Landesman apparently didn't know about Roy Scott or Barry Dennen.)

During Barbra's engagement, Landesman recalled, 'I created a little revue-type format for the brothers, and Barbra began to do their sort of patter between her numbers. Her raps went on as long as my introductions. I thought her heavy Jewish material distracted from the mood and delivery of the subtle songs that followed.' Landesman called Barbra into his office and told her to cut the patter. 'But I get so bored doing the same thing every night,' she replied.

'You've been in the business two weeks and you're bored already!' an astonished Landesman replied.

By now Barbra was not only bored but homesick. Being away from New York, she wrote Schulenberg, was 'strange. I'm sort of depressed. Forgive me.' Bob called her, and the two of them talked for nine hours. 'She had such a vulnerability. She could seem hard, but she was really just trying to protect herself. She was just trying to keep things going.'

On that score, Barbra was doing all right. She gave her last performance in St Louis on Monday, May 8, and the next day flew back to New York. That night she opened her second stint at the Bon Soir, this time behind two comedians, Renee Taylor and Phil Leeds. Barbra shared a tiny dressing room with Taylor, and one pair of stockings. Barbra would slip into them, do her act, come back to the dressing room, slip them off, and return them to Renee. They reversed the procedure for the second set.

On opening night, Phil Leeds invited a friend of his to see his act. Marty Erlichman was a dark-haired, Bronx-born, boxily built, quintessentially New York personal manager who represented the Irish folk singers the Clancy Brothers. Erlichman never got to see his friend perform. 'I was just mesmerized by Barbra,' Erlichman recalled. 'She sang five songs, and I got chills on all five of them. And everyone in the place was enchanted too, except for the rest of the people at my table, who were industry people. They started talking to each other in the middle of her first song. And one of them, an agent, said to me after the first number, "Boy, that girl has a lot to learn – you don't *open* with a ballad." That was a problem in Barbra's life. When you initiate, when you're different, most of the world is frightened of it and doesn't understand it.'

When Barbra completed her set, Erlichman rushed backstage and found her next to the coffee urn in the Bon Soir's kitchen. He told her how wonderful he thought she was and wound up talking with her until she had to go on again. He missed Phil Leeds's act in the process. 'I told her, "Barbra, the first time out of the box, you're going to win every award that this business has to offer – the Tony, the Emmy, the Grammy, the Oscar." She looked at me and said, "The Oscar?" and I said, "That's going to be the biggest one, because you're going to be the biggest movie star of them all." She giggled and said, "I think I'm going to be a star, too."'

Barbra liked Erlichman's direct – some would say gruff – manner, so akin to hers. He asked her if she had a manager. She told him she was unhappy with Ted Rozar, who wouldn't accompany her on the road because he had a wife and young children, but that she had a contract with him. Her agency was always telling her, Marty later said, 'to change your nose, change your clothes, and stop singing those cockamamie songs.' She asked Erlichman if he would suggest she change anything about herself. He replied, 'Not a thing,' then offered to work for her for a year without commission in order to prove himself. Barbra liked that, and she told Erlichman that if she could wrangle out of her contract with Rozar, he could be her manager.

BARBRA CONTINUED TO give a lot of thought to her act, and to her audiences. She wondered whether she needed to explain where a new song came from in order for the audience to enjoy it fully. She plotted to vex the customers by whispering something to just one side of the audience. She told Jimmy Daniels she wanted to be introduced as 'the ugly, untalented, lousy Barbra Streisand.' She came up with a withering put-down for a heckler: 'I'd tell you to shut your mouth but it might ruin your sex life.'

She talked to Barry about singing songs as theater characters she wanted to play – Juliet, Ophelia, the young girl in *The Rose Tattoo* – and about putting together an act in which she would begin the set as a little girl and end it as a jaded woman. She worried, though, that she wouldn't be able to pull off the older woman because of her youth.

As it turned out, Barbra was soon able to sing torch songs with hard-earned personal conviction – thanks to Barry Dennen. According to Bob Schulenberg, while Barbra lived with Barry he treated her 'like a secondclass citizen.' Dennen told her not to answer the phone because he didn't want anyone in his family to know they were living together, and the doorman thought Barbra was Barry's cousin.

The relationship began to unravel in May of 1961 when Dennen went back to California to visit his family. Barbra hadn't been able to speak with him for the entire time he was away, and she missed him badly. The night he was due to return, she and Bob planned an elaborate welcome-home celebration. They bought champagne and all of his favorite foods, and left a note for him: 'Eat up, we'll be back after the show.'

When Barbra finished her last set at the Bon Soir she rushed home, thrilled that she would see Barry again after so long. He wasn't there. 'She worried that he'd missed the plane,' Bob recalled, 'but she couldn't call his family.' They sat up until three in the morning, but there was no call from Barry. 'This had to be so hard on her,' Schulenberg said. 'She planned this joyous welcome, and then nothing.'

Dennen's absence, and his silence, continued for a week, during which Bob felt 'Barbra ate up all her emotion for Barry.' When he finally returned, she adopted a defensive coolness toward him. A few weeks later Schulenberg figured the romance was really over when Barry had a group of male friends over to the apartment while Barbra visited her mother. One of the men riffled through a closet, put on some of Barbra's clothes, and started to imitate her singing 'Keepin' Out of Mischief Now.'

'Barry was laughing,' Schulenberg recalled, 'and I thought, You schmuck! Those are her clothes! I thought Barry should have gotten up and punched the guy in the nose. So I wondered, Can this relationship survive? And the answer I came up with was no.'

Barbra carried bitterness toward Barry for some time, and she used it for her biting rendition of 'Cry Me a River.' Schulenberg could tell the minute he heard it that 'Barbra was singing about Barry – all that bitterness and anger – "Now you say you're *sorry!*" I mean, she's not acting in that song, she's *feeling* it.'

BARBRA'S BON SOIR engagement extended through June 6, but once the gig lapsed, she got no new job offers. Most of the booking agents approached on her behalf had never seen her perform, and they repeated the usual litany of complaints about her. Her income had dried up, and after the breakup with Barry she had no place to live. She went back home to Brooklyn for a few weeks, but she couldn't stand her mother's harping about how she should get a *steady* job, something she could *count* on, not this on-again-off-again nightclub nonsense.

She fled back to Manhattan and spent the night wherever she could, most often in friends' apartments, where she usually slept on the couch. Sometimes, if someone else had beaten her to the available bed, she slept on the floor or in the bathtub. Finally she paid $12.95 at a Whelan Drug Store for a cot, which she lugged around with her everywhere she went. That way, no matter where she crashed, she could sleep on a bed of her own. For a time a friend let her sleep in his office, but she had to wait until the place was closed before she could come in and had to be out again by eight in the morning.

At last Irvin Arthur got her another sight-unseen booking, this one July 3–16 at the Town & Country Club in Winnipeg, Ontario, and a one-month return booking at the Caucus Club to begin on July 17. Meanwhile she needed money so badly she took a job as a switchboard operator at Ben Sackheim, an advertising agency where her brother, Sheldon, worked in the art department. 'The regular switchboard operator was away on vacation and Barbra was supposed to take her place,' Sheldon recalled. 'Well, for those two weeks none of us could get a call either in or out. Barbra was so bored with the work that she'd talk in these made-up foreign languages to everyone who called.'

Joe Battaglia, the vice president in charge of broadcast advertising for the agency, recalled Barbra as 'a moody kid. If she felt like saying good morning, she would. If she didn't, she'd ignore you. She was a little bit slovenly in her appearance. You looked at her and wondered whether she had bathed that day.'

One morning Sheldon went to Battaglia's office with a kinescope of Barbra's appearance on the Paar show, which had cost him $125 to obtain, and asked if he could help Barbra get work. 'I've had a lot of trouble with her,' Shelly told Battaglia. 'She has no home. She's almost uncontrollable. I can't make her do anything.' Battaglia said he'd see what he could do. He sent the kinescope to writers he knew at *The Steve Allen Show* in Hollywood. After a long delay, the response came: They thought Barbra's voice was 'great,' but they considered her 'too undisciplined' for prime-time network television.

Battaglia talked Barbra up to a few other people he knew in the business but had no success. Although the results had been disappointing, Battaglia expected that Barbra would express some gratitude for his efforts. She did not. 'She was aware that I had made efforts on her behalf with Steve Allen, but she would never thank me. She never so much as came up to me and said, "Listen, Joe, thanks for trying." Nothing like that at all.'

WHILE SHE PLUGGED calls into the switchboard at Ben Sackheim, Barbra got herself another permanent living situation. She had stayed briefly at a seedy single-room occupancy hotel near the Bon Soir, but now her acting school classmate Elaine Sobel came to the rescue. Elaine had a one-bedroom walk-up on Thirty-fourth Street near Second Avenue, and she offered Barbra her couch in exchange for help with the rent. 'It was a lot better than the street or bathtubs,' Elaine said.

Living together created a deep intimacy between Barbra and Elaine. 'We spent hours talking about our problems, until early in the morning,' Elaine reminisced. 'We were both trying to escape our past. We shared a core of pain that was nonpareil. I would cry, but Barbra wasn't a crier. Usually we talked about Barbra's problems. She never took much interest in mine.'

They talked a lot about men. 'She'd ask me about guys, but I wasn't any more sophisticated than she was, fellas-wise. She'd tell me about some guy she liked and she'd ask, "Do you think he's cute?" It was always more "Do you think he's cute?" than "Do you think he's talented?" Barbra used to moan, "Will I ever get a guy? Do you think anyone could ever love this face?"'

The roommates went to see Jean Genet's controversial play *The Balcony*, and Barbra recognized the Executioner as Stanley Beck, who had found her so interesting when they were both at Malden Bridge. She went backstage to see him, and the two began to date. 'Barbra told me she couldn't believe how well built Stanley was,' Elaine recalled, 'but she had rather ambivalent feelings toward him. When he was around, she felt she could take him or leave him. But when he was away, she missed him. At any rate, she told me he was *so* well built that she had bought herself a diaphragm just in case she gave in to temptation!'

Barbra was impressed, too, by an insight into her character that Stanley had shared with her. 'Stanley told her that she didn't like herself,' Elaine recalled, 'and that she thus couldn't accept it when someone else liked her. He said that was why she was attracted to guys who paid no attention to her, because they confirmed that she was nothing. She said to me, "Maybe he's right. I don't know."'

Elaine soon discovered that she and Barbra shared an odd phobia, one that might explain why so many people felt Barbra often looked as if she hadn't bathed. 'We both were frightened of taking showers. I found out later that mine came from the Holocaust, from what I'd heard about the gas chambers. Barbra's fear was of water falling on her head. I don't know where that came from.'

Elaine's biggest problems with Barbra revolved around the housekeeping. 'Barbra was just not a *balebosteh* – she wasn't neat around the house. No domestic talents. She never did any cooking, no, sir. It was always other people's food and drink.' Elaine also found that Barbra could be 'ruthless – in the sense that nothing would stop her. She could be thoughtless toward innocent people. She could be inconsiderate – like not returning calls, or not paying her share of the phone bill on time or not returning my coat that she borrowed. But when she wanted something, it was "Pack it, do it, move it, *now!*"'

Barbra and Elaine spent long spells in front of the mirror. 'She'd call herself *mieskeit* and say, "Who the hell wants me?" She'd look at me and say, "You're beautiful, Elaine. Look at your nose!" I was one of the first people to tell her, "Don't change your nose!" Barbra was very insecure about who she was. She kept repeating, "Ya think this is right? Ya think this is good? Whaddya think?" Over and over again. I told her that when something touches me deeply I get tingles on my left side. I call it "the truth chill." And when I heard her hit some notes in the bathroom my left side started to go crazy. I shouted to her, "It's happening, it's happening!"'

Whenever Barbra sang after that, she would ask Elaine, 'Ya gettin' any tingles?'

BARBRA'S ENGAGEMENT AT Auby Galpern's Town & Country Club in Winnipeg turned into a disaster. Perhaps because she was so far away from home, Barbra apparently decided to be as outrageous and experimental as possible in Canada. According to Marie Lawrence, a waitress at the club, Barbra came out on opening night in a brashly colored outfit that looked like a sarong, with thongs on her feet, carrying a bongo drum. 'She started playing the bongos and was chanting and singing in a foreign language. She would bend her body forward all the way to the floor, with her hair flying up and down with her movements.

'Mr Galpern went into a frenzy. He could hardly wait for the show to finish. The people just sat there staring at her, almost hypnotized. They were an older Jewish crowd and they didn't know what to make of her. Mr Galpern told her that if she didn't change her style of dress and singing she could take the first transportation back to where she came from. She changed her style after that – sometimes she'd sing Yiddish songs – but Mr Galpern hardly stayed around to watch any of her performances.'

Gene Telpner, a critic for the *Winnipeg Sun*, recalled that Galpern 'didn't like the way she dressed, that's for sure. She wore things that you'd wear when you were cleaning up the house. It was astonishing. That turned a lot of people off. She was poor, she was staying at the YWCA, but Galpern wasn't a very forgiving type. He kept telling her to get decent clothes, and she just ignored him.'

According to Auby Galpern's brother Myer, there was more to it than that. 'He was being polite later when he said it was her clothes, but really it was her slip. She wore this slip that you could see and it was dirty. She wore it day after day and never cleaned it. He didn't know how to tell her. Finally he did and she was insulted.'

All might have been forgiven if Barbra had been a bigger hit with her audiences. She told Elaine Sobel that she found Canadians 'a sour lot – emotionless and dull.' Still, she envied the girls she met, all of whom seemed to have good relationships with their parents. 'I wish I was like that,' she said. 'I'm getting very depressed.'

Auby Galpern was eager for an excuse to fire Barbra, and he got it a week into her engagement when she stalked offstage after four songs because the audience wouldn't quiet down. Galpern told her to pack up her things and leave. Barbra couldn't believe it. The next day she told Elaine Sobel, 'I don't know if I'm really fired, but I think I am.' She was. This would stand as the only time in her life that Barbra Streisand was dismissed from an entertainment job.

Nine years later, when Barbra was in Ottawa as the guest of Canadian Prime Minister Pierre Trudeau, whom she was dating, a reporter from Winnipeg asked her about her stay there.

'I've never been to Winnipeg,' Barbra replied.

'Yes, you have. You sang at Auby Galpern's Town & Country Club.'

'I've never met anyone named Auby Galpern,' she insisted, and turned away.

BARBRA'S THIRD AND last sojourn in Detroit was far more successful; after Winnipeg, the Caucus Club must have seemed to her like a family bosom. She stayed at the Hotel Wolverine, quite a step up from the YWCA, and was welcomed with enthusiasm by old friends and by new fans during her four-week stint between July 17 and August 12.

Barbra wrote to Elaine Sobel from Detroit to ask about something that had left her troubled: she wasn't sure what was expected of her when a man took her out after the show. Should she invite him to her room? Let him kiss her? Sleep with him? When she did invite a man up, she confessed she didn't know how to tell him to leave if she decided he wasn't quite right for her: 'I never know when to say when!'

While she was in Detroit, Barbra managed to extricate herself from her contract with Ted Rozar when her agency lent her $700 to 'buy him off,' as she put it, although Rozar insists Barbra owed him the money in commissions. Their main problem, Rozar said, was that 'she wanted someone who would always be there and act more as a personal assistant than a manager. With Barbra, there was a lot of hand-holding.' She telephoned Marty Erlichman, who was in San Francisco, and told him he had a client. They never signed a contract, and thirty-four years later, with a ten-year separation between 1977 and 1986, Erlichman is still Barbra's manager.

One sticking point remained with Rozar, however. Barbra had left several suitcases of clothes in his office, and she told friends he was holding them as ransom until he got paid. Rozar insists she was free to pick them up whenever she wanted to: 'Her wardrobe wasn't worth *anything* at that point!'

Still, Barbra showed up at Rozar's door, he said, accompanied by 'a big fat guy' and told him, 'I want my stuff!'

'I guess I was supposed to be intimidated by this goon,' Rozar said. 'I just said, "Fine, it's right there." I told the guy, "I oughta kick your butt outta here." And he said, "I'm a lawyer, and if you lay a hand on me I'm gonna sue you for five hundred dollars for every time you hit me." I just laughed. I could have shot the son of a bitch for trespassing. I don't know why she felt she had to bring this henchman with her. I'd already been paid.'

TRY AS SHE might, Barbra couldn't persuade Mike Wallace not to eat smoked foods. It was December 1, and she was making her fifth appearance on *P.M. East*, Wallace's late-night East Coast talk-variety show. Since her first guest stint on the show in June, Barbra had become its resident eccentric, spouting off amusingly on everything from the evils of milk to the benefits of Zen Buddhism. That she could also stagger the audience with the purity and power of her voice quickly made her one of Wallace's most popular guests. In New York, gay bars offered two-for-one drink nights whenever she appeared on the show, and Wallace's ratings swelled nationwide as well. Between June 1961 and June 1962 she appeared on the show thirteen times – five times in one five-week period. On various shows she sang a duet with Mickey Rooney ('I Wish I Were in Love Again'); confronted David Susskind, who had been an agent, over the fact that he had kept her waiting in his office and never granted her an interview; debated the merits of fallout shelters; sang 'Ding-Dong, the Witch Is Dead' from *The Wizard of Oz*; and kibbitzed with Eartha Kitt and Katharine Anne Porter.

The smoked foods controversy erupted during a party-themed show on which Woody Allen, the actor Paul Dooley, and the trombone-playing nightclub singer Lillian Briggs were also guests. Wallace's co-host, Joyce Davidson, had prepared an elaborate spread of food, most of which, Barbra protested, could kill you. She knew the health food pioneer Robert Rodale and sometimes slept in his office. She had taken to heart many of his warnings about the health risks posed by much of the food Americans ate. One Streisand fan's audiotape of the show preserves the dialogue for posterity:

BARBRA: I'll tell you, I'm very hungry . . . Oh, wait a minute! Wait a minute! Don't you understand? They're all smoked foods. You're not allowed to eat that stuff! [Laughter from the others.] Don't eat it, I'm *telling* you!

MIKE WALLACE: Aw, c'mon, you used to buy it all the time. It looks wonderful.

BARBRA: No, you wanna hear something? The highest cancer rate is in Iceland. [More laughs] No, wait a minute. People think there's nothing doing up in Iceland. Did you know there was a big medical university in Iceland?

JOYCE DAVIDSON: Eat the sandwich.

BARBRA: It's a fact. Up in Iceland there's a big medical university, and they made tests on these things . . . A lot of people in Iceland don't have refrigerators, so they have to smoke the food. They can't eat raw meat. They gotta smoke—

PAUL DOOLEY: No cigarettes?

BARBRA: Cut it out! Don't you care if you die or not?

WOODY ALLEN: Streisand's a little sick, folks.

BARBRA: You know what happens? They get a lot of cancer up there in Iceland.

LILLIAN BRIGGS: From what?

BARBRA: Smoked foods!

WALLACE: Barbra, why don't you *sing?*

MARTY ERLICHMAN DIDN'T take long to prove himself to Barbra. From the outset it was clear that he was willing to devote all his energies to the care and feeding of the Streisand career and to hold her hand as much as necessary to keep her on an even keel. And he took no guff from anybody about Barbra. When Abel Greene, the influential owner of the show business bible *Variety*, wrote that Streisand should consider 'a schnoz bob,' Marty hit the roof. Against all advice, he called Greene. 'Would you do that to your own daughter?' he railed at the startled publisher. 'You can say nose job or have the nose fixed, but where do you come off saying "schnoz bob"? It's vulgar and tasteless.' Greene apologized, but not in print.

Erlichman had very little money and no office. Barbra later said that his headquarters was a phone booth on Fifty-third Street and his capital was a pocketful of dimes. She was only half joking. What Erlichman did have in abundance was belief in Streisand and a willingness to pound the pavement day and night to get the word out about her. Perhaps an even more important contribution of Marty's to Barbra's career was his insistence that she deserved only the best. 'I always treated Barbra like a star,' he recalled, 'not by giving her limousines but by making decisions for her as if she *were* a star, not settling, but demanding the best treatment for her by everyone.'

Erlichman felt Barbra was overdue to move up from the Bon Soir to one of the classier uptown Manhattan nightspots. One of the poshest was Herbert Jacoby's Blue Angel on Fifty-fifth Street near Third Avenue, a gleaming den of sophistication with a red-carpeted entrance where celebrities like Tallulah Bankhead, Beatrice Lillie, and Truman Capote came to hear Pearl Bailey, Eartha Kitt, Johnny Mathis, and other top-notch performers.

Barbra had already auditioned for Jacoby on March 27, but he had found her 'too weird' for his tastes. Late in August Marty started to badger him to give Barbra another look, and finally he relented. In September she auditioned again, with toned-down material and a dressed-up look. This time Jacoby liked what he saw, and he scheduled Barbra for a two-week engagement beginning that November.

STILL, WHAT SHE really wanted was to get back on a theater stage. After several rejections, Marty got her an audition for *Another Evening with Harry Stoones*, an irreverent, wacky off-Broadway revue with music written by Jeff

Harris, a brash twenty-five-year-old newcomer, and partially backed by *Guys and Dolls* composer Frank Loesser. Harris already had as his star Diana Sands, the beautiful actress who had scored a major hit on Broadway as the feisty daughter in *A Raisin in the Sun*. 'It was an anti-revue,' Harris recalled. 'All the sketches kind of made fun of everything.'

Harris and his director, G. Adam Jordan, asked Barbra to audition twice. 'Both times she came in with Marty Erlichman,' Harris recalled. 'Marty wore the same suit to both auditions; it had a hole in the left sleeve.' Barbra's singing greatly impressed Harris. 'She certainly was hot, clearly talented, and very different.' Abba Bogin, the show's musical director, found Barbra's voice 'startling' and her personality 'funny, kooky. You asked her something and she answered funny. It was perfect for the show.'

Still, Harris and Jordan turned her down at first. They saw her as a singer, not as an actress, and the show had a limited number of songs, most of them earmarked for Susan Belink, who went on to renown as the opera singer Susan Belling. The rest of the cast – Dom DeLuise, Sheila Copelan, Virgil Curry, Kenny Adams, and Ben Keller in addition to Diana Sands – were all primarily straight or comic actors.

The auditions continued for a fourth girl to round out the cast, but Harris and Jordan found they couldn't keep the memory of Barbra Streisand from gnawing at their minds. Finally they called her in for a second audition, and she impressed them so much once again that Harris decided that if his show didn't have enough songs for Barbra Streisand to sing, he'd just have to write a few more. Abba Bogin recalled that they told Marty Erlichman on the spot that they wanted Barbra, 'and we told him what the deal was. The deal was terrible. This was off Broadway. There was practically no money involved. [Barbra would be paid $37.50 a week.] But it was a chance for her to do something in an important revue, a chance to be *seen*.'

When Barbra arrived for the first day of rehearsals at the Gramercy Arts Theater on East Twenty-seventh Street the second week of September, she was so nervous she vomited in the ladies' room. As rehearsals got under way, Bogin discovered that Barbra 'had no theatrical discipline at all. She always showed up late. The stage manager would admonish her, and she'd say, "I couldn't get here" or "I overslept" or something like that. But she'd also say, "Don't worry, I'll be ready," and she always was.'

Harry Stoones featured thirty-eight sketches, songs, and comic blackouts that ran the gamut from sophomoric to brilliant. Fourteen featured Barbra, including three solo numbers, two of which ('Jersey' and 'Value') Harris wrote specifically for her. In 'Jersey' she lamented the fact that her boyfriend had left New York and moved to the deep, dark wilds of the Garden State. 'It was a full-blast jungle number right from a movie,' Harris explained. 'She worries about all the dangers that can befall you in Jersey, and there are native jungle rhythms. She resolves to go after him – even though she may die – and bring him out.' At the end of the song, Barbra sang, 'I won't yell, I won't scream, I won't squawk – because it's better to die together in Jersey than be single in New Yawk.'

In 'Value' she comically compares the finances and automobiles of her two rich boyfriends, Harold Mengert and Arnie Fleischer. Another tune had her singing nothing but 'I've got the blues, I've got the blues, boy, do I have the blues' over and over again for three minutes until finally she announces, 'Now I feel better!'

In her comic sketches, Barbra played a klutzy ballet-dancing Wendy in a *Peter Pan* spoof, an Indian maiden during Columbus's discovery of America, and a mousy secretary sitting through boring dictation until she stands up, looks amorously at her boss, played by Dom DeLuise, and drops her skirt. Another sketch, 'Big Barry,' takes place in the girls' and boys' bathrooms of a high school. Ace, a macho jock, is bragging to his friend Jimbo and a nerdy little fellow, Barry, about his conquest of the night before. In the girls' room, Tina and Jo Jo are waxing poetic about their romances while mousy Nancy, played by Barbra, listens quietly. Finally mousy Nancy and nerdy Barry meet in the hallway. 'Barry,' Nancy whispers, 'I'm pregnant.'

Another Evening with Harry Stoones opened on Sunday evening, October 21, 1961, after five weeks of rehearsals and two weeks of previews. For the opening sketch, 'Carnival in Capri,' the entire cast rushed onstage, called out 'Hello, Good-bye, and Thanks!' and rushed off again as the lights went out. It was an unfortunately appropriate bit, because the show never had another performance. The Monday morning reviews in *The New York Times* ('not exactly unbearable if nonetheless none too stimulating') and the *Herald Tribune* ('callow . . . too predictable to be inspired') were enough to kill the precariously financed show before later positive reviews appeared in *The New Yorker*, *Women's Wear Daily*, and elsewhere.

Barbra's reviews were uniformly good. 'Barbra Streisand is a slim, offbeat, deadpan comedienne with an excellent flair for dropping a dour blackout gag,' *Variety's* reviewer wrote. Michael Smith in the *Village Voice* felt that 'Barbra Streisand can put across a lyric melody and make fine fun of herself at the same time.'

After the show, Jeff Harris had scheduled a potluck party for the company in his Riverside Drive apartment. 'Everybody came except Barbra. It was a real downer because of the notices. Everybody left and I got ready for bed. The doorbell rang, and it was Barbra. She brought a loaf of rye bread, and she was so proud because it had been freshly baked and sliced. That was the level of affluence we all shared at that point. I had to explain to her that the party was over – in more ways than one.'

ON NOVEMBER 16, Barbra opened fourth on the bill at the Blue Angel. When she arrived at the club that Thursday night, Herbert Jacoby stressed to her that she needed to be *sophisticated* – she wasn't in Greenwich Village any longer. 'Don't worry, I'm sophisticated,' Barbra told him. 'I'm gonna close with a Cole Porter number.'

Decked out in a simple black cocktail dress, Barbra certainly *looked* more sophisticated than she had at the Bon Soir. But the Cole Porter number, it turned out, was the outrageous ditty 'Come to the Supermarket in Old Peking' from *Aladdin*, a show written for television's *DuPont Show of the Month*. Barbra sang frenetically of that weird emporium where one could buy 'gizzard cakes, lizard cakes, pickled eels, pickled snakes, almost anything!'

As ever, her beautiful voice and her kooky material captivated her audiences. Barbra was a smash hit at the Blue Angel, and Jacoby extended her two-week engagement to four. Her success there proved that Streisand could appeal to chic audiences as much as she had to largely gay crowds and those in the vanguard of hip.

Pleased as she was by her latest breakthrough on the nitery circuit, Barbra still had her sights securely focused on the stage. On the morning of the day she opened at the Blue Angel, she walked into an audition for *I Can Get It for You Wholesale*, a Broadway musical to be presented by David Merrick, the red-hot producer of *Gypsy* and many other smash hits.

That audition would make its way into theatrical legend and result not only in Barbra's first Broadway show but in her marriage as well. It would also mark the beginning of one of the most phenomenal rises to superstardom in show business history.

PART 2

A Great Big Clump of Talent

'Some ain't got it, not a lump,

I'm a great big clump of talent.'

—*Barbra Streisand as Fanny Brice in* Funny Girl

7

A voice boomed out 'Miss Barbra Streisand' as she walked across the stage of the St James Theater under the harsh glow of a bare-bulb work light. She wore a mottled honey-colored 1920s caracul coat trimmed with thick fox fur at the knees and neck, which she had bought for ten dollars. Her feet were adorned by smudged tennis shoes; her unwashed hair spilled out in tangles from beneath her wool knit cap. Vigorously she smacked on her chewing gum.

She carried a bright red plastic case stuffed with sheet music, and as she approached the piano she dropped the briefcase. It landed with a thud and burst open, spilling sheet music at the feet of Peter Daniels, her accompanist. 'Oh, dear!' she exclaimed, and pounced on the mess. When she swooped down, her bag fell off her shoulder, and the strap got tangled up in the sleeve of the coat. Finally she got it together and turned to the amused audience – the show's director, Arthur Laurents; its author, Jerome Weidman; and its composer, Harold Rome. As Weidman recalled the scene in 1963, Barbra told them, 'Listen, my name's Barbra Streisand. With only two *a*'s. In the first name, I mean. I figure that third *a* in the middle, who needs it. What would ya like me to do?'

At first they had thought, Oh, God, here comes another loser, but by now they were laughing out loud. This girl was captivating, a real character. 'Whaddaya, dead or something? I said, what would you like me to do?'

'Can you sing?' Laurents asked.

'Can I sing?' She rolled her eyes toward the work light and back again. 'If I couldn't sing, would I have the nerve to come out here in a thing like this coat?'

'Okay, then, sing!'

'Sing!' She turned to the work light as if to say, Can you believe this?

'Even a jukebox you don't just say "Sing." You gotta first punch a button with the name of a song on it! What should I sing?'

'Sing anything.'

Barbra turned to Peter Daniels. 'Play that one on top.' Then she turned back to the seats, where assorted assistants watched along with the principals, and Marty Erlichman sat alone, eight rows back. 'Listen,' she called out. 'I'm real tired. I got ta bed real late last night. Can I do this sittin' on that chair over there?' She pointed to a secretarial chair on wheels.

'Sure, whatever you want,' Laurents replied.

'Great!' She plopped herself onto the chair, took off her shoes, pulled the wad of gum out of her mouth, and stuck it underneath the seat. By now everyone was fairly helpless with laughter. Then she launched into 'Value,' comparing the cars and bankbooks of Harold Mengert and Arnie Fleischer while she careened across the stage on casters. When she was done, Laurents, Weidman, and Rome burst into applause. 'It may not have been the funniest song ever written,' Weidman recalled, 'but it certainly came out that way when filtered through Miss Streisand's squint, fur coat, gestures, and vocal cords.'

Still laughing, Laurents asked her, 'Do you have a ballad?'

'Do I have a ballad!' By the time she finished the haunting, plaintive 'Have I Stayed Too Long at the Fair,' the *I Can Get It for You Wholesale* creative team's jaws were slack. Harold Rome leaned over to Arthur Laurents and whispered, 'Isn't she *something?*'

'She's terrific,' Laurents agreed. 'But what can we do with her? She's not right for the ingenue, and Miss Marmelstein's fifty years old.'

'Maybe Miss Marmelstein doesn't have to be fifty years old,' Rome mused. 'The way this girl looks, people would believe her as a spinster. She could be any age.'

Laurents thought a few moments. 'Let's have her back for Merrick to take a look.' He asked Barbra if she could return that afternoon.

'Gee, I don't know.' She shielded her eyes and sought out Marty Erlichman. 'Marty, what time's my hair appointment?'

'Two o'clock.'

'Ya see, I gotta get my hair done because I'm opening tonight at the Blue Angel. I'm singing there. Maybe you'll come and see me.'

Finally she promised to be back at four, and after she left, Arthur Laurents asked his assistant, Ashley Feinstein, to check under Barbra's chair for the wad of gum. As he had suspected, there was none. 'She had the gift of thinking something out and then, when she did it, making it look spontaneous,' Laurents said.

When Barbra returned, the first thing she asked was how everyone liked her hair. All agreed it looked smashing. This time David Merrick was in the audience, and Barbra sang five songs. Afterward she said to Marty, 'I don't think they liked me.' Everyone had liked her just fine, except Merrick. He thought she was ugly, he told Laurents, and 'too weird.'

Laurents, Rome, and Weidman did go to the Blue Angel that night, without Merrick, and they asked Barbra to audition four more times, all the while trying to convince Merrick she was right for the part. Finally, the producer yielded to the judgment of his creative team, and on the day after Thanksgiving they told her she would be their Miss Marmelstein. Barbra Streisand, at last, would make her Broadway debut in a top-flight production at a salary of $150 a week. 'Oh, goody!' she exclaimed. 'Now I can get a telephone.'

BASED ON JEROME WEIDMAN'S 1937 novel, *I Can Get It for You Wholesale* tells the story of brash, opportunistic Harry Bogen and his rise to the top of the garment industry in the late 1930s. Along the way he strains his relationships with his mother, his partner, and his girlfriend. As a new David Merrick musical, the show was virtually assured of success – in 1960 Merrick had six hit shows running simultaneously. Arthur Laurents had written the librettos for two of Broadway's biggest recent hits, *Gypsy* and *West Side Story*; this show would mark his debut as a director. Harold Rome, a twenty-five-year Broadway veteran, had more than doubled the existing record for the longest-running Broadway show in 1937 with the 1,108 performances of his sprightly paean to unions in the garment trade, *Pins and Needles*.

Cast in the pivotal role of Harry Bogen was twenty-three-year-old Elliott Gould, whose previous career height had been kicks in the choruses of *Rumple*, *Say, Darling*, and *Irma la Douce*. Rounding out the cast were Lillian Roth as Bogen's mother, Jack Kruschen as his boss, Marilyn Cooper as his girlfriend, and Sheree North as a hooker he keeps on the side.

On the first day of rehearsals, as Barbra sat in a half circle with the other actors for the initial reading of the play, Jerome Weidman noticed that she seemed preoccupied with something she was writing. When the reading ended, she rushed over to David Powers, the show's press agent, thrust a piece of paper at him, and began an animated discussion of her effort. Weidman ambled over, and Powers handed it to him. 'Look what this dame gives me.'

Powers had asked the cast members to compose their biographical notes for *Playbill*, the theater program magazine, and what Barbra wrote left him skeptical: 'Barbra Streisand is nineteen, was born in Madagascar and reared in Rangoon, educated at Erasmus Hall High School in Brooklyn and appeared off Broadway in a one-nighter called *Another Evening with Harry Stoones* . . . She is not a member of Actors' Studio.'

'Was it hot in Madagascar?' Weidman recalled he asked Barbra.

'How the hell should I know?' she replied. 'I've never been to the damn place.'

'That's my point,' Powers spluttered. 'It's a phony. Nobody reading that will believe you.'

'What the hell do I care? I'm so sick and tired of being born in Brooklyn, I could plotz. Whad I do? Sign a contract I gotta be born in Brooklyn? Every day the same thing? No change? No variety? Why get born? Every day the same thing, you might as well be dead!'

After a protracted struggle, Barbra got her bogus bio published in *Playbill*. It made a little piece of theater history and added to Streisand's growing reputation as a kook. As with most of her apparent madnesses, though, there was method behind it. 'I figured the audience would read it before I came on and notice me more,' she had reasoned. 'I played the part of a Brooklyn girl. How boring it would have been to say I was from Brooklyn.'

As rehearsals progressed, the *Wholesale* company learned that Barbra Streisand was anything but boring. At times she drove Arthur Laurents to distraction with her behavior, often the opposite of what one would expect from a young actress getting her first big break. For one thing, she repeatedly arrived late for rehearsals and out-of-town performances, and harsh admonishments from the stage manager and Laurents didn't solve the problem. Finally, during the Broadway run, after she had been officially late thirty-eight times, Merrick filed a complaint against her with Actors' Equity. The newspaper columnist Sidney Fields reported that as Barbra prepared to appear before the Equity board she asked him what he thought of 'an elaborate set of alibis she'd prepared to excuse her tardiness.' Fields advised her not to lie but to apologize and promise never to do it again. And that, presumably, is what she did.

Elaine Sobel recalled the reason for at least one of Barbra's latenesses. 'She had a meeting with David Merrick. She was sitting at our dressing table staring into the mirror. I said, "Barbra, you're gonna be late. You can't keep a man like David Merrick waiting." She just said, "Yeah, I know. He'll wait."'

BARBRA WAS DETERMINED to create her Miss Marmelstein entirely on her own. 'I listened to what they wanted me to do,' she recalled, 'and I argued. I almost got fired, but I did it the way I wanted to, finally. I didn't want help.'

A serious disagreement between Arthur Laurents and Barbra arose around her one solo musical number, 'Miss Marmelstein,' the comic lament of a drudge whom no one ever calls 'bubelah' or 'passion pie.' Barbra wanted to do it sitting in a secretarial chair, just as she had when she sang 'Value' at her audition. Laurents preferred that she stand while she delivered the number, but when she rehearsed it for the first time she grabbed the chair, settled herself into it, and started to sing before Laurents could stop her. When she finished, he told her to do it again – on her feet this time.

Her second performance was perfunctory, and Laurents exploded in anger. He dressed her down in front of the cast, and Jerome Weidman recalled that his heart went out to her. 'There she sat, head down, her face concealed by that curtain of tumbled hair, her hands making small twitching motions in her lap. The sight of Miss Streisand's suffering filled me with so much pity and horror that I could neither speak nor move.'

Finally it was over, and after Laurents left, Weidman recalled he walked over to Barbra and said, 'I'm sorry, kid.'

'Listen, Jerry,' she said, 'whaddaya think of this?' Her hands had been twitching while she scratched a pencil across a diagram of a new apartment she had just rented. 'Here's where I wanna put the couch,' she said without looking up, 'but the fireplace is all the way over here on *this* wall. Where the hell would *you* put the couch?'

At that moment Weidman decided that Barbra possessed the vital ingredient for success: 'She was made of copper tubing.'

She wasn't, of course, but she'd be damned if she'd let anybody see her uncertainty, her vulnerability, her fear. And no matter what, she had made up her mind that if she felt something was right for her, she wouldn't let anyone talk her out of it. Not a producer, not a director. No one. She was too afraid of failure to do something that went against her instincts. 'The reason I talked back to the director was that I sincerely felt I'd be better off walking out of the show if I couldn't play the character my own way. I just didn't care what happened. I could go out and work in a nightclub again.'

As the rehearsal came to an end, Barbra ran around handing out slips of paper to anyone who would take one. 'I just got a phone installed in my new apartment,' she announced. 'Call me!' That night the telephone rang just once. A male voice on the other end of the line said, 'You asked for somebody to call, so I called. I just wanted to say you were brilliant today. This is Elliott Gould.' Before Barbra could say anything, he had hung up. Later Gould would say that when he watched her perform 'Miss Marmelstein,' she had reminded him of his mother.

IT WAS DURING out-of-town tryouts in Philadelphia that the company first noticed something was going on between Barbra and the show's tall, dark, handsome, and teddy-bearish leading man. Wilma Curley, a dancer in the chorus, recalled that Barbra frequently made her entrance from the wrong side of the stage, which would put the other actors off kilter. 'Harold Lang [a cast member] would go to a door and call for Miss Marmelstein, and she'd come in from the opposite side. He got pretty annoyed because it would throw his timing and staging off.'

After a while the company realized that Barbra's errant entrances were always made from the direction of Elliott Gould's dressing room, the side of the stage opposite hers. 'It was like, "Ah, she's in Elliott's dressing room,"' Wilma recalled. 'We were a little surprised, because he had been dating Marilyn Cooper. Marilyn wasn't very pleased when Barbra stepped in. She said to me, "I really like this guy, but Barbra's out to get him." And of course she did get him.'

Barbra hadn't liked Elliott initially, and he had been too shy to ask her out at first. But he would sometimes walk her to the subway after rehearsals. When he finally asked for a date, Barbra recalled, 'I thought he was being funny because he was always joking around and doing nutty things.' Their evening out consisted of dinner and coffee in a diner after a late rehearsal. 'I found myself always laughing when Elliott was close by,' Barbra said. They talked until the small hours of the morning, and as they spent more and more time together, Elliott opened up his heart to her. She was amazed at how much alike they turned out to be, far beyond the surface similarities of their profession, their Jewish faith, and their Brooklyn upbringing.

Insecure about his appearance, Elliott had spent his childhood thinking that he had 'a fat ass' and wishing he looked like Robert Wagner. He had always had difficulty being on time. He had adored Jerry Lewis and pantomimed to his records. He had escaped from hot Brooklyn summers inside movie houses. They were, he said, 'my sanctuary.'

He had needed sanctuary from the stifling two-and-a-half-room apartment he shared with his parents, Bernard and Lucille Goldstein, in the Bensonhurst section southwest of Flatbush, where he had slept in the same room with them for eleven years, listening to their ever-worsening battles. 'That's the place where I was most vulnerable, where I began to withdraw and become self-conscious,' he told *Playboy* in 1970. 'I would have loved to have taken a bat and just destroyed every wall and every shelf and everything else in it.'

He could have been talking about Barbra and Louis Kind and apartment 4G. But as much as their commonalities captured Barbra's imagination, it was the one major difference between them that fascinated her the most: from the age of nine, Elliott Goldstein had spent his childhood singing and dancing, pushed into lessons and auditions and recitals by his ambitious mother. He had appeared on television – an assignment for which his mother changed his name without telling him 'because it sounded better' – and at thirteen had been part of a vaudeville bill on the stage of New York's fabled Palace Theater, playing a singing bellboy.

'Oh, that must have been wonderful,' Barbra burbled.

'I hated every minute of it,' he replied.

'But *why*?' Barbra couldn't imagine how anyone could have hated doing what she had so longed to do as a girl.

He explained that he'd had no choice, that he was constantly pushed, pushed, pushed. He had never harbored a deep ambition to be a performer. Yet here he was, the leading man in a Broadway show at twenty-three, and it amazed Barbra that she and Elliott had arrived at this point via such different avenues.

The more she saw him and the more they talked, the more enamored she became. The feeling was mutual. 'I was fascinated with her,' Elliott recalled in 1964. 'She needs to be protected. She is a very fragile little girl. She doesn't commit easily, but she liked me.' Just as Roy Scott had four years earlier, Elliott found Barbra 'absolutely exquisite. She was the most innocent thing I'd ever seen, like a beautiful flower that hadn't blossomed yet.'

'I was beginning to feel something for the guy, and it scared me half to death,' Barbra recalled. 'I found myself talking gibberish . . . One night I even went onstage with half my face made up . . . I guess I was in love.'

Their romance took on the trappings of a Manhattan fairy tale. They'd walk around the city in the night cold, duck into Forty-second Street theaters for midnight showings of low-budget horror movies about giant ants and caterpillars that ate cars, seek out all-night diners on Ninth Avenue for rice pudding and coffee ice cream, play Pokerino in penny arcades off Times Square.

One night, Barbra recalled, 'we were walking around the skating rink at Rockefeller Center when he chased me and we had a snowball fight. He never held me around or anything, but he put snow on my face and kissed me, very lightly . . . It was great. Like out of a movie!'

On the opening night of *Wholesale* in Philadelphia, Barbra sent Elliott a note: 'To my clandestine lover.' They had not yet been intimate, but that would change a few days later. Was Elliott still a virgin? That depends on which of his stories one chooses to believe. In one interview he said that he had 'become a man' at fourteen with a very fat girl wearing a girdle who fell asleep on top of him. In another interview he said his first sexual experience was in a Boston hotel room in 1958, when he was nineteen.

But in a proposal for his autobiography that made the rounds of publishers in New York, Elliott claimed he had 'surrendered' his virginity to Barbra in a room at the Bellevue Stratford Hotel in Philadelphia. 'Barbra was the one I chose,' he wrote. 'I was excited, but I was frightened.' Just as he and Barbra were reaching heights of ecstasy, Elliott said, a bunch of his pals showed up. 'I was trying to become a man, and these guys were pounding on the door. I wouldn't open it. This was my moment, and I wasn't about to let anyone take it from me.'

If Elliott was a sexual neophyte, he and Barbra evidently made up for lost time. They spent most of their free hours in his room, and their activity disturbed Wilma Curley, who had the room next door. 'I'd be trying to get to sleep and their bed would start bouncing,' she recalled. 'One time I had to go over, rap on the door, and tell them to keep it down. One night I heard Barbra pounding on the door and screaming at him to let her back in. I peeked out and there she was, stark naked. Finally he let her back in.

'They were like high school kids. They'd have food fights in restaurants, they giggled all the time, he'd lock her out of the room. None of us thought of them as having an affair – it wasn't mature enough to be an affair.'

ARTHUR LAURENTS HAD come to doubt that Barbra Streisand was mature enough to be an actress on Broadway. He had given in to her on the issue of the chair, and when she stopped the show on opening night in Philadelphia by whirling on casters across the stage while she sang 'Miss Marmelstein,' he was glad to concede she'd been right. But the next night she altered her inflections, her movements, her timing, and Laurents was furious. 'I gave the director a bad time,' Barbra later admitted. 'He insisted on blueprinting exactly how I should do everything. I can't work that way . . . I find it very difficult to do anything twice in exactly the same way.'

Consistency, of course, is the essence of the theater – without it there's anarchy – and Laurents put his foot down. 'She didn't know very much about the stage,' he recalled. 'she was very undisciplined. She's inventive, but it never occurred to her that the invention should be for rehearsals and not for onstage. She would throw the other actors off cue. I had to be rather sharp with her just before we opened in New York, and from that point on, the performance was solid and stable.'

From David Merrick's standpoint, Barbra's employment was far from stable – and so was Elliott's. 'I had a battle every night with Merrick,' Laurents said. 'He wanted to fire them because he thought they were both unattractive, and he didn't think Barbra was funny.'

Laurents thought Barbra was funny. 'We kept giving her more to do in the musical numbers, taking what was a group number and highlighting her. Merrick wasn't that concerned with Barbra after a while because she wasn't the lead. But Elliott was, and he wanted me to fire him.' Elliott's out-of-town reviews didn't help his cause; most of them criticized his singing and his character's unlikability. 'I was terribly green, and I was trying too hard,' Elliott admitted. Merrick kept up the pressure on Laurents to dismiss Gould. 'In Philly and Boston, Merrick kept bringing in every leading man in town' to find a replacement for him, Laurents said, but the director held his ground. 'I thought he was fine in the role. When Merrick finally said he was going to fire Elliott, I threatened to quit. Elliott stayed.'

ELEVEN WEEKS AFTER its first rehearsal, *I Can Get It for You Wholesale* opened on Thursday, March 22, 1962, at the Shubert Theater on West Forty-fourth Street. Barbra made her greatest impression about ten minutes into the second act. She had had just a few lines and had sung just snippets in two musical numbers in the first act. But now out of the wings she rolled, whizzing across the floorboards on her swivel chair, arms and legs aflail, pencil stuck in her beehive hairdo, her face framed by a huge white collar like the subject of a portrait by Holbein the Younger.

She stopped the chair in the middle of the stage by planting her feet squarely in front of her. She lowered her head into her hands, then looked up imploringly at the audience as the music began. 'Oh, *why* is it always Miss Marmelstein?' she fairly sobbed, her Brooklyn accent unrestrained.

The girl who hadn't wanted to be laughed at put her audience into hysterics. She was hilarious. She was touching. She whined, she mugged, she belted. The audience laughed with her, rooted for her, adored her. When she finally came to a defeated conclusion and fairly spat out, 'Ooooh, I could *bust!*' they jumped to their feet to cheer and applaud her for a solid three minutes – an eternity in the theater. She had stopped the show cold. At that moment – 9:35 P.M. on the fourth Thursday in March 1962 – Barbra Streisand became a Broadway star.

Friday morning's reviews of the show ran the gamut from raves to pans. The majority of the critics found the story and its hero too unpleasant to be enjoyable, but Barbra's performance garnered unanimous raves. 'Brooklyn's Erasmus Hall High School should call a holiday to celebrate the success of its spectacular alumna, Barbra Streisand,' Norman Nadel wrote in the *World Telegram & Sun*. 'As a secretary, she sets the show in motion and hypos it all the way.'

Theatre Arts critic John Simon, who would later write witheringly of Barbra's looks and personality, praised her 'Chekhovian brand of heart-breaking merriment. Gifted with a face that shuttles between those of a tremulous young borzoi and a fatigued Talmudic scholar . . . she can also sing the lament of the unreconstructed drudge with the clarion peal of an Unliberty Bell.' The critic for *The Nation* likened Barbra to 'an innocent

Modigliani model. Her Miss Marmelstein – a screaming, hysterical, efficient, harassed, nervously giggling secretary – is a delightful comic miniature.'

Overnight, Barbra became the toast of Broadway. On April 4 she appeared on *Today*, hosted by John Chancellor. After she sang 'Much More' and 'Right as the Rain,' Chancellor asked her whether she missed the *a* in her name and what she was made of – 'sugar and spice and everything nice?' Barbra winced slightly and replied, 'No.'

'What, then?' Chancellor pressed. 'Songs?'

'Flesh and bones,' she said weakly.

Within weeks *Life* magazine had featured her prominently as one of that season's 'Broadway Showstoppers.' *Mademoiselle* chose her, along with Barbara Lang, Barbara Harris, and Sue Lyon, 'Most Likely to Succeed.' *The New Yorker* called her a 'coming star' and ran an interview in which she bragged about finding a hundred-dollar dress marked down to twelve-fifty in Filene's Basement in Boston.

She spoke of her mother too, and frankly. 'She did come to the opening night of *Wholesale*, but I don't think she understood what I was trying to do in it. Why should she? The things that interest her about me are whether I'm eating enough and whether I am warmly enough dressed. She's a very simple, nonintellectual, nontheatrical person who lives and breathes.'

Elaine Sobel had walked with Barbra's mother from the theater to the opening-night party at Sardi's. Along the way she turned to Diana and said, 'You must be thrilled – your daughter's a Broadway star.'

'Yes, that's nice,' Diana replied. 'But I still think she'd be more secure working in a school as a *real* secretary.'

THE SWORD OF her new success, as it often does, had two edges for Barbra. 'I was the most hated girl on Broadway,' she said. 'Elliott was the only one in the show who liked me. No one could understand how a girl like me could suddenly come off with all those raves. Everyone expects you to slave in seventy plays before you make it.'

Barbra's unpopularity had less to do with her raves, in fact, than with her behavior. Her lateness and unpredictable entrances annoyed the company, and her occasional childishness grated on them. Wilma Curley recalled finding some makeup missing from her dressing room. 'Who has my stuff?' she yelled into the hallway.

'Oh, I do,' Barbra called out. 'I needed it.'

'She wanted it, she needed it, she took it,' Wilma said. 'It wasn't a gigantic problem, but it annoyed me because she had gotten some-one to open my dressing room door. And she'd never return anything unless I asked for it. She was self-engrossed. Everything was just me, me, me.'

Already Barbra had become the subject of bitchy repartee. At a cocktail party Elliott and Barbra attended, one young lady told anyone who would listen, 'Barbra Streisand thinks she's flat-chested so she's got the front of her dress stuffed with tissue paper. You can hear it crackling! Go look!'

Any animosity that existed toward Barbra among the *Wholesale* company surely deepened when she became the only member of the cast or crew to win a nomination for the coveted Antoinette Perry Award (the Tony). At the April 29 ceremonies in the ballroom of the Waldorf-Astoria Hotel, she vied for Best Featured or Supporting Actress in a Musical with Elizabeth Allen in *The Gay Life*, Barbara Harris in the revue *From the Second City*, and Phyllis Newman in David Merrick's other new show that season, *Subways Are for Sleeping*.

Merrick managed to insult both of his young nominees that night. He sat at Newman's table rather than Barbra's, but as the list of nominees was read, he turned to Newman and said, 'Streisand's going to win, and I voted for her.'

In fact the winner was Newman, and Marty Erlichman's prediction that Barbra would win every major award would have to wait. Why didn't Barbra, who had clearly made the biggest impact among Broadway neophytes that year, win the Tony? That *Wholesale* was her first show hurt rather than helped; she was correct that many people prefer to honor someone who has paid some dues. And word of Barbra's reprimand by Actors' Equity for her repeated latenesses surely didn't help.

Barbra did collect the New York Drama Critics Circle Award and the lion's share of that Broadway season's acclaim and publicity. She also won the leading man. Shortly after *Wholesale* opened, Elliott moved into Barbra's apartment above a seafood restaurant on Third Avenue.

✳

IT WAS A tiny one-bedroom cold-water flat. The only window in the living room looked smack out onto a brick wall. The bathtub sat in the middle of the kitchen, the floor was so uneven that visitors felt they were listing, and there were no closets. Barbra didn't mind, though: the rent was only $67.20 a month, and for the first time she had an apartment all her own.

By all accounts, the place was a wonder. 'The smell of fish!' Elaine Sobel exclaimed. 'And the *shmattehs* hanging everywhere!' (*Shmattehs* are rags, or inexpensive clothes.) A close friend of Barbra and Elliott's, who spoke on the condition of anonymity, said it was 'the filthiest apartment I've ever seen. Awfully, awfully dirty. I'd go over there to play cards with Elliott and I used to kid him and say, "Where the hell are you fucking this girl?" Because they slept on a *folding cot*. For two people! And Elliott's a big guy. No mattress cover or anything like that. God! And her idea of art was a toilet seat hung on the wall.'

Whenever she or Elliott bathed, they had to boil four large pots of water on the stove for hours to keep the water hot. The rest of the time they covered the claw-footed tub with a piece of plywood and piled stacks of dirty dishes on top of it to free up counter space.

In the living room, feather boas hung from Tiffany-style lampshades, and an old wooden sewing machine cabinet doubled as the dinner table. Beaded bags hung from gilt picture frames with nothing in them. *Harry Stoones* creator Jeff Harris recalled that 'she had this one amazing thing that looked like a World War II oxygen mask – but to this day I'm not sure what it was.' In the bedroom, dozens of shallow drawers in an old wooden dentist's cabinet held sheet music, costume jewelry, belt buckles, fabric swatches. An apothecary jar housed Barbra's collection of paste-on beauty spots. She plastered the bathroom walls with a collage of photos, articles, ads, and words or phrases she'd cut from newspapers and magazines, then shellacked it to a burnished sheen. Her guests tended to spend inordinate amounts of time in the room – reading.

Such decor would not have been everyone's cup of tea, but Elliott loved it. When he moved in, he said, he thought of himself and Barbra as Hansel and Gretel, ensconced in an enchanted cottage. 'The happiest memories I have of Barbra are when we were living together before we were married. We were having a really romantic time.' They worked together, lived together, played together 'like kids in a treehouse,' one friend said. They watched late-night horror movies on a temperamental old television set. Seated at Barbra's sewing machine, they gobbled Swanson's frozen fried chicken dinners and bricks of Breyers coffee ice cream. Late at night they'd munch on kosher salami, fried matzos, and pickled herring.

They read scenes together from Greek dramas – Barbra as Medea, Elliott as Jason. They made up their own language, a variation on pidgin English, so that no one else could understand what they were saying to each other. It was Hansel and Gretel against the world.

'I wanted to take care of Barbra,' Elliott recalled in 1964. 'Every morning I'd wake her up, saying, "Barbra, come get your chicken soup."' One evening, as the two slept on their cot, Elliott heard 'a gruesome squealing and scratching. It sounded like a rat the size of an elephant. I looked under the tub and I saw a tail about a yard long . . . I closed the door and called the fire department.' There was nothing the firemen could do, and after spending the rest of the night in a hotel, the couple learned to live with their uninvited guest, which they named Gonzola.

'We used to laugh about that a lot,' Elliott has said. 'I look back to Third Avenue with sublime affection.'

NO MATTER HOW hard he tried, Marty Erlichman couldn't get Barbra a recording contract. Since the fall of 1961 he had been badgering every record industry executive in New York to listen to her. He never sent a tape; he insisted on live auditions. Barbra would schlep to the offices of Columbia or RCA or Capitol Records with a trio Marty would quickly patch together – Peter Daniels on piano, Barbra's bass player from the Bon Soir, Bobby Short's drummer – and she would sing two or three numbers, usually 'A Sleepin' Bee,' 'I Stayed Too Long at the Fair,' and 'When the Sun Comes Out.'

The responses were uniform. 'She has a beautiful voice,' Marty recalled the bigwigs telling him, 'but it's more Broadway than records, and certainly the voice and the material are not what's being bought right now. We don't think she'll sell records.' The main problem was that in this era a new singer was expected to have three or four hit singles on release before the label would get behind an album. Because her looks and her sound were so different – she wasn't likely to be booked on *American Bandstand* – no one could foresee Barbra Streisand as a singles seller.

Precisely the elements that made Barbra so unforgettable in a nightclub – her esoteric material, her jazzy playfulness, her histrionics – worked against her in the minds of the recording industry decision-makers. The popular vocalists of this era were bland, unthreatening, homogeneous balladeers. The biggest-selling non-rock 'n' roll singles were prettily sung melodic ballads like 'Moon River' and 'A Taste of Honey.' And auditioning live actually may have hurt more than it helped. Barbra didn't look like Patti Page or Julie London or Doris Day, and her sometimes overwrought performing style tended to turn off hidebound traditionalists, which included most record executives.

Marty had his heart set on signing Barbra with Columbia, the Cadillac of record labels, and after her live audition for the company's president, Goddard Lieberson, he played a tape he'd made of his client at the Bon Soir. 'Listen to the applause,' he urged. 'They loved her. They gave her standing ovations, flowers, the works.' He asked Lieberson to hold on to the tape and 'listen to it when the phone ain't ringing.'

Lieberson listened and then played the tapes for others in the company. They agreed with his opinion that Barbra was too special. Sure, the Bon Soir audience loved her, but they were sophisticated New Yorkers, and many of them were gay at that. To sell records in numbers that mattered, Barbra would have to appeal to mainstream America, and Lieberson didn't think she would. He sent her a note to say she had a beautiful voice but he didn't see the kind of commercial potential for her that the economic realities of the music marketplace required.

Shortly after Barbra's *Wholesale* audition, Arthur Laurents sent Lieberson a note, unbeknownst to Barbra or Marty, urging him to sign her. Lieberson asked Marty to bring Barbra in again, and this time he recorded her audition at Columbia's Studio B at 799 Seventh Avenue in order to see how she would sound when her voice was professionally taped. But he still felt she was too eccentric.

Barbra soon appeared on two Columbia albums anyway. The label specialized in original-cast Broadway recordings, and on Sunday, April 1, Barbra joined the rest of the *Wholesale* cast to commit the score to vinyl. She arrived late, as usual, dressed in jeans, a tatty sweater, and dirty sneakers, and made a beeline for Lieberson the minute she saw him. 'Goddard! Goddard!' she called out. 'I got a great idea for the album!'

According to the album's musical director and vocal arranger, Lehman Engel, Barbra stopped singing in the middle of 'Miss Marmelstein' and complained that she didn't like the orchestration. 'Goddard could have spoken to her over the intercom,' Lehman wrote in his memoirs. 'Instead, he left the control room and walked over to her. He put his arm around her shoulders and gently led her away to the sidelines. Out of earshot of the orchestra and the rest of the cast he spoke to her. I don't know what he said to her, but when she came back, she sang the song as it was charted, straight through, in one amazing take.'

Marty and Barbra hoped that the *Wholesale* album would change Lieberson's mind about signing Barbra, but Harold Rome's score did little to enhance the unique qualities of the Streisand voice. And while 'Miss Marmelstein' amply demonstrated her comic talents and her ability to belt, it didn't showcase the beauty, purity, and range that made her voice so special.

Barbra's appearance on a second album – a twenty-fifth-anniversary edition of Rome's first big success, *Pins and Needles* – came about in spite of Lieberson's opposition to using her. Rome felt so strongly that she was right for it that he threatened not to do the record at all unless Barbra participated. Lieberson relented, and Rome's instincts proved unassailable. The cheery, lilting score celebrating the joys of union membership in the garment trade gave Barbra some marvelously funny turns that left the listener wishing the show had been revived on Broadway as well. Arguably, it would have been more successful than *Wholesale* and made Barbra an even bigger sensation.

After *Pins and Needles* and the publicity barrage that had attended Barbra's triumph in *Wholesale*, both Capitol and Atlantic came back to Marty with contracts in hand. He turned them down. 'The first company that wanted to sign her was Atlantic,' he recalled to *Billboard* in 1983, 'but that label was basically jazz. I told them that I thought she had great potential as an album seller, and since Columbia was the best album-producing company, I had my heart set on them. I told Capitol the same thing. It was a difficult thing to do, turning down offers after we'd waited so long, because neither of us had any money. But we both thought it would be better to hold out for the best than to jump at the first offer just because we were hungry.'

To keep the Streisand buzz hot and to ensure that 'Miss Marmelstein' wouldn't typecast her as an ethnic comedienne, Erlichman booked her into a two-week return engagement at the Bon Soir beginning May 22. This time she was the headliner, billed as 'Barbra (*I Can Get It for You Wholesale*) Streisand.' Every night after the show, Marty had a taxi ready outside the theater at eleven-thirty to whisk her downtown.

On May 29 she appeared on the popular TV prime-time variety hour *The Garry Moore Show*. She stepped out onto a balcony set, dressed in an elegant black cocktail dress, and sang a highly charged, thrilling rendition of 'When the Sun Comes Out.' Later in the show, during a 'That Wonderful Year' segment set in 1929, she sang a slowed-down, ironic version of the traditionally uptempo Democratic Party theme song 'Happy Days Are Here Again' as a wealthy woman who has lost all her money in the stock market crash of that year. With forced gaiety, she sat in a deserted barroom, paying for each successive glass of champagne with her earrings, rings, and bracelets.

Barbra also appeared on *PM East* five times between April and June, and one of those appearances finally turned the tide for her at Columbia. For months Marty Erlichman had urged David Kapralik, the sprightly director of Columbia's artists and repertoire department, to catch Barbra's act in the hope that Kapralik would report back favorably to Lieberson. Kapralik never got around to it, but late one night he returned to his apartment and switched on *PM East*. A girl was singing, Kapralik recalled, 'and I was knocked off my feet. When she finished and Mike Wallace said her name, I made the connection: this was the girl Marty had been bugging me about! She was in command of the full spectrum of human emotion from comedic to tragic, and she just blew me away.'

As Marty had hoped, Kapralik relayed his enthusiasm to Lieberson, whose opposition to Streisand had already begun to soften. Everywhere he turned, it seemed, people were talking about 'this girl.' At cocktail parties he would listen to Harold Arlen rave about the way she sang his songs, 'A Sleepin' Bee' and 'Right as the Rain.' Whenever Lieberson spoke to Harold Rome or Arthur Laurents, they'd marvel, 'You haven't signed her yet?' Even within the hallowed halls of Columbia Records, Barbra converts were becoming legion. Kapralik, by now a self-described 'Streisand groupie,' dragged his co-workers to the Blue Angel nearly every night. Few remained unmoved by her, and Kapralik made sure the word always got back to his boss.

Finally Lieberson, who was referred to in hushed tones by his employees as 'God,' deigned to descend to the Blue Angel for Barbra's closing performance on Friday, August 17. He left impressed. Not only had her voice become richer and more mature in just a few months but there was a new elegance to her look and style that boded well for mainstream acceptance. As if to underscore that, Lieberson noticed that the audience around him, cheering and stomping after Barbra's every number, encompassed a far wider range of ages and types than he had imagined it would. The following Monday, Lieberson called Marty Erlichman. 'It takes a big man to admit a mistake,' he said, 'and I made a mistake. I would like to record Barbra.'

And so, after more than a year of struggle, of auditions, of campaigning and cajoling, the most prestigious record company in the world asked Barbra Streisand to join its roster of artists. Any other young hopeful would have jumped for joy and exclaimed, 'Where do I sign?' Not Barbra. To her and Marty, Lieberson's green light only signaled the beginning of negotiations. Several more months would pass before the details could be hammered out, because an issue of paramount importance to Barbra, of course, was the little matter of creative control.

B arbra sat at the huge oak table in the Columbia Records conference room. It was Monday, October 1, 1962, and as a photographer's flashbulbs popped, she and Goddard Lieberson scrawled their names at the bottom of her contract. She was wearing a simple black wool dress set off by a string of pearls, her hair perfectly bouffant. She had been groomed by Columbia's hair and makeup specialists, and she looked precisely the way so many people had told her she needed to look in order to succeed in show business.

It was one of the few concessions she had been willing to make to Columbia. The document she signed that day would have been the envy of many an established star, much less a newcomer with questionable commercial potential, for Barbra's contract granted her full creative control. The label could not dictate what she would record or could not record, and it guaranteed that anything she recorded would be released. Further, the company had to release at least two Streisand albums in the first year.

How did Marty Erlichman win such concessions from a label that not much earlier hadn't wanted to sign Barbra to any contract at all? 'You give up something for that,' he explained in 1983. 'You give up the front money. We were offered a lot more of a guarantee from several of the other companies. But they weren't willing to give us creative control. When you break the mold, you have to make sure you have creative control because they'll try to make you into what they think you should be. That's how you show whether you believe in yourself or not. Only if her records *sold* would she make any money, and she had the final say about what went on her albums, so she was taking all the responsibility for that.'

Dave Kapralik recalled that once the label agreed to sign Barbra, Columbia decided to sink or swim with what it had. 'We realized she had created a very successful nightclub career with material of her own.' The one-year contract (with four annual renewal options at Columbia's discretion) gave Barbra a $20,000 advance per album (small by industry standards but a fortune to her) and a 5 percent royalty against 98 percent of records sold after all recording expenses were earned back.

Although few expected Barbra to be a strong singles seller, such success could be so important to album sales that the label rushed her into the recording studio to cut two sides for release as a single. Two weeks after she signed her contract, Barbra stood in front of thirty musicians in Columbia's Thirtieth Street studio, shaking with nervousness, and performed 'Happy Days Are Here Again' and 'When the Sun Comes Out.'

'Happy Days Are Here Again' would become one of Barbra's signature songs, but the Columbia sales department so lacked faith in its sales potential that they ordered only a minuscule five hundred discs be pressed. They distributed the record only in New York and didn't even send any demo copies to disc jockeys.

To some observers it seemed that certain people within the Columbia hierarchy actually wanted the record to fail, as certification of their lack of faith in Barbra's commercial appeal. The head of the label's sales department, Bill Gallagher, preferred Anita Bryant's bland white-bread warbling to Streisand's hyperemotionalism, and most of his staff agreed. To many of them, Barbra and Bob Dylan were 'the two the fags and radicals brought in.' Whenever Barbra's name came up, they most often asked, 'Why doesn't someone give her a bath, wash her hair, and buy her a new dress?'

With no demos mailed to radio stations, rhythm-and-blues DJs across the country – including Sly Stone, who was then a disc jockey in San Francisco – had to discover 'Happy Days' on their own. When they did, they played it. 'Barbra's singing really reached the black DJs,' Dave Kapralik said, 'because it was real. Her emotion came from an authentic place within her, which is where the most soulful music always comes from.' But when listeners went out to their local stores to buy the record, there were no copies available. 'Happy Days' bombed.

Barbra and Marty fumed, and Erlichman put pressure on Columbia to release another Streisand single as soon as possible. A month later they did – 'My Coloring Book,' Fred Ebb and John Kander's downbeat torch ballad. This time the company put more resources behind the record, mainly because of widespread positive reaction to the song. They pressed twenty thousand first-run copies and mailed demos to DJs across the country.

Still, Marty was livid that the label did not advertise or promote the record, especially when he saw a full-page ad in *Billboard* for another Columbia single, 'Shake Me I Rattle, Squeeze Me I Cry.' He stormed into the

Chinese restaurant off Columbia's lobby and threw the magazine down in front of Bill Gallagher. 'You take out an ad for *this* cockamamie song and not for Barbra?' he thundered. 'I'll match her career against anybody's. I'd bet my year's commission that she'll outsell, outlast, any of the people you're pushing.' He stopped, red-faced, to catch his breath.

'Marty, take it easy,' Gallagher said, laughing. 'You'll give yourself a coronary.'

Barbra's second single went on to sell 60,000 copies, helped along by her performance on Ed Sullivan's popular Sunday-night television variety show in December. 'This was an impressive number for an unknown at that time,' Dave Kapralik said. Still, 'My Coloring Book' hadn't dashed up the pop charts, so Columbia abandoned its halfhearted efforts to build Streisand singles momentum. All thought now focused on how best to present Barbra on an album. Everyone agreed that since her singing success had been in nightclubs, the LP should capture the excitement and spontaneity of a live performance. With Barbra in the middle of a one-month stand at the Bon Soir, the pieces fell neatly into place.

GOD HIMSELF INTRODUCED her: Goddard Lieberson stood before a raucous crowd of Streisand fans and Columbia employees at the Bon Soir on November 5 and explained that the evening's performance, and the next two nights' as well, would be live recording sessions for Barbra's first Columbia album. The somewhat boozy throng, sitting at tables specially decorated with flowers and gingham tablecloths, cheered and hooted. 'For me and everyone at Columbia, she's a singular artist. You can't put her in any category,' Lieberson said, touting as a virtue what he had long considered a Streisand vice.

She rushed down to the Village by taxi as soon as the night's *Wholesale* performance ended and hopped onstage to cheers and stomps and whistles. She sang Leonard Bernstein's 'My Name Is Barbara,' then 'Much More.' A fuse in a microphone blew out. 'You're kidding!' she exclaimed. Lieberson apologized. Barbra asked the photographer to stop snapping pictures of her because 'it really distracts me and I can't concentrate.' The fuse was replaced. 'Can you hear now?' Barbra asked the crowd. 'We can hear you, babe,' someone called out.

After Harold Arlen's 'Napoleon,' Leonard Bernstein's 'I Hate Music (But I like to Sing),' and 'Right as the Rain,' Barbra told the audience she was wearing 'my boyfriend's old suit.' Then 'Cry Me a River,' 'Value' from *Harry Stoones*, 'Lover Come Back to Me,' and an announcement that she wanted to pay tribute to her favorite singer, the spectacularly untalented

Florence Foster Jenkins. The session ended with 'Soon It's Gonna Rain,' 'Come to the Supermarket in Old Peking,' 'When the Sun Comes Out,' and 'Happy Days.'

The audience – and the next two nights' crowds as well – left happy and satisfied, but Barbra, Marty, and Lieberson were far less pleased. When they listened to the tapes, they realized that *Barbra Streisand Live at the Bon Soir!*, while a great idea in theory, wasn't going to work. The sound quality of the tapes proved far inferior to what could be achieved in the studio. The rowdy audience reactions distracted from rather than augmented the intimacy Barbra wanted to convey. Worst of all, her voice didn't sound as good as it could under the quality controls of studio recording. Barbra Streisand's first solo album would have to wait.

On November 18 Barbra completed the Bon Soir gig, her fourth and last. The critic Leonard Harris's comments in the *New York World Telegram & Sun* echoed the prevailing wisdom now about Streisand: 'The star of *I Can Get It for You Wholesale* is the best – no maybes, no "young" or "old" or other qualifiers needed. She's twenty; by the time she's thirty she will have rewritten the record books. Her voice has sweetness, range, color, and variety. Pick the best singer of any style, and Barbra can challenge her on her home ground. And Barbra's own style – elfin, humorous, but packing a real punch – is original and unforgettable.'

Now it was time to crank up the Streisand juggernaut. Marty knew the best way to sell Barbra's first album would be for her to perform live in as many venues as possible around the country. He immersed himself in plans for a tour that would result in a triumphal Streisand musical march through seventeen cities and make Barbra a nightclub superstar within a year.

The about-to-explode Streisand career had dissipated some very different plans of Barbra's that one New York newspaper had published back in August: 'Barbra Streisand has applied to all-male Dartmouth College in Hanover, N.H.,' the item said, 'to become one of the first women to be admitted in the summer of 1963. Barbra wants to major in economics and languages at the college which, for the first time in its history, will be accepting female students next year.'

ALSO THAT AUGUST, Barbra had been desperate to appear on *Tonight*. The show's casting director, Bob Garland, recalled in 1968 that he didn't think she was right for it, and had repeatedly turned her down. Finally Barbra telephoned Garland and pleaded with him to see her in his office. 'Everybody in the business says you're so sensitive and understanding,' she cajoled, 'and I need your advice. It's terribly important.'

When she showed up, she was visibly upset. She wrung her hands in anguish as she explained why she had asked to see him. 'You really don't know much about me,' she began haltingly. 'I'm from Cleveland and, well, my mother is back there and she's not well. As a matter of fact, she's dying, Bob.' She choked back a sob. 'It would mean so much to her to be able to see me on *Tonight*. If you could please just give me *one chance* . . .'

'Well,' Garland sighed as he summed up the story, 'she got her *Tonight* booking and went on from there.'

Barbra made her debut on *Tonight* with guest host Groucho Marx on August 21. The first thing she did was complain that the announcer had pronounced her name 'Streesand.' Just as she had on *PM East*, she quickly established herself as an audience favorite, and she was brought back roughly once a month between October 4, 1962, and March 5, 1963.

The October 4 show was her first with Johnny Carson, the regular host. Carson asked her if she planned to marry someday. 'Of course,' Barbra replied.

'But not until you fulfill your career? Or does it make any difference?'

'No, that doesn't matter at all. I might give up my career, if my husband wants me to.'

'You're not that dedicated to the theater, then?'

'No.'

'You'd give it up if you got married. I think that's a smart move.'

'Yeah.'

During her appearance on February 1, 1963, Johnny mentioned that *Time* magazine had done an article on Barbra the week before. Then he added, 'I suppose when you get to be a big star we'll never see you again.'

'No,' Barbra replied with a laugh. 'Never.'

'That will be it, huh?'

'Never. I will never come here again!'

'You know,' Johnny concluded, 'she probably means it, too!'

ELLIOTT PACED BACK and forth in front of the open door to Barbra's dressing room after a performance of *Wholesale*. Whenever one of the chorus girls passed by, he whistled and patted her backside and asked, very loudly, whether she had any plans for later in the evening. Barbra ignored him while she dabbed off her makeup in front of her mirror and chatted with Bob Schulenberg, who had come backstage to pay her a visit. Bob listened to Elliott for a while, then had to ask: 'What on *earth* is he doing?'

Barbra peeled off a false eyelash. 'Getting back at me, I suppose.'

'What for?'

'I told him he was flat on his last note tonight.'

Finally Elliott huffed off. Barbra and Bob went out to eat, and afterward Barbra invited Bob up to her apartment for coffee. When she opened the door, they saw Elliott sitting alone in the darkened living room, illuminated only by the rose light filtering through a red glass lampshade. He didn't move or say hello. Barbra turned to Schulenberg. 'I think we'd better not have that coffee,' she said, and closed the door behind her.

Working together and living together often put a strain on Barbra and Elliott's relationship. 'We fought all the time,' he said. 'I wasn't always sure about what.' After one disagreement, Barbra locked Elliott out of the apartment and refused to answer the door or pick up the phone to talk to him. He went home to Brooklyn. Another time he locked her out in the rain until four in the morning before he opened the door to a wet, cold Barbra, her face awash with tears.

But always they would kiss and hug and make up, and later they'd laugh about it all. 'I was madly in love with her,' Elliott said.

BY THE FALL of 1962 *I Can Get It for You Wholesale* had been running for six months, mostly on half-price twofers (the musical ultimately lost money). Barbra couldn't wait for the show to close. She hated the interpretive strait-jacket that tied her into the same performance as Miss Marmelstein every night. Only three months into the run she had said, 'I see the part differently now from the way it was written and directed, and I'd like to do it differently, but I can't.' She missed the wild improvisation she had done in acting class, longed for the delicious chance to surprise even herself.

Her boredom, the sameness of it all, caused her performance occasionally to flag. 'Every time she did "Miss Marmelstein" I'd go to the back of the theater and watch her,' said her dresser, Ceil Mack. 'Once in a while she wasn't so good. Her performance wasn't big enough, it lacked that *ruff!* she gave it on a good night. But the audiences never knew the difference. She stopped the show cold every night.'

That was part of the problem for Barbra, too. She had proven herself in *Wholesale*. She knew she could wow an audience even on an off night. She wanted fresh challenges, wanted to conquer unknown worlds. So many opportunities lay before her as 1962 drew to a close. She longed to begin new journeys.

In October a tremendous challenge and a nearly unprecedented opportunity were laid at Barbra's feet when she was chosen over far more established actresses to star as the legendary Ziegfeld Follies comedienne and singer Fanny Brice in a major new Broadway musical, *Funny Girl*. It seemed a perfect part for her: Fanny Brice was Jewish, had a prominent nose, struggled up from poverty, and combined humor with pathos to make her audiences laugh and cry and adore her.

Marty had lobbied for her to get the part for over a year, and Barbra wanted it so badly that when she learned she had it, standing in Broadway's Shubert Alley, she felt almost numb. 'Because I cared so much,' she said, 'I didn't care at all. Deep down I knew the part belonged to me, but for that reason I made myself think nothing of it . . . I always think the worst. Actually, it's a combination of positive and negative thinking, superego and complete insecurity. Things come to me . . . if I think of the worst.'

THE LAST PERFORMANCE of *I Can Get It for You Wholesale* fell Sunday, December 9, and when the curtain came down, Barbra ran backstage yelling, 'I'm free! I'm free!' The next morning she met with Marty Erlichman to discuss her appearance one week later on *The Ed Sullivan Show*, plan her nationwide concert tour, go over the songs for her first album, and figure out when she would have the time to start rehearsals for *Funny Girl*. Marty told the show's producers that she probably wouldn't be available full-time until the end of 1963. They didn't see that as a problem, since the show's score and book needed a great deal of work. Besides, they reasoned, if Marty's plans for Barbra panned out, they might be getting a big star to play Fanny Brice after all.

Elliott had pressing business too that Monday morning. He walked down to East Fifty-eighth Street, took his place in line, and applied for fifty dollars a week in unemployment benefits.

OVER THREE DAYS late in January 1963, Barbra laid down the eleven tracks that would make up her first album, essentially a studio version of her nightclub act. For weeks she had rehearsed in the West End Avenue apartment of Peter Matz, a gifted young arranger-conductor whom Harold Arlen had recommended to her, and the two of them hit it off well. Every day she rushed over to Matz's place, her lunch in a brown paper bag. (One day she was so late she ran out of her apartment wearing only blue jeans and a bra under her raincoat.)

'It was a delight to work with her,' Matz recalled. 'She didn't know how to read music, but she could follow it up and down on paper. With her instincts she didn't have to read. People credit me for those early arrangements, but really most of the ideas and the songs came from Barbra and Peter Daniels. They made my job very easy.'

Barbra found studio recording far less satisfying than live performing. 'The exciting thing about being a performer, the really creative thing,' she said, 'is going onstage or stepping in front of a microphone in a nightclub and creating something just for the people who are there. You may be great or you may be lousy that night, but that's the exciting thing about creating it all over again each time. But when you go into a recording studio, you've got three hours . . . You can never do your best under those conditions. The way I'd like to record would be to have an indefinite closing time on the session.'

Barbra decided to include three songs on this album that she hadn't sung during the three nights of taping at the Bon Soir, including 'Who's Afraid of the Big, Bad Wolf?' That song caused Columbia executives some consternation. Peter Matz recalled that the album's producer, Mike Berniker, 'was walking a tightrope between the upstairs guys, me, and Barbra. He would go upstairs and tell them, "She's doing 'Who's Afraid of the Big, Bad Wolf.'" They would say, "What!" and he would come down to me and say, "Do you have to do that?" And she'd say, "Yes, goddammit, it's on the album!"'

Still unsure of Streisand's commercial potential, Columbia had budgeted the album at a paltry $18,000, which forced Matz to use very small combinations of musicians. For one session he had just a rhythm section and four trombones, for another only a small string section. Whenever Barbra wanted more, Mike Berniker would tell Matz, 'Look, we can't spend a lot of money on this! We don't know if this woman is going to sell records!'

At first she didn't. Columbia released *The Barbra Streisand Album* on February 25, after toying with titles like *Hello! I'm Barbra Streisand; From Brooklyn to Broadway . . . Barbra Streisand!*; and *Sweet and Saucy Streisand*. 'They loved that alliteration – *Sweet and Saucy Streisand*,' Marty Erlichman recalled. 'When I suggested it to Barbra, she got nauseous.'

The album provided listeners with nothing less than a roller-coaster ride of emotional highs and lows. Anyone who had heard Barbra only on the *Wholesale* cast album or *Pins and Needles* would have been astounded by the richness and maturity her voice had gained in less than a year. The reviews were largely ecstatic, typified by Stanley Green's comments in *Hi Fi/Stereo Review*: 'The eagerly awaited Barbra Streisand album turns out to be a fascinating package. Miss Streisand is a compelling stylist with a full, rich vocal quality that may give you goose bumps when you hear her more dramatic arias.'

Despite such fulsome praise, sales of the album languished through March, and it looked as though Columbia's fear that Barbra would appeal only to gays and 'hip urbanites' might be well founded. Barbra wrung her hands, but Marty soothed her with the assurance that her national tour and the television appearances he had begun to line up for her would, surely if slowly, put the album over the top.

FOR THE REST of 1963, Barbra barely stopped for a deep breath. The year had begun with two appearances on *Tonight*, on January 2 and February 1, and a triumphant three-week return engagement at the Blue Angel that began January 8. On February 5, with Elliott in tow, she kicked off her tour in the Boston area with a five-night stand at the Frolic, a nightclub in Revere Beach. Then she and Elliott schlepped on the train to Cleveland, where Mike Douglas welcomed her as his co-host for the week of February 11 on his nationally syndicated afternoon variety show.

Over the five days Barbra sang every song from her album, and kibbitzed and clowned with Douglas. 'She was brilliant,' he recalled. 'We kidded around, doing Nelson Eddy-Jeanette MacDonald duets in costume. We got down on the floor and played a game she'd played as a child – kind of tiddlywinks with bottle caps. Those shows were classics.' They no longer exist, however, because a few years later a technician at the station erased them to tape commercials.

Demand for Barbra's album skyrocketed after her appearances on Douglas's show, but hopeful record buyers couldn't find it. Columbia's initial pressing of just a few thousand had sold out quickly, and the company lagged behind in getting out new ones. Marty hit the roof. He called Bill Gallagher and started to yell. 'How dare you do this to us? After we went out on a limb, taking less money, building a following, and you guys don't have records out there?' Gallagher apologized and explained that the company's printing plant in Pitman, New Jersey, was on overtime pressing new albums, and he promised to have all back orders filled within five days. Gallagher also said that the company would send several sales representatives to San Francisco to 'work the album' in anticipation of Barbra's opening there at the trendy hungry i nightclub. Placated, Marty hung up.

After she completed her week with Mike Douglas and a simultaneous stint at the Chateau in Lakewood, Ohio, Barbra and Elliott returned to New York, where she did two more *Tonight* appearances. At home they were able to relax for a few weeks, perhaps for the last time for months to come, because Elliott had been cast in a London revival of the Leonard Bernstein-Betty Comden and Adolph Green Broadway and movie hit *On the Town*, and if the show was a success, he'd likely remain in England for the better part of a year. Barbra had had to decide whether to embark on her tour as planned or accompany Elliott to England. When she chose to go with her man, he told her she shouldn't derail her career at this critical juncture and insisted that she stay in America.

The lovers said a tearful good-bye as Barbra hopped a plane to Florida for the next stop on her national tour, the Cafe Pompeii in the Eden Roc Hotel in Miami Beach. The engagement proved inauspicious. She shared the bill with the romantic Italian singer Sergio Franchi, and as Jack Anderson pointed out in the *Miami Herald*, 'It's unfortunate that two such disparate talents should have to share the same bill. It's debatable whether the same audience can respond with the appreciation they equally deserve.' Barbra didn't appeal to the Eden Roc's well-heeled older Jewish clientele— 'the rocks and lox crowd,' she called them. She was too strange, her emotions too raw, her material 'cockamamie.' They stayed away in droves.

Larry King, then a Miami radio interviewer, got a frantic call from the owner of the hotel. 'Look,' he said, 'you gotta help me. I've got this wonderful singer, and nobody's coming. Honest, the place is empty. The waiters are standing on the tables applauding, and there's nobody here. Would you interview her?' King did, and he recalled asking her to describe how she sang. 'I'm not Ella Fitzgerald,' she replied, 'but you're going to hear from me. You're going to know about me.'

On Sunday morning, March 24, Barbra flew back up to New York for an appearance on *The Ed Sullivan Show*, then returned to Miami Monday morning. Business picked up considerably after the Sullivan appearance, but it was too late to turn the engagement around, because Barbra was set to open at the hungry i in San Francisco on Wednesday, March 27. She finished her last two shows at the Eden Roc on Tuesday night; on Wednesday morning she rushed to the airport to catch a plane for the West Coast. She arrived in San Francisco with scant hours to spare before she had to take the stage again.

Barbra came into the hungry i with a bit of history with its owner, Enrico Banducci. She had first met him early in 1962 in the office of her agent, Irvin Arthur. Upset that Arthur had nothing for her, and aware that Banducci had turned her down, Barbra vented her spleen. 'Look, why don't you give me a job?' she asked the startled Banducci. 'I hear that you're supposed to give unknowns jobs. I don't really wanna work for you in your dirty old nightclub anyway. But actually I'm gonna be a big star, so you might as well grab me now and get me cheaper.'

Barbra so hated asking for work that the only way she had been able to pull this off was to pretend to be a character in a play asking for a job. 'It worked!' she marveled. 'Twenty minutes later we signed a contract. He's the only one that would have done that, though. Everybody else would have thought I was nuts. But *he's* such a nut. He's a delightful guy. I love him.'

With her commitment to *Wholesale*, Barbra hadn't been able to fulfill her contract with the hungry i for over a year. The wait was expensive for

Banducci – her salary jumped from $350 a week to $2,500 – but ultimately proved worth it. Her four-week engagement as the club's headliner 'set this town on its ear,' according to the *San Francisco Chronicle* columnist Hal Schaefer. The Bay Area's hippest audiences, led by the city's fast-growing population of gay men, flocked to see her shows at eight and eleven o'clock nightly. On opening night, Marty Erlichman pulled a publicity stunt that would have made a studio flack from the 1940s proud. With the club already jammed and crowds milling around outside on Jackson Street waiting to get in, Marty called the police and the fire department, and the ensuing excitement made the newspapers the next morning.

The critics were effusive in their praise. One told his readers, 'Don't miss Barbra Streisand at the hungry i. You'll regret it if you do.' But as usual Barbra's performances were her best publicity. As word of mouth about 'this phenomenal girl' spread, Banducci had to turn the customers away.

BARBRA HADN'T SEEN Elliott in nearly a month, and she missed him terribly. They spoke at least once a day by transatlantic hookup; he would call her from his hotel after his show around midnight or so – late afternoon Pacific Standard Time, and they'd talk for hours, running up enormous bills. Sometimes, though, Elliott would telephone much later than usual, or not at all. Barbra would call him and discover that he had not yet returned to his room. When she asked him about it, he made jokes. Barbra found herself wondering, What is Elliott doing over there? Perhaps to bolster her confidence in the relationship, Barbra told a *Chronicle* reporter, Joan McKinney, that she and Elliott had just gotten married.

Her vocal cords presented an even more pressing worry for Barbra. The strain of the tour had begun to affect her voice, which sometimes failed her as she sought to reach a high note. Her audiences rarely noticed it, but she did. Barbra couldn't abide this inability to deliver as much as she wanted to, and she feared her singing would continue to deteriorate until only a hoarse croak remained. She went to a throat specialist, who told her she had nodules on her vocal cords and would have to rest them.

That diagnosis turned out to be wrong, but when Barbra got to San Francisco a psychological problem took the place of her physical concerns. 'I was in trouble,' she recalled to *People* magazine. 'People [had been] asking me, "How do you hold your notes so long?" I told them it was my will – that I just *wanted* to hold them. Subsequently I started to consciously think, How *do* I hold these notes so long? And voilá! One night I just couldn't hold them anymore. My consciousness of an unconscious thing had made me impotent.'

Barbra went to see a voice teacher, Judy Davis. Apprehensive after her last go-round with a coach, Barbra was pleasantly surprised by Davis. 'I was frightened and she reassured me that I was doing everything right, but I was like a person who was paralyzed in their legs having to relearn how to walk. Judy showed me pictures of the area, showed me physiologically what the process was.' In her sessions with Davis, Barbra learned how to achieve through conscious effort what before she had just left to chance. 'I will always remain grateful to her,' Barbra said.

ON APRIL 13 *The Barbra Streisand Album* broke into *Billboard* magazine's Top 100 Albums chart, bolstered by Barbra's March 24 appearance on *The Ed Sullivan Show* and by huge sales in San Francisco. A week later her hungry i gig ended. Enrico Banducci hated to see her go, but he couldn't extend her engagement because he had earlier booked another act to follow her. 'In another year,' he told a columnist, 'no one will be able to afford her at all.'

After Barbra's last show, Banducci bounded onstage, his violin in hand, and joined her in a parody of an Italian opera in which the characters are dying but continually manage to summon up one last ounce of strength to continue singing. As Barbra coughed and wheezed, prone on the floor, Banducci floridly sang to her in flawless Italian. She gamely responded with a mixture of Italianate gibberish and Yiddish. The audience loved it, and Barbra left San Francisco on April 21 awash in applause, laughter, and love.

9

B arbra returned to New York in time to celebrate her twenty-first
birthday on April 24 with Marty Erlichman and a few close friends. As
thrilled as she was by her success so far, she desperately missed Elliott
and longed to fly to London to see him. She could have – her engagement at
New York's top supper club, Basin Street East, wouldn't begin until May 13
– but Elliott asked her not to. 'The show needs a lot of work, Barb,' he told
her. 'I have to concentrate. You'd be a distraction.' She understood, sort of.
When she next spoke to him, she told him she wanted to start looking for a
new apartment – 'Something big, like a duplex, and nice, like on Central Park
West or something.' Elliott said he didn't think he'd be able to afford that.
'That's okay,' Barbra replied. 'I'm making enough for both of us now.'

ON MAY 13, the night after her appearance on Dinah Shore's NBC variety
show, Barbra began a triumphant three-week stand at the posh Basin Street
East in the Shelton Towers Hotel on East Forty-eighth Street, a booking that
signaled like a clarion peal that she had *arrived*. She opened for the legendary
swing man Benny Goodman, whose All Star Sextet joined Peter Daniels
behind her. As the New York *Daily Mirror* columnist Jack Thompson
pointed out, 'It takes an immensely courageous girl to allow herself to
be booked on the same bill with Benny Goodman, and even expect to be
noticed. To appear on the same program with the great clarinetist and to run
away with the show reveals something akin to show business supremacy.'

In many ways this was a homecoming for Barbra, and her fans descended
on the club to welcome back the local girl who was making the big time.
The lines stretched a block down Forty-eighth Street to Third Avenue.
Astounded by Barbra's drawing power, Barney Ward, the manager of the

club, reportedly offered her a five-year contract to appear there exclusively. She turned him down.

Barbra's more demonstrative fans caused Benny Goodman some chagrin when they chanted 'We want Barbra! We want Barbra!' during his set. Barney Ward told an employee of the hotel, 'I've got a real problem with her. When Benny Goodman comes on, there's no interest, they can't wait for him to get off and for her to come back. They're unruly. They heckle him. They heckle *Benny Goodman!*'

Marvin Stein, Barbra's former Flatbush neighbor, worked in the Shelton Towers health club, and he recalled that Barbra asked him if she could use the steam room 'because I have nodules on my vocal cords and the doctor says steam will help.' Stein told her to be his guest. A few days into Barbra's engagement, Mrs Kind came into the hotel and ran into Stein. 'Marvin, you have to do me a favor,' she said. 'Barbra won't tell me what she's earning for her appearance here, and I really want to know. Could you find out for me?' Stein asked Ward, who told him that Barbra's salary was $2,500 a week. 'Mrs Kind was flabbergasted,' Stein recalled. 'That was an awful lot of money, and obviously Barbra wasn't giving any of it to her mother. The woman was in that lobby *every day*, trying to hustle Barbra.'

BARBRA TOOK FOUR days off in the middle of her Basin Street East stand to fulfill some commitments. The first took her to Washington, where she sang for President John F. Kennedy at the annual Press Correspondents' Dinner at the Hilton Hotel, the closest thing America has to a royal command performance, on Friday, May 24. She had tingled with excitement over the invitation for weeks; in San Francisco early in April she told a reporter that she couldn't decide what to wear. 'Something Empire? Something Napoleonic? Something – *Caligula?*' She decided on the Empire, accessorized with long white gloves and a feather boa and topped off with the new pageboy-and-bangs hairstyle fashioned for her by the popular stylist Fredrick Glaser.

She stole the show that night with five numbers, including 'Happy Days Are Here Again,' during which she rarely took her eyes off the handsome young president. Afterward she stood in a reception line to meet Kennedy, and emcee Merv Griffin told her that protocol didn't allow the president to be 'detained' as he made his way down the line. There were to be no requests for autographs.

When Kennedy wended his way down to Barbra, he stopped and asked her how long she'd been singing. 'About as long as you've been president,' she replied. Then she blurted, 'Mr President, my mother in

Brooklyn is a big fan of yours, and if I don't get your autograph she'll kill me.'

Several people winced, but Kennedy just laughed. He asked to borrow Peter Daniels's back for support and signed the program Barbra had handed him. 'Thanks,' Barbra purred. 'You're a doll.' The next morning at breakfast Merv Griffin admonished her. 'They specifically asked us not to stop the president.'

'But I wanted his autograph,' Barbra replied. 'How many times would I get the chance to have the president sign an autograph?'

In his autobiography, Griffin says that when he asked Barbra if Kennedy had written an inscription, she said that he had scribbled 'Fuck you. The President.' Barbra of course was joking. Years later she admitted that JFK had actually penned, 'Best wishes – John F. Kennedy.' She also confessed that she misplaced the signature before she had a chance to give it to her mother.

Later that Saturday, Barbra hied herself off to London to catch Elliott's opening in *On the Town* the next night. He was worried about the show, he had told her, and she wanted to be there to lend him moral support. As matters turned out, he needed it. Although Barbra led boisterous cheers at the opening, the reviews on Monday morning were lukewarm at best and full of insidious comparisons to the movie version that had featured Frank Sinatra, Gene Kelly, and Jules Munshin. Clearly *On the Town* wouldn't last very long, and that prospect fell over Barbra's reunion with Elliott like a soggy mantle. She had to leave on Tuesday to resume her Basin Street East engagement, so there was little time to discuss their future. Barbra tried to keep things light as they drove through picturesque villages north of London, stopping at tiny antique stores where she burbled with excitement about the treasures she found.

In the few days she was in England, Barbra learned what Elliott had been doing those nights when he called her later than scheduled, or not at all: he had been gambling. The news didn't faze her much, as long as he didn't overdo it.

WHEN BARBRA RETURNED to New York, Marty gave her the thrilling news that her album had jumped into the top twenty nationally. Within a few weeks it peaked at number eight, and at that point Barbra became the best-selling female vocalist in the country. Marty resisted the urge to call everyone at Columbia and bray 'I told you so,' but he did roll his eyes whenever one of the label's salesmen insisted he had known all along that Streisand would be a sensation.

The Barbra Streisand Album ended up the most successful debut album in history released without singles support. The disc remained in the Top 40 for a phenomenal seventy-four weeks and, eighteen months after its release, received the coveted gold certification from the Record Industry Association of America, signaling that it had achieved $1 million in sales at the manufacturer's wholesale price (33⅓ percent of the retail list price). Thus, Barbra's first album sold approximately 700,000 units in both monaural at $3.98 and stereo at $4.98; in 1963 sales of the two formats were about equal.

The album for which Barbra had been paid a $20,000 advance earned her royalties of approximately $140,000 in a year and a half and enriched Columbia's coffers by more than $750,000. Now the company wanted Barbra back in the recording studio. With her schedule virtually nonstop for the next six months, the only time she had to spare was the first week of June. She had hoped to rejoin Elliott in London, but this was pressing. He would be home soon anyway, she told herself.

Barbra recorded eleven tracks over four days in early June. The record's sound engineer, Frank Laico, saw a difference in Streisand from her previous sessions. 'It's like she got her feet wet with that first album,' he said, 'and now she was ready to take over. She came into the control room and started asking, "Why don't you do this? Why don't you do that?" I listened and then said, "Hey, Barbra, you didn't know anything with that first album, and look how successful it's become. I'm still the same person. I have the same ears. I'm not going to let you down."'

After the first session, Laico found himself flanked at the control board by Barbra on one side and Marty on the other, each giving him advice on how to mix the tracks. Laico went to Mike Berniker, who was again producing, and threatened to quit unless they let him do his job as he saw fit. Berniker replied, 'We've got to be careful. We don't want to upset them.'

The Second Barbra Streisand Album crammed all of the most dramatic and emotional of Streisand's nightclub arias into one startling package. Barbra gave even the quieter numbers a raw emotional intensity that often stunned her listeners on first hearing and left them knowing they had not just listened to a record, they had had a theatrical experience. Compared to Barbra Streisand, most of the other pop stars of the day – Patti Page, Doris Day, Julie London – seemed somnambulant.

The album, released late in August as the Streisand juggernaut built up more and more steam, jumped into the Top 10 in a matter of weeks and spent three weeks in the number two position. It was certified gold five months before Barbra's first album. Now Barbra Streisand wasn't just a sensation in nightclubs and on Broadway; she was a phenomenon on records as well.

The music industry trade publication *Cashbox* said what many were already thinking: 'The Streisand name could be the biggest to hit show business since Elvis Presley.'

By now observers had begun to call 1963 'The Year of Barbra Streisand.' After another appearance on *The Ed Sullivan Show* on June 9, she took off for Chicago for a three-week gig at the popular nightspot Mr Kelly's. In the middle of the stand, on June 25, Barbra again basked in the national spotlight with a previously taped appearance on *The Keefe Brasselle Show*, a highly touted summer replacement series. The show wasn't a hit, but Barbra was. *Variety* noted, 'Miss Streisand was remarkably effective. She looked like a misplaced teenager in a long, would-be sexy tubular gown, but this strangely aided her performance.'

The day after her closing in Chicago, Barbra – accompanied by Elliott, who had returned from London quickly as expected – flew halfway across the country in the hope of conquering a strange and challenging new milieu: Las Vegas.

OH, GOD, THIS is going to be another Eden Roc, Barbra thought as she stood on the stage of the Riviera Hotel and faced an audience of well-heeled middle-aged couples who had come to see Liberace. She was the opening act for the flamboyant pianist, a glamour-and-glitz Vegas favorite. The crowd didn't know what to make of her. After her first song she announced that she had made her gingham dress herself out of a tablecloth for four dollars. Murmurs abounded. 'That was a joke, right, Harry?' a woman asked her husband. Liberace's fans couldn't relate. As he put it, 'Everything I had on cost more than four dollars, including my shoelaces.'

As Barbra's accompanist, Peter Daniels, recalled, 'We went out and did twenty-five minutes. No response. It was very upsetting. The second show, the same thing, and the same thing the next night. So on the fourth day, Liberace called a meeting and said, "I think maybe she's too much for my audience at this particular point. Here's what we're gonna do: I'll go out and open the show, do about ten or fifteen minutes, and then I'll introduce Barbra as my discovery. Give it the old schmaltz."' The gambit worked, according to Daniels. 'That fourth night, after he gave her that stamp of approval, she came out and did the same exact show she'd done before and got a standing ovation.'

Barbra ended her month-long stand at the Riviera on August 4. The engagement had turned out to be so successful that the management offered her an open-ended contract for as many return engagements as she cared to make at $10,000 a week (she had been getting $7,500).

She signed the contract, but she put the commitment off for seven years.

On August 5, Elliott and Barbra returned to New York, where she did two one-night stands, one at the Lido Country Club on Long Island on August 9 and the other at the Concord Hotel at Kiamesha Lake in the Catskills on the tenth. They used a week-and-a-half hiatus from her tour to move into their new home, a two-story penthouse apartment on the twentieth floor of a posh building on Central Park West.

This sumptuous duplex, which had once belonged to Lorenz Hart, contrasted spectacularly with the Third Avenue flat. The monthly rent of $450 brought Barbra and Elliott six sprawling rooms with high ceilings and crown moldings, chandeliers, and a grand staircase winding down from the master bedroom, which was located in a tower. 'I can make an entrance,' Barbra said, 'you know what I mean?' There was an office, a huge rooftop terrace off the bedroom, and another fifty-five feet of terraces circling the apartment's lower level. The view of a brick wall on Third Avenue had been replaced by panoramic vistas of Central Park, upper and lower Manhattan, and the Hudson and East rivers.

Another of Barbra's dreams had come true. This was the kind of home that glamorous women in the movies always seemed to have. What a far cry from apartment 4G! Barbra longed to decorate every room in a different classic style, to wallpaper and drape and furnish the apartment until it became her own Xanadu. But there was no time; she would be on the road for most of the rest of the year. She did buy one extravagant piece of furniture: a 'fabulous' three-hundred-year-old carved-wood French canopy bed, which she installed on a two-step-high marble platform. Next to it she placed a small refrigerator covered with black patent leather. 'So I can lie in bed all day and eat coffee ice cream.'

Such leisure would be a rarity for the rest of the year. On August 20, Barbra, Elliott, Marty Erlichman, and Peter Daniels flew to Los Angeles for her most important engagement to date: a two-week stand at 'the legendary Cocoanut Grove.'

IF YOU WERE a hit at the Grove, all of America sat up and took notice. Over the years, Mae West, Jean Harlow, Rudolph Valentino, Cary Grant, Bette Davis, Joan Crawford, Elizabeth Taylor, and Marilyn Monroe had all come to hear hundreds of other superstars perform there. With six months of raves behind her, Barbra was the club's most anticipated headliner since Judy Garland's comeback in 1958. Newsreel cameras recorded the excitement (Barbra covered her face and tried to shoo the cameramen away)

as Hollywood's crème de la crème turned out for Streisand's opening night: Henry Fonda, Natalie Wood, Danny Thomas, John Huston, Kirk Douglas, Ray Milland, Edward G. Robinson. Barbra could barely believe it. 'It wasn't that long ago when I was sitting in a candy store in Brooklyn eating ice cream and reading movie magazines. Now all of a sudden I'm appearing before those very stars – and I'm now one of them.'

She acted like a star, too. She kept the audience waiting a full hour before she appeared, dressed in a white satin midshipman's blouse and black skirt. She looked out at the record-breaking, standing-room-only crowd of fifteen hundred people that nearly surrounded her as she stood on a stage that jutted out into the audience, and quipped, 'If I'da known you were going to be on both sides of me I'd have gotten my nose fixed.'

Then she started to sing, and one of the most jaded audiences in the world realized they were witnessing the birth of an extraordinary new star. Over the course of her engagement, just about every celebrity in Hollywood came to see Barbra. Jack and Mary Benny sent her a telegram: 'You were magnificent Friday night. We love you.' Danny Thomas threw her a pizza party in his home and offered her a guest spot on his television sitcom, as did Bing Crosby and Bob Hope on their planned specials. Judy Garland – who turned to her companion after Barbra's first song and muttered, 'I'm never going to open my mouth again' – asked her to appear on her variety show, set to premiere that fall.

Her commitments allowed Barbra to accept only the Hope and Garland offers and forced her to turn down what would have been her first movie. The producer Sam Goldwyn Jr offered her the lead in his film *The Young Lovers*. She longed to say yes – the starring role in a movie! – but she couldn't. Her tour wouldn't be over until December 7, and she would have to begin rehearsals for *Funny Girl* immediately thereafter. 'There'll be time for the movies,' Marty told her. 'Don't worry about that.' As if to underscore the point, while Barbra was in Hollywood she acquired new agents: the team of David Begelman and Freddie Fields, who had just formed Creative Management Associates, which would evolve into International Creative Management. Unlike Barbra's former representatives, CMA had a thriving division devoted to motion pictures.

BARBRA HAD CHEATED on him, Elliott was convinced. While he was in London, reports had filtered over to him that Barbra wasn't being faithful. While they were in Las Vegas, he had confronted her with the rumors, and to his shock she not only made no attempt to deny them but told him that if he insisted on monogamy he couldn't remain her lover. 'I really can't stay with you,' he recalled her saying. 'It's not comfortable. I have to sow my oats. What if I was with you and I wanted to be with Marlon Brando?'

Stunned, Elliott had decided that the best way to have Barbra all to himself would be to marry her. He began to apply pressure; she hemmed and hawed and told him maybe. Perhaps her cavalier comments about monogamy had been an act, designed to test how much Elliott truly wanted her? If so, she discovered he wanted her very much indeed.

Barbra closed at the Grove on September 8; the next day she was in Lake Tahoe to begin a two-week gig at Bill Harrah's hotel-casino, again opening for Liberace. On Friday the thirteenth she said yes to Elliott's latest proposal of marriage, and the two of them drove twenty-five miles to Carson City on the spur of the moment, accompanied by Marty Erlichman and Marty Bregman, Barbra's new business manager, hired to help handle all the money she was raking in. (Barbra's handlers had advised her to marry Elliott in Nevada, which has no community property laws.) They exchanged vows in front of Justice of the Peace Pete Supina. After Barbra changed 'Love, honor, and obey' to 'Love, honor, and feed,' she kissed Elliott and then it was back to Harrah's to complete her engagement.

A few days later Barbra decided to throw a party in the grand house that Bill Harrah had provided the Goulds for the duration of their stay. Her new status as a wife must have brought her a sense of domesticity, because she decided to bake a cake for her guests, who included Liberace. Throughout the dinner, Barbra kept saying, 'Wait'll you taste this cake. It's gonna be great.'

Finally, Liberace recalled in his memoirs, she brought out a separate fullsized cake for every one of her twelve guests. 'I used the Betty Crocker recipe,' she explained, 'and I didn't know how to adjust all the ingredients for a real big cake. So I made lots of regular-sized ones.'

Everyone dug in. Brows furrowed. Mouths twisted. No one said anything. 'Well,' Barbra pressed, 'how *is* it?' Elliott spoke up first. 'Barb, there's something wrong with the frosting,' he ventured. 'It's sort of . . . tough.'

'Oh, yeah, well, I guess that's because I had a little problem. I ran out of confectioner's sugar, so I used flour instead.'

'Well,' Liberace wrote, 'we all peeled the frosting off and ate the cake – a little of it, because she'd obviously done some substitution on that, too. We took the rest home with us, saying we'd eat it after the show . . . It makes a great doorstop.'

BARBRA AND ELLIOTT repaired to Los Angeles, where they had the closest thing to a honeymoon they were likely to get. Ensconced in the posh Beverly

Hills Hotel – the 'Pink Palace' – they frolicked in the pool, went out on the town, and lolled about in their luxurious suite phoning for room service at all hours. The photographer Bob Willoughby captured them in the pool as Elliott hoisted the bikini-clad Barbra onto his shoulders. At one point Barbra put her hand over Elliott's face, obscuring it, as Willoughby snapped their picture.

For Barbra it was a working honeymoon. She taped *The Bob Hope Comedy Special* along with Dean Martin, James Garner, and Tuesday Weld, which aired September 27. Wearing a simple black scoop-necked dress, she sang a rousing 'When the Sun Comes Out' and a feverish 'Gotta Move.' Then she, Bob Hope, and Dean Martin did a funny bit in which they played a trio of country bumpkin musicians. Barbra, wearing a frilly print dress and a floppy ribbon in her hair, strummed a washboard.

On Friday, October 4, Barbra arrived at the CBS studios at Fairfax and Beverly in Los Angeles to tape her appearance on *The Judy Garland Show*. The variety series had debuted the week before to positive reviews and strong ratings. But with eight shows in the can, CBS worried about the program's future. The writing was uneven, the humor often strained. Worse, Judy had proved typically unreliable at times, her singing strong and vibrant on one show, weak and wavery the next.

Streisand's appearance created a surge of excitement that ran all the way from the show's dancers up through the top management at CBS. William S. Paley, the network's founder and chairman of the board, and James Aubrey, its president, both planned to attend the taping.

No one was more excited, or more nervous, than Judy. On the one hand, she sensed that her teaming with Streisand had the potential to set off fireworks. On the other hand, Barbra abounded in youthful high spirits, possessed the loveliest voice Judy had ever heard, and was frequently heralded as 'the new Garland' – which implied that the old Garland was on her way to superannuation. As much as Judy admired Barbra's talents, she'd be damned if she'd let this newcomer upstage her. She would match Barbra Streisand every step of the way or fall over trying.

The minute Judy walked into rehearsal, the crew knew something was up. Often she had dragged herself into the studio after a night of booze and pills and insomnia, barely able to function. This morning she strode in crisply, her hair done, totally pulled together. Barbra was a different story. The show's pianist, Jack Elliott, recalled to the author Coyne Steven Sanders that during rehearsal 'in walk[ed] this very unattractive, dirty, scruffy, barefoot girl with stringy hair. We were surprised that she would get a spot on the Garland show . . . But when Barbra started to sing, it was an electrifying moment, and instantly, everybody realized we were listening to a star.'

Barbra's nonchalance stemmed from her growing self-confidence as a performer. She seemed to be riding an inexorable wave of adulation to superstardom, so much so that gushing praise failed to impress her much anymore. When a crew member told Barbra how magnificent he thought she was, she replied, 'You too, huh?'

'I was feeling all full of myself,' she later admitted. 'You know, like "Wait'll they *see me!*"' As she and Judy rehearsed one of their duets, Barbra couldn't understand why Garland was so frightened. 'My heart went out to her. She was holding on to me, tight. She was scared. Somehow you get more scared as you get older, maybe. When you're young, you have nothing to lose.'

As BILL PALEY and Jim Aubrey watched the taping, they knew they were witnessing a once-in-a-lifetime show business pairing. Two great singers, a thirty-five-year veteran and the greenest of newcomers, were performing at their peak, and the electricity in the air was palpable. As soon as the taping ended, Paley ordered that the show be aired the next Sunday, just two days hence, instead of an earlier show that had already been announced. Editors worked around the clock until 5:00 A.M. on Sunday to make it happen.

The show opened with Judy's customary 'Be My Guest' introductions. When she told Barbra, 'You can have anything you want, dear,' Barbra replied, 'Can I replace you?' Judy did a comic double take, then sang, 'Be my guest, be my guest.' One writer later suggested that Barbra had ad-libbed the line as a dig at Judy, but of course the whole bit was written, rehearsed, and meant to be a joke.

Barbra then sang 'Bewitched, Bothered and Bewildered.' Never before or since has her voice sounded so pure, so bell-like. Her vocal cords could have been a Stradivarius as she caressed them into the highest, cleanest, sweetest notes imaginable. She then wasted barely a moment before she ripped into a scathing, sardonic, raucous version of 'Down with Love' with grimaces and bitter laughter and clenched fists and ironic smiles that grabbed viewers anew not only with its intensity but by its complete departure from what Barbra had just sung.

The performance left Judy ecstatic. 'You're *thrilling*,' she told Barbra when she finished the second number, 'so absolutely *thrilling!* You're so good that I *hate* you!'

'Oh, Judy,' Barbra replied, 'that's so sweet of you, thank you. You're so great I've been hating you for years. In fact, it's my ambition to be great enough to be hated by as many singers as you.'

Next came an exciting duet in which these two talents spurred each other on to a superlative performance. It had been Judy's idea to combine 'Happy

Days Are Here Again' with one of her own theme songs, 'Get Happy,' and the result was grand. They matched each other note for note, emotion for emotion, belt for belt.

During Judy's regular 'Tea Time' segment, she and Barbra were engaged in chitchat when a huge voice boomed out of the audience singing 'You're Just in Love.' It was the queen of the belters, Ethel Merman. She bounded onstage and exclaimed, 'How about this Barbra? Isn't this great? The new belter! There aren't that many of us left.'

Judy told Ethel she couldn't go away without singing a song with her and Barbra. Ethel burst into 'There's No Business like Show Business,' and her companions followed suit. But no one could compete with Merman, who drowned out both women so thoroughly that Barbra slapped her forehead in feigned despair. As the song came to an end, Barbra pumped her arms at her sides as if to summon up more volume. But the contest went to Merman, vocal cords down.

Another Streisand-Garland medley topped off the hour in exuberant high style. The two women were so clearly out to knock 'em dead that their performance still stands as one of TV's most memorable moments.

Barbra was so impressive, in fact, that for the first time, a guest star was nominated for an Emmy Award for Best Variety Performance, in competition with four stars of their own weekly shows: Andy Williams, Perry Como, Danny Kaye, and Judy Garland. Barbra, unhappy to be competing with Garland, told the press she thought it was silly not to put her in a different category. The point became moot when Danny Kaye won the award.

Prize or no, Barbra had put a remarkable cap on her career as a television guest star. She wouldn't make another such appearance for six years. 'Once she did *The Judy Garland Show*,' Marty Erlichman said, 'I told her, "There's no more reason to be a guest artist on these cockamamie television shows. You just couldn't top that."'

BARBRA HAD JUST paid for a brooch in an antique shop in Manhattan when the news came over a radio: President Kennedy had been shot and killed as he rode in a motorcade in Dallas, Texas. It was early afternoon, November 22, 1963. At first, like everyone else, she couldn't believe it. 'It must be some kind of Orson Welles hoax,' she whispered to her companion, recalling Welles's 1938 radio presentation of H. G. Wells's Martian-invasion novel *The War of the Worlds*, so realistic it set off panic. 'It just can't be true.'

It was true, and Barbra was devastated. John F Kennedy was not only an inspirational leader, he was also a man she had met and liked. She had been looking forward excitedly to singing for him again at the White House on December 5. Now he was gone, shot to death, and Vice President Lyndon Johnson had succeeded him. What kind of president would Johnson be? Barbra, like many Americans, knew little about him. What would happen to this country? she wondered.

Rushing home in a cab, Barbra spotted Elliott in another taxi. They hopped out of the cars and embraced each other, then spent the rest of the afternoon at home with a few friends, reminiscing, wondering, worrying about the state of America. That night Barbra went to a rehearsal with Peter Daniels to try out several new arrangements. One of them was 'Happy Days Are Here Again.' A few phrases into the song, she started to cry and couldn't go on.

BARBRA CLOSED OUT her phenomenal year in a rush. She had appeared with Sammy Davis Jr. at the Hollywood Bowl the night after she taped the Garland show, and between November 29 and December 7 she did a series of one-and two-night stands in Chicago, Indianapolis, San Jose, Sacramento, San Francisco, and Los Angeles.

On December 28, New York's *Cue* magazine chose Barbra as its Enter-tainer of the Year. It was the perfect end to a remarkable year, but Barbra had no time to bask in the glory. She was now deeply enmeshed in rehearsals for *Funny Girl*, the most eagerly awaited Broadway musical in years. The ensuing months of backstage tribulations, personality conflicts, script problems, and creative struggles would test Barbra's talent, her mettle, even her health. And the hard-won results would make it clear that the Year of Barbra Streisand had been a mere warm-up.

On the first day of rehearsals for *Funny Girl*, on the stage of the Winter Garden Theater on December 10, 1963, Barbra came perilously close to being fired. Milton Rosenstock, the show's musical director, recalled in 1990 that during the initial read-through with the cast a few days earlier, Barbra had sung Jule Styne and Bob Merrill's score so beautifully, 'she broke everybody's heart.' But now, as Barbra struggled with blocking and phrasing and breathing, Rosenstock was amazed at what he saw. Christ, he thought, she can't even walk across the stage properly. What's going on with her? And when she sang, Rosenstock felt 'it was like some kid out of high school. It was all gone. Something had happened.'

The producer, Ray Stark, and several of his associates watched from a few rows back. Styne and Merrill took notes. The director, Garson Kanin, studied Barbra carefully from beneath furrowed brows as his wife, the actress Ruth Gordon, whispered comments into his ear. Barbra was supposed to end a line of a song with a dismissive 'Ecch,' but she was overdoing it. 'It's too much,' Kanin called out.

Barbra froze. 'What do you want?' she asked.

'Make it more natural.'

She tried again; Ruth Gordon whispered to Garson Kanin; Kanin asked Barbra to do it once more.

'Just tell me what you want and I'll do it!' she pleaded.

'Well, Miss Streizund—'

'My name is Strei*sand!*' Barbra snapped.

At that Ray Stark stood up and started toward the stage. Barbra seemed near tears. 'I'm trying to do everything you say. I've lost my confidence. I don't know how to sing anymore because I'm doing what *you* say, not what I *feel!*'

'You're doing okay,' Ray Stark soothed. 'You're doing good!'

'I didn't take this to be *good!*' Barbra exploded. 'I have to be great or nothing! Either you tell me how to be great – not good, *great* – or don't tell me *anything!*'

Stark called off the rehearsal, and as everyone said perfunctory good-byes, Milt Rosenstock feared the farewells might be final. 'I knew they had someone else lined up to replace her if she didn't work out,' he recalled. The next morning at eleven, everyone regathered 'in dead silence,' according to Rosenstock. 'It was like a morgue. Barbra seemed unfazed. I asked her if she was okay, and she said, "Yeah." Kanin announced we'd pick up with "Don't Rain on My Parade," then looked at Barbra and said, "Are you ready, Miss Strei*sand?*"'

Barbra began to sing, and as Kanin called out directions to her it became clear that nothing had changed. 'If she was supposed to stand still, she moved,' Rosenstock said. 'If she was supposed to move, she stood still. If she was supposed to breathe this way, she breathed that way.' Finally one of Stark's partners leaped from his seat and ran toward the stage. 'He was going to stop her. That was going to be it. She was out. Jule Styne sees the guy, runs after him, and tackles him. He pushes the guy into a seat and tells him, "Leave her alone!" Streisand's singing, she doesn't know any of this is going on. She's building steam, and the magic is working. Styne whispers to me, "She's on fire! She's on *fire!*" She was burning up the stage, hitting every glorious note, really cooking.

'When she got to the end of the song, there was a point where she had to take a breath or she wouldn't be able to hold the final note on that great big finish – "Nobody, no, nobody is gonna rain on my pa-a-a-rade!" She didn't take the breath, and when she got to the note she didn't make it. She stood there and started to cry. She said "I'm sorry" and walked away. She thought for sure she was through.

'But the performance was so brilliant, and in a way not being able to make the final note added to the intensity of the emotion she was conveying. Everybody just burst into applause and cheers and bravos. She came back onstage and she couldn't believe it. From that moment on, she *was* the greatest star.'

Well, not quite yet. Over the next three months this roller-coaster ride of Streisand incompetence and near-firing mingled with stunning brilliance would be repeated again and again. And the show itself had so many problems and received such bad reviews out of town that Ray Stark seriously contemplated closing it. The vehicle that Stark had struggled for more than a decade to produce, the show that would make Barbra Streisand an international superstar, almost didn't come off.

FANNY BRICE, THE beloved Jewish comic and singing star of the Ziegfeld

Follies from 1911 to 1923 and a popular radio personality in the 1930s with her Baby Snooks character, was born Fanny Borach on Manhattan's Lower East Side in 1891. By her early teens she was appearing in stage shows in Brooklyn. At eighteen she embarked on a short-lived marriage to a much older barber – 'Doesn't he smell good?' she asked a friend – and later married the suave, charming gambler and con man Nick Arnstein, who was born Julius Arndstein. Plain-looking, with a prominent nose and only an average voice, Fanny built her success around low ethnic humor and heart-tugging torch songs like 'My Man.'

It was her volatile, unhappy marriage to Arnstein, one of the great Broadway tragic romances, that was most fascinating about her. The two met while Fanny was on the road with the Follies in Baltimore in 1912. She was twenty-one, he thirty-three. She fell in love with his manicured, mustachioed good looks and his dapper style. He, by most accounts, fell in love with her money. The first thing he did when he saw her apartment in New York was decide to redecorate it. He ordered $10,000 worth of new furniture from Gimbel's and charged it to Fanny. 'He was a suave con merchant who talked about millions,' Jimmy Breslin wrote, 'but mostly you found him hanging around the parking lot across from the Forrest Hotel on Forty-ninth Street, with Fanny Brice's money in his pocket and larceny in his head.'

They lived together for six years, and as Fanny's success mushroomed, Nick got into trouble. Fanny hocked her jewels to pay for his lawyers when he was arrested for embezzlement, but he went to Sing Sing anyway. They married in 1918, after Nick divorced his first wife, and had two children, Frances and William. A new con landed Arnstein in Leavenworth, and Fanny borrowed $80,000 from another gambler, Arnold Rothstein, to pay his legal bills.

'Why do you stay with the guy?' Rothstein asked her.

'Because I love him,' Fanny replied. But it all became too much for love to conquer, and Fanny divorced Nick in 1927. She went on to marry and divorce the Broadway impresario Billy Rose and, later in life, became an interior decorator and art collector of exquisite taste. She died in 1951 of a cerebral hemorrhage.

In the late forties, urged on by her friend Goddard Lieberson, Fanny decided to dictate her memories for an autobiography. The galleys for the ghostwritten book had already been sent to reviewers after her death when her son-in-law, Ray Stark, paid $50,000 to have the plates destroyed. Stark's wife – Fanny and Nick's daughter, Frances – didn't like some of the book's frankness. ('She sat like a queen,' Katharine Hepburn said in its pages, 'and could swear like a truck driver.')

Ray Stark, strawberry-haired, medium built, a hard-driving businessman, became a Hollywood agent with Marilyn Monroe and Richard Burton among his clients. His original plan was to turn his mother-in-law's story into a movie, but he couldn't get financing from any of the Hollywood moguls, who were less impressed than Broadway veterans with Fanny Brice's long-ago stardom.

By early 1961 Stark had decided to tell the Brice-Arnstein story as a Broadway musical, as a sort of out-of-town tryout for the movie. 'It seemed wise to open it halfway as a trial,' he said, 'before going the whole way with a film.' Only the best would do. Stark enlisted David Merrick as his co-producer and Jule Styne and Stephen Sondheim, hot off *Gypsy*, as composer and lyricist. He then sent the script – fashioned by Isobel Lennart from a screenplay she had written – to Mary Martin. The star indicated her interest, but Sondheim balked. '*Mary Martin* is going to play Fanny Brice?' he said to Stark. 'You've gotta have a *Jewish* girl! And if she's not Jewish she at least has to have a *nose!*'

'Oh, c'mon, Steve,' Styne answered. 'We're not going to find any girl with a nose.'

Sondheim withdrew, largely because he didn't want to do another back-stage musical after *Gypsy*. Mary Martin departed as well after reconsidering the wisdom of playing a famous ethnic comedienne. She also realized that it would be difficult for her, at nearly fifty, to carry off the play's early scenes of Fanny as a teenager.

Three months went by without Styne hearing a word from Ray Stark, and it was during this period, the spring of 1962, that Styne found the girl with a nose. When Marty Erlichman became aware that *Funny Girl* was in the works, he began to badger David Merrick to give Barbra the part. 'Who would be better as Fanny Brice?' he argued. But Merrick felt that despite her talent, Barbra wasn't mature or sophisticated enough to play the older, wiser Fanny of the show's second act. Marty insisted that Merrick catch Barbra's opening night at the Bon Soir in May, and Merrick sat through both shows. Impressed by her growth as a performer, he turned to Erlichman and said, 'Tell Barbra I think she's aged.'

Merrick urged Styne to catch Barbra's act, and she excited the composer so much that he attended every night of the engagement save one. Styne had seen Barbra in *Wholesale* but hadn't thought of her for *Funny Girl:* 'She was very funny in that show, but it didn't look like she had the quality for a romantic story like the one Isobel Lennart had written.' Seeing her at the Bon Soir changed his mind. Now he fantasized about this marvelous voice singing his songs, and he found himself writing new tunes with Barbra in mind, even though there was no guarantee she'd get the role. 'I was writing the score for someone with that range, that dynamism, that sense of fun.'

When Styne next heard from Ray Stark, the producer told him that he had a director, Jerome Robbins *(West Side Story, Gypsy)*, the most acclaimed director-choreographer on Broadway, and a star, Anne Bancroft, who had created a sensation on Broadway as Annie Sullivan, Helen Keller's teacher, in *The Miracle Worker* in 1959.

Bancroft, a brilliant actress, possessed little more than a fair singing voice. Jule Styne and his new lyricist, Bob Merrill, played her four songs they had written for the show, including 'I'm the Greatest Star' and 'Don't Rain on my Parade,' which Styne had composed with Barbra's voice in mind. Anne Bancroft blanched. 'You'll never get *anyone* to sing those songs,' she protested, and bowed out.

Styne conveyed his excitement about Barbra to Ray Stark, but Stark wanted to cast a name star who would guarantee the show a solid initial box-office take. While the producer sent out feelers to Carol Burnett, Eydie Gormé, Kaye Ballard, Shirley MacLaine, and others, Styne began a public-relations campaign to win the role for Barbra. Column items popped up in the New York papers naming Streisand as the front-runner for the part. When Barbra made her first appearance on *Tonight* on August 21, 1962, Groucho Marx mentioned that Jule Styne had told him Barbra would be 'great for that show he's doing . . . the Fanny Brice story.' A few days later an item appeared in a New York paper announcing that Barbra had been 'chosen' to play Fanny Brice.

At last, the following October, Ray and Fran Stark went down to the Village to see Barbra at the Bon Soir. Styne was sure that would do the trick. It didn't. Both Starks thought Barbra 'too sloppy,' 'not chic,' too undisciplined, to play the refined older Fanny Brice they best remembered. 'That girl will never play my mother,' Fran said. 'My mother was something special.'

But after Jerry Robbins saw Barbra's act, he too began to argue for her, and he persuaded Stark to have Barbra come in for an audition. It did not go well. 'I can't tell you how horrible she looked,' Jule Styne recalled. 'She wore a Cossack uniform kind of thing she'd picked up at a thrift shop . . . In the scene she read, she was supposed to get emotional and weep. She didn't. Robbins said, "Barbra, that's not what we worked on." She sighed and shrank in her chair. Marty Erlichman heard Stark say, "She's terrible. Look at that chin. She'll never play my mother-in-law."'

Still, like Allan Miller before him, Robbins found Barbra fascinating despite her apparent dramatic deficiencies, and he understood when she explained that she couldn't weep where he wanted her to because the words as written hadn't touched her. With that kind of emotional honesty, he felt,

Barbra had the potential to achieve *anything* with the proper direction. He called her back to read seven times, and with some outside coaching from Allan Miller that helped her convey more maturity in one of the play's later scenes, she won Robbins over. 'As far as I'm concerned,' he told her, 'you *are* Fanny Brice.'

Ray Stark finally saw her potential, too. Despite the enormous risk of casting a relative unknown in such a pivotal role, Barbra clearly had to play Fanny. When her signing was announced in July 1963, her comments to the press gave a clue to why: 'We're very much alike,' she said. 'It's like me talking. Like Miss Brice, I find it hard to take advice from anyone. [She] was a woman who refused to heed her mother, or Florenz Ziegfeld.'

Stark knew that if the Streisand gamble worked, the rewards could be phenomenal. With Anne Bancroft, he had told Marty Erlichman, the show would be guaranteed one million dollars in advance sales. With Carol Burnett, two million. With Barbra, next to nothing. But if the show made Streisand a Broadway sensation – which Stark strongly suspected it would – she could bring in five million over the course of the run. And so, Stark decided, 'We go with the kid.'

BY THE TIME *Funny Girl* went into rehearsals, Barbra's meteoric rise to stardom as a singer over the prior year had brought the public's interest in her and the show to a keen pitch, and advance bookings were already in the millions of dollars. Casting had been completed with Sydney Chaplin, the handsome thirty-eight-year-old son of the screen legend Charlie Chaplin, set to play Nick Arnstein, and Kay Medford cast as Fanny's mother, Rose. By then, too, the show had a new director in Garson Kanin – who stepped in after Jerome Robbins quit over book problems and Bob Fosse had come and gone – and just one producer when David Merrick sold his share of the show to Ray Stark after a bitter disagreement between the two men. 'It was a serious falling-out,' Garson Kanin recalled. 'They quarreled, had a big row. I don't know if it was about percentages or the movie rights or what. But David called me one day and said, "Just talk to him. Don't talk to me anymore because I'm out."'

Merrick's departure created a potentially disastrous problem because Barbra had signed her contract with him, not with Ray Stark. Without Merrick, *Funny Girl* had no Streisand, and Stark likely had no show. David Begelman and Freddie Fields, Barbra's agents, smelled an opportunity, and they upped the ante for her to re-sign with Stark on the theory that she was a far more valuable commodity now than she had been six months earlier when she signed her contract. They told Stark that Barbra wanted an increase in her weekly salary from $1,500 to $7,500, a chauffeured limousine to take her to and from the theater, a personal hairdresser, and free daily meals for her and Elliott.

The demands insulted Stark. 'Ray was terribly angry about the whole thing,' Kanin remembered. 'He was a very proud man and a shrewd businessman, and he wasn't going to give in to a lot of pressure. There was a period when we didn't know what was going to happen, and I was desperately attempting to hold this thing together and not let everything go down the drain.'

Stark finally agreed to raise Barbra's salary to $5,000, largely because of the huge advance ticket sales, which were attributable mainly to her. But he agreed to none of her other demands, and the sometimes acrimonious negotiations left each wary of the other. Stark resented what he saw as Barbra's agents' hardball tactics; Barbra thought him niggardly in light of how important she clearly could be to the success of his long-held dream to bring his mother-in-law's story to life. The volatile love-hate relationship between Barbra and Stark, which would extend from Broadway to Hollywood and cover more than twelve years and seven productions, had begun.

ON JANUARY 13, 1964, *Funny Girl* had its first out-of-town tryout at the Shubert Theater in Boston. The performance started an hour late because of a snowstorm, and the audience was restless and unresponsive. By twelve-thirty in the morning, the curtain still had not fallen, and half of the audience had left the theater. The show finally ended at 1:00 A.M., and in the early-morning hours, the dispirited cast read the reviews in a deserted tavern. The notices made Isobel Lennart weep.

Clearly *Funny Girl*, as it stood, was a fiasco. Just about everything that could be wrong with the show, was. It was too long (the next night, twenty minutes of songs and scenes were cut out). It was unfocused, loose, rambling. Many of the musical numbers didn't work. The book didn't seem sure whether Nick Arnstein should be portrayed as the reprehensible ne'er-do-well he was or fictionalized beyond recognition as a charmer forced into an embezzlement scheme only because of his embarrassment at being considered Mr Fanny Brice. The former concept gave the show a richer, more multidimensional leading man, but the latter elicited more audience sympathy. Jule Styne and Garson Kanin argued for Arnstein as he really was, but Ray Stark was unwilling either to offend his wife's memories of her father or to stir any litigious anger in the eighty-three-year-old Arnstein. He held out for what Styne called Nick's 'candyization.'

Audiences might have forgiven all of this if Barbra's performance had been better. There were flashes of brilliance, to be sure, but on the whole she seemed ill at ease. Her performance was often flat and one-dimensional; she behaved essentially the same with her friends and family onstage as she did with Arnstein. And Barbra was trying too hard with the comedy.

The Boston reviews terrified her. She had given up nearly one million dollars in cabaret and television bookings to do this show, and now she feared the whole thing would be a disaster. She had never had to carry a hugely budgeted Broadway show on her shoulders. For the first time in her career, she doubted her abilities. Her stomach twisted into knots; she couldn't keep food down. Her doctor put her on Donnatal, a prescription drug to control her stomach.

Her employment was still tenuous and she knew it. Erasmus Hall High School alumna Lainie Kazan, Barbra's understudy, confirmed that Ray Stark interviewed actresses to replace Streisand at this point. Kazan was privy to that, she said, 'because I was one of the people they talked to.' For Lainie, a Broadway novice, the experience of working on *Funny Girl* was an eye-opener. 'It was like going to war. There were hirings and firings and accidents. There were a lot of power struggles. I was in shock. And it must have been overwhelming for Barbra. But she got through it because she was a strong-willed, feisty little thing.'

Fearful of being dismissed, Barbra became more obsessive than ever about being 'great.' After one of the Boston matinees, Kanin returned to the theater and was surprised to find Barbra kneeling on the apron of the stage, singing 'Don't Rain on My Parade' at full throttle. He went down to the footlights and called out, 'Barbra, wait a minute.' She stopped, startled. 'Barbra,' Kanin said, 'you've just played a whole tough, long matinee. And in about an hour and a half you'll have to be back here again starting to get ready. You should be in your hotel room, resting.'

'Goddammit!' Barbra shouted. 'I gotta get this fucking thing right! Jesus Christ!'

Kanin backed off. 'All right. It's your life and your career. Do what you want.'

That evening, Kanin recalled, Barbra apologized for blowing up at him. 'I didn't mean to do that,' she said. 'But that whole number was getting so fucked up. And the tempo! Jesus, I thought it was my fault. But it was that goddamned asshole in the pit. Jesus Christ!'

✦

'KANIN'S NOT TELLING me what to do!' Barbra wailed to Marty. 'I need direction! All he ever tells me is everything's fine!' Erlichman sat down for a drink with the director and relayed Barbra's concerns. 'When are you going to tell her more – like what to do?'

'She doesn't need to be told what to do,' Kanin replied. 'She knows what to do. I'm only gonna tell her what *not* to do.' Kanin's theory was that once he coupled an actor or actress to a role successfully, the rest would take care of itself. 'In forty-five years,' he said in 1980, 'I have never read a line for an actor. And I have very seldom given anyone a physical direction about where to go, what to do. I believe that you create an atmosphere in which the creative work can take place, and then the players – if you have the right players – will respond.'

Although Barbra was clearly the right player, she didn't have enough experience to call on in the absence of a strong directorial hand. Kanin's approach might have worked with a veteran like Mary Martin or Ethel Merman, but it wasn't working with Barbra. Something had to be done, and Barbra knew what it was: she needed Allan Miller to coach her.

Ray Stark gulped when she told him this. 'Okay,' he replied, 'but you can't let Garson know. I don't want to offend him.'

'But Allan will have to come to the theater and watch the performance,' Barbra protested.

'Well, tell everyone he's your cousin or something.'

MASQUERADING AS BARBRA'S lawyer-cousin from California, Miller watched a performance, and his heart sank. 'She looked like a rank amateur,' he recalled. 'It was pitiful. Nothing had been discovered for her; she didn't know what her emotions were supposed to be based on. She was just told, "Could you do this? Could you move like this?" She covered up her deficiencies by relying on what we call "indicated acting." She wasn't feeling anything, she was just *pretending* to feel something. The scenes between her and Sydney Chaplin were awful. They stood onstage during these supposedly intimate moments and there was a *chasm* between them.'

For one scene, Miller coached Barbra and Sydney in the theater rest room, with Chaplin's wife, Noelle, standing guard lest Garson Kanin find them out. It was the moment that Fanny first sees Nick, backstage after a performance. Both actors had played the scene awkwardly, stiffly. Miller asked Chaplin to wait outside the bathroom, then told Barbra to put herself in Fanny's place. 'You've just done a performance. How long do you think you've been in those dancing shoes?' he asked her. Barbra picked up his train of thought immediately. 'Oh, God! My feet are probably swollen!'

'That's right. And so what are you gonna do the minute you get back to your dressing room?'

'Take off my shoes.' Barbra sat on one of the toilets, undid her shoelaces, and started to massage her feet.

'That's good,' Miller told her. 'Your feet are killing you, they're swollen, so how are you gonna get out of the theater?'

'On my hands and knees!' Barbra exclaimed as she fell to the floor and started crawling.

Miller then left the room to talk to Sydney. 'When you come in, you like what you see,' he told Chaplin. 'This is a young girl, she's uninhibited, you're drawn to her. So you want to join her. When you go in there and see what she's doing, let's see what you do.'

Chaplin came upon Barbra crawling around on all fours, her shoes tied by their laces around her neck. First she saw his legs, and she let out three woofs. Then she looked up and said the famous line from the script, 'Gorgeous.'

'I beg your pardon,' Chaplin said, reciting the dialogue.

'Your shirt. It's gorgeous.' At that point Chaplin got into the spirit of things. 'This?' he said, and pulled the shirt out of his pants and took it off. Then he sat down on the floor with Barbra for the rest of the scene. 'It was a wonderful moment,' Miller recalled. 'You could see why she'd fall instantly in love with the guy.'

According to Miller, another major problem was that audiences weren't responding to Barbra's rendition of 'People.' There was a real risk that the song, which Jule Styne expected would top the pop charts, might be dropped from the show. 'Barbra was singing it the same way all the way through, with no connection at all to the lyrics,' Miller said. 'And she was singing it out to the audience, rather than to Sydney. We worked on all that, and the next night – all of this exploration had to be done before live audiences in Boston – she sang the song very differently. Sydney Chaplin looked at her like "What the hell's going on?" And Milton Rosenstock didn't know what she was going to do. She was so halting in the beginning – which was right for the song – that Rosenstock didn't know how to keep the orchestra in sync with her. He just had them stop playing and she sang a cappella.

'When she got to the phrase, "two people, two very special people," she turned to Sydney and sang the rest of the song only to him. It was magical, touching, *real*. I could see Sydney smiling; he really got caught up in what this girl was doing. At the end of the number, the audience was on their feet. It stopped the show.'

Although Barbra's performance improved, *Funny Girl* remained in chaos around her. The book still presented a major problem; Isobel Lennart would sit in the wings during rehearsals, type new pages of dialogue, and hand them to the cast. Whole scenes were added, then discarded. Musical numbers came and went with alarming speed. Most of the abandoned songs had belonged to Sydney Chaplin, and as Barbra's performance gained steam, it became clear that more and more of *Funny Girl* would have to revolve around her. Jule Styne wasn't happy about that. 'This is turning into An Evening with Barbra Streisand,' he groused. But Ray Stark and Garson Kanin knew that if Barbra continued to grow into the role, her star quality would propel the show's box-office grosses into the stratosphere. Thus, anything that didn't serve Barbra was expendable.

'She was the whole show,' said Chaplin's understudy, George Reeder. 'It didn't matter who else was in it. Finally they told Sydney, "You look great. Just come on in your tuxedo, walk around, and look nice. Let Barbra do the show."'

SYDNEY CHAPLIN MAY have been so sanguine about Barbra taking over *Funny Girl* because by the time the show got to Philadelphia early in February, the two of them were enmeshed in an affair. Barbra had said to Elliott six months earlier, arguing against marriage, 'I have to sow my oats,' and Sydney Chaplin – handsome, dapper, charming, a ladies' man – proved too attractive for her to resist. With Noelle Chaplin back in France and Elliott at home in New York a good deal of the time, Chaplin and Barbra began a discreet romance, dining alone after the show and having rendezvous in each other's hotel rooms.

Garson Kanin recalled that 'They were extremely chummy . . . He was a very waggish fellow. He always made a lot of jokes and talked dirty, and she used to laugh and respond to that.'

Ceil Mack, Barbra's wardrobe lady, said, 'I was aware of it, their little affair. They weren't obvious about it, but if you already knew about it you could pick up on things, like the way he looked at her.'

Rumors of the affair rippled through the company in Philadelphia, and George Reeder recalled that one night after the show he and several other male cast members were sitting around a table in a restaurant with Chaplin when someone mentioned 'a rumor going around.'

'What rumor?' Chaplin asked.

'Nobody wanted to tell him,' Reeder recalled. 'So I piped up and said, "Well, the rumor is that you and Barbra are having an affair." None of us really believed it, so we were pretty surprised when he laughed and said, "Oh, that's nothing," in a way that told us "Yeah, it's true."'

Years later Elliott said that when he first heard of the liaison he confronted Barbra, and she readily admitted that she and Chaplin were involved. Barbra's infidelity, needless to say, put a strain on the Goulds' barely five-month-old marriage. George Reeder recalled that Barbra and Elliott 'didn't act like a happily married couple. He wasn't around very much.'

Another rumor that emanated from Philadelphia said that Barbra was expecting a baby. Had she been, it would have spelled disaster for the show. 'She really did look like she was three months pregnant,' Larry Fuller, a dancer in the cast, recalled.

The first press mention of the rumor appeared in Earl Wilson's *New York Post* column on February 8: 'Producer Ray Stark, denying his *Funny Girl* star, Barbra Streisand, is expecting, says he'll give $1,000 to charity if he's wrong.'

On March 2, Barbra herself denied the rumor to Wilson. On March 11, Wilson reported that 'Barbra Streisand lost five pounds last week, helping squash rumors she's expecting.' That news, of course, prompted fresh speculation that Barbra had had an abortion.

Ceil Mack, involved in the day-to-day fittings of Barbra's costumes, denied Streisand ever was pregnant. 'What made her look that way was her posture. When she stood, her belly protruded. Irene Sharaff, the costume designer, had to design loose-fitting outfits and Empire dresses for her to disguise it. I would have known if she was pregnant and then got an abortion. She looked the same from the beginning of rehearsals. She didn't gain any weight. The rumors weren't true.'

Still another rumor came out of *Funny Girl*'s Philadelphia tryout – that Barbra Streisand's performance had evolved into a stunner. The reviews were good, and word of mouth was now so positive that by the third week, when the company moved from the Forrest Theater to the Erlanger, *Variety* reported that the show was making 'big news' with $30,000 in ticket sales the first day on sale at the Erlanger 'despite a snowstorm.' For the next two weeks in Philadelphia, the show was a sellout.

It was at this time that Allan Miller saw Barbra give 'the most surpassingly beautiful performance I've ever seen on a musical comedy stage.' He had been working with her daily, refining her interpretation of Fanny, developing the nuances that make a characterization memorable. The night before, he had suggested that Barbra dedicate her next performance to her father, in the hope that the deep feelings she had for him would translate into a richer emotional outpouring from her.

It worked. After the performance, Miller recalled, Ray Stark, Jule Styne, Bob Merrill, and Milton Rosenstock went to Barbra's dressing room. 'They said to her, "Barbra, if we ever had any doubts about you, please forgive us. You are golden. Anything you want is yours." And they literally bowed down in front of this twenty-one-year-old girl for this incredible performance.'

Miller remained after the others left. 'So what did *you* think?' Barbra asked. Miller simply hugged her.

'No notes tonight?' Barbra asked.

'No notes. You were flawless. Let's go out and celebrate.'

The next night, as he watched Barbra's performance, Miller was even more stunned. 'She tried to do everything the same from the night before, and it was a travesty. It was unhuman, unfeeling. Nothing worked. She was back to indicating, not feeling. Ray Stark stormed out of the theater in the middle of it, and later in her dressing room it was just her and me.'

'Don't say anything,' Barbra said softly. 'I know, I know.'

'So what are you gonna do?'

'I don't know.'

'We're going to go over what we worked on.'

'Oh, God.'

'Yes, we are. We're going to go over everything we worked on the other night to get you back into focus. You can't do this again.'

The next night Miller felt Barbra had brought the performance about two-thirds of the way back, but that evidently wasn't enough for Ray Stark. According to Miller, 'Stark came zooming back to her dressing room and flung open the door. He barreled in and barked at me, "You get out of my way!" Then he *screamed* at Barbra. "You bitch! You goddamn fucking little bitch! How did I trust you? You'll never work in the theater again! I want Monday night's performance back!"'

'What are you yelling at me about?' Barbra wailed.

'I'm yelling at you because it's my show. I own you.'

'You do not own me! You get out of here. My throat is hurting and I don't want to yell. Fuck you! Get out!'

Stark was shocked. 'You can't say that to me!'

'This is my dressing room. And I'm saying it to you! *Fuck you!* Get out!'

Stark stormed out, slamming the door behind him. Barbra looked at Miller wide-eyed. 'Did you hear what I said to him?'

'Good!' Miller said.

Barbra giggled. 'Do you think I should call the others in and say it to them, too?'

'No, you don't need to do that,' Miller replied.

'Wow,' Barbra whispered. 'I really said "Fuck you!" to Ray Stark!'

STREISAND'S INCONSISTENCY, unresolved book problems, the lack of a firm directorial hand in Garson Kanin – as *Funny Girl* plodded toward its Broadway previews, all of these problems convinced Ray Stark that he had to bring in another director to 'whip the show into shape.' He asked Jerome Robbins to come back. Robbins caught a performance in Philadelphia and he agreed to return as 'production supervisor' only because 'Streisand has gotten so good, I want the rest of the show to live up to what she's doing.'

Robbins lost no time. He pushed back the Broadway opening, which had already been postponed twice, from March 14 to March 24. He immediately restaged most of the dance routines Carol Haney had created for the show, and jettisoned even more of the musical numbers and scenes that didn't highlight Barbra. 'They wanted every number to stop the show,' Garson Kanin said. 'And who can blame them?'

Robbins was amazed at how much Streisand had grown as a performer in less than a year. She had soaked up every ounce of advice from Allan Miller, and she had honed her theatrical instincts to the point where she was able to make the right interpretive decisions on her own. She seemed to thrive on the creative chaos that drove all around her to distraction. Robbins later wrote, 'She accepts the twelve pages of new material to go in that evening's performance and pores over them while *shnorring* part of your sandwich and someone else's Coke. She reads, and like an instantaneous translator, she calculates how all the myriad changes will affect the emotional and physical patterns . . . When she finishes reading, her reactions are immediate and violent – loving or hating them – and she will not change her mind. Not that day. During the rehearsal, in her untidy, exploratory, meteoric fashion, she goes way out, never afraid to let herself go anywhere or try anything . . . That night onstage, in place of the messy, grubby girl, a sorceress sails through every change without hesitation, leaving wallowing fellow players in her wake . . . her performances astound, arouse, fulfill.'

W hen Barbra opened on Broadway,' Shana Alexander wrote in a *Life* magazine profile, 'the entire gorgeous, rattletrap show business Establishment blew sky-high. Overnight critics began raving, photographers flipping, flacks yakking and columnists flocking. Thanks to such massive stimulation the American public has now worked itself into a perfect star-is-born swivet.'

The opening-night audience was stunned by this starburst of talent. Onstage Barbra seemed to possess a pulsating life force, unbound by theatrical convention. She was gangly and defiant as the young Fanny Brice surrounded by a chorus of nay-saying neighbors who mocked her show business ambitions because 'If a Girl Isn't Pretty . . .' Then she rattled the Winter Garden to its rafters with one of the most powerful statements of a dream and a belief in oneself ever written for the musical theater, 'I'm the Greatest Star.' She reduced her audience to helpless hilarity as the pregnant bride in 'His Love Makes Me Beautiful.' She touched every heart during her awkward and nervous introduction to the 'gorgeous' Nick Arnstein and with her yearning rendition of 'People.' She ended Act One with a thrilling anthem to the power of love, 'Don't Rain on My Parade.'

By now the audience members, awed by the power and versatility of this twenty-one-year-old Broadway tyro, knew they were seeing an extraordinary melding of performer and role. Barbra's background had become well known enough that the similarities between her life story and Fanny Brice's were lost on very few. As the audience cheered Fanny on through poverty to stardom and love and loss, they also cheered Barbra's incredible rise from a housing project in Brooklyn to the top of her profession. It was the start of the Streisand cult.

The reviews could have been written by Barbra's press agent.

'If New York were Paris,' *Time*'s critic felt, 'Broadway could temporarily consider renaming itself the Rue Streisand. Some stars merely brighten up a marquee; Barbra Streisand sets an entire theater ablaze ... Actress, songstress, comedienne, mimic, clown – she is the theater's new girl for all seasons.'

On this memorable night – March 26, 1964 – yet another of Barbra Streisand's girlhood dreams came true.

THE FAME AND the adulation that *Funny Girl* brought Barbra staggered her. Two weeks after the show opened, an evocative portrait of her by the artist Henry Koerner graced the cover of *Time* magazine, placing her among a select group of entertainers so honored by a publication that then generally featured scientists and statesmen on its cover. The six-page article, complete with color photos, rare in that era, was headlined simply 'The Girl.'

Six weeks later *Life* did its own cover story on Barbra, entitled 'A Born Loser's Success and Precarious Love.' Reporter Shana Alexander's perceptive and glowing profile described Streisand as 'Cinderella at the ball, every hopeless kid's hopeless dream come true ... Her show is a sellout and her albums are a smash. Even more remarkable is the sudden nationwide frenzy to achieve the Streisand "look." Hairdressers are being besieged with requests for Streisand wigs (Beatle, but kempt). Women's magazines are hastily assembling features on the Streisand fashion (threadbare) and the Streisand eye makeup (proto-Cleopatra).'

The success Barbra had dreamed about for so long left her exhilarated yet oddly unfulfilled. 'The reality can never live up to the fantasy, can it?' she mused to a reporter. 'The excitement of life lies in the hope, in the striving for something rather than the attainment.' In her fantasies there had been no stress, no exhaustion, no poor performances, no stomach aches from nerves, no battles with co-stars and producers, no disappointments.

She took little joy in the hosannas thrown her way by everyone from gossip columnists to august national publications. In the most glowing review, she would fixate on the one reservation the critic expressed about her performance. Again and again she would ask reporters, 'So am I great or am I lousy? I gotta know!'

She mistrusted the effusive praise. In the syndrome her former boyfriend Stanley Beck had first pointed out to her, she thought less of anyone who considered her great. How much can they know? she would think. Tonight's performance was lousy! She didn't understand that what she considered lousy was still enthralling to anyone seeing her for the first time.

She had been told for so long that she was unattractive, that her clothes were ugly, that she would never make it. Now that she was described as beautiful, named a fashion trendsetter, and celebrated as the toast of Broadway, she couldn't quite bring herself to believe it. 'The trouble with Barbra,' Elliott later said, 'is that she can't seem to let herself be happy.'

Of all the disillusionments Barbra had suffered on her way to the top, Marlon Brando supplied one of the worst when she finally met her girlhood heartthrob. 'I wanted to say to him, "Let us speak to one another because I understand you. You are just like me." So one night I'm waiting to go on at a benefit, and somebody comes up behind me and starts caressing my shoulder and nuzzling my neck. I turn around, and there he is! It's Brando. And he says, "I'm letting you off easy," and I laugh and say, "Whaddaya mean, easy? This is the best part!" And then, I don't know, what the hell was there to say? It was kind of sad, because he wasn't like me at all.'

The kids who waited every day outside the stage door for a glimpse of Barbra, an autograph, perhaps a picture, felt that she was like them, too. Some of them were homely, some overweight, some homosexual, some just different in one way or another. All of them felt like misfits, and Barbra Streisand was the most gloriously successful misfit since James Dean. If she could triumph, capture the spotlight, win fame and wealth, maybe they could too. She became a symbol to them, proof that they were indeed what they felt like inside: not strange but special.

They were prepared to idolize her, but she didn't want to be worshiped. As Barbra finished an evening's performance and got ready to leave the theater, she would ask her dresser, Ceil Mack, 'Are they out there?'

'They're always out there,' Ceil would reply. 'You know that.'

'Tell them I've already left.'

'They know you haven't left.'

'Oh, God, I wish they'd leave me alone,' Barbra would sigh. Then she'd put on dark glasses, a babushka over her hair, and an oversized coat and leave the theater through the front door, unrecognized among the last of the audience as they filed out.

While she waited for a cab in the rain one day, a teenage fan took off his coat and threw it over a puddle in the gutter for her to walk on, a Broadway Sir Walter Raleigh. 'Don't do that for me!' Barbra exclaimed, shocked. 'Pick your coat up!' Chagrined, the young man did as he was told. Barbra looked back at him as she got into the cab and said, 'Have more respect for yourself than that.'

Sometimes she found the fervor of her fans frightening, even threatening. Her arranger Peter Matz, working with her on a new album, recalled walking with Barbra to the theater one evening. 'We approached the backstage entrance, and it was mobbed by those autograph people. Many of them are very weird. When they saw Barbra coming, they started screaming, "Here's Barbra! Here's Barbra!" and they headed toward us en masse. Barbra dug her fingers into my arm to the point that blood was coming out. Her face was totally drained white. She was terrified of this assault. The doorman cleared the way and we got inside, but she was shaking and sweating.'

A FEW WEEKS after *Funny Girl* opened, Barbra scratched one of her corneas, and although she went to the theater she was advised not to perform because the tremendous exertion her role required might aggravate the injury. 'My understudy was getting ready to go on in my place,' Barbra said. 'Then I got this little dish of candy from my stepfather – he was out in front, in the audience.' Although Louis Kind and her mother had never divorced, Barbra had not seen or heard from him in the eight years since he had walked out on the family. The minute she heard Kind was in the audience, Barbra told the stage manager, 'I'm going on!'

Her doctor gave her some anesthetic for the eye, and she walked onstage determined to show her stepfather how wrong he had been about her. 'I never did a show like that,' Barbra said. 'It was the best performance I ever gave.' Afterward she went to her dressing room and refused all visitors, waiting for Lou Kind to come backstage and finally tell her that she had done something well. She waited for over an hour, but he never appeared.

Barbra kept the dish of candy – the only thing Kind had given her since that doll when she was six – for twenty-three years. Then, in 1987, she said, 'After all these years I just threw it out. So I got rid of him.'

Knowing whether she had finally impressed her stepfather was especially important to Barbra because her mother, even after all the acclaim – the cover of *Time* for goodness' sake! – still hadn't come around. 'I wish I could convince my mother that I'm a success,' Barbra told an interviewer. 'Even today she calls me and says, "So-and-so in the office says he read something nice about you in the papers." But it never seems to mean anything to *her* personally.'

Mrs Kind subscribed to the theory that if she praised her daughter too highly to her face she'd get 'a swelled head.' She did express pride in Barbra's accomplishment to a reporter, however: 'One of the big thrills for me was seeing her open in Philadelphia in *Funny Girl* . . . I was so nervous before the show – I seemed to feel everything Barbra was going through. I was so overwhelmed that I just couldn't sit still. I had to leave my seat and stand in the back of the theater. As I heard Barbra singing, I got emotional. She was so terrific it upset my balance – my feelings just welled up in me. I felt fearful for her – and excited and proud, all at the same time.' But for whatever reason, Mrs Kind never said any of this directly to Barbra.

Barbra's grandparents Anna and Isaac, whom she hadn't seen for years, came to see the show a few weeks into the run and proudly posed for a picture with her in her dressing room. Later that year Isaac died at the age of eighty-five; Anna lived another ten years. Barbra didn't attend either funeral. Other, more distant, members of her family clamored to get free passes to *Funny Girl*. 'Oh, God,' she said to Ceil Mack, 'I've got more cousins than I ever dreamed. They're coming out of the woodwork.'

Her sister, Roslyn, now thirteen and totally starstruck by Barbra's success, saw forty Saturday matinees of *Funny Girl* in a row. After each show she would hang around outside the stage door like all the other Streisand fans in the hope of seeing Barbra. 'Roz was a little shy,' her mother explained, 'and she didn't know how to approach a big sister who had gotten so famous.' Roslyn, timid, awkward, very fat – 192 pounds on a five-foot-two-inch frame – fit right in with the hangers-on. She appeared so matronly that when the others found out she was related to Barbra, one of them asked, 'Are you her aunt?'

When she told them who she was, the fans were skeptical. 'If you're really her sister,' someone asked, 'why don't you go inside instead of hanging around here with the rest of us?'

'I would like to,' she replied softly, 'but I don't want to impose.'

Her obesity caused Roslyn deep unhappiness. 'I was encased in fat,' she said, 'wrapped up in it. You get in a shell and after a while you want to stay there. Total disaster. Kids at school called me Fatso. I had no boyfriends.' At the *Funny Girl* opening night Barbra, who hadn't seen her sister for months, looked at her and said, 'Gee, you really look like a *big* girl now.'

'That hit me right in the heart,' Roslyn said. Still, she worshiped her celebrated sister.

'At home,' Mrs Kind said, 'Roslyn would play the *Funny Girl* album day and night and imitate Barbra. She was really her best imitator.'

AND THEN THERE was Elliott. Barbra's phenomenal success had swept him up in its tide, and often now he felt adrift on the crest. He could laugh, he professed, about being called Mr Streisand, but her total professional dominance over him was harder to accept. 'To have a relationship with someone as successful as Barbra made it difficult for me to face or find myself,' he said.

Their world revolved around Barbra now. Everything seemed to be in her service, including Elliott. He waited for her in their car every night after the show, ready to drive her home. 'I felt sorry for him,' Ceil Mack said. 'I remember thinking, What is he, her chauffeur now?'

When Barbra bought a used Rolls-Royce, Elliott actually put on a chauffeur's cap and drove her around town. It was meant as a goof, but there was more symbolism inherent in the gesture than either of them probably realized, because Elliott had allowed himself to buy into Barbra's fantasies. 'A person with the romantic emotions of an actor can be unduly impressed by limousines and living in big places,' he said.

Later he added, 'I hated Barbra supporting me. It is essential for a man to support his woman.' But how was he to do that without work? He had wanted the role of Nick Arnstein but 'couldn't get the job. I'm more talented than all the guys who played Nicky Arnstein put together.' Barbra could have insisted that Elliott be given the part, but she didn't. Asked if she wanted him to play the role, Elliott replied, 'I don't know.'

He had a lot of time on his hands, time he often spent playing three-man pickup basketball games in Manhattan school yards. He also became deeply involved in gambling on sporting events. 'I bet on every game on the boards, thousands on a game,' he told *Playboy*. 'I wasn't very successful.' Eventually he would lose $50,000 on one football season. And every night on Broadway his wife played a woman whose success overshadowed that of her husband, an inveterate gambler on a losing streak. Art was imitating Fanny and Nick's life onstage, and Barbra and Elliott's life was imitating art offstage. Elliott told himself that his idleness was in service to his love, that he needed to attend to his marriage. 'Possibly that gave me an excuse not to look for work,' he admitted. 'I was afraid I wouldn't get it, afraid to go out on my own.'

As if to complete this sorry syndrome, Elliott's few efforts to strike out on his own failed. Less than a month after Barbra opened in *Funny Girl*, he flew to Jamaica to appear in a film, *The Confession*, along with Ginger Rogers and Ray Milland. The budget was low, his part as a deaf mute who is miraculously cured at the end of the story was small, and the picture was shelved for seven years until it came and soon went under the title *Quick, Let's Get Married*. It later turned up on television renamed yet again as *Seven Different Ways*. Later, Elliott did not list it among his credits.

In June 1964, *Once Upon a Mattress*, a television version of the Princess and the Pea legend which Elliott had taped in March, was aired over CBS. It was a ratings success, but Elliott's role as the Prince was largely forgotten in the glow of Carol Burnett's hilarious comic performance as the princess. While Barbra negotiated a $5 million dollar deal with the same network for a series of specials of her own, Elliott received no other offers of television work.

BARBRA WAS JUST about to reach the moment in 'People' when she would look at Nick Arnstein and turn the song from a generalized statement to a personal expression of her feelings for Nick. Just then her eyes fell on Sydney

Chaplin's face and she lost her concentration, and very nearly her place in the song. Chaplin, his back to the audience, was grunting and mumbling obscenities at her, loudly enough so that she feared the audience would hear him. Shocked and disconcerted, she barely got through the song. 'He would actually be talking to try to upstage her while she was singing "People,"' cast member Linda Gerard recalled. 'He would be doing things that were so ridiculous and so amateur-night-in-Dixie.'

A few days earlier, Barbra had ended her affair with Chaplin, and the gentleman was highly displeased. He reacted with a year of contentious behavior that culminated in Barbra's bringing him up on charges before Actors' Equity and, finally, his early departure from the show. 'It was a scorned affair,' Chaplin's understudy George Reeder recalled, 'and they were at each other's throats.'

Nearly every night Chaplin muttered sotto voce obscenities at Barbra during their intimate scenes. He changed bits of business and dialogue on her, throwing her off stride. When they passed each other leaving or entering the stage, George Reeder recalled, Chaplin would purposely brush up close to her. 'Not a big, obvious thing, but enough to knock her off balance.'

According to Larry Fuller, 'Sydney was extremely angry at her. He'd grumble and say things behind the set about her as she waited to go on. I never spoke to her at those moments out of respect for her preparation as an actress. But Chaplin would complain to me about her loud enough for her to hear. I could quite often feel the tension onstage between them because his anger was so voluminous.'

In August, Chaplin gave an interview to the New York *Daily News* that revealed some clues to his state of mind. His words tinged with bitterness, Chaplin said of his role as Nick Arnstein, 'I'm sort of nobody – a straight man for Barbra Streisand. I'm a guy in white tails, a snob – the audience doesn't root for me. At the end of the play, I kick the dog, slap the baby – I leave Fanny. I'm lucky the audience doesn't wait outside the theater to lynch me.'

Chaplin continued to vex Barbra, and in September Ray Stark called the two stars into a meeting. Barbra pleaded with Chaplin to tell her what she was doing wrong. All he would say was that the writing of the show was terrible. But, George Reeder recalled, he had refused to accept any new dialogue in rehearsal, saying, 'I don't have to learn these lines – my uncle just gave me one million dollars.' He also would no longer accept notes criticizing his performance, notes he knew originated with Barbra. 'I'm tired of doing the show her way!' he barked. 'I'm going to do things *my* way!'

Backstage at one performance, Chaplin shouted, 'Christ, what a vulgar audience!' loud enough for a good portion of that audience to hear him.

Furious, Barbra picked up a prop and threw it on the floor. 'Just shut up and follow the script!' she hissed.

During intimate scenes, George Reeder recalled, Chaplin took to whispering '*nose*' in Barbra's ear. At one intermission, she ran back to her dressing room in tears, and the stage manager, Tom Stone, had to use all his powers of persuasion to get her to take the stage again for the second act.

The battles escalated. 'We would actually hear shouting in the halls,' George Reeder said. 'Yelling and slamming of doors, that kind of thing.' Lainie Kazan recalled that Chaplin 'had a foul mouth. Every other word was a four-letter word. I'm sure he couldn't understand this young girl usurping him and his position in the theater or his position with the producers . . . I heard Sydney saying some things that were not very kind about Barbra.'

Larry Fuller added, 'I never saw him do anything threatening to her. I just saw him be extremely angry.'

Finally Barbra decided that she had no recourse but to bring Chaplin up on charges before Actors' Equity. There was a hearing, but no action was taken against him. According to George Reeder, 'Sydney could be such a charming and witty man that he just went in and charmed the pants off the Equity Committee. Barbra was angry, and she came off a little bit aggressive and abrasive, and here was this tall, handsome, ingratiating man giving his side of things. Barbra didn't have a chance.'

But she got her revenge, Reeder recalled. At the end of the 'You Are Woman, I Am Man' number, after Fanny falls back on the chaise longue and Nicky starts to kiss her, a blackout curtain would come down as the set moved upstage to make room for the next scene. 'There was a heavy lead pipe sewn into the bottom of the curtain,' Reeder recalled, 'and Sydney and I were warned to keep our heads down, because if we lifted them up too soon we risked getting conked on the noggin with this pipe as the curtain fell.

'Well, this one performance, as Sydney was pretending to nuzzle and kiss Barbra's neck at the end of the scene, he said "nose" to her again. She bit his neck really hard and he reared his head up. The pipe hit him. Everybody was going "Are you all right?" and he said, "Yeah, I'm fine." But then when he came down from his dressing room for his next scene, he stopped on the stairs and said, "Oh, my God, I don't think I can do this." He felt really dizzy, and it turned out he had a concussion. So I had to go on for him.'

In June 1965 Chaplin left the production. Stark agreed to continue to pay him his $2,100-a-week salary through the end of his contract – a total of $84,000 – and told Chaplin he was to say his problems had been with Stark, not Barbra. Chaplin lived up to the agreement and gave his final performance on June 19. Few among the cast were sorry to see him go.

Years later Chaplin remained bitter toward Barbra. In a 1989 interview he said, 'It seemed clear to me that Barbra didn't find herself attractive and was compensating with this enormous drive to succeed. I thought those qualities were rather attractive – until the charm became overbearing. Barbra thought she knew everything. When she started directing me, I told her she should stop mugging like Martha Raye, leave me alone, and concentrate on her own lines . . . She's not a generous person. Whatever niceness may be there is pretty deeply hidden. You'll see – she'll end up sad.'

Johnny Desmond, younger and even better looking than Chaplin, stepped into the Arnstein role. Desmond had begun his career as a big-band singer with Glenn Miller and had starred on Broadway in another Jule Styne show, *Say, Darling*, in 1958. Unlike Chaplin, he knew from the beginning exactly what he was getting into playing Nick Arnstein. What he didn't expect was the flurry of notes on his performance that Barbra kept sending to him through the stage manager. 'I asked for a meeting with her to talk things out,' Desmond recalled. 'We talked for two hours onstage, and I told her I was happy in my work and I wanted a good working relationship. I couldn't steal the show from her if I stood on my head and yodeled . . . I wanted her to feel secure in my performance.' After things got thrashed out, the two stars got along just fine, and most of the company much preferred Desmond to Chaplin.

MONTHS BEFORE CHAPLIN left, another classic backstage drama had cost Lainie Kazan her job as Barbra's understudy. On Tuesday, February 2, 1965, Elliott called the theater to say that Barbra had laryngitis, and for the first time she would not be able to go on. The stage manager frantically telephoned Kazan and told her to come in and rehearse with Sydney Chaplin. 'I had career ambitions,' Lainie said, 'and the people in the press kept saying to me, "If you ever go on, let us know." So I kept a list of critics and columnists, and when I found out I'd be going on that night, I had a girlfriend call them.'

While Lainie rehearsed the role that afternoon, a reporter for *The New York Times* called Barbra and told her what Kazan was up to. Barbra reportedly replied, 'Over my dead body!' and showed up at the theater at seven-thirty ready to give her performance. The next day's newspapers had a field day with the story of an insecure star who had dragged herself out of a sickbed to keep her understudy from stealing any of her limelight. 'Show Goes On, but Lainie Doesn't,' one headline read.

'I think Barbra was probably upset,' Lainie understated. 'She was very protective of that role. I wanted her part, but she didn't want me to do it.'

By the next day, however, Barbra was even sicker, and Lainie got her chance to go on twice, during the matinee and the evening performance. Reporters for *Time* and *Newsweek* attended. Publicly, Barbra appeared gracious; she sent her fellow Erasman a telegram: 'We were told trees grow in Brooklyn. But we know better. Stars do.' However, Ray Stark fired Kazan, possibly as a result of pressure from Barbra.

'Ray Stark called the replacement auditions for Barbra's understudy between the two shows that Lainie did that day,' George Reeder recalled. 'That was a really nasty thing to do, because it let Lainie know that that night was the last time she was going to be doing that role.'

For the record, Lainie denied that she was fired. 'I got so much publicity that within a week I was swamped with offers,' she said. 'I had a record contract and a nightclub offer. So I asked Ray Stark if I could have my release.'

'Lainie likes to say she left, but she was fired,' her replacement, Linda Gerard, said. 'Barbra was really upset about what she had done. In fact, when I signed my contract, part of my deal was I could not alert the media if I ever went on.'

Not long after this, Peter Daniels, who had been assistant conductor for the show, was fired by a furious Barbra when she learned that he had given some of the arrangements he had prepared for her to Lainie, whom he later married, for her nightclub act.

★

BARBRA'S RECORDING CAREER kept pace with her Broadway stardom throughout 1964. *Barbra Streisand/The Third Album*, released in February, rose to number five on the pop charts and went gold within a year. The most cohesive of her first three efforts, the mostly classic songs highlighted the beauty of her voice as much as her second album had showcased its theatricality.

Two months later the original-cast recording of the *Funny Girl* score hit the stores. The excitement the show had generated and Barbra's growing legion of fans propelled the album to number two. The sales of all four of Barbra's albums were bolstered considerably in May when *The Barbra Streisand Album* won the Grammy Award as Album of the Year and Barbra was chosen Best Female Vocalist for her work on the album. She remains the youngest recipient of both awards.

One of Marty Erlichman's predictions had come true, but another would have to wait. Despite the stunning impact Barbra had made on Broadway, the Tony Award eluded her again when the Best Actress citation went to Broadway veteran Carol Channing for her role as Dolly Levi in David Merrick's production of *Hello, Dolly!* Channing's win was part of a nearly clean sweep for her show. The only one of its eight nominations *Funny Girl* won was for Kay Medford as Best Supporting Actress. Barbra was sorely disappointed, but she felt better the following night when her audience jumped to their feet upon her first entrance, and her fans in the balcony cheered and shouted, 'You're the best actress to us, Barbra!'

ON SUNDAY, JULY 12, 1964, Barbra tried out some material for a new album on the concert stage at the Forest Hills Music Festival in Queens. The crowd gave her a thunderous ovation as she stepped out on the stage, and a gathering summer storm gave her some literal thunder just as the music began for her first number. 'Quiet down!' she said, looking skyward. 'I haven't done anything yet!'

Between songs, shouts of 'Come closer, Barbra!' echoed through the night air. The arena, a tennis stadium, had been set up with a large expanse of grass between the stage and the first row of seats. At intermission Barbra decided to honor the request. And so, as she sang 'People' to open the second act, she walked across the grass, which was still wet from an afternoon downpour, trailing the microphone cord behind her. 'She had been warned that she could be electrocuted on the wet grass,' Peter Daniels said, 'but she did it anyway. She had to win back the crowd. And she did. They jumped to their feet after that number.' The show proved that Barbra hadn't lost any of her ability to weave concert magic, and she repeated the triumph at the following year's festival.

Barbra reached a new recording milestone in September when her fourth studio album, *People*, climbed to the number one position on the *Billboard* Top 100 Albums chart, helped along by the sales and airplay of Streisand's first bona fide hit single, a new recording of the title tune. It was a remarkable accomplishment in an era dominated by the Beatles – Barbra knocked *A Hard Day's Night* out of the top spot – but understandable both in terms of the excitement surrounding Streisand and the album's quality. Arguably her best recording to date, *People* featured songs of unusual musical and narrative depth which highlighted the richness that her voice continued to acquire. Had there been any thought that Streisand might be a flash in the pan, *People* put it to rest. The record won Barbra her second consecutive Grammy as Best Female Vocalist.

BY THE END of 1964 Barbra Streisand had become a very rich woman. Her *Funny Girl* salary tallied up to more than a quarter of a million dollars a year, and the annual royalties from her record sales amounted to at least that. On top of it all she had just signed a $5 million contract with CBS to star in five television specials.

She was nearly a millionaire, but Barbra considered her new wealth 'play money'; the figures bandied about by her agents and manager were too fantastical for her to take seriously on an everyday basis. Marty Erlichman recalled relaying an offer to her to sing for one night for fifty thousand dollars. Barbra told him no, then asked, 'Why does it cost twelve-fifty to send a messenger across town?'

'Barbra,' Marty replied, 'you just turned down fifty thousand and you're worried about twelve dollars?'

'You know me better than that, Marty,' she replied. 'I can *relate* to twelve dollars.'

For Barbra, the best part of having this kind of money was that it allowed her to do anything she wanted to do with the duplex on Central Park West. Its decoration and renovation became a year-long project that occupied just about all of her spare time. She hired a decorator, Charles Murray, 'to help me realize my vision.' She and Murray haunted the thrift shops for 'great old things,' but now she could afford to reupholster a couch in the finest, most expensive fabrics, and anything she couldn't find, she could have custom-made. She loved many different eras and styles, and now she could afford to live with them all – sometimes in the same room. Describing the apartment in an interview, she said, 'My dining room and my living room and my foyer [are] French, and my kitchen and my office [are] sort of crazy Victorian and American – early American – and the den is contemporary Victorian and Modern, and the bedroom is English Tudor and Jacobean and Italian.'

Every surface of the bathroom was covered with red patent leather; chandeliers hung in six of the rooms, including the bathroom. 'Sure it's expensive,' Barbra told the columnist Earl Wilson. 'Everything good is expensive.'

THE WINTER GARDEN remained dark on Monday night, January 18, 1965, so that Barbra could perform at Lyndon Johnson's inaugural gala. Johnson had helped America heal itself in the wake of John Kennedy's death, and to the delight of Kennedy admirers who feared that with his southern conservative background Johnson would reverse many of Kennedy's progressive policies, he had created the Great Society program, the most liberal package of government aid to the poor since Franklin Roosevelt's New Deal. To even greater surprise he worked for and signed into law the most sweeping civil rights legislation in the country's history. In November of 1964 he had been elected to his own full term as president by an overwhelming majority over the conservative Republican Arizona senator Barry M. Goldwater. On January 20 he would be sworn in, and Barbra had been asked to be a part of the week-long celebration in Washington.

Barbra was delighted to accept, and she appeared along with Margot Fonteyn and Rudolf Nureyev, Alfred Hitchcock, Julie Andrews, Carol Channing (who sang 'Hello, Lyndon!'), Harry Belafonte, the comedy team of Mike Nichols and Elaine May, Carol Burnett, Johnny Carson, and Woody Allen, among others. During the rehearsal she took a wad of gum out of her mouth and stuck it under a wooden three-legged stool. When she left, two young girls rushed up to the stage and retrieved it.

Glittery in a beaded dress in shades of gold, orange, and red, she held the audience in the National Armory spellbound with a stunning rendition of 'People' despite a minor mix-up in her lighting cues. The columnist Dorothy Kilgallen observed that 'Barbra Streisand came on and sang flawlessly, moving her arms sinuously, using her hands with maximum effect, turning her elaborate beehive wig toward all parts of the auditorium as she made "People" sound like the most important song next to the National Anthem.' Walter Winchell concurred: 'No other star won such rapt attention and respect.'

On Sunday, April 4, Barbra participated in a three-hour benefit to raise money for civil rights groups. The event – attended by eighteen hundred people including the Reverend Dr Martin Luther King Jr. – raised $150,000, the most ever for a one-night fund-raiser. Barbra sang Harold Arlen's 'That's a Fine Kind of Freedom.'

AS THE MONTHS onstage in *Funny Girl* dragged on, Barbra began to dread doing the show night after night. The out-of-town tryouts, as stressful as they were, had exhilarated her. She had learned the sometimes hourly changes in a flash; she had thrived on the excitement, the danger, of doing a scene for the first time while in front of a paying audience. She was handed a new version of the show's final scene twenty minutes before the curtain went up on opening night in New York – and she loved it. But as the months wore on, and *Funny Girl* continued to sell out, thoughts of her run-of-the-play contract made Barbra cringe. 'My last year on stage in *Funny Girl* was a nightmare,' she said. 'It drove me into analysis. I felt like I was locked up in prison . . . It was very trying to be at the whim of every audience, to have to go out and try all over again every performance. If the laughs were smaller at one performance than another, then I'd worry why they were smaller. I'd worry during the performance. I'd keep thinking, I can't seem to please these people enough. It was very, very exhausting.'

Sometimes she wasn't up to doing the whole two and a half hours eight times a week. George Reeder recalled that there were three versions of the show, and which one they did at any given performance depended on Barbra. 'There was the full version, then a shorter version where she wouldn't do one or two of the reprises. In the shortest version we'd eliminate entire scenes and all of the reprises except "Don't Rain on My Parade" at the end.'

Early in 1965 the cast found themselves doing the shorter shows more frequently, because Barbra was preoccupied with filming *My Name Is Barbra*, the first television special in her multimillion-dollar contract with CBS.

I n March of 1965 Marty Erlichman, David Begelman, and CBS program-
ming chief Michael Dann gathered for a meeting at the Four Seasons
restaurant in Manhattan. Dann had just screened *My Name Is Barbra*,
and as Marty slid into the leather banquette he wondered just how effusive
Dann's praise would be.

'Let me get this out of the way,' Dann began. 'I just saw the special, and
in one fell swoop you're gonna ruin this girl's career.' Marty's eyes widened
and his astonished gaze went from Dann to Begelman and back again.

'That show is gonna do *daytime* ratings,' Dann went on. 'It's gonna be
blasted by the critics. We've got a firm air date that we can't move, so
here's what I think you should do to save the show. I would rearrange the
three sections of it and put the second one first, where she does the comedy
monologue. I mean, how dare you take this girl, with a name nobody's even
gonna be able to pronounce, and allow her to open up a TV show by singing
for seventeen straight minutes before she even says hello to the audience?'

Maybe I should have expected this, Marty thought, because once again
Barbra was trying to break the mold. Television specials always had guest
stars, usually performers who were under contract to the network airing the
special. Months earlier, Dann had suggested that Barbra have Frank Sinatra
and Dean Martin on her show.

'I saw that show,' Marty had told him. 'It was called *Judy Garland and
Friends*.'

'You're right,' Dann had replied. 'Let's go instead with two big CBS stars,
Dick Van Dyke and Andy Griffith.'

Barbra wouldn't give that idea a second thought. 'Why didn't I want guest
stars?' she said later. 'It's that idle, silly talk you have to indulge in on TV
shows. It doesn't interest me.'

Now Marty couldn't believe that Dann, who must have been speaking for others at CBS as well, hadn't seen the quality of Barbra's show. He told Dann he was dead wrong and offered to void the entire CBS deal. 'Daytime numbers? She'll double them. It will be the highest-rated variety special this year. And reviews? She'll win every award.' Marty could afford to hold his ground because Barbra had complete creative control over her special and was answerable only to the network censors. *My Name Is Barbra* would be aired as it was or not at all.

Barbra's contract with CBS called for one special a year for three years, a possible series in the future, and further specials to stretch over a ten-year period, for which she would reportedly earn $5 million. 'I'm fuzzy on the details,' she told the Associated Press. 'But it gives me creative control over my programs. That's the main thing. I don't have to get sponsor approval.' Indeed, shortly after the contract was announced, Chemstrand Carpeting agreed to sponsor the first special sight unseen.

'I want to do something vital,' Barbra said, 'something important.' She and Marty assembled a pool of innovative young talent that included director Dwight Hemion, scenic designer Tom John, and the thirty-four-year-old Joe Layton, credited with the conception of the production numbers. Peter Matz would arrange and conduct the music. 'We all decided,' Marty said, 'that the whole show [with the exception of a brief comic monologue] would be Barbra just singing. We didn't want to worry about getting that funny piece of sketch material that may or may not work.'

Rehearsals and production began in January, scheduled around Barbra's eight weekly performances at the Winter Garden. The first act of the special, taped at a Midtown CBS television soundstage, had Barbra rush around a multilevel set to the strains of 'I'm Late,' stopping only to sing lovely renditions of 'Make Believe' and 'How Does the Wine Taste?' before cavorting as a five-year-old in an oversized playground while she sang of tigers and polar bears and giraffes. The second act took place at the elegant Bergdorf Goodman department store on Fifth Avenue and featured Barbra singing songs of poverty and deprivation while she pranced around the store in fur coats, diamonds, and fancy hats. For the third act Barbra sang in concert.

On April 25, three nights before the show aired, Barbra made a rare promotional appearance on the venerable quiz show *What's My Line?* As the mystery guest, Streisand signed in on a blackboard, and she immediately managed to plug her special by boldly scrawling 'My Name Is Barbra.' Before a blindfolded panel composed of the actors Tony Randall and Arlene Francis, the publisher Bennett Cerf, and the columnist Dorothy Kilgallen, Barbra attempted to obscure her voice by responding in Italian to questions designed to determine her identity. It didn't work; she was recognized quickly, thanks in part to continuous cheers from the studio audience. At the conclusion of the segment, host John Charles Daly announced, 'Our camera and sound men worked with Miss Streisand [on part of her special], and they think it's gonna be one of the great successes of all time.'

THE FOLLOWING WEDNESDAY, April 28, Barbra and the entire *Funny Girl* cast crowded into her dressing room to watch the first fifteen minutes of the special during their intermission. 'Finally the big moment came – nine o'clock!' Barbra said. 'But there was no *singing*, there was no *picture*. My first television special and the engineer had forgotten to push the button to start the show! I couldn't believe it!' Streisand the perfectionist recalls the moment as being more dramatic than it really was. Only the first second and a half of the show was missed, and it was barely noticed by anyone but Barbra.

After she completed that night's performance of *Funny Girl*, Barbra, accompanied by Elliott and Marty, swept into a swank cocktail party in her honor hosted by Bergdorf Goodman owner Andrew Goodman in his twenty-two-room penthouse above the store. Sybil Burton, Bill Blass, and Arlene Francis joined most of Manhattan's high society in singing Streisand's praises. Wearing a jeweled evening gown in paisley voile, 'and beautiful silver-painted fingernails to match,' Barbra accepted the compliments graciously, but soon repaired nervously to a bedroom, where early reviews of the show were read to her over the phone. The first one was an ecstatic rave, but Barbra's reaction to it surprised the guests. 'They must be more specific,' she fretted to no one in particular. 'I want to know everything.'

'Everything' turned out to be all that Barbra could have hoped for. The majority opinion was echoed by a review by Rick DuBrow of United Press International that has become a milestone in the Streisand lore. The special, he felt, was 'a pinnacle moment of American show business, in any form, in any period. She is so great, it is shocking, something like being in love . . . She may well be the most supremely talented and complete popular entertainer this country has ever produced . . . She sang . . . but that is as complete as saying Tolstoy was a writer . . . She touches you to your toes, and then she knocks you out.'

For days afterward critical raves continued to pour into Marty Erlichman's office, but his favorite response came from Mike Dann, the man who weeks earlier had told him the show would ruin Barbra's career. Dann's phone call was the first one he got the morning after the show aired. 'I apologize,' Dann said simply. 'I was wrong.' By the end of the week it was clear Marty had been right about the viewership, too. *My Name Is Barbra* garnered a terrific 35.6 percent share of the viewing audience, topping its competition.

The importance of *My Name Is Barbra* to the broadening appeal of Barbra Streisand can scarcely be overstated. In a single hour she cemented the already passionate loyalty of her existing fans and won millions of new admirers. Gone forever was the unkempt gum-chewing *mieskeit* in secondhand finery who sometimes shrieked the climaxes of her songs. She had been replaced by a silkily assured performer who despite her youth could now be placed confidently in the same league as such esteemed veterans as Garland and Sinatra. For those who hadn't seen Barbra on television since the days of *PM East*, the transformation was nothing short of jaw-dropping.

Not everyone, though, was entranced. Following the showing of *My Name Is Barbra*, Streisand became one of the most controversial women in America. Almost everything about her became fodder for intense debate: her looks, her fashions, her fingernails, her dramatic vocal delivery, her Jewishness, her sex appeal, her lack of it. What some considered vast, wondrous talent others saw as shameless showing off. She made the best-dressed list and the worst-dressed list. She was regarded as exotically beautiful by many, hopelessly ugly by many others.

The allure of Barbra's glitzy success was especially inspiring to youngsters who didn't fit into the WASPish mold of cheerleader or captain of the football team. If she could turn homely into exotic and a prominent 'schnoz' into a classic profile, and make the cover of *Vogue* in the bargain, maybe they could, too. Within days of the airing of *My Name Is Barbra*, teenage girls in high schools across America proudly sported exaggerated eye makeup and blunt-cut pageboys while they struggled to grow their fingernails to 'dragon lady' lengths. Barbra Streisand had truly become a national phenomenon.

TO NO ONE'S surprise, *My Name Is Barbra* received six Emmy nominations, and at ceremonies held simultaneously in New York and Hollywood on September 15, 1965, the show won five of the awards, including Outstanding Program Achievement in Entertainment and Outstanding Individual Achievement by an Actor or Performer. Looking a bit zaftig but tanned and glowing, Barbra accepted her Emmy with relaxed good cheer. 'I think I have a run in my stocking,' she quipped. 'Of all nights!' She told the audience that she used to watch award shows as a little girl only 'to see who showed up drunk.' She then announced that she had figured out she would have to perform in *Funny Girl* for fifty-six years to be seen by as many people as had watched *My Name Is Barbra*. She closed her remarks by recalling a letter she had received shortly after the special was aired. 'Of all the people on your show,' a young fan wrote, 'I liked you the best.'

'BARBRA'S FAVORITE SUBJECT is Barbra,' Elliott said. 'It bugs me a lot and I get bored by it sometimes.' She had always been self-centered, but now that she was one of the entertainment industry's most celebrated women there often seemed to her to be no outside world. The Columbia Records art director John Berg described an evening he spent with Barbra in her apartment going over some photos for an upcoming album. He arrived with color slides and a light box at around five-thirty in the afternoon. Barbra greeted him in a housecoat; she and Elliott were expected for a formal dinner at eight at the home of the composer Richard Rodgers.

'We went into the library to make the final selection,' Berg recalled to the author Shaun Considine. 'After a while Elliott came into the room, naked except for his Jockey shorts, and he said, "Barbra, we've got to get dressed to go out." And she said, "Elliott, don't worry, we've got plenty of time." Then seven P.M. comes 'round and we're still editing . . . Elliott comes in dressed in a shirt, his shorts, and socks, and says, "Barbra, come on, now.' She kept looking at her photos – yes to this, no to that, and eight P.M. comes around . . . Elliott is beginning to rage. Barbra is still looking at the slides and says, "Just a minute, hon, just a minute." And she means that! She thinks it's just a minute, but Elliott is completely tuxed up, and it's nine o'clock. I'm beat, worn out . . . And Elliott is thoroughly pissed off. He's going around the apartment yelling, kicking the furniture. Until finally Barbra holds up one slide and says, "John, this is it! This is the one.'

'She's happy. She has chosen her photo . . . She sweeps off to change for dinner.'

✴

AFTER MORE THAN a year of professional inactivity, Elliott got another job in the fall of 1965, as the leading man in a Broadway musical, *Drat! The Cat!* Having been put through three months of auditions and uncertainty before he got the part, Elliott later said, 'They tried very hard to find someone else, but they couldn't.' The story concerned the unlikely love affair between a cop, played by Elliott, and a cat burglar, played by the lovely eighteen-year-old newcomer Lesley Ann Warren.

Barbra and Elliott had high expectations that the show would be a hit and finally establish him with a star identity of his own. She reportedly invested $100,000 to help keep the show afloat through its out-of-town tryouts. Elliott denied this, saying they had each invested just $750; others have disputed the denial.

In any event, Elliott's hopes were dashed yet again. *Drat! The Cat!* opened on Sunday, October 10, in the midst of a New York newspaper strike. The magazine reviews were lukewarm, and the show closed six days later. The production would have been completely forgotten except that Barbra had recorded a song Elliott had sung in it, 'She Touched Me,' which was released as the single 'He Touched Me' in September in an effort to help the show. Barbra's impassioned performance of the soaring ballad made it a fan favorite.

Elliott again faced the stinging reality that he had failed while everything Barbra touched seemed to turn to gold. 'I cried for a week because I couldn't bear *Drat! The Cat!* closing,' he said. It left him in a sorry state and drove him into psychoanalysis. 'I was terribly confused. I lacked confidence, and I subordinated myself to [Barbra] because I always felt, What did I have to offer her? What I did give Barbra wasn't healthy for either of us – it was my self-respect.'

ON SUNDAY, DECEMBER 26, 1965, Barbra gave her last performance on Broadway as Fanny Brice. The show continued to run for another year and a half with Mimi Hines as Fanny, but Ray Stark had let Barbra out of her contract in return for her agreement to reprise the role in London the following spring. The English production had also figured in Barbra's negotiations with Stark over the film version of *Funny Girl:* she had told him she wouldn't take the show across the Atlantic unless he guaranteed she could do the movie. Stark refused. Barbra asked Marty Erlichman what she should do. 'Stick to your guns if you're prepared to lose the movie,' he told her.

'I wasn't prepared to lose the movie,' Barbra said, and she agreed to star in the West End production with no film guarantee from Stark. Of course the producer never seriously considered anyone else for the movie, especially after *My Name Is Barbra* proved how lovely Streisand could look on film. Shortly after the special aired, Stark announced that Barbra would indeed be his silver-screen Fanny and had signed to do three additional movies for Stark as well.

Barbra's final performance on Broadway turned into a standing-room-only love fest as her most loyal fans packed the theater to the rafters to bid her au revoir. None of them realized they were really bidding her adieu, because she would never return to the Broadway stage.

Her performance that night, one critic felt, was 'sublime, one of the more incandescent of Streisand's career.' When she sang 'People,' she recalled, 'it was as if I had just discovered the meaning of the song. As I sang it I deliberately looked out into the audience. That used to frighten me before, but this night it was like a farewell, and I sang the song to them. I got very emotional.'

When she finished her reprise of 'Don't Rain on My Parade' and the show was over, the audience leaped to their feet in a cheering, stomping, screaming ovation. When her turn came to take a solo bow, Barbra spoke haltingly. 'I feel as though tonight signals the end of an era in my life,' she began. 'Thank you all so much for your support. I'd like to pay tribute to a great performer, the woman I play in the show. Oddly enough I'm standing on the same stage where she did her last Broadway show. So as a tribute to her I'd like to sing this song that she made so famous.'

Barbra then delivered a rendition of 'My Man' that left the audience in a frenzy. 'God, did she sing that song!' Larry Fuller said. 'When it was finished she was crying and we were crying and the audience was crying.'

Then strangers held hands with each other as the audience sang 'Auld Lang Syne' back to Barbra.

'I was sitting in the front row,' Elliott recalled, 'thinking about that line, "People who need people are the luckiest people in the world." . . . Everybody was with her. Everybody was pulling for her.'

13

B arbra rushed to her dressing room in tears and slammed the door. Amid the vividly colored surroundings of a whimsical circus set, she had been rehearsing and taping her second television special, *Color Me Barbra*, for over fifteen uninterrupted hours. The animals had caused upsetting and expensive delays. A baby elephant named Champagne trumpeted so loudly that a young llama panicked and bolted, dragging his trainer after him. A frisky monkey tried to make a meal of three of Barbra's fingers. A lion broke free and roamed about the set growling menacingly for several tense moments. Worst of all, a penguin, unaccustomed to the hot studio lights, had withered and died. At that point Barbra, tired and stressed out, lost her composure and fled to the sanctuary of her dressing room.

A year earlier she had found working on her first special a joyful experience, but the punishing demands of this one brought her close to collapse. The death of the penguin seemed to symbolize every unforeseen mishap the production had encountered, and Barbra still had a full concert sequence to shoot two days after she completed the circus segment. Her discomfort was magnified by a battalion of magazine writers, newspaper reporters, and photographers who were there to scrutinize every moment of the taping for profiles in *Life, Look, Newsweek,* and *The New York Times,* among others.

Barbra's frame of mind didn't help. The crushing expectations that her fame and her relentless pursuit of excellence had placed on her brought on her most negative mind-set to date. She distrusted the intense devotion of her growing legion of admirers and was convinced that others came to her performances with a 'show me' attitude. 'It makes me feel that they're the monster and I'm their victim,' she said. Less guarded around the press than she should have been, Barbra seemed to do nothing but complain. She told

Rex Reed, 'I always used to dream of a penthouse, right? So now I'm a big star, I got one and it's not much fun. I used to dream about terraces, now I gotta spend five hundred dollars just to convert mine from summer to winter . . . It's just as dirty with soot up there on the twenty-second floor as it is down there on the bottom.' For many of those who were still 'on the bottom,' such comments seemed little short of ungrateful whining.

JUST DAYS AFTER she closed in *Funny Girl*, Barbra had reported to the CBS studios to film a short color test. The success of *My Name Is Barbra* had prompted the network to agree to shoot Barbra's follow-up production in color, still a television rarity in 1966. For this show, which Barbra envisioned as a bookend to the first, most of her collaborators from the previous year regathered.

Filming commenced the third week of January. Once again the show revolved around a three-act blueprint, and the problems had begun almost immediately. Soon after three special Marconi color cameras arrived in Philadelphia, where Barbra was to film Act One in the Philadelphia Museum, two of them broke down. Because they were so new as to be practically experimental, there were no repair technicians available outside New York, so the blocking and choreography of the entire segment had to be redesigned for a single camera. Luckily, a snowstorm hit Philadelphia that weekend and the museum, expecting only minimal attendance, agreed to let the *Color Me Barbra* troupe stay on for an extra day. 'I got a kick out of asking them to move a million dollars' worth of paintings,' Barbra told one writer, 'simply to provide an appropriate backdrop for a song. It was fun, but it took so much time. Technicians were falling asleep.'

Many onlookers were astounded by Barbra's stamina, which often lasted into the smallest hours of the morning. Others noted that her energy was fueled by a gastronomically challenging diet of kosher pickles, stuffed derma, pretzels, potato chips, sour green tomatoes, stuffed gefilte fish, hamburgers, and a variety of sandwiches, all washed down with coffee, orange juice, ginger ale, and cream soda and topped off with coffee ice cream, jelly beans, peppermint sour balls, and petits fours.

The sustenance proved necessary. 'Barbra worked almost thirty-two hours straight,' marveled one reporter. 'She began Saturday at noon: try on costumes, submit to hairdresser, apply rhinestones to upper eyelids. At 6:00 P.M. she stepped before the camera. The shooting went on all night [and all day Sunday]. Lights blew out, cables snapped . . . but nothing fazed Barbra's remorseless preoccupation with self.' *Look* also duly reported that Elliott was on the set and that he 'rubbed her back and held her hand' during breaks.

After less than a day's rest, Barbra returned to Manhattan to record the songs needed for the circus sequence, and on Tuesday, January 25 she reported to CBS Studio 41 to rehearse and tape the segment. A minute of screen time of Barbra jumping on a trampoline required three hours of intense rehearsal and nine takes before the camera. After a few awkward flops, Barbra finally got the hang of it, although on one landing she crashed heavily to the canvas and bounced uncontrollably as Joe Layton and Marty Erlichman held their breath. 'What I won't do for the television audience,' Barbra gasped as she climbed down from the trampoline.

'It's not for them,' Layton replied. 'It's for you.'

As the hours dragged by, the animals proved to be a handful, and Barbra grew more and more tense. Horrified when the penguin died, Barbra finally gave in to exhaustion and frustration and stormed off the set. Rex Reed was unaware of the bird's death and grew resentful, as did the other reporters, at being kept waiting three hours to see Barbra and then have her say, 'Okay, ya got twenty minutes. Whaddya wanna know?' Reed characterized Barbra's behavior in *The New York Times* as typical star temperament, a petulant ego run rampant. Peter Matz felt Reed was unfair. 'Sometimes people don't want to accept a simple explanation for something happening because the person involved is too powerful, too big a star,' he said. 'Barbra is intensely vulnerable, and yet people want to go right past that and say, "Aw . . . she's just being a star."'

Back on the set, Barbra dug in her heels and performed the circus medley and a comic monologue flawlessly, though it would ultimately take another thirty-hour workday to complete the taping. Her nerves were shot. At one point, overwrought, she screamed that there were 'too many people not connected with the show' milling around the set, 'too many people staring at me!'

On Friday evening Barbra returned to the studio, which had been converted from the circus set into an elegant concert stage, to tape the final act of the show. Members of several East Coast Streisand fan clubs were recruited to fill the theater seats, and they applauded wildly in response to the five songs Barbra performed to close the show. But when Dwight Hemion asked her to do two of the numbers again, Barbra demanded that the audience be dismissed.

'Tell them to go away,' she reportedly told Marty Erlichman. 'I hate them. I *hate* them!' Marty and Hemion argued with Barbra for half an hour while the fans waited in their seats unaware of what was going on. Finally they convinced her that without the audience the sound quality of the new takes wouldn't match that of the earlier ones. Returning to the stage to a thunderous ovation, Barbra sang the two songs and, after a brief bow, headed for the control room to watch a playback.

As with many projects that are strife-ridden during production, *Color Me Barbra*, telecast on Wednesday, March 30, 1966, at 9:00 P.M. showed few signs of its production *meshugass*. Only during the brief concert that closed the special were the tensions of the prior week evident in Barbra's performance. Despite the enthusiastic audience, she seemed uncomfortable as she attacked the material. The orchestra sometimes had trouble keeping up with Barbra's tempo, and during the orchestral bridge on 'Where Am I Going?' Barbra turned away from the microphone as though she were about to halt the performance. It's possible that she distrusted the audience's unrestrained reactions to some of these less-than-perfect performances and that this provoked her desire to repeat the songs in an empty theater.

Reviews for *Color Me Barbra* echoed, for the most part, those of the first special. Although *Time* magazine's assessment was harsh – 'The show proved that one full hour of Streisand's particularly nasal voice is about forty-five minutes too much' – and there were scattered minor carpings about the show's 'overblown production,' the vast majority of critics raved. *Newsweek* called the special 'a one-woman tour de force of song and sex appeal,' and *The New York Times* added, 'In color, the museum settings were magnificent, the circus was happy, and Miss Streisand looked gorgeous.'

Indeed, the most important contribution *Color Me Barbra* made to Barbra's career might well have been the color itself. She had looked interesting and exotic in black and white, but the lighting required for the color camera softened her looks, producing a lavender tint in her eyes and a porcelain glow on her skin. *Color Me Barbra* offered further evidence that Streisand's unconventional looks would likely prove no barrier to her expected leap to movie stardom.

Color Me Barbra was another ratings champ, but the Sunday before the show was aired Rex Reed had dampened the glow with a profile of Barbra published in *The New York Times*. The article, 'Color Barbra Very Bright,' established Reed as a sharp-witted, incisive celebrity chronicler, but it also single-handedly launched the Barbra-as-monster legend. It was the first high-profile piece to paint Streisand as an unreasonable perfectionist who was demanding, paranoiac, rude, driven, arrogant, and contemptuous of her fans. While no one connected with the production of *Color Me Barbra* would have denied that there were elements of truth in Reed's article, many felt, as Peter Matz did, that the huge pressures Barbra shouldered – and the vulnerability that her apparent arrogance was meant to conceal – had been grossly ignored.

'Why should I write nice things about Barbra?' Reed protested privately.

'She never invites me to any of her parties.' A few years later, when Reed was at the peak of his fame, he sent Barbra an apology for the piece. She spurned the olive branch. 'Fuck him,' she snorted. 'I had more respect for him when he hated me.'

ELLIOTT WAS DETERMINED to make love to Barbra. She had returned to their Savoy Hotel suite anxious and wound up after a *Funny Girl* rehearsal at the Prince of Wales Theater in London. She had been jittery for weeks, worrying before they arrived in England about the impending broadcast of *Color Me Barbra*, and now that they were there she had become even more frantic about the play, fretting about lighting and sound problems at the theater, the inadequacy of her dressing room, and a conductor she found incompetent and would soon have fired.

'By then the star thing was really going hard,' Elliott told the authors Donald Zec and Anthony Fowles. Barbra's frazzled state made it nearly impossible for her to relax, and the Goulds hadn't had sex in weeks. But this night Elliott set his mind to it. 'I really had to talk her down' in order to get her to relax, he said. 'I talked her all the way down through the whole encounter.'

Elliott used no contraceptive protection that night because he wanted Barbra to get pregnant. He felt 'it would be the best thing' for Barbra to have a baby and '[bring] her mind back down to life.' And his baby was the one thing Elliott could give Barbra that she couldn't get by herself, that no audience could give her, no amount of money could buy her, and no other man could give her. It was his way of reclaiming some of his self-respect – and reclaiming his wife and his marriage, too. But to his way of thinking, it was a selfless act. 'I was thinking of Barbra, not thinking of [the baby] or myself. The best thing I could give her was a child.'

Barbra seems not to have had any say in the decision. When Elliott found out from her doctor that she had indeed conceived, he asked the man not to tell her, because he didn't want her to know until she had successfully opened her show. In the meantime he tried to hide his Cheshire Cat grin. That night of lovemaking in an elegant suite overlooking the River Thames, he felt, 'was the best bit of talking I have ever done.'

STREISAND HAD ARRIVED in England on March 20, 1966, accompanied by her hairdresser, her secretary, and Marty Erlichman. Elliott had arrived a week earlier to find a place to live. He could have been a part of the production, because at Barbra's behest he was offered the role of Nick

Arnstein. But after having wanted the role so badly he turned it down out of pride. He feared it would be said that he'd been hired only because of the power his wife wielded, and he couldn't have that.

Such talk wouldn't have been much worse, however, than the slings and arrows he now suffered at the hands of Fleet Street's journalistic archers, always eager to find a soft underbelly and stick it with barbs. They dubbed Elliott 'Mr Streisand' and 'the guy who came to London with Barbra.' Whatever his position, the shadow Barbra cast over him would have been unavoidable, because her arrival generated the biggest wave of publicity England had seen since Marilyn Monroe set foot on its shores in 1956. The newspapers followed Barbra everywhere, took pictures incessantly, asked endless questions. Front-page articles heralded her as the most talented American performer in a generation and the highest-paid entertainer in the world. A *Daily Mirror* article began, 'Rarely in the whole bedazzled history of live and lusty entertainment has one box of assorted vocal cords been awaited with such pent-up, electrifying excitement.' All of this generated such a lather of anticipation of *Funny Girl*'s April 13 opening that the show was already sold out for the entire fourteen weeks Barbra had agreed to appear in it.

Barbra adored the gentility of English customs. Serving as hostess in the plush town house flat at 48 Ennismore Gardens that Elliott had found at a rent of $1,600 a month, she would ask visitors, with just a hint of a British accent, 'Shall we go into the drawing room?' Then she would grandly offer them tea and avocado sandwiches.

At the Prince of Wales Theater, though, things weren't so hunky-dory. She really didn't want to do *Funny Girl* again, but if she had to do it, everything would be exactly the way *she* wanted it to be. The columnist Sheilah Graham reported that the moment Barbra entered her dressing room she walked right back out. Marty Erlichman called the theater to say Barbra wouldn't return until she had a suite worthy of 'a star of her stature.' The management tore down a wall to make the room larger, put up new wallpaper, and brought in some antique furniture to make the place more to Barbra's liking.

When she returned, she struggled with the sound problems, that unsatisfactory conductor, who was replaced by Milton Rosenstock, and her own lack of excitement. The English actor Michael Craig, cast as Nick Arnstein, recalled seeing Barbra outside her dressing room standing still and looking forlorn after a problem-plagued out-of-town performance. He asked her what was wrong. 'Two and a half years ago when I started this show in Philadelphia,' she replied, 'it was such fun and everything was marvelous. Now it's all so difficult and I don't get any fun out of it anymore.'

She continued to accentuate the negative and take little joy in the positive.

She was disappointed with what she perceived as a lackluster reaction from the first-night crowd. 'I remember worrying opening night, "I don't think it's electric out there,"' she said. 'They were so quiet I only felt the things that were going wrong.' But that silence was just typical British reserve; the audience loved the show and gave Barbra six curtain calls. Even at that she wasn't sure they really liked her: 'Maybe they were only being polite.' She fixated on the few negative reactions to her in the next day's newspapers, most of which joined in a rhapsody of praise.

One critic wrote 'A star is a girl whose voice, face and talent are all familiar and who can still set the blood tingling by the impact of her personality. A star is a girl who can hush a thousand people into silence and a second later make them explode with joy. By these tests and any other you can think of, Barbra Streisand is a star, and *Funny Girl*, which had its official opening after the biggest build-up since D-Day, is her show.'

A second critic weighed in with 'Miss Streisand is a miracle. Energy spurts out of every inch of her like electric sparks. She is hardly ever still, but she never makes a conventional movement; every gesture is new and original and unexpected . . . How glad I am that I never saw her until now; to have all this talent unleashed on one at the very moment that one has been brought to the highest pitch of expectation is something to remember all one's life.'

The London audiences never did rouse themselves to the level of ecstasy that her New York audiences had, but Barbra got used to that. Then Princess Margaret and the Earl of Snowdon came to see the show, and their presence further dampened the proceedings. In keeping with custom, no one in the audience laughed or applauded until the royals did so, and few in Britain are less prone to outbursts of enthusiasm than the Windsors. For Barbra, whose performances tended to ebb and flow with her audience's reactions, the occasional laughter and mild applause proved disheartening.

After the performance, still dressed in the fringed suede dress she wore in the final scene, Barbra stood in a receiving line to be introduced to the princess and Lord Snowdon. When Margaret told Barbra how much she had enjoyed the show, Streisand replied, 'You should come back some night when you're not here.'

IMMEDIATELY AFTER THE opening-night performance, Elliott told Barbra that she was pregnant. Her first reaction was horror: how could she have a baby now? She was committed to a twenty-city American concert tour of one-night stands, scheduled to commence in a few months, that would guarantee her $50,000 a performance – one million dollars. She had planned a television special built around the Parisian world of haute couture. And how could she continue to perform such a strenuous role every night? She'd put the baby in danger!

Once again Elliott 'talked her down.' Being pregnant didn't mean she'd have to stay in bed twenty-four hours a day. She could do the 'short' version of the show and have some of the livelier numbers like 'Cornet Man' and 'Rat-a-Tat-Tat' rechoreographed to save her energy. She could keep the early concert dates; she would just have to cancel the others. She didn't need the money. And she could do the special anytime.

The more she thought about it, the more Barbra liked the idea of motherhood and of taking a break from show business. She had been hurtling forward on a nonstop career express for nearly six years now, working herself close to exhaustion to achieve goal after goal. But there was an unreality about it all, and at times she must have wondered whether her thirst for more, more, more wasn't her way of avoiding real life. 'I was beginning to feel like a slave to a schedule,' she said. 'I had to *schedule* in my free time!' As Elliott had put it, it was high time that Barbra brought 'her mind back down to life.'

The announcement made news on two continents. The New York *Daily News* gave the story its entire front page with the headline, 'Barbra Awaits Million $ Baby.' The emphasis on the lost income her pregnancy would cost her appalled Barbra. 'Why do they have to measure everything in money?' she complained. 'Is that important? I'll tell you what's important. Having a healthy baby, that's what's important. For that matter, what's success? A million dollars doesn't automatically give you happiness. I used to live well on twenty dollars a week.'

BARBRA PLUNGED INTO impending motherhood with the same gusto she had brought to her career. 'I went to Harrods and bought skeins of wool, all different shades of pink.' Within a week she met reporters in the Ennismore Gardens house with knitting needles and wool in hand. Her industry didn't last long. 'I knitted like mad for a week, and then I got bored. I think I'll just have the baby and be done with it.'

Although she claimed that she didn't care about the sex of her child, it seems clear that Barbra wanted a girl. Not only was there that pink wool, but whenever she referred to the child she almost always used the pronoun 'she.' She told Gloria Steinem that if the child was a girl, her name would be Samantha. Should the child be a boy, she and Elliott had agreed on Jason Emanuel, after their friend the artist Jason Monet and Barbra's father.

Barbra became an adherent of Britain's Dr Grantley Dick-Read, a pioneer in the modern natural-childbirth movement. 'I can't understand how some women can just say, "Give me an injection,"' she explained in an interview with *Cameo Baby Magazine*. 'That attitude is based on fear and on a lack of knowledge of the process of birth . . . Believe me, I hate pain, but delivering a baby is a natural thing that the body is designed to do . . . For me, it's too important an experience to be uninvolved.'

ON JUNE 12, showing just a little, Barbra headlined a benefit performance at the American embassy in Grosvenor Square called 'A Very Informal History of the American Musical Theater: 1926–1966.' In the two-hundred-seat embassy theater, Barbra sang 'Where Am I Going?' accompanied on piano by the tune's composer, Cy Coleman. Then she told the audience, which included Yehudi Menuhin and Noël Coward, that when it came time for her to choose what songs to sing at the event, 'It was a very hard decision because, I don't mean to brag, but our country really has produced some terrific music. I was looking for one hunk of music that would sort of represent or embody – express, you know – sort of capture America. And so I decided that would be – for me anyway – George Gershwin's *Porgy and Bess*. When you think of it, I mean, in terms of its many facets: being a folk opera, having the influence of the American Negro blues, spirituals, jazz, pop music, and grand opera, also with a little trace of Georgie's own Russian Jewish background. I think it sort of represents America, which is a beautiful mishmash. That's it, kid.'

The next day *The New York Times* called the evening 'an extraordinary one-night stand. Miss Streisand, looking sleek and a little pregnant in a glittering long evening gown, won the hearts of the audience even before she sang . . . [She] made even the familiar numbers from *Porgy and Bess* distinctively her own.'

BARBRA GAVE HER nine hundredth and last stage performance in *Funny Girl* on Saturday, July 16, 1966. And for her, not a moment too soon. By then she was not only thoroughly sick of the show intellectually but barely able to keep up physically with even its reduced demands. New blocking had cut down Fanny's 'running around on stage,' Barbra said, 'and you can bet I don't do a flying leap to the couch in the love scene anymore!' Still, at the completion of every show she was near exhaustion. 'I'm so tired all the time,' she said. 'All I want to do is sleep.'

She didn't have much time to rest, however, once she returned to the United States on July 18. After just two days at home, she flew to Las Vegas to appear at a Columbia sales convention and perform several numbers from her upcoming album *Je m'appelle Barbra*, in which she would sing French songs in both English and French. The Columbia brass had prevailed upon her to show up because they were concerned about the sales potential of the esoteric project.

Just over a week later, on July 30, Barbra made the first stop on her concert tour, which had been reduced from twenty cities to six – and then to four – because of her pregnancy. Accompanied by Elliott, Marty Erlichman, her friends Dr Harvey and Cis Corman, a fifty-foot dressing trailer and her own orchestra, Barbra sang and joked on a cool moonlit night at Festival Field in Newport, Rhode Island, site of the Newport Jazz Festival. Wearing a diaphanous gown – the left side orange, the right side brown – with one orange and one brown shoe and earrings to match, Barbra beguiled the sixteen thousand people in the audience, who had paid a top ticket price of fifteen dollars – expensive in 1966 – and listened to her in rapt silence. 'You're so quiet,' she said at one point. 'Are there really sixteen thousand of youse out there?'

She sang a selection of her standards, some songs from the French album, and some new special material. As a prelude to a folk song parody, she started to tell an absurd story of a girl from Cambodia who was going to kill herself when she lost her lover to her sister, but the audience didn't respond as she had hoped they would. Barbra stopped. 'You're not laughing,' she said, 'so I'm not singing.'

She saved the night and sent the audience home with a dose of magic by ending the balmy summer evening's concert with 'Silent Night,' sung as a haunting hymn. She left the Boston *Herald American* columnist Bruce McCabe beside himself with admiration. 'Listening to Barbra ... is something like having your soul massaged. Like being infused with an electric charge ... That's Barbra. Barbra of the thunder and lightning, wind and rain, spring and fall, darkness and light. One is captured, enslaved by her.'

The one-night stand netted $121,000, which was $41,000 more than Frank Sinatra had attracted in Newport a year earlier. By now Marty Erlichman was on a crusade to make sure that Barbra made more money per gig than any other performer ever had. For her second appearance at Forest Hills the year before, he had gotten Barbra one dollar more than the Beatles had been paid at the same venue. Ticket prices at all of Barbra's concerts now were calculated to ensure that she would break records wherever she performed.

Barbra repeated her Newport triumph in Philadelphia on August 2, in Atlanta on August 6, and in Chicago on August 9, raking in a total of $406,618 at the four venues and taking home $200,000 for four nights' work. In Philadelphia, a death threat against her was phoned in to JFK

Stadium. Phyllis Dorroshow, who was in the audience, recalled that 'Elliott Gould was standing up front with the security guards. He was keeping an eye out, and he looked like he was ready to jump anybody who pulled a gun out. Of all the guards he was the most intent on scanning the crowd.' There were no problems.

Barbra's performance at Soldier Field in Chicago marked the last time she would appear in public for the next eight months. Now it was time to go home, relax, and turn her attention to becoming a mother.

'WHEN I WAS pregnant, at least the last four months,' Barbra said, 'I was a woman. No deadlines or curtains to meet. Whenever I thought of what was growing inside me ... it's a miracle, the height of creativity for any woman.'

She had worried about morning sickness, but never experienced it. She sat around a lot eating brownies, and her inactivity caused her to gain weight. 'I think I've always had a secret desire to be fat. Skinny kids are always being pestered about eating – especially if you have a Jewish mother.' Mrs Kind was delighted, of course, but Barbra's pediatrician wasn't. The weight gain was excessive, he thought, and he told Barbra to watch her calories. 'My first diet!' she marveled.

Barbra told Gloria Steinem that when she was a child she couldn't envision having a normal life. 'I would try to imagine my future, like other kids, but I couldn't. It just stopped. There was a big blank screen, no husband, no children, nothing.' Now, amid all of her achievements, she viewed her impending motherhood as her greatest triumph. As Elliott had hoped, Barbra had come back down to earth. She had stationery printed that put the third *a* back in her name, as if to say, 'Now I'm a wife and mother first and foremost. Barbra is a creation, an image, a show business commodity. Barbara Joan Streisand, the little girl from Brooklyn, is the *real* me.'

Elliott told a reporter that he expected Barbra would give up her career for her family – if not immediately, then before very long. His hope sprang eternal even as she went back to work. Throughout September she spent long hours at Columbia's recording studios putting the finishing touches on the *Je m'appelle Barbra* album. The idea for Barbra to sing French songs, some of them in the original French, most in English translations, had popped up in the spring of 1965 when she began to work with the gifted thirty-four-year-old French composer Michel Legrand, whose score for *The Umbrellas of Cherbourg* had just been nominated for an Academy Award.

Barbra and Legrand had established a special rapport as they worked into the early hours of the morning in the deserted Winter Garden theater after her *Funny Girl* performances. 'Some nights we laughed so much together, we had so many amusing moments in common,' Legrand said, 'that upon leaving I would suddenly look at my watch and realize that we hadn't felt the hours pass. It was four A.M., five A.M. Time no longer existed. [It was] a euphoric time.'

Barbra learned the songs phonetically, and Legrand was impressed by how good her French accent became after a few months of work to tone down her Brooklyn inflections.

Legrand, a married man, admitted to a fellow Frenchman, the author Guy Abitan, that his relationship with Barbra became 'almost intimate,' and there are those who say it indeed evolved into an affair. 'We became inseparable,' Legrand said. 'I didn't have time – nor did she, evidently – to understand what was happening all of a sudden to us.' Certainly Elliott felt threatened by his wife's closeness to this attractive, sophisticated Parisian who shared a musical affinity with her that he could never hope to approach. Legrand wasn't very sympathetic toward Gould's plight: 'This gawky, bearlike ninny did not seem to take great pleasure in my conversations with Barbra. Nothing must be more boring (for a bear) than the sight of two birds constantly occupied with singing the same tune.'

This proximity between Barbra and Legrand couldn't have helped the underlying strain in the Gould marriage. Barbra's pregnancy helped smooth over some of the rough edges, but it didn't alleviate all of the problems, and Elliott's jealousy of Legrand was likely one of them. 'First we talked about having [the baby],' Elliott said. 'Then we had arguments about him – and arguments about many things; arguments that seemed to be about one thing but were really about something else.'

Early in November they had a major blowup; Barbra ran into the bathroom in tears, locked the door, and refused to come out as Elliott pounded on the door. 'I don't want your child!' she sobbed.

At that Elliott lost control. 'Barbra is infantile in some ways,' he said, 'no matter how brilliant she might be. But it was wrong of me at that point in her pregnancy to kick the door down.'

WHILE MICHEL LEGRAND'S initial exposure to Barbra had been nothing but positive, as they got down to the serious work of recording her tracks he saw a different side of her. 'I watched her during certain rehearsals becoming incredibly angry because someone had forgotten to put out his cigarette or because she had seen someone in a corner somewhere whose presence she didn't feel was necessary. It's unbelievable – Barbra in anger – when we've had the pleasure of seeing only the happy and passionate Streisand of other times. An angry Barbra is all of a sudden a usually courteous and delicate woman seized with fury and capable of the most foul vocabulary . . . Her tantrums are *torrential.'*

Je m'appelle Barbra, released at the end of October, drew mixed reviews. Some critics felt it was Streisand's best album to date, showcasing well her new sophistication. Others found it pretentiously arty. The collection featured Barbra's first musical composition, 'Ma Première Chanson,' with words in French by Eddy Marnay. The album's producer Ettore Stratta, however, has claimed to the author Shaun Considine that 'I actually co-wrote that song with her, but my name is not on it.' According to Stratta, Barbra whistled a tune for him one day, a melody he found 'small and uninteresting. But as she whistled it, I rewrote it, harmonized it. I made it better . . . I never asked for credit. Today I would.'

The album rose to number five on the pop charts, a solid hit, but it didn't have the same staying power of her earlier efforts, and it became the first Streisand album not to be certified gold.

As HER PREGNANCY progressed, Barbra decided that her sprawling six-room penthouse wouldn't be big enough for her family once the baby arrived. She sent Marty Erlichman across the hall to speak to her neighbor Gerry Blumenfeld, who occupied the only other apartment on the floor with her husband, the news picture editor of United Press International. Marty, Blumenfeld recalled, 'said that Barbra was pregnant and would we mind moving because she wanted to have the whole top floor for herself. He said Barbra would pay all our moving expenses. Well, there was a bigger place opening up in the building so we decided we would move. A while later she and Elliott came into our house and just started measuring rooms even before we moved out. They were rude and didn't offer any conversation at all.

'Even though it wasn't very far, we had a lot of big, expensive furniture, and it cost us ten thousand dollars to move. They didn't pay us a cent, so we had to sue them. They wanted to settle for five thousand, and we agreed rather than keep dragging it through court.'

Even before this disagreement, Blumenfeld had little use for her famous neighbor. 'Barbra treated people at the place very poorly. She would run out and yell "Get me a cab!" without saying please or thank you or anything polite. One day I had a cab hailed for me, and she came running out into the street and grabbed my arm as I was getting in and she practically yanked me out and said, "I'm late" and pulled me out and jumped in to get to her show on time. One day she came over to ask my husband if he could tell his photographers at UPI not to take any pictures of her while she was pregnant. Of course, he couldn't.

'But the worst thing Barbra did showed how cruel she could be. There was a little girl in our building named Allison who was the daughter of an opera singer. She was a dwarf with a bad heart, and very sensitive and sweet. We didn't allow soliciting in the building, but we allowed her to collect for the Red Cross every once in a while. She came to our floor one day, and I gave her a couple of bucks and then watched as she knocked on Barbra's door.

'Well, Barbra opened the door and looked over at me and down at little Allison, who was holding the Red Cross can up in front of her face, and then she slammed the door right in the little girl's face. The child started crying and I had to take her in and comfort her. You just don't do that to a child, any child. But it was typical of the way Barbra treated people around the building.'

AS THE BABY'S delivery approached, Elliott helped Barbra every morning with her breathing exercises in anticipation of the natural delivery. Barbra turned her cluttered sewing room into a temporary nursery, with a violet-colored tiled floor and pointillist wallpaper. She picked out matching fabric and painted the accessories herself.

Once everything was ready, all that remained to do was wait. And wait. And wait. Although she expected the baby around December 20, Barbra didn't go into labor – despite two false alarms – until six in the morning on Thursday, December 29. Certain within two hours that this was the real thing, Barbra checked into Mount Sinai Hospital at nine. Nearly six more hours of labor followed. 'It was very traumatic,' Elliott said, 'but Barbra was very brave. We held hands and talked about a son or daughter.'

When her doctor discovered that the baby was in the breech position (feet first) inside Barbra's womb, they decided that a cesarean section would be necessary to avoid any possible damage to the child during delivery. The incision through the muscles and walls of Barbra's abdomen and uterus, of course, dashed her hope of experiencing a natural birth, and she was unconscious when the baby, a healthy seven-pound, three-ounce boy, made his entrance into the world at 2:55 P.M.

When Jason Emanuel Gould was brought to his mother in room 507 – with the name Angelina Scrangella on the door – she could barely trust her eyes. 'I could not believe he grew inside of me.' She held the child with trepidation and awe, feeling more love flow from within her than she ever had before.

She and Elliott fairly burst with pride. 'You know,' he told the press, 'my baby didn't cry. All the other babies were crying and had their eyes closed, and this woman next to me said, "Look at that brand-new baby with its eyes wide open," and it was *my* baby!'

At home Barbra doted on the boy. 'I take his picture every Thursday, on his birthday,' she said. She also tape-recorded his every giggle, gurgle, and hiccup. She hovered over his crib, murmuring, 'Who's that gorgeous thing? What's his name?' Whenever she fed him, she saved the last spoonful for herself. 'I love baby food.'

She opened up easily to reporters whenever the subject was Jason. Did she sing to him? 'No, I never sing around the house,' she replied. 'Silly people say, "I hope your son has a good voice." Who cares? The last thing I want him to do is go into the theater.'

Having a boy child, Barbra said, taught her a great deal about men. 'You realize that they are these little people, and they want to be held, and they cry, and they get hurt, just like women. Unfortunately society has put these pressures on men to be *strong*, and it's quite unfair. It's nice to find a man who's as vulnerable as he is strong.'

Asked whether she found it strange to think that her baby, as the child of vastly wealthy parents, would have an upbringing so different from hers, Barbra smiled and replied, 'I can't suddenly get poor, can I?' Then she went on to say, 'I don't want a child who has nothing but toys from F.A.O. Schwarz. Kids like simple things to play with: a piece of paper, a walnut shell. They should be dirty and basic when they want to be.'

After giving Jason a bottle during an interview for a *Look* magazine photo layout on America's most famous new mother, Barbra patted his back rhythmically. Soon he let loose with a robust burp, and Barbra laughed with delight. 'Isn't he a *gas?*'

Frank Teti

A radiant Barbra sweeps into the New York premiere of her first film, Funny Girl, *September 1968. The picture made her a Hollywood superstar.*

Douglas Kirkland/Sygma

The Philip Arms on Pulaski Street in Brooklyn, where Barbara Joan Streisand lived with her mother, brother, and grandparents after her father died.

Barbra's father, Emanuel Streisand, at twenty-two, 1929. His death at thirty-five, when his daughter was only fifteen months old, left her with an obsessive feeling of loss.

Laura Van Worner

Barbara graduated from P.S. 89 in Brooklyn in June 1955. She was already determined to be an actress.

Author's collection

Below: Appearing as the office vamp in a summer stock production of The Desk Set *in 1957, when she was fifteen, Barbara dances with Paul Bressoud. A critic called her "a fine young comedienne."*

Right: Barbara rehearses with Herb Evans for the way off-Broadway production of Driftwood, *December 1958.*

Courtesy Emily Cobb

Charles Biasiny-Rivera

January 1959: Barbara graduated from Erasmus Hall High School half a year early, and with a 91 average. She shocked her classmates by dating a black boy.

Courtesy Kevin Burns

Another summer stock performance: as Hortense in The Boy Friend, *1960. She took a break from nightclub singing to appear in the show.*

The first newspaper article about Barbra Streisand (she had just removed an "a" from her first name) appeared in Flatbush Life, *August 21, 1960.*

Flatbush Actress Heads for Stardom

Barbra Streisand, who, as a child was determined to become a dramatic actress, now finds herself in the rather enviable position of being considered for her singing ability as well.

Barbra, though only 18, has already appeared in important roles in summer stock and off-Broadway, playing Millie in "Picnic" Elsa in "Desk Set," both at the Maldenbridge Playhouse, Ellie Mae in "Tobacco Road," at the Clinton Playhouse, and more recently, in the key role of Clythia, the butterfly in the Karel Capek play "Insect Comedy" at the Jan Hus. August 16th through 30th she'll be appearing in "The Boy Friend" at the Cecilwood Theatre in Fish-

BARBRA

A photo session for the second album on which Barbra sang, Pins and Needles, *spring 1962. Columbia Records executives didn't want to use her at first.*

Opposite, bottom: Barbra poses with the cast of the one-night wonder Another Evening with Harry Stoones, *October 1961. Diana Sands and Dom DeLuise are in the right foreground.*

Photofest

"*Oh why is it always Miss Marmelstein?*" *Barbra's Broadway debut in* I Can Get It for You Wholesale, *March 1962. She stole the show and married the leading man, Elliott Gould.*

Opposite: Barbra wows the audience at the famed Cocoanut Grove in Los Angeles, August 1963. The gig brought her a movie offer she had to turn down because of prior commitments.

Globe Photos

Barbra's guest appearance on The Judy Garland Show *in October 1963 won her an Emmy nomination. The veteran and the neophyte brought out the best in each other.*

Richard Giammanco collection

Elliott Gould congratulates his wife on her triumphant Funny Girl *opening night, March 26, 1964. Before long their private life would parallel several of the show's plotlines.*

Barbra as Fanny Brice and Sydney Chaplin as Nick Arnstein in Funny Girl. *Their extramarital affair turned into a battle royal.*

Singing "A Kid Again/I'm Five" on her phenomenal first television special, My Name Is Barbra, *April 1965. One critic called the hour "a pinnacle moment in American show business."*

Nefertiti Streisand? Barbra's second television special, Color Me Barbra, *March 1966. The production was rife with problems.*

Barbra shows off her Emmy for "Outstanding Individual Achievement in Entertainment" for My Name Is Barbra, *September 12, 1965.*

La Streisand primps before filming a sequence of The Belle of 14th Street, *her third and least successful special, spring 1967.*

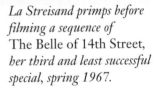

"A Happening in Central Park": Barbra sings "Marty the Martian" in front of 135,000 people, June 1967.

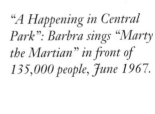

"Hello Gorgeous!" Barbra makes a dazzling screen debut in Funny Girl,
September 1968.

Barbra rehearses the "You Are Woman" number with Omar Sharif, cast as Nick Arnstein. Once again she and her leading man played love scenes off stage as well as on.

"I was appalled by every move she made," Walter Matthau said of his Hello, Dolly! *costar.*

On the set of Hello, Dolly! *with her eighteen-month-old son Jason, summer 1968. One of Jason's first words was "hat."*

Barbra and Eugene McCarthy leave a Hollywood fund-raiser after Barbra endorsed the senator's presidential bid, May 1968.

Streisand opens the International Hotel in Las Vegas, July 1969. She had to wear a hard hat during rehearsals because the showroom wasn't completed.

Posing with her Best Actress Oscar for Funny Girl, *April 1969. With her are Jack Albertson (right), and Anthony Harvey (left), who accepted for Barbra's co-winner, Katharine Hepburn.*

PART 3

Being a Movie Star

'To me, being a star means

being a movie star.'

—Barbra in 1967

14

U nder an enormous tent covering Ray and Fran Stark's sprawling Holmby Hills backyard, three hundred guests, including dozens of America's biggest movie stars, listened to an all-girl band, chomped on Polynesian canapés, drank mai tais, and waited impatiently for Barbra Streisand. It was May 14, 1967, and Barbra, just turned twenty-five, had been in Hollywood for four days. The Starks were throwing her a welcome party to befit the woman who was there to re-create her role in *Funny Girl* for Columbia Pictures, and who had already signed contracts with Twentieth Century-Fox and Paramount Pictures for two other big-budget movie musicals based on Broadway shows, *Hello, Dolly!* and *On a Clear Day You Can See Forever*. She was the only performer in history to have signed for three movies (with combined initial budgets of over $30 million) without ever having faced a movie camera.

All of Hollywood wanted to meet its heiress apparent, and close to five o'clock in the afternoon, the appointed hour, its *haute société* jammed into Ray Stark's backyard lanai and garden. John and Pilar Wayne were there, and Marlon Brando with Mrs Louis Jourdan. The legendary beauties Merle Oberon and Jennifer Jones kibbitzed with funny lady Bea Lillie. Veteran stars Rosalind Russell, Janet Leigh, Cary Grant, Gary Cooper, Ginger Rogers, Robert Mitchum, Gregory Peck, and Jimmy Stewart mingled with Hollywood's young royalty, including Steve McQueen and Natalie Wood.

'Where's Barbra?' the guests kept asking their hosts. She was half an hour, then an hour, then an hour and forty-five minutes late. 'She'll be here any minute,' Stark assured them hopefully. 'She must have gotten stuck in traffic or something.' Unlikely on a Sunday, and Barbra had to travel less than a mile from the eighteen-room, six-bathroom mansion on Chevy Chase Drive, a former home of Greta Garbo, that she had rented for $3,250 a month.

While Hollywood's elite waited for her, Barbra, just about shaking with fear, couldn't decide what to wear. She tried on dozens of outfits and accessory combinations while Marty Erlichman and Elliott kept reminding her how late it was getting. As Marilyn Monroe had often done before attending a party, Barbra was stalling, frightened to meet these important people, unwilling to have them size up her nose and compare her looks to Merle Oberon's or Natalie Wood's.

Finally, already hopelessly late, she decided on a short strapless silver-sequined dress with matching sequined jacket and shoes and wore her hair piled high atop her head. Elliott and Marty practically pushed her out the door. 'When I'm performing I'm not afraid of anything or anybody,' she said. 'But when I'm just me I have this fright of being a disappointment to people . . . I can't shake the feeling they're going to look at me and think, "What's so special about her?"' When she arrived at the Starks' at seven o'clock, she tried to camouflage her nervousness with humor, complaining about the unflattering early-evening sun. 'What's the idea of starting me off in this terrible lighting?' she joked.

Things went downhill from there. Barbra felt overwhelmed by the megawattage of star power that surrounded her, even though as the guest of honor she should have been the brightest light there. 'I was frightened,' she said years later. 'Everybody in Hollywood was there, all these people I'd never met. I was never a very gregarious kind of person. I was always shy.' She sat at her table under the tent for just a few minutes, during which Cary Grant, Rosalind Russell, and Natalie Wood came over to say hello. Rather than make small talk, Barbra picked their brains about film technique. When a photographer for *Women's Wear Daily* aimed his camera at her and started snapping, she stiffened up. 'I didn't know any pictures would be taken,' she muttered. Then she retreated inside to the Starks' library, where she remained for the rest of the evening. She didn't mingle; anyone who wanted to meet Barbra Streisand that night had to go to her. Someone nudged William Wyler, set to direct Barbra in *Funny Girl*, and said, 'That will give you an idea of what you're in for.'

The next day's press reports were devastating. This arrogant, untested newcomer, they said, had kept some of America's greatest film legends waiting for *two hours*. Then she had snubbed them. How dare she? Perhaps the kindest comment came from Judy Jacobs of *Women's Wear Daily:* 'Hollywood loves Barbra. But is the feeling mutual?'

Barbra had too much pride to explain how frightened she felt, so the perception of Streisand as an aloof prima donna stood. Even after the bad press, she made no effort to play the Hollywood game. Rock Hudson invited her to a party for Carol Burnett at his home, attended by four hundred celebrities. She and Elliott arrived late, said a few words to Carol, and left. 'It was revolting,' Barbra told a reporter. 'All those photographers. I didn't know people invited photographers to parties in their own homes. Elliott and I went to a drive-in and ate hamburgers, then went home and played bridge.'

Hollywood denizens shook their heads over comments like that, but during the ensuing months 'ingrate' and 'hypocrite' were added to the litany of complaints about Barbra when she made a series of derisive comments about Tinseltown. 'People are so self-centered [here],' she told the reporter Norma Lee Browning. 'Such utter self-concentration. It's very boring. Here performers are images and commodities . . . [Hollywood] is like a small town. It has its own set of values, narrow and small . . . I wouldn't want to raise my son here, in a town where people are judged by the size of their swimming pools.' She said she had rented the Greta Garbo house because 'it has class, style. Something very unusual for Hollywood.'

'How *dare* she?' Hollywood's elite muttered. Self-centered? She could make Narcissus look modest. Narrow values? What was she using the eighteen rooms for, her pets? Class and style? She had shown little of either at Ray Stark's party. It seemed clear to many that Barbra Streisand felt disdain for the town that had been ready to embrace her. She had little interest in courting insiders and less interest in pleasing the press. Interviewer Glenna Syse reported that when she visited the *Funny Girl* set to interview Barbra a few days after filming began, Streisand 'slumped into her white canvas chair, sighed, scrutinized her long catlike fingernails, gave me a desultory glance, and asked, "Whaddayawannaknow?" . . . So in my best Brooklyn accent I replied, "Whaddayawannatellme?"

'"Nuttin," said La Streisand . . . She looks the other way when you talk to her, and she often answers with a shrug or a monosyllable. Another interview? What a drag.'

Barbra had said that, to her, 'being a star means being a movie star.' She couldn't have made a much worse impression on the industry she hoped would make her that star, or on the press that would be so important in shaping her new silver-screen image for the American public. Now the knives were out for her. And the bad feelings Barbra stirred up during her first few months in Hollywood would haunt her for the rest of her career.

BARBRA HAD SIGNED a four-picture deal with Ray Stark in 1965, guaranteeing her the movie version of *Funny Girl* for a salary of $250,000 and a small percentage of the box-office take and subsidiary-rights income. Stark formed a production company, Rastar, and shopped the project around Hollywood.

The same old story ensued. Columbia Pictures expressed interest, but they weren't sure about Streisand. They didn't think she'd look good onscreen. She was too kooky, too Brooklyn. Her television triumph with *My Name Is Barbra* wouldn't necessarily translate to the big screen, and most of the great Broadway stars – Mary Martin and Ethel Merman came immediately to mind – hadn't been able to make a successful transition to motion pictures. The Columbia brass told Stark they'd be interested if Shirley MacLaine played Fanny.

Stark refused, not only because he had a contract with Barbra but also because he was certain she was the only woman who could do the role justice. In his own mind, he told the writer Pete Hamill, 'There was no question about who would do the movie. I just felt she was too much a part of Fanny, and Fanny was too much a part of Barbra to have it go to someone else.' Stark stuck to his guns and finally was able to persuade Columbia to take the project, and Barbra with it, by agreeing to a comparatively small budget for a musical, $8.5 million. On December 17, 1965, Columbia announced that they had acquired the movie rights to *Funny Girl*.

Barbra told Stark that she wanted a nonmusical director for the film. 'I'm confident about the singing, Ray,' she explained, 'but I'm not so confident about the acting. I want a strong director.' Stark agreed, especially since the plotline of *Funny Girl* had always been its weakest element. After considering Mike Nichols and George Roy Hill, Stark signed Sidney Lumet, who had impressed critics with his direction of *The Pawnbroker*, but within six months Lumet had departed, blaming 'artistic differences.'

An executive at Columbia suggested William Wyler, who had directed *The Collector* for the studio two years earlier. Barbra, who had very little knowledge of Hollywood history, didn't know who Wyler was. Told he had won the Academy Award as best director of 1959 for *Ben-Hur*, Barbra reportedly said, 'Chariots! How is he with people, like women? Is he any good with actresses?'

Wyler, sixty-five and deaf in one ear, had directed some of Hollywood's greatest actresses to Oscars, Barbra was told, including Bette Davis in *Jezebel* in 1938 and Audrey Hepburn in her first American film, *Roman Holiday*, in 1953. 'Yeah, but that was years ago,' Barbra said. 'Give me someone recent.' Samantha Eggar had been nominated as Best Actress for *The Collector*. 'Okay,' Barbra finally agreed. 'I guess he'll be all right.' Wyler accepted the assignment, he said, mainly because of Streisand. 'I wouldn't have done the picture without her. She's an interesting performer and represented a challenge for me because she's never been in films, and she's not the usual glamour girl.'

Herb Ross, who had staged the musical sequences for *I Can Get It for You*

Wholesale and for the films *Inside Daisy Clover* in 1965 and *Doctor Dolittle* in 1967, came aboard to direct and choreograph a dozen full-scale musical numbers and four shorter musical interludes that constituted more than one-third of *Funny Girl*'s running time. Wyler welcomed Ross's uncredited directorial help: 'I'm no choreographer, that's not my business.' With the signing of the sixty-five-year-old Academy Award-winning cinematographer Harry Stradling *(My Fair Lady)*, an MGM alumnus renowned for making actresses look their best on film, *Funny Girl*'s behind-the-scenes creative team jelled.

Barbra's concern about looking good on the silver screen bordered on the obsessive. When she first met with Stradling, she came armed with slides of herself to show how much better her face photographed from certain angles, and particularly from the left side. She also had *Color Me Barbra* blown up to motion-picture proportions to see how she would look. She was particularly concerned about scars on her cheeks caused by her teenage acne, but Stradling assured her that he would use a sliding diffusion lens – a device usually used to make aging stars look younger – over his camera to camouflage any imperfections. 'Barbra has youth,' Stradling said, 'but she's a difficult girl to photograph.' He noticed that when she grew fatigued her lazy left eye would wander toward her nose and make her appear cross-eyed. Whenever that happened during filming he would call out, 'Barbra, you're tired. Let's take a break.'

Despite – or perhaps because of – her concern about her appearance, Barbra had refused to submit to a screen test. When Ray Stark had tried to persuade the studios to finance the picture with Barbra as star, they asked that she test for them, and Stark begged her to do so. He went so far as to offer her $25,000 as an incentive. She wouldn't budge.

But when Stradling told her he wanted to shoot some footage so that he could better judge how to light and photograph her, she agreed. Herb Ross directed the tests. 'We spent hours shooting her to test her in different lights, different makeups, different hairdos,' Ross said in 1983. 'I was with her the day she saw the first set of dailies. She was terrified – it was the first time she'd ever seen herself on film. Well, onscreen she looked a miracle. How could anyone have known that her skin was going to have that brilliant reflective surface, that she was going to look radiant – that was just a wonderful *plus*. She was holding my hand real tightly, and as the tests unreeled, I could feel her relax and start to enjoy herself. Then she turned to me and said, "This is just like going to the movies, isn't it?"'

ANOTHER DEEP CONCERN for Barbra was her clothes. Irene Sharaff, who had designed the costumes for the Broadway production, did the same for the movie, and many of the outfits remained the same except for minor changes. Barbra would turn up for fittings, Sharaff recalled, decked out like various movie stars from the twenties. 'The best was when she imagined herself as Garbo, dressed like and giving a full performance of that unique star. She adored clothes and wore them with a flair.' For the most part, Sharaff found Barbra's 'brazen assurance' to be 'tiresome,' but she was amused by one of Streisand's quirks: 'She liked to vary the size of the padding in her bras . . . [which] was maddening to the fitters.'

As LATE AS the spring of 1967, with *Funny Girl* scheduled to go into production within weeks, Barbra still had no leading man. None of the actors who had played Nick Arnstein on the stage had been considered for the picture, and the names of some of Hollywood's handsomest leading men had been bandied about – Tony Curtis, Sean Connery, Gregory Peck, David Janssen, James Garner. Barbra fantasized about Marlon Brando playing the part, but Ray Stark convinced her he would be all wrong.

The main problem with each of these possibilities was that none of them could sing, and Jule Styne had a fantasy of his own: Frank Sinatra as Nick Arnstein. 'What a powerhouse bill that would be!' he exclaimed. 'Streisand and Sinatra together!' Styne called Frank in Las Vegas, and he expressed tentative interest if the composer would write a few new songs for him to sing, if his part could be beefed up, and if he received top billing. Barbra balked at the billing, and Ray Stark balked at Sinatra's price tag – reportedly $750,000 – which he thought was too big a chunk of his tight budget. He also felt that Sinatra, at fifty-two, was too old to play Nick Arnstein and wrong for the role. 'We need a big, attractive man, someone with Cary Grant class,' Stark told Styne.

As a joke, someone suggested Omar Sharif, an Egyptian of Lebanese descent who was under contract to Columbia. This was during the height of the tension between Israel and Egypt, which would soon erupt into war, and the idea was clearly ridiculous. But Wyler saw Sharif every day in the studio commissary, and started to think about it. Sharif, thirty-five and swarthily handsome, had set hearts aflutter in the romantic melodrama *Doctor Zhivago* two years earlier. A gambler himself, completely at home in a tuxedo, he cut the same dashing figure Nick Arnstein had. Soon Sharif joined in the joke, asking Wyler every day at lunchtime, 'When do I sign the contract?' Within a few weeks, at his wit's end for a leading man, Wyler looked at Sharif while he ate his lunch and asked him, 'How would you like to play Arnstein?'

It turned out that Sharif could sing well enough to be presentable in a musical, and Ray Stark liked the idea that under the terms of Sharif's contract with the studio his services would cost barely $20,000. Everyone agreed that Sharif would be an unlikely but fine Arnstein, but Barbra wasn't sure. She wanted to meet him first. Arthur Laurents, the director of *I Can Get It for You Wholesale*, heard about the encounter from Ray Stark. 'Stark told me that Sharif came in, oozing Continental charm,' he recalled. 'Then Omar bowed elegantly, kissed Barbra's hand, and told her, "In America you are the woman I have most wanted to meet." Naturally he got the part.'

Within days, the Arab-Israeli Six-Day War erupted, and suddenly Sharif was on shaky ground. 'All the investors in the production were Jewish,' Sharif said in his autobiography. 'The atmosphere of the studio was pro-Israeli . . . A wave of panic swept over the set . . . Ray Stark spoke of breaking my contract.' William Wyler, a Jew, reacted strenuously: 'We're in America, the land of freedom, and you're ready to make yourselves guilty of the same things we're against? Not hiring an actor because he's Egyptian is outrageous. If Omar doesn't make the film, I don't make it either!'

Barbra weighed in with her own opinion of the controversy to the columnist Dorothy Manners: 'We people of the theater don't think of ourselves by race or creed. We have our own little world, our own standards of judging each other – and that's by talent! I just somehow feel ashamed that I have to say these things – anything else is so ridiculous, so unfair, so hateful.'

Sharif stayed, and Stark decided to make the most of the publicity value this odd pairing generated. A rehearsal photo of Omar nuzzling Barbra's neck turned up on the wire services and nearly created an international incident. The Egyptian press, smarting from their country's quick defeat in the war, condemned Sharif for kissing Barbra – who had recently participated in a fund-raiser for Israel's defense, pledging all the proceeds of her next album – and began a campaign to strip him of his citizenship. A reporter called Sharif to ask his opinion of the controversy. 'I don't make a point of asking a girl her nationality, her occupation, or her religion before kissing her – either on the screen or off,' Sharif said.

Ray Stark, who subscribed to the theory that any publicity was good publicity, rubbed his hands with glee, but the controversy cost him in the end because from that point on, all of Barbra's films were banned throughout the Arab world.

★

'I HATE ANYTHING that could lead one group of people to have contempt for another group of people,' Omar Sharif wrote. 'How do we overcome this religious, patriotic, and racist conditioning? . . . By love.'

Sharif practiced what he preached, and widely. As Anne Francis, cast in the film as a Ziegfeld girl put it, 'He had quite a reputation for chasing women around the studio. He was considered something more than a womanizer in those days.' Sharif had been married to the Egyptian movie star Faten Hamema for twelve years, and they had one son, but their marriage had evolved into a convenience. They agreed to lead separate lives but would not divorce unless one of them wanted to marry someone else. This gave Sharif a wide berth. 'The truth is, I worship women . . . the kind who can use both her intelligence and her femininity . . . The woman must give the impression that she needs a man.'

Barbra Streisand might have been tailor-made for this self-confessed male chauvinist who said, 'A woman mustn't contradict me openly.' Because as independent and opinionated as Barbra could be, when she felt attracted to a man she could revert to a seemingly helpless femininity. Given her growing reputation as a barracuda, this side of Streisand usually surprised and delighted any man who saw it.

Initially Sharif had not found Barbra attractive. After he first met her, he called his agent and asked, 'How is this girl going to be a leading lady?' The next day, he recalled, 'I looked at her again and I found her not bad. I thought she looked quite nice from certain angles. The third day of rehearsals I started to find her more and more attractive. About a week from the moment I met her, I was madly in love with her. I thought she was the most gorgeous girl I'd ever seen in my life . . . I was *lusting* after her.'

Barbra proved ripe for Sharif's picking, because her marriage had become rockier than ever. She and Elliott had already separated once for several months, and now he had gone back to New York to appear in the Jules Feiffer play *Little Murders* and then to play a supporting role in the film *The Night They Raided Minsky's*. His departure left Barbra alone in that eighteen-room mansion – and alone with another handsome actor to play love scenes opposite, just as she had with Sydney Chaplin. It was a classic Hollywood setup, and history repeated itself.

'It got so I couldn't wait to get on the set in the morning,' Barbra told a reporter shortly afterward. 'The days I knew I was going to work with Omar were happy days. The days he didn't have to work were miserable. I know Omar knew I was going gaga over him, but he was too much of a gentleman to make a play for a married woman. I would read in the columns where he took this girl and that girl out. It used to make me feel actually sick. I fell hopelessly – madly – in love with my leading man. It sounds like the old

Hollywood story – a B-movie script – but it actually happened. And I don't care who knows it. I loved every second of it.'

Like many of Barbra's public statements, this one hid a deception amid seemingly remarkable candor. Sharif did in fact make a play for this married woman, and she responded. 'She was so fresh and zestful and full of life, like a little kid who was told she could do whatever she wanted,' Sharif said. 'I was married, and so was she – which made the glamour more intense.'

Their affair began in Sharif's Beverly Wilshire Hotel suite, with script conferences that he turned into seduction dinners complete with Dom Pérignon champagne, oysters, and imported caviar. To Barbra's horror, the Hollywood gossip columnist Jim Bacon began reporting these cozy tête-à-têtes, even down to the brand names of the wines. 'Barbra always wondered how I knew those things,' Bacon said. 'Next time when getting room service in a man's room, ask the waiter if he knows Jim Bacon, Barbra.'

To better ensure their privacy, the lovebirds moved the center of the action to Barbra's place. 'We were not having an affair,' Sharif said. 'It was a romance, really . . . We would go [to her house] and have dinner in the evening and maybe have a glass of wine and we would just sit around; she would cook something that she liked, and I would cook sometimes.' Sharif would prepare Italian specialties, particularly pasta, but Barbra could muster only TV dinners. 'We led the very simple life of people in love,' Sharif said. 'We seldom went anywhere for supper.'

Perhaps bored with such discreet domesticity, Barbra and Omar ventured out after a few months, first attending a fashion party at a Hollywood discotheque, then dining out together at one of Los Angeles's trendiest restaurants. Inevitably word got back to Elliott, and this time the reports were more difficult for Barbra to laugh off as nonsense than Jim Bacon's column items had been. Sheilah Graham telephoned Elliott for his reaction. 'I'm furious with Barbra and told her that,' he said. 'I'm a very secure person, but as a man I have certain reactions.' He said that when he had asked Barbra, 'Why in hell did you go to that fashion show with Omar?' she replied, 'Because the ticket would have cost me two hundred and fifty dollars.'

It may have been Elliott's anger that prompted Barbra to end the affair; despite all their problems she wanted to keep the marriage together. Or perhaps the reason was, as Omar put it, that their romance was 'one-sided. I was in love with her. She had a lot of affection for me, but it didn't go beyond that.'

Like Sydney Chaplin before him, Sharif was infuriated by Barbra's rejection. Suddenly her incessant questions and suggestions on the set and the shortcomings of his role as Nick Arnstein, which he had tolerated while enmeshed in the affair, became prickly thorns. After the filming ended, Sharif told Rex Reed, 'She's a monster. I had nothing to do but stand around . . . Sometimes I just stood on the sidelines and watched her. I think her biggest problem is that she wants to be a woman and she wants to be beautiful, and she is neither.'

AS THE SUN came up over Manhattan on Saturday, June 17, the crowds began to stream into Central Park, carrying pillows and blankets and picnic baskets and thermos bottles. They were ready to camp out for more than fourteen hours to be as close to the stage as possible for a free Barbra Streisand concert scheduled to begin at nine that evening in the ninety-three-acre Sheep Meadow.

Ray Stark had agreed to give Barbra a three-day weekend off from *Funny Girl* filming so that she could fly back to New York for this much-heralded 'Happening in Central Park.' She took an overnight flight from Los Angeles on Thursday, arrived early in the morning, slept for a few hours in her apartment, then prepared for a full dress rehearsal, which was set to begin at eight-thirty Friday night.

The logistics were nightmarish, made worse by the fact that CBS was taping the concert as a television special. There were seven cameras, miles of cable, huge lights, and twenty-eight microphones scattered around near Barbra, the orchestra, and the crowd, which was expected to exceed sixty thousand, most of them in 'festival seating,' which meant no seating at all, hence the pillows and blankets.

As she prepared to begin the dress rehearsal, Barbra still hadn't decided what to wear for the concert. The show's director, Robert Scheerer, pleaded with her not to change outfits between the two acts, so that if he needed to he could rearrange numbers for the television special. But Barbra felt that it would be visually boring for her to wear the same dress for over two hours. The journalist Martha Weinman Lear attended the rehearsal and recorded what she saw for a profile of Streisand in *Redbook* magazine. Barbra wore a pink copy of a red pleated gown Irene Sharaff had designed for *Funny Girl*, covered with a chiffon cape that fluttered like giant butterfly wings in the breeze when she spread her arms, as she began the first strains of her opening number, 'Any Place I Hang My Hat Is Home.'

'Close your eyes and she was totally immersed in the song,' Lear observed. 'Open them and she was totally preoccupied with the gown, playing with it, studying the effect in two television monitors. The orchestra moved into "Cry Me a River." She sang it with heart and gut, and with her eyes fixed on the monitor, holding a sparkling lavaliere at her waist, at her bosom, at her shoulder, pondering each effect intently. Then she retired to her trailer to choose a gown for the second half of the show.

'"What am I going to wear?" she said, glumly eyeing two gowns . . . "Marty, they've got to give me another light – up here. I can't see the top of my head in the monitor. My face loses proportion. Fred [to her hairdresser, Fredrick Glaser, who stood with several hairpieces at the ready], my hair isn't right this way. Let's try it with the part in the middle, huh? Marty, I saw a new angle on the monitor we never used before. It's this way, three-quarters to the left [assuming the angle in front of the mirror]. It's *good*, huh? . . . Listen, what the hell am I going to *wear?*"'

The rehearsal lasted until midnight, when the orchestra had to quit by order of New York City so as not to disturb the residents along Central Park West. 'There was only enough time for us to block out maybe six to eight songs of a program of twenty-eight numbers,' Robert Scheerer recalled. 'The rest I would just have to wing the next night when we taped. I really had little idea of what Barbra would be doing at any given time, what movements she'd make. It was tremendously scary. Nobody had to remind me of how much could go wrong.' Indeed, during the rehearsal Barbra's audio 'conked out,' Scheerer said, 'and we all panicked.'

Marty Erlichman fretted about the weather. 'It had rained lightly on Friday,' Scheerer recollected, 'and Marty was terrified that if it rained any more heavily there'd be so much mud in the park that nobody would want to come to the concert. He got insurance for the rain itself [Lloyd's of London and GoodWeather, Inc., covered the concert for a four-hour period on Saturday night], but he couldn't get mud insurance. All we could do was pray.'

BY EIGHT O'CLOCK the largest crowd ever assembled for a single performer – 135,000 people – had streamed into the Sheep Meadow, overflowing into the Sixty-seventh Street entrance to the park. The concert was scheduled to begin at nine, but the skies were still too light for the television cameras. While they waited, the crowd danced to radios, played baseball, kicked soccer balls, and flew kites. Overnight, some furtive hippies had painted 'Flower Power' on the rocks beneath the huge Plexiglas stage constructed by the set designer Tom John.

Robert Scheerer feared that if the crowd were kept waiting any longer they might riot. 'I couldn't bring myself to think about it.' At nine forty-five, under a hazy moon, with a warm breeze stirring, the overture began. The restless throng quieted. Fredrick Glaser bit his nails, worried that if the fans tried to get too close to Barbra they might go out of control and trample her to death.

Sheer terror swept over Barbra as she waited in the wings, and it wasn't just her usual stage fright. A few hours earlier someone had telephoned a death threat against her because of her support of Israel in the Six-Day War, which had ended the week before. Barbra felt a very real fear that a bullet would rip through her as she stood in front of this enormous crowd.

As the overture swelled, Robert Scheerer's wife had to push Barbra onto the runway that led up to the stage. As she appeared the audience rose to its feet in a thunderous ovation, and Barbra shrank away in mock horror: 'I didn't do nothin' yet!' She ripped into 'Any Place I Hang My Hat Is Home,' then sang 'The Nearness of You,' 'My Honey's Lovin' Arms,' 'I'll Tell the Man in the Street,' and 'Cry Me a River.' As she sang, residents of Central Park West on one side of the park and Fifth Avenue on the other hung out their windows to hear her, and motorists slowed down for blocks.

'That opening portion was no good,' Robert Scheerer said. 'Barbra was too tight, still nervous. It took four or five songs to get her warmed up.' During her sixth number, 'Value' from *Harry Stoones*, she stumbled over the lyrics. 'Wait a minute,' she cried. 'I forgot the goddamn song!' She began again, but soon stopped and looked at her conductor, Mort Lindsay, for help.

Lindsay called out the next line of the lyric: '"A car is just a car!"'

'Oh, yeah, that's right!' Barbra said and finished the song.

Barbra has said that she tried to keep moving during the concert on the theory that by darting around she would make a more difficult target for a gunman. But the tape of the show indicates otherwise; her movements seem entirely appropriate for each song. 'How much could she move?' Robert Scheerer confirmed. 'She's too much of a pro to do that.'

As the concert progressed, she relaxed and warmed to the audience, performing nine more numbers, including 'I Wish You Love,' 'What Now My Love?' and 'Free Again.' She ended Act One with 'When the Sun Comes Out.'

A limousine then whisked her a quarter mile to her house trailer, where she had about seven minutes to put on a towering new wig, freshen her makeup, and change into another diaphanous chiffon gown, this one mostly red with a large multicolored pattern. She did her own makeup while Fredrick Glaser frantically adjusted, teased, and sprayed the wig. She was angry with herself for forgetting lyrics and for the less-than-perfect early performances. 'She was in a foul mood during the break,' Glaser said. 'She began cursing and swearing at people in her trailer. Everyone fled and left me with her ... I got her out of the trailer and we drove back in a golf cart to the back of the stage. She continued to rant and rave. She said the crowd had moved too close to the stage.'

None of this trauma was apparent as Barbra swept back onto the Plexiglas stage. 'I feel like I'm walking on a coffee table!' she quipped. The thirteen songs in the second act – including 'Stouthearted Men' and 'I'm Always Chasing Rainbows' – proceeded smoothly, except for a false start on 'Love Is a Bore.'

In the middle of 'Second Hand Rose,' Barbra turned over the second half of the song to the audience, attempting to re-create a magical moment during the sound check when the audience began to sing the song along with her. 'It didn't quite come off,' Robert Scheerer recalled, 'because it wasn't the same kind of thing. It wasn't spontaneous.' Still, most of the crowd did know the lyrics, and Barbra seemed genuinely to enjoy the interplay with her fans.

The concert ended just before midnight and 135,000 Streisand fans went home happy. They left behind five tons of trash, including a sterling silver champagne bucket, a Scrabble game, someone's upper plate, a jar of quail eggs, a miniskirt, and a Merry Widow bra.

The evening was a triumph for Barbra and further solidified her legend as America's most celebrated singer. For all the tension, Robert Scheerer found working with Streisand a pleasure. 'I had heard all the stories about Barbra being difficult,' he said, 'but I got none of that. She was delightful to work with. I had no problem whatever with her.'

Fifteen months later CBS aired about half of the concert in an hour-long special that nicely captured the excitement of the Happening, won solid ratings, and elicited largely favorable critical response. UPI critic Rick DuBrow wrote, 'She is fantastically theatrical, but it is for real, and the countless young persons in the crowd – giving her standing ovations – were the proof of how her genuine, wholly personal talent and demeanor are regarded by the toughest audience of all: youth . . . Robert Scheerer's producing and direction captured the romance in the love between audience and performer. Miss Streisand looked beautiful, as always . . . There has never been anybody quite like her.'

DAVID SHIRE, WHO had worked in the pit as assistant conductor of *Funny Girl* after Peter Daniels left, performed the same task for Barbra's Happening. He recalled that it was around this time that Barbra met Maharishi Mahesh Yogi, the Indian spiritual leader who had gained celebrity as guru to the Beatles.

Marty Erlichman, who arranged the meeting, joined Barbra and Shire on a pilgrimage to see the maharishi late one night after a party, with Barbra still dressed to the nines. As Shire recalled it, 'the maharishi, who was supposed to renounce everything material, was staying at the Plaza Hotel! But his room was tiny, barely big enough to hold his bed. When we entered the room, he was sitting in the middle of the bed in the lotus position, holding a single flower under his nose.'

He was a small man dressed in white ceremonial robes, his long hair falling greasy and unkempt around his shoulders. Barbra stood at the foot of the bed, waiting to be enlightened by his words of wisdom. When he spoke, it was in a thin, high-pitched voice interspersed unpredictably with giggles. He spoke of the power of transcendental meditation and proclaimed, 'Rejuvenation is here!'

'Whaddaya mean by *that?*' Barbra interrupted him. 'Why *is* that?'

'Barbra would question Jesus,' Shire said with a laugh. 'Finally she asked him to sum up his philosophy. He held up the flower he was holding and said, "If you let de consciousness go where it wants to go, it will go toward its greatest happiness. Like de sap of de tree or de stem of de flower, it goes to its source of greatest happiness.'

'Well,' Shire went on, 'Barbra thought a minute and she said, "Well, I normally go toward the point of greatest *un*happiness, so that must mean that unhappiness is the source of my greatest happiness." I'm sure the maharishi had never heard that one before. He just sat there nodding, holding his flower.'

S he was a bit obstreperous in the beginning,' said William Wyler. 'But things were ironed out when she discovered some of us knew what we were doing.' Back on the Columbia lot in Hollywood to resume *Funny Girl* filming, Barbra argued with Wyler about virtually everything – her interpretation, how she should be photographed, whether or not she could see the results of each day's filming. Wyler let her, but when Ray Stark told her one afternoon that she couldn't see the dailies because there wasn't time, she walked off the set. 'Girls like Bette Davis, Barbra Streisand, are not easy,' Wyler said. 'They're very demanding.'

Reports from the set painted Barbra, in the words of the writer Joyce Haber, as 'a full-fledged girl monster' who treated Wyler like 'a butler whose professional skills one respects, up to a point, but who must know his place.' Streisand, of course, had played Fanny Brice nine hundred times and had definite ideas about how to do so. 'I think I knew more about *Funny Girl* than Mr Wyler,' she said. 'I remember every line of every script.' Not all of her ideas, however, were as appropriate for film as they had been for the stage. 'She's got ideas on how to perform,' Wyler said. 'Some are good, some are not good.'

Wyler admitted that Barbra 'frightened me to death' because 'who *knew* her? She was twenty-two years old [*sic*], and she was telling everybody how she wanted to be photographed and everything . . . when everybody was saying, "Don't let her get away with that! Who the hell does she think she is?" I had sense enough not to argue [with her], because film is cheap. You can run it and do it her way, then change the lighting or whatever. But, my God, she was *right!* Where she got the knowledge, I don't know.'

Barbra explained her ideas to Wyler. And explained them and explained them and explained them. As Anne Francis recalled it, 'I just loved the way Barbra handled Wyler. She would get him so confused because she intellectualized incredibly about her character and what she thought she should be doing at this moment, and did he feel she should be doing this or what? She would give him so many ideas at one time that he would just roll his eyes and say, "Go ahead, Barbra, go ahead." It was wonderful. She just knew how to handle him completely. She's a very smart woman.'

Wyler, known as 'ninety-take Willie' because of his tendency to shoot and reshoot until he felt satisfied, came to appreciate Barbra's determination to be as good as she could possibly be onscreen. 'I'd much rather work with someone like Barbra, a perfectionist insisting on giving her best at all times and expecting it of everyone else, than a star who doesn't give a hoot. I've never known an actress so careful of detail. She even checked with me about the color of her nail polish!' As Ray Stark joked, 'She's the only dame who ever asked Willie Wyler to do another shot!'

Once Barbra realized that Wyler shared her goals, she relaxed a bit. 'What interested me,' Wyler said, 'was this girl, this fascinating creature, and how to present her on the screen. My principal job was to present her in the most advantageous manner possible. Not to draw attention to myself, but to draw it to her.'

Barbra couldn't have agreed more, and when she felt Wyler was straying from this focus, she didn't hesitate to balk. Over time Wyler grew more sanguine about Barbra's attitude, but others did not. There is a scene early in *Funny Girl* in which Fanny Brice has just been hired as a Ziegfeld girl and the legendary impresario gives her two important numbers in his new show. Fanny looks over the sheet music for the second number and tells Ziegfeld, 'I don't wanna be in the finale.' A shocked hush falls over everyone onstage behind her: My God, she's contradicting the great Ziegfeld!

Most of the cast and crew of *Funny Girl* had a similar reaction whenever Barbra Streisand disagreed with William Wyler, a man who had made sixty-seven films that had won forty Academy Awards. Before long the shock turned to resentment. One of the assistant directors, Jack Roe, summed up the prevailing sentiment: 'Here was this young whippersnapper telling a very noted director how to do his job.' During one heated exchange between them, one grip said to another, 'Willie shouldn't be so hard on her. After all, this is the first picture she's ever directed.'

Barbra couldn't understand the resentment. 'I don't know what other actresses do,' she said. 'Do they just sorta stand around like mummies, get dressed, get told what to do, move here, move there? That can be pretty boring for the actress and the director, besides what it does or does not do for the performance.'

Barbra's co-workers might have been more indulgent of her quest for perfection if they had liked her more. But most of the company found Barbra distant, unfriendly, self-involved, and inconsiderate. Jack Roe recalled that 'Barbra was very aloof when she arrived. I picked her and Elliott up at the airport and took them to the studio. He was charming, but she didn't give me the time of day. And then we were walking down an alleyway between soundstages and Harry Stradling came out of one of the doors. Now, he was gonna shoot the picture, and he was an Oscar winner, one of the best cinematographers in the business. I stopped to introduce her to this wonderful man, and she barely stopped walking long enough to say a little hi. She didn't shake his hand or anything. I thought it was very rude. But then, I thought she was rude during the whole shoot . . . I didn't like the way she treated people, from Wyler and Stradling all the way to her personal maid, Gracie.'

Anne Francis had an odd experience with Barbra as they shot the scene that leads up to 'Don't Rain on My Parade' when Fanny announces that she's going to follow Nick Arnstein to Europe, and the Follies girls try to talk her out of it. 'I was next to Barbra,' Anne recounted, 'and I'm saying "Don't do it" or something like that, and I touched her on the arm. When the camera stopped rolling she turned to me and said, "Don't touch me." I said, "What?" She said, "Don't touch me. I've been told that a star is never touched in a scene like this." I looked at her and said, "Oookay, Barbra."'

Streisand's tardiness, Jack Roe recalled, frazzled a great many nerves. 'She was late all the time, not just in the morning. When she was through with a scene, she would go to her trailer and a little red light would come on [over her door] that meant she was on the phone and couldn't be disturbed. Omar Sharif got so tired of waiting for her for every shot that he took it upon himself to teach her how to play cards. That way he could keep her on the set rather than letting her go back to her trailer and get on that phone.'

In the middle of *Funny Girl* filming, on October 11, 1967, CBS-TV aired Barbra's third special, *The Belle of 14th Street*. She had taped the show in April, just before flying to Los Angeles for the film's rehearsals.

'OH, MY GOD,' a receptionist at Marty Erlichman's office whispered as she hung up the telephone. 'I thought that guy with the deep voice on the phone was Elliott Gould. It was Barbra!' Lying weakly in her Jacobean bed, Barbra hacked and sneezed and sniffled through one of the most miserable colds of her life. Worst of all – considering that in two days she was scheduled to record tracks for *The Belle of 14th Street* – her throat was sore and so severely constricted she could barely speak. Taping of the show was set to commence on Wednesday, April 26, at CBS's

Studio 41 on Fifty-seventh Street, after months of planning and a number of delays.

Barbra couldn't postpone the special because Ray Stark had threatened to charge her a hefty daily penalty if she didn't get to Hollywood for *Funny Girl* rehearsals in early May. She had originally hoped to complete the TV show by the end of March, but she found to her distress that her cesarean operation had left her abdominal and diaphragm muscles so weak that she could not project her voice. David Shire, the assistant conductor for the special, recalled his shock at finding that Barbra's range had fallen a full tone and a half after Jason's birth. 'We had to rewrite dozens of charts for her,' he said.

Now, with the taping pushed back as far as it could be, Barbra found herself unable to sing because of her cold. She considered postponing the special, but its sponsor, Chemstrand/Monsanto (which had invested $580,000 in the program), the network, and Columbia Records all had considerable interest in airing it that fall. Barbra felt a keen responsibility to these corporate giants who had been so instrumental in her unprecedented rise to superstardom and who she felt had treated her exceptionally well. Cold or no cold, she vowed to get *The Belle of 14th Street* in the can before she left for Hollywood.

For this special, Barbra preferred not to reprise the one-woman format that had worked so well on her first two outings. Part of the reason was her desire to try something new, but she also feared that she might reach the point of diminishing returns if she repeated herself. Instead she opted to recreate a turn-of-the-century vaudeville revue with all the songs, skits, and costumes derived from the era. 'We weren't looking to make fun of it or camp it,' Barbra said, 'but to do it as they did.'

Almost a year of preparation ensued, during which Barbra sought the reminiscences of vaudeville veteran George Burns for verisimilitude. The revue format was designed to be less demanding for Barbra than her one-woman showcases had been. Although she planned to perform a dozen songs, she would sing one as part of an ensemble and would be offscreen entirely for two long numbers performed by others. She reportedly hoped to land Marlon Brando or Richard Burton as her co-star, but dropped the idea when she realized that both men commanded fees that approached the show's entire budget. Instead, the respected actor Jason Robards Jr stepped in, along with Lee Allen, who had played Eddie in the London production of *Funny Girl* and would do so again for the film, and veteran song-and-dance man John Bubbles.

The first day in the recording studio, Barbra was so hoarse she could barely hum in order to set tempos for the orchestral tracks. Two days later, she struggled with her voice again, and showed only minor improvement the next day. A throat specialist examined her and strongly recommended a week of bed rest with absolutely no talking, much less singing. That was impossible, so the doctor offered to drop cortisone on Barbra's vocal cords to lessen the inflammation. Fearful of the drug's possible side effects, Barbra rejected the treatment.

When rehearsals began on April 26, Barbra could muster up only a fraction of her usual energy. Flying across the set in a harness for a planned parody of Shakespeare's *The Tempest* nearly did her in. When she smashed against a backdrop during one trial landing, she shot a dirty look at the director, Joe Layton, and said wearily, 'At least you could pick me up.' She couldn't sing or dance, and couldn't speak above a whisper. Marty Erlichman summoned another doctor, and this time Barbra agreed to the cortisone. She gamely forged ahead, but the treatment helped only a little, and the delays caused by her infirmity added five hours of expensive overtime to the rehearsal.

Barbra's inability to perform satisfactorily the following day resulted in even more overtime. Marty and Joe Layton tried to persuade her to postpone the show, but she insisted that she was feeling the first stirrings of recovery. Over the next two days – until 5:00 A.M. the first day and 2:00 A.M. the second – Barbra managed to deliver some passable performances with the help of vocal coach Maurice Jampol. Most often she just mouthed the lyrics to songs she would have to record again later when her full vocal power returned. The taping took so much longer than planned that Barbra had to cancel an appearance on *The Ed Sullivan Show* scheduled for Sunday, April 30.

When Marty Erlichman viewed a rough cut of *Belle* culled from over fifty hours of exposed tape, his heart sank. Barbra's illness wasn't the show's only problem. What had seemed like a smashing idea on paper didn't come across on the screen with the impact he had expected. He reportedly told one CBS executive that they should shelve the show. But after Barbra went back into the recording studio a few days later, fully recovered, and laid in some superlative vocal tracks, the network decided the show was fine.

The Belle of 14th Street won decent ratings but confused most viewers and left critics grumbling. The vaudeville theme had been done to death on television variety shows, and for all of the attention to period detail, including an audience made up mostly of Monsanto employees in 1900s costumes, the entire enterprise had a flat, uninspired look and feel.

The first number, set in an Art Nouveau theater, had Jason Robards and a 'bevy of beefy beauties' – each weighing two hundred or more pounds – singing an overlong 'You Are the Apple of My Eye' while the overstuffed chorines threw apples into the audience.

Barbra then took the stage for a coy version of 'Alice Blue Gown,' which developed into a comic striptease as wires gradually pulled off her frilly dress to leave her in a Merry Widow and tights, hiding behind a twirling parasol.

John Bubbles then strode out wearing, for unexplained reasons, black rooster feathers and chicken feet to perform an uninspired 'I'm Goin' South.' Then Barbra came back with Robards, Lee Allen, and eleven-year-old Susan Alpern to sing, in a thick Irish brogue, an ode to patriotism, 'We're Four Americans.' Barbra's vocal problems were noticeable in this number, especially during the spoken bits when her voice cracked more than once.

The second act of the show opened with Barbra as a formidable prima donna, Madame Schmausen-Schmidt. In the hand-wringing style of the period, Barbra comically sang 'Leibestraum' with a surprisingly strong operatic voice. A clever challenge-duet of 'Mother Machree' followed, between Schmausen-Schmidt and a wide-eyed youth in the audience, also played by Barbra.

The scene from *The Tempest* came next with 'the quick-change artistes, the Mungers' (Streisand and Robards) playing, respectively, both Prospero and Caliban and Miranda and Ariel. Even fans of Shakespeare found the scene tiresome. At the conclusion of the skit, the Mungers take a curtain call, and Barbra, wearing a tacky backstage kimono and a huge bouffant wig, got some of the few laughs in the show as the southern-accented Roberta Lee Booth-Munger: 'Thank you very kindly . . . Why, ah'd just like to throw y'all a big honeykiss. Y'all been such a captivated audience. I 'specially want to thank all those big strong stagehands back there who give me such assistance . . . Now, after a refreshin' intermission there's a young lady goin' to come out here and sing for y'all . . . so y'all hurry back here, hear?'

Barbra concluded the show with a mini-concert, one of the few format holdovers from the first two specials. This time all of the songs were germane to the vaudeville period. Barbra sang while standing on a brightly colored bandstand next to her accompanist, David Shire. With hand on hip, wearing an elegant black velvet gown and a matching picture hat trimmed with white ostrich feathers, she leaned on a jeweled walking stick and toyed with a feather boa in the best tradition of Lillian Russell.

Critics were not forgiving. *Newsday* called the special 'a jarring, stylistic jumble,' and *The New York Times* labeled it 'an embarrassing outing, a concoction of deranged productions.' Two weeks later Ben Gross, writing in the New York *Daily News*, said, 'Barbra Streisand, the cult idol, did herself tremendous damage by appearing in that recent ill-advised special.'

A year later Barbra spoke defensively about *The Belle of 14th Street*, 'My third [TV special] wasn't as good as the other two. But if it had been my first it would have been [considered] damn good, you know?' Because of the poor reaction, plans for a sound-track album were scrapped.

As Barbra's first big professional misstep, *The Belle of 14th Street* proved to some that she was at her best when unfettered. To others it suggested that her talent and taste had been grossly overpraised. Most of her fans yearned for Barbra to return to the one-woman format, where she would simply sing and clown over the course of an hour. With her next television special, the tape of her Central Park concert aired in 1968, she would regain their admiration by doing precisely that. But CBS would not air another Streisand television special for six years. She was too busy becoming a movie star.

AFTER A WEEK of filming on *Funny Girl*, Harry Stradling threatened to quit unless Barbra stopped telling him how to photograph her. 'She argued with Harry about how to light her,' Jack Roe recalled. 'She wanted the key light on one side and not the other. It wasn't so much whether she was right or wrong, but she was just starting in the business and she was very pigheaded about things that she really didn't know anything about.'

It wasn't just her appearance that concerned Barbra. She thought that parts of the film should have the grainy look that cheaper film stock brought to European films like the ones she used to watch back in Flatbush. Stradling disagreed, but Barbra wouldn't let up. Finally he told her, 'Okay, Barbra, I'll tell you what we'll do. I'll go ahead and shoot the picture like we usually do, and afterward we'll scratch up the film for your grainy look.'

Barbra's stubbornness was rooted in both her fear that she would fail on film and her certainty that she knew what was best for her. She couldn't allow anyone, no matter how talented or accomplished, to present her in anything less than the best light – literally and figuratively. Just as she had in the stage version of *Funny Girl*, she wanted to be great, not just good, on the screen. She'd had the chutzpah to tell a reporter shortly after she arrived in Hollywood, 'I'll be the brightest star there ever was.' Now she had to put up or shut up – many would have welcomed the latter – and she certainly wasn't going to fail because of someone else's shortcomings, real or perceived.

'When I came out here,' Barbra said, 'everybody thought, Oh, she's got to be a bitch and have temper tantrums, be demanding and nasty. I had no intention of being that. But it's funny. Circumstances make you behave like they expect you to sometimes. Like, on the morning of a scene, my dress isn't here yet, my hair isn't fixed properly, and they want me to go out anyway and film it. *For posterity!* Listen, once it's on film, that's it. It's got to be perfect when the cameras are turned on you.'

Stradling came to accept the fact that Barbra Streisand considered herself a collaborator on every aspect of *Funny Girl*, and, like Wyler, he welcomed some of her suggestions and ignored others. He found himself agreeing with her more and more often when he realized that she had nearly unerring instincts about the best light and the best angles for her. 'I *feel* things like lights,' Barbra said. 'I *know* a light should be two inches to the left and so on.'

Harry Stradling Jr recalled that his father 'could never stop raving about what a smart woman Streisand was, about how she would notice if he changed the lights, if he didn't quite do it the same way as he had. She would bring it to his attention. He liked her, and he said that she was very, very right about a lot of things.'

Unsurprisingly, Barbra was most often right about the film's music; while some might have questioned her filmmaking expertise, no one doubted her musical instincts. Still, Walter Scharf, the film's musical supervisor and conductor, had his share of problems with Streisand. 'They warned me that she was temperamental and stubborn,' he said. 'She was. As an artist Barbra is very sensitive, terribly, terribly sensitive. But she has a remarkable intuition about the sound of music. It was a challenge to adapt the music from the Broadway *Funny Girl*. I wanted to keep the mood of Fanny Brice's time alive and yet contemporize the music. Barbra and I developed a healthy and lasting respect for each other's contributions to the job we set out to do. It wasn't always easy or peaceful.'

Barbra's perfectionism, her desire to do things 'just one more time,' extended beyond the final day's filming on December 1. That afternoon she completed the movie's last scene, a heart-wrenching version of 'My Man' sung after Nick Arnstein has come back from prison and told Fanny he wants a divorce. The next day, while most of the cast and crew dispersed, Marty, Barbra, Ray Stark, William Wyler, Herb Ross, Columbia Pictures president Leo Jaffe, production chief Mike Frankovich, and half a dozen other studio executives gathered to watch the dailies of *Funny Girl*'s final musical number.

When the song ended everyone burst into applause. The performance was brilliant, they told Barbra, and it made for a killer ending to a picture they all knew would be a smash. But Barbra wasn't pleased. 'I know everybody in this room is going to be angry except Marty,' she said, 'but I really would like to redo that scene.' Silence fell. All eyes turned to Ray Stark. 'But, Barbra,' he sputtered, 'everybody's gone home. It would be very difficult. Besides, the number is great! What's the problem?'

'Ray, I recorded that song three months ago, before we even started the movie. Now I'm lip-synching to it on film and it just doesn't look right. My whole life is pouring out and the audience is going to be distracted by the lip-synching. It isn't *real*.

'And you know what else?' she concluded. 'The whole song should start in close up and *then* pull back, not the other way around.'

Stark swallowed hard and said, 'Okay, Barbra, you're probably right.' He spent the next three days rounding up the cast and crew, including Omar Sharif, whom Barbra wanted on hand so that just before she came out to sing 'My Man' she could perform the heartbreaking scene that leads into it, in which Nick tells Fanny he's leaving her for good.

The scene aroused strong emotions in Barbra, both for her character and herself. It was not only Fanny Brice saying good-bye to Nick Arnstein but Barbra Streisand saying good-bye to Omar Sharif – and possibly to Elliott Gould as well, for by now she feared that their marriage might be unsalvageable.

'My Man' – or rather the first half of it – became the first movie musical number to be recorded live since the early talkies. When Barbra tentatively talk-sings the lyrics at the beginning of the song in dramatic close-up, she is singing live. But when she rips full-throttle into the remainder of the song, she is lip-synching, and that nearly destroys the intimacy Barbra has created. One wonders why she didn't do the entire song live after going to all that trouble.

WHILE BARBRA REMAINED narrowly focused on her career, the outside world reeled toward turmoil. After his inauguration, despite having run in part as an antiwar candidate, Preisdent Johnson had dramatically increased American troop and artillery support for South Vietnam in its effort to avoid a takeover by Communist North Vietnam. As more and more American boys died for a cause many of their countrymen did not support, Johnson's popularity plummeted. Peaceful antiwar demonstrations on college campuses across the country grew increasingly more violent. In October 1967 thousands marched on the Pentagon; hundreds were injured and arrested. Many carried 'Dump Johnson' banners.

On January 21, back in New York, Barbra participated in a 'Broadway for Peace 1968' rally at the New York Philharmonic, a fund-raiser for members of Congress who opposed the war and were up for re-election. Co-hosted by Leonard Bernstein and Paul Newman, the event raised $50,000. Alaska's Democratic Senator Ernest Gruening gave the keynote address, in which he said, 'If the American people only knew the facts, they would end this unconstitutional, illegal, indefensible, and monstrous war.' Dressed in an unattractive gingham smock and fisherman's hat and accompanied by Leonard Bernstein, Barbra sang 'So Pretty,' an antiwar ballad by Bernstein with lyrics by Betty Comden and Adolph Green.

After little-known Democratic Senator Eugene McCarthy of Minnesota, challenging Johnson as an antiwar candidate, won a startling 40 percent of the vote in the New Hampshire primary, the president's vulnerability led New

York Senator Robert F. Kennedy, also an opponent of the war, to challenge him for the nomination as well. On March 31, 1968, the president announced in a nationally televised speech that he would not run for re-election. His vice president, Hubert Humphrey, then threw his hat into the ring.

Both the McCarthy and the Kennedy camps wooed Barbra in an effort to get her to publicly support their candidate, but she admired both men and couldn't make up her mind. Her friends Marilyn and Alan Bergman, staunch McCarthy supporters, arranged a private meeting between the senator and the singer in the hope that meeting McCarthy would help Barbra make up her mind. It worked. Later the Bergmans told friends, 'We don't know what he said to her in that room, but she's willing to do anything in the world for him now.'

In May, Barbra – dressed in a jejune gingham outfit with a bow at the neck and a matching hat – attended a cocktail party fund-raiser for McCarthy at Paul Newman and Joanne Woodward's home and afterward was photographed driving away with the candidate. The Robert Kennedy camp wasn't pleased, but in spite of McCarthy's big-name Hollywood support, Kennedy and Hubert Humphrey were considered by most pundits the front-runners for the nomination.

FUNNY GIRL WOULD not be released until September 1968, plenty of time for the Hollywood rumor mill to spew out reports of Barbra the Monster before anyone could see whether all the grief she had apparently caused so many people had been worth it. The film had barely wrapped when Doris Klein reported in the *Hollywood Reporter* that Anne Francis had asked that her name be removed from the picture because her part had been whittled down from 'three very good scenes and a lot of other ones to two minutes of voice-over in a railroad station.'

Klein quoted Francis at length: 'I had only one unpleasant meeting with Barbra Streisand during the entire five months of *Funny Girl*, but the way I was treated was a nightmare . . . Every day Barbra would see the rushes, and the next day my part would be cut. Barbra ran the whole show . . . She had the Ziegfeld Girls' scenes changed – one day she told Wyler to move a girl standing next to her because she was too pretty, and the girl wound up in the background. Eventually the Ziegfeld Girl scenes were eliminated altogether.'

Klein's column, read or discussed by almost everyone in Hollywood, cast a pall over the film and further sullied Streisand's budding stardom. That a respected actress like Anne Francis would speak out so forcefully against Barbra, many felt, proved that Streisand must truly be the arrogant, egomaniacal ogre that rumor had it. It is an image that Barbra hasn't been able to entirely shake to this day.

For years Anne Francis refused to comment about the sentiments attributed to her in Klein's column, but she revealed for this book that she never said, nor did she believe, anything of the kind. 'I had no reason to think that Barbra had anything to do with my scenes being cut,' she said. 'I think that was entirely Wyler's decision. He didn't like the character I was playing, didn't think she added anything to the picture. There were a lot of scenes that were cut on the very day I was to shoot them. I would sit in my dressing room, all ready to be called, and then a note would be slipped under the door saying, "Omit scene such and such." It was *very* strange.'

So where did the published quotes come from? Francis's public relations woman, Peggy McNaught. 'Peggy was infuriated by the whole thing,' Anne explained, 'and she felt it was all Barbra's fault. She talked to Doris Klein and said it was okay for Klein to attribute her sentiments to me. When I read it I thought, *Oh, God*, but what could I do? Peggy was an old, dear friend. I couldn't very well go public and say, "I didn't say those things; my publicist did." It was just a very awkward situation all around.'

A few months later Joyce Haber's article in the fledgling magazine *New York* appeared. Entitled 'Barbra's Directing Her First Movie,' it further cemented Streisand's reputation as a terror. Haber wrote that 'Barbra Streisand is working quite energetically ... at becoming a monster,' that people in Hollywood were 'terrified' of her, and that Ray Stark had presented her with a ten-minute trailer for the movie with the credits, 'Written, Produced and Directed by Barbra Streisand.'

Barbra suspected that Stark, who was cozy with Haber, had orchestrated much of the bad press on the theory that any publicity would bolster interest in the film. 'Everything in the papers was such an out-and-out lie,' Barbra protested. 'Even my producer of that film was out to get as much publicity as he could, even if it was negative or cruel.'

Omar Sharif spoke up in Barbra's defense. 'She wasn't bad to work with at all when you understood her. She didn't just think she was plain – she thought she was ugly. So no wonder that insecurity. There *was* trouble – in wardrobe, in makeup, and so on. But when you play important parts like these, when the whole film sinks or swims on you, you have to be a little bit selfish.'

Barbra's next leading man wouldn't be so gallant. If the $10 million *Funny Girl* production had been a frying pan of seething resentment against Streisand, the making of the $24 million film version of the Broadway smash *Hello, Dolly!* – begun a scant two months after *Funny Girl* wrapped – proved to be a hellish fire.

16

The sweltering heat at the *Hello, Dolly!* location in Garrison, New York, threatened to undo everyone. Whenever she wasn't before the camera, Barbra tried to keep cool and protect her makeup by pointing a small portable electric fan at her face. Tensions had been rife throughout the shoot, which had begun in April after two months of rehearsals. But on Thursday, June 6, 1968, tempers reached the exploding point after a national tragedy stunned America: in the early morning hours of June 5, shortly after winning California's Democratic presidential primary, Senator Robert Kennedy had been shot, and twenty-five hours later, early Thursday morning, he died.

Although Barbra had supported Eugene McCarthy, she sympathized with most of Kennedy's positions and would very likely have campaigned for him had he won the nomination to run against the Republican standard-bearer, former vice president Richard Nixon. When she heard the news of the shooting, she felt nearly as devastated as she had when the senator's brother, President Kennedy, had been killed.

Barbra's co-star, the hangdog comic actor Walter Matthau, was appalled by the latest instance of rampant violence in America. 'I was in a mean, foul mood. I took it hard,' he said. 'I was knocked out. It was one hundred degrees. Giant brutes [lights with tremendous wattage] surrounded us in a complicated outdoor scene. My head felt as though it was being smashed.'

The film's director, the former MGM musical star Gene Kelly, brought Barbra, Matthau, several extras, and the crew together to shoot a scene in which Barbra's character, Dolly Levi, and Matthau's character, Horace Vandergelder, are sitting in a wagon outside Vandergelder's hay-and-feed store. As Kelly explained what he wanted everyone to do, Barbra made a suggestion. She had an idea for a humorous exchange between the characters. 'Why don't we say something like this?' she piped up, and recited some lines of dialogue. She remembered that most of the crew laughed with appreciation.

Walter Matthau, however, blew his top. 'Who does she think she is?' he bellowed. 'I've been in thirty movies, and this is only her second – the first one hasn't even come out yet – and she thinks she's *directing!*'

Gene Kelly grabbed Matthau's arm and tried to pull him away. 'I went into a wild, furious, incoherent tirade about her,' Matthau recalled. Barbra stood speechless as her co-star railed on. 'Why don't you let *him* direct?' Matthau shouted, waving in Kelly's direction. 'You don't have to be great *all* the time!'

Barbra fought back tears. 'Why don't you learn your lines?' she shot back. 'You're just jealous because you're not as good as I am!'

'You might be the singer in this picture,' Matthau roared, 'but I'm the *actor!* You haven't got the talent of a butterfly's fart!'

'I couldn't believe it,' Barbra said of Matthau's harangue. 'I had no defense. I stood there and I was so humiliated I started to cry, and then I ran away.'

'Everybody in this company hates you!' Matthau shouted after her. 'Go ahead, walk off! But just remember, Betty Hutton thought she was indispensable, too!'

Barbra ran to her dressing room and telephoned the film's writer-producer, Ernest Lehman. 'She was sobbing,' Lehman recalled, 'and she said, "Please come over right away." I came rushing down, and she poured out all of her sorrow at the way Walter talked to her and the things he said about her. I did my best to soothe her.'

'Barbra cried for a long time,' Gene Kelly recalled. 'I said, "Cut the lights," stopped everything. We went into a little store and straightened it out.' Three hours later the still-seething stars completed the scene.

FROM THE VERY outset, Barbra's participation in the film version of *Hello, Dolly!* had stirred up resentment. When Ernest Lehman announced her casting on May 8, 1967, Streisand faced a wave of outrage from fans of the show, who felt that Carol Channing, who had played Dolly Gallagher Levi on Broadway for over two years, then had taken the show on the road and helped make it the highest-grossing touring musical in history, should have been given the chance to immortalize her performance on film. In 1967 Carol Channing was as much identified with the character of Dolly Levi as Barbra was with Fanny Brice.

What made Channing's slight all the worse was that the twenty-five-year-old Barbra seemed so clearly wrong for the part of the irrepressible middle-aged Irish widow trying to get back into the swing of life fourteen years after the death of her husband, Ephraim. The fact that Barbra was a totally untried commodity in movies added insult to injury, especially when Twentieth Century-Fox trumpeted the fact that her signing – at a salary of $600,000, Lehman recalled – was 'the largest single film deal in history with a performer who has never before appeared in a motion picture.' In the past, when a Broadway star was denied a chance to re-create a role on screen, the rationale had usually been that the project required a proven movie box-office draw to guarantee its commercial success.

Channing desperately wanted the movie version of *Dolly*, and in the hope that a successful film performance would boost her chances, she took the supporting role of a zany heiress-aviator in George Roy Hill's comedy *Thoroughly Modern Millie*, which starred Julie Andrews and Mary Tyler Moore. 'I really wanted to use Carol Channing in the picture,' Lehman recalled. 'I mean, who else would you use? But then I saw a rough cut of *Thoroughly Modern Millie*. I thought she looked a little grotesque, cartoonish. I felt very guilty because Carol is a lovely woman and she and her husband had been so nice to me and my wife. But I honestly felt I couldn't take a whole movie in which Carol was in practically every scene. Her personality is just too much for the cameras to contain.'

Lehman then considered Elizabeth Taylor, with whom he had just worked as the writer and producer of *Who's Afraid of Virginia Woolf?*, but Richard Zanuck, Twentieth Century-Fox's head of production, had called that notion 'the single worst casting idea I've ever heard.' Zanuck felt similarly about Julie Andrews, to whom Lehman had sent the *Dolly* script. Lehman had run out of ideas when he had dinner with Mike Nichols, the director of *Virginia Woolf*. According to Lehman, 'Mike said to me, "Why don't you cast Barbra Streisand as Dolly? She'd be great." I said, "Gee, I don't know. What is she, twenty-four?" But the more I thought about what her voice could do with that score . . . Then I'd think, "But she's not right for it." Then I'd tell myself, "Forget that she's not right for it. Just forget that."'

Richard Zanuck, who loved the idea of Barbra as Dolly, arranged a meeting for himself, Barbra, her agent Freddie Fields, and Lehman at Hollywood's Bistro restaurant a few days after Barbra arrived in town in May 1967. 'It was the first time I'd seen the Hollywood Miss Streisand,' Lehman recalled. 'She wore a broad-brimmed hat, and I kept peeking under it and saying, "Do you mind if I look at you?" And all she kept saying was, "Why me? Why me? I'm too young for the role."

'I kept coming up with all the reasons she should do it: she was such a vivid personality, her voice was one of the all-time greats, she was going to be a tremendous star in pictures. I gave her every reason I could think of. I never had any doubt that she could do it, or that she would be a huge movie star.

We never even tested her. She was a known quantity as one of the greats of all time. Making the transition to movies was only a formality. Finally she said yes, and I was ecstatic.'

When the announcement was made, Carol Channing sent Barbra flowers and a gracious note of congratulations. When the bouquet arrived, Barbra told a reporter, 'I called Elliott right away and told him about it, very excited. He said, "Yes, I already read about it in the paper."'

The press came down firmly on Carol's side. The *Washington Post* called Barbra's casting 'knuckle-headed.' Other observers called it 'cynical,' 'mercenary,' 'unfathomable.' Lehman defended his choice and pointed out that Thornton Wilder, who wrote *The Matchmaker*, the play on which *Hello, Dolly!* was based, had described Dolly as a woman of 'uncertain' age. 'She could well be in her thirties,' Lehman suggested.

Barbra attempted to defend her selection as well, but her customary bluntness rebounded to her further detriment. 'It's so ridiculous and boring,' she said of the controversy. 'They can cast anyone they want in a picture. I can't help it if I get the part. I don't know whether I'm right for it or not. I haven't even read the script. If they pick the wrong person for a part, that's their problem. Everbody wants to be a casting director.'

To round out the cast, Lehman hired Michael Crawford and Danny Lockin to play Vandergelder's clerks, and Marianne McAndrew and E. J. Peaker as Irene Molloy and Minnie Fay, the milliners they take out on the town in New York. Lehman had tested a number of actresses to play Irene Molloy, among them Phyllis Newman, Yvette Mimieux, and Ann-Margret, before deciding on the unknown McAndrew. 'One reason we didn't hire Ann-Margret was that she had too sexy an image for such a sweetness-and-light character as Irene Molloy,' Lehman said.

EVEN AFTER SHE signed for the part, Barbra harbored deep reservations about her casting. When she saw the show on Broadway she had considered it 'a piece of fluff' and felt the audience sat through it waiting to hear the title tune, which had become a number one hit for Louis Armstrong in 1964. 'I wasn't gonna do it. I tried to convince them that it would be more emotional if it were the story of an older woman whose time is running out and she has to make the most of it. I thought Elizabeth Taylor should play it.'

But Barbra got over her concern that Dolly Levi had traditionally been played as middle-aged. 'This woman is a widow, but this doesn't mean she has to be old,' she said. 'After all, she could be a widow of nineteen, married a year, who'd lost her husband in a war.' But some of the meddlesome Dolly's characteristics made Barbra uncomfortable because they hit a little too close to home. 'I was reluctant to show the part of me that is very Dolly Levi-ish,' she admitted, like 'searching for bargains and all that.'

Still, the excitement of the opportunity to star in the film versions of both of the two biggest Broadway hits of 1964, not to mention her salary and a percentage of the box-office take, had finally convinced Barbra that she should accept the role. 'It was fun thinking about the jewelry I'd wear, stuff that I had and loved that I thought would be good for Dolly. And I liked the idea of being able to laugh and smile a lot, which I usually don't do – I mean, I'm not much of a laugher.'

IT WAS SYDNEY Chaplin who had poisoned his friend Walter Matthau's mind against Barbra. Chaplin had given Matthau such an earful of his complaints about her during the *Funny Girl* run that by the time Matthau met Barbra, at a Broadway revival of *The Glass Menagerie* in 1965, he felt he had to avenge his friend's agony. He walked up to Streisand at intermission and said, 'Oh, you're Barbra Harris. I see you've had your nose done.'

'I was so shocked I couldn't even answer him,' Barbra later said.

When he was cast as the grumpy Yonkers hay-and-feed merchant Horace Vandergelder, the 'well-known unmarried half a millionaire' on whom Dolly sets her sights, the forty-seven-year-old Matthau felt 'a strange kind of attraction to the fact that I was going to work with Streisand. I almost knew that I was going to blow up at her.'

As soon as the rehearsals got under way, Matthau started to seethe. 'I tried very, very hard to be civil, but it's extraordinarily difficult to be civil to her. When she "acts" – and I say that in quotes – she likes to tell the director when the other actors should come in. She pretends as though she's asking, but she's overstepping her boundaries. She should simply be the instrument of the director, and not be the conductor, the composer, the scene designer, the acting coach, et cetera.'

Matthau became furious with Barbra when he recorded the title tune, which Horace sings to Dolly at the end of the film. 'She laughed,' he said. 'She would break up every time I sang a line in the recording booth. I had to re-record everything.'

'I was laughing at Vandergelder the character,' Barbra explained later. 'I *wasn't* laughing at Walter. Actually, I like the way he sings very much.'

Less than a week before filming began on April 15, 1968, Barbra appeared at the Academy Awards ceremony to present the Best Song Oscar. She wore the high, tightly curled 'Colette' hairstyle she had been partial to for a while. The next day Matthau asked her, 'That hairdo you wore – was that supposed to make the audience laugh?'

'Why are you so cruel?' Barbra responded. 'That hairdo is the latest fashion.'

'I just wondered if you meant it to be funny.'

'You are a very hostile person,' Barbra told him and walked away.

Once filming began, Matthau's antagonism grew with every suggestion Barbra made, every one of her requests for a retake. 'The thing about working with her was that you never knew what she was going to do next and were afraid she'd do it. I found it a most unpleasant picture to work on and, as most of my scenes were with her, extremely distasteful . . . I was appalled by every move she made.'

Ernest Lehman took Barbra's side in almost all of her disputes with Matthau, and still does today. 'Walter's a grump. He's a great guy, but he's a grump, a complainer. He scowls a lot. He resented that she would speak up and make suggestions to the director, which was something that he wouldn't do. And he felt kind of shunted off to the side. He was an old pro and he thought, "Who's this upstart kid who's getting all this attention?" And boy did she get attention. When she was around, you knew she was around. I couldn't very well ignore her and say, "Yes, Walter, what can we do for you, Walter?"

'Barbra wasn't full of herself; she didn't have an ego. I think just the opposite. If she were full of herself she wouldn't have been so concerned about everything being just right. She's never been a person who feels her own perfection. She was a very insecure person, doubting her own worth, especially interpersonally. She dabbled in everything. Her opinion was "We're all in this together, and it's the result that's gonna count, not how we got there."'

Matthau thought Barbra should keep her own counsel, but when he went to Richard Zanuck to complain about her ('Do I need a heart attack? Do I need an ulcer?'), Zanuck replied, 'I'd like to help you, but the film isn't called *Hello, Walter!*'

Lehman seems to have been somewhat infatuated with his star. 'I couldn't take my eyes off her. There's something very beautiful about her as a woman,' he said. 'Elizabeth Taylor was a very beautiful woman when I made *Virginia Woolf* with her, but I never had the same feeling about her.' During the first meeting in his office with Barbra, Matthau, and Gene Kelly, Barbra said to Lehman, 'Ernie, why do you keep looking at me?'

'I don't know,' Lehman replied, flustered.

'Well, please stop looking at me all the time.'

'I can't help it,' he said sheepishly.

'When she was in a room with other people,' Lehman said, 'you wanted to look at her. It was the same way when she was on screen.'

Lehman found charming a habit of Barbra's that grated on those who were less kindly disposed to her. 'Barbra used to eat food off my plate. I'd be hungry, and she'd eat the food right out from under my mouth. She has all kinds of little things that she does. She doesn't say to herself, "Oh, I mustn't do that, that wouldn't be proper." She does whatever she feels like doing, whatever comes to her mind. I found it sort of friendly; there's an intimacy to someone eating off your plate. I liked Barbra a lot.'

Doubtless this affection led Lehman to welcome – and to miss, on the rare occasions when they didn't come – the dozens of late-night telephone calls from Barbra during the filming, calls that most other producers would have considered a nuisance. 'She used to call me every night for hours,' Lehman recalled. 'She'd talk to me about the day's events. She'd say, "Walter did this to me, Gene did that to me." "Why doesn't Dolly say so-and-so instead of so-and-so?" "Will you please tell Gene to do so-and-so?" "I wish he wouldn't do so-and-so all the time." The calls didn't annoy me because I stay up real late anyway. When she *didn't* call I'd think, Call and harass me, *please!*'

WHILE BARBRA AND Walter Matthau worked in an atmosphere of mutual distaste, she and Gene Kelly got along only marginally better. 'Who would get along with Gene Kelly?' Ernest Lehman asked. 'He's a tough guy. He would grin and smile and laugh and all that, but he was no pussycat. Once I made a suggestion to Michael Crawford about how he should play a close-up, and Kelly said to me, "If you ever talk to another one of my actors on the set I'll kick your fucking teeth in."

'Kelly didn't like Barbra . . . They were not meant to communicate on this earth. They didn't even like being around each other. She complained a lot to me about Kelly in those late-night telephone calls. She didn't like him. She didn't like the fact that he didn't care enough about directing her.

'Barbra was a frightened woman. She had had William Wyler and Herb Ross to guide her through her insecurities on *Funny Girl*, and she was familiar with that role. She was unsure how to play Dolly, and Gene Kelly wasn't helping her any.'

Kelly has admitted that he let Barbra down. 'If there had been more time,' he said, 'I'd have tried to help her work out a clear-cut characterization, but we had a tight schedule, and I left it up to her. With the result that she was being Mae West one minute, Fanny Brice the other, and Barbra Streisand the next. Her accent varied as much as her mannerisms. She kept experimenting with new things out of sheer desperation, none of which really worked. And as she's such a perfectionist, she became terribly neurotic and insecure.'

Kelly resented most of Barbra's suggestions, and usually ignored them. At the end of the huge 'Before the Parade Passes By' number, which utilized nearly 3,800 extras, Lehman's script called for a rolling shot that would leave Barbra in the center of the screen and then go wide to show most of the parade around her. Kelly shot it differently. Barbra complained. He would not reshoot the number, Kelly told her – that was the way he liked it. Barbra started to argue. Kelly walked away.

Barbra called Lehman that night and told him, 'Ernie, I think you should know that Gene didn't shoot the last part of the parade number the way you wrote it. He shot straight down so all you could see are a few people marching by the camera. It would be much better the way you originally intended it.'

Lehman immediately telephoned Kelly. 'He was very angry,' Lehman recalled. 'But I told him that he'd better shoot it the way I wrote it – I thought that was understood. He gave me all the reasons why he did it his way. I said, "No." He said, "Okay, you know what, you direct it! Tomorrow morning at nine o'clock you be out there. I'm calling back all the extras and you're gonna direct the shot!"

'I had never directed traffic! But I went out there and Kelly called out over the bullhorn, "We're ready for you, Mr Lehman," and I shlumped into my jacket and walked over and climbed up on the boom and did the shot. It's that fabulous shot of Barbra holding that last note seemingly forever while the parade marches on. And I did it!

'The next day Gene and I were watching the dailies. His shot came on and he didn't say a word. Later he told me, "Jesus, my shot was awful. I'm glad you redid it."'

Barbra brought Jason to the set often, and the eighteen-month-old toddler watched wide-eyed as his mother cavorted around in enormous hats and glittery dresses. 'He came when we were doing the "Hello, Dolly!" number,' Barbra recalled. 'There I was, his *mother*, in a red wig and a gold dress, with a strange man on each side of her, and he got upset. He didn't like it. I got embarrassed with him watching me. It was like having my mother watch me – because she *knows* I'm just pretending and it's not really me at all.'

Jason got used to his mother as Dolly Levi, though, so much so that one of his first words was 'hat.' For Mother's Day in May, Elliott decided to surprise Barbra by having Jason sing to her. He rehearsed the boy and then coached him from the sidelines as he sang 'Hello, Dolly!' to his delighted mother.

Walter Matthau didn't act very kindly toward Jason – largely, it seems, to annoy Barbra. He insisted on talking baby talk to the child, even after

Barbra explained that she didn't approve of that sort of thing. 'The only way to bring up kids,' Matthau announced, 'is to talk baby talk to 'em and beat 'em.' Barbra grabbed Jason and said she was taking him for a ride. 'Gonna make poo-poo in the car, Jason?' Matthau taunted. Mother and son hurried off.

Matthau seemed to take great delight in harassing Barbra. With his sweat suit soaking wet one day after a jog, he said to her, 'I don't have anything on under this. Doesn't that excite you?'

THE FILMING OF *Hello, Dolly!* grew more and more nightmarish. Twentieth Century-Fox's original budget projection of $10 million had already ballooned to $15 million and would wind up in excess of $24 million, expensive today but staggering in 1968. Lehman walked around the set looking morose, worried about everything. Egos slammed into each other like prize-fighters' fists. Irene Sharaff designed Dolly's 1890s wardrobe, including the sparkling gold gown she wears for her return to the Harmonia Gardens and the 'Hello, Dolly!' number. As Barbra rehearsed her dance steps for the scene while wearing the gown, she and the film's choreographer, Michael Kidd, realized that the dress's lengthy train hindered her ability to dance.

Lehman called Sharaff down to the set. Kidd explained the problem. Sharaff said she didn't see why there should be a problem. Kidd asked Barbra and the waiters to go through the number. As before, both she and the other dancers tripped on the train at several points. Sharaff puffed on a cigarette and suggested that Kidd change the choreography. Kidd said he couldn't do that. Barbra agreed that he shouldn't do that. Lehman took Barbra's side.

Ultimately, the train went, and so did Sharaff. 'Irene announced to me and Barbra,' Lehman said, 'that she never again would make another picture with either of us. She won three Oscars on pictures of mine, and here she was never gonna work with me again because of that infernal gown.'

The only time Ernest Lehman challenged Barbra was during a recording session. He listened to her sing one of the show's tunes, then said, 'To hell with all this being polite stuff. You didn't sing the melody on that final word in the second chorus.'

Barbra looked at him coldly. 'Do you realize, Mr Lehman, how much people pay me not to sing the melody?'

ONE POTENTIAL PERSONALITY clash never occurred. It was Lehman's idea to use the legendary sixty-eight-year-old trumpeter and vocalist Louis 'Satchmo' Armstrong in the 'Hello, Dolly!' number. 'Satchmo had such a huge hit with that song,' he recalled. 'He was more associated with it than Carol Channing was. I thought it would be great to have him join Barbra in the middle of it – a real audience-pleaser. Barbra didn't like the idea.'

Barbra has said that she felt using Armstrong in the film smacked of exploitation, but Lehman suspects her reasoning was more selfish. 'I'm sure she was afraid that this guy was gonna take her big moment away. She didn't get to sing two of the best songs in the score ['Ribbons Down My Back' and 'It Only Takes a Moment'], but this one number made up for that. And here I wanted her to share it with Louis Armstrong. She never dug in her heels and refused to work with him or anything. She just said she didn't think it was a good idea. But she loved Satchmo, and they got along great. And of course his appearance just makes an incredible number even more incredible. It's great to have the two of them onscreen together.'

Finally, in July, after eighty-nine grueling days, *Hello, Dolly!* was in the can. Everyone dispersed, and Ernest Lehman waited nervously for Gene Kelly to show him his cut.

Barbra called late one night and asked Lehman if she could keep the expensive Victorian antiques that the studio had bought to grace her dressing room during the shoot. 'The studio said absolutely not,' Lehman recalled, 'so I had to say to Barbra that I couldn't do it. She said, "What do you mean you can't do it? You're the producer." She didn't understand that it didn't matter that I was the producer. It was the studio that owned what she wanted, and they didn't want to give it to her.

'As a result, she was no longer friendly toward me. I asked her why, and she said, "Because you never gave me what I wanted. The most valuable possession I own is my friendship, and therefore I'm withholding it from you."'

Several years later Lehman ran into Barbra at a play. 'She greeted me warmly,' he recalled. Apparently she hadn't held a grudge.

WHEN LEHMAN SAW Kelly's cut, he was thrilled with both Barbra's and Matthau's performances but thought the movie, filled as it was with Michael Kidd's brilliant, obligatory dance numbers, was too long. Knowing the next-to-impossibility of making any drastic cuts, Lehman decided to defer to the creative decisions of studio heads Richard Zanuck and David Brown. The film, they felt, should be released exactly as it was.

The big question was when. In 1965, when Fox purchased the movie rights from David Merrick for $2.1 million and a large percentage of the gross, Merrick had insisted on a contract clause that said the film could not be released until the show had closed on Broadway. At the time studio executives didn't think that would present a problem. But here it was nearly four years later, the film would soon be ready for release, and *Hello, Dolly!* was still going strong on Broadway even after Channing left it, thanks to Merrick's showmanship in casting stars like Ethel Merman, Ginger Rogers, and Pearl Bailey (in an all-black version) to replace her. There was no end in sight to the Broadway run, the studio wanted to start recouping its enormous investment as soon as possible, and the only way they could do that was for Brown to persuade David Merrick to alter the deal. While the two men negotiated, the movie version of *Hello, Dolly!* stayed on the shelf.

17

I nside Manhattan's Criterion Theater, Barbra sat with Ray Stark and Marty Erlichman and fidgeted nervously. It was September 18, 1968, and *Funny Girl* was about to have its world premiere. She had arrived with Elliott looking every inch the movie star in a nude-colored net gown and cape designed by her favorite couturier Arnold Scaasi and a towering wig in the French Directoire style. Surrounded by a dozen burly bodyguards, she made her way regally up the red carpet leading to the theater entrance as fans cheered, flashbulbs popped, and reporters hurled questions.

How would the public like the film? How would they like *her?* Advance word from screenings in the Midwest had been excellent, and Columbia had launched one of the most ambitious publicity and promotion campaigns in Hollywood history to support the picture. The film would be an exclusive 'road show' attraction, with advance reservations required for tickets at a sliding price scale topped at a hefty (for 1968) six dollars. Six months before the film opened, it had drawn the largest advance ticket sale in history. There were fashion and merchandising tie-ins, including a *Funny Girl* wristwatch, long before such things were commonplace, and audiences could purchase a slick, colorful, picture-packed forty-eight-page program.

Still Barbra had good reason to be nervous. With all the excitement that surrounded the film, she had never seen it with an audience, and she honestly didn't know how people would respond to it. It didn't take long to find out. After her first song, 'I'm the Greatest Star,' the Criterion viewers burst into spontaneous, prolonged applause. And they did so again after just about every number. No one had seen anything like it. 'Audiences *never* do that!' Ray Stark marveled. 'At the *end* of a movie I've seen people applaud, but not all through it! This was like an opening night on Broadway!'

Barbra's motion picture debut turned out to be the most dazzling in show business history. Not only was this $10 million movie built around her diminutive shoulders, but she had thrillingly succeeded at everything the script asked of her. She sang breathtakingly, mugged hilariously, and then broke audiences' hearts with dramatic scenes in which she never hit a false note.

The public flocked to the picture. It grossed $66 million in the United States alone, an enormous sum for the period, and *Funny Girl* remained among the top twenty all-time moneymaking movies for years.

Many of the reviews criticized the film's sometimes 'irritatingly fake' look, Wyler's often 'ponderous' direction, and the talky letdown of the second half after a thrilling first hour of song and comedy, but almost to a man and woman they praised Streisand. To Martin Knelman of the *Toronto Star*, Barbra's performance was 'one of the greatest events in the history of movie musicals.' Joseph Morgenstern of *Newsweek* felt that 'a star is not born in *Funny Girl* . . . a star comes of age . . . Miss Streisand has matured into a complete performer and delivered the most accomplished and enjoyable musical comedy performance that has ever been captured on film.'

'Every age has its Super Lady,' Rex Reed wrote in *Women's Wear Daily*. 'Other ages had Lillian Russell and Sarah Bernhardt and Gertrude Lawrence and Helen Morgan and Judy Garland. Well, we've got ours. Her name is Barbra and whether we like it or not, all those monstrous things she keeps doing to people out of fear and insecurity only make her more exciting on screen. When all that talent comes to a boiling, raging, ferocious head of fireball steam, as it does in *Funny Girl*, bad publicity pales in the glow of her extraordinary genius.'

A series of equally successful premieres followed in Hollywood, London, and Paris. In London, Barbra crossed paths again with Princess Margaret following the screening, and she seemed just as ill at ease as she had two years earlier. Omar Sharif lent a hand by chatting charmingly with the princess. Margaret laughed. 'I see that your co-star is helping you out again,' she said to Barbra. At a benefit gala at Claridge's afterward, Barbra conversed with guests rather than heed a musical cue ('People') to enter the main ballroom. Margaret nudged her: 'I think you ought to go in, dear. They're playing your tune.'

At the gala that evening, Barbra met the attractive, Continentally dashing forty-nine-year-old bachelor prime minister of Canada, Pierre Elliott Trudeau. As keen observers watched them deep in conversation, they couldn't help but wonder, Were those *sparks* they saw?

Barbra next moved on to Paris, where the legendary boulevardier Maurice Chevalier escorted her from her suite at the Plaza Athenée Hotel to the Paris Opéra. 'We set off like two newlyweds in a Rolls-Royce provided by Columbia,' Chevalier wrote in his memoirs. 'We had to take an extra turn around the block when we got to the Opéra in order not to make our entrance too soon.'

When they arrived, bedlam broke out. As they began to ascend the grand stairs of the opera house, one hundred and fifty photographers from nearly every European country crashed through police barricades and pushed Barbra along a wave of humanity up the stairs, flashbulbs bursting, curses flying in five languages. 'Finally we made it to the top,' Chevalier recalled. 'We'd been hoisted up . . . almost without touching the ground.'

Barbra had been terrified of being crushed to death in a stampede, and she would remember that fear far more clearly than the accolades and hosannas thrown her way. 'I could see that she was a bundle of nerves just barely under control,' Chevalier said. Still, the evening was 'a triumph. Paris, the toughest of judges, was enchanted. Judaism's loveliest flower had captivated the hearts of Paris as completely as young Lindbergh did many years ago.'

THE ENORMOUS SUCCESS of *Funny Girl* propelled the sound-track album from the film to number twelve on *Billboard*'s Top 100 Albums chart for the week of January 25, 1969. The charting was noteworthy in light of the dramatic shift in pop music taste that had occurred by the second half of the 1960s, a phenomenon Barbra would soon have to confront. Hers was the best-selling album of traditional pop music that week; artists charted above her included the Young Rascals, the Beatles, the Rolling Stones, Steppenwolf, Janis Joplin, and Iron Butterfly.

Prior to *Funny Girl*, Barbra had produced two studio albums of varying concept and quality. The first, *Simply Streisand*, allowed her to put her personal stamp on a collection of (mostly) great American standards, but the arrangements were at once too much and not enough. A mellow jazzlike orchestration introduced almost every song, but soon gave way to soaring strings and brass in support of Barbra's patented vocal crescendos. The background choruses on some of the tracks bring uncomfortably to mind the kind of generic, middle-of-the-road sound Barbra and Marty had fought against when she signed her Columbia contract five years earlier.

Just weeks after the release of *Simply Streisand*, Barbra signed a new contract with Columbia. Clive Davis had taken over most of the label's business dealings from Goddard Lieberson, and he recalled the Streisand negotiations as 'intense.' Marty Erlichman was adamant that Barbra should receive a much larger slice of the financial pie this time. He eventually won a guaranteed advance of $850,000 per album, a royalty of forty cents for each disc sold, and ten cents for every single. The new Streisand contract drew press attention when it was revealed that her per-album royalty exceeded that of the Beatles by one cent.

Released almost simultaneously with *Simply Streisand* was a package that struck many as a surprise: *Barbra Streisand/A Christmas Album*. Holiday albums were almost de rigueur for popular singers, but because of Barbra's renowned Jewishness, some observers raised an eyebrow, especially since many of Streisand's song selections were religious rather than secular ('Silent Night,' 'Ave Maria'). Columbia rushed the album into release in October 1967, and Barbra's fans and music critics alike greeted it warmly. As it turned out, there were few objections from either Jewish or Christian organizations. By now Barbra Streisand had become so interwoven into the broad fabric of American popular culture that her religion mattered not a whit when it came to what she sang.

FUNNY GIRL PLAYED for over a year at its exclusive-run theaters in the United States before going into wider general release, an unprecedented run. Barbra had achieved her greatest dream: now she was indeed a *movie star*. She had conquered every major realm of show business, and she might have been the happiest woman in the world. But in a sadly real Hollywood cliché, her marriage had come to an end.

The Goulds made a joint announcement of their separation on February 13, 1969. Barbra seemed to hope for an eventual reconciliation. 'We are separating not to destroy our marriage but to save it,' she told a reporter. Conventional wisdom had it that the Gould marriage was destroyed by one partner's career exploding while the other's languished. Certainly this was part of the problem. 'Her success was painful to me,' Elliott admitted to *Playboy* in 1970. 'When Barbra became an enormous celebrity, I tried my damnedest not to take seriously the fact that I wasn't . . . But when we went out in public, which was seldom, it was devastating to me. I didn't want to be there. I wanted to go someplace as *me*. And yet I felt an obligation to attend to my wife, no matter who the fuck people thought I was . . . Mr Streisand or whatever.'

Elliott might have been able to live with the inequality of his professional success and that of his wife, he said, if Barbra had been more attentive to him. 'She was so in love with her work and the image of herself she was creating, there was no time for me,' he told Trudi Pacter of the London *Sunday Mirror*.

Years later Elliott intimated that the failure of his marriage had more to do with Barbra's deep-seated psychological problems than with her success. 'I don't think she knew how to love me back,' he told another British reporter,

Corinna Horan. 'She was incapable of real love because she never had it from her father.' He said he had once told her, 'Your mother thinks affection is something people use to get something,' and she had replied, 'That's why I am the way I am.'

His love for Barbra was 'pure' and 'never exploitative,' Elliott insisted, but he felt he had been 'taken in' by the 'trap' of believing Barbra was vulnerable. 'She uses her vulnerability and insecurities as a seduction,' he told Horan. 'But she's not vulnerable . . . She is very cold, smart and acutely business-oriented and she keeps herself isolated to maintain the status quo of her situation . . . She must be the most miserable person I've ever known. She keeps herself occupied with so many things because she's so afraid to fail, so afraid of the truth.'

To Diana Lurie of the *Ladies' Home Journal* Gould said, 'One side of Barbra needed me. The other was disdainful of men – and competitive toward them. Barbra has ambivalent feelings about men . . . She has a problem that she can't reconcile – [she feels] that men are no good and can't be trusted. My adoration of her caused her to lose respect for me, to think less of me. She wondered how I could like her when she didn't really like herself.'

Elliott revealed his bitterness when he was asked about a comment he had made years earlier, that being married to Barbra was like 'a bath of lava.'

'It was never that hot,' he said.

Over the years, Barbra has been as silent on the reasons for the breakup as Elliott has been talkative. Her only comment was that she was 'so deeply wounded' during her marriage that 'I thought I would never give myself to any man again . . . We did nothing but battle day and night.'

One can certainly speculate about the difficulties Barbra faced being married to Elliott, above and beyond the problems created by her success. There was his gambling, which had grown worse with every passing year. 'I lost a great deal,' Elliott said, most of it on football games. 'I bet on every game on the boards, thousands on a game,' he told *Playboy*. 'I wasn't very successful. I lost close to $50,000 on the football season before last.' Since Elliott had no income of his own, it seems a safe assumption that the money he was losing was Barbra's.

A close friend of Elliott's, who spoke on the condition of anonymity, said that Gould's gambling 'had to affect his marriage to Barbra; I'm a recovering gambler myself, so I know how it can affect one's personal life. And I bet it didn't help their sex life, either. If you know anything about gamblers, sex is the last thing on their minds. Gambling was kind of an escape for him because it must have been awful frustrating for him to be Mr Streisand. Some guys turn to drugs and booze; other guys turn to gambling.'

Elliott did turn to drugs as well. The mid-sixties marked the beginning of a social revolution in America: drugs like marijuana and amphetamines – earlier found only among jazz-club denizens, the ultrasophisticated, and hardcore addicts – had by 1968 made their way to most college campuses, where students considered drug experimentation a badge of honor. Fearful, Barbra shied away from any mind-altering substances at this juncture, but Elliott developed a heavy pot and upper habit. He admitted that he sometimes smoked while he worked but would abstain when he needed to be sharper.

In his *Playboy* interview he described taking mescaline, a hallucinogen, and then going to Disneyland, where he watched for hours as Indian dancers did the same act every twenty minutes. On the way home he 'put on a fantastic demonstration' of driving over winding canyon roads, feeling that his senses and reflexes were incredibly sharp. But he became paranoid, he said, and grew convinced that there was a monster in the back seat of his car. 'I scared the shit out of myself. I had to really assure myself that I didn't want to do me any harm and that what was going on was something promoted by my subconscious.'

It could not have been easy for Barbra to be married to Elliott at this time.

DESPITE THE BREAKUP, Barbra asked Elliott to escort her to the forty-first annual Academy Awards ceremony at the Dorothy Chandler Pavilion on April 14, 1969. *Funny Girl* had been nominated for eight Oscars, including Best Picture and Best Actress. Barbra desperately wanted the award, yet another facet of her lifelong dream and, as Marty Erlichman had told her in the kitchen of the Bon Soir nine years earlier, 'the biggest one of all.' She wasn't at all confident that she would win because the competition that year was unusually strong. The other nominees were Katharine Hepburn in *The Lion in Winter*, Patricia Neal in *The Subject Was Roses*, Joanne Woodward in *Rachel, Rachel*, and Vanessa Redgrave in *Isadora*.

Unquestionably, 1968 felt like 'Streisand's year,' but there was animosity toward Barbra among many of the 2,900 Academy voters, and that surely would hurt her chances, since the Oscars have often been based as much on popularity as on merit. For all these reasons, the Oscar derby in 1968 proved extremely difficult to handicap. Streisand and Hepburn were considered the front-runners, but who could be sure? Barbra had, in fact, convinced herself she wouldn't win, and she tried not to think about the awards. 'I'm very Jewish,' she said. 'I always think negative. You never think about things like that – bad luck!'

At the event, Barbra sat nervously for over two hours – the Best Actress award was the second-to-last, before Best Picture. *Funny Girl* hadn't won a single award all evening, and Barbra grew surer than ever that she wouldn't either. She was also nervous about Elliott. He had arrived to pick her up high on marijuana, and she hoped no one would notice. Elliott needed to get stoned, he said, because 'I was terribly self-conscious about being with a woman from whom I had just separated and about being among people I felt weird about, people who thrive on the dramatic implications of that kind of situation,' he told *Playboy*. 'It was a difficult night for me, a trauma.' No one noticed Elliott's condition, except a friend whom he had told to watch for a signal: if he was stoned, he'd tug on his ear twice when the camera first panned to him and Barbra. He did so.

Finally the elegant Ingrid Bergman began to read the Best Actress nominees. Barbra stared numbly straight ahead. Bergman opened the envelope and gasped. 'It's a . . . It's a tie! The winners are Katharine Hepburn . . . and Barbra Streisand!' It was the first Oscar tie since 1932. Barbra turned joyfully to Elliott and ran up to the stage, tripping briefly over the hem of her sequined see-through black net pantsuit.

Jack Brodsky, Columbia's head publicist, had suggested her opening line – the same she had used in the film. 'Hello, gorgeous!' she exclaimed as she held the gold-plated statuette aloft. 'I'm very honored to be in such magnificent company as Katharine Hepburn. Gee whiz, it's kind of a wild feeling. Sitting there tonight I was thinking that the first script of *Funny Girl* was written when I was only eleven years old. Thank God it took so long to get it right, you know? I would like to thank my co-producer, Ray Stark, for waiting until I grew up.' She thanked the film's creative team, then concluded, 'Somebody once said to me – asked me if I was happy, and I said, "Are you kidding? I'd be miserable if I was happy!" And I'd like to thank all the members of the Academy for making me really miserable. Thank you!'

At the Governors Ball following the ceremony, Barbra seemed a little stunned. She sat quietly at her table, showing no emotion but repeatedly running her long-nailed fingers up and down the Oscar. Elliott sat uneasily next to her and remained silent, drawing little circles and squares with his fork on the tablecloth, answering yes or no and then clamming up whenever a reporter asked him a question. Barbra didn't eat any of her dinner, but she picked cherry tomatoes off the plate of everyone else at her table.

Controversy marred Barbra's triumph the next day when many commentators roundly criticized her outfit, designed for the Oscar ceremonies by Arnold Scaasi. 'Inappropriate,' they called it, 'a monumental salute to bad taste.' Barbra looked 'like a fugitive from a harem,' sniffed one fashion maven, and another expressed horror that 'Miss Streisand was naked as a jay bird, the "loincloth" having narrowed to the width of a garter belt in back, leaving her plump bare rear exposed to the audience who had to witness her ascent to the stage.'

Scaasi considers the criticism unjustified. 'The outfit seemed see-through, but it wasn't really,' he said. 'It was underlined with nude-colored georgette crepe. There were pockets over the bosom with double and triple fabric – if you look closely at the outfit there's nothing indecent about it at all. But none of us considered what would happen under glaring lights, or when the flashbulbs went off. The lights eliminated the black net covering [and] made it seem that you were seeing Barbra's skin.'

Before the ceremonies, Barbra and Scaasi had attended a small party at the Starks'. 'Fran Stark was a very elegant woman, on the best-dressed list,' Scaasi said, 'and when she saw Barbra walk in wearing this pantsuit with little white kid gloves and a black satin bag, she said to me, "You've just made her look spectacular. She looks like a great model! She reminds me of Jean Shrimpton." What I tried to do was present Barbra as the modern young woman she was. Young girls were wearing things like that all over the world. Barbra had an older image because of *Funny Girl*, but this night she could be herself, her own person, youthful and current. We just never realized what would happen when those flashbulbs went off!'

ON APRIL 21, 1969, Louis Kind died of congestive heart failure at the age of seventy-six in the Veterans Administration Hospital on First Avenue and Twenty-fourth Street in Manhattan. He had been barely well enough the week before to watch the stepdaughter he had treated so cruelly win her profession's highest accolade.

Roslyn attended her father's funeral with Diana, who had legally remained Lou Kind's wife. Barbra stayed away. Months later Kind's will was made public. He left an estate worth about $93,000, which he divided among Roslyn – 'my world, my beloved daughter' – and his three children from his first marriage. He expressly excluded Diana from the will and made no mention of Barbra.

A few days after his death, the *New York Post* ran a prominent obituary of Louis Kind. They did so, of course, only because of his relationship to Barbra Streisand.

18

Huge movie lights illuminated the banquet hall of the magnificently baroque Royal Pavilion in Brighton, England, built in the early eighteenth century as a seaside playground for King George IV. Dozens of extras, dressed in sumptuous Regency period costumes designed by Sir Cecil Beaton, sat around an enormous table set with gold decanters, fine cut glass, silver bowls overflowing with fruit, and place settings that cost a total of $75,000. Capons, lobsters, and suckling pigs dotted the table, and dozens more were kept at the ready in the wings for retakes. Actors dressed as waiters in black uniforms with gold braid and white gloves waited for the director to yell 'Action!' In the meantime, all eyes were on *her*.

Barbra looked breathtaking, a vision in white, dressed in a resplendent low-cut pure white crepe gown sprinkled with thousands of tiny beads and diamonds. She wore a diamond-studded choker and a white turban festooned with cameos and strings of pearls that dangled across her forehead and down the sides of her neck.

Her director, Vincente Minnelli, waited for her to signal that she was ready to begin the scene for *On a Clear Day You Can See Forever* in which Melinda Winifred Waine Moorepark, a buxom, sensual courtesan, seduces Robert Tentrees, a dazzling young aristocrat, across the banquet table with her eyes, her wineglass, and her sexual allure while she sings 'Love with All the Trimmings' as an interior monologue.

The handsome blond English actor John Richardson played Tentrees, and he sat across the table from Barbra, waiting along with everyone else for her to be ready. Suddenly she signaled to Minnelli that she needed to talk with him. The sixty-year-old creator of some of the most joyful and elegant MGM musicals of the 1940s and 1950s came down from his loft next to the camera boom and huddled with his leading lady. They whispered for a few moments, then Minnelli walked over to the producer, Howard Koch, and conveyed a message.

Koch approached Richardson, who got up from the table and left. Several crew members scurried around and erected a black screen across the spot where Richardson had been sitting. 'Barbra didn't want to do this highly sexual emoting while she looked at John Richardson,' Koch recalled. 'She didn't think Richardson was masculine enough, so she wanted to think of somebody else. We set the black up so that she wouldn't be distracted by anything, and I took Richardson out onto the street and told him, "Come on, it's a close-up of Barbra; you don't have to be there." He wasn't upset or anything, he was a hell of a nice guy.'

Minnelli filmed the scene in adoring close-up, and Barbra brought to it a steamy sensuality that nearly melted the film stock. 'She imagined her own man that she was playing it to,' Koch said. 'Later on I said to her, "Tell me who you were thinking of!" She said, "I'll never tell!" And she never did.'

ON A CLEAR DAY had been a financial failure on Broadway during the 1966 season. With lyrics and script by Alan Jay Lerner (*My Fair Lady, Camelot*) and music by Burton Lane, the show starred Barbara Harris as Daisy Gamble, a college student from Mahwah, New Jersey, who asks a psychology professor who specializes in hypnosis to cure her addiction to cigarettes. While under hypnosis she reveals a prior incarnation as Melinda Tentrees. The professor, although annoyed by Daisy's chatty, vapid personality and 'Joisey' inflections, finds himself falling in love with the elegant, sexy, willful, and soignée Melinda.

When Daisy, who is attracted to the professor, finds out about his feelings for 'the previous me' she is furious and refuses to be hypnotized again. He persuades her to go under one more time, during which she reveals prior and future incarnations as his wife. He's not sure he wants to hear more and lets her leave. 'So long, Doctor,' she says. 'See ya later.'

Despite the failure of the stage version, Paramount Pictures bought the film rights for $750,000 in the Hollywood frenzy for musical properties that followed the blockbuster success of *The Sound of Music*. The studio's vice president in charge of production, Howard Koch, decided to personally produce the film, with a budget of $10 million. He knew immediately who should play Daisy. 'I'd seen Barbra on Broadway,' he said, 'and thought she was stunning. She'd already been signed for the movie version of *Funny Girl* so it was pretty clear that she was going to be a success in Hollywood. We figured she'd be great in *Clear Day*.'

Koch approached Barbra while she was in London doing *Funny Girl*. She had liked the show on Broadway, but she was so preoccupied with the impending birth of Jason that the last thing she wanted to think about was work, and she turned him down. Koch then offered the role to Audrey Hepburn, but she declined as well because she felt that the Regency sequences were too close to her role in *My Fair Lady*. Unwilling to give up on Barbra, Koch came back to her in 1967, and in addition to a salary of $350,000, he offered her the chance to choose or approve the film's entire creative team. She agreed to make the movie.

Koch had been close to signing the Irish actor Richard Harris, who had made a strong impression as King Arthur in the 1967 screen version of *Camelot*, to play the professor when the actor 'walked out on it because he got a better deal or something,' Koch said. When Frank Sinatra and Gregory Peck turned the part down, Koch turned to the romantic French balladeer Yves Montand. Montand was a huge star in France, but he had failed to make much of an impact on American audiences, most notably opposite Marilyn Monroe in *Let's Make Love* in 1960. Still, he seemed perfect for the part, which had originally been written as a Frenchman. Koch brought him to meet Barbra.

Montand, like Omar Sharif, turned on his charm for Barbra. He kissed her hand and told her he considered her 'incomparable.' She had listened to some of his French recordings and liked his warm, masculine singing. She told Koch that Montand would be just fine. Rounding out the cast were Larry Blyden as Daisy's stuffy fiancé and the struggling thirty-one-year-old Jack Nicholson in the small role of Tad Pringle, her free-spirited former stepbrother.

Vincente Minnelli, famous for his exquisite taste and an Oscar winner as director of the elegant 1958 Best Picture, *Gigi*, also seemed to Koch a natural for the film, especially the sequences in Regency England. 'I had worked with him at Metro when I was an assistant director, and I knew that if anybody could do a picture with that kind of style it would be him.' For the same reasons Barbra asked that the period costumes be created by Cecil Beaton, who had won Oscars for his designs for *Gigi* and *My Fair Lady*. The contemporary outfits would be designed by Arnold Scaasi.

The regression sequences of *On a Clear Day* offered Barbra the kind of movie glamour she had always dreamed about. One of the reasons she hadn't been eager to play Dolly Levi was that she considered the character too plain. 'I'd really like to play very exciting women,' she had said. 'Nineteenth-century courtesans who had ten lovers, that sort of thing. That's my fantasy.'

Melinda was exactly that, and Barbra worked excitedly with Cecil Beaton to create the most gorgeous gowns for her character to wear. The flamboyantly stylish sixty-three-year-old royal photographer and confidant of Greta Garbo came to respect and adore Streisand. 'She was charming to work with,' he said. 'Almost literally, like a hypnotist. Barbra and I talked our way into everything, and I trusted her judgment . . . I've never met anyone so young who had such an awareness and knowledge of herself. Pleasing her was very difficult, but it pleased me inwardly because I myself am extremely hard to please . . . She is an ideal mannequin and compelling actress in elegant period costumes. Her face is a painting from several historical eras. She is a self-willed creation.'

When Barbra arrived on the set for the banquet sequence swathed in white and 'looking like an Arabian princess,' she had clipped a diamond to one of her nostrils. No one liked it. 'I was careful not to draw attention to her nose,' Beaton said. 'The diamond got vetoed. But I admired her very much for having wanted it. I always admire people daring to be different and individual. It isn't the easiest way to go about life, but it is the most interesting.'

Barbra and Vincente Minnelli liked each other immediately. That his accomplishments commanded respect and admiration went without saying, but he was also the ex-husband of Judy Garland, who had touched Barbra so deeply when she appeared on her show in 1963, and the father of her friend Liza Minnelli. Like Beaton, the MGM veteran much admired Barbra's instincts. 'You have to work with people who respect your opinion,' Barbra said. 'Now, Vincente is terrific that way. Even before he saw *Funny Girl* I guess he must have liked my work or something. He didn't come in as the old-time director of many hits and you're just a little girl with one picture, two pictures. He's so open and he trusts my instincts.'

ON A CLEAR DAY proceeded as Barbra's least troubled production to date. There were no blowups between her and Yves Montand, no walk-offs, no standoffs between star and director. Part of the reason, of course, was that with the release of *Funny Girl* Barbra had proven herself as a movie star; she won her Oscar during *Clear Day* filming. No longer could anyone wonder, 'Who does she think she is?' By now everyone knew exactly who she was – the biggest female star in Hollywood – and they treated her accordingly.

That Barbra had mellowed a good deal helped as well. No longer was she so insecure that she refused to back down from an argument. 'I have to compromise,' she said. 'A little. I know that now. I've even come to understand that a little bit of compromise is part of the perfection. Know what I mean? A little bit of imperfection is part of the perfect, because perfection is lifeless and dull.

'I used to have just the instinctive reaction – this is right, or this is wrong – and I couldn't tell why. Now I can tell why. And I'm in a position where I can easily say, "No, not this way." But I hate to. It's much more satisfying to work with someone who gets it. You know, someone who sees it my way or can prove me wrong.'

The *Clear Day* company spent ten days in Brighton for the sequences at the Royal Pavilion. Barbra was fascinated by the ornate, eclectic architecture of the beach palace, reminiscent of the Taj Mahal. 'It's a combination of the grotesque and the beautiful,' she said. 'And it's grotesquely beautiful.'

Barbra had decided not to bring Jason with her such a long way from home, creating their first prolonged separation. 'I miss him terribly,' she said, and she ran up enormous phone bills listening to his baby talk from five thousand miles away.

During the Brighton filming Barbra developed a crush on the dashing thirty-year-old Australian actor George Lazenby, a former model who was starring as James Bond in *On Her Majesty's Secret Service*. 'He would come down on his motorcycle just to see her,' Howard Koch recalled. When the day's work was finished, Barbra – dressed in bell-bottoms and a halter top – would hop up on the seat behind him and they would roar off along the seacoast to have dinner. After a few days of this Barbra invited him up to her hotel suite. They chatted for a while, Lazenby said, then 'I took her in my arms. But something stopped me from going much further. I didn't want her to think little of me . . . But she was very disappointed.'

The next time he was alone with Streisand, Lazenby said, it was Barbra who stopped him when he began to kiss her. 'She wasn't interested, she said, in a casual affair,' he recalled. 'She wanted me to be her one and only.' Although Lazenby found Barbra 'beautiful,' he did not want to commit himself 'body and soul' to anyone, and he left.

A few months later, Lazenby ran into Elliott at a party. 'Gould went red in the face,' Lazenby said, and threatened him with a kitchen knife. One of the other guests grabbed Elliott and pushed him away. Lazenby never saw Barbra again.

THE *CLEAR DAY* company returned to New York in the middle of May 1969 to film a campus demonstration scene at Fordham University. But the school balked at the last minute because actual student demonstrations against President Nixon and the Vietnam War had broken out on campuses across the country; administrators didn't want to risk inciting their students to riot. When Columbia also refused to lend its facilities, Koch shut down filming while he scurried to find a college that would. Finally the University of Southern California agreed, but the company would have to move back to Los Angeles to film the scenes, extending the production schedule.

This created a problem, because Barbra had been guaranteed a finish date in May so that she could begin rehearsals for her return to Las Vegas at the International Hotel early in July. With *Clear Day* behind schedule, her contract expired, and the movie legally had no star. There were rumors that Barbra would hold out for a huge additional salary, but that wasn't what she wanted. 'She asked for certain things that were not in the contract,' Koch recalled, 'like items on the set that she wanted to become her possessions.' Unlike their counterparts at Twentieth Century-Fox, Paramount executives were receptive to the idea. 'We didn't want to pay her more money, so we made a deal with her,' Koch explained. 'It was strange. One of the things she wanted was a trailer . . . and all the furniture in it. All the wardrobe that she wore. Some stained-glass windows we used on the set. I think she probably took seventy to eighty thousand dollars' worth of stuff to her home. It was good for us because those things were expendable anyway.'

'I made some real money on those windows,' Barbra later boasted. 'The studio rented them back from me for five hundred dollars to use in *The Great White Hope*.'

WHILE BARBRA WAS in New York working on *Clear Day*, the Friars, the exclusive all-male theatrical club founded in 1904, paid tribute to her as its entertainer of the year with its annual roast. She was only the second woman so honored; Sophie Tucker had been the first. The star-studded event at the Waldorf-Astoria Hotel on May 16, 1969, attracted hundreds of Barbra's friends, family members, business associates, and colleagues including Ed Sullivan, Ray Stark, Marty Erlichman, Leo Jaffe, Charles Bluhdorn, Howard Koch, Danny Thomas, Ethel Merman, Julie Budd, Steve Lawrence, and Eydie Gormé.

The evening's souvenir program featured written tributes to Barbra, some serious, some tongue-in-cheek, from Erlichman (who signed his name 'Maarty'), Alan Jay Lerner ('She happens to be a miracle'), Jackie Gleason, Joe E. Lewis ('*Time* magazine ran her nose on the cover, and *Newsweek* ran the rest of her'), Jule Styne ('She scares and overpowers you with the magic of her talent'), and Ernest Lehman.

Lehman's tongue-in-cheek essay poked fun at Barbra's penchant for perfection. 'To her, midnight isn't too late to phone the screenwriter and discuss lines. If he happens to be the producer, too, even one o'clock in the morning is all right. But to talk to him for an *hour?* . . . *Two* hours? . . . Just to make a few scenes *better* . . . Just to make the *whole picture* better? What kind of nonsense is that? . . . She'll stay up till four in the morning figuring out how to make it better while she's doing her nails and eating too much chocolate ice cream. But who needs all that passion for excellence? Who needs thrills? Who needs fun? Who needs memorable experiences? I mean, after all, it's only a *movie. Who Needs Barbra Streisand!'*

A highlight of the evening's entertainment program was the serenade to Barbra by seven legendary composers who sang parody lyrics, written by Sammy Cahn, to some of their most famous tunes. Richard Rodgers concluded the musical tributes with his own touchingly re-crafted lyrics to 'The Sweetest Sounds.'

'This was an incredible evening,' Barbra later said. 'To get a sense of what that meant to me, just think about the sweep of those seven careers [that] have given us some of America's most beautiful, moving, and enduring popular music. For them to sing me their songs . . . was an unforgettable honor . . . what fun it was!'

The evening came to a hilarious close when Don Rickles delivered a lengthy monologue of his patented insult humor, liberally sprinkled with Yiddish. 'I'm so fed up with this *feckuckteh* affair,' he began. (*Feckuckteh* is an all-purpose put-down meaning 'silly,' 'useless,' or 'screwed up.') 'Barbra, I say this publicly: I never liked you. Omar Sharif has been my whole life . . . When I first met Barbra [in 1963] I was at the Riviera Hotel and she kept asking me, "Is Liberace queer?" . . . As soon as the career slips, she'll be back to her old job on Coney Island going, "Psst, sailor!" . . . But really, Barbra, God made you a great star. Steve Lawrence and Eydie Gormé kept leaning over to me saying, "We sing better," but unfortunately they're failures . . . As Ed Sullivan has said many times, "Let's really hear it for Barbra Straysang . . . Straymancraitz . . . Barbra Straymaynan!"'

SIX WEEKS LATER Barbra stood in the wings of the concert theater of the spanking-new International Hotel in Las Vegas, waiting to go on. She felt nearly paralyzed with fear. One of the hotel's talent coordinators tried to help. 'Is there anything I can do?' he asked.

'Nothing, thanks,' she replied, her eyes fixed in a vacant stare.

'Look, Miss Streisand. You started in nightclubs. You were a hit on the Broadway stage. You won an Emmy. You won an Oscar your first time out in a movie. Who else ever did all that?'

This was probably the worst thing the man could have said to her at that moment. For it was the audience's exalted expectations that most frightened her. 'All I kept thinking about was, What am I supposed to be? My God, all these people are going to watch me sing. What about what they've read in the papers and what they believe and think . . . the envy and the kind of pedestal they put you on and the negative things they've read about you.

The moment I stepped out onstage I was in shock. It was like, What am I doing here?'

What she was doing was fulfilling a five-year multimillion-dollar contract with the International, entrepreneur Kirk Kerkorian's $60 million, thirty-floor, 1,500-room hotel and casino, the largest in the world. Kerkorian wanted the country's biggest star to open this lavish playground in style, and he first approached Elvis Presley. Presley's manager, Colonel Tom Parker, turned the offer down, unwilling to let his client take the risk of appearing at a brand-new facility before all the inevitable problems with sound, lighting, acoustics, and logistics had been ironed out. 'Let somebody else stick his neck out,' Parker said, then agreed that Elvis would follow whoever opened the hotel. When Kerkorian offered Barbra $100,000 a week and enough stock in the hotel to make her four-week engagement worth $1 million, she decided to stick her neck out.

Barbra liked the idea of being the first act at the heralded new showplace as much as Elvis hadn't. 'We wouldn't have played the hotel,' Marty Erlichman said, 'if she weren't the opening act.'

For some time Marty had been urging Barbra to go back to live performing. She wouldn't consider a tour, with its backbreaking travel schedule, different problems at every stop, weather uncertainties, and likely security lapses. Las Vegas, as much as Barbra loathed it, offered a far more predictable, secure, and comfortable environment. Or at least she *thought* it would.

When she began rehearsals in June, the hotel was so far from completion that Barbra had to wear a hard hat to protect herself against falling plaster and welders' sparks. The drummer Don Lamond was a part of Barbra's thirty-seven-piece orchestra, and he recalled that 'a few days before we opened they hadn't even finished laying the carpets. They were hammering, and things were dropping, and electric drills were humming – all the sounds of a construction site. And Barbra didn't squawk one bit about that. She just went ahead with rehearsal. I know a lot of people I've worked for who would have flipped over that, but she didn't.'

According to Dennis Ritz, the advertising director for the International, when Barbra arrived 'the showroom wasn't ready, and the penthouse she was supposed to stay in definitely wasn't ready, so they got her a little house on the golf course. Marty Erlichman was a wreck. He kept running around going, "She's gonna blow her stack!" But she got here and she was *wonderful*. She never complained a bit.'

'There were no chairs, tables, or booths in the theater,' Marty recalled. 'She was rehearsing in a totally empty room.' So that Barbra could 'get the feel of things' in Vegas, Erlichman took her to some of the other shows around town. At a Dean Martin performance, a heckler got tossed out by two burly security guards. 'If they do that to *him*,' Barbra said, 'What'll they do to *me*?'

Such icy fear gripped Barbra as she prepared to go onstage on her opening night, July 2, that she considered lying on a chaise longue as the curtain went up in case her knees gave way. She nixed that idea, and as the orchestra completed the overture, she summoned up the courage to stride out in front of an anticipatory audience that included Cary Grant, Rudolf Nureyev, Andy Williams, Joe Louis and Sonny Liston, Tony Bennett, Rita Hayworth, Natalie Wood, and Peggy Lee, who was appearing in the hotel's lounge. Barbra had no opening acts, and would not perform while the audience ate dinner. Most of the patrons, seated for dinner at eight-thirty, had grown impatient by the time she appeared at half past ten.

The curtain rose. There was no set, no glitter, no dancing girls. Just Streisand – in denim overalls and a wrinkled shirt. The columnist May Mann described the audience's reaction as 'shock and cold disbelief.' Barbra had meant to make fun of the unfinished condition of the hotel, but because she didn't explain that before she began her first song – 'I Got Plenty of Nothin',' also meant to be a joke – many patrons wondered whether she meant to insult them. 'There was some noise in the audience,' Dennis Ritz recalled. 'I wouldn't say [there were] boos exactly, but it was clear a lot of people thought she was being rude and got offended.'

The audience reaction worsened when Barbra still said nothing to them before she began her second number, the exquisite but languid Rodgers and Hart tune 'My Funny Valentine.' Then she sang four *more* numbers without saying a word between songs. Muted, almost grudging applause followed each number. Barbra sang to perfection, but she didn't seem to care that there was anyone else in the room. There was no kibitzing, no self-effacement, no warmth. And as she felt the lack of response – her worst fear realized – she froze up even more.

'I wanted to be with my audience,' Barbra said, 'and what did I do? I turned them off! I felt hostility coming up on the stage in waves. I worked, but it was total fear time. Of course it showed. They thought I was a snob, but I was really just scared!' By the time Barbra began to talk and joke, she had lost most of the patrons' goodwill. 'The jokes she cracked at the unfinished condition of the hotel,' May Mann wrote, 'rather than making the audience laugh, alienated them. They settled into a cold resentful disgust. If Dean Martin had said the things she had, everyone would have laughed . . . It was embarrassing all the way around. Many people began to walk out as soon as she stole off for a brief intermission to change her costume. She came back wearing a rose pleated chiffon, about which she said, "This was my bedspread. I just thought I'd put it on and make a costume!" Again silence, not laughter.

The harder Barbra tried for sympathy with her audience, the more reserved they became.'

The show ended with a thud, and Barbra, devastated, cried in her dressing room afterward. 'I was in a state of shock. I could feel the hostility of that audience.' She didn't need reviews to tell her that she had just flopped more completely than she had since the Town & Country debacle in Winnipeg nine years earlier, but the next day the critiques appeared anyway. Charles Champlin of the *Los Angeles Times* summed up the general reaction: 'Even allowing for the opening-night tension, Miss Streisand's appearance was a curious, cold, and intensely disappointing eighty minutes' worth. As her admirers know, she has a superb voice, and a spiky directness of manner. The trouble was that manners had become mannerisms. Her performance had been finely calculated, but that magic rapport which Sinatra, Tony Bennett – and [Peggy] Lee – can establish with their audiences never really got going for Barbra . . . Miss Streisand seemed a dazzlingly efficient but chillingly impersonal machine . . . who still has some lessons to learn.'

Barbra knew she had to do something. As Don Lamond recalled, 'One of the critics wrote that Barbra could pick up some pointers from Peggy Lee. Well, don't you know, the next night she went to listen to Peggy. She's never too big to learn something. I really respected her for that . . . And the critics said she laid a big egg because she started the show with "My Funny Valentine" and in Vegas people aren't used to that kind of opening. They like the slam-bang stuff. So she said to us, "I know we got a bad write-up after the opening. Don't let it get to you. We're just going to have to change the opening number." So we changed it to a real roaring start, and then she changed the whole show.'

The next night Barbra began with 'Don't Rain on My Parade.' The rousing anthem excited the audience and put them on Barbra's side immediately, reminding them as it did of her wonderful performance in *Funny Girl*. She followed that with 'People' and 'My Honey's Lovin' Arms' before she got to 'My Funny Valentine.'

She still offered no patter between the first few songs, but this time it didn't matter: the audience burst into wild applause after each number. The chemistry between a performer and an audience is a fragile thread, as Barbra had learned to her chagrin the night before. Put an audience off, and it may be impossible to win them back, no matter what. Put them in the palm of your hand and everything that didn't work the night before will leave them laughing and cheering.

Now they laughed at her jokes. 'This is an absolutely *feckuckteh* place, you know?' she said. 'There are no clocks here. They want everybody out in the casino, so the television sets in your rooms don't work, right? There are no Bibles in the rooms. Even the rooms that have Bibles there's only five commandments. The Jewish Bible, six tops!'

The laughter loosened Barbra up. Before long she had established a warm rapport with her audience. 'And now for your yentatainment pleasure!' she called out at one point. She described her friends Marilyn and Alan Bergman as a 'nice Jewish couple' before she sang their song 'Ask Yourself Why.' Then she described 'Punky's Dilemma' as 'a song by Simon and Garfunkel, another nice Jewish couple.' She said she thought it would be 'the ultimate in chic' to use just a performer's initials on a marquee. 'Of course, that might not be such a good idea for me – or for Tony Bennett!'

The crowd loved it; Barbra had turned everything around. Over the ensuing weeks, Charles Champlin heard such persistent reports that Barbra's show had improved he went back and reviewed it again. This time he found the concert 'a scintillating display of her gifts . . . she seemed to be having a ball, relaxed, amiable and in charge.' The *Los Angeles Times* columnist Joyce Haber agreed: 'I discovered a very improved show. La Streisand got a standing ovation. It was a concert to remember.'

Now Barbra could relax and have fun. 'She had a custom '57 Thunderbird she brought with her, and she used to drive it around town,' Don Lamond recalled. 'She'd wave to people. She was having a ball, once she got settled in.' The bass player Milt Hinton recalled that after her shows Barbra would say, 'Let's go around to the jazz joints,' and they would hop in her car. 'We'd go hear Cannonball Adderley and Joe Williams. She'd sit in the back so no one would recognize her and she could just enjoy the musicians. Joe Williams came to see her show, and she introduced him from the audience. He was one of the few she did that with – she wasn't into that Hollywood thing of lots of back-slapping at all.'

DURING BARBRA'S INTERNATIONAL engagement, an issue of *Ladies' Home Journal* appeared on newsstands containing an interview in which Elliott Gould spoke freely, frankly, and often bitterly about his relationship with her. 'Barbra is really fourteen years old,' the article quoted Gould. 'Here is a girl who is a major star, who makes a fortune, but who is unhappy. It is a pain to hear her complain constantly.' The interview continued at length in a similar vein, and when Barbra read it she became red-faced with fury. According to her hairdresser Fredrick Glaser, she threw everyone out of her dressing room and 'proceeded to tear the place apart.'

ALSO DURING HER Vegas stint, Barbra's twelfth solo album was released. *What About Today?* proved an unsuccessful attempt to move Streisand into the rock genre that had revolutionized popular music. When she was asked about rock 'n' roll in 1965, Barbra had replied, 'Musically, I love it, but there's nothing in it for me to sing.' This album came close to proving her right.

In 1966 a funky new era had dawned at Columbia Records when Clive Davis took over many responsibilities from Goddard Lieberson. Davis wanted to make the label more of a competitor in the pop and rock scene that had exploded in the wake of the 'British invasion' spearheaded by the Beatles in 1964. At the close of 1967, with the relative failure of *Simply Streisand* fresh in his mind, Davis felt it was time the company's top female artist considered singing, if not rock 'n' roll, at least more contemporary pop music. The sales slump Barbra was in, although minor compared to the career-threatening drop-offs suffered by other artists, indicated to Davis that even staunch Streisand fans would be pleased to have their idol take her recording career in a new direction.

Davis was thus delighted when he learned that Barbra had cut some pop singles that were unlike any of her prior efforts. Unfortunately the songs Barbra chose provided little indication that she could make such a transition successfully. The single 'Our Corner of the Night,' backed with 'He Could Show Me,' was released in February 1968 and received scant radio attention, sold abysmally, and confused Barbra's admirers.

Although this first contemporary pop effort of Barbra's failed, Clive Davis was impressed by her willingness to go along with the requirements of the song, no matter how alien they might have seemed to her. She sounded legitimate on the record, not at all like a Broadway diva doing a bit of slumming. It was clear that with the proper material, the Streisand voice and talent could produce a successful contemporary sound.

While the *Hello, Dolly!* company was stationed in Garrison, Davis had paid Barbra a visit, ostensibly to get her approval of photographs to be used in the packaging for the *Funny Girl* sound-track album. He suggested that she continue her efforts to update her musical profile because she was too young and too vital an artist to allow her recording career to stagnate.

Barbra argued with Davis at first, unsure that she should or could make such a dramatic switch in her musical style, but her instincts told her he was right. Aside from the financial rewards that broadening her fan base would surely bring, singing contemporary music would give her a chance to prove to the public that she wasn't just a singer of sound tracks from old-fashioned musicals.

The release of *What About Today?* while Barbra performed at the International symbolized the uneasy mix of old and new on the album, which contains no cut that could in any way be called rock. In brief liner notes, Barbra dedicates *What About Today?* to 'young people who push against indifference, shout down mediocrity, demand a better future and write and sing the songs of today.' Oddly, the songs she chose from Lennon and McCartney, Buffy Sainte-Marie and Paul Simon had nothing to do with relevant issues of the day, while most of the timid protest cuts on the album were from the pens of such establishment composers as Harold Arlen, Michel Legrand, David Shire, and Richard Maltby. Only 'Little Tin Soldier,' a grim antiwar statement by Jimmy Webb, could qualify as any kind of a message from a young artist.

Reviews for *What About Today?* were mixed. 'Because she has adapted these lyrics without altering her distinctive pop style,' *Variety* enthused, 'she retains her vast adult appeal and delivers the young message to rock-deaf ears.' Others felt either that Barbra seemed uncommitted to the material or that the songs weren't up to her usual standards. 'A powerhouse singer like Barbra Streisand thrives best with powerhouse programs,' Greer Johnson wrote in *Cue*. 'She tends to overwhelm flaccid and semi-professional ephemera.'

Commercially, *What About Today?* was a bust. It managed only to reach an unimpressive thirty-one on *Billboard*'s chart, making it Barbra's poorest selling studio album to that date. To Clive Davis's chagrin, *What About Today?* did nothing to help what he hoped would be Streisand's transition to contemporary pop idol. It would be two more years before the right mix of material and talent would come together to ensure Barbra's placement among that hierarchy.

ON JULY 30, 1969, Barbra gave her last performance at the International. Both Don Lamond and Milt Hinton adored Barbra and knew they would miss her. 'I was lucky to work with her,' Hinton said. 'It was amazing to watch her work. If she didn't like an arrangement, she would tear it apart. The arrangers wouldn't like it, but she knew what she was talking about. I was very grateful that she thought enough of me to introduce me during the show. Once she told me that whenever I went into the bar and ordered a drink, I should put it on her tab. "Don't give them your money," she said.'

Don Lamond considered Barbra 'a wonderful person. There were a lot of rumors going around that she was very hard to work for and all that, but to me she wasn't. She just knew what she wanted. She meant no harm to anybody. That engagement in Vegas was one of the best times I ever had in my life.'

Of course, not everyone reacted so positively to Barbra. Joy Simmons, a cocktail waitress in Las Vegas for twenty years, found Streisand 'rude,' 'demanding,' and with 'no respect' for the hotel staff. 'You get to know who is nice and who isn't,' Simmons said. 'The word gets spread around town like wildfire. There are four people who waiters, bartenders, and service people of all kinds hate in Vegas . . . and Barbra Streisand [is one of them] . . . Barbra is rude and will pretend like she is deaf rather than wave to and acknowledge someone who calls to her or asks for an autograph. She would have a drink once in a while but would never ever tip. She never tipped for room service. No one wanted to take food up to her because the toast might be too cool, too hot, or too light and she'd have you fired, especially if she suspected the least bit of sarcasm in your tone when you delivered something to her. She's had a lot of people fired from their jobs. Sinatra gets moody and may get mad at you, but later he'll feel guilty and has been known to tip a hundred dollars even if you've spilled a drink on him by accident. Barbra wouldn't even give us a dollar or a free album when we asked for one.'

ELVIS PRESLEY WAS scheduled to follow Barbra at the International – an engagement that would be a triumphant comeback – and he caught her next-to-last show. She introduced him to the audience, and afterward he went backstage to meet her. Don Lamond passed him in the hallway and was impressed by how good the thirty-four-year-old Presley, who had been out of the public eye for a while, looked. 'I think he was the handsomest guy I ever saw. This was before he got bloated and all that stuff. My wife said she couldn't believe how fantastic he looked. He went into Barbra's dressing room, and they got together.'

Years later Barbra's longtime lover, Jon Peters, revealed in an unpublished interview the extraordinary scene that followed, recounted to him by Barbra. She was alone, sitting at her dressing table. After Elvis closed the door behind him, he said simply, 'Hi,' and an awkward silence followed. Suddenly he reached over and picked up a bottle of red nail polish from the vanity table. Without a word, he fell to one knee, took Barbra's hand in his and began, slowly and painstakingly, to apply the bright crimson varnish to Barbra's tapering fingernails.

The intimacy of the gesture, the supplication of it, stunned Barbra, who stared in fascination as Elvis worked, and when he finished, she mumbled 'Thank you.' An associate of Presley's, who spoke on the condition of anonymity, revealed that the intimacy between Barbra and the King of Rock 'n' Roll didn't end there. 'Elvis told me that he spent the night with Streisand in her suite. I guess he was kind of bragging. There was that kind of wink-and-a-poke-in-the-ribs way he talked about it.

'Elvis didn't say how long he and Barbra stayed involved, and I made it a policy never to press him for details about anything. But I have the feeling it was a pretty fleeting thing. Not necessarily just a one-night stand, but probably no longer than two or three. One of the books about him said that when he saw her show he said, "She sucks," but that's bull. He talked as though he worshiped her.

'I was absolutely amazed by what he told me. Barbra Streisand and the King! Wow. I wish I'd been a fly on the wall.'

PART 4

Very Today

'Now I can make a movie [with] no
songs, like a normal person . . .
It's just going to be me,
the me that's natural and very today.'

—*Barbra in 1970*

19

Barbra squiggled her bare toes into the deep white carpeting, pulled the collar of the plush terry-cloth robe up around her neck, and shivered as she stared anxiously at her reflection in the full-length mirror. She turned and sank into a vinyl beanbag chair that along with a mélange of chrome-and-glass furnishings made up the modish decor of her small dressing room. A few steps away was the bedroom set where her co-star, George Segal, her director, Herb Ross, and a minimal crew waited impatiently for her to shoot the one scene in *The Owl and the Pussycat* she had been dreading: a sexual tumble with Segal that she had agreed to film topless.

Just days earlier she had told a reporter that her non-singing, contemporary role as Doris, a 'hopeless, hapless hustler' who fancies herself 'a model and an actress,' would allow her to shed the elaborate trappings of her first three films and appear on screen for the first time as 'the me that's natural and very today.' Now she was faced with just how natural the script demanded that she be. When she finally emerged from her dressing room, bundled up in her robe, Barbra took Herb Ross aside and admitted that she had cold feet, among other things, about shooting the scene.

'Herbie, I can't,' she whispered, 'I've got goose bumps and they'll show. What will my mother think of this?'

Ross responded patiently, 'But, Barbra, it *is* a story about sexual passion.'

'Yeah,' Barbra said, 'but I don't think I have that great a body. My mother will be unhappy. I don't think I'm ready for it.'

Buck Henry, the film's scenarist, recalled that 'Ross told her not to worry, she had a great body. They went into a closet and she showed him why she thought she didn't have what it takes. Well, it happens that Barbra has a great figure. And Ross laughed and said, "Well, you're nuts. You've got to

trust me."' For nearly an hour, while George Segal catnapped, Ross pleaded
with Barbra to go through with the brief scene as planned. He assured her
that the nudity was appropriate for the uninhibited Doris. Besides, he cajoled,
didn't she want to make a dramatic break from her current screen image as
queen of the old-fashioned musicals? Wasn't she serious about moving into
the new decade as a hip, daring young actress?

Worn down by the wheedling and reassured by Ross's promise that he
would delete the scene in the editing room if she wasn't happy with it,
Barbra finally muttered, 'Oh, what the hell, I'll try it once.' As Harry
Stradling's camera rolled, Streisand dropped her robe to reveal her pert
breasts, crossed the room, and climbed into bed alongside a now completely
alert George Segal.

'It was perfect,' Ross recalled. 'I yelled, "Cut and print. Beautiful!" But
Barbra *is* the perfectionist. She wanted a retake! I think we were all shocked,
because everybody burst into laughter, including Barbra. We did the retake.'
When Barbra's mother visited the set a few days later, she took one look
at Doris's X-rated pajamas and sighed, 'I'm shocked by all those things
actresses have to do today. But I guess it's part of the job.'

IN ITS MOVIE version, *The Owl and the Pussycat* is a raucous romantic
comedy about two self-deluded opposites who, after a series of verbal
confrontations, sexual escapades, and role reversals, discard their pretensions
and form an unlikely love match. Felix Sherman is an uptight, snobbish,
pseudo-intellectual would-be writer who clerks in a bookstore. Doris is a
street-wise, loud-mouthed, defensive prostitute who changes her last name
on a whim to Washington or Waverly or Wellington. She claims she only
hooks part-time and that she is, in fact, a model and an actress who has 'been
in a movie' – which turns out to be a pornographic S&M epic entitled *Cycle
Sluts*. By story's end, he admits that his real name is Fred and she reveals that
her real last name is Wilgus. As they cast aside his writing aspirations and
her vices, the couple set out to share an apartment and a new life together,
both now based firmly in reality.

The Bill Manhoff play *The Owl and the Pussycat* had opened on Broadway
in November 1964. Starring Alan Alda and Diana Sands, the gifted African-
American actress who had played in *Harry Stoones* with Barbra, the show
ran for over four hundred performances before moving to London's West
End, where Barbra caught it while she was there in *Funny Girl*. As one of
the backers of the play through his Seven Arts production company, Ray
Stark easily acquired the movie rights for $100,000 and in 1965 announced
plans to cast the most expensive, publicized, and sought-after movie stars in

the world at that time, Elizabeth Taylor and her husband Richard Burton, in the film version. Burton rejected the idea almost immediately, and Stark turned to beefy, rough-hewn Rod Taylor as his replacement. But Rod soon backed out, and finally so did Liz.

Stark then thought of Streisand, who owed him three pictures. The prospect excited her; she longed to do a non-singing contemporary role and thought that playing Doris would be a perfect way to make the transition. Stark announced Barbra's signing for the film on November 25, 1968, after reportedly agreeing to pay her $1 million, plus 7 percent of the net profits – a dramatic raise from their original contract agreement.

After some thought was given to casting Sidney Poitier, George Segal was signed to play Felix. Segal's Oscar-nominated supporting performance in *Who's Afraid of Virginia Woolf?* in 1966 had established him as one of Hollywood's most talented young dramatic actors, but he had a lesser-known knack for comedy as well. In 1960 he had garnered laughs in the off-Broadway satirical revue, *The Premise*, in tandem with the comedy actor and writer Buck Henry, who remained a pal. When Henry signed on to write the *Pussycat* screenplay, he suggested Segal to play Felix.

One of the first decisions Henry made in refashioning *Pussycat* for the screen was to change the story's locale from San Francisco to Manhattan in order to better showcase the unique personality of the leading lady. Of his script Henry said, 'Lots of stuff in it was written for Barbra's rhythms, and for that ingenious New York ear and accent which lends itself to certain patterns of speech that other actresses wouldn't sound good doing.'

With the screenplay in Henry's capable hands, Stark turned to Herbert Ross to direct. Ross had made his full-scale directorial debut in 1969 with the well-received musical remake of *Goodbye, Mr Chips* and had guided Peter O'Toole to an Oscar-nominated performance. Because of their long history together, Barbra trusted Ross completely, as she did her 'beloved' Harry Stradling, whom she insisted she wanted for the fourth straight time. The small supporting cast was completed with Robert Klein, a swarthy, cerebral young stand-up comic who would play Felix's friend Barney, and Roz Kelly as Eleanor, Doris's gum-chewing platinum-tressed cohort.

Discord between Barbra and Ray Stark over the film's music erupted during preproduction. When Barbra signed for the film, Stark had issued statements to the press that Doris would be portrayed as a 'folk hooker' and that Barbra would sing two songs. To his chagrin, she flatly refused to do so, determined as she was to prove that she could carry a picture without a song. Hoping for a compromise, Stark commissioned Martin Charnin to compose 'The Best Thing You've Ever Done,' a dramatic ballad for Barbra to sing over a montage of scenes depicting an estrangement between Doris and Felix. But Barbra held firm. 'When the showdown came,' she recalled, 'I said there was no way I would sing. I was pushed around, made to feel like I was a bad girl or something. There was no reason for that.'

PRODUCTION ON *The Owl and the Pussycat* began on October 6, 1969, on soundstages leased by Columbia Pictures just north of Manhattan's theater district. George Segal, who like everyone else had heard the stories of Barbra's temperament, was surprised to find her nothing like the ogre he had been told about. 'She's the easiest person to work with,' Segal said. 'She's warm and even and a real professional. She knows exactly what she's doing. *I* was the troublemaker on that set. One time I got upset over working late hours. Ray Stark and I had a big screaming fight in my dressing room.' Barbra liked Segal, too, and loved it when he said, 'I think there's Brando and then there's Barbra.'

According to Robert Klein, Segal had all he could do to keep up with Streisand's performance pace. 'The comedy came naturally to Barbra,' Klein recalled. 'She was much more adept at how to be funny, she seemed more sure of herself . . . her virtuosity really forced George to work hard at being funny. She was thinking *all the time* about how to do a particular thing, and she was completely thorough. Ultimately, though, I think George was quite effective with her. And like him I never, ever saw that side to her that I had heard a lot about. She was not only thoroughly professional, but she was very accommodating in making me feel at home.'

THE SCRIPT OF *The Owl and the Pussycat* provided Barbra with many firsts, not the least of which was a certain phrase she uttered in one memorable scene. While Doris and Felix take a walk, she shows him a dictionary she now totes around to consult when she hears an unfamiliar word. Proudly she manages to use 'assimilated' and 'impeccable' conversationally as proof of her newly expanded vocabulary. Impressed, Felix tells her to 'remember that language is power.'

This is played against a barrage of catcalls to Doris from a car full of obnoxious young hoods on the make ('Hey, baby, wanna go for a *ride?*'). Finally fed up, Doris recalls that language is power and steps over to the curb. She stares the offenders down and says, 'I beg your pardon, boys, but you are intruding on my privacy and I would appreciate it very much, if you don't mind, if you would just *fuck off.*'

The outburst leads the boys to chase Doris and Felix through the bowels of the Lincoln Center parking garage. Actor Tom Atkins, who played 'Tough

Guy #1,' recalled Barbra's 'cute, sassy face when she had to say "fuck off." Herb Ross had her do it again and again. It got to a point where it was funny and we were all cracking up – except for Ross! Then it got tense, and it went on and on. I don't know if he ever got exactly what he wanted from Barbra, but he certainly got enough variations. She never complained; she did it as many times as he wanted. She was just as determined as he was.'

Barbra was the first major star to utter that expletive on film, and some theaters refused to book the picture unless it was removed. Thus some prints of *Pussycat* have Barbra saying, 'Up yours!'

EIGHTEEN MONTHS AFTER her Happening in Central Park, Barbra went back to the Sheep Meadow to film *Pussycat*'s final scene, her most challenging dramatic moment in the film. It was a piercingly cold Tuesday, December 16, and just hours before the New York premiere of *Hello, Dolly!* scheduled for that evening. In the middle of still another loud argument, Doris and Felix notice several dogs around them, playing, fighting, and copulating. Felix becomes agitated and compares his and Doris's behavior to that of the canines. He soon humiliates a confused but compliant Doris by forcing her to kneel in front of him and beg like a dog: 'I assimilated impeccable,' she offers to him in a tearful, childlike defense. He realizes how cruel he is being, and after taking a well-deserved slap from Doris, he apologizes. The scene made many audiences uncomfortable, and Buck Henry would have preferred to delete it. 'I wrote about ten [alternate] endings,' he says. 'But Barbra really wanted to play the dog thing . . . because she's an actress and it is really a playable moment for an actor to do. I was opposed to it because I think it made [Felix] so unsympathetic that no one can recover from it.'

With this tricky scene in the can, and with only three weeks of filming to go, Harry Stradling stunned the *Pussycat* company by quitting the production and returning to California. 'I'll never leave the [Los Angeles] soil to do another location film,' he announced. Although no one recalled hearing him complain of any specific malady on the set, the long hours of *Pussycat* production coupled with the frigid temperatures had apparently taken a toll on the sixty-eight-year-old cinematographer, who had suffered a coronary several years before.

Ray Stark hastily called Herb Ross and Barbra together over the Christmas weekend to view samples of other cinematographers' work. They chose the forty-three-year-old Hungarian-born Andrew Laszlo, whose work on *You're a Big Boy Now* and *The Night They Raided Minsky's* had been well received.

The remaining days of filming on *The Owl and the Pussycat* went smoothly, with Laszlo ably matching his predecessor's style, but Barbra was heart-broken when she learned that Harry Stradling had died suddenly on February 14, just two days before he received his fourteenth Oscar nomination for *Hello, Dolly!*

ALTHOUGH THE PROPERTY had been knocking around for years, *The Owl and the Pussycat* could have been designed specifically to ease Barbra Streisand through a crucial career transition. While some conservative moviegoers who thought of Streisand as Brooklyn's answer to Julie Andrews were offended by the film's language and its frank view of sexuality, others – particularly young people – were captivated by what they perceived as not only the 'new' Streisand but the real one as well. *Pussycat* helped Barbra regain a measure of the 'hipness' that had been an integral element of her early nightclub career.

She was not hip enough, however, to allow her topless moment to remain in the finished print of *Pussycat*. 'When she saw the scene,' Buck Henry recalled, 'she said, "No, I can't take my family looking at it. You have to fog the film." And she had the right to have that done.' Later Barbra said that her decision wasn't based solely on modesty. She also felt the sight of her bare breasts would detract from the comedy of the fumbling lovemaking scene that followed, and she was probably right. Although she was assured that the film and negative of the only nude scene of her career would be destroyed, as so often happens they weren't. Almost a decade later they would return to haunt her.

AT FIVE IN the afternoon on December 16, Barbra rushed home from filming to prepare for the world premiere of *Hello, Dolly!* at the Rivoli Theater on Broadway at eight o'clock that evening. A few minutes before the hour she emerged from her building, bundled up against the cold in an Arnold Scaasi-designed white leather midi-coat embroidered in burnt orange and edged with white fur, and a white-and-orange Turkistani pillbox hat, and hopped into a royal blue limousine with Marty Erlichman.

The picture had been ready for release since early summer, but because the show was still running on Broadway – it would go on to set the all-time longevity record with 2,844 performances – David Merrick had stuck to his contractual right not to allow the movie to open. He finally changed his mind when Twentieth Century-Fox, eager to capitalize on Barbra's *Funny Girl* popularity as soon as possible, agreed to reimburse the producer for any decline in the show's box-office revenues attributable to the movie's release.

With this roadblock cleared, Fox gaudily launched the two-hour-and-twenty-eight-minute film as a road show production, with a $6.50 top ticket price and a souvenir program. The studio was convinced that they had a blockbuster with the potential to equal the staggering box-office success of *The Sound of Music.* 'We were all working on the assumption that *Hello, Dolly!* could never be a failure,' Lehman said. 'Everybody in the world wanted to see it. It had Barbra Streisand and Walter Matthau and Louis Armstrong. How could it fail?'

THE PREMIERE INVIGORATED everyone's optimism and frightened Barbra to death. Close to one thousand fans mobbed Broadway outside the Rivoli. They had waited for hours in sub-freezing temperatures to catch a glimpse of Barbra, one of America's few genuine superstars. When the crowd spotted her limousine two blocks away, pandemonium erupted. In a scene that could have been lifted from Nathanael West's apocalyptic Hollywood novel *The Day of the Locust,* hundreds of fans broke through the police barricades and surrounded the car, screaming 'Barbra! Barbra!' as they pounded on the hood and pressed their faces against the windows to catch a glimpse of La Streisand.

Barbra sat in the back seat and cringed as the mob got more and more out of control and the press of their numbers on either side began to rock the limo back and forth. Police on foot and horseback forced the crowd away from the car; still, it took the chauffeur fifteen minutes to drive the few feet to the red-carpeted Rivoli entrance.

One fan recalled that as soon as he spotted Barbra's car, he began to run along with it, peering in at Streisand. 'She looked gorgeous, but she had an expression on her face like a deer caught in headlights,' he said. 'She kept pulling up her fur collar and sort of sinking into it. Every so often she'd put up her white-leather-gloved hand and make the V-shaped peace sign with her fingers next to the window. Maybe she thought that would help calm the crowd down. It got pretty hairy. One crazed fan jumped on the front hood of the limo and started pounding on the glass and screaming. At one point people behind me were pushing so hard my face was smashed against the window. I motioned to Barbra that she shouldn't get out of the car.'

Afraid to leave the limo, Barbra stayed put until the police had cleared the way into the theater. When she finally stepped out onto the red carpet, people screamed and shoved and surged toward her. Flashbulbs popped in her face. Fans screamed her name, threw flowers, waved their autograph books at her. A flying wedge of burly police and private security guards surrounded her and Marty and inched them from the curb toward the

theater. Streisand looked petrified. It took another fifteen minutes to get
her through the Rivoli's doors, and as soon as she was inside, the barricades
collapsed and a sea of humanity lunged against the theater entrance.

In the lobby crush, frenzied photographers jostled so viciously for advantage that scuffles broke out. One photographer had his camera smashed by
several fans who had shoved past the ushers and cops behind Barbra. Marty
Erlichman and a photographer collided, fell to the floor, and scrambled back
up punching and kicking each other. The man's camera knocked Erlichman
in the head, opening a gash that splashed blood all over his shirt collar. 'Oh,
my God, what's *happening?*' Barbra screamed. 'Marty! Marty! Are you okay?
What did they do to you, Marty?'

The film's publicist Pat Newcomb later said, 'I was with Marilyn Monroe
and Elizabeth Taylor at premieres, but this was the worst.'

Afterward, at a party at the Pierre Hotel, a badly shaken Barbra vowed
to the columnist Earl Wilson that she would never attend another premiere.
'It's inhumane,' she said. 'I was devastated by what happened to Marty.'
Wilson asked her how she had liked the movie. 'I'm not sure I even saw
it,' she replied.

Although frightening, the pandemonium seemed to indicate tremendous
interest in the film and its star, and the reviews further heartened studio
executives. 'It is grand, it is spectacular, it is lavish, it is sentimental, it
is buoyant, it is swift,' Charles Champlin raved in the *Los Angeles Times*.
'Walter Matthau, baying like a dyspeptic elk, is a figure of infinite charm
and interest . . . The principal attraction is, of course, Barbra Streisand. And
I presume no one will be shocked to hear that she is superb . . . The parade,
and indeed the "Hello, Dolly!" orgy amidst the splendors of the Harmonia
Gardens, are unqualified triumphs of the several arts of make-believe. Not to
be awed by them is not to be awed by the motion picture as an art form.'

'*Hello, Dolly!* is not invulnerable to criticism,' Vincent Canby wrote in
The New York Times, 'but I suspect that Barbra Streisand is. At the age
of twenty-seven, and for the very good reason that she is one of the few
mysteriously natural, unique performing talents of our time, she has become
a national treasure.'

There were dissenters, both to the movie and to Barbra, but they were
in the minority. At first it seemed that *Hello, Dolly!* would more than live
up to Fox's lofty expectations for it. The first two weeks' box-office receipts
surpassed those of *The Sound of Music*, a fact that was trumpeted by the studio
in double-page advertisements in the Hollywood trade papers.

But then attendance dropped off. Seven Oscar nominations in February,
including Best Picture, but not Best Actress, didn't help much, and neither
did the three technical awards the film won in April, for Art Direction,

Sound, and Score. It soon became clear that *Hello, Dolly!* would not earn the blockbuster grosses necessary to compensate for its enormous budget. The picture took in $38 million at the box office domestically, enough to make it the fourth-highest grossing film of the year, and another $20 million worldwide, but that simply wasn't enough. In order for Fox to recoup its initial investment and the money it had spent on promotion, *Hello, Dolly!* would have had to gross over $60 million. By that yardstick, the movie was a flop.

What had happened? Why had a film with so much going for it failed to reach the audience that had flocked to *Funny Girl?* The answer lay mainly within the rapidly changing American culture itself. Just as the Vietnam War and the youthful counterculture had revolutionized popular music, by 1969 the movie industry largely reflected the profound changes taking place in American society. *Midnight Cowboy*, John Schlesinger's gritty portrait of a bisexual hustler, became the only X-rated film ever to win the Best Picture Oscar. Sydney Pollack's *They Shoot Horses, Don't They?* offered a nihilistic view of life's futility. *Bob & Carol & Ted & Alice* satirized the trendy practice of wife-swapping. And *Easy Rider*, the archetypal sixties protest film, celebrated drug use and galvanized many young people against bigotry and mindless savagery.

In this climate *Hello, Dolly!* seemed to many like so much idiotic fluff, and most young moviegoers – always the backbone of box office – preferred to buy tickets to more relevant films. Other old-fashioned musicals released around the same time met with even less success than *Hello, Dolly!* Pundits declared the movie musical dead, and for a time they were right.

No one blamed Barbra for the financial failure of *Hello, Dolly!* On the contrary, her popularity likely pulled in most of the people who did buy tickets. Had a lesser draw starred in the picture, it surely would have fared far worse. Ernest Lehman, in fact, feels that the film failed because there wasn't enough of Barbra in it. 'At the premiere in New York it was so clear that all those people had come out to see no one but Barbra. And I thought, My God, they're expecting this to be a Barbra Streisand picture. And it really wasn't. There were long stretches when she wasn't on the screen, when all you saw was those idiot clerks and their idiot girls. I firmly believe a lot of people were disappointed that there wasn't more Barbra, and that hurt the film.'

Unquestionably Streisand provides the most enjoyable elements of the movie. Her Dolly Levi is funny, vibrant, compelling, a comic locomotive barreling through scene after scene. Yes, her characterization meanders wildly, from Mae West to Lena Horne to Fanny Brice, but that's part of the fun and the humor of the performance. Barbra may have been miscast, but she turned it into a very entertaining miscasting.

There's sparkling comic chemistry between Barbra and Walter Matthau in spite of all the unpleasantness during filming. What they lack, however, is romantic chemistry. Harry Stradling's camera makes Streisand look so lovely – with her peaches-and-cream complexion, her vivid blue eyes, her upswept auburn Gibson Girl hairdo, and her hourglass figure – that it's hard to believe she couldn't snare a more attractive 'half a millionaire' than the ill-tempered, sour-faced Horace Vandergelder.

Hello, Dolly! finally prevails as a comic and musical triumph for Barbra. It is a film that is remembered primarily because she starred in it, just as its composer, Jerry Herman, had predicted. As Richard Cohen observed in his review of the film for *Women's Wear Daily*, 'There she stands at the head of the great ornate stairway, her glorious merry-widow figure draped in a ton of jeweled gold, a spray of feathers in her belle époque topknot. She is smiling her sly, secret, Brooklyn-Jewish-girl-who-made-it-big smile. The film is at its climax, she is the champion female movie star of her time and she is poised for the most played, the most familiar, the most parodied song of the decade. We are expectant. Will she bring it off? Will she top all the toppers? Boys, the kid's a winner. The whole thing is a triumph. She was smiling that sly smile because she knew all along she was going to kill us.'

B arbra tapped her feet, clapped her hands, and called out encouragement as she watched the man with the fiddle dance the Red River
jig, a traditional Canadian folk dance. She was at the National Arts
Center in Manitoba, Canada, attending a celebration of the province's
centennial on January 28, 1970. Few people in the audience were watching
the performance, however. Most eyes were on Barbra and her escort: the
country's prime minister, Pierre Elliott Trudeau.

Trudeau – tall, attractive, erudite, unmarried, a youthful and unconventional fifty years old – had been the head of the Liberal Party and Canada's
head of state for two years. He had first charmed Barbra when they met in
London at the *Funny Girl* premiere, and a year later he had flown to New
York for a series of weekend dates with her. On Friday night they shared an
intimate dinner at Casa Brasil on Manhattan's East Side, then danced until
the early-morning hours at Raffles, a private discotheque on Fifth Avenue.
After spending Saturday night in seclusion, they attended a play on Sunday.
When a reporter asked Trudeau how long he had known Barbra, he replied,
'Not long enough.'

Gossips had a field day. 'What is more fitting for a superstar,' Joyce Haber
declared in her *Los Angeles Times* column, 'than to cotton to a handsome,
swinging super-politician? Barbra plays the Matchmaker in *Dolly*. In real life
she's given us a match to watch.'

Two months later, a week after she completed principal photography
on *The Owl and the Pussycat*, Barbra flew to Canada's capital city of
Ottawa, accompanied by three huge trunks, two of them crammed full
of fur coats, stoles, and hats to protect her from the wintry chill. The
prime minister escorted his glamorously bedecked paramour to the ballet,
and at a party afterward they held hands. Then Trudeau invited a few

close friends to meet Barbra at a cozy candlelit dinner in the executive mansion.

A few days later Barbra attended a session of Parliament, during which she and Trudeau exchanged waves and glances. George Hees, a frustrated member of the Tory opposition, stopped at one point and said, 'I should like to ask a question of the prime minister – if he can take his eyes and mind off the visitors' gallery long enough to answer it.' Trudeau blushed; Barbra laughed and tapped the railing in front of her seat with her umbrella.

Then Barbra moved on to Manitoba, where she and Trudeau were driven separately to the National Arts Center for the centennial gala. When Barbra arrived, Trudeau bounded out of his limousine, pushed past some Royal Canadian Mounted Police, and opened Barbra's car door with a flourish. They entered the concert hall amid much buzz from the crowd.

Ed Schreyer, the governor general of Winnipeg and a political rival of Trudeau's, recalled Barbra's delight as she watched the show. 'The guest list was crammed with prominent Manitobans,' he said, 'and I remember it struck me what an honor it was to have her there. We exchanged pleasantries for just a short period of time when some of the entertainment started and she became fascinated. She kept exclaiming enthusiastically as the fiddler danced the Red River jig, which I explained to her was like the Virginia reel. Everyone was watching her reaction because it was quite funny and quite genuine.'

Schreyer felt that Trudeau 'certainly took a political risk in dating Barbra Streisand. Some people were impressed, but they weren't the majority. He was seen with Barbra in coffee shops and taverns, and it was quite the topic of conversation.'

Many Canadians were concerned. Where would their prime minister's obvious affection for this glamorous movie star lead? Would she be willing to give up her career and become Canada's first lady? If so, what kind of first lady would she be? Or would Trudeau renounce his position for the woman he loved? During a nationally televised interview, a reporter confronted Trudeau with the question of the day: 'I think everybody is interested in the fact that you have seen Miss Streisand not just once as a casual encounter but three or four times while she has been in the city. I think the public is entitled to know whether you are developing a serious relationship with her.'

'It's none of your business or the public's business,' Trudeau replied.

Barbra probably didn't know it, but Trudeau had been seeing another young woman, twenty-one-year-old Margaret Sinclair, before Barbra arrived in Canada. In an attempt not to have the whirlwind of publicity surrounding his dates with Barbra upset *that* apple cart in case things with Streisand didn't work out, Trudeau called Margaret several times while Barbra was in town. Each time Sinclair shouted 'Go back to your American actress!' and slammed the phone down.

Trudeau married Margaret Sinclair in March of 1971; the tempestuous union ended in 1977. In her 1977 *Playboy* interview, after responding 'I don't want to answer that' when asked if Trudeau had proposed to her, Barbra made it clear that she had seriously contemplated life as Canada's first lady. 'I thought it would be fantastic. I'd have to learn how to speak French. I would do only movies in Canada. I had it all figured out. I would campaign for him and become totally politically involved in all the causes, abortion and whatever.'

But 'certain realities' kept her from marrying Trudeau, Barbra said – most likely Trudeau's Catholicism and the impossibility of maintaining her career while performing the duties of a first lady. She had never considered asking Trudeau to give up his career, she said, because 'His life was too important to a whole country, to a world. I don't feel mine is that significant. It's significant in that it gives people a fantasy life or some pleasure, but it's not like being the prime minister of a country.' Barbra and Trudeau remained close friends through his marriage and beyond.

BEFORE SHE LEFT for Canada, Barbra had attended the New York nightclub singing debut of her not-quite-nineteen-year-old sister, Roslyn, in the elegant Persian Room of the Plaza Hotel. Throughout 1969 Roslyn had been on a fourteen-city tour sponsored by RCA Records to promote the release of her first album, *Give Me You*, late in 1968. RCA executives told the press that they were giving Roslyn 'the biggest push any artist has received in years.'

Roslyn had nurtured her own singing ambitions for years as she imitated Barbra and sang along to her albums. But the closest she had gotten to show business before this was her position as president of the Barbra Streisand Fan Club and editor of its newsletter, *The Streizette*. It was an angle played up in the press by Barbra's public relations people: Adoring Kid Sister Runs Fan Club for Superstar.

'I didn't actually *run* it,' Roslyn later said. 'Barbra started getting so much mail that they gave it to a fan club service [to answer]. Then I was voted into the position [of president of the fan club]. I was *told* that I'd be doing it, by my sister, I think. I had no idea. I said, "You mean somebody else is signing my signature on these letters? How dare they!" I take things seriously, so I actually went to work on it. I used to do it one day a week after school.'

As much as Mrs Kind had discouraged Barbra's show business ambitions she encouraged Roslyn's. Barbra had proven nothing if not that lightning could strike in the most unlikely places, and Diana felt Roslyn had a far better chance to succeed than Barbra had at her age. Roslyn was more conventionally pretty – she had dropped sixty pounds and was now just 'pleasingly plump,' as she put it – she wasn't the least bit kooky, and she had a pleasant voice that brought Barbra's to mind without any of the histrionics that put some people off.

Barbra, busy with her career, still bitter toward her mother, rarely kept in contact with her or Roslyn; both of them practically had to make an appointment with her secretary to talk to her on the phone. 'There hasn't been too much communication between us,' Roslyn said. 'She really didn't know I had a career going.' Barbra rarely sent the family any money. Her daughter was a multimillionaire by now, but Diana Kind wasn't much better off for it. Roslyn, though, was a devoted daughter who still lived at home, which was now an apartment on West Fifty-eighth Street; she and her mother had moved to Manhattan from Brooklyn in 1967 so that Diana could be near her job as a school clerk. If it didn't seem probable that Barbra would support Diana in her old age, Roslyn more likely would. Mrs Kind was willing to let her younger daughter do anything she needed to in order to earn even a fraction of the income Barbra did.

Roslyn's career, launched with great optimism, never amounted to much. Her first album sold poorly, and after a second effort did even worse, RCA dropped her. The main problem for Roslyn was, unsurprisingly, Barbra. Try as she might not to, she sounded like Streisand. Only she wasn't as good, and the comparisons were always to her detriment.

A few years later Roslyn spoke bitterly about what she saw as Barbra's lack of help with her career. 'If only Barbra would say something nice about me when she's asked. I feel she's hurting my chances with her silence.' When Barbra did put in a word to get Roslyn booked into a club in Las Vegas, Roslyn said, 'It was the worst place you've ever seen . . . absolutely nobody knew it existed.'

Some felt that Barbra resented how easy it had been for Roslyn to get her start – a recording contract right out of high school! All Barbra would say was 'The trouble with Roslyn is that when she's not invited back to a place she thinks I'm somehow behind it. That's nonsense; that's sad.'

Roslyn considered quitting the business altogether. 'I don't want to, singing is my life, but without my sister's endorsement I cannot see my getting much further.'

✯

'I LOOK FORWARD to working less and simplifying my life, to fulfilling some of my potential as an individual and as a woman,' Barbra told *Life* magazine late in 1969. 'My little-girl fantasy of being a recording star, a theater star, a concert star, and a movie star is impossible to maintain; each of them suffers. There is so much else to learn, so much more to do. What I'd like is more time – time not only to read the stacks of political journals that have been piling up, but also time to read *Good Housekeeping* to find out different ways to decorate my son's sandwiches.'

She was exhausted after she finished *The Owl and the Pussycat*, and with good reason. In the last two and a half years she had made four movies, three of them elephantine musicals; produced two television specials, one of them a live concert before 135,000 people; and put out seven studio and sound-track albums. She *needed* a rest, and she was determined to take one. Scheduled to return to the Riviera in Las Vegas in August to fulfill her 1963 contract with the hotel, Barbra asked to postpone the date until November. She already had an obligation to return to the International (now the Hilton) in December; that way, she reasoned, she could kill two Vegas birds with one stone. The Riviera agreed, and Barbra settled back and tried to return to a private life.

She read those political journals, listened to classical music, worked at improving her questionable culinary skills. 'I think cooking is so fascinating,' she said. 'It's like chemistry or math, and I love math because it's based on logic. It's not like life. I like anything that's tangible – you follow the recipe carefully for baking a cake and it comes out right; that's terrific.'

Whenever possible she shopped, usually for antiques. 'I love art glass,' she said. 'My day is made when I find a piece of mold-blown Gallé. I love the flowing, unending line of Art Nouveau furniture. It makes me cry it's so beautiful.' She spent time with her best friends, the lyricists Marilyn and Alan Bergman, playing bridge, singing around the piano, walking on the beach, staying up late into the night talking and giggling.

Mostly, of course, her newfound free time allowed her to dote on three-year-old Jason, who brought her no end of joy. She delighted in his every move, his every word. She proudly told a reporter that when Jason bit into a grapefruit he complained, 'Oooh, sour,' and that he always said 'Okay' with a questioning inflection – 'Okay?' – just like his mother. And Jason was learning how to deal with fans. When Barbra brought him to a matinee performance of the Joffrey Ballet, autograph seekers approached Barbra at intermission. She sank into her seat and tried to discourage them. Jason stood up and declared, 'No autographs today!'

✪

SHE SPENT TIME house-hunting, too. In California she had found a 9,600-square-foot, two-story Mediterranean-style villa with five bedrooms and seven baths on Carolwood Drive in Holmby Hills, just west of the Beverly Hills Hotel. She first rented it, then purchased it for $295,000 in July of 1969. She still lives in the house, which in 1993 was assessed at $2,447,000.

She didn't have such good luck in New York. She started looking for another apartment when she was denied permission to break through the walls separating her two apartments on Central Park West and make them one. Unless she moved, she said, 'Jason will have to sleep in a separate apartment. Can you imagine him telling his analyst about *that* twenty years from now?'

She found an elegant twenty-room place she liked near Eighty-sixth Street on Park Avenue, and applied to the building's board for permission to purchase it for $240,000. She was turned down. The reason, the wife of a board member said, was that 'we don't want flamboyant Hollywood types' in the building. She denied that the turndown had anything to do with Barbra's being Jewish. 'We have three or four Jewish families in the building,' she said.

It was the second time in a year that Barbra had been denied the chance to buy a co-op. After a story about the rejection appeared in *The New York Times*, the New York State attorney general launched an investigation into the practices of the city's co-op boards. 'It's an unbelievable experience to be discriminated against,' Barbra said. 'You know, the board didn't even give me an interview. They apparently think theatrical people are noisy. Let me tell you, it's the society people who are swinging from the chandeliers. I happen to lead a very quiet, conservative life. I hardly ever entertain.'

Barbra gave up on a co-op and bought instead a five-story, seventeen-room Art Deco town house on East Eightieth Street, built in 1929, for $420,000. She needed all that room, she explained, because 'I have so much stuff that I've been collecting for years. Most of it is in storage because our apartment is so small. I want to give all those things a home.' The 'things' included a collection of cranberry glass, an ice-cream-parlor bar, a gum machine, and penny candy and spool cabinets.

On June 9, 1970, before she had moved in a stick of furniture, Barbra invited three thousand guests to the house for a political fund-raiser to benefit the primary campaign of the liberal Democratic congressional hopeful Bella Abzug. A handwritten note from Barbra invited all those who wished to contribute $25 or more to the cause of sending 'that very special lady running for Congress who is dedicated to peace' to 'drop in' between five and eight in the evening. 'There will be stars of stage, screen and radio! – drinks – canapés – but no furniture! You must *abzug*lutely come!'

An army of young 'Bella Boosters' mopped the floors and washed the windows in preparation for the event, which was a smashing success and raised more than $50,000 for the candidate. A week later Streisand joined Abzug to campaign on the streets of Manhattan's Lower East Side, startling passersby as she orated through a bullhorn from the back of a flatbed truck.

Bella Abzug won the primary, and on November 1, two days before the general election, which Abzug also won, Barbra headlined a 'Broadway for Bella' benefit at the Felt Forum in Madison Square Garden. That show featured performances from *Cabaret*, *Purlie*, *Fiddler on the Roof*, *1776*, *Company*, and *Hair*, and Barbra's performance of 'People' brought the house down. A Streisand fan who crashed the party recalled, 'She was so great she had everybody in tears. Even the stagehands were crying, and they must have seen everything ever to go onstage. The crowd got kind of hysterical and they started to storm the stage, and she yelled into the microphone, "Who do you think I am? Tom Jones?" It was okay, though. Nothing got out of hand. Afterward people sneaked into her dressing room and took things like wire hangers and bits of soap to save as souvenirs.'

Barbra soon became disenchanted with the town house, which she discovered needed a new roof and heating system and which she was unable to sell. At a dinner party a few months later, she met Steve Ross, the head of Warner Communications. As she complained about the place Ross asked, 'How much do you want for it?'

'Four hundred and fifty thousand,' Barbra replied. Ross agreed to buy it on the spot.

ON JUNE 17, 1970, *On a Clear Day You Can See Forever* opened. Quietly. There was no premiere, no road-show engagement, no souvenir booklet. Paramount, nervous about the decline in audience interest in big old-fashioned musicals, had decided to cut its expected losses on the film and forced Vincente Minnelli to snip nearly fifteen minutes from it, including two complete musical numbers – one of them a Streisand duet with Jack Nicholson! Few of the cut scenes involved Yves Montand, but he still expressed unhappiness with his share of the screen time after the film's release. 'It was to have been a more equitable sharing of the movie,' he said. 'That was what I thought. There was very little give [from Streisand]. I worked with Monroe, and she knew she was beloved of the public, but she didn't bring it with her on the set. They gave Streisand everything she wanted, and more. It was eventually decided to change it from a movie version of the play into a picture for her: a Barbra Streisand picture.'

Paramount spent as little as possible on publicity and promotion. This lack of studio belief in the film's box-office potential, as it almost always does, became a self-fulfilling prophecy. With decidedly mixed reviews – Montand's stiffness and sometimes unintelligible English prompted particularly harsh assessments – *On a Clear Day* brought in only $13.4 million at box offices around the country. But because Minnelli had provided the film's lavish production values without going over his $10 million budget, *On a Clear Day* was able to break even with foreign receipts and its sale to television.

Just as *What About Today?* reflected Barbra's uneasy transition to pop music, *On a Clear Day* proved an equally uncomfortable segue to contemporary characterization for her onscreen. How to play Daisy Gamble, the first present-day role she had acted since summer stock, clearly puzzled Streisand; her Daisy resembles no known species of late 1960s college girl. In her early scenes she seems, in the words of *Time* magazine, like 'Jerry Lewis in drag.' She makes actressy, 'indicating' decisions, like turning her feet toward each other when she sits down, that make Daisy seem buffoonish.

Her haute couture contemporary wardrobe, designed by Arnold Scaasi, doesn't help. With her huge white hats, short Empire-style dresses with matching half coats, cute little pinafores with Peter Pan collars, and a nightgown in paisley material that matches her bedroom wallpaper, Daisy Gamble was the most precious coed who never lived. 'That's where Minnelli's love of beauty occasionally fails him,' wrote the critic Joel E. Siegel. 'If the contrast between her present and past lives had been even sharper, I think it would have solved most of what was wrong with the film.'

If Barbra should have played Daisy more like the entirely believable college girl she played in *What's Up, Doc?* two years later, her Melinda Tentrees in *Clear Day* emerged as her most exquisite cinematic creation. Modeling Cecil Beaton's sumptuous Regency costumes to stunning effect, she's gorgeous, sexy, funny, imperious, coy, beguiling, and compelling as this willful, irresistible courtesan. Her performance and Minnelli's presentation of it provide some of the most enchanting Streisand moments ever captured on film, particularly the banquet scene, during which Barbra's seductiveness often proved literally arousing to those who appreciated her sex appeal.

ON A CLEAR DAY sounded a death knell for the MGM Golden Era-inspired musical, and for Streisand movie musicals as well, at least for the next five years. Barbra had professed her determination not only to contemporize her image but to prove that she could be effective in movies without singing a line. With the release of *The Owl and the Pussycat* on October 30 she did both.

That Barbra's new movie nearly got an X rating proved it was as 'very today' as Barbra felt, and she expressed delight that the film deserved the MPAA's most restrictive rating. But Ray Stark knew that many theaters refused to show X-rated films, even if they were not truly pornographic, and many newspapers refused to carry ads for them. Somehow he was able to persuade the ratings board to give the film an R rating without removing Doris's four-letter put-down. Some newspapers did refuse to run the *Pussycat* ads, though, because they showed Barbra wearing her 'model outfit' with two hands and a heart sewn over strategic spots, so Columbia prepared a G-rated campaign without them.

The Owl and the Pussycat won wide critical approval, especially for the comic teamwork of Barbra and George Segal. Most critics, especially New Yorkers, considered the movie a homecoming for Streisand. 'There she comes, right where she belongs, in a real New York street,' wrote Jack Kroll in *Newsweek*, 'ducking through the sleazy rain in a fake-fur minicoat, white boots scrambling, tote bag swinging, cussing out a departing bus in her interborough voice and with a shrug and a chomp on her Juicyfruit, flopping into a passing car . . . Streisand [displays] the most amazing comic energy seen on the screen in a very long time.'

Pauline Kael added, 'She may never again look as smashing as she did in that high-style champagne bit [in *On a Clear Day*], but if the price of that glamour is the paralysis of talent, it isn't worth it. Streisand, who is easily the best comedienne working in American movies, is better when she isn't carrying all that deadweight. She can be trusted when she cuts loose, because she has the instinct and the discipline to control her phenomenal vitality. She is like thousands of girls one sees in the subway, but more so; she is both the archetype and an original, and that's what makes a star.'

The Owl and the Pussycat grossed $29 million in the United States, which placed it among the top-grossing pictures of the year. Its success, along with the grosses of *Funny Girl* and *Hello, Dolly!*, put Barbra on the male-dominated Top Ten Box-Office Attractions list for the first time. She had made the transformation from dinosaur Dolly to dirty-mouthed Doris, and for Barbra there would be no looking back.

WHILE SHE RESTED from filmmaking during the summer of 1970, Barbra's thoughts turned again to the legitimate stage. The prior April 19 she had been voted an honorary Tony award as Broadway's Star of the Decade, finally completely fulfilling Marty Erlichman's prediction, and the recognition started her fantasies whirring. She mulled over an opportunity to appear in a repertory production of *Romeo and Juliet*. 'I'd like to play Juliet while I'm still young enough,' she told the columnist Radie Harris.

'And whom would you like as your Romeo?' Harris asked.

'Robert Redford,' Barbra replied without missing a beat. 'He's one of the best young American actors around.'

She fantasized about playing Medea, just as she and Elliott had dreamed of doing when they first met, and Hamlet – Sarah Bernhardt had done it, why couldn't she? But her stage fright and her inclination toward laziness won out over her ambition, and she never did return to live theater. 'That's why I love being in movies,' she said at the time. 'I'm performing all over the world – while I'm home taking a bath.'

HER RECORDING CAREER presented an entirely different problem. She hadn't had an original studio album in release since *What About Today?* a year earlier. The *Hello, Dolly!* sound track and the compilation album *Barbra Streisand's Greatest Hits*, despite their release during the holiday season, had sold anemically, and the sound track to *On a Clear Day* bombed: it never even entered *Billboard*'s Top 100 Albums list. Even considering the failure of the picture, it was shocking that an album containing six lovely new Streisand performances of songs by Burton Lane and Alan Jay Lerner would chart so poorly. Where were her fans?

Apparently she had fewer of them now. Unlikely as it might have seemed even two years earlier – the *Funny Girl* sound track had risen to number twelve, after all – Barbra was the latest victim of a revolution in mainstream pop musical tastes that was now complete. If most young people regarded her musical films as quaint relics of a past age, they considered her records scarcely more modern. Clearly she would have to update her musical image or risk losing forever her position as a pop music force.

Surprisingly, considering Streisand's career savvy, she resisted. Perhaps she feared a repeat of the failure of *What About Today?* Even more to the point was that Barbra didn't feel comfortable with or understand most of the pop-rock music she had heard. She related to classic ballads or new material in the standards mold. Thus despite renewed pressure from Clive Davis to do another contemporary album, Barbra had begun work earlier in the year on *The Singer*, a collection of what she called 'good music,' written mostly by Michel Legrand and her friends Alan and Marilyn Bergman.

She recorded 'The Best Thing You've Ever Done,' which she had refused to sing for *The Owl and the Pussycat*, and two Legrand-Bergman compositions, 'Summer Me, Winter Me,' and 'What Are You Doing the Rest of Your Life?'

The first two were released as a single, which went nowhere. Undeterred, Barbra proceeded with plans for *The Singer*.

Then Clive Davis stepped up the pressure. Barbra, he felt, would be making a big mistake if she released the album. He requested a meeting with Marty Erlichman. 'I was aware of her resistance to change,' Davis said. 'She was against the composers of the day because she did not understand their music.'.Davis sensed that the material was more frightening to Barbra in the abstract, so he promised Erlichman that he would come back to Barbra with specific material he thought would be right for her.

Davis got in touch with Richard Perry, a staff producer at Warner Brothers Records who had recently struck out on his own and produced a record of Ella Fitzgerald singing songs from the Beatles and Smokey Robinson. The thought of working with Streisand excited Perry; he hadn't thought much of *What About Today?* but felt Barbra could make a successful transition to pop with the right material and the right approach. 'Here was the greatest vocal instrument of our generation,' he said, 'not at all relating to popular contemporary music.'

When Perry and Barbra got together, he saw that she 'wasn't into any of the contemporary figures around. She didn't have a really good stereo in her home or anything like that.' Perry played a few songs for her, including Harry Nilsson's 'Maybe,' which she liked.

'You really think I can do this?' she asked.

'Sure,' Perry replied. 'Why not?'

Over the next few months, Barbra would call Perry late at night to say, 'I want the new Van Morrison, the new Joni Mitchell, Randy Newman, Marvin Gaye . . .' To Perry, this was a sure sign that Streisand had 'totally immersed herself in the pop culture.'

Finally she agreed to lay down enough tracks for an album, but she reserved the right to have them destroyed if she didn't like them. The night before the session, Perry recalled, 'she called me up, freaking out. She said, "I can't do it. This isn't me. I don't feel it."' Perry tried to soothe her. 'You've come this far, you've gotta do it,' he told her. 'Trust me that you're gonna love it. It's gonna blow your mind as soon as we get into it a little bit.'

The first session on July 30, during which Barbra recorded five songs, lasted from seven in the evening until five-thirty in the morning, the longest in the history of the Los Angeles branch of the American Federation of Musicians. Barbra recorded 'Maybe,' Joni Mitchell's 'I Don't Know Where I Stand,' Randy Newman's 'I'll Be Home,' Cynthia Weil and Barry Mann's 'Just a Little Lovin'' – all rather gentle pop songs – and Laura Nyro's rocker 'Stoney End.' As she listened to a playback of that last number, Barbra smiled, turned to Perry, and whispered, 'You were right and I was wrong. But it's nice to be wrong.'

Barbra 'was going through a metamorphosis,' Perry said, 'not just musically but in a lot of ways.' But she still had a long way to go, evidently. When Perry, in Los Angeles, sent a mix of 'Stoney End' to Barbra at her apartment in New York, she called him to say that the tape had no background vocals. 'That's impossible,' Perry replied. 'They're there.'

'I don't hear any,' Barbra said.

'Look, I'm coming to New York tomorrow,' Perry told her. 'I'll come over and we'll listen.'

When Perry listened, he turned to Barbra and said, 'No wonder there's no background vocals – one of your speakers is out.' Three months later, Perry paid a visit to Barbra's house on Carolwood Drive and found that she had had state-of-the-art audio equipment installed, including a complete professional tape deck with huge stereo monitors built into the walls. 'When she goes,' Perry said, 'she goes all the way.'

When Clive Davis heard 'Stoney End,' he felt it had hit potential, but he encountered opposition to the idea, beginning with his own staff. Three versions of the song had been released, sung by Darlene Love, Peggy Lipton, and Nyro herself, and none had done all that well. Barbra hadn't had a hit single since 'People' six years earlier, and radio stations rarely played her songs. Many within the company felt they should wait to see how the album did before releasing a single. Others found Barbra's voice unrecognizable on the record and suggested a radio contest: 'Guess who this singer is?'

Undaunted, Davis authorized the single release of 'Stoney End,' backed by 'I'll Be Home,' in mid-September. Marty Erlichman went on the road with two of Columbia's promotion men to push it. They traveled to seven cities in ten days, visiting the major radio stations and key record stores in each city. The stores featured a life-sized cardboard cutout of Barbra next to a telephone – an idea of Marty's. When customers picked up the phone, they would hear a greeting from Barbra and a few snippets of 'Stoney End.'

In spite of the promotion, disc jockeys resisted the song; by the end of October no major radio station had included it on its playlist. Doggedly, Columbia persisted. They 'reserviced' the record, shipping it again to stations around the country. Barbra made rare personal appeals. She wrote letters to disc jockeys, placed several phone calls in selected cities, and hosted a reception for DJs at the Fairmont Hotel in San Francisco.

Finally 'Stoney End' started to get airplay, and when it did, the public responded. The record inched its way up the charts through December and January until it reached number six nationally, a startling turnaround for the commercially moribund Streisand. In some cities it fared even better.

Richard Perry recalled driving in his car with Barbra down Sunset Boulevard one night. 'The guy on the radio says, "And now the number one record in L.A. this week: 'Stoney End!'" It was such a thrill for us, like a fantasy.'

The success of 'Stoney End' convinced Barbra that she should scrap *The Singer* and proceed with plans for a contemporary album. In February, Columbia released *Stoney End*, which featured the songs she had initially recorded in July, plus six others. Columbia's print ads confronted the issue of Barbra's transformation head on: 'A new album by a young singer' blared the headlines, and the copy read: 'It's easy to forget how young Barbra Streisand is. After all, most people in their twenties haven't made two plays, four TV specials, four movies, and sixteen albums. Now on her new album . . . Barbra sings the songs of today's best young composers.' Lest Barbra's long-time fans worry, the ad reassured them that 'while other performers her age sing the songs of young composers to people even younger, Barbra sings them for everyone.'

Stoney End won nearly uniformly favorable reviews and rose to number ten on the pop charts. One critic felt that 'this album is going to impress a whole lot of people who were never very much impressed by Miss Streisand and her attitudes . . . Streisand doesn't sound like Streisand here. She sounds like one hell of a singer belting her guts out, and the effect is immediately appealing.'

With the success of *Stoney End*, Barbra Streisand was back on top of a radically changed musical world. Not everyone was pleased, though. Some of her earliest fans felt she had betrayed them; they hated pop and rock music and thought she should continue to interpret Harold Arlen and Richard Rodgers. Others felt she still hadn't made the grade with this album. One of these was Peter Matz, who had arranged and conducted *What About Today?* 'They were all good songs,' he said, 'and the album was consistent – *What About Today?* wasn't consistent. But I was bothered by the fact that many of those songs were just duplicates of other people's versions.'

Five months later Barbra released another album of music by contemporary songwriters, and this one proved, as Stephen Holden put it in *Rolling Stone*, an 'uneasy mix.' The album commingled the hard rock primal scream of John Lennon's 'Mother' with the traditional sound of Michel Legrand and Marilyn and Alan Bergman's 'The Summer Knows.' Richard Perry felt that the album's eclecticism reflected 'the fact that we were, on the one hand, experimenting further into the rock idiom, and on the other, there were still other songs Barbra liked. "The Summer Knows" didn't work with the other material, but it was like, "What the hell?"'

Barbra Joan Streisand equaled the success of *Stoney End*, and seemed to show that although Streisand was still finding her way with pop and rock, she had established a new, youthful fan base strong enough to support any number of future rock efforts. But Barbra, having proved she could do it, wouldn't release another album of pop-rock music for three years. And in an ironic twist, two years later she would release a more traditional collection that would become her first number one album in nine years.

ONSTAGE AT THE Las Vegas Hilton, Barbra got stoned on marijuana. She had done a comic 'pot bit' in the show from the beginning of her triumphant return engagement, which had started at the Riviera on November 27, in fulfillment of her 1963 contract with the hotel, then moved over to the Hilton on December 13. Smoking pot had become so commonplace by 1970 that even though it was illegal, more and more people made little effort to hide their use of the drug. Elliott Gould had, in fact, freely smoked a joint during his *Playboy* interview. For the most part, authorities looked the other way, especially for celebrities.

Barbra had decided to use a fake marijuana cigarette as part of a comic monologue about confronting one's anxieties. 'Last year I was so nervous about working in this town,' she would tell the audience. 'I went to see Dean Martin, and I couldn't believe how calm he was, how relaxed. Of course, he drinks. And there are performers, I'm told, who take pills. I can barely swallow aspirin, so that's out. Besides, I don't think people should use any kind of crutch for their nervousness. I believe we should be strong' – here she would stop and take a long, theatrical drag on the 'joint' – 'and face our nervousness head on, you know?'

It was a funny bit, and everyone knew that Barbra was only kidding. But during her last show, late on the Saturday night of January 2, she wasn't kidding. 'I started lighting live joints, passing them around to the band, you know?' Barbra said later. 'It was *great*. It relieved all my tensions.' It also came close to sending her act right down the drain, as a tape of the performance made by a fan indicates.

As soon as Barbra took her first drag that night, after she had sung three songs, the Borscht Belt comedian Shecky Greene came onstage and announced that he had been sent by the Las Vegas narco squad to arrest Barbra. She pushed a joint at him and told him, 'You'll love it, Shecky.' They kibitzed for a while, and then Barbra told him, 'I want to see you work this room.' For the next fifteen minutes Greene took over the show while Barbra stood idly by, occasionally interjecting a comment or two.

Once Greene left the stage, Barbra sang three more songs, but then she began to ramble, her mind wandering all over the place while she laughed and giggled a lot.

'What am I doing?' she asked after about fifteen minutes of this. 'Oh, my God . . . This is the same show that I started about an hour ago . . . Where were . . . What do . . . What do I usually do here? Oh, yeah. I talk about some *feckuckteh* thing here . . . I'm so bored with it!'

A few minutes later she apparently thought her stool was someplace it wasn't. 'There are evil spirits among us,' she said to the band. 'You didn't do that? What is this? That was spook time. This moved by itself. Did it move by itself? Did you see it? Who moved that? Who moved it? Howard Hughes moved it. Oh, my God.'

Then she began a monologue she had delivered in every show, essentially the silly story about Pearl from Istanbul's lost button, which she had told on her first television special, but with a lengthy new introduction about searching for artifacts in the desert near Las Vegas. This evening she spent four minutes on the introduction, building to the gist of the story. Then she completely lost her train of thought and never mentioned Pearl from Istanbul again. Instead she started offering her observations about Shecky Greene's act, leaving her audience completely mystified about why she had started the monologue in the first place.

Some considered this a surprising lapse in Streisand's usual professionalism, but the frat house atmosphere she had created didn't end with her. As she introduced the members of the band, the one female musician, a harpist, stood up and took her bow. As she did so the front of her dress fell down, revealing her naked breasts.

According to the hotel's advertising director, Dennis Ritz, the whole thing had been planned as a practical joke by Marty Erlichman. Marty had asked Ritz to pay a showgirl $500 to replace the actual harpist at the last minute and bare all as Barbra introduced her. When Barbra saw this, all her joviality left her. She gasped and asked the woman, for all the audience to hear, 'Why would you do that to yourself?'

'Barbra was *pissed*,' Ritz recalled. 'I had never seen her react that way before. Afterward there was a reception, and I came into the party with the girl. Barbra said to her, "I don't even want to look at you. How could you *do* that?"'

After her own performance that night, it was a question many in Barbra's audience wanted to ask her, too.

From all appearances, Elliott Gould had flipped out. In February 1971 he turned up at the Manhattan location of his new comic fantasy film, *A Glimpse of Tiger*, with a six-day growth of beard, chomping an old cigar butt and wearing a knee-length navy pea coat with an American flag where the belt should have been. Elliott was producing the picture with his partner, the former publicist Jack Brodsky. The esteemed director Anthony Harvey (*The Lion in Winter*) was at the helm, and the twenty-four-year-old actress Kim Darby had been cast as the teenage sidekick to Elliott's con man.

By the end of the day, depending on which report one believes, Elliott had either threatened to or had actually struck either Harvey or Darby or both of them. He fired Harvey in midafternoon, and his violent, irrational outbursts left Darby trembling in fear. Word got back to Warner Brothers that Elliott probably had a drug problem, and if he didn't, he must be losing his mind. 'I was very unstable, but it wasn't drugs,' Elliott later insisted. 'Sure, I smoked grass and did psychedelics a little, but I was *not* a druggie or a crazy. Gimme a break. I was a *lamb*, unaware of the laws of the jungle.'

A frantic Brodsky called Barbra, hoping she could settle Elliott down. She talked to him for thirty minutes; he calmed down and apologized to everyone. An hour later Brodsky called Barbra again with some new horror story.

Sometimes Elliott would blow a shrill whistle while other actors were performing, ruining take after take. He fired Brodsky, then rehired him. By the third day of filming, the location resembled an armed camp as uniformed security guards encircled the set. Explained Paul Heller, the Warner executive assigned to watch the *Tiger* set, 'Kim Darby was quite afraid of Elliott, so we hired several [security people] to calm her.'

'I was threatened by men with weapons on my own movie set,' Elliott said years later. 'I was forced to stay away.' Warner executives had decided that if Elliott didn't have his act together by the next day they would shut down production. The following morning Elliott failed to show up, and Heller informed his bosses. They told him to call them back if Elliott didn't turn up in an hour, and the movie would be off. When Heller tried to make the call, he found that 'every phone booth in the area had had the wires cut.'

Warner Brothers canceled the film and sued Elliott for its production costs. In order to recoup some of its expenses from an insurance company, the studio compiled a dossier on Elliott's behavior and sent it to several psychiatrists. 'Without even examining me,' Elliott said, 'they came to the conclusion the person in that dossier must be mad. That way the producers were able to collect insurance on the film.'

Gould has admitted, 'It was a difficult time . . . To be considered mad was an unnerving experience . . . Even Elvis Presley, who'd said he was an admirer of mine, sat down in front of me, a gold forty-five in his belt, and told me, "You're crazy."'

Elliott agreed to repay Warner Brothers for a large portion of its loss. He didn't have much money, though, because in the two years following the *Glimpse of Tiger* debacle no producer would touch him, and he didn't work at all.

It was a spectacular crash landing to one of the most meteoric rises to stardom in movie history. In the year and a half following the announcement of his separation from Barbra early in 1969, Elliott's career had skyrocketed until he was a bona fide movie star and an antihero to the youthful counter-culture. He received an Oscar nomination as Best Supporting Actor in 1969 for *Bob & Carol & Ted & Alice*, his third film, and made the cover of *Time* after his next picture, the smash hit antiwar black comedy *M*A*S*H*. Proclaiming him a 'star for an uptight age,' the magazine predicted that Elliott would have a bigger and longer-lasting career than his estranged wife. The National Association of Theater Owners named him Star of the Year for 1970. 'Sometimes I think I must have sold my soul to the devil,' he said of his success at the time, 'and that he's going to be around soon to collect.'

ACCORDING TO ELLIOTT, in the summer of 1970, about sixth months after they entered into a legal separation, Barbra decided she wanted him back. Perhaps she felt that his success would put their relationship on a more even footing. Perhaps, as he said, 'She didn't want to be alone.' Or perhaps she realized how much she loved him after all. Elliott was in Sweden, where he had been cast as the first non-Swedish star of an Ingmar Bergman film, *The Touch*. Barbra flew to Stockholm and told Elliott she wanted to give their marriage another try.

But Elliott was now deeply involved with Jenny Bogart, the lovely eighteen-year-old flower-child daughter of the director Paul Bogart, whom he had met in Dustin Hoffman's apartment. Unambitious, yielding, Jenny represented the polar opposite of Barbra. 'I'd like to marry a beautiful woman who isn't in show business,' Elliott said. 'That would be the double opposite of Barbra.' Jenny, he felt, had a certain 'hopelessness,' and he felt he 'could be of help.'

'Barbra wanted us to get back together immediately,' Elliott said, but he told her that he couldn't leave Jenny. 'I didn't know that was my last opportunity [with Barbra], and I don't know if it would have made a difference if I had known.'

Barbra came home, and on June 30, 1971, she and Elliott jointly filed for divorce in the Dominican Republic, where the matter was finalized quickly and with a minimum of publicity. There were no recriminations, no requests for alimony on either side. Barbra was granted custody of Jason and allowed Elliott liberal visitation rights. Still, the most difficult aspect of the divorce for Elliott was his separation from Jason. 'It's unnatural to *visit* your son,' he said. 'God, it's hard.'

To make things worse for him, he didn't approve of the way Barbra was raising Jason. Despite her statement while she was pregnant that children should be allowed to be 'dirty and basic when they want to be,' Elliott was appalled to find that Barbra had hired someone to teach Jason etiquette – at two years old. He also didn't like the fact that his son was cared for primarily by a nanny and was surrounded only by females. 'I like getting Jason away from Barbra's house,' he said. 'He's got so many women around him, I feel like I've done a service to take him away for an hour.'

AFTER THE *Glimpse of Tiger* fiasco, Barbra worried about Elliott. During a meeting with Warner executive John Calley, whom she had dated over the prior year, Barbra asked if there was anything she could do to dissuade the studio from suing Gould for punitive damages. Calley suggested that *A Glimpse of Tiger* be rewritten so that Barbra could take over Elliott's role and play a female con artist with a young male sidekick.

The idea intrigued her, and she told Calley she had the perfect director: Peter Bogdanovich. She had seen a preview screening of his first major film, *The Last Picture Show*, a stark character study set in a small Texas town in the 1950s, which went on to garner eight Oscar nominations. Barbra considered it brilliant and felt that Bogdanovich could help her turn *A Glimpse of Tiger* from a lightweight comic fantasy into a serious exploration of relationships and social issues.

Bogdanovich had other ideas. The intense thirty-one-year-old wunderkind had gotten his start as an uncredited second-unit director and screenwriter on Roger Corman's *The Wild Angels* in 1966, then had directed some sequences of a cheap Russian import, *Voyage to the Planet of Prehistoric Women*. In 1968 he won acclaim for *Targets*, a cult cheapie with Boris Karloff, and was given the opportunity to make *The Last Picture Show*. An inveterate movie fan, Bogdanovich adored the screwball comedies of the 1930s, especially those by Howard Hawks and Preston Sturges, and he wanted his next picture to be a homage to them and a light change of pace for him.

Suddenly he was presented with the chance to work with Barbra Streisand, arguably the best film comedienne of the day. *A Glimpse of Tiger* didn't interest him, however. 'It was kind of a comedy-drama with a lot of social overtones,' he said, 'and I didn't like it at all.' But he very much wanted to work with Streisand. He told her he wanted to do a slapstick comedy and would have his friends David Newman and Robert Benton, who had written the brilliant Oscar-nominated script for *Bonnie and Clyde*, write it.

'It'll be just like *Bringing Up Baby*,' Bogdanovich told her. 'You know, the Howard Hawks picture with Katharine Hepburn and Cary Grant. You'll play this free-spirited zany girl who meets this stuffy scientific-type guy and turns his life upside down. It'll be great.'

'Well, I guess so,' Barbra had replied. 'As long as Ryan O'Neal plays the guy.'

BARBRA HAD MET the blond, boyishly handsome twenty-nine-year-old O'Neal at a dinner party in Hollywood a year earlier, and sparks had flown between them immediately. She found herself attracted to Ryan's healthy physicality and surfer-boy looks, which fit right in with her new image as a slim, tanned, long-haired, blond-streaked California girl. An ex-boxer, O'Neal made her feel physically safe when they went out together. And he had quite a reputation as a sexual swordsman. 'He's an incredible lover, totally devoted to giving a woman pleasure,' vouched his first wife, the actress Joanna Moore.

O'Neal had gained a strong fan following in the mid-sixties by appearing in over five hundred episodes of television's popular night-time soap opera *Peyton Place* as stud-louse Rodney Harrington. In 1970 he got his big break in movies and made the most of it: his role in the wildly popular tearjerker *Love Story* won him a Best Actor nomination.

Because O'Neal had not yet divorced his second wife, the lovely actress Leigh Taylor-Young, Barbra and Ryan attempted to keep their relationship under wraps. They were successful for a while, but when they showed up together at a party, then attended a James Taylor concert together in Los Angeles, a buzz began. On January 10, 1971, they went to a private dinner party, then to the Santa Monica Civic Auditorium for a Mama Cass Elliot concert. Ryan's younger brother, Kevin, went along as a beard: he was supposed to be Barbra's date, and Ryan their chaperon.

Peter Borsari, one of the Hollywood paparazzi, tried to take a picture of Barbra and Ryan together as they left the party, but they refused and ran to their car. Borsari followed them to the concert, waited until they came out, and tried again. Kevin O'Neal grabbed Borsari's camera.

'Don't fight me. I can sue!' the photographer yelled.

'You can sue me for as much as you want,' Kevin shouted back, throwing a punch. 'I don't have any money anyway.'

Borsari's camera was damaged, and Barbra and Ryan wound up splashed across the front pages of the national tabloids. The more cynical Hollywood gossips tittered that Barbra Streisand had found herself a toy boy, a cute hunk with a hard body and not much upstairs, and that Ryan O'Neal had linked himself up with the most powerful actress in Hollywood to further his career.

The cynics had it wrong. 'Barbra's far too bright to ever be with somebody just because he's a hunk,' said Steve Jaffe, Ryan's public relations man at the time. 'And Barbra had a lot of choices of men she could have dated. I'd be at her house and the phone calls that would come in! Extraordinary men would be on the line. But she wanted Ryan, and it wasn't just for his body.'

Although Jaffe saw 'a wonderful physicality between the two of them, like two fighters sparring,' he felt that Ryan's attractiveness to Barbra was based on 'his wit, his charm, his mind, and *then* his good looks. Ryan has an incredibly quick wit, and the mental sparring between him and Barbra was fantastic because she's incredibly responsive to quick-witted people. Ryan made her laugh a lot, which she loved, particularly because most people were afraid to be themselves around her, and that deprived her of a lot of humor.' Barbra loved the fact that Ryan rarely used her real name; instead he'd call her Ceil or Hilda or Sadie.

According to Jaffe, Ryan had a lot to teach Barbra. 'Ryan O'Neal is a philosopher by nature. He liked to expound on things, and his opinions sounded like they'd been tested. He knew where the bodies were buried and how you could get into trouble in Hollywood. Barbra would soak it all up like a sponge.'

'Ryan and I had an argument on our first date,' Barbra said. 'He won. I never felt better losing ... Ryan isn't afraid of my image; he respects my talent, but he's not in awe of my career. I guess that's what made me like him first.'

The romance blossomed through the early months of 1971. The couple held hands at parties, went shopping together, and played on the beach in Malibu with Jason. On June 14, Barbra performed five songs and her marijuana routine at a Los Angeles fund-raiser to benefit the Motion Picture and TV Relief Fund. For most of the show she and Ryan sat in the front row, holding hands and watching performances by Jimmy Durante, Bob Hope, Pearl Bailey, the Fifth Dimension, and other acts. After Barbra's performance, the next-to-last of the evening, she rejoined Ryan to watch Frank Sinatra give what was billed as his farewell performance. (He later un-retired.)

Four nights later Ryan escorted Barbra to the opening of his latest film, *The Wild Rovers*. This time the couple let themselves be photographed, and newspapers across the country ran the pictures under headlines like 'A New Love Story?' By now neither Barbra nor Ryan cared who knew about their relationship. They were young, in love – and about to start a movie together.

'*WHAT'S UP, DOC?!*' Barbra exclaimed when Peter Bogdanovich told her the title he'd come up with for their film. 'I'm not going to be in a picture called *What's Up, Doc?!*' In the ensuing weeks Barbra's conviction that she had made a mistake in agreeing to do a slapstick comedy hardened. She didn't think the movie Bogdanovich was fashioning was funny, and she didn't think the classic comedies the director wanted to model it after were very funny, either.

The screenwriters David Newman and Robert Benton, friends of Bogdanovich's since the mid-sixties, whipped up the script of *What's Up, Doc?* in a week and a half that February. Newman recalled, 'Peter said he needed it fast because he had a "pay or play" deal with Streisand and O'Neal. If he didn't have a script ready to shoot by July, they were gone. So we flew out to Los Angeles and went into these intensive sessions with Peter where we hashed out the story. Peter would talk to Howard Hawks every night, and he'd come in the next day and say, "Howard thinks we should try such-and-such."'

Barbra had a lot of influence on the script as well. 'Peter talked to her every night,' Newman recalled. 'He'd tell her the story so far, then the next morning he'd say, "Barbra loved this, she didn't like that, she thinks it would be funny if she got to do that."'

Bogdanovich arranged for Barbra and Ryan to see a steady stream of his favorite screwball comedies, and Newman recalled the night he, Benton, Bogdanovich, Barbra, and Ryan watched Preston Sturges's *The Lady Eve*, starring Barbara Stanwyck and Henry Fonda, in Barbra's basement screening room at Carolwood. 'Peter, Benton, and I *loved* this movie. We knew it frame by frame. It's a hilarious, classic, fall-down slapstick comedy.'

Newman had never met Barbra or Ryan before, but when he did, he felt they'd be great together in the movie. 'There was a lot of funny bantering between them,' he recalled. 'They kidded each other a lot. There was a *Thin Man*, Nick and Nora Charles feel about them.'

When *The Lady Eve* unreeled, Peter, Barbra, and Ryan sat behind Newman and Benton. The two writers started laughing right away, and every so often Bogdanovich would guffaw. Soon Newman realized that he hadn't heard so much as a giggle from either Barbra or Ryan. 'Then I heard Barbra say, "That's four for her and only two for him." I turned around and asked, "What?" It turned out she was counting the close-ups. And Ryan said, "Oh, there's another one for him; that makes it four to three."'

A short time later Barbra stood up and said, 'Okay, that's enough, I know what you mean,' and halted the screening. Newman felt that the essence of her reaction was 'I hope we can do better than *this*.' He walked out of the film 'feeling stunned because we had just seen one of our favorite movies and Barbra didn't think it was any good. And when Peter screened *Bringing Up Baby* for her, she thought that was awful, too.'

Undeterred, Bogdanovich and his writers began to work on a second draft of *What's Up, Doc?* They came up with the story of Judy Maxwell, a free-spirited girl with a near-genius IQ, who has been thrown out of innumerable universities for things like accidentally blowing up the chemistry lab, and the tumultuous effect she has on the life of Howard Bannister, a staid young musicologist from Iowa. Howard and his fiancée, Eunice, have come to San Francisco, where Howard hopes to win the $20,000 Frederick Larrabee Grant for a theory he has formulated about early man's musical relationship to igneous rocks. His chief competitor is Hugh Simon, a villainous, pompous Hungarian inspired by the vitriolic New York film and theater critic John Simon, who had recently given both Bogdanovich and Barbra scathing notices.

As Judy barrels her way into Bannister's life, calling him Steve and pretending to be Eunice at a welcoming luncheon, four identical plaid overnight bags supply sublime slapstick humor. Judy's contains her clothes, Howard's his igneous rock formations and his tuning fork. A third carries the very rich Mrs Van Hoskins's collection of jewels, and the fourth hides top-secret documents stolen by a government reformer. The hotel's security chief and desk clerk want the jewels, and a secret agent wants the papers back. No one very much wants Judy's undies or Howard's rocks, but their cases add much to the confusion and mayhem, which includes a fire in Howard's hotel room.

A lengthy chase takes car after car through the streets of San Francisco, through a huge pane of glass, down hundreds of stone steps, into a Chinese dragon, past a frantic cement layer, and finally into the bay. When all is said and done, Howard regains the Larrabee Grant, which he had forfeited to Hugh Simon because of all the trouble Judy caused, when she reveals that Simon is a plagiarist. Eunice ends up with Frederick Larrabee, and Howard winds up with Judy, who just happens to be seated in the row behind him on the plane back to Ames, Iowa.

Bogdanovich wasn't entirely happy with the Newman-Benton script, so he called in Buck Henry for a rewrite. 'There was just six weeks before we were supposed to begin filming,' Henry said. 'I didn't think I could do it in six weeks, but Barbra was going to walk off and so was Ryan, and they were right. The script was in no condition to shoot. Peter asked me, "Can you do something about Barbra's part?"'

'Well, I couldn't rewrite Barbra without rewriting Ryan, and I changed so much of Ryan that I caught her up a little short. And when Barbra saw the script, like most actors she counted the pages. There's a very long period in there where she doesn't say anything – the whole chase scene and the court scene, and all the stuff between Howard and Eunice. She, understandably as a movie star, thought, Where am I? How did I get lost?'

Whenever Barbra expressed her growing misgivings about this project, Bogdanovich would invariably tell her, 'Trust me.' And, dazzled as she was by *The Last Picture Show*, she did. 'I gave up script approval, costume approval, everything, to him,' she said. Once Bogdanovich was happy with the script, he showed it to Barbra. 'This doesn't seem very funny to me,' she told him. 'It'll play funny, Barbra, you'll see,' he assured her. '*Trust me.*'

ON THE FIRST day of rehearsals Barbra *really* started to worry. Bogdanovich had assembled a sterling cast of mostly New York-based theater comic actors to complement his two stars: the droopy-faced Austin Pendleton as Frederick Larrabee, the veteran Mabel Albertson as Mrs Van Hoskins, the histrionic Kenneth Mars as Hugh Simon, and the brilliant comic actress Madeline Kahn, a Broadway star who had never before appeared in a film, as Howard's fiancée, Eunice Burns.

Buck Henry recalled that 'these guys were really hot' at the first reading of the script around a huge table on a soundstage at the Warner Brothers Studios in Burbank. Madeline Kahn gave Eunice a hilarious whine, Austin Pendleton's Frederick Larrabee had a sublime obliviousness, and Kenneth Mars brought to Hugh Simon a delicious dollop of malice. 'Ken got ahold of some old tapes of John Simon on television,' Pendleton recalled. 'He watched them over and over again until he got the accent and behavior down pat. John

Simon never forgave anyone involved in the movie for that.' At one point, as she listened to Mars impersonate Simon, Barbra called out with delight, 'Meaner! Make him meaner!'

Buck Henry felt that 'Barbra and Ryan were already nervous, and I think Barbra really got twitchy about it because all those other people were going to be very good.' But Ryan thought Barbra was the funniest of the lot: 'God, she was wonderful!' he said. Among this group Ryan, not a comedian and an actor of limited range, clearly had his work cut out for him. Steve Jaffe recalled seeing Ryan 'dancing around like Muhammad Ali before a fight, just getting ready for a scene with Barbra. He was trying to act at his absolute peak. Not only because Barbra's so great and such a perfectionist but because he was in love with her. He wanted her to respect him. He wanted to be as good as he could be.'

Filming of *What's Up, Doc?* began on location in San Francisco on August 16. Barbra adopted a look for the picture that wasn't far different from the way she looked in everyday life in this period. She was thinner than she had been in nearly ten years, and deeply tanned; both the weight loss and the color in her face heightened her cheekbones and gave her face a lovely chiseled quality. She wore light makeup; her long blond-streaked hair, parted in the middle, tumbled past her shoulders. She wore tight slacks and little halter tops that revealed her smooth, creamy shoulders. Unlike Daisy Gamble, and much more than Doris Wilgus, Judy Maxwell was a child of the seventies.

The cast and crew stayed in sixty rooms at the San Francisco Hilton, which Bogdanovich used for the numerous hotel scenes in the film. But Barbra and Ryan shared a suite of rooms at the far posher Huntington Hotel on Nob Hill. They were so discreet about their affair, and Barbra and Bogdanovich were so affectionate with each other, that observers wondered whether Barbra had thrown over her leading man in favor of her director. The writer Pat Rogalla, a visitor to the set, watched Bogdanovich discuss an upcoming scene with Streisand. 'Bogdanovich frequently calls her "gorgeous," holds her hand, kisses her cheek, and once patted her backside. Barbra responded to him with warm smiles and hugs.'

There was no romance, but the director took good care of his star. During a scene where she picks up a telephone immediately after an extra has used it, Bogdanovich called 'Cut!' in the middle of take after take just after the man hung up the receiver. Each time a crew member would rush over and spray the telephone with disinfectant, and only then would Barbra pick it up.

Barbra seems to have gotten along well with everyone in the cast. Between takes they would all sit around in a circle and talk about themselves, almost as though they were in group therapy. 'I've never been on a film where there was such a group feeling,' Austin Pendleton said. 'We'd talk about acting, mostly. I think Barbra was a little in awe of us because we were New York stage actors. She talked about how impressed she'd been with Bibi Andersson's performance in *The Touch*, the Ingmar Bergman film Elliott had just done. She said she wanted to attain that kind of simplicity, which was incredibly complex without being acted out or demonstrated.

'Barbra talked about things in her life, about seeing Pierre Trudeau, that kind of thing. I got the impression they still saw each other occasionally. And it was funny because she was so famous most of us had already read about the things she was telling us. We wanted to say, "Yeah, yeah, Barbra, we know all about that." But she wasn't like some superstars who get bored the minute the subject isn't them. Barbra was interested in our lives and ideas and problems, too.'

One of the reasons the cast couldn't wait to take breaks and continue their discussions was the extreme stress of acting in *What's Up, Doc?* 'I have never been in a more difficult film,' Pendleton asserted. 'The intricacy of the line cueing was exhausting. Peter would do everything in master shots, and he wanted everybody to talk fast, fast, fast. We couldn't do it fast enough for him. And we had overlapping dialogue. The pressure was tremendous, because if you blew a line, the entire shot would be ruined and everybody – not just you – would have to do the whole scene again.'

It may have been this difficulty that made Barbra doubt that anything in *What's Up, Doc?* was funny. As Pat Rogalla put it, 'Barbra appeared to be working with gritted teeth.' After nearly every scene, she would nudge O'Neal and say, 'We're in a piece of shit, Ryan!' She never let up. Again and again she told O'Neal, 'This is not funny, Ryan. I know what's funny, and I'm telling you this movie isn't funny.'

PETER BOGDANOVICH HAD a tendency to play out every scene himself in order to show his cast exactly what he wanted them to do. This approach worked well with O'Neal. 'He let Peter place him, his body and his voice,' said Buck Henry. 'Ryan was playing Peter.' But the first time Bogdanovich showed Barbra how he wanted her to recite some dialogue, she looked at him as though he had lost his mind. 'Are *you* giving *me* line readings?' she asked.

Bogdanovich might have been the strongest, and certainly the most hands-on, director Barbra had ever worked with. That she put herself as much in his hands as she did is quite remarkable. 'He was opinionated and autocratic,' she said. 'He knows how he wants to do things, and he doesn't waste a lot of time.' While Bogdanovich coddled Barbra in many ways, he didn't take any nonsense from her. He always won their battles over a line reading or the arc of a scene. 'She tried to direct me, but we put a stop to that real quick,' he said. Sometimes he seemed to take a particular course just to keep her in her place. After a dozen takes on one scene she said to him, 'You should print that last take, Peter. It never will get better.' Bogdanovich demanded one more go, and after that take he shouted, 'Print it!'

One day, out of the blue, for no apparent reason, Bogdanovich demanded of Barbra, 'Sing something!' She responded with about four bars of 'People.'

THE COMPLICATED FARCICAL chase that takes up a large portion of the film's second half posed physical dangers to the cast and crew. For everything but the close-ups, Bogdanovich used stunt doubles for both Barbra and Ryan. Ray Gosnell, one of the film's assistant directors, recalled that 'The first double for Barbra broke her ankle, so we had to use a man as a double for Barbra in the scene where she and Ryan ride the cart down those steep streets. But for the close-ups we needed Barbra, and the cart had to be moving as fast as it was in the long shots. She wasn't happy about it – it was a little cart going down a steep hill, and it was stressful for her, and a bit frightening.'

Later in the chase, as Barbra and Ryan ran through an alley after changing into costumes to disguise themselves, Ryan wrenched his back. In the finished film he can be seen at the moment of injury as he nearly loses his balance and then hops on one foot for a few moments before the camera switches to pursuing cars. His injury was serious enough that several months after filming ended he needed spinal surgery.

By then he and Barbra were no longer an item. 'Ryan had a very highly attuned libido,' Steve Jaffe said. 'Barbra and everyone else knew it.'

Ryan's roving eye likely doomed his relationship with Barbra. Neither has ever spoken about the reason for their breakup, but she was reportedly miffed when Peggy Lipton, the exquisite young star of television's *Mod Squad*, visited him on the *Doc* set. Later he wooed the Playboy bunny and actress Joyce Williams as well as Lana Wood and Bogdanovich's estranged wife, Polly Platt. Barbra dated the Czech director Milos Forman and Steve McQueen – in retaliation, some conjectured.

Still, Barbra and Ryan remained good friends. While he recovered from his surgery at St John's Hospital in Santa Monica in December, Barbra was appearing in Las Vegas, and she flew down twice to visit him. 'Poor Ryan,' she said at the time. 'I feel so terrible for him; you know they've removed two disks from his spine.' During her visits, Barbra said, 'Ryan's spirits were good. He was in a lot of pain, but he was very valiant about it all. He was lying in bed, and you know, he has that terribly irresistible little-boy quality

about him. I have that terrible Brooklyn Jewish need to mother. Maybe that's
why we get along so well.'

'I found Barbra very sexy,' Ryan said somewhat later. 'A terrific girl.' Then
he added, in mock dismay, 'but I think she *used* me!'

TOWARD THE END of 1971 Barbra met with the director Jerry Schatzberg
to discuss his directing her next film, *Up the Sandbox*. They never came to
an agreement on that, but Schatzberg did spend a memorable evening with
Streisand. 'We were at this party,' he recalled, 'and Mae West was there.
Barbra was all excited to see her and went over to talk to her. Everyone in
our group was dying of curiosity about what these two Hollywood giants of
their generations would say to each other. A few minutes later Barbra came
back, laughing. She said she had asked Mae what she felt the difference
was between the Hollywood of Mae's heyday and today. Mae gave her one
of those looks and in her inimitable way said, "Well, honey, the biggest
difference is, today there are no stars."'

BARBRA RETURNED TO the Las Vegas Hilton between December 24, 1971,
and January 13, 1972, at a salary of $125,000 a week. It was the last time
she would perform in Vegas for twenty-two years. She put on essentially the
same show as she had the prior holiday season, adding a few songs from the
Barbra Joan Streisand album.

The reviews were excellent. Barbra seemed finally to have learned the
knack of *seeming* to enjoy performing in front of a Las Vegas crowd. But
she was determined never to do it again. Robert Klein was her opening act,
and he remembers her telling him that she found the engagement 'a drag.'

Barbra offered Klein her friendship and moral support, and he provided
her with companionship. 'She was lonely,' he recalled. 'The nanny had taken
Jason to New York to see Elliott, and Barbra was all alone in this nine-room
suite at the Hilton. We were good company for each other. She would invite
me to her dressing room after the show, and sometimes we'd smoke a little
grass.' That may have helped Barbra get through the three weeks, which she
couldn't wait to be over. 'I was in the dressing room when Al Shoofey, the
president of the Hilton, came in and *begged* her to extend her three-week
engagement,' Klein said. 'She was of no mind to.' Shoofey did everything
he could to woo her into giving the hotel another week, including a $6,000
watch and six complete tennis outfits with her name on each piece. Barbra
wouldn't budge. She had had her fill of Las Vegas.

✴

A FEW WEEKS after Barbra closed in Vegas, she attended a small private screening of *What's Up, Doc?* with Ryan, Marty Erlichman, Peter Bogdanovich, John Calley, and various Hollywood insiders. As the movie unreeled, there were pockets of sporadic laughter, but for the most part the reaction was deadly, even allowing for the notorious taciturnity of industry audiences. Barbra muttered to anyone who would listen, 'I *told* you this wasn't funny,' and she offered to bet John Calley $10,000 that the movie wouldn't even gross $5 million. Calley refused the bet because he knew Barbra wasn't likely to pay, but he did accept her offer to sell back to him the 10 percent share of the profits her contract guaranteed her.

This turned out to be one of Barbra's worst business missteps, because for one of the few times in her career she was dead wrong. When the movie was shown to a general audience at a preview, the laughter was so loud and so continuous that many of the lines got lost and most of the audience said they wanted to see it again to get all the jokes. When the film opened at Radio City Music Hall in New York on March 9, it won mostly rave reviews, and it went on to draw over $70 million in box-office receipts to become Barbra's biggest grosser to that date. The film's huge success propelled Streisand to her first designation as Box Office Champ of the Year.

In many ways *What's Up, Doc?* is a watershed film for Barbra. Despite all the departures from Streisand's movie past *The Owl and the Pussycat* had provided, Doris Wilgus was yet another loud-mouthed, aggressive fantasy woman with little relationship to reality. Judy Maxwell, for all her eccentricities, is someone audiences can imagine having as an acquaintance, a girl whose pushiness as she pursues Howard Bannister is swathed in a softly appealing contemporary femininity. Tanned and slim as she is, Barbra looks prettier than ever, and she exudes a healthy California Golden Girl vitality that seems light-years away from her origins in the concrete canyons of New York.

Two major critics had diverse opinions about this new Streisand approach. 'Not the least of Bogdanovich's triumphs is his success in scaling down Miss Streisand's superstar personality to fit the dimensions of farce,' Vincent Canby wrote in *The New York Times.* 'Although she never lets us forget the power that always seems to be held in uncertain check, she is surprisingly appealing, more truly comic than she's ever been on film.'

Pauline Kael disagreed: 'Streisand sings a sizzling "You're the Top" behind the titles, and there's a moment in the movie when the audience cheers as she starts to sing "As Time Goes By," but it's just a teaser, and it has to last for the whole movie. Why? Nothing that happens in the movie – none of the chases or comic confusions – has the excitement of her singing. When a tiger pretends to be a pussycat, that's practically a form of Uncle Tomism.'

Most critics and audiences sided with Canby. What is most fascinating about Streisand in *What's Up, Doc?* is that even scaled down, she is still the most compelling performer amid a company of comic geniuses. While the others have wildly hilarious moments, Barbra saunters through the film, funny in some scenes, sexy in others, but always captivating, the kind of movie star that audiences cannot take their eyes off. This film proved once and for all that Barbra didn't have to rely on lavish production numbers, glittery costumes, or larger-than-life characters to capture an audience's attention. There could be no doubt now that Barbra Streisand was a movie natural.

W hile Barbra was in San Francisco filming the final scenes of *What's Up, Doc?*, she was already poring over the script of her next picture, *Up the Sandbox*, which she envisioned as exactly the kind of movie she had hoped *A Glimpse of Tiger* would evolve into: a gentle comedy with social and political overtones that addressed the confusion many modern women felt about their place in a rapidly changing but still male-dominated society.

In 1970 Anne Richardson Roiphe's second novel, *Up the Sandbox*, was published to good reviews and national press attention. At a time when radical groups advocated abandonment of traditional family-oriented roles for women, Roiphe said, 'These days I feel a cultural pressure *not* to be absorbed in my child. I am made to feel my curiosity about the growth of my babies is somehow counter-revolutionary.'

Roiphe's *Sandbox* heroine, Margaret Reynolds, is a young Manhattan housewife who is outwardly content as the loving mother of two young children and the supportive mate of her husband, a well-regarded professor at Columbia University. But when Margaret learns she is pregnant again, and before she reveals her condition to her husband, she begins to question whether she wants another child. She wonders what she might be missing in the world outside her cluttered Riverside Drive apartment. As a result of this soul-searching, she pictures herself in elaborate, outlandish fantasy scenarios that Roiphe contrasts with Margaret's mundane everyday world.

In the movie version of the story, Margaret's fantasies include unmasking Fidel Castro as a woman, blowing up the Statue of Liberty with a group of black revolutionaries, shoving her domineering mother's face into a cake at an obnoxious family reunion, having her husband rescue her from a sinister abortion clinic, and being menaced by a tribe of spear-toting female

African natives. Finally Margaret decides to have the baby after her husband reassures her that her role as a nurturing mother is of the utmost importance. 'Our children will be a credit to the world,' he tells her. 'They'll make it less crazy.'

Robert Altman competed for the movie rights to *Sandbox* with producer Irvin Winkler who, with partner Robert Chartoff, had produced *They Shoot Horses, Don't They?* and *The Gang That Couldn't Shoot Straight*. At a ceiling of $60,000 Altman dropped out of the bidding, and the rights went to Winkler, who later said wryly, 'It wasn't a best-seller, but I thought it would be. If I had waited, I could have gotten it for a lot less.' Prior to engaging a screen-writer, Winkler and Chartoff sent a copy of the novel to Barbra, whose first reaction was ambivalent. 'I liked it well enough, but I'd just finished working and I wasn't so crazy to start again. But then you're pulled together and you want to do something and it becomes *ahhhh*.'

One of the reasons Barbra wanted a break from filmmaking was to spend more time with her adored Jason. She implied as much when discussing her attraction to *Sandbox:* 'I feel for Margaret. Part of me wants to be a mother and a wife, and I feel for women who have this kind of predicament. I wanted to have them heard. There is something in between the radicals and the women who go around proselytizing for women staying at home.'

To shape *Sandbox* into a screenplay, Chartoff and Winkler hired Paul Zindel, a novice screenwriter, but a recent Pulitzer Prize winner for his play *The Effect of Gamma Rays on Man-in-the-Moon Marigolds*. Zindel's first challenge was to distinguish Margaret's fantasy scenes from those in her real life. (In the novel, the fantasies had been set off as separate chapters.) Zindel was loath to depend on cinematic clichés such as a wavy screen or corny musical motifs to tip off the audience that a fantasy was about to commence.

Irvin Kershner, who knew Barbra socially, was chosen to direct the film primarily because she admired his handling of the 1970 George Segal-Eva Marie Saint vehicle *Loving*, which explored the emotional complications of a romantic triangle. *Loving* had been photographed beautifully by Gordon Willis, and Barbra approved Kershner's suggestion that Willis shoot *Sandbox*.

David Selby, a young actor who had made an impact on *Dark Shadows*, a gothic-horror TV soap opera, and had earned strong notices in *Sticks and Bones* on Broadway, was chosen to make his film debut as Margaret's husband, Paul. Though pleasantly attractive, with tousled dark hair and striking blue eyes, Selby was no glamour boy. 'I didn't want a big, beautiful, handsome man,' Kershner said, 'who'd make [the audience say] "Oh, man, he's great, what is her problem?" I wanted just a guy who looks like the guy next door.

He's nothing special. Love is not about special people; it's about ordinary people who feel special because they're in love.'

Selby felt anything but ordinary about the prospect of starring opposite America's top female box-office attraction. 'Until we were introduced at the rehearsals in Hollywood,' he said, 'I had to content myself with a symbol of a sort of queenliness that her voice timbre reflected to me.' Barbra laughed off Selby's iconic image of her, and by all accounts was helpful to him, but Irvin Kershner felt that even after filming began, Selby remained in awe of his leading lady. 'You can't blame him,' Kershner said. 'To suddenly play opposite Barbra Streisand and be new to the screen is pretty overwhelming. It affected his work, in fact; in places he had to try very hard to just be there on the screen with her. It was tough on him.'

UP THE SANDBOX provided an opportunity for Barbra to officially wield power behind the scenes for the first time. In June 1969, Barbra, Paul Newman, and Sidney Poitier had joined forces to establish a film production company, First Artists, in order to 'create a new enterprise, distinct from both major film studios and independent production companies, for the development and production of theatrical motion pictures.'

The new company, which owned no production facilities, had an arrangement under which the distributor, usually a major studio, advanced a substantial portion of each film's production costs upon delivery of the film and shared a portion of its distribution fee with the company. The process afforded the three stars the opportunity to exercise complete creative control over their productions. Streisand, Newman, and Poitier agreed to star in three films each by June 1976 with a per-film budget not to exceed $3 million, or $5 million for a Streisand musical. They would not take an up-front salary but would be paid between 25 and 33 percent of each picture's gross. In 1971 Steve McQueen joined the company; he was followed a year later by Dustin Hoffman.

Barbra's company, Barwood Films, produced *Sandbox* through First Artists, in conjunction with Chartoff and Winkler. Perhaps to ease her transition into the business end of the film industry, Barbra surrounded herself with trusted colleagues. Marty Erlichman, who was on the First Artists board as a vice president and director, was named associate producer, and Barbra's close friend Cis Corman launched her career as a casting director. Even Jason wound up playing a small part in the picture.

Fundamental story flaws in *Up the Sandbox* surfaced early in pre-production. 'I liked it as a book,' recalled Kershner, 'but it wasn't the kind of material I would choose for a film. There wasn't enough drama in the main story. All the drama was in the fantasies, which didn't work because you knew it wasn't really happening. I was unhappy going with it, but I had been warned by Barbra's agents not to tell her that I was unhappy with the story because she would just walk off the picture.

'Now, once we were working and we got to know each other in a professional capacity, I revealed to her one day that the reason we were struggling every day and every night was because we never made the story work as well as it should. She said, "Did you know this before we started?' I said, "Of course, I did." "Well, then, why did you start?" "Because I was being pushed, and I was told that if I didn't start, and made you aware of my doubts about the material, I'd lose you." She said, "That's ridiculous. We just would have kept working until we got it right."'

Although it's not clear how much input Barbra had in the final *Sandbox* script, she seems to have worked intensely enough with Paul Zindel for him to have strong memories of the experience. 'I really should have hauled off and socked her a few times,' he said in 1982. 'A good uppercut would have done her wonders, I think.'

☆

Before she left Los Angeles for location shooting in New York, Barbra fulfilled a promise that she had reportedly made to Warren Beatty months earlier in his Beverly Hills bedroom. Perhaps partly because she hoped to land Beatty as her co-star for her next movie, *The Way We Were*, she had indulged in 'one of my flings' with the sensuously handsome actor, whom she had known since they had met in summer stock when she was sixteen.

Beatty's renowned passion for women and filmmaking was matched by his love of politics. Avowed liberal Democrats, he and his activist sister, Shirley MacLaine, had strongly supported the presidential aspirations of Robert Kennedy in 1968. When George McGovern, running on a fierce antiwar platform, became the Democratic front-runner in 1972, Beatty and MacLaine threw their considerable clout behind the soft-spoken senator from South Dakota and his effort to defeat Richard Nixon, whose duplicitous stand on the Vietnam War and on many domestic issues had divided the nation.

When Beatty learned that Barbra supported McGovern as well, he approached her about headlining a concert to benefit the campaign. The Streisand-Beatty romantic liaisons took place in Warren's notorious suite of rooms, El Escondido ('The Hideaway'), at the Beverly Wilshire Hotel.

Barbra and Warren reportedly spent most of their time in bed negotiating for him to co-star in *The Way We Were* and for her to sing for McGovern. The author Shaun Considine claimed that an unidentified 'studio production executive' gave him details of the coupling. The account is a hilariously unlikely scenario laden with crude double entendres: 'Warren was relentless. He worked on her head. And on her hands, feet, and shoulders. Barbra matched him stroke for stroke. He'd get her into bed and he'd turn on the famous Beatty charm and he'd slip in a plug for the concert. He'd whisper, "Barbra, you *should* do it. You *have* to do it. It's your civic duty. For me, baby, come on, come on." And Barbra would moan and sigh and say, "Oh, I know, Warren, I know. I *am* considering it. Now let's read some more of the script." And he'd say, "Okay, Barbra. You want to take it from the top or the bottom this time?"'

Barbra never was able to persuade Beatty to make *The Way We Were*, but she did agree to join pop superstars Carole King and James Taylor for the George McGovern fund-raiser at the Forum, an 18,000-seat stadium in the Los Angeles suburb of Inglewood. Although she had just begun work on *Sandbox*, Barbra was able to pull a show together quickly with the same musical charts she had used three months earlier in her final Vegas appearances.

Barbra soon began to have second thoughts. Although her forays into pop rock had been welcomed by all but the most hardened rock critics, and in spite of the fact that she had included four of King's songs on her last two albums, Barbra convinced herself that she would be booed off the stage of the Forum by irate rock fans, as though she were Ethel Merman facing a mob of Led Zeppelin fanatics. 'They're coming to hear James Taylor and Carole King,' she fretted to Beatty. 'They won't stay and listen to me.'

As the concert date approached Carole King's representatives said they wanted King to close the show, a spot traditionally held by the headliner. But Marty Erlichman wouldn't budge: Barbra would close the show or would not appear at all. King backed down, but Barbra, more frightened than ever, vacillated. 'Maybe I should just go on first,' she mused, 'and then get outta there.'

The myth that Streisand was the musical odd man out for this concert is based almost entirely on her own publicly expressed insecurities. Her participation had been advertised from the outset, and she hadn't appeared in a full concert in the Los Angeles area since she became a movie star. Many of the ticket buyers would be there specifically to see her.

Barbra's performance anxiety led to excruciatingly tough last-minute rehearsals. 'She was very uptight during those final run-throughs,' recalled Marty Erlichman. 'She kept yelling at me during rehearsals, "I shouldn't be here!"' Barbra's intense rehearsals took up so much time that King and Taylor were forced to cram their onstage run-throughs into only thirty minutes.

By the night of the concert, Saturday, April 15, Quincy Jones and his orchestra had been added to the lineup. Tickets ranged in price from $5.50 to $100, and ushers on the ground floor included Julie Christie (with Warren Beatty), Jack Nicholson, Gene Hackman, Goldie Hawn, Jon Voight, Carly Simon, and James Earl Jones. The audience was no less star-studded for what was later called 'the most glamorous pop concert in recent history.'

King and Taylor each performed to enthusiastic response and brought down the house with a spine-tingling duet of 'You've Got a Friend,' with King on piano and Taylor on guitar. Following intermission, Quincy Jones conducted his orchestra in a jazz-flavored set. Backstage, Barbra practically bolted for the door when someone in the audience yelled 'Rock 'n' roll!' during one of Jones's quieter numbers. Although otherwise politely received, the thirty-minute Jones segment slowed the pace of the show, and didn't allow Barbra to begin her set until well after 11:00 P.M.

She strode onstage in a simple black pants outfit, her hair streaming to mid-back, and she established an immediate rapport with the roaring crowd when she launched into a disarming medley of 'Sing' from *Sesame Street* coupled with 'Make Your Own Kind of Music.' Calmer as she realized that she wouldn't be hooted off the stage, she delivered powerful versions of many of her standards. The crowd cheered the pot monologue, which took on new meaning in a venue where marijuana smoke had wafted noticeably through the air all evening.

Barbra cemented her bond with the audience when she let them decide whether she should sing 'Second Hand Rose' or 'Stoney End.' When their applause indicated they preferred the latter, Barbra admitted that she hadn't sung it in a while so she had had the lyrics written on the floor of the stage. By the time she finished her one encore, 'People,' the audience had accorded her seven standing ovations in the course of a forty-minute performance. George McGovern then joined Barbra, King, Taylor, and Quincy Jones onstage and greeted the crowd with brief remarks. Barbra announced that the evening had raised more than $320,000 to further the senator's campaign, though it was later reported that after all of the expenses of promoting and staging the concert were paid, the campaign received just $18,000.

The evening turned out to be a triumph for Barbra. *Rolling Stone* magazine, which a year earlier had ridiculed her attempts to modernize her image, now praised her 'jolting rock 'n' roll voice on "Make Your Own Kind of Music" . . . Streisand is a star and, on this night, *the* star.'

When George McGovern lost the presidential race in a landslide to

Richard Nixon – even as the Watergate scandal that would bring Nixon down unfolded – Barbra said, 'I thought me and my friends were for the right things, and it's very disappointing that we turned out to be such a small bunch. In terms of lower- and middle-class groups, McGovern would have been much better for them. But I guess they just couldn't see he was really their man.'

BARBRA RELAXED FOR a few days after the concert, then flew to New York to resume filming *Up the Sandbox*. In Manhattan, crowds of gawkers gathered at Broadway and 125th Street in Harlem to watch Barbra-as-Margaret shop at an open-air grocery. Another location shot placed Barbra near the corner of Madison Avenue and Eighty-third Street. 'It was quite close to the school where her mother worked,' recalled a friend of Diana's, who spoke on the condition of anonymity. 'We were watching the filming, and the principal asked if she could have her picture taken with Barbra and Diana. I asked Barbra, and she said, "My mother works here?" She didn't even know where her mother was working.'

As a production assistant on the film, Howard Koch Jr was responsible for making sure Barbra's well-known penchant for tardiness didn't slow down the tightly budgeted production. 'I would go to her trailer, knock, and say, "Barbra, they're ready for you," and she'd stall and say, "Just a minute." And then I would remind her that she was one of the producers on the film and that it was her money that was being wasted. "You're right!" she'd say and fly out of the dressing room.'

BARBRA SAT UNDER a giant tree on a small hill overlooking the dry terrain of Archer's Post in Kenya. Draped in a vivid blue sarong with matching turban and colorful beaded earrings, she closed her eyes as a young local woman from the Samburu tribe carefully applied homemade color to her eyelids. 'She broke a twig from a tree,' Barbra recalled, 'took a long thread from her husband's skirt, made like a Q-Tip, broke off a piece of soft blue rock, spit on it, and put that on my eye with the Q-Tip.'

In June, shortly after she completed location filming in New York, Barbra had flown to equatorial Africa to shoot one of the movie's most complicated fantasies: Margaret has returned to her apartment after attending a noisy cocktail party in honor of Dr Beineke, an eccentric anthropologist newly arrived from the Dark Continent. Suddenly knocked unconscious by a would-be mugger in the laundry room of her building, Margaret imagines that she and Beineke are schlepping through the plains of Kenya in search of a painless method of childbirth practiced by the Samburu natives. The segment as written and filmed was elaborate and overlong; what little remains of it in the finished film is practically indecipherable.

To capture what turned out to be less than eight minutes of screen time, the *Sandbox* company was based outside of Nairobi for close to a month. Barbra found the natives fascinating, and they found her intriguing as well. 'At first, we were suspicious of them and they were suspicious of us,' she said. 'Do you know that these women are not permitted to show pain? They can't even scream when they have a baby. They seem happy, but wow! Who am I to say anything . . . to preach?'

Barbra's looks, of course, contrasted greatly with those of the Samburu women, and many of the male warriors were drawn to her. Their method of showing appreciation caused Streisand some embarrassment. When a tribesman found a woman attractive, he would smile broadly, pull aside his wraparound skirt, and expose his excitement. After a week of this, Barbra claimed with a giggle that she found it easy to measure which of the men liked her best.

Actor Paul Benedict, who was playing Dr Beineke, recalled one of the numerous times when he and Barbra were killing time between scenes. 'Kershner and the camera crew were stationed about one hundred and fifty yards off, and Barbra and I were just sitting around waiting. The native women grew restless and started chanting in the Samburu dialect. Barbra really got into the melody and began humming it. Then she picked up the words and sang along with the tribeswomen. During this performance, Kershner came up to us to discuss something, and Barbra stopped singing. When he left, she began again. I was so impressed with that because you knew she wasn't showing off; she just really appreciated the music and wanted to be a part of it.'

SLATED FOR A Christmas 1972 release, *Up the Sandbox* had its first preview in San Francisco in October. Barbra, on a brief break from filming *The Way We Were*, attended the screening and was distressed at the audience reaction. 'There was laughter,' she told a friend, 'but it was nervous laughter, often in the wrong places.' She and Kershner set about cutting almost twenty minutes from the film, and they changed the ending. 'I had originally shot the ending so that it was a fantasy within a fantasy within a fantasy,' the director said. 'It was three fantasies removed from reality, so you didn't know where you were anymore. Everyone got scared, and at the last minute it was redone so it was clearer.' With these alterations, Kershner felt confident that the film would go over big. 'I remember sitting with the agents and producers and we all thought, sixty million dollars!'

Barbra was upset and mystified when the ninety-seven-minute film was rated R by the Motion Picture Association of America, mainly because of the bare-chested Samburu women and the fantasy in which Fidel Castro exposes his breasts to reveal that he is really a woman. Even though actor Jacob Morales wore obviously fake breasts, the rating board was firm. 'What kind of morality do you have,' Barbra pondered, 'when people would rather have children see blood and gore than a woman's breasts?'

To promote *Up the Sandbox*, Barbra appeared at press junkets in Los Angeles and New York at which she talked to upwards of sixty reporters from across the country. 'I care about *Sandbox*,' she said. 'I think it is a provocative film and I want to help it.' She felt it was vital that the public read about the movie before seeing it. 'We're against polarization,' Barbra told writers assembled at Manhattan's 21 Club. 'We're saying a woman shouldn't feel guilty about going out into the world or about staying at home. She should feel it's right to stay wherever she can be fulfilled.' About producing for the first time she said, 'As a producer, I had to be above all the on-set situations. If I was late, it wasn't because I was a prima donna, but because I was late. Sometimes the actress in me fought the producer in me. I was a lax producer and I let the actress in me win out.'

Despite the rare Streisand publicity, when the picture opened, it quickly became clear that the $60 million grosses Irvin Kershner expected would never materialize. Most audiences were disappointed and mystified by *Sandbox* after being misled by a wacky ad campaign to expect a zany comedy like *What's Up, Doc?* Paul Zindel's determination to avoid obvious setups left many viewers unsure where the fantasies began and ended. Others seemed to prefer a zanier, larger-than-life Barbra in a comedy. And the ambiguous stand the movie took on the 'modern woman's dilemma' failed to please either the radical feminists, the traditional homemakers, or the millions of other women who fell somewhere in between.

While most critics complained about the film's shortcomings, many were impressed with Barbra's work. 'It's a likable, honest performance,' said Alan Howard in the *Hollywood Reporter*, 'and in its subtle way, a bold one.' Writing for the New York *Daily News*, Rex Reed said that *Sandbox* 'provides her with her finest role to date and she rises to the challenge cunningly. There is a new vulnerability in her work here, a touching sweetness that makes you want to know the character instead of the actress.' Pauline Kael's thoughtful review offered a pithy tribute, 'She's a complete reason for seeing a movie, as Garbo was.'

For all of its problems, *Up the Sandbox* has a certain appeal that comes not only from Barbra's restrained performance but also from the distinctive, almost European style in which it is filmed. There are several memorable scenes, especially the family reunion, which Barbra suggested be filmed in black and white with a hand-held camera for the sake of realism – just as her brother, Sheldon, always did at family gatherings.

Up the Sandbox remains refreshing as the most audacious Streisand film to date, but its message about the plight of contemporary women, somewhat naive even at the time, has dated badly. 'It was very discouraging,' Barbra said of the film's failure. 'I remember taking a friend to a theater in Westwood and there were *four people* there. It sure made me feel bad.' A few years later she was more defensive: 'I liked *Up the Sandbox*. That was my statement about what it meant to be a woman. It's what I wanted to say, and I'm glad I said it, even if it didn't make a nickel.'

Up the Sandbox grossed $10 million, which nearly returned its original investment, and earned a small profit from television and video sales. 'I love the film,' Irvin Kershner said. 'I think it's so unusual for her. She's wonderful in it, she shows the full range of what she can do . . . I'm very glad I made it, even though I couldn't get another assignment for three years . . . I never told Barbra, but I went broke on account of that film.'

Barbra professed not to care if the film made money. She was proud of it, and that was what mattered to her. '*Up the Sandbox* was my tribute to my son, and it exposed me as a real person,' she said. 'I'm a serious person, and not just the zany person that people expect me to be because of movie and stage roles.'

R obert Redford was worried that he'd get too excited lying in bed
next to Barbra. They were about to film a scene for their new film,
The Way We Were, in which Barbra's character, Katie Morosky,
undresses and slides into bed next to Hubbell Gardiner, a former campus
golden boy she has lusted after for years and who has just passed out, drunk.
She caresses his hair, and he rolls over to her, becomes aroused, and makes
love to her quickly before falling back to sleep on top of her. The director,
Sydney Pollack, had ordered everyone off the set for the scene except the
cinematographer, Harry Stradling Jr.

Barbra was nude from the waist up when she undressed, her back to the
camera. The next shot would show her already in bed, and she wore a thin
mesh bikini and brassiere under the sheets. With his character supposed to
be nude as well, Redford was taking no chances. According to Moss Mabrey,
the film's costume designer, 'Redford put *two* jockstraps on for that scene.
He's a very modest man. He was afraid of getting an erection.'

The bulky athletic supporters caused a problem, however, when their
outline became visible through the sheets. 'Finally,' Redford said, 'I took
them off under the cover, slid them under the bed, did the scene, picked
them up, and put them back on under the cover.'

The look of ecstasy on Barbra's face in the scene likely reflected reacting
more than acting. Because by this time her feelings for Redford were just
as strong as Katie's for Hubbell.

THE WAY WE WERE came into being in 1971 when Ray Stark asked Arthur
Laurents, who had directed Barbra in *I Can Get It for You Wholesale*, to
write a movie for her. He came up with the story of Katie Morosky, a

dowdy, frizzy-haired, politically ardent Jewish coed of the late 1930s who supports communism because she believes it to be a force for peace, and her ill-fated marriage to the handsome, apolitical, golden-haired WASP Hubbell Gardiner amid the backdrop of the Hollywood Blacklist.

The passionate, questioning Katie Morosky has many similarities to Barbra, and the character was written for her to play, but Arthur Laurents did not base her on Streisand. Rather he was inspired by a girl he had known in college and a woman he knew later, and he combined the two of them. 'Barbra certainly has been involved slightly politically,' Laurents said, 'but she's unsophisticated politically, unlike Katie. The connecting tissue is Barbra's passion and her sense of injustice. But I don't think she's like that character.'

In preparing for *The Way We Were*, Barbra's main concern was her leading man, and she immediately thought of the actor she had wanted to play Romeo to her Juliet, Robert Redford. Ray Stark sent a fifty-page treatment of the script to the actor, who turned it down because he considered Hubbell Gardiner a two-dimensional character. Laurents then suggested Ryan O'Neal, but Stark didn't think audiences would be keen on a re-teaming. Next in line was the big, blond, and good-looking Ken Howard, and Laurents made arrangements for a tennis match to see how Howard and Barbra would get along. Laurents and Nora Kaye, Herb Ross's wife, played doubles against Ken and Barbra. 'You've never seen bad tennis playing until you've watched Barbra on the court,' Laurents told the authors Donald Zec and Anthony Fowles. 'We were wiping Ken and Barbra out, but she was delightful, taking the beating with a great sense of humor. At one time the ball hit one of her breasts and she quipped, "Don't worry, I have another one."'

Streisand and Howard seemed to be meshing well, Laurents recalled, 'until a very beautiful girl drove down to pick up Ken Howard. Barbra froze. Next day she told me there was no sex appeal between them . . . Howard was out.' After rejecting Dennis Cole, and with the supply of blond male stars exhausted, Barbra turned to Warren Beatty, whom she kept after during their affair, constantly badgering him for a commitment to the film. He didn't feel that the character gave him enough to work with, however, and Barbra's assurances that the part would be beefed up failed to change his mind.

Barbra and Ray Stark had reached a dead end. When Barbra moaned, 'God, if only we could convince Redford,' Stark had an idea. He would try to get Sydney Pollack to direct the picture. Pollack and Redford had been close friends since they appeared together as actors in *War Hunt* in 1962, and Pollack had directed Redford in *This Property Is Condemned*, a Ray

Stark production, in 1966 and in *Jeremiah Johnson* in 1972. If anyone could persuade Redford to change his mind, Stark reasoned, it was Pollack.

Stark sent Pollack the galleys of Laurents's novelization of his screenplay. He liked it and signed to direct the film in April of 1972. 'I was very moved by it,' Pollack said, 'and I thought right away, This would be great for Bob.' But when he mentioned it, Redford said, 'Aw, that piece of junk.'

As Pollack worked on some script revisions, he became more and more convinced that only Redford could do justice to Hubbell. Ray Stark put renewed pressure on the director to deliver Redford, and Pollack sent him the revised script. 'No, it doesn't work, Pollack,' Redford said. They argued for hours, but Redford remained unmoved. 'I don't know what you see in this,' he finally said.

Stark was getting angry. 'We have Barbra, and what do we need Redford for?' he told Pollack. 'Ryan O'Neal will do it.' Finally, at a meeting with Ray Stark and Arthur Laurents in Stark's apartment in the Dorchester Hotel in New York, matters came to a head. 'I'm going to give Redford one hour and then fuck it,' Stark announced. 'I'm just not going to chase my life around Robert Redford. Who the fuck does he think he is?'

Pollack found this 'a real vindictive, ego conversation. I said to him, "Ray, don't do it." I got Bob on the phone and told him I had to come over to his apartment and settle this.' As Pollack left, Stark told him 'You've got an hour.'

Pollack used every argument he could think of to change Redford's mind: the picture wouldn't start filming until the fall, it could be shot mostly in New York so that Redford could stay with his family. Pollack also assured him that the script would be rewritten to give Hubbell a stronger point of view.

'What is this picture *about*, Pollack?' Redford wanted to know. 'Who *is* this guy? He's just an object. A nothing. He runs around saying, "Aw, c'mon, Katie, c'mon, Katie." He doesn't want anything. What does this guy *want*, Sydney? *What does he want?*'

'He's a very moving guy, Bob,' Pollack replied.

Redford was asking, 'What's moving? What's moving?' when the phone rang. It was Stark, telling Pollack his hour was up. 'Come back. That's it. We're hiring Ryan O'Neal.'

'No, you're not. I'll call you back in ten minutes!' Pollack slammed the phone down and turned to Redford, who was cradling his head in his hands. 'All right, Pollack,' he finally said. 'I'll do it. I'll *do* it!'

'The reason I finally decided to do the picture,' Redford said, 'was that I had faith that Pollack and [the screenwriters] Alvin Sargent and David Rayfiel would make something more out of that character than was in the script. As it was written, he was shallow and one-dimensional. Not very real

– more a figment of someone's imagination of what Prince Charming should be like. What emerged out of the rewrites were glimpses of the darker side of this golden boy character – what his fears were about himself.'

Once Redford signed – at a reported salary of $1.2 million, which was $200,000 more than Streisand received – Barbra eagerly awaited their first meeting, a customary procedure where two co-stars sit down to get to know each other and discuss their roles. Redford wanted no part of it. 'He wouldn't meet with Barbra for the longest time,' Pollack recalled, 'until she began to develop a complex: "Why can't I sit and talk with Bob Redford? I'm going to act with him in the movie!" Finally it started to get destructive. I told him, "You've got to go, because she's starting to take it personally."'

Redford said he would meet with Barbra, but only if Pollack came along. 'So the three of us sat down at her house and we had dinner and talked, and we got together maybe twice more before we started rehearsals. That's all.' The reason Redford didn't want to get too familiar with Barbra, Pollack said, was that 'he believes very strongly that the strangeness contributes to the chemistry in a movie. And I must agree that the fact that they didn't know each other inside out worked for what was going on in the college scenes, where she was supposed to be awkward with him.'

At that first dinner, Barbra found Redford dazzling. 'She was simply mesmerized by him because she found him so beautiful,' Arthur Laurents said. But there was more to it than that. Redford had a quiet strength, a keen intelligence, and a strong commitment to political and environmental issues. 'He always has something going on behind his eyes,' Barbra said. 'He's not just an actor, he's an intelligent, concerned human being, so that whatever you see has many layers underneath.' Barbra considered Redford well nigh a perfect man and Lola, his wife of nearly fifteen years, a very lucky woman. 'Why can't I find a man like Redford?' she sighed to a friend.

At that first dinner Barbra peppered Redford with questions, as is her wont, and some of them were quite personal. Redford, charming if taciturn up to that point, became a little sharp. 'Barbra,' he said, 'if we're going to be able to work together, you have to keep in mind that anything I tell you about myself will be volunteered because I *want* you to know it. Not because you think you have some kind of right to know it.'

With that Redford completely won Barbra over. Not only did she love the fact that he had stood up to her, but she knew he was right. If there was one thing Barbra hated it was people who pried.

BARBRA WAS AS comfortable with her character as Redford had been uncomfortable with his, which is probably why she seemed to Laurents far less concerned with how to play Katie Morosky than with how she would look in the film. When they first discussed the script, Laurents was stunned to discover that Barbra's main concern revolved around how many costume and hairdo changes the script provided her.

While Barbra didn't discuss her characterization with Laurents, she did with Pollack, and she was pleased to discover that they saw eye to eye on nearly every detail. 'I wanted Barbra in this picture to really act,' Pollack told Zec and Fowles. 'I did not want her to rely on any of the Streisand mannerisms . . . I really wanted to get her back to a kind of simple truth in her performance that I knew she was capable of. It wasn't a problem because Barbra is like any other enormously talented person. They are never a problem if you can create an atmosphere of trust.'

Apparently Barbra got along far better with her director than she did with her costume designer. She was so concerned about her appearance in the picture that Dorothy Jeakins, a three-time Oscar winner, quit in frustration with Streisand after designing three-quarters of her thirty costumes. Barbra would approve a design, then change her mind, approve another design, then change her mind again. Jeakins told her replacement, Moss Mabry, that she left the picture because 'I can't stand all this confusion and indecision.'

Barbra asked Mabry to design outfits that accentuated her bust and behind. 'She loves her derriere,' he recalled. 'She's got wonderful buns. And one of the most beautiful busts in Hollywood. And beautiful skin.' At Barbra's behest, Mabry designed a backless halter-top pantsuit that revealed and accentuated these attributes very nicely.

One of the reasons Barbra had to be so concerned with her wardrobe, according to Mabry, was that Sydney Pollack didn't seem to care very much. 'A lot of people got the impression that Pollack really favored Redford,' Mabry said. 'I would go to his office with sketches and swatches, and he couldn't have cared less what she wore. It surprised me, because I hadn't run into that kind of attitude before.'

In fairness to Pollack, he was immersed in what he described as 'the nightmare' of trying to retool the script to his and Redford's liking. 'We were rewriting all the time,' Pollack said. 'While we were shooting we were rewriting. We were getting so much pressure. Columbia was going under at the time; they hadn't had a big hit in years, and the picture was going over budget. Bob didn't get along with Ray Stark, and neither did I. We didn't know how to mix the politics and the love story and make it work. There were just a lot of problems.'

Stark, who was being pressed by the studio, leaned hard on Pollack. 'Hurry up, hurry up!' the director recalled Stark telling him. 'You can't do this! You can't do that! Hurry up! Get it done! Cut this, cut that! Don't do it with more than one car! Shoot up angles so you don't have to fix the streets.'

'Truthfully, nobody had any faith in the picture,' Pollack said. For Redford, making the movie was like 'doing overtime at Dachau.'

Finally Pollack swallowed hard and asked Arthur Laurents to come back. According to Laurents, eleven screenwriters had come and gone before he was asked to save the script and the movie. 'They made a lot of silly mistakes,' Laurents said of the writers who had followed him. 'None of those people knew anything about that period. I lived through it . . . They just kept cutting the political stuff because Stark said to me that he had to make a choice between the romance and the politics. That's balderdash. I think they're constantly underestimating the public.'

If Sydney Pollack was too busy trying to solve his film's script problems to concern himself with Barbra's appearance in the picture, the cinematographer, Harry Stradling Jr., more than took up the slack. His main goal, the son of Barbra's favorite cameraman said, 'was to make Barbra Streisand look good . . . whenever there was an outdoor scene we had to build a canopy to shade her because with direct sunlight on her nose, it looks terrible . . . every now and again, Robert Redford would get a little grouchy because every shot was always lined up to suit Barbra.

'But she was the only person I had to please. If she was happy, that was all that mattered.'

✵

ONCE FILMING BEGAN on September 18, 1972, at Union College in Schenectady, New York, Barbra began to fret. Redford's subtly effective acting impressed her so much that she feared her performance would suffer in comparison. 'Barbra was very intimidated,' said Bradford Dillman, who was cast as Hubbell's best friend. 'There was a lot of stuff that Bob and I did that was total improvisation. Barbra was very, very new to that, and I don't know how comfortable she would have been.'

Her insecurity led her to want to discuss her scenes in even more detail than usual before she acted them. 'She called me up – oh, my God – every night!' Pollack said. 'She called out of compulsive worry – "Should I do this?" "Listen, I was reading back five drafts earlier and I found this line." It was all pushing and testing and trying to cover every base – worrying it, worrying it, worrying it.'

Before she would do a scene, Barbra wanted to talk it out so thoroughly that sometimes she seemed to be stalling. This drove Redford, who prefers to plunge into a scene and see what happens, to distraction. 'There comes a time when you're ready to go,' he said. 'You learn too much in rehearsals.

Things start to get pat, and film is a medium of behavior and spontaneity. Barbra would talk and talk and talk and drive me nuts. And the amusing thing was that after she'd talk and talk and talk, we'd get down to doing it and she'd do just what she was going to do from the beginning.'

Pollack found himself caught in the middle. 'She'd get in there and want to talk, and Bob would want to do it. And Bob felt the more the talk went on, the staler he got. She would feel he was rushing her. The more rehearsing we did, she would begin to go uphill and he would peak and go downhill. So I was like a jockey trying to figure out when to roll the camera and get them to coincide.'

Regardless of how the two actors came around to their performances, each thought the other was doing a better job. 'She would call me at night,' Pollack said, 'and ask, "How does he do it?" She would see the dailies and think he was wonderful and she stunk. But they're very alike in that respect, because he would see them and think that she was wonderful and he stunk . . . I had to calm both of them down.'

If Barbra's infatuation with Redford practically trumpeted itself, it was clear that Redford found her intriguing as well; once again life imitated art. She made him laugh a lot, throwing Yiddish words at him and needling him for being such a WASP. Their interaction offscreen, Redford said, helped them 'create an inner life of enjoyment between the two characters.'

'Whenever he would say anything Jewish,' Pollack recalled, 'she would get hysterical. There's one scene that's almost all improvised in the beach house where he was trying to learn some Jewish words and she was breaking up. A lot of that we photographed and tried to keep in.'

WHEN THE TIME came to film the sex scene, it was clear to Harry Stradling that the chemistry between Streisand and Redford extended beyond their roles. 'They were very close,' Stradling said. 'During the scene where they were both in bed, it was very arousing . . . more so than just actors acting.'

It is unlikely that Streisand and Redford ever consummated their mutual attraction, but word filtered back to Lola Redford about the romantic sparks flying between her husband and his leading lady. One evening, after the two stars lost track of time during an impromptu rehearsal, Redford missed dinner with his family. Lola hit the roof. Their son Jamie went to school the next day, a columnist reported, and told his classmates, 'Mommy threw a glass of milk at Daddy. They had a fight about Barbra Streisand.' When he was asked about the accuracy of the report, Redford replied, 'That sounds about right.'

AFTER A MONTH on location in New York, the production moved to Hollywood on October 11 and filming wrapped on December 3. Everyone was worried: Barbra because if this film failed after the public's rejection of *Up the Sandbox* she might never be able to establish herself as a straight dramatic actress; Redford because he wasn't at all sure his characterization was compelling enough to hold its own against Streisand's; and Pollack because he feared he hadn't successfully mixed the politics and the love story.

Over the next nine months Pollack and Margaret Booth edited the film, and they took out most of the political scenes, almost all of which involved Barbra. At the first of two previews scheduled for a Friday and Saturday in September of 1973 in San Francisco, Pollack discovered he hadn't cut enough. When the film began to unreel, a buzz rose among the audience as they realized they were going to see the new Streisand-Redford film. For two-thirds of the picture they seemed enraptured. Then the blacklisting scenes began to unfold and, Pollack recalled, 'We lost the audience completely.' He grabbed Margaret Booth, went up to the projection room, took out a razor blade and snipped an entire sequence in which Katie was about to be named as a Communist, eleven minutes in all. 'The politics just got too complicated for the audience,' he said. 'They wanted us to stick with the love story.'

The following night the audience reaction to the shorter version was strongly positive. 'All of a sudden everyone was ecstatic about it,' Pollack said, 'and morale turned around.' Now all Barbra could do was wait to see whether this troubled production would result in a hit.

The Way We Were opened around the country on October 16, 1973. The reviews were mixed; most critics praised the acting and chemistry of the two stars but faulted the film's parboiled politics. 'Pollack and Laurents are so busy working on the dubious proposition that politics can kill a good marriage,' Paul D. Zimmerman wrote in *Newsweek*, 'that they barely have time to establish the political atmosphere that is meant as a catalyst to the connubial collapse, sketching it in hurriedly in bits of cocktail gossip and snippets of radio reports and newspaper headlines.'

In spite of that, *The Way We Were* proved a runaway hit through the holiday season and beyond – it grossed $56 million domestically – largely because audiences responded to its nostalgic sheen, its star chemistry, and its moving love story. There had been few sentimental, big-star movie romances since the 1950s, and fewer still that had succeeded. The opinion of Norma McLain Stoop, the reviewer for *After Dark*, encapsulated the main reason that the film went on to become Columbia's second-highest-grossing film of all time to that date, next to *Funny Girl:* 'The measure of the success of this brilliant motion picture is that it draws the viewer so deeply into its web of character and plot that one . . . leaves the theater feeling as one often does when close to a couple who resort to divorce – wondering "Which one was right? Which one should I see in the future?"'

In a subtler and more profound way than *Up the Sandbox*, *The Way We Were* is a feminist film. Katie is the central, the aggressive, the committed character. Hubbell is the passive, more creative, prettier love object. Katie pursues the relationship, creates the situation that leads to their having sex, and later promises Hubbell, 'I won't touch you.' Katie is the one whose commitment to ideals undermines her marriage in the face of her spouse's ambivalence. Arthur Laurents had turned the traditional Hollywood notion of male-female roles on its head, and many Americans were ready for the liberation from stereotypes he had thus offered both sexes.

More than ever in *The Way We Were* Barbra Streisand was America's Everyperson, acting out onscreen what each audience member had at some time experienced: the longing for an unattainable love object. Many women and gay men certainly related to her lust for Hubbell, but millions of others, heterosexual men included, also identified with her. Who at some point hasn't felt unattractive, been mocked, or been hurt by love?

The film was an unqualified triumph for Barbra and hoisted her to another plateau of movie stardom. She won a Golden Globe as World Film Favorite, and she had now succeeded artistically and commercially in films as a musical comedy star, as a non-singing comedienne, and as a romantic leading lady in a drama. No performer before her had conquered such disparate movie genres so successfully in so short a span of time.

THIS LATEST FILM triumph of Barbra's, ironically, resulted in her first number one single. Marvin Hamlisch, the erstwhile rehearsal pianist for *Funny Girl*, had achieved success scoring films, and he not only scored *The Way We Were* but also wrote the title tune, with lyrics by Marilyn and Alan Bergman.

Sydney Pollack and Hamlisch wanted Barbra to sing the song over the credits, but she resisted because she didn't want to steal any thunder from her acting. She also didn't much like the melody. 'She said it was too simple,' Hamlisch recalled, and she insisted that he write another tune. She liked the new song, and so did Pollack. 'We recorded both versions with a piano accompaniment,' said Hamlisch. 'Then we took the cassette player into the projection room and played each song against the film.' As Alan Bergman explained it, 'The second didn't work *at all* with the images on the screen. But the original song worked beautifully . . . So that was our answer, plain and simple.'

Although one critic called the tune 'weak and plaintive,' preview audiences responded so strongly to it that Columbia released it as a single, redone with a more 'pop' arrangement, three weeks before the film opened. Radio disc jockeys resisted playing it because Streisand hadn't had a hit single in three years. But as the film's popularity grew, more and more stations added the song to their playlists. A month after its release the record climbed into the Top 100, and fourteen weeks later it hit the number one position, where it remained for weeks. *Billboard* named 'The Way We Were' the top pop single of the year, and the record was certified gold, signaling that it had sold over one million units, in February 1974.

In January Columbia released, simultaneously, a sound-track album and a new Streisand studio collection also called *The Way We Were*. The sound track did well; it rose to number twenty and was certified gold in September 1975. The studio collection, propelled by the success of the single even though its second side consisted primarily of material left over from *The Belle of 14th Street* and the aborted *The Singer* project, went to number one, the first Streisand album to do so since *People* ten years earlier. For the first time, Barbra was on top of the heap with both her movies and her music.

THIRTEEN-YEAR-OLD David Hirsch wanted Barbra Streisand to sing 'People' to him over the telephone during his bar mitzvah celebration. This impossible dream was a fantasy other Streisand fans had harbored without success; she once turned down an offer of $100,000 from a father to sing in person for his son. But David got lucky. His bar mitzvah fell on April 7, 1973, and Barbra was taking requests to sing to people over the phone to raise money for the Pentagon Papers Legal Defense Fund. She had already turned down one request to sing 'People' for a donation of $1,000 because she preferred to sing songs that evening that she hadn't performed live before. But when David's uncle, Miles Rubin, offered $10,000, Streisand warbled and David got his wish.

The Pentagon Papers case had been a cause célèbre to liberals since 1971, when a former Defense Department analyst and antiwar activist named Daniel Ellsberg leaked a forty-volume study of America's involvement in the Vietnam War to *The New York Times*. The documents showed, among other things, that the military and the government had misled the American people about their conduct of the war. After two installments of a series based on the papers, the Nixon administration won a restraining order against the newspaper, citing national security concerns. But the Supreme Court reversed the decision and the publication was allowed to proceed.

Nixon's attorney general, John Mitchell, then went after Ellsberg, indicting him for theft, conspiracy, and espionage. The president's chief domestic adviser, John Ehrlichman, organized a break-in at Ellsberg's psychiatrist's office in order to gain damaging information about him. Ellsberg's legal fees were enormous, and Hollywood's liberals came to his aid.

The April fund-raiser, held in a tent in the backyard of Universal Studios executive Jennings Lang, featured only Barbra, singing for donations to the crowd and to people over the phone. The event drew two hundred guests, including Joni Mitchell, Hugh Hefner and Barbi Benton, Rod Steiger, Burt Lancaster, Yoko Ono, and all of the Beatles except Paul.

Barbra's agent Freddie Fields offered $5,000 for her to sing 'My Melancholy Baby.' Carl Reiner telephoned; he and Barbra sang 'Twinkle, Twinkle, Little Star.' A caller asked Barbra to surprise a man called Stanley in New York. When she got him on the line, she said, 'Hi, Stanley, this is Vicki Carr.' Stanley hung up.

Another caller asked that Barbra join the three Beatles in attendance on 'With a Little Help from My Friends.' John Lennon called out from the audience, 'We don't even know it. That's why you're up there and we're down here.' She sang the tune on her own.

In a magical three hours, Barbra sang twenty songs, including 'In the Wee Small Hours of the Morning,' 'Long Ago and Far Away,' 'Time after Time,' and 'The Very Thought of You.' The event raised over $50,000 for Ellsberg. The following month the charges against him were dropped. John Ehrlichman went to jail in July 1974 for his part in the break-in at Ellsberg's psychiatrist's office, and the following month President Nixon resigned under threat of impeachment for his part in the Watergate scandal.

After most of the guests had left the fund-raiser, George Harrison cornered Barbra and told her he wanted to write some songs for her next album. She and Harrison sat at Jennings Lang's dining room table until five in the morning, chomped on leftover hors d'oeuvres, and discussed song ideas. They never did work together.

THE CAMERAMAN DOLLIED in for a close-up of Barbra. 'Dwight!' she yelled to Dwight Hemion, the director in charge of her fifth television special, *Barbra Streisand . . . and Other Musical Instruments.* 'If you close in on my nose I look cross-eyed. If you close in on my eyes my nose looks too big.' A different angle didn't help. 'How many times do I have to say it?' she barked. 'That camera is nearly in my teeth!'

It was July 18, 1973, Barbra was in the third day of filming at the Elstree Studios north of London, and her duet with Ray Charles on his song 'Cryin'

Time' wasn't going well. She and the blind jazz great had spent five hours and twelve takes trying to get it right. If Barbra or Dwight Hemion didn't like anything about her appearance or performance, they'd do it all over again. Charles, sitting patiently at the piano, took it all in stride. 'She's a bitch,' he had said privately of Barbra, but he also felt she was 'the greatest living white female singer. She doesn't just sing notes, she sings feelings.'

Six-year-old Jason, bored, scribbled on a notepad under the watchful eye of Barbra's personal maid, Grace Davidson. Finally 'Cryin' Time' was in the can, and Barbra went right into 'Sweet Inspiration.' After innumerable takes, her temper grew short as a technician struggled to adjust one of the spotlights. 'I'm not going to have what happened the other night,' she said, 'having to do a complicated song at five to eight.' The tension grew thick. The light still wasn't ready. Barbra waited a few more minutes, got up, said, '*C'mon*, Dwight,' and started to walk off the set.

'Just a minute, Barb,' Hemion called after her.

'What!' she shouted angrily.

'Oh, forget it, Barbra,' Hemion said.

'I am tired. Either you're gonna do this or you're not,' she said as she swept off. 'I want to go and change.'

She returned ten minutes later wearing a black velvet pantsuit. As she cooled herself with a battery-powered fan, Hemion called out, 'Barb, I don't like the dress.'

'What's wrong with it?'

'It looks like a rehearsal costume.'

'Well, I like it.'

After Hemion told her to take a look at herself in the monitor, Barbra tramped back to her dressing room and changed into an off-white satin pantsuit left over from *What's Up, Doc?*

A disagreement about camera angles followed, and finally Barbra snapped, 'Dwight, *you* are going to have to adjust to *me*. I am not going to adjust to you. I'm not going to screw up my whole performance over this.' Then she began to munch on a large chocolate cake, one of many brought to the set every day for her to choose from. In a balcony above the set, Jason licked a cone-shaped cream-filled pastry. 'Isn't that good, J.J.?' Barbra called up to him. 'You sleepy, honey? We're gonna go home soon.'

Several more hours and twelve takes elapsed before she and Hemion pronounced themselves happy with 'Sweet Inspiration.' A relieved Ray Charles tinkled out a few bars of 'Jingle Bells' on the piano. At nine o'clock Barbra's limousine took her back to the house she had rented in central London. 'I don't know how she does it,' her maid, Gracie, said. 'She's worked the whole day, and when we get back I just close the door and say good night, but she's on the telephone, phoning home for hours. She only gets five hours' sleep.'

One of the 'concepts' of *Barbra Streisand . . . and Other Musical Instruments* was 'The World Is a Concerto,' in which Barbra would sing along with the 'music' of a blender, a vacuum cleaner, a steam kettle, a sewing machine, a washer, an electric shaver, and other noisy household appliances. It was the last segment filmed, and when Barbra arrived on the set on the morning of July 28, she called out to Hemion, 'I'm going to be nice to you today, Dwight.' But her mood soured after a series of mechanical failures and other problems. The washing machine didn't spin, the toaster didn't pop up on cue, and the tea kettle refused to whistle.

Eleven hours and twenty-three takes were required to get footage to everyone's satisfaction. At lunchtime Barbra soothed her frazzled nerves with food. 'She's been very good today,' an employee of Elstree's commissary said. 'She's supposed to be on a diet, you know. You should have seen her the other day. She fancied fish, so she had prawn cocktail, poached halibut, plaice [flounder] off the bone, Dover sole, and rice pudding. She eats like a horse.'

BARBRA STREISAND . . . and Other Musical Instruments was aired over CBS on Friday, November 2, 1973, and proved a very mixed bag creatively, as well as a ratings disappointment; it scored only a 30 share opposite a roast of Johnny Carson on the *Dean Martin Comedy Hour*, which in contrast won a 41 share. The reviewers weren't kind. John J. O'Connor in *The New York Times* praised the Ray Charles segment but called the show 'overproduced, overorchestrated and overbearing to the point of aesthetic nausea.' Morton Moss in the *Los Angeles Herald Examiner* felt that 'all the dazzle and incessant cartwheels are a distraction . . . The effects of *Instruments* might on occasion be accused of brilliance . . . but brilliance and unusual theatricality are irrelevant when they act as disgression to the major interest.'

Barbra Streisand . . . and Other Musical Instruments was Barbra's last special produced specifically for the home screen. Within two years of its telecast, her CBS contract expired. Released from that obligation, she was free to work for any other network. She opted to work for none. 'It takes a lot of time to do a special,' she explained. 'In the time it took me to do this special, you could do a whole movie . . . I don't like to work that hard. I don't have the time or the interest.'

WHILE SHE WAS in London to make the special, Barbra's attention to her work was often distracted by the presence of a new paramour, an Arizona businessman and entrepreneur named Sam Grossman. Attractive and strong-willed, Grossman wound Barbra around his finger. 'I like to accompany him on his business travels,' she told a reporter. 'I feel terribly guilty having to work. He doesn't want to be around when I'm working, and I don't want him to be because my concentration goes right out the window. The other day he came to rehearsal, for instance, and the musical director asked me if I wanted three bars or four in a certain spot. I didn't know and I didn't care. Yet if he hadn't been there I would have known exactly. It's a terrible thing, but I actually enjoy being subjugated to him. Not in a personal or physical sense – I still need to be respected in my own right – but in terms of our work. It's far more important to a man's ego to have a career than it is to a woman's. I don't need to work anymore to feed my ego. I get all the ego nourishment I need from him.'

In another interview she said, 'I like to be taken care of, but I also like to take care of. I'd love to be a sex object to the right man. I'm old-fashioned.'

The relationship with Grossman ended within a few months, but before long Barbra met another man, one who would sweep her off her feet, turn her private and professional worlds upside down, make her feel like the sex object of all time, touch 'a deeper place in my heart,' and become the love of her life.

◆ 24 ◆

J on Peters wouldn't leave Barbra alone. The darkly good-looking, cocksure twenty-eight-year-old hairdresser, the millionaire owner of several salons, had met Streisand, now thirty-one, in the summer of 1973 when she asked him to design a hairdo for her to wear in her new film. He had found her 'the most beautiful woman that I've ever seen in my life' and a 'sexy little ball of fire.'

Barbra was taken aback by Jon. The day he came to her house on Carolwood to discuss the assignment, Barbra said, 'Jon drove up in his red Ferrari. I was shocked by his appearance, because he was wearing a low-cut shirt with an Indian necklace and tight jeans. I thought, What is this person?'

She kept him waiting for forty-five minutes, and when she finally came down the stairs to greet him he told her, 'Don't you ever do that again. Nobody keeps me waiting.' Later, when she turned her back to him, he muttered, 'You've got a great ass.'

Barbra liked that. 'He made me feel like a woman, not like some famous thing.' She later said that meeting Jon was love at first sight, but she was leery. He seemed like the kind of wily hustler she had seen too many of in her business. When he asked her out, she declined.

He wouldn't take no for an answer. 'Jon doesn't let up going after something he wants,' she said. 'He wore me down. I would say to him, "Stop coming after me; you're not my type. I like men who smoke pipes and are more distinguished. I want to be with a doctor or a lawyer."' (According to Jon, Barbra had just returned from a visit with Pierre Trudeau when he first met her, which perhaps had prompted that description of her ideal man.)

The next day Jon pulled up to the house in a dark green Jaguar. When he got out of the car Barbra saw that he was wearing eyeglasses and a velvet smoking jacket over his jeans and T-shirt. Amused and touched, she accepted his invitation to dinner that night. And thus began the great love story of Barbra Streisand's life.

✮

'THERE WERE AREAS that were sketchy about Jon's background,' said Steve Jaffe, who would become Jon and Barbra's personal publicist. 'And Jon wanted them to remain a mystery.'

He was born John Pagano Peters on June 2, 1945, in a lower-class section of Los Angeles County's San Fernando Valley, the son of an Italian mother and a half-Cherokee father. When he was nearly eight, his father died in front of him. 'My world fell apart,' he said. 'I was angry, confused. My mother was working. I was alone.'

His mother remarried, and he despised his stepfather. 'I started to get into trouble,' he told the British reporter Rosalie Shann. 'They called it "being incorrigible."' He was small-boned but strong and pugnacious; he strutted like a bantam rooster and got into so many fights with classmates that 'I got thrown out of every school in the Los Angeles system.' He hung out with motorcycle gangs, and although he was intelligent he was put into 'the retarded class' at school 'because I'm an emotional guy.' He ran away a number of times and once stole a car.

A juvenile court judge sentenced him to a year in a reform school in the San Bernardino Mountains ninety miles northeast of Los Angeles – 'a kind of kids' jail,' he called it. Every day he did grueling work, often breaking up rocks, and at night he was chained to his bed. 'I'll never forget that. It sure toughened me up.' And, he added, 'it gave me a healthy respect for what society could do to you if you crossed it.'

When John came home he told his mother he'd rather die than go back to eighth grade. Her family, the Paganos, owned a string of beauty parlors in Los Angeles, and she suggested he go to beauty school. 'I was only twelve, but mature for my years,' Jon recalled. From the outset, he knew it was a life he wanted to pursue – especially when he saw all the beautiful girls who frequented the shop. 'I loved playing with their hair.'

After two years his mother sent him to New York with $120 in his pocket. He worked the night shift in a Fifty-seventh Street salon, dyeing the hair of hookers to match their poodles. The following year, not yet fifteen, he married a girl named Marie Zambatelli, age fifteen and a half. 'I was in a hurry to grow up . . . My folks gave their consent. They were only too glad to get rid of me.'

The newlyweds lived in Philadelphia, where John worked as an apprentice hairdresser by day and moonlighted as a bouncer in a nightclub at night.

When he was nineteen, in 1964, John and Marie divorced, and he returned to California. He smooth-talked a real estate agent friend into lending him $100,000 to open his own salon in Encino in the San Fernando Valley. His talent and his sex appeal made the shop an immediate hit; suburban housewives and movie starlets alike clamored for his professional – and sometimes his personal – attention. He took the *h* out of his first name, and by the early 1970s had three Jon Peters Salons, one of them in Beverly Hills. Along the way he became a millionaire.

In May 1967 Jon got married again, this time to Lesley Ann Warren, who had starred opposite Elliott Gould in *Drat! The Cat!* in 1965. Lesley Ann was a big Barbra Streisand fan. 'I was totally fascinated with her,' she said. 'I asked Elliott how she did her makeup. I vocalized to her albums.'

Two months after she married Jon, Lesley Ann 'dragged' him to see Barbra at the Hollywood Bowl. 'Jon had never heard of her,' she recalled. He found Streisand mesmerizing. 'The moment I saw Barbra – wow! She blew my mind. She was fantastic, staggering . . . I couldn't take my eyes off her.'

In the early seventies, Jon began to boast that Barbra was one of his clients. 'I've done Streisand, everybody,' he told a reporter at the time. As a result, his business increased 40 percent. 'All these women would come in and want Barbra's hairstyle,' he said. Finally he decided that he must meet her, and he sent word via mutual friends, the Joe Laytons, that he would go anywhere in the world at any time to cut her hair – free. Barbra ignored the offer.

Peters soon found himself distracted by marital problems. He and Lesley Ann had a son, five-year-old Christopher, but their marriage floundered. They separated, and Jon began a hedonistic whirl during which he saw a number of women including Sally Kellerman, Leigh Taylor-Young, and Jacqueline Bisset. 'I had dozens of affairs,' Jon told Rosalie Shann. 'I couldn't relate to any one woman. I had to have several on the go at once. It wasn't an enviable state to be in. It was a tragic one. I was kind of scared of becoming involved.'

Then, in August of 1973, while Jon was in London staying with a young actress, the telephone rang. It was Barbra. 'I got your message,' she said. 'When you get home, come and see me. I want a new look for my next film.' Barbra had seen a woman at a party with a short, boyish hairstyle that she liked. When she was told Jon Peters had designed it, she decided to call him.

If Jon's mode of dress put Barbra off when she met him, he found himself pleasantly surprised by her. 'I expected this big woman, and this little bitty girl came down the stairs. She was vulnerable and beautiful. Immediately the chemistry starting working between us.' It was mostly confrontational chemistry. After Jon dressed Barbra down for keeping him waiting, he balked when she told him she wanted him to style a wig, not her hair. 'I don't do *wigs!*' he snapped. 'How insulting!'

Barbra wasn't used to being called on her behavior like that, and she was intrigued. (Had Jon not been so attractive, however, one suspects she would have thrown him out.) She batted her eyelashes and pleaded with him until he relented.

'You're the only person in the world I'd do this for,' he told her.

'Listen,' she said, 'will you take a look at these clothes I'm gonna wear in the picture? Tell me what you think.' She pulled out some photographs and spread them out on her coffee table.

Jon frowned as he studied them. 'I don't like them,' he said.

'I hate them too!' Barbra exclaimed.

'Okay, then, let's go shopping,' Jon replied. Two days later they spent an entire day scouring Beverly Hills boutiques. 'He saw me as a young, hip chick,' Barbra said. 'At the time, I wore Dior clothes; I appeared older than I was . . . He just made me feel very young and beautiful, and he said, "The public should see this side of you – the sexy side, your legs, your ass, your breasts."'

She was starting to like this guy, but not enough to give herself to him. 'It was four months before we became lovers,' Jon said. 'But it was already there – that intense feeling.' The relationship had to develop long distance, because in September Barbra flew to New York to begin location shooting for her new picture.

WHAT CAN ONE say about *For Pete's Sake?* For years Barbra had talked about wanting to make 'significant' films. She longed, she said, to play characters by Shakespeare and Euripides, but by mid-1973 Barbra seemed more interested in remaining a strong box-office attraction than in becoming a classical actress. Devastated by the failure of *Up the Sandbox*, and unsure whether the public would support the as-yet-unreleased *The Way We Were*, she felt she couldn't risk another arty flop.

What she needed to do, Marty Erlichman kept telling her, was another zany comedy, the kind that moviegoers flock to in the summer. There weren't enough good scripts for Barbra, he felt, so he went to Stanley Shapiro, who had written several of those will-the-virgin-or-won't-she? sex comedies for Doris Day and Rock Hudson in the late fifties and early sixties.

The story Shapiro and his writing partner, Maurice Richlin, came up with could make one's teeth ache: Brooklyn housewife Henrietta Robbins – nicknamed Henry, which prompted Barbra's desire for a boyish haircut

– is so upset about her husband Pete's financial worries that she borrows money from the Mafia to allow him to purchase pork belly futures on the stock exchange. When the porcine abdomens fall in value, the Mob threatens to feed her to the fishes. Frantic, she sells her debt to Mrs Cherry, a homey Jewish mama who's also a madam, and goes to work for her as an afternoon hooker. But when Pete comes home unexpectedly, she shoves a kinky judge into her closet and he almost dies of a heart attack.

Disappointed in Henry, Mrs Cherry sells her contract to two 'business-men.' They tell Henry to disguise herself in a curly platinum-blond wig and sunglasses and deliver a package. She is interrupted by undercover cops and chased through the subway by a police dog, but she finally brings the package back to the men. All three manage to escape before it explodes. Next her debt is sold to cattle thieves, and Henry winds up rustling a herd of cows and riding a bull along the streets of Brooklyn, through a china shop, and finally into a movie theater where she crashes through the screen during a cattle stampede scene. Marty Erlichman is in the audience and turns to the camera to comment about the realism of the film he's watching.

For Pete's Sake offered precious little realism, of course, but that's expected of a slapstick comedy. What is far worse about the film, which Marty produced with Shapiro and which is very funny in spots, is its political incorrectness. Many of its situations and characters are objectionable, especially in a film starring Barbra Streisand, who is supposed to have higher sensibilities. Henrietta's willingness to do anything, even prostitute herself, for her husband flew in the face of Barbra's professed feminism. Henry's household help is a droll but lazy black lady who calls herself 'the colored woman.' Henry tells a flamboyant, lisping grocery clerk, 'You keep the Froot Loops, you'll love them.' Even in 1973 the film was a throwback to the bad old days of the 1950s, with enough insults to offend just about every minority. In the 1990s the film would never have been made as written.

But Barbra 'liked the script,' and she wanted to help Marty break into producing. (Because he was a novice, Erlichman enlisted Ray Stark to oversee the production, which Stark agreed to do only on the condition that *For Pete's Sake* not be considered the last of his four-picture deal with Streisand: Stark wanted her to do a sequel to *Funny Girl*.) The fact that the picture would be made in New York also appealed to Barbra because she 'didn't want to be in L.A. any longer.' Ironically, by the time production began in Brooklyn, Barbra wished she had stayed in California, near Jon Peters.

BARBRA HAD GOTTEN into the habit of calling Jon every night to ask his advice, and their conversations sometimes stretched into hours. After they had discussed the day's filming problems, they often opened up about their innermost feelings. 'I can't get over Barbra,' Jon told Steve Jaffe. 'She's such an amazing person. We talked all night.'

He told her about his background, and more and more she felt she had found a soul mate. She could understand Jon's youthful alienation, his desire to grow up quickly, to 'get out.' She felt his pain over the early death of his father; she related to his dislike of his stepfather. She even believed that his dropping the *h* from 'John,' just as she had dropped an *a* from 'Barbara,' proved that there was some kind of 'cosmic connection' between them.

She wanted Jon close by, so she hired him as an uncredited wardrobe consultant on the film, and the production flew Peters to New York and put him up at the Plaza Hotel. Within a few days he went home angry. 'I had feelings for her, and she kept me waiting a lot. I decided I wasn't talking to her ever again.'

Two weeks later Barbra telephoned him and pleaded, 'I need you. I was taking a bath and my wig fell in the tub. You have to come.'

He went back. 'It was always these silly things that would get us together,' he said.

PETER YATES, RENOWNED for his direction of *Bullitt* and *The Friends of Eddie Coyle*, found Barbra 'absolutely delightful' to direct in *For Pete's Sake*. 'She was a strange, strange girl. She has a sort of unusual attraction about her. It's not only her talent, which is enormous, but she has this extraordinary personality which comes through, even when you first meet her and talk to her. She's far more friendly than her reputation would lead one to believe.'

Yates felt Barbra was 'extremely generous' to her leading man, Michael Sarrazin. 'If a star is selfish, he or she can do things to cut down on the time spent shooting the other person. But Barbra wasn't selfish. If it was his scene, she would give it to him and help him with it.'

But the film's third lead, Estelle Parsons, had less affectionate things to say about Barbra. Playing Henry's nagging mother-in-law, the Oscar-winning actress called the filming 'not the happiest experience. Miss Streisand is not a warm human being. Of course, our characters were at odds anyway, but she carried that over into real life . . . she's a very inward-looking person. Perhaps that's the nicest way I can put it. She doesn't believe in sharing a picture, even a comedy, which has to be a team effort.'

BARBRA LOATHED BEING back in Brooklyn, which held such unpleasant memories for her. During the scene in which Henry takes a subway train to escape the police dog, the film's second assistant director, Stu Fleming, noticed that Barbra had a 'faraway look' in her eyes. 'Do you remember when you used to take the subway?' he asked her.

'Yeah,' she replied. 'I hated it.'

Every day, vociferous New York Streisand fans disrupted the production and drove Barbra to distraction. At each location they lined the streets behind police barricades, took pictures, shouted comments at her, and generally became obstreperous. The assistant director, Harry Kaplan, 'got hoarse' yelling at the onlookers to keep quiet and not interrupt scenes. During one brief shot of Barbra coming out of a manhole, things got out of hand. Three camera-toting fans had dogged Streisand for days, taking pictures of her between takes, and calling things out to her. 'Sing "On a Clear Day" for us, Barbra!' one insisted.

'Yeah, right,' Barbra replied, 'I'll stop the picture and sing for you right here.'

Between shots of the manhole scene, one of the fans started taking flash pictures. The clicks and flashcube bursts broke Barbra's concentration, and she asked the girl to stop. She didn't, and the constant pops of light sent Barbra over the edge. She climbed out of the manhole shouting, 'I told you to stop taking pictures, goddammit!' and lunged for the fan's camera. The girl dodged Barbra's grasp; a crew member calmed Streisand down and took her to her dressing room. (The fan has souvenir photos of a wild-eyed star on the attack.) The incident upset Barbra so much that she told Marty she could not continue to film in Brooklyn. The company returned to Los Angeles a week early, where the shoot was completed at the Burbank Studios on December 12, 1973.

When *For Pete's Sake* opened the following June, with an ad campaign that trumpeted 'Zany Barbra,' audiences responded well enough initially, but poor word of mouth kept the box-office receipts to $26.5 million, just over one-third of the grosses for *What's Up, Doc?* The reviews were largely negative, although Vincent Canby of *The New York Times* liked the film. He called it 'often a boisterously funny old-time farce . . . The star barges through the movie with a self-assurance that is very funny, because it seems always on the edge of farce.' Of the film's sometimes leering tone and the ill-tempered black maid, Canby said, '*For Pete's Sake* courts disaster, but most of the time manages to sidestep it.'

More typical was *New York* magazine's view: 'Everyone involved in *For Pete's Sake* owes not only the audience but also his colleagues an apology for perpetrating this piece of schlock, certainly the worst Barbra Streisand package yet . . . Doris Day our Barbra isn't, and we are not the setups we used to be . . . Stale television frenzy does not a mad, mad comedy make.'

Barbra later called the picture 'stupid,' but Peter Yates defended his movie. 'People want me to say it's the one film I regret making, but it isn't. It was made to be frothy and light and charming and amusing, and I don't think there was anything wrong with that. It's wrong to call it stupid, because to call something that a lot of people have enjoyed "stupid" is to criticize the taste of those people . . . At the time, Barbra loved it. And she liked it even more, I'm sure, when the checks came in. She had a big piece of it.'

BARBRA AND JON were falling in love. When she got back from New York, they spent most of their time together, and Jon has admitted he was attracted to Barbra's show biz megawattage. 'I didn't fall in love with Barbra independent of her star trip,' he said. 'I was fascinated by her and, of course, by Hollywood.' But what he found most appealing was her femininity and her vulnerability. 'She's a little baby underneath. The sweetest girl I've ever known in my life.'

He was surprised, as many other Streisand suitors had been, at how yielding she could be to his masculine prerogatives. 'Jon has always had women cater to him like a king,' Barbra said. 'He is a very, very strong personality, and he wasn't the least bit intimidated by me. I used to say, "Hey, come on, be a little intimidated." He never was . . . Jon likes me in the kitchen. But that's okay. I enjoy cooking for him.'

The strength of Jon's body appealed to Barbra, too. His friend Geraldo Rivera described him as 'built like a barroom bouncer . . . He had Popeye-like forearms . . . and a meticulously shag-cut head of hair . . . Even with the pretty-boy locks, Jon came across as rough-and-tumble.'

The sexual kineticism between Streisand and Peters finally led them to consummate their attraction to each other, four months after they met, at Jon's rustic ranch house on Valley Vista Boulevard in Sherman Oaks. 'My house has a Jacuzzi,' he said at the time. 'People take their clothes off.'

Barbra found that Jon expanded her sexual horizons. She told *Playboy* in 1977 that she had become a 'sexually aggressive woman just in the past three years, in my relationship with Jon.' Asked how often she initiated sexual activity, she replied, 'We're equal, honey, we're equal.' How innovative was she sexually? 'Well, I do have some erotic art books,' she replied, laughing. She and Jon sometimes watched pornographic movies together, but they found *Deep Throat* boring and fell asleep in the middle of it. Nevertheless, Jon told *Playboy* in 1978 that 'Good in bed means giving head.'

Before long, Jon said, 'It just seemed to be the natural thing to do to start being together all the time.' Barbra liked Jon's place, which he had largely built himself out of aged wood and stucco. What impressed her most about

the house was its lace curtains. 'When I first went to see his house on Valley
Vista I thought, Wow, this man is so creative and so original. Here was
this smallish house – two thousand square feet – with burnt wood walls,
mirrors, lace, and chandeliers. This combination of masculine and feminine.
That made me realize that Jon was secure enough in his masculinity to be
comfortable with his feminine side.'

ON FEBRUARY 19, 1974, nominations for the forty-sixth annual Academy
Awards were announced. *The Way We Were* garnered six, including Best
Actress for Streisand. Jack Haley, the producer of the awards ceremony,
asked Barbra to sing 'The Way We Were,' which had been nominated
as Best Song. Afraid to perform live in front of a worldwide audience of
millions, she declined. Haley turned to Peggy Lee, who agreed to cut short
a Canadian engagement to make the appearance. Shortly before the telecast,
Barbra changed her mind, but Haley told her he wouldn't cancel Peggy Lee
at the last moment. Barbra was reportedly angry, and Lee's performance
during the April second telecast proved a disappointment. Her voice did
little to enhance the melody line, and she reversed two stanzas. The song
did win the award, as did Marvin Hamlisch's score.

The Best Actress competition that year wasn't nearly as strong as it had
been in 1969. Also nominated were Joanne Woodward for *Summer Wishes,
Winter Dreams*, Marsha Mason for *Cinderella Liberty*, Ellen Burstyn for *The
Exorcist*, and Glenda Jackson for a light comedy role in *A Touch of Class*.
Handicappers predicted either Streisand or Woodward would triumph, and
Barbra thought her performance deserved the award: 'I felt it was the best
of those five for the year.' She declined to appear as a presenter, and she
didn't want to sit in the audience, where the camera could telecast her
disappointment around the world if she lost. Instead she waited backstage
with Jon, and when Glenda Jackson's name was announced in an upset,
Barbra picked herself up and went home.

Streisand's bad reputation among Hollywood insiders undoubtedly cost
her a second Best Actress Oscar, but Arthur Laurents feels that she was hurt
as well by the fact that many of the scenes Sydney Pollack had cut from
the film contained some of her best acting. In one, she catches Hubbell in
flagrante delicto with his former girlfriend, and in another she drives past a
student demonstration, stops, sees an ardent coed who is remarkably similar
to her younger self, and starts to weep.

Laurents also felt that Barbra had blown her big dramatic opportunity
in the scene where she telephones Hubbell in tears and begs him to come
back to her. 'She kept her hand in front of her face, and it looked like she

was trying to hide [the fact] that she wasn't acting very well,' Laurents said. 'She *was* acting beautifully, but you couldn't see it.' According to Laurents, he pleaded with Barbra to redo the scene and argued that her eyes were not red enough for a woman who had been weeping for hours. 'She was surprised at my suggestion and said, "But I look so beautiful in that scene."' Laurents felt that had the scene been reshot, Barbra would have won the Oscar.

Pollack countered Laurents's assertions. 'That scene was done in one take, and she was really crying . . . Her eyes were plenty red. Maybe we didn't have a pin light picking it up because it was a dark night scene.'

SHORTLY AFTER THE new year began, Jon and Barbra had decided to live together. First, though, Jon needed seven-year-old Jason's approval. 'I knew the big test would be when Jason met him,' Barbra recalled. 'Finally I invited Jon over to the house, and he and Jason kind of stared at one another for a long time. Then Jason said, "Are you a good swimmer?" and it was as if Jason just knew that Jon would be the kind of man he would like, for soon after, Jon and Jason were out in the pool. Jon was teaching Jason how to do the breaststroke. They've been friends ever since.'

In October 1973 Peters had purchased a small parcel of land in the secluded, heavily wooded Ramirez Canyon area of Malibu, and in March 1974 he and Barbra, buying separate lots, picked up three and a quarter additional acres at a cost of $250,000. Within two years they would buy up another sixteen acres for $600,000.

Over the next year, Jon expanded the small main house on the property with mellow wood salvaged from old barns in New York. Built almost entirely of wood and stone, the house took on the same eclectic, masculine-feminine look Barbra had admired in Jon's Valley Vista home when she decorated the place with many of the antiques she had collected over the years. 'Jon deals with the structure,' she said, 'and I come along with the detail.' Tiffany lamps coexisted with Navajo rugs, lace was juxtaposed with macramé, distressed wooden sideboards held silver tea services, and Barbra's treasured beaded bags hung from rusted hundred-year-old nails.

The stained-glass windows Barbra had commandeered from the set of *On a Clear Day* bounced splashes of multicolored sunlight around the loft bedroom, whose centerpiece was a huge four-poster bed handmade by Jon. The bathtub, set among river stones, resembled a mountain pool. Outside, a waterfall designed by Jon tinkled, an old wine vat housed the Jacuzzi, and a garden tended by Barbra sprouted tomatoes, corn, herbs, and sunflowers. Roaming the property were a Doberman, a stallion named Shot, and a mountain lion named Leo.

All of this outdoorsy living would have given the old Barbra an asthma attack, but she insisted that knowing Jon had changed her. 'I love it here,' she said. 'You are very much in touch with the earth, with the natural things that happen. I never used to walk or ride a bike. I never breathed deeply before. The pressures of this business can destroy you . . . The thing that keeps me sane is living here. It's away from it all.'

LOVING JON PETERS, Barbra said, 'has made me the happiest I've ever been.' She appreciated how much he had opened her up to new experiences, she adored his energy and his boyish rambunctiousness. 'In the beginning he was really crazy, a nut,' she said. 'He took me to a party once and said he wanted to go for a walk with me, then put me on his shoulders and wouldn't let me down. He was so vital, so verbal, really terrific and alive.

'He's the strongest person I've ever met,' Barbra went on. 'I don't mean physically; I mean in his presence, his sense of self, in his perceptions of other people, of other things, of his sensitivity, of his vitality, in his unconventional conventionalism. Like me. It's fabulous to find somebody who's like you. When I didn't like myself as much as I do now, I was always drawn to people who were not like me.'

'Obviously I love Barbra,' Jon chimed in. 'She's powerful. She's gentle. She's beautiful. She's fun to be with. She's ten different people, and I love them all. On our good days we could fly over the universe. Our bad days are pretty low, too.'

On their bad days they fought, they scratched, they clawed. Jon had a temper forged on the mean streets, and when Barbra got angry she took no guff from anyone. 'Our life together is fiery, really fiery,' Jon admitted. They found themselves arguing frequently about who was going to pay for what. 'Money doesn't really mean that much to me,' he said. 'It means much more to Barbra.'

One night, Jon revealed, they had a terrible fight. 'We were like wild animals. In the end, Barbra sat on my chest and spat at me. I spat back. Finally the resentment started to turn into something else, something sensual and sexual. It was very real, for it showed that on an emotional level people who love each other deeply occasionally really hate each other, too.'

That realization, Barbra said, 'was a very liberating thing for me, because now I can say I hate without destroying love.'

Jon's volatility sat less well with those who didn't love him. When Elliott Gould visited the Malibu ranch, he and Jon got into an argument over Elliott's visitation rights to Jason. As Steve Jaffe recalled it, 'Elliott could be very vague. He would act dumb when he wasn't hearing what he wanted to hear, like he didn't understand English or something. It frustrated the hell out of Jon. This one time Elliott was acting particularly dense, and finally Jon lost it and he threw Elliott down on the hood of his car and yelled, "Listen, don't give me that bullshit! We're going to take good care of Jason!" They came to blows, and suddenly Elliott was as alert as could be. They worked things out, and Jon said, "Now I'm ready to be friends with him." That was typical Jon.'

Jon's divorce from Lesley Ann Warren was still pending. In June 1974 Lesley petitioned the Santa Monica court to issue a restraining order against Jon for 'annoyance.' She won the order, which stated that 'Peters is restrained from annoying, harassing, molesting and making disparaging, derogatory comments about the mother, and she about Peters, to or in front of the minor child.' The final divorce decree gave custody of Christopher to his mother, and ordered Jon to pay $400 a month in child support. The judge also ordered Jon to pay Lesley $1,000 a month in alimony until January 1, 1983. In petitioning for the alimony, she testified that she had only one hundred dollars on hand for living expenses. 'My lifestyle is used to higher standards,' she told the court.

JON AND BARBRA loved together and lived together; to work together seemed a logical extension of their relationship. From the beginning Jon had been after Barbra to 'get with what's happening' musically. He had caught Bette Midler's wild and woolly show in New York in the fall of 1973, and he told Barbra, 'I don't know anything about music, but Bette Midler was terrific and you're better than she is, and if you could get involved with some young people and use that instrument in a contemporary way . . .'

Columbia wanted a new album from Streisand in time for Christmas, and Jon kept suggesting songs for Barbra to sing on it. One day she said to him, 'Why don't you design the album cover?'

'How about if I produce the whole thing?' Jon replied.

At the first recording sessions Barbra, braless and wearing a tight T-shirt, hung all over Jon, sat on his lap, and kissed him as her favorite photographer, Steve Schapiro, snapped away. Schapiro didn't record the battles, however. 'She'd get as tense as a prizefighter,' Jon recalled to Julia Orange of *Woman's Day*. 'We fought about it. I quit, she quit, I'd fire her, she'd fire me.'

Barbra and Jon had selected songs 'no one was particularly thrilled about,' she later admitted. And when Columbia heard the cuts – which included Carole King's 'You Light Up My Life,' the sixties Drifters hit 'On Broadway,' and an R&B song called 'Turn Me On (It's a Funky Type Thing)' – the label's artists and repertoire director Charles Koppelman called in the producer Gary Klein and gave him the unenviable job of sitting down with Barbra and Jon to tell them the cuts just didn't cut it. 'Charles and I didn't think it was up to Barbra's standards,' Klein recalled, 'and he wanted me to go out to California, sit down with them, and tell them why. It was very difficult to meet her for the first time to criticize an album that her boyfriend, who was sitting right there, had produced. But I went over the album cut by cut, and I was very specific about what I thought was wrong with it, and they knew I knew what I was talking about, so I gained their respect.'

The recording engineer Al Schmitt came in to remix the tracks, but he quit within three days when Jon refused to share the producing credit with him. The whole thing blew up into a barrage of bad publicity about 'Barbra's hairdresser boyfriend' when Schmitt gave an extended interview to Joyce Haber of the *Los Angeles Times*. 'This album has a flat, one-dimensional sound,' Schmitt said. 'Peters is a nice guy, but he's not a record producer . . . Essentially, Peters wanted all the money and I'd be doing all the work . . . Streisand has this tremendous thing of knowing exactly what's right for her. But now, it seems, that's gone out the window. She's never let anyone direct her career this way.'

The morning Haber's column appeared, Barbra got the reporter on the phone, waking her, to defend Jon and the album. 'Is Schmitt trying to imply that I've given up my career for Jon Peters?' she asked. 'I don't even know this Schmitt. The only thing he said that's true is "Barbra has this thing of knowing exactly what's right for her." This is possibly the best singing I've ever done. That's what Al Schmitt told Jon.

'I'm an artist. Jon and I have to deal with ourselves on two levels – as creative people and as lovers. The reason we're calling [the album] *ButterFly* is that when we first met he said I reminded him of a butterfly. He gave me this one-hundred-year-old Indian butterfly [brooch]. Both of us gravitate toward butterflies. Jon designed the album cover . . . My attitude has changed toward people. I'm less afraid. That's Jon. It kills me to have him put down more than to have me put down.'

Those comments provided fodder for ridicule. Jon, with no experience, had not only produced the album but designed the cover too? And what was all that about gravitating toward butterflies? Cynics chuckled that Barbra Streisand appeared not only to have been blinded by love for a fledgling Svengali but to have become a spacey flower child in the bargain.

'Do they think I would let Jon produce a record if I wasn't absolutely sure he could do it?' Barbra retorted. 'I believe in instinct, I believe in imagination, I believe in taste. These are the important ingredients, and they're all the things he has.'

Jon jumped to his own defense as well: 'Barbra is far too much of a professional to get involved with me professionally just as a romantic gesture. And of course they're going to think I hit the jackpot by being with Barbra ... What they forget is that I made a lot of money before I met Barbra.'

MOST CRITICS WERE lying in wait when *ButterFly* was released in October 1974. They mocked the album's cover (a fly alighted on a stick of butter), its back cover (a rendering of Barbra's face on a Maxfield Parrish-like field of butterflies), its inside photo spread of Barbra hanging all over Jon, and Barbra and Jon's choice of material. Traditionalist critic Hugh Harrison admonished Streisand, writing that *ButterFly* was 'not only your worst public exposure ever but may well be one of the worst albums ever made by a major talent' and that she should never have trusted Jon to produce the album.

Not all the reviews were negative, though. Shaun Considine, writing in *The New York Times*, said, 'Beyond the fashionable cracks at Peters's profession ... his role as producer certainly has enhanced this album. *ButterFly* is one of Streisand's finest albums in years. It is a revelation of what this performer can do when she leaves her legend outside the studio doors ... Love becomes the lady.'

The truth about the quality of *ButterFly* lies somewhere in the middle. The album, like all of Streisand's pop-rock efforts, has high points and low. Barbra does the most soulful wailing she has ever done on the stirring 'Grandma's Hands,' and brings such steamy sensuality to 'Love in the Afternoon' and 'Guava Jelly' that one can imagine her needing to take a private break with Jon after laying down each track. But her mechanical rendering of David Bowie's 'Life on Mars' is, as Bowie himself put it, 'bloody awful,' and 'I Won't Last a Day Without You' is just as saccharine and dull as it was when Karen Carpenter sang it.

ButterFly proved criticproof. It rose to number thirteen and received gold certification three months after its release. Commercially, at least, Jon had proved himself, but the *Stereo Review* critic Peter Reilly took the wind out of even those sails when he wrote, 'saying that one "produced" a Streisand album is like saying that one pumped up the tires for Henry Ford.'

Whatever the merits of *ButterFly*, Jon had had enough. 'I've had it with producing records,' he said. 'I made my mark. Barbra and I are now going on to bigger stuff, like doing big concerts and movies.'

25

T hat's the most disgusting idea I've ever heard!' Barbra shouted at Ray Stark. 'You can't capitalize on something that has worked before. You'll have to drag me into court to do that picture!'

The picture Barbra refused to do was *Funny Lady*, a sequel to *Funny Girl*, which would take Fanny Brice from just before her divorce from Nick Arnstein through a second marriage and into the 1940s. Many observers joined Streisand in the opinion that Stark would be foolish to attempt to re-create her greatest film triumph, but Stark saw the sequel as a guaranteed box-office blockbuster. Barbra hadn't appeared in a musical in five years, and many moviegoers hungered to see her sing onscreen again. She would be returning to her Oscar-winning Fanny Brice characterization, under the aegis of a producer who would spare no expense to package the film with the most lavish production values. How could it lose?

Barbra kept telling Stark 'There is no way I will do this movie' – until she read a witty, insightful script rewrite by Jay Presson Allen, the scenarist of *Cabaret*. 'There was wonderful material available,' Allen said. 'Fanny Brice did an oral history two years before she died that was just a mine, an embarrassment of riches.' Allen also admitted he had tailored some of the dialogue to fit Barbra's 'powerful personality and singular pattern of speech and pace.' Allen's partly fictionalized account began in the early days of the Depression and focused on Fanny's life following her painful divorce and on her second marriage to producer-hustler-songwriter Billy Rose. Though Brice and Rose start off as bickering antagonists, they eventually marry after developing an affection for each other that is rooted in companionship, a shared sense of humor, and mutual business interests rather than in romantic passion.

The marriage runs smoothly until their careers impose a lengthy separation. On the road with an aquacade, Billy takes up with his star swimmer

Eleanor Holm while Fanny, in Hollywood to begin her stint as radio's Baby Snooks, unexpectedly encounters Nick Arnstein. Ultimately, Brice and Rose part, leaving Fanny sadder but free of romantic illusions about men.

Barbra felt an empathy for the older Fanny Brice. 'I understand her whole thing with Billy Rose,' Barbra said, 'and what it means to fall in love with somebody who is like you. You can only do that when you accept yourself and feel yourself worthy of being loved . . . Otherwise it's always your fantasies – like hers with Nicky Arnstein . . . In the second part of Fanny's life, I feel she starts to discover herself . . . and finally lets go of her illusions and fantasies about men. She grows up.' Barbra could, of course, have been describing herself since she met Jon Peters.

Along with her admiration for the script, Barbra agreed to make *Funny Lady* mainly to put an end to her obligation to Ray Stark, to whom she owed one final film on the contract they had drawn up nearly a decade earlier. She also saw the project as an opportunity to play a grown-up Fanny who was tougher, wiser, and truer to the original than the one portrayed in the first film. 'The Fanny Brice of *Funny Lady* is a marvelous character that I didn't play in *Funny Girl*,' she admitted. 'That Fanny Brice was more like me. Even the numbers were written for me. Now I'm more of an actress and less of an ego. It's more of a real acting job for me in this picture.'

VINTAGE PHOTOGRAPHS SHOW that Fanny Brice, even in low heels, towered over the four-foot-eleven-inch Billy Rose. With this height discrepancy in mind, the first actor to read for the part was short, stocky, pugnacious Robert Blake, who had played a television gumshoe in *Baretta*. Invited to read a scene with Barbra at Carolwood, Blake asked instead if they could run through the entire script. Barbra complied, and she was impressed with his reading. But contrary to press reports, Blake was not offered the role on the spot. Al Pacino's name surfaced briefly in some columns as a likely candidate, but it was his *The Godfather* co-star, James Caan, who was signed to play Billy at the end of 1973. Tall, athletic, and ruggedly handsome, Caan seemed the polar opposite of Rose. With an eye to the box-office potential of a Caan-Streisand teaming, Ray Stark went on the defensive about the casting. 'If Arnstein could be played by an Arab,' he offered, 'then Billy Rose didn't have to be short.'

Barbra rationalized the choice from another angle. 'It comes down to whom the audience wants me to kiss. Robert Blake, no. James Caan, yes.'

Omar Sharif, whose box-office appeal had slipped considerably since *Funny Girl* with missteps like *Che!*, *The Tamarind Seed*, and *The Mysterious*

Island of Captain Nemo, agreed to return as Nick Arnstein in three brief but pivotal scenes.

To no one's surprise, Herb Ross was signed to direct *Funny Lady*, and his suggestion of Vilmos Zsigmond *(McCabe and Mrs Miller)* for cinematographer met with everyone's approval. Bob Mackie, highly publicized for the glitzy, sometimes outlandish designs he whipped up for Cher's and Carol Burnett's television shows, was engaged to create the film's costumes in tandem with his partner Ray Aghayan. *Funny Lady*'s musical score would consist of old standards, some penned by Billy Rose, and new songs by John Kander and Fred Ebb, who were at the peak of their careers following the success of their razor-sharp score for *Cabaret*.

Ray Stark budgeted *Funny Lady* at $7.5 million (less than the original). In an unusual move, all fourteen of the film's musical numbers were rehearsed one after the other and filmed in sixteen days in the early spring of 1974 at Metro-Goldwyn-Mayer's theater soundstage, which featured a fully rendered proscenium, theater seats, and backstage space equal to that of a typical Broadway theater. The first number shot, 'Great Day,' was given an elaborate design that placed a sequin-draped Barbra at the top of a stylized altar, where she belted out the song, gospel-like, as black dancers writhed below her.

When Ray Stark viewed the footage of the number the next day, he was shocked at Vilmos Zsigmond's approach to the cinematography. Zsigmond had opted for a dark, realistic, almost gritty look to a scene that cried out for glossy Hollywood glamour. According to the film's assistant director, Jack Roe, 'Vilmos did a terrible job. When I saw the rushes, all I could see was the one dancer right in front of the camera. Vilmos blamed it on the lab, but it was a joke. I don't know why they hired him anyway. He wasn't the right person for the movie.'

Sensing disaster, Stark fired Zsigmond, to the surprise of his star. Gossips claimed that the firing was instigated by Streisand because she didn't feel Zsigmond's photography had flattered her looks, but Barbra was apparently not told of Zsigmond's dismissal until after the fact. Zsigmond, who went on to win an Oscar for *Close Encounters of the Third Kind*, later defended himself: 'I wanted the movie to look less like *Funny Girl* and more like *Cabaret* . . . They wanted the old concept of musicals. They were not interested in art, but in making it safe.'

Stark then begged the two-time Oscar-winner James Wong Howe, seventy-six and five years into retirement, to take over the photography of *Funny Lady*. Intrigued by the idea of shooting his first musical since *Yankee Doodle Dandy* in 1941, Howe agreed to the job, even as he learned that he would have to begin the following morning at seven-thirty without any preparation. 'I'm sure if I hadn't had fifty-seven years of experience in the film industry, I wouldn't have been able to jump into such a big project on twenty-four hours' notice,' he said.

Funny Lady production progressed smoothly except for one incident that might have proved tragic. 'The second day of filming,' remembered the second assistant director Stu Fleming, 'a sandbag fell from up high and missed Jason by *that* much. It was *so* close. Barbra didn't know about it. We've never talked about it. I doubt she knows about it today. Nothing was ever said, because that would have freaked her out. She would have been gone.'

After several weeks at MGM the company moved on to the Columbia soundstages in Burbank for the majority of the interior shots. It was soon obvious to bystanders that James Caan and Barbra were developing a pleasant, even playful, working relationship. Their first important scene together proved to be tough sledding only because the two stars couldn't keep from breaking up.

Wayne Warga, on the set for the *Los Angeles Times*, observed, 'Everything on [the sixth take] is going perfectly. Streisand, disdainfully smoking while Caan promotes [his song], is solidly in character and remains so as a piece of tobacco gets stuck on the tip of her tongue. She carefully reaches up to pick it off just as Caan, in the passion of promotion, grabs her hand to emphasize his point – and shoves her hand into his mouth. The entire company – several dozen extras in the club, the crew and various supporting people – explodes in laughter, and from then on, neither Caan nor Streisand can look at one another without giggling. "I'm sorry, I'm sorry, I'll get it right this time," she says.

'"Time is money, time is money – and no, you won't," Caan replies.'

'From that day on,' Caan later said, 'I was yelling at her, putting her down, and calling her a spoiled rotten thing, and she would call me [names] and we'd carry on and we'd laugh . . . I just remember giggling quite a bit.' In a later scene, Fanny, looking flawless in an elegant shimmering gown topped with cock feathers, has words with Billy in her dressing room. As the argument escalates, Rose picks up a full carton of loose dusting powder and threatens to throw it in Fanny's face. Barbra told Herb Ross, 'I don't think that Jimmy should hit me . . . with this powder; [it's] toxic, you know, and I'll get it in my lungs.'

Caan winked at Ross and said, 'I think you're right . . . I'll go to hit you with it and then I won't.' Of course he ended up hitting Barbra full in the face with the chalky powder, and she was stunned. 'I really felt bad for a minute because she was so shocked,' Caan said. 'She called me names. She said, "You lied to me!" I was hysterical. And then she laughed too.' As good a sport as Barbra turned out to be about the incident, she would not agree to a second take.

When Omar Sharif played his scenes with Barbra, there was less levity, but in its place came an easy rapport shared by the older and wiser ex-lovers and co-stars. 'For the first two days,' the now gray-haired Sharif recalled, 'she seemed a little different to me. But then, I'm sure I appeared somewhat different to her, which is natural. [In 1967] she was married and had led a somewhat sheltered personal life. She has broadened considerably in the intervening years. I think it shows in her performing as well.'

Jon's presence on the set as an uncredited creative consultant kept Barbra on a fairly even keel, and Ray Stark was happy to have him there, principally because Jon pushed her to be more punctual. 'Her lateness drove Jimmy Caan nuts,' Jack Roe recalled. 'One day he yelled at me about it, and I said, "What am I supposed to do? Sleep with her to make sure she gets here every morning?" She would be anywhere from twenty minutes to an hour late for each setup. I don't ever recall her being on time once.'

BARBRA HAD TO film a scene at the Santa Monica airport in which Fanny, after realizing she is through with Nick Arnstein for good, impulsively hires a 1937 biplane to fly her to Cleveland, where she plans to surprise Billy, who is on the road with his aquacade. For the shot, she was required to run to the plane, climb into it, and ride in the open cockpit as the pilot guided it off the ground and into the air for several minutes. 'It took Herb Ross almost the entire picture to talk Barbra into doing it,' Jack Roe recalled. 'She was obviously frightened.' Ross finally convinced her that if a double was used in the air, it would be obvious to the audience.

'Herb was wonderful,' Roe recalled. 'He could really finesse actors. She had a right to be scared; it was, after all, only a two-seater plane. But he talked her into the shot. I had set it up with the airport for the plane to take off and turn around and then land; she wasn't supposed to be up in the air very long. But it got messed up and the control tower couldn't let it land. It was bizarre. She was up there for almost half an hour, scared to death, and you could hear her screaming bloody murder from the minute the plane touched down until it taxied to a stop. She said she thought she was being kidnapped. It was terrible. But amazingly, Herb was able to talk her into doing it *again!*'

Funny Lady wound up production in the second week of July 1974. At a lavish wrap party, Barbra dispensed close to two hundred parting gifts, each with a handwritten note of gratitude, to the cast and crew. She gave James Caan a sterling silver rodeo belt buckle and James Wong Howe, who would die within a year, an antique camera with a plaque that read, 'Thank you for your talents, generosity and cha siu bao' – Barbra's favorite Chinese dish.

Barbra gave Ray Stark a gift that perfectly symbolized the conflicting dynamics of their relationship. Across the face of an antique mirror, she scrawled 'Paid in Full' in vivid red lipstick. Yet on the accompanying plaque she had had this sentiment engraved: 'Even though I sometimes forget to say it, thank you, Ray. Love, Barbra.'

SCHEDULED AS COLUMBIA'S major release for Easter 1975, *Funny Lady* began previews in January, and it became apparent that there were problems with the ending. As originally written, Fanny, after arriving unannounced in Cleveland to reaffirm her marriage to Billy, discovers him in bed with Eleanor Holm. Rose accompanies her to the train station and admits that his love for Eleanor is genuine and reciprocated: 'To her . . . I'm Nick.' Understanding, Fanny asks to be left alone while she awaits her train back to California. The film ends as the camera pulls back from a forlorn Fanny sitting in a darkened station as her vocal of 'Am I Blue' plays on the sound track.

Audiences found the scene too downbeat, so Stark called Streisand and Caan back to the studio to shoot an alternate ending, set a decade later, when Fanny and Billy are reunited after many years. Rose, it turns out, wants Fanny to appear in a revival of a Ziegfeld-type revue he is planning. She promises to let him know, and while the film ends on an ambiguous note, it's clear that Fanny is at last her own secure grown-up person. This second ending, though hardly memorable and marred by silly aging makeup on the stars, proved more popular with test audiences. Its inclusion in an already long movie, however, forced Ross to trim some of Barbra's musical numbers.

Perhaps because they were hungry for a Streisand musical, most critics greeted the film with lavish praise. '*Funny Lady* wins over its predecessor, *Funny Girl*, on all counts,' raved Judith Crist. 'You have to be crazy not to love *Funny Lady*,' said Rex Reed, while Richard Cuskelly, writing for the *Los Angeles Herald Examiner*, added, '*Funny Lady* . . . defies the laws of gravity to prove that you can still move upward from the top.' Many of the critics were even more enthusiastic about Barbra's performance. John Barbour, reviewing for KNBC television, said, 'Barbra Streisand's incredible artistry as an actress and singer deserves more than an Oscar; it deserves a Nobel Prize.' James Caan's notices were nearly on a par with Barbra's, and the opening week's box-office receipts matched the reviews. *Funny Lady* was a hit, and went on to gross over $48 million.

There were, of course, dissenters. Pauline Kael, the doyenne of American film critics, used her review of *Funny Lady* to launch into an elaborate critique of Barbra's entire career that ran seven pages in *The New Yorker*. 'Streisand's performance,' Kael wrote, 'is like the most spectacular, hard-edged female impersonator's imitation of Barbra Streisand . . . It's a performance calculated to make people yell without feeling a thing – except adoration.'

Why so many critics went so far overboard in their praise of the picture is hard to fathom. In truth, the movie is cumbersome and often flat; it lacks two of the most exciting elements in *Funny Girl* – the struggle of a young performer to reach the top against all odds and the compelling romance between Nick and Fanny. While Barbra and James Caan have a sparkling comic chemistry, their mild love story never gives off much heat. Worst of all, the new songs were not nearly on a par with those of *Cabaret*, and there are only sporadic moments of genuine electricity in the musical productions, several of which are frustratingly truncated.

Almost a year after *Funny Lady* opened, Herb Ross said, 'Up until *Funny Lady*, I thought Barbra's possibilities were limitless, but that film was a curious experience. She was in love at the time, and she didn't seem to want to make the picture or play the part. It was a movie that was made virtually without her. She simply wasn't there in terms of commitment, and one of her greatest qualities is to make a thousand percent commitment.'

In a Columbia Studios publicity interview, Barbra admitted as much. 'I'm a bit of a perfectionist, but not a whole one. I'd say to Herb, "Look, that's good enough," and he'd say, "No, it's *not*." I'm very changed . . . When I had a lack in my private life I cared more about my work. It was like a fill-in, sublimation. Now I don't. Now it's only a movie.'

Still, there is no evidence on screen that Barbra wasn't as committed as always. Her performance is believably consistent, and for better or worse she was unafraid to show Fanny Brice's harder edges. 'I don't try to be liked,' she said. 'I don't know if she's likable, this character.'

BARBRA DIDN'T WANT to rehearse. It was Sunday, March 9, 1975, the afternoon of a planned live, nationally-televised concert in front of President Gerald R. Ford, Senator Edward M. Kennedy, and hundreds of other government dignitaries at the Kennedy Center in Washington, D.C., to promote *Funny Lady* and to benefit the Special Olympics. Barbra was nervous and cranky; she had a sore throat and didn't want Ray Stark telling her what to do.

At first Barbra had refused to promote the picture at all. In the nine months since filming wrapped she had done little but supervise the construction and decoration of the ranch, tend to her garden, and enjoy her life unfettered by professional responsibilities. Stark had planned an ambitious international promotion tour that included a premiere in New York, a royal command performance in London, and a reception with the president of France in Paris. Streisand, of course, was the key to the whole thing, but she told Stark no. The last thing she wanted to do was perform live in front of millions of people, face another potentially dangerous mob of New York fans, then travel all the way to London and Paris for more of the same. According to her publicist Steve Jaffe, 'She was terrified of getting crushed by these fans who were full of adulation but could squeeze the life out of her.'

Nevertheless, Stark told Barbra her participation in these promotional activities was vital to the success of the movie. He offered her $100,000 to sing five songs at the Kennedy Center event. She wouldn't budge. Stark pleaded with Jon to reason with her. Jon told Barbra she *had* to do it, if not for herself and the movie then for him. He was in the middle of negotiations with Stark to produce a film, and if he could deliver Streisand for this publicity blitz, his stock would surely rise with the producer. She at last agreed, but she didn't like it.

'Barbra had celebrated the end of her contract with Ray Stark,' Steve Jaffe offered, 'and here she was now having to do this grueling tour for him. She wasn't happy. There was this kind of one-upmanship between them. She would do something to get at him, and he would follow it up. They were like two prizefighters – one gets a jab in here, the other lands a punch there.'

Jaffe recalled that when Barbra told Stark from her Watergate Hotel suite that she had a scratchy throat and wanted to rest her voice rather than rehearse the songs she was scheduled to sing that night, a 'heated argument' ensued. 'Ray was *pissed off* with her. He said, "Listen, this is really serious. This is the meat of the whole tour. You have to be there for rehearsal!" But she wasn't gonna do it. I thought, Boy, Streisand's the one in charge here.'

Later, as the rehearsal got under way, Jaffe stood and chatted with several Secret Service men who were there to scope out the Kennedy Center in anticipation of President Ford's arrival. 'Barbra's not going to rehearse,' Jaffe told the men. But within moments Streisand appeared. 'She walked out, looking casual but very elegant in jeans and a beautiful silk shirt, and started to rehearse two or three of the numbers,' Jaffe recalled. 'I thought, That's very interesting. Here it had seemed that she was in charge, and now it was clear that Ray Stark was calling the shots.'

Peter Matz, who was conducting the orchestra, recalled that 'Barbra was very upset by the time we started rehearsals. She had agreed to do [the show] only because it was for the Special Olympics – she had vowed never to do any more television. Then, when it was too late, she realized that it was really a Ray Stark promo for the movie, a hype. Barbra gets crazy when she feels she's been hyped. It was a bad situation.'

Funny Girl to Funny Lady, broadcast live over ABC, proved a triumph for Barbra despite her anger at Stark and a case of nerves that left her retching in the bathroom moments before she took the stage. She had expected the audience of government officials to be stuffy, but when she strode out in a lowcut black gown, her straight blond hair flowing to mid-back, the officials jumped to their feet for a two-minute ovation. 'Men in tuxedos and women in high-fashion gowns stood up and carried on like bobby-soxers of old,' a UPI reporter wrote, 'shrieking and screaming above the thunderous applause. When Streisand started crooning "The Way We Were," it all started again.'

'If you applaud too much we'll run out of time,' Barbra told the audience, but to no avail. The frequent and lengthy interruptions put the show behind schedule, and at the end of the hour there was no time left for Barbra to sing 'People,' which she had planned to do in tribute to the children and volunteers of the Special Olympics. 'Oh, that's it?' she asked when she was told she had to wrap things up. 'That's a live show for you!'

The event, a promotional masterstroke, prompted grumbling from some critics. Frank Swertlow of UPI was incensed. 'If this show was for charity, why was Miss Streisand paid $100,000 for her appearance? Wasn't an hour of prime time advertising enough? . . . People who turned in to see Barbra Streisand were cheated. They sought entertainment, but what they received was plugola. There is something very wrong about this, very wrong indeed.'

BARBRA AND JON traveled by train to New York on Monday morning; on Tuesday afternoon she and James Caan met the press at the Hotel Pierre. She hadn't wanted to do that either. 'Barbra hated talking to reporters,' Steve Jaffe said. 'She felt that they'd only twist what she had to say, or write bad things about her no matter what she said. She felt that it wouldn't help her career any, because her work basically sold itself.' But once again Ray Stark had prevailed.

At the premiere that evening, just as she had feared, Barbra and Jon were mobbed by fans outside the Loew's Astor Plaza. Once again it took fifty policemen and a phalanx of burly bodyguards to inch them through the screaming, madding crowd, Barbra looking stricken and Jon hovering protectively nearby.

A friend of Barbra's mother, who spoke on the condition of anonymity, escorted Diana to the screening. 'It was strange,' he recalled. 'No one seemed to want to come over and talk to Diana. Barbra didn't, and I went up to Marvin Hamlisch and asked him to say hello, and he hesitated but finally did. Ray Stark did come over, and he said to her, "Your daughter and I have had ten good years. If only someone would talk to her, we could have ten more."

'After the screening, an announcement was made that people with yellow roses on their chairs should board the bus and go to the party. Diana didn't have a yellow rose on her chair. I guess she wasn't invited.'

FRIGHTENED ANEW BY the New York mob scene, Barbra ordered Steve Jaffe to tell Ray Stark that she would not go on to London. Stark, understandably, hit the roof. 'I'm not going to talk to her,' he shouted at Jaffe. '*You* talk to her! Get Jon to mediate. Just make sure she's *there*, goddammit!'

Jaffe telephoned Barbra with Stark's message. 'Ray! I *hate* him!' she cried. Jaffe told her she had to do this, that the Queen of England and the president of France were expecting her, and that she owed it to Stark. 'She felt such bitterness toward him,' Jaffe recalled. 'She felt as though she'd been an indentured servant to Stark for ten years, and she was sick of having to do what he wanted her to do.'

Jaffe pleaded with Barbra to go on to London as planned. 'Ray's been responsible, at least in part, for your career, Barbra,' he told her. 'Maybe he didn't pay you what you wanted to be paid, but if you got paid what you wanted to be paid, there wouldn't be any gold in Fort Knox.'

Jaffe found that 'I could actually talk to her like that, and she would laugh. She handled the truth as well as any of the major egos that I've encountered. She finally said she'd go to London, but she and Stark still weren't talking. I thought, This is going to spell trouble for the rest of the trip.'

In London, although all of the others, including James Caan, registered at the Dorchester Hotel under their own names, Barbra and Jon signed in as 'Mrs B. Gould and party.' On the evening of March 18, Barbra met Queen Elizabeth for the first time, and the encounter went par for the Streisand-and-royalty course. Upset that Jon hadn't been allowed to stand next to her in the receiving line to meet the Queen, Streisand asked Elizabeth, 'Why do women have to wear gloves and not men?'

Taken aback, the Queen muttered, 'I'll have to think about that. I suppose it's a tradition.' Then she quickly moved on.

After the command performance, Ray Stark hosted a celebratory dinner at a posh London restaurant. Just as Steve Jaffe sat down to eat, the maître d' told him he was wanted on the phone. It was Jon. 'Barbra's not feeling well,' he said. 'Tell Ray we're not going to Paris.'

In the background Jaffe could hear Barbra calling out, 'I'm tired. I don't want to do this anymore!'

Jaffe swallowed hard and went over to Stark. 'Ray, I just got a call from Jon. Barbra's not feeling well.'

'That's okay,' Stark replied. 'Tell her to rest up a bit, and she can join us later. We'll still be here.'

Jaffe couldn't bring himself to relay Barbra's actual message, so he got Peters back on the phone. 'Jon, I think Ray would react very badly if I told him you weren't going to Paris. Why don't you just rest up tonight—'

'No, Steve, she's not going,' Peters replied.

Then Barbra grabbed the phone: 'Tell him I don't feel well. I'm sick, and I'm not going.'

Jon took the phone back. 'You got that?'

'Yeah, I got it,' Jaffe sighed.

When he gave the message to Stark, the producer said quietly, 'Tell her she's going.'

Jaffe called Barbra back. 'No way,' she insisted.

Stark then told Jaffe, 'Tell Barbra that I will provide her with a hospital plane if I have to, and I'll send doctors to the hotel. *But she is going to Paris tomorrow.*'

'There isn't a way in the world, Steve,' Jon thundered at his hapless publicist.

When Jaffe relayed this latest message to Stark, the producer stood up and left his own party. 'He was *real* pissed off,' Jaffe recalled.

The next morning Jaffe found out that Stark had somehow persuaded Barbra to go to Paris. 'I think Ray owed her one last payment or something, and he threatened to withhold it unless she got herself to France.' When Jaffe arrived at the Plaza Athénée Hotel, he learned that Barbra and Jon had stopped at an Italian restaurant on their way to Paris from the airport. 'They ate everything in the place,' he marveled. 'They just *stuffed* themselves. A quarterback would have been sick eating all the food they did. They made sure that by the time they got to the Athénée Barbra was sick as a dog.'

When Stark heard about Barbra's distress, he came to her suite. As she ran back and forth to the bathroom, Stark yelled, 'She's coming tonight! She's going to show up tonight. The president of France is going to be there and he expects to see her.'

'But you can see she's sick,' Peters pleaded.

'I've got two doctors on the way right now. They'll examine her. If they report to me that she's too ill to appear, then she doesn't have to appear.'

As far as Jaffe was concerned, 'Barbra's one of the greatest actresses on the planet. I figured all she had to do was act sick and she'd be in the clear.'

When the doctors arrived, they examined Barbra in her room for a few minutes as Stark, Jaffe, Jon, and Marty Erlichman waited. When they came back out, one of the physicians announced, 'She has zee stomach problem.' As the doctor spoke, Jaffe noticed Barbra peering around the edge of the bedroom door, trying to hear what he was saying.

'How serious is it?' Stark wanted to know.

'It weel go away. She weel be okay.'

'Are you going to give her any medication?'

'Ah, *oui*, I can geeve her zee medication.'

Finally Ray lost his patience. '*Well, what's wrong with her?*'

'As you Americans say,' the doctor replied, 'she has zee gas.'

Marty and Jon shifted their feet uncomfortably. Steve Jaffe put his head in his hands. 'The limo will be here at seven,' Stark said softly as he left. 'The screening starts at eight. She should be there by seven-thirty.'

Barbra never did go to the gala. 'She found out the French president had canceled his own appearance due to pressing business,' Jaffe said, 'and she figured that let her off the hook. But there were hundreds of people from the highest levels of French society who were disappointed. They expected to see Barbra Streisand, and all they got was Jimmy Caan, Ray Stark, and David Begelman.

'Stark never stopped steaming, and Barbra decided she was never going to talk to Ray again. He felt she had let him down. She resented being forced to go on this grueling tour to promote a movie she didn't even have any profit participation in. As we were at the airport getting ready to leave, there was ice-cold silence between Barbra and Ray. But finally he went over to her. I couldn't hear what he said, but it was obviously some sort of apology. Barbra seemed to be saying, "I wasn't so easy to deal with myself." It was like the end of a movie.

'A cynic might say that Stark didn't want to burn his bridges with the biggest box-office star in the country,' Jaffe concluded. 'And Barbra knew that Stark had all the financing power in the world. If she wanted to make a deal with Columbia, it was Ray who was in charge. She's really smart when it comes to money. So she patched things up.'

BARBRA WOULD NEVER be able to patch things up with Johnny Carson, though. The host of *Tonight* had been after her for years to appear on the program; her last stint had been in March of 1963. Finally, when Ray Stark, Jon, and Steve Jaffe all told her she should do it, Barbra agreed.

'Barbra was afraid to do live television interviews,' Steve Jaffe said. 'She never wanted to put herself in a position where she wasn't in control. She was afraid of losing the public's admiration by saying something she couldn't cut out later. And she wanted to control how she looked. She kept trying to redesign the show, do the lights herself. She kept changing the musical arrangements, and here you're dealing with some of the finest musicians in the country. They just aren't used to putting up with someone making tremendous demands on them because it's a very well produced show.'

Still, Carson's producer Fred deCordova was so eager to have Streisand that he capitulated to all her demands, and the appearance was scheduled for Wednesday evening, July 9. On Monday the show began a publicity blitz to promote the appearance, even though no one could reach Barbra to make last-minute preparations. On Tuesday Marty Erlichman called the show to say that Barbra had changed her mind and would not appear. Ray Stark called deCordova to apologize: 'You know what she's like. There's nothing I can do.'

Johnny Carson was livid. During the Tuesday night show, he told his millions of viewers, 'I was informed prior to going on the air that we'll have a cancellation tomorrow night. Barbra Streisand will not be with us. We don't know why. Nobody has been able to reach her . . . Although she doesn't owe the show anything in particular, we thought it only fair to tell you, so when you tune in, you don't get mad at us. I would rather you get mad at her. Streisand will not be here Wednesday night, nor will she be here in the future.'

The next night Carson's audience was surprised to hear him introduce Barbra. 'I got Madlyn Rhue,' Carson later recalled, 'and we dressed her up in a Streisand getup, and she started to do "People." For a moment you couldn't tell if it was Streisand or not because she was lip-synching. I walked over and said, "Thank you, but we don't need you." And she walked back to the curtain and it was wonderful.'

Twelve years earlier, Johnny had said to Barbra, 'I suppose when you get to be a big star we'll never see you again.'

'No,' Barbra had replied. 'Never.'

'You know, she probably means it, too!' Johnny had exclaimed. Apparently she did.

JON WAS STILL after Barbra to create a more youthful public image. 'You can't spend the rest of your life playing Ray Stark's mother-in-law!' he had told her in exasperation. He had seen a script he liked, a rock remake of the classic Hollywood romantic tearjerker *A Star Is Born*.

Barbra laughed when he told her about it. 'You idiot! That's been made three times already!'

But this will be different, Jon argued. 'You'll play a sexy young girl, an aspiring singer. It's exactly the kind of thing you should be doing in movies.'

'Well, maybe,' Barbra replied. Her decision to go ahead with the project would nearly destroy her relationship with Jon and nearly break her, body and soul. It would also make her a more popular star than she had ever been before.

PART 5

Her Own Visions

'Now I want to take the
responsibility for my own choices and
my own visions. I've grown up.'

—*Barbra in 1976*

26

Barbra's eyes narrowed to slits as she contemplated the question. She sat surrounded by dozens of reporters at a large round white table on the twenty-yard line of Arizona State University's Sun Devil Stadium. It was late morning, and the temperature had already soared into the mid-nineties as a harsh sun glinted off the tiny beads of sweat on Barbra's forehead. She wore white slacks, a floral silk tunic top, a tightly curled new hairdo, and an unhappy expression.

Warner Brothers had flown one hundred and fifty journalists to Tempe on a publicity junket to promote Streisand's new movie, *A Star Is Born*, currently filming on location. She and Jon, her co-star Kris Kristofferson, and Frank Pierson, the film's director, had made themselves available to the media by hopping from one table to the next. It was a risky, perhaps even foolhardy, promotional ploy. For not only were the cast and crew in the middle of a logistical nightmare – preparations to film a live rock concert sequence in front of fifty thousand young people – but rumors of discord and ego battles on the film had been rampant for months, prompted by a *New Times* magazine cover story that ridiculed Barbra's personal and professional relationship with Jon and dubbed the picture, which Peters was producing and Barbra unofficially co-directing, 'Hollywood's Biggest Joke.'

Malicious glee prompted one reporter to ask, 'What do you think of your co-star, Barbra?'

She began to answer, but Kristofferson, who had overheard the question while he sat at an adjacent table, interrupted her. 'She said I was an asshole,' he called out.

The not-easily-shocked newspeople gasped. Barbra Streisand had called her leading man, a music superstar, an *asshole?* This was juicier than they could have hoped.

'Why did you call him an asshole?' the reporter pressed.

'I don't know,' Barbra said, embarrassed. 'I forget. He's a beautiful man, let's just stay with that.'

'Shit,' Kristofferson mumbled. He was wearing a brown cotton shirt open to the waist, and his rumored heavy daily intake of tequila with beer chasers already seemed to have taken effect.

Barbra glared at him as she mentioned that Bruce Springsteen's music had served as the inspiration for that of Kris's character.

'You should have hired him for the part,' Kristofferson sniped.

The reporters' taste for blood was soon satisfied again as Kris and Barbra filmed a scene on the huge stage that had been erected for the concert. Kristofferson's head had been swimming for weeks as he wondered to whom he should listen: Pierson, whom Barbra wanted to fire on the second day of filming; Streisand, who seemed to see the film as a way to experiment with every other idea that popped into her head; or Peters, who had never made a movie before but was on hand for just about every take.

'Nobody seemed to know what they were doing,' Kris reflected later. 'Barbra was a pain in the ass. Jon and I were like a couple of dogs growling at each other. I wish she had told me up front who was in charge so I wouldn't have had to go through the crap of wondering why she kept opening her mouth. We'd spend four hours setting up a scene, go out there, and have her say, "No, man, it's all wrong."'

That's just what Barbra told Kris this afternoon, and to the reporters' delight, an open microphone broadcast their exchange throughout the stadium.

'You're not doing what I tell you to!' she told him.

'Shit!' he shot back. 'I got Frank telling me one thing and you tellin' me another. Who's the director? Get your shit together!'

He turned his back to her, and she exploded. 'Listen to me! I'm talking to you, goddammit!'

'Go fuck yourself,' Kris responded.

Barbra stalked away, and Jon Peters moved toward Kris. 'You owe my lady an apology.'

'Listen,' Kristofferson growled before he stormed off, 'if I want any shit out of you I'll squeeze your head.'

'If we didn't have a movie to make I'd beat the shit out of you!' Peters bellowed after him.

And all the while the scribes scribbled furiously. Maybe this movie wasn't Hollywood's biggest joke. Maybe it was Hollywood's biggest brawl.

A STAR IS BORN had taken a tortuous three-year path to production that began on July 1, 1973, in a car on a Hawaiian roadway when screenwriter John Gregory Dunne said to his wife and writing partner, Joan Didion, 'James Taylor and Carly Simon in a rock remake of *A Star Is Born*.' The Dunnes took the idea to Dick Shepard, their former agent, now head of production at Warner Brothers. Warners had owned the rights to the story of a young actress on the ascent and her alcoholic actor husband on the way down since the last remake in 1954, starring Judy Garland and James Mason.

Shepard loved the idea. The tale had proven audience appeal, the rock elements would update it nicely, and the sound-track possibilities were so strong that the box-office take of the movie, as one music bigwig told Dunne, might just be 'gravy.' The Dunnes were hired to write the screenplay, and there then ensued, in Dunne's words, 'three drafts, an arbitration, a threatened breach-of-contract suit, and a sizable legal (read "cash") settlement ... As closely as I can figure, we were followed by, officially and unofficially, fourteen writers.'

John Foreman, a 'hot' producer after the success of *Serpico* in 1973, signed on as producer of the project. It soon became clear that the music people at Warners were less excited about James Taylor, whose film and music careers were in the doldrums, than they were about his wife, Carly Simon, who had never made a film but whose records were flying out of the stores. 'Don't worry about James if you don't use him,' one executive told Dunne. 'We can always find something for him to do, maybe a house in Malibu.' That line wound up in one of the Dunnes' subsequent drafts.

As worries built that hiring Carly Simon would result in a 'multimillion-dollar screen test,' word came that she and Taylor weren't interested in the project, reportedly because its plot hit a little too close to home. The script then settled on the ICM desk of Sue Mengers, who had replaced David Begelman and Freddie Fields as Barbra's agent. Mengers immediately sent it to Streisand, her top client. 'I don't want to do a remake,' Barbra told her, and passed.

With Streisand and the Taylors out as potential stars, just about every musical name in Hollywood was bandied about to play the film's main characters, John Norman Howard and Esther Hoffman: Elvis Presley and Liza Minnelli, Diana Ross and Alan Price, Cher and her husband, Gregg Allman.

The director Mark Rydell joined the project, then left after three months of work without pay. Foreman called Jerry Schatzberg, whose *Scarecrow* had won a prize at the Cannes Film Festival, and asked him to direct. Schatzberg signed a development deal with Warner Brothers, and Foreman told Schatzberg that Kris Kristofferson had agreed to play the male lead. But still there was no female star.

Soon thereafter, Jon called Schatzberg to see if he would be interested in directing Barbra in *Wait Till the Sun Shines, Nelly*, a Ray Stark project that she had turned down in 1968 but was now reconsidering. Schatzberg replied that he was committed to *A Star Is Born*. 'What's that?' Jon asked. When Schatzberg told him, Jon said, 'It sounds interesting. Can we read it?'

JON STOOD IN front of a full-length mirror, checking himself out and waxing enthusiastic about *A Star Is Born* to the reporter Marie Brenner. '*I* discovered this project. *I* was the one who found if for Barbra and convinced her to do it. She'd just done *Funny Lady*, and I thought, Why should a young girl be playing an old lady? She's a young, hot, sexy woman.'

Barbra remained resistant to the idea for some time, but as Jon talked the project up, she liked it more and more. When she read the Dunnes' script, she became convinced that her and Jon's involvement in the project must have been preordained, because 'the male character was named John, he drove a red Ferrari and had a red Jeep, which my Jon does, and he was a Gemini, which Jon is. It was kind of a mystical thing – it was destined to be.'

John Foreman called a meeting with Jon and Barbra, Kris Kristofferson – who hadn't yet signed a contract – Jerry Schatzberg, and the Dunnes, who had wanted out of their contract but reconsidered when Streisand entered the picture, because with her involved, they said, 'we knew we weren't going to get poor.' But as discussions progressed, the writers grew uneasy. Barbra didn't feel the love story was strong enough, and she worried that the male part was the better one. As Jon and Barbra expressed their ideas about how to punch up the love angle, the Dunnes realized that what the couple wanted to put on screen was *their* love story. 'The world is waiting to see Barbra's and my story!' Jon exclaimed, jumping up and waving his arms as he often did in moments of epiphany.

The Dunnes flinched, and before long they were pushed out of the project with a deal guaranteeing them $125,000 and 10 percent of the gross. Schatzberg, however, seemed to be on the same wavelength with Streisand and Peters. By now Barbra had persuaded Warner Brothers to allow First Artists and Barwood to produce *A Star Is Born*, making her the film's executive producer. She would take no salary either for producing or starring, but stood to make a great deal of money with a 25 percent cut of the film's box-office net. Then she hit the moneymen with a bombshell: she wanted Jon to produce the picture.

When word of this leaked out, most Hollywood observers chuckled.

Streisand wants her boyfriend, a hairdresser, to produce a $6 million musical? Surely Warner Brothers would laugh at the suggestion. When the studio agreed, the amusement turned to chagrin. The Warner executives' reasoning, word had it, was that a Streisand musical was foolproof box-office gold. 'It doesn't matter if the picture is good,' one executive said. 'Shoot her singing six numbers and we'll make $60 million.' But underlying the agreement was Warners' assumption that Jon would be a figurehead producer, someone who would defer to the experience of Foreman and Schatzberg.

The assumption proved wrong as Jon began to speak about '*my* concept, *my* picture.' Every night he and Barbra sat up until the early morning hours discussing what approach the film should take, how to make the screenplay right for Barbra, how to update the plot to the seventies. They screened the Judy Garland-James Mason version, and both were impressed. But something about the picture bothered Barbra. Later she would verbalize her misgivings: 'The female character was so passive in the earlier versions. All she did was love him and watch him come apart. But this is the seventies. I don't believe it. She shouldn't stand around and watch him disintegrate. I want her to say, "Fight for me, goddammit. Protect yourself or *I'll* kill you!"'

These private tête-à-têtes between Barbra and Jon disturbed Jerry Schatzberg. 'His influence over her was very strong,' he said. 'We'd talk about one thing, and then I'd come in the next day and everything would be changed, and I wasn't privy to their conversations. He was like Rasputin or Svengali with her. She ogled him, aahed over him. She was a woman in love. He would come up with something, and she would say, "I think that's a great idea," and she'd come back to me.'

KRIS KRISTOFFERSON'S AGENT was holding out for equal billing with Streisand, but she wasn't sure she wanted to give it to him. Barbra called Schatzberg and asked, 'What do you think of Jon playing opposite me?' She explained that Jon had told her, 'Hey, I can do this part. I got the looks and the energy!'

'You can do anything, Jon,' Barbra had replied.

Schatzberg assumed she was kidding, but she persisted. He told her he would think about it, in the hope that she wouldn't bring the subject up again. But the next day she pressed him on it. This is completely ludicrous, Schatzberg thought as he asked for a meeting with Barbra and Jon at the Malibu ranch.

'I don't want to shoot a documentary about you two,' he told them. He also reminded them that Kristofferson, although he still hadn't signed a contract, was considered part of the package.

'You mean Warners would rather have *him* than *me?*' Barbra demanded.

Schatzberg then cut to the core question: 'Can Jon sing?'

'No,' Jon admitted. Then he leaped up. 'But you could shoot around me, just like you were going to do with Kristofferson.'

'Look,' Schatzberg replied, 'you can do that with a singer to make it look like his acting has more energy. You can't do it with an actor to make it look like he's a singer.'

The wind whistled out of Jon's sails, and the idea was dropped. Later he and Barbra would claim the notion was little more than a joke, but Schatzberg isn't sure. He remains astonished that Barbra ever supported the idea. 'If you think of Barbra Streisand, that's not normally what she would do, because she's much too clever for that. But that was at the height of their affair, and her judgment was clouded.'

Kristofferson had heard about Jon's desire to replace him, and when John Foreman called him to say, 'Disregard everything you've heard about Jon Peters playing your part,' Kris replied, 'Is Barbra's still up for grabs? I'll try for *that* one.'

Now Jon felt that what the film needed was a young, hip new writer, and Sue Mengers suggested one of her clients who was barely into his twenties: Jonathan Axelrod, the stepson of the screenwriter George Axelrod. He hit it off well with both Jon and Barbra. 'I found them fantastic, very gentle and sensitive to my feelings and to my age,' he said. He was in awe of both of them, and attracted to Barbra: 'I thought she was very sexy, and I had a big crush on her.' The three of them spent hours in story conferences at the ranch; Jon considered Axelrod 'my interpreter.'

Jerry Schatzberg turned crimson when he heard about this. 'They were having meetings with this writer without my knowledge,' he said. 'Now, maybe that's a Hollywood thing to do, but in New York we have respect for the director and his input.'

Shortly after Axelrod appeared, Schatzberg quit the film. 'When I told Barbra my decision, she genuinely didn't understand it. But I didn't think, under the circumstances, that I could perform the way I should have. Jon was a little immature as a producer, and he tried to fake his way through in certain ways. I thought I had enough experience to help him along, but in the end I just felt I couldn't direct Barbra properly under the circumstances.'

Jon continued to work closely with Axelrod – so closely that when the writer presented a script after four months, Jon told his associates, 'I wrote it.' But he and Barbra still weren't satisfied. The movie, they felt, needed 'meatier dialogue' and 'a real writer.' After nine months Axelrod was off the project, but he feels no bitterness because he himself wasn't satisfied with the script he had produced. Rather, he's grateful to Barbra for helping him stretch his talent. 'Don't limit yourself,' she had told him. 'Be an artist.'

JON AND BARBRA forgot about finding another writer for a while and interviewed a string of potential directors, including Arthur Hiller and Hal Ashby. None seemed to understand their vision for the film; most, Jon said, 'bored' him. During one dead-of-night discussion in bed, Jon turned to Barbra and said he should direct the film. 'Nobody understands this better than I do!'

'You're *right!*' Barbra exclaimed.

This time Warner executives resisted, and negotiations dragged on for three months before they gave in to this notion, too. By then a new problem had popped up: bad press. The *Los Angeles Times* columnist Joyce Haber wrote a series of articles ridiculing the film, Barbra, and Jon's pretensions to being producer, star, and director of a major movie musical. This put considerable added pressure on the studio, and on Barbra and Jon, who were shocked by the criticism.

Still, they remained adamant. 'Directing is a thing I've done all my life!' Jon exclaimed to Marie Brenner, who was doing a piece on the peregrinations of the project for *New Times* magazine. He and Brenner were dining with some studio people and Steve Jaffe at the Warner commissary. 'It's getting people to do what I want them to do!' He got too excited to eat as he told Brenner, 'This is a young movie, young ideas, young talent. People in this town have it in for me because I'm young, you know what I mean? And I'm a bit uptight about directing this film. This is a big project, you know?'

Jaffe piped up that with a good editor, script, and cameraman, Jon would be as competent as half the directors in Hollywood, even with no experience.

'That's what I think!' Jon responded. 'That's why my editor is Dede Allen!'

Marie Brenner was impressed: Allen was renowned as the best editor in Hollywood. But Brenner later learned that Jon had never spoken to Allen, and when he did so later in the day, she turned down his offer to edit the picture. But she suggested her young former assistant for the job, and Jon loved the idea. 'Great! This is a *young* movie. We need young ideas, we need young talent.'

WHEN BRENNER'S *New Times* article appeared in March 1975, it stunned Barbra and Jon. Barbra had declined to be interviewed, but Jon had given

Brenner his full cooperation. He and Barbra both felt that Brenner had betrayed them. The cover of the magazine featured a rendering of a bald Barbra with the headline 'A Star Is Shorn.' The article portrayed her and Peters as egomaniacal children with an expensive new plaything, and called the movie 'Hollywood's biggest joke.' Barbra was shattered. This project was difficult enough without being made a laughingstock. According to Steve Jaffe, Brenner 'snowed me like you can't believe. She made it seem as though she would not write a bad word. She said all the right things to persuade Jon to cooperate. I consider it the classic journalistic deception of my career.'

The bad publicity soured the notion of Jon directing *A Star Is Born*, and later Barbra insisted that it was merely a fleeting thought, like his playing John Norman, that had been blown out of proportion by the press. And yet during an interview by Barbara Walters on *Today* in February 1975, Barbra had stated unequivocally, 'He's going to direct it.'

WITH KRIS KRISTOFFERSON'S participation still uncertain, Barbra and Jon turned their attention to finding an alternative co-star. They considered Mick Jagger, but the studio bigwigs felt that he'd had his shot at movie stardom and blown it. They considered Bob Dylan, but the word came down from studio executives that Dylan wasn't 'aesthetically pleasing' enough to co-star opposite Barbra. (Kristofferson heard about this and assumed they meant Dylan 'looks too Jewish.') Barbra, as always, wanted the most attractive leading man possible; most of her biggest movie successes had paired her with 'gorgeous *goyisher* guys.'

Barbra's thoughts turned to Elvis Presley. Jon loved the idea: 'The man's been an idol of mine since I was nine! Imagine Barbra Streisand opposite the King of Rock 'n' Roll!' But Elvis had changed dramatically since Barbra's affair with him in Las Vegas in 1969. He was over the hill, she worried, and he had gained an alarming amount of weight.

'Perfect!' Jon exclaimed. 'He'll really understand the part!'

Presley agreed to meet with the couple in Las Vegas. When he entered their hotel room, both Barbra and Jon were shocked. Elvis looked far worse than either had expected. 'He was so fat he looked almost pregnant,' Jon recalled. He also seemed lethargic, unfocused, out of it. 'He was dying, really.' They spent two hours sitting on the floor, talking, drinking wine. Jon suspected it would be difficult for Elvis to get back up.

At one point a boozy Presley looked at Barbra and said, 'You know, you're the only woman who has ever intimidated me.'

On the flight back to Los Angeles, Barbra and Jon remained quiet, dispirited. 'He *was* John Norman Howard,' Jon said.

'And that's why he wouldn't be able to play him,' Barbra responded.

Elvis was out of the running.

AT AN IMPASSE with co-star possibilities, Jon and Barbra looked again for a writer and a director. Both came in the person of Frank Pierson, whom Warner Brothers had asked to do a 'fast rewrite' of the *Star Is Born* script. Pierson – tall, snowy-bearded, fifty – was a hot screenwriting commodity in Hollywood; his script for *Dog Day Afternoon* would win an Academy Award the following year. 'In a moment of mad ambition,' Pierson said, he accepted the assignment.

'He was going to be only the writer,' Barbra recalled, 'and then at the last minute he said he wouldn't write it unless he could direct it. I said, "Well, I'll let you direct it if you let me collaborate with you."' According to Barbra, Pierson agreed.

Although Pierson's directing experience was limited to television and one unsuccessful feature film – *The Looking Glass War*, in 1969 – Barbra warmed to the idea of his directing *Star* when he seemed to agree with her primary goal for the film: to update the story and bring the male-female relationship more in tune with the various social revolutions that had taken place since the last version in 1954.

As they discussed casting at the ranch, Pierson recalled in a memoir of the experience, Barbra asked, 'What about Brando? I've always wanted to work with Brando. Why does it have to be a musical?'

'Brando was here!' Jon shouted, jumping up. 'He was cute! The son of a bitch, he wanted to screw Barbra – I was ready to kill him! I take him off [her], and I kiss him. He's beautiful! I love him, the bastard! They'd make a great pair. Imagine. Streisand and Brando!'

Pierson reminded Barbra that the studio's forbearance all this time had been based on her *singing* in this picture, and he gently added that the idea of remaking *A Star Is Born* without music was absurd. The Brando idea evaporated.

Barbra told Pierson she agreed with Jon that the public wanted to see their love story. 'People are curious,' she said. 'They want to know about us. That's what they come to see.' She and Jon then confided to Pierson the most intimate details of their life, their lovemaking, their fights. But when Barbra read those details in Pierson's first draft script, she got cold feet. The movie, she said now, 'was not our life. You don't want to make it too real. I don't want to use too much ...

because someday they'll want to do my life story, and I don't want to use it up.'

Because Barbra felt strongly that for the sake of realism the music for *A Star Is Born* should be filmed live, Pierson would not consider anyone but Mick Jagger or Kris Kristofferson as her co-star. Finally forced into a decision, Barbra chose Kristofferson. 'He's an actor. He's beautiful to look at. He can sing and play the guitar. And he's a Gentile, which seems to work with me – the Jew and the Gentile.'

What Pierson didn't know was that Barbra and Kristofferson had enjoyed a brief affair in 1970, before he met his future wife, Rita Coolidge, and while Barbra was separated from Elliott, so Barbra knew the chemistry between them would likely be special. Kristofferson later told a reporter that during their affair 'she was being a superstar and I was being a country shitkicker, both playing games.'

Kris met with Barbra at the Malibu ranch to discuss the role, and he liked her ideas, but he wasn't told that she considered herself the film's co-director. 'I knew Barbra was writing the script and the picture's big songs and had total control of everything,' he said, 'but Frank was *called* the director, an' I figured I'd just do my usual tap dance between two haystacks, tryin' to keep both star and director happy. I'd never been in no movie where they were the same person.'

At one point in the meeting, Barbra asked Kristofferson, a former Rhodes scholar, if he was willing to stretch himself as an actor. Kris replied, 'Are you willing to get down? I'll stretch as far as you get down.'

THE TWENTY-SEVEN-YEAR-OLD singer-songwriter Rupert Holmes stood in the middle of Barbra's music room at Carolwood for the first time, while his debut album, *Widescreen*, played in the background. As Barbra walked in to greet him, she casually sang along with the album. 'She knew the words to all the songs!' Holmes later marveled. Barbra was working on her new album, and she had tracked Holmes down in his New York studio. When they met, Barbra told Holmes that she was particularly impressed with his album's dramatic title tune, with its imagery of movie-fueled fantasies that were so much like her own when she was a girl in Brooklyn.

By April 1975, Streisand and Holmes were in the studio laying down tracks for what would become Barbra's thirtieth album, *Lazy Afternoon*. They established such an easy working rapport that both sides of the disc were recorded in just three six-hour days. Holmes treasures the experience. 'She took the risk [of hiring a relative neophyte], and she never once doubted or lost confidence in me. Barbra gave me many gifts besides giving the gift of her talent and voice to my songs.'

When *Lazy Afternoon* was released in October 1975, it emerged as one of Streisand's most consistent and satisfying pop albums. Holmes's imaginative musical settings complemented Barbra's kaleidoscopic vocals beautifully. 'Shake Me, Wake Me' marked her first foray into the effervescent disco sound, and a lengthened version of the song, with a funkier arrangement, proved popular in dance clubs.

The majority of critics, many of whom had loathed *ButterFly*, welcomed *Lazy Afternoon* as a first-rate effort. 'In restoring her to the pop mainstream,' said Robert Hilburn in the *Los Angeles Times*, 'Holmes ironically has given Streisand her most authentic connection yet with contemporary pop influences . . . The steady drum emphasis and closing guitar shading on her version of "My Father's Song" is an example.'

Lazy Afternoon peaked at number twelve on *Billboard*'s album chart, and went gold in April 1976. By then, however, Rupert Holmes had been practically flattened by the volatile *Star Is Born* juggernaut.

By OCTOBER 1975, scant months before the February start date Warner Brothers had insisted upon so that *A Star Is Born* could be released by Christmas 1976, this musical had no music. Rupert Holmes had come aboard the prior March as musical supervisor and had written a dozen songs for the film, but he found the experience frustrating. 'I read about twelve different scripts before I tried to write the score,' he complained, and thus his tunes had little dramatic cohesion. Barbra wasn't satisfied with most of them, and during a meeting to discuss alterations, Jon lost his temper with the composer. According to Pierson, Holmes grew frightened of Jon's fury and took the first plane back to New York. He never again communicated with anyone about the movie and didn't work with Barbra again until 1988.

As part of her preparation to play Esther Hoffman, Barbra immersed herself in the rock milieu, attending every concert within a hundred-mile radius of Los Angeles. Jon installed a $20,000 sound system at the ranch and bought an entire catalog of the latest rock albums. Barbra took guitar lessons; since Esther Hoffman was a musician and songwriter, Barbra wanted her strumming to look realistic. Night after night, Jon said, she sat 'alone in our living room until one, two, three o'clock in the morning, plucking away on her guitar.'

When Barbra heard that her guitar teacher wrote her own songs, she grew 'very emotional and very insecure and very upset.' She thought, God, I only sing these songs that other people write; I've got to try to do something like that. Bored during one lesson, she began to 'fool around with chords,' and eventually a brief melody emerged. It would evolve into 'Evergreen,' the film's love theme.

Barbra put in a call to Paul Williams, co-writer of 'I Won't Last a Day Without You,' which she had recorded for *ButterFly*. She wanted Williams to write the film's final song, which she saw as an anthem much like Williams's 'You and Me against the World.' He came on board as musical supervisor, and Pierson later recalled that when Williams began to supply his lyrics, along with melodies composed by his collaborator Kenny Ascher, Barbra 'reshape[d] them, attacking lyrics with a logician's mind. She insist[ed] on precision and simplicity, on lyrics meaning exactly what they say and saying what they mean. It [was] an education.'

Barbra's obsessiveness proved an ordeal for Williams. She would call him at all hours of the night to ask, 'How's it coming? When will you have the new lyrics?' When he stopped taking the calls, Pierson confronted him. Williams shouted back, 'How can I write when I have to talk to her all the time and nothing ever gets finished because before I finish the damn song she's already asking for changes?'

Williams flinched when Barbra told him she wanted him to write lyrics to a melody she'd written. But when he heard the tune, he adored it and exclaimed, '*This* is the love melody!' When he didn't deliver the lyrics over the next few weeks, Barbra began to press him. He stalled her. 'I know what I want to do with it,' he explained. 'I'm gonna call it "Evergreen" because when I listened to it I went, "Love, ageless and ever, ever green."' But that was as far as he would go, he told the frustrated Barbra; he wanted to concentrate on the rest of the score. '"Evergreen" was the last thing I wrote, and that totally pissed her off.'

Williams would come to think of working with Streisand and Peters as 'having a picnic at the end of an airport runway.' When he again became incommunicado, Barbra panicked. Was he still working or had he quit? When he re-emerged, he had the score completed. Barbra told him she liked most of it, but then she hired Phil Ramone to produce all the film's music, a move that incensed Williams. He disappeared again.

Throughout all this musical *meshugass*, the one person who wasn't consulted was Kris Kristofferson. Although he was the most successful singer-songwriter of the entire ensemble, Barbra felt that his country-flavored music wasn't right for the film; she had envisioned John Norman Howard in the Bruce Springsteen mold since the publicity blitz that had put Springsteen on the cover of *Time* and *Newsweek* simultaneously the previous March.

An angry Kristofferson asked for a meeting, which included Williams and took place in an empty rehearsal stage on the Warner Brothers lot in Burbank. It quickly became clear that Kris hated Williams's music and wanted to use his own. When Jon attempted to talk him out of that, Kris jumped up and yelled at him, face flushed, arms flailing. 'Who shall I say says my music isn't rock – Barbra Streisand's hairdresser?'

'It's crap! I don't care who says it!' Jon screamed back. Barbra and Pierson shouted at Jon to ease up, but Kris stormed off. Williams then confronted Jon with what he saw as a betrayal: Jon, he felt, hadn't stood up for Paul's music. Jon thought he had, and he lashed back: 'Where were *you?* You didn't say a goddamn word!' Furious, the diminutive Williams leaped up, knocked over a music stand and some chairs, then took an upward swipe at Peters. Jon grabbed his arm; a guard called for help. Paul stalked out before the reinforcements arrived and sent the rest of his rewrites by messenger.

Shooting was just a few weeks away, and already everyone was exhausted. Barbra and Jon went to New York, where they caught a Muhammad Ali fight at Madison Square Garden. Pierson wrote in his journal that their absence was 'a blessed relief. Without the endless questioning and explaining, we are able to set schedules and locations. Sets are designed, casting is locked in.'

To photograph the film, Pierson chose the sixty-nine-year-old veteran Robert Surtees, a three-time Academy Award winner, most recently for *Ben-Hur*. Jon and Barbra thought he was too old, and Pierson was amazed to realize that neither of them knew who he was – 'What does he know about backlight?' Barbra wanted to know. But their objections came too late; Surtees had already been signed.

PRINCIPAL PHOTOGRAPHY WAS to begin the next day at a Pasadena nightclub. The scene was Barbra's first musical number, and precious rehearsal time had been eaten up in the effort to get the music right. To his concern, Pierson noticed that Barbra's weight was down and she had broken out in a rash. It seemed to him that her 'driving angry force' had faded. 'She is resigned to fate,' he recalled thinking. 'Tomorrow the options to change stop; everything will be frozen on film.'

27

B arbra was beside herself. She and Frank Pierson had worked out the camera setups for the first day's filming – a scene in which the audience would be introduced to Esther Hoffman performing in a small club – and Pierson had changed most of them without telling her. The changes disconcerted her and made her angry. What on earth did Pierson think he was doing? They were supposed to be collaborators!

She found even more troubling Pierson's seeming inability to help her with her characterization. When she asked him his opinion of two interpretations, he replied, 'I'm neutral.'

'Frank,' she told him, 'if you ever want to be a director, you can never be neutral – lie, make it up, explore your feelings, anything – because the actor has to have some feedback, some mirror, some opinion, even if it's wrong.'

That night Barbra and Jon sat up in bed until the early-morning hours and agonized over what to do. Pierson, Jon felt, had gone from director in name only to tyrant. Barbra was frightened, worried sick that the movie would be a disaster. Finally Jon decided that there was only one reasonable course of action: he would fire Pierson.

Later that morning he told the Warner Brothers executive John Calley what he planned to do. Calley talked him out of it. 'This movie has already had such bad publicity, Jon,' he said. 'This could be devastating. You and Barbra can work something out with him. These things happen on movies all the time. It'll be okay, you'll see.'

Stuck with Pierson, Barbra decided to work around him. The next day she attached a video camera to Robert Surtees's main rig so that she could instantly review a scene's lighting, composition, and pace, and scrutinize the performances. Pierson found the move 'meddlesome,' and Kris Kristofferson was caught firmly in the middle.

'Pick up the phone and look at her,' Pierson would tell him.

'Don't pick up the phone and look away,' Barbra would counter. As Kristofferson readied himself for one take, his every move already blocked out, Barbra told him, 'You're supposed to be over *there*.'

By now Kris had learned simply to stand and wait until Pierson and Streisand stopped arguing. But this seemed to be happening with every take, and finally Kris lost his temper. 'You two have got to get your shit together!' he barked. 'I don't care which of you wins, but this way, with two commanders, one sayin' retreat, the other advance . . . it's demoralizing the crew and puttin' me into *catatonia!*'

This last condition was helped along by Kris's prodigious intake of tequila with beer chasers, which usually began at midmorning, continued throughout the day, and was buffered, in his words, by 'massive quantities of laughin' tobacco.'

Concerned, Pierson took him aside. 'The booze, Kris, I got to talk to you about it.'

'What?' Kris replied. 'Is it making me sloppy?'

Later he would admit, 'I was so drunk at times, if I'd been Barbra and Jon I'd've fired me.' Instead, Pierson noticed, Barbra had become 'watchful, judgmental' of Kris's performance, just as she had of Pierson's work and of the entire film. She began to push herself close to exhaustion; she often didn't get to sleep until three or four in the morning, then woke up at six or seven.

Pierson looked on the project as a job, not a mission, and went home every evening at a reasonable hour. To Barbra, this was tantamount to betrayal; by now she had convinced herself that her career was on the line with this film. She grew constantly tense, quick to anger; her mistrust of Pierson made her confrontational with him. One day she arrived on the set and saw a group of extras on one side rather than the other. She didn't understand, Pierson later said, that they would be moving.

'Why are they here?' she shrieked. 'They should be over *there!*' Pierson tried to explain, but Barbra wasn't listening. 'I *want* it!' she cried, in a wail that to Pierson 'had the power of primitive will, deep and full of loneliness.' He ignored her.

At first Kristofferson had directed his resentment at Barbra, thinking the 'endless changes' she demanded were the result of her whims or a lack of attention. Later he realized that many of the problems resulted from the fact that Pierson hadn't, as he put it, 'listened or remembered. He was out to lunch from the first day.'

Barbra's obsession with the film, and with herself in it, became clear to all during screenings of the daily rushes. Her mood would swing violently from joy if she liked something to despair if she didn't. Her rage when she saw something that displeased her shocked Pierson, he wrote, because it was 'vomited back in savage attack: "I told you not to do that. *Why* did you do it? It's *wrong!*" Everything is seen in terms of right and wrong; there is no personal preference, nuance, or shading.' After a while, fewer and fewer of the company attended the dailies. Finally even Robert Surtees dropped out, and only Barbra and Pierson remained. Then he stopped going, preferring to work in the morning with the film's editor, Peter Zinner.

JON WAS OFFERING some suggestions before a scene when Frank Pierson demanded, 'Jon, be silent or leave!'

'How dare you!' Jon yelled back. 'I'm the producer on this movie—'

'Jon, get out of here!' Barbra hissed, and Peters stalked off.

Later Pierson explained to him that input from a producer can only interrupt the flow of an actor's creativity.

'It's all right,' Jon replied. 'It's not you I'm pissed off with. It's her.'

Pierson soon realized that Barbra was in physical fear of Jon. Quick to lose his temper, quick to resort to fisticuffs, Jon had injured a hand punching a door during one fight with Barbra, and he regaled Pierson with stories of a scene at Madison Square Garden when he and Barbra went to see the Muhammad Ali fight. A man heckled Barbra, Jon related excitedly. 'Pow! I let him have it! He made a motion like he's gonna touch, maybe he's gonna hit Barbra: he's gonna hit my woman! I go crazy! *Bam! Pow!* They're pullin' me off him. The cops come take him away. You can't go anywhere with her! That's the meaning of "star"! We gotta get that in the picture!'

As Pierson walked to his car at the end of filming one evening, he saw Barbra scurry out from behind a hedge, crouched low, and run along behind some cars. 'For God's sake, take me home,' she pleaded. In the car, she cowered in a corner, trembling. 'He gets so furious,' she said. 'I don't know what to do.' Pierson suggested Barbra spend the night at his house, but since Jon wasn't at Carolwood when they arrived, she went in. Pierson watched her as she walked to the front door. She seemed to him 'small and tired and scared.'

'YOU THINK IT'S easy, some dude making love to your woman?' Jon asked Pierson. Barbra and Kris had already shot the film's first sex scene, in which Barbra made a point of being on top and taking off *her* belt first, 'like a man would.' Now they were ready to film a love scene in which Esther and John Norman share a candlelit bath and, in another reversal of sex roles, Esther paints his face with makeup and glitter and tells him how pretty he is. 'We took that from real life,' Jon said. 'Barbra and I have an enormous stone tub at home with a big broad rim on which we put lighted candles when we bathe together.'

Barbra and Jon both worried that Kris might take a Method approach to the scene and wear nothing. 'I insisted on Kris wearing a little pair of flesh-colored underpants,' Jon recalled. 'He yelled "*What!*" but I told him to put them on.'

'For God's sake,' Barbra told Pierson as she got ready for the scene, 'find out if he's going to *wear* something. If Jon finds out he's in there with nothing on . . .' As a precaution, Pierson barred Jon from the set for the duration of the scene.

Wearing a short half-slip and nude from the waist up, Barbra climbed into the tub, where Kris was waiting for her. Feeling mischievous, Kristofferson wrapped his legs around her, and she soon realized he indeed was not wearing a thing. Furious, Barbra pulled away from him and screamed at Pierson to 'make him put something on!' The director fetched the flesh-colored shorts, Kristofferson wriggled into them, and the scene came off without any further hitches.

PIERSON WORRIED DEEPLY about the upcoming rock concert in Phoenix, the film's centerpiece. The plan was to fill Sun Devil Stadium with fifty thousand rock fans, who everyone hoped would remain orderly through hours of tedious filming of a John Norman Howard performance in order to see acts such as Peter Frampton, Montrose, and Santana. Jon was excited about the concert, hopping around the office and talking about hiring Evel Knievel to do a stunt where John Norman Howard drives a motorcycle off the stage. 'This is the heart of the picture,' he burbled. 'This is the action part for people like me!'

Barbra seemed to Pierson not to hear. 'Listen,' she said finally, 'where are the close-ups? There are never any close-ups in this picture. When I worked with Willie Wyler, we had close-ups in every scene.' Pierson had vowed to himself not to discuss things like this with Barbra, but he nonetheless pointed out some recent close-ups they had shot. 'Soon we are embroiled in exactly how close up a close-up has to be to be called a close-up.'

Three weeks before the scheduled shoot in Phoenix, Pierson claimed, he learned to his dismay that for all of Jon's enthusiasm about the concert, he had done nothing to arrange it. 'This is a disaster of such magnitude that I cannot think about it,' Pierson wrote. 'All I can do is shoot whatever is there the day we arrive.'

This fatalism of Pierson's irked Barbra most about him. Jon finally came through by hiring the rock promoter Bill Graham to organize the concert, which Graham accomplished in record time. Acts were signed, posters were printed, everything was set. Now all the *Star Is Born* crew had to worry about was that fifty thousand young rock fans wouldn't turn into a raging mob while Pierson and Streisand bickered over setups.

Everyone was nervous, including Phil Ramone, who was there to record Kris's performance live. 'Christ, my ass is on the line!' he said at the time. 'And to make matters worse, the film crew doesn't really understand what I'm doing or how this is coming together. They're used to having sound prerecorded so it usually doesn't matter what the music sounds like during a shoot. But when Kris goes out on that stage, we'll be filming it, sound and all. What you hear in that stadium is what you'll hear in the film. What we don't get we'll never get. It's like driving on slick pavement!'

'I just want to tap-dance and fart my way through,' Kris joked, but he was worried, edgy, and angry at Barbra. After first opposing the use of Kristofferson's own band, Barbra had changed her mind. 'I have *always* relied on my band to make me look good when I didn't on my own,' Kris would explain, 'an' I figured for this movie, I'd need them in the *worst* way.'

But the moment Kris's boys got off the plane at Phoenix, Barbra commandeered them to audition for her. 'They're stuffed in this little room playing stuff they've never heard before,' Kris told *Rambler* magazine. 'Barbra listened and instantly said we gotta get studio musicians, the kind who read charts, like in Vegas shows.'

Kris wanted to kill somebody. 'I ain't trusting my career to no Vegas singer and her hairdresser!' he bellowed before storming out to the parking lot and into his publicist's car to take a ride and cool off.

Barbra agreed to keep Kris's band in the movie, then monopolized so much of their rehearsal time practicing her own numbers that Kris had virtually no rehearsals of his own. His concert loomed a day away. Kris slammed his trailer door and refused to come out. 'Goddammit!' he screamed. 'I've been trying to make this stuff sound like music. I've got to go out and play in front of thousands of people, but she doesn't give a damn!'

He later said, 'She just assumed, since I'd worked with my boys forever, that I didn't need 'em. And it was my fault I never said to her, "Hey, Barbra, goddammit, I'm in this movie too. You're working with the band on stuff you shoot next week. I gotta shoot tomorrow. *I need my boys!*"'

Pierson was more tired than he had been 'since World War Two,' and on the most important day of filming, he overslept. This infuriated Barbra, who had risen at 4:00 A.M. She saw this as another example of Pierson's lackadaisical attitude toward the film. Everyone was uptight. Would enough people show up to fill the huge stadium? Would they remain civilized? Would

As the elegant Regency-era courtesan Melinda Tentrees, one of Barbra's dual roles in
On a Clear Day You Can See Forever, *1970.*

Barbra greets admirers as she attends an Ottawa arts festival with her rumored new paramour, Canadian Prime Minister Pierre Trudeau, January 1970. Barbra and Elliott had separated a year earlier.

George Segal as Felix, uptight would-be writer, and Barbra as Doris, foul-mouthed hooker-cum-actress, in The Owl and the Pussycat, *1970.*

Ryan O'Neal and Barbra clown around during the filming of Peter Bogdanovich's slapstick comedy What's Up, Doc?, *1971.*

With her divorce from Elliott final, Streisand and O'Neal make their affair public at the Hollywood premiere of O'Neal's film The Wild Rovers, *June 1971.*

While in Africa to film fantasy sequences for the feminist comedy Up the Sandbox *in 1972, Barbra led the natives in song.*

Flanked by Barbra and James Taylor, Democratic presidential candidate George McGovern says a few words after a fundraising concert at the Forum in Los Angeles, April 1972.

Steve Schapiro

Steve Schapiro

Barbra's blissful expression mirrors her reported romantic feelings for Robert Redford, her costar in The Way We Were, *1973.*

Barbra's dress seems to be caught in the washing machine during a novelty number in her television special Barbra Streisand…and Other Musical Instruments, *1973. Marty Erlichman assists her.*

Opposite, bottom: Barbra creates a stir at a Madison Square Garden boxing match when she shows up with her new love, hair stylist Jon Peters, January 1974.

Back in Brooklyn, Barbra shows her displeasure with obstreperous fans during filming of For Pete's Sake, *1973.*

Bob Scott

Prince Charles pays Barbra a visit in Hollywood, 1974. The future king of England called Streisand "my only pin-up…she is devastatingly attractive and with a great deal of sex appeal."

Archive Photos/Express Newspapers

James Caan jokingly gets Barbra in a choke hold during a publicity tour for their film Funny Lady, *1975. The picture's producer, Ray Stark, often wanted to do the same thing to Barbra for real.*

After a year of struggle and strife making A Star Is Born, *Barbra shares a laugh with Jon Peters and her leading man, Kris Kristoffer-son, as the film breaks box-office records, December 1976.*

Archive Photos/Fotos International

Barbra and Jon celebrate as A Star Is Born *wins five Golden Globe Awards, including Best Picture, Best Actress, Best Actor and Best Song, March 1977.*

Barbra poses prettily with her sister, Roslyn Kind, and her mother, Diana Kind, after Roslyn's opening night cabaret performance at West Hollywood's Studio One, August 1977.

Bob Scott

Bob Scott

O'Neal and Streisand reunite for another hit summer comedy, The Main Event, 1979. *Barbra's proximity to her former lover made Jon Peters jealous.*

Gene Hackman as troubled drugstore manager George Dupler and Barbra as ditzy Cheryl Gibbons in the box-office dud All Night Long, *1981.*

Streisand confers with Mandy Patinkin and Amy Irving on location for Yentl, *her first directorial effort, 1982. "I don't know how I survived it," Barbra admitted.*

Amy Irving as Hadass and Barbra as Yentl masquerading as Anshel in Yentl, *released in 1983 to critical acclaim. Of the three stars, only Amy received an Oscar nomination, which created an uproar.*

Musician and ice cream heir Richard Baskin became Barbra's live-in lover in 1984 after she broke up with Jon Peters. They separated in 1987 but have remained friends.

Kevin Winter/DMI

Madonna visits Barbra and her costar Richard Dreyfuss on the set of Nuts, *1986. Streisand played a prostitute accused of murder.*

Chris Nickens collection

Bob Scott

Barbra's affair with Miami Vice *hunk Don Johnson sent press and fans into a tizzy. Here, they attend the Los Angeles premiere of Johnson's film* Sweethearts Dance, *September 1988.*

As the director of The Prince of Tides, *Barbra led her costar Nick Nolte to his first Oscar nomination, 1991.*

Jason Gould escorts his mother to the Academy Awards ceremonies in 1992. Although The Prince of Tides *was nominated for seven Oscars, including best picture, Streisand was again overlooked in the best director category.*

Streisand discourages a photographer from snapping her with her rumored new love interest, the tennis heartthrob Andre Agassi, after the U.S. Open Tennis Tournament at Forest Hills, New York, September 1992.

President-elect Bill Clinton embraces Barbra after her performance at his inaugural gala, January 1993.

Barbra acknowledges the cheers of her hometown fans during her 1994 concert tour stop at Madison Square Garden. Reportedly, one of her reasons for touring was that she needed the money.

Osamu Honda/AP

Fidgety and nervous, Barbra delivers an address on "The Artist as Citizen" to students at the John F. Kennedy School of Government at Harvard University, February 1995.

Arthur Pollock/*Boston Herald*

Phil Ramone get the sound quality he needed? Would Robert Surtees get enough usable film footage?

The fans, most of them students at Arizona State University, began to file into the stadium at three in the morning. By nine o'clock, fifty thousand of them were writhing under the hot sun, smoking pot, making out, discarding more and more clothing. They cheered as various acts came out to perform, but there were long delays between sets. Pierson's skin prickled when the crowd began to chant, 'No more filming! No more filming!' before he had shot a thing. Finally he got ready to shoot, but a series of technical problems caused more delays. 'The noise, the pandemonium, the incipient panic are all but overwhelming,' he wrote.

Against the advice of just about everybody, Barbra appeared onstage to try to calm the crowd. 'We're gonna do *rock and roll* today!' she shouted above the din. 'And we're gonna be in a *movie!* In our movie we're *real.* We fight, scream, yell, we talk dirty, we smoke *grass!*' Now she had the crowd. 'So, listen, what we're gonna do now is meet my co-star, Kris Kristofferson. A great performer. So when he comes on, I know you all love him anyway, but you have to love him even *more*, you know, so we won't have any problems. So, in the lingo of the movie, I say, all you motherfuckers *have a great time!*'

Some observers found Barbra's comments patronizing, but the kids loved it, and they 'performed' their ecstatic reaction to John Norman Howard's act – and their horror over his motorcycle accident – flawlessly. Then there were more delays. Barbra and Pierson quarreled over a shot, more time elapsed, the crowd began to chant anew. Graham couldn't believe it. 'Don't you know what you're doing?' he screeched at both of them. 'They're going to *kill* us!'

Barbra took the stage again, this time to perform. She was 'petrified,' half convinced she'd be booed off the stage. She wasn't. Her movie star magic wove its spell as she sang 'People' and 'The Way We Were' to prerecorded accompaniment ('I didn't bring any strings with me'). The crowd – the women especially – cheered the film's feminist anthem 'Woman in the Moon,' and then Barbra announced that she would sing a song she'd written for the movie. 'I hope you like it. If you don't I'll be *crushed.*' She sang 'Evergreen,' and even on first hearing it was clearly a classic. The crowd stomped, yelled, applauded. Barbra didn't seem able to accept the adulation. 'Do you *really* like it?' she pleaded. More roars. 'I'm really glad you like it, because that's the first time I ever sang that song in front of people.'

More acts, more filming, more delays. Then the day was over. The crowd hadn't stampeded the stage, no one had been killed, and Pierson had gotten most of the shots he wanted. But the dailies turned out to be disjointed, unrepresentative. 'You've ruined it!' Barbra exploded. 'How could you do that? We can never do it again!' Pierson explained that the basics were there, the film just needed to be judiciously edited. Barbra remained unconvinced.

Pierson then realized that Barbra was frightened not only for the success of the movie but for her relationship with Jon. 'If this film goes down the drain,' she told him in a moment of candor, 'it's all over for Jon and me. We'll never work again.'

Pierson reminded her that even if the film flopped all she had to do was agree to sing again 'and they'll fall all over you to do another picture.'

'I know,' she replied. 'But what would happen to Jon?'

MANY OF THE crew members had had their fill of Barbra and Jon. He later admitted that his behavior was sometimes intentionally provocative: 'I was terrified, but I couldn't show them that, could I? I had to get things done . . . so I walked through people.'

As Kristofferson later put it, 'Barbra was like a general who can't trust any of his officers to do their job.' By now Kris was 'narrowing [his] peripheral vision with more tequila and laughin' tobacco than's even usual.' Pierson, he thought, looked 'like a sunstroke victim, and if you'd said to the crew, "Shove this movie, we're all going to Mexico," they'da yelled, "*When?*"'

The company moved to Tuscon, where Barbra sang soaringly for two Esther Hoffman concert sequences, then on to the outskirts of town for scenes at John and Esther's desert adobe, which Barbra had had constructed to resemble the Malibu ranch, complete with a loft bedroom like Jason's. When she told Pierson she wanted John and Esther to wrestle in the mud, he thought it would look like a 'bad comedy routine . . . like whores wrestling in a mud bath.'

Barbra, as usual, got her way, but someone in the crew decided to play a practical joke on her. As Kris remembered it, 'Barbra's wearing this white pantsuit, an' she's supposed to be covered with mud. The prop man smears this brown stuff all over her, an' Barbra calls to me, "Come over here, smell this stuff." I did. *Whew!* I went over to Frank and said, "They're puttin' crap on Barbra." He said, "I don't want to hear about it." Well, the crew said the smell was from some preservative they'd put in the mud to keep it moist, but, man, by then they hated Barbra so much I *know* what it was they smeared on her – and so did Barbra! But we both broke up laughin' – an' Barbra's laughing harder than me! I mean, she coulda thrown a whole tantrum.'

ON MARCH 29, Pierson won an Academy Award for writing *Dog Day Afternoon*. A few days later Jon returned from a trip back to Los Angeles and confronted the director about his continued disagreements with Barbra.

'You don't listen,' Jon yelled. 'You've never listened. You just go ahead and do it your way. You've never doubted, never asked a question.' He continued with a litany of complaints, and Pierson thought that Jon was either trying to force him to quit or had been sent by Barbra to fire him. Frustrated by Pierson's lack of response, Jon stalked out, yelling, 'I'm not afraid of your Oscar!'

To Pierson it was a nightmare that didn't end, even when it was over. The day after filming wrapped, he received a note telling him that his director's cut of the film was due in four weeks. His lawyer got the deadline extended to six weeks. Barbra, who had final approval of the cut, asked to be included in the initial process; in exchange she offered to consult Pierson throughout her own editing. He refused.

Pierson and Peter Zinner labored over the film 'feverishly' to produce what Pierson considered a 'rough but serviceable cut.' He showed it to Barbra and Jon and a few others at a special screening. Barbra seemed pleased, but the next day Pierson got word that she had commandeered the film and would re-edit it.

According to Jon, 'Warners panicked' when they saw Pierson's cut because they didn't think Kristofferson's performance was strong enough. Pierson claimed that Barbra's version favored her over Kris at many key moments and that only after he wrote her a detailed letter about the slights did she restore Kristofferson's establishing scenes and many of his reaction shots.

Barbra bristled at Pierson's charge. 'Many times I cut my own shots out if Kris was better in his,' she said.

Ralph Sandler was one of Peter Zinner's assistant editors with whom Streisand worked on the film. She spent eighteen-hour days at the Todd-AO studios in Hollywood tinkering with every frame as it passed on a huge screen. As they worked, Sandler noticed that Barbra was indeed, as Pierson had said, removing many of Kristofferson's reaction shots.

Some of the other changes she wanted were minuscule; occasionally she would want to change her pronunciation of a single word. 'I don't like the way I said "careful,"' she would tell Sandler, and it would be his job to snip enough of the rolled *r* to clean the word up without the cut showing. Sandler came to realize that Barbra didn't trust him – or anyone else, for that matter. 'She would watch everything I did. She'd tell me what to do, and I'd do it, but she was always looking to see, did I *really* do it?'

Jon was frequently present at the editing, but he said little. 'He had pretty much learned by then that she was the boss,' Sandler said. One night Sandler saw them cuddling on a folding chair. 'Oh, Jon, you're the greatest,' Barbra cooed. Later that night Sandler saw a national tabloid with a headline about Barbra and Jon breaking up.

Sandler found himself amazed by some of Barbra's foibles. Whenever doughnuts were delivered to the studio for the crew, Barbra would rush over to them and break a piece off a chocolate one, a cream-filled one, a sugar-coated one, until few were left untouched. The crew was not amused. 'They didn't want to eat a doughnut that her hands had been all over,' Sandler said.

Barbra worked such long hours on the film that Jason had to be driven to the studio to see her by one of her maids; they were usually accompanied by a friend of Jason's, a pretty girl of about his age. One day as they came into the editing room the maid said, 'Jason, go kiss your mother.' He refused and rushed back out to the car. After a few similar visits, several members of the editing crew took Sandler aside to tell him that whenever they saw Jason in the car with his young friend he invariably had his hand up her dress. 'We didn't dare say anything to Barbra,' Sandler said, 'because we were sure we'd be fired.'

Soon thereafter, Jon caught Jason in the act. He came into the editing room and told Barbra with a laugh, 'Jason's got his hand up that girl's dress.'

'*What?*' Barbra exploded. '*What!* I'll *kill* him!'

Very late one night, Barbra called a break, and everyone left the editing bay. When Sandler went back to get something he needed, he saw Barbra sitting alone at the console, fiddling with the dials. 'This was a major infraction of union rules,' he said, 'but she figured she could do whatever she wanted.'

Barbra hadn't heard Sandler come in. She was intently watching herself, as Esther Hoffman, sing 'Evergreen,' her face ten feet wide on the screen. As Esther hit a high note, Barbra let out a cry: 'Sing it, bitch! *Sing it!*'

IT WAS NOVEMBER, the film was set to open in a matter of weeks, and still Barbra fiddled. Eventually she screened a 'final' cut of the picture for all involved, but she was ready to tinker some more with it if necessary. This was the first time Kristofferson had seen the film, and he was deeply moved. He found the movie 'beautiful,' and he even liked his own music in it. 'It's a sad love story, but a real one,' he said. 'All you heard in the screening room was the blowin' of noses.'

But no sooner did the lights come up than Barbra accosted Kris. 'Are you happy with it?' she implored. 'What *didn't* you like?'

'Barbra,' Kris replied, 'would you relax for crissake? It's a great picture, a two-person picture. You gave me *more* than equal time.'

She wasn't listening; she was scribbling notes. 'When did you start to cry?' she asked. 'I mean, in which *frame* did you start?'

It was all too nerve-racking for Barbra. 'Every time I go to see a screening of it I think I'm going to die of palpitations,' she said. When Warner Brothers informed her she could make no more changes, she said, 'It was the most horrible experience to let it go.'

Barbra soon learned that Frank Pierson was circulating among major magazines a forty-three-page article about his experiences directing *A Star Is Born*. She finagled a copy and was stunned. The piece was a startlingly intimate exposé that painted her as megalomaniacal, frightened, indecisive, rude, disruptive, and monstrously self-absorbed. Jon emerged as a brash hot dog, jumping up and down, threatening violence, full of 'mad schemes,' and incompetent.

Barbra couldn't believe her eyes: she considered the article a staggering betrayal of the implied confidentiality between an actress and her director. She called Pierson to beg him not to put 'a black cloud over the film' before it opened. According to Barbra he assured her he had no intention of publishing the piece, that he had written it only for the amusement of his friends, and accused her of stealing a copy from his office. A few weeks later a shortened but still quite lengthy version of the article appeared simultaneously on both coasts, in *New York* and *New West* magazines.

When she saw 'My Battles with Barbra and Jon' splashed across the full cover of *New West*, Barbra collapsed into tears. The article was the second major journalistic strike against the film before its premiere, and Barbra was terrified that it would so prejudice the public that *A Star Is Born* would never get a fair hearing. Barbra wrote a letter to Pierson, telling him that he had portrayed her and Jon as 'idiots' and had 'distorted' the facts. He couldn't face his own limitations, she went on, and that was why he had done so 'destructive' a thing to all concerned. She concluded that he was a 'sick, vicious' person with 'no scruples.'

Later, on national television, she was no less blunt. She told Geraldo Rivera, 'Pierson's article was so immoral, so unethical, so unprofessional, so undignified, with no integrity, totally dishonest, injurious. If anyone believed it, without examining who that person was, to try to put a black cloud over a piece of work before it's even released . . .'

NOW THERE WAS nothing left to do but wait. Barbra was jittery, coiled, short-tempered. Pierson's article had her terrified that the film would be a colossal flop, that she and Jon would come out of it looking like fools. They fought more and more frequently; they came perilously close to breaking up.

The first reviews, from the West Coast, were disarming. *Daily Variety* raved that the film was 'a superlative remake. Barbra Streisand's performance . . .

is her finest screen work to date, while Kris Kristofferson's magnificent portrayal of her failing benefactor realizes all the promise first shown five years ago in *Cisco Pike*. Jon Peters's production is outstanding, and Frank Pierson's direction is brilliant. Selznick himself would be proud of this film.'

But with the reviews from the East Coast and most national magazines, the roof caved in. Rex Reed's notice bordered on vicious but wasn't atypical: 'If there's anything worse than the noise and stench that rises from [the sound-track] album, it's the movie itself. It's an unsalvageable disaster. This is why Hollywood is in the toilet. What the hell does Barbra Streisand know about directing and editing a movie? So many people have disowned this film that I don't even know who to blame. But I do blame a studio for giving $5.5 million to an actress and her boyfriend to finance their own ego trip . . . the result is a junkheap of boring ineptitude . . . every aspect of the classic story has been trashed along with the dialogue . . . Kristofferson – paunchy, dissipated, stoned and looking like the Werewolf of London – sounds like a pregnant buffalo in labor pains. To hear Streisand at thirty-four trying desperately to sound like Grace Slick . . . is laughable and sad and ultimately infuriating. She is wrecking her image, talent, and femininity, and I cannot stand around applauding while she does.'

John Simon, writing for *New York*, was more vicious still. 'O, for the gift of Rostand's Cyrano to evoke the vastness of that nose alone as it cleaves the giant screen from east to west, bisects it from north to south. It zigzags across our horizon like a bolt of fleshy lightning, it towers likes a juggernaut made of meat. The hair is now something like the wig of the fop in a Restoration comedy; the speaking voice continues to sound like Rice Krispies if they could talk . . . Kris tells Barbra, "When you hook into an incredible marlin, that's what it felt like hearing you sing." Funny, it feels like that to me when I see her face . . . And then I realize with a gasp that this Barbra Streisand is in fact beloved above all other female stars by our moviegoing audiences; that this hypertrophic ego and bloated countenance are things people shell out money for as for no other actress; that this progressively more belligerent caterwauling can sell anything – concerts, records, movies. And I feel as if our entire society were ready to flush itself down in something even worse than a collective death wish – a collective will to live in ugliness and self-debasement.'

Barbra burst into tears when she read these reviews, her fear of failure threatening to undo her. 'I couldn't even control myself. It was *so* devastating to me . . . it hurt me deeply that the reviews were so personal.' Jon tried to console her, but he too was scared. His dreams of Hollywood success and power – and his relationship with Barbra – had suddenly begun to feel looser in his grip.

But as he later put it, 'We planned on breaking up, and then the movie was a hit.' Despite the harsh reviews, audiences – young people, especially – flocked to *A Star Is Born* when it opened nationally on Christmas day; reports came back to Warners of people standing in line for hours in snowstorms to see it. The film grossed $10 million in its first ten days of release, an enormous take in 1976, and it ultimately grossed over $92 million domestically and another $66 million internationally. It remains Barbra's most successful movie and one of the most profitable musicals of all time.

The sound-track album of the film's troubled and controversial musical score, which Rex Reed hated so much, surged to number one, sold four million copies, and became the largest-selling movie sound track to that date. The single release of 'Evergreen' also rocketed to the top of the charts and sold over one million copies.

In February, *A Star Is Born* won five Golden Globes in the Musical or Comedy category: Best Picture, Best Actress, Best Actor, Best Song, and Best Score. Accepting his award, Kris Kristofferson thanked 'the lady.'

AFTER ALL THE bad press and all the critical vitriol, Barbra had been vindicated, and so had the executive who told Pierson, 'Shoot her singing six numbers and we'll make $60 million.' But why the stunning chasm between the way so many critics and journalists saw the film and the way the moviegoing public embraced it? The reasons are complex, and Barbra had her own opinion: 'The media loves to build you up when you're new on the scene, but after you become a star they're always trying to tear you down.' There was, of course, an element of that in the press's reaction to Barbra and Jon, but the couple undoubtedly played into the hands of the cynics with their grandiose, often ill-advised statements about the film, Jon's abilities, and the public's desire to see their story on the big screen.

A remake of a beloved classic is always a risky proposition. No matter how excellent it may be, it can never totally please fans of the original. There was no way that Rex Reed, an unreconstructed fan of Judy Garland and of traditional pop music, would ever have liked a rock version of *A Star Is Born*.

The quality of the film *is* uneven. It careers from scenes of soaring music and touching drama to passages of embarrassingly inane dialogue, unbelievable situations, and mawkish sentimentality. Barbra's characterization of Esther Hoffman wobbles badly in the film's early reels: she's self-possessed enough in her first scene to approach John Norman Howard during one of her songs and tell him angrily, 'You're blowing my act,' but moments later, alone in a car with him, she acts like a nervous schoolgirl. At the end of the film, when Esther hears a tape of John Norman that has accidentally been turned on, she believes for a few moments that he might still be alive. It is a scene that makes the suspension of disbelief difficult.

But the film works well as a musical love story. Streisand's singing is breathtaking at times, especially with the rousing 'Woman in the Moon,' the lyrical 'Evergreen,' and the at first heartbreaking, then raucous seven-minute one-shot finale, 'With One More Look at You/Watch Closely Now.' Kristofferson's performance is layered and touching; he rarely hits a false note as a man in self-destruct mode who fights, does drugs, and cheats on his wife. It is a tribute to his attractiveness and his ability to move us that he never loses our sympathy despite all that. The chemistry between Barbra and Kris clearly worked; most viewers found them both sexy, attractive people.

The overriding reason for the film's popularity, however, must have been the contemporary nature of the love story. Barbra was correct to feel that for her character to be as submissive and docile as the previous incarnations would have been fatal to the film in 1976. Young people grappling with the issue of sex roles could relate to Esther's taking the dominant role during sex and making John Norman up with glitter and rouge in a bathtub. This was what was happening in the front lines of the sexual revolution, and if the Reeds and Simons of the world didn't get it, the young moviegoing public did.

WHEN KRIS KRISTOFFERSON saw his lifeless body lying on the ground at the end of the movie, he gave up drinking. 'I realized it was my own life I was seein' on the screen. It was like seeing myself through [his wife] Rita's eyes – when I saw the corpse at the end, I had a weird feeling of sadness, like a character in *The Twilight Zone* who sees a coffin with his name on it. I feel so goddamn lucky to have found out in time – I'd been drinking for twenty years.'

His lyrics to 'Evergreen' won Paul Williams an Academy Award when the song was chosen as the best of 1976. Accepting her trophy, Barbra said, 'Never in my wildest dreams could I have imagined winning an Academy Award for writing a song.' Williams thanked Barbra for writing 'a beautiful melody' and Dr Jack Wallstader for giving him 'the Valium that got me through the whole experience.'

The months of wrenching work on *A Star Is Born* left Barbra exhausted but exhilarated. She had put her artistic vision on the line, and while the results were mixed, she had proved to herself that she could do it. Her head had long been aswim with cinematic visions of light and color and composition, but 'I had always been afraid before,' she said. She had put many of those visions on film in *A Star Is Born*. Some had worked, some had not. But the film left Barbra certain she could someday be a director.

'*A Star Is Born* was the beginning of Barbra's examining her own power,' Jon Peters told the author Karen Swenson in 1984. 'It was the discovery period for her. And she started to realize that she could do it, she could take control of her life. I was the tool, in a way. The halfback. I was the one who ran interference for her – because there were a lot of changes she wanted to make, but she couldn't always articulate it . . . I remember Jane Fonda calling her up after she saw the film and saying, "Congratulations. Not only for the movie, but for leading the way for all of us."

'In retrospect,' Jon concluded, 'I have to say that the most creative experience I've had in my life to date was *A Star Is Born*. I've never worked with a more compelling, imaginative person.'

I'm very tired,' Barbra said early in 1977. 'This film has taken up two and a half years of my life. I can't even look at it anymore. I don't want to hear about it, I don't want to know about it.'

The filming and the eighteen-hour days she had spent getting the picture ready for release took a toll on Barbra physically; the steady barrage of negative press she and Jon had endured almost since they met had left her emotionally drained. 'I wish I could say that I've risen above it,' she said, 'but that would be a lie. I cry a lot, I can tell you that. I get so *wiped out* sometimes that I think, It's not worth it. And then all of a sudden, someone will see me in the street, you know, and grab my hand and say, "I love your work" or "I love you, Barbra." The people bring me back to a kind of reality, because the people's reaction is so different than what I read.'

The Malibu ranch provided rest and relaxation for Barbra for most of the next two years; she wouldn't start work on a new film until the fall of 1978. She certainly didn't need to make another movie to keep the bills paid; her and Jon's share of the *Star Is Born* box-office bonanza amounted to over $15 million, and Barbra's royalties on the sound-track album brought in over $5 million more.

Barbra spent a good deal of the money to buy up additional land in Malibu and construct houses in order to create a lavish compound of five separate residences, each decorated in a distinct style. The eclectic and rustic main house, known as 'the barn,' contrasted sharply with the 'Deco house,' a cool, streamlined example of 1930s Moderne with chrome-and-glass fixtures, gray and red lacquer, and geometric patterns. A third house might have been lifted right out of America's Colonial era, and the 'peach house' contained guest quarters, a projection room, and a gym.

Jon worked mostly on the grounds because when he and Barbra had tried to renovate one of the houses together they fought constantly. He planted trees, built stone waterfalls, and landscaped the property in order to 'help get rid of his hostility,' Barbra said. To the dismay of the neighbors, Jon redirected Ramirez Creek so that it would babble closer to the house. Bulldozers moved earth, stonemasons created a new riverbed, and nature's will was thwarted. The downstream neighbors complained that the creek now swelled more dangerously during rainstorms, but Jon wasn't about to undo the change.

When all of the rustic comfort and luxury of Ramirez Canyon wasn't enough, Barbra still had her house on Carolwood and a cottage on the Pacific Ocean in Malibu Colony that she had bought for $564,000 cash in May of 1978. 'On the beach we have a little shack,' Barbra said. 'I mean, a real tiny little beach house. Which I like in contrast to the space of this place. It reminds me of my past ... I always lived in apartments until I was really grown up. And it's like a little apartment. I'm doing it like a Victorian dollhouse. [All these houses] are the dollhouses I never had. We spend different parts of the year in different places. Because there's so many different environments that I like.'

Despite all this excess, Barbra professed to want a simple life. She had proven herself more than ever the most popular actress in the world; in 1977 she was second only to Sylvester Stallone in the Quigley Poll of top box-office attractions. Now, she insisted, she wanted merely to live, to enjoy her new family and her lavish new compound, to be as normal a person as she could be.

'I don't go to openings and premieres and wear beaded gowns,' she said. 'I don't live that way. I go home and I cook dinner. I wash dishes and do the laundry. I haven't done that in years. This is my new kind of life ... I really like that kind of small, basic responsibility – taking care of people that you love.'

A Malibu neighbor, Joe Kern, recalled that Barbra 'was very charming, very retiring, and very shy' whenever she visited him. 'She walked the canyon a lot and she didn't like it when people approached her. It wasn't that she was snobby or anything, just scared. When she'd pass a group of us she'd be relieved if no one said anything to her or tried to stop her. She would just say hi and go on.'

'In the mornings,' Jon recalled, 'she works in the yard – she raises begonias, orchids, and the best vegetables in Malibu.' More accurately, she supervised the gardener's efforts: 'I have a very weak back, so any time I've done it, I'm paralyzed for a week afterward, but I really like to *plan* gardens, you know. I spent the summer just going to nurseries finding the most exotic varieties of perennial plants.'

In the afternoons Barbra might play tennis or walk along the beach and the mountainside. On weekends a number of neighbors would meet at her house at ten in the morning, cook breakfast, then embark on a five-mile hike. 'The other day we were walking back,' Barbra recalled, 'and this big white limousine with blackened windows went past. We were all looking in, wondering who the movie star might have been in the car.' When the same thing happens to her, she admitted, she hates it. 'I always wonder what people are staring at. Then I realize, "Oh, yeah, I'm what's-her-name."'

That realization came rudely to Barbra one day when a man began to stalk her. Another neighbor, Ruth White, recalled that 'there was a stalker at one point. I worked very closely with the police on that. I gave them information, and I spoke to Barbra's office as well. This is a very closely knit neighborhood; whenever there's a situation we kind of close ranks. I was in charge of dealing with the police about this stalker. Barbra wasn't the only celebrity in the area [Don Henley, Geraldo Rivera, and Mick Fleetwood also lived in the canyon], and the others sometimes had stalker problems, too.'

The threat made Barbra nervous and Jon wary. They erected a No Trespassing sign at the entrance to their property, punctuated by another: 'Danger! Beware: Guard Dogs Trained to Attack.' They meant it, too. Geraldo Rivera, who became close buddies with Jon after he purchased a house nearby, recalled in his autobiography that Jon's Doberman pinscher, Big Red, was 'the scariest dog in captivity. This Doberman was always pissed off. Once, he tried to rip the fender off my 1954 Jaguar.' Big Red also attacked a woman who had come to the ranch for a meeting, resulting in a lawsuit, and he 'tore up' Joe Kern's schnauzer. 'Jon paid all the vet bills,' Kern said, 'but he didn't really apologize.'

Barbra went to the dog trainer Michael Kramer to learn how to control Big Red and two German shepherds. 'At first she was a little nervous,' Kramer said, 'but once she became familiar with the dogs she was very relaxed and applied herself diligently. Now she is able to have the dogs attack whenever she needs to, using her own special commands.' Kramer recalled vividly how upset Barbra could become when recognized by strangers. One time she was sitting in Kramer's waiting room with some of his other clients. 'All of a sudden there was a pounding on the door and Miss Streisand was yelling at me to let her in. She was shaking. When I asked her what was wrong, she said she had to get out of the waiting room because the other clients had recognized her. The funny thing was that no one had actually approached her.'

Jon and Geraldo acted like fraternity brothers when they were together. 'We'd work out, talk about women, and get drunk together,' Rivera wrote. 'We were each involved with very dominant ladies, and we commiserated and compared notes. We dreamt of our younger days, when we were free to roam and plunder and raise hell.' Whenever they could, they tried to relive those wilder days. They drag-raced their powerful motorcycles through the winding hills of Malibu until they nearly went over a fifty-foot cliff. 'I had to sort of lay the bike down to keep it from going over,' Geraldo said. It came to a stop with one wheel hanging over the edge of the cliff. 'Jon missed going over by about half a foot . . . We never rode those bikes again.'

According to Geraldo, 'Jon was wild in those days . . . I watched him deck a crazed fan who was stalking Barbra on the ranch. Jon wasted him with a rising left hook. I bailed him out of that one when I told sheriff's deputies that he had merely acted in self-defense.'

Jon's hair-trigger temper sometimes got him into legal trouble. In 1977 he gave a deposition in a lawsuit filed against him by Philip Mariott, an automobile salesman, charging him with assault and battery after an incident at the Terry York Chevrolet lot in Encino on December 1, 1974. According to Jon, he and Barbra were shopping for a car when Mariott approached them, asked if he could be of assistance, and 'stated to my companion [Barbra] that she looked like Barbra Streisand. My companion stated that others had told her the same. The salesman then became persistent in talking with us although we asked to look at autos ourselves.

'He insisted on telling us about his personal dislike for Barbra Streisand movies and records, and he became more and more abusive in his comments until we finally had to leave. He became hostile and aggressive to Barbra Streisand, stating that he hated her movies and records and in general disliked her and found her unattractive, and her singing was terrible.' Finally, Jon alleged, Mariott placed himself next to Barbra 'in a space of an amount that he knew would annoy her.'

At that point, Mariott alleged, Jon attacked him, injuring him so badly he could no longer work. The matter was settled out of court on December 12, 1977.

On March 5, 1978, Barbra had to bail Jon out of jail after he was arrested for reckless driving and resisting arrest. The incident and what led up to it, Jon told a reporter, 'was a nightmare from beginning to end.' Southern California had been battered by torrential rains for days, and Jon, Barbra, Jason, Jon's son Christopher, and a group of their neighbors had worked around the clock to build sandbag barriers against the swelling of that redirected creek, which now threatened to flood their homes. When Jon and Christopher drove off to pick up additional sandbags from the fire department, Jon said, he informed patrolman Patrick Meister, who was standing guard, and Meister gave him permission to return.

When he got back, Jon alleged, Officer Meister 'started hassling me, saying I had to have proof of identification and proof I lived in the area. Hell, who had identification? I was wearing the same muddy, rain-soaked clothes I'd had on for days. I told him I had to get back to my home, to Barbra and Jason. When he wouldn't let me, I drove through the roadblock, and when he caught up with me, he dragged me out of my car, slammed me against the hood, put a gun to my head, and started hitting me with his club, while I kept screaming, "Why are you hurting me?" Then he took me away in handcuffs.'

Meister's supervisor, Sergeant Rodney Yates, said that Meister pursued Jon for three miles before he was able to stop him and that the officer was justified in hitting Jon: 'He hit him on the legs with his baton after Peters came at him in an aggressive manner.' Barbra paid $500 to spring Jon from jail, and he made noises about suing Meister for assault and false arrest. He never followed through on the threat, however, and the charges against him were ultimately dropped.

On Barbra's birthday in 1977 her cook, Bing Fong, prepared a cake, but by the time of her party the icing had become too hard for Jon's taste. He told Fong to replace the icing, but the chef protested that to attempt such a thing would ruin the cake. According to Fong's attorney, Leonard Kohn, Jon then pushed Fong against the sink so violently that the cook seriously injured his lower back. 'They settled for $5,000, but with the doctor reports and testimony I think we could have gotten a lot more,' Kohn said. 'But Bing Fong wanted to just settle it and take the money and not have it drawn out in court. He was very afraid of Peters.'

In Aspen a few years later Geraldo Rivera came to his friend's aid again when Jon faced 'possible felony charges for sticking his antique Colt revolver in the ear of his gardener, who had become abusive over an unpaid bill,' Geraldo wrote.

Failure to pay their bills in a timely fashion was apparently a habit with Barbra and Jon, who were slapped with numerous mechanic's liens over the years, according to court documents. Among the complainants were a pool contractor, a masonry supply company, and a general contractor hired to do work at the Malibu ranch. In all cases either Barbra or Jon contended that the work hadn't been done to their liking; the unpaid amounts ranged from $4,500 to $50,000. The liens were removed from the properties once the bills were paid.

JASON GOULD, ELEVEN in 1978, and Christopher Peters, two years younger, had been leery of each other at first, but soon became fast friends. They went tearing through the canyons during Chris's weekend visits, first on bicycles, then on motorbikes, and finally on motorcycles as they got older. Their neighbor Trude Coleman recalled that Jason was 'a sweet kid, but Christopher was a real pistol. He took after his father. I wouldn't go so far as to say he was a troublemaker, although he certainly was loud around the canyon, which was a perfect place to go motorbiking. It's a great place for boys to grow up, a fun place. There are lots of trails and woods and places to play and build forts, and that's what the Streisand and Peters boys did together. They'd go up into the trails for hours.'

Both Lesley Ann Warren and Elliott Gould fretted about the influence Barbra and Jon's sumptuous Shangri-la would have on their sons. 'I worry that Christopher's not going to want to come back home to me after he's spent time there,' Lesley Ann said. Elliott groused that 'Barbra lives in a fantasy world. That's one of the reasons I want to take Jason back to live with me. I just don't want to take chances with his head . . . I don't want him to grow up in a world of fantasy. I find that when he's with me he's very natural. I want to keep him that way.' Barbra, however, might have argued that her life in Malibu provided a more stable environment for Jason than his father's with Jenny Bogart, who had borne him a child out of wedlock, then left him, had come back, borne another child, and finally married him in December 1973.

Why didn't Barbra and Jon get married? 'I've asked her about three times, but she turned me down,' Jon said. 'Now I'm waiting for her to ask me.'

To Barbra, marriage represented not an institution but 'a final commitment, a beautiful, romantic gesture . . . But there is also a kind of excitement in not being married – you can never take each other for granted.' Neither felt any pressure to legitimize their love affair for the sake of the boys. 'The children look to see what you feel about each other,' Barbra said. 'They don't check to see if you've got a piece of paper.'

Steve Jaffe, whom Jon had fired as his publicist late in 1975 after Jaffe declined to fly from New York to Los Angeles on a few hours' notice to attend a meeting, recalled that Barbra and Jon would talk about marriage 'almost as if it was a running joke, because neither of them needed the ceremony, and neither one was going to be changed by it. They were both pretty savvy individuals and knew that there was a good chance that the relationship wouldn't last.'

'I *hope* I'll be with her for the rest of my life,' Jon said. 'Most mornings I wake up here with her and I *laugh*, it's so good.'

IN JULY 1977 Roslyn Kind returned to the club circuit with engagements at the Grand Finale in New York and the Backlot at Studio One in West Hollywood. She had given up her singing career in the early 1970s; in 1976 she had gone to work as a purchasing agent for Hollywood General Pictures. After losing that job and collecting unemployment, she decided to take another stab at performing, helped along by an encouraging friend, Richard Gordon, a Streisand fan who had befriended Diana Kind. 'I got Roslyn the Grand Finale booking,' Gordon recalled, 'and she was a hit, got a lot of attention, television shows, that kind of thing. She was the toast of the town for two or three weeks.'

At the Backlot, Elliott Gould introduced his former sister-in-law with the words, 'Now we're going to hear somebody who can *really* sing.' Barbra arrived late and alone, wrapped in an ivory-colored shawl and looking like a fragile porcelain doll. During intermission, when a woman mentioned to Barbra that her husband was out of town, Streisand replied, 'So is mine.'

At the end of Roslyn's act, the audience applauded heartily, but no one stood up. After about thirty seconds, a man rose to make room for someone to get out of his seat. Barbra took this as a cue and jumped to her feet. Everyone followed suit, and Roslyn got a standing ovation.

She also got excellent reviews, but nothing came of the comeback. Over the next few years Roslyn made sporadic club appearances, but she still had the same problem with comparisons to Barbra, something she seemed to invite by wearing the same hairdo and singing similar songs. As Richard Gordon put it, 'When Barbra was blond, Roslyn got a blond wig. When Barbra's hair was red, she got a red wig.' Roslyn still protested that she didn't want to be compared to Barbra, but her actions spoke louder than her words.

Gordon felt that Roslyn's inability to forge a singing career was largely her own doing. 'Barbra could have helped Roslyn more, but the fact of the matter is Roslyn's lazy,' he said. 'She doesn't have the ambition that Barbra had at her age. Never did. She also expected things to happen to her because of who she is. She thought her relationship to Barbra would open doors. Then she saw that it didn't.'

By the early 1980s Roslyn had gone to work in a bakery in Westwood owned by her manager and his wife, with whom she was living. She worked mostly behind the scenes, reportedly because she considered serving customers beneath her. The name of the bakery was 'Butterfly.'

BARBRA ALLOWED WORK to intrude on her Malibu idyll when she returned to the recording studio to give Columbia its annual Streisand album, which the company wanted as soon as possible to capitalize on the enormous success of the *Star Is Born* sound track. Gary Klein produced the package, entitled *Streisand Superman*; apparently his trial-by-fire introduction to Barbra when he criticized the *ButterFly* album wasn't held against him. 'The concept was to keep Barbra Streisand on the pop charts,' Klein said, 'not have people think of her as just an MOR [middle-of-the-road] artist.'

Klein suggested an eclectic mix of songs, from Billy Joel's bluesy 'New York State of Mind' and Kim Carnes and Dave Ellington's 'Love Comes from Unexpected Places' to the hard-rocking 'Cabin Fever' and 'Don't Believe What You Read.' Barbra composed the latter tune's lyrics when she became incensed by a *Los Angeles* magazine gossip item that reported the contradictory news that she had a germ fetish and that she had pet birds flying free around her home, leaving their droppings everywhere.

The cover and inside packaging of *Streisand Superman* featured Barbra clad in skimpy white shorts and a T-shirt with the Superman logo emblazoned across the front, an outfit she had worn briefly in *A Star Is Born*. The *Stereo Review* critic Peter Reilly wrote: 'Streisand's newest features, among other goodies, several rearview photographs of her in an abbreviated track suit that permits an ample display of tushie. And a very pretty and appealing tushie it is, too. *And* also probably aimed directly, for bussing purposes, at the critics.'

Those critics were kind to *Streisand Superman* upon its release in June of 1977; Stephen Holden considered it 'among the finest of Streisand's thirty-plus LPs.' The album shot up to number three, and a single, 'My Heart Belongs to Me,' hit number four on the pop charts.

The playfully sexy photographs of Barbra published in the album led *Playboy* magazine to feature her on its cover in October to accompany an extended interview. She had posed in a bunny outfit, but the picture chosen had her wearing the Superman outfit with the *Playboy* logo across her chest. She was the first female movie star pictured on the magazine's cover since Marilyn Monroe more than twenty years earlier.

Larry Grobel spent months interviewing Streisand, and the experience, he said, left him drained. 'Barbra Streisand is the most intense woman I've ever met. Whenever I'd ask her a question that had even the nuance of being critical, she would take the question apart to see if it was fair to have asked it . . . [S]he carefully dissected the words "power" and "control" each time I used them . . . she felt "control" had "negative implications" and was too broad a term. She narrowed it to "artistic responsibility," elaborating, "If you mean that I am completely dedicated and care deeply about carrying out a total vision of a project – yes, that's true."'

IN OCTOBER 1977 Barbra signed a new five-year contract with Columbia Records. Negotiated by Jon, the pact called for five albums over the next five years plus a 'Greatest Hits' package, and guaranteed Barbra an advance of $1.5 million for each album against a royalty rate of approximately 20 percent of the retail price, about $1.50 per album. The budget for each record was set at $250,000, a considerable improvement over the $18,000 spent on Barbra's first effort for Columbia. The label's president, Bruce Lundvall, found Jon 'very smart,' with 'a good street sense. I never found him to be an adversary.' Although other labels had expressed interest in wooing Barbra away from Columbia, Lundvall doubted that Jon had spoken seriously to any of them. 'It became one of those things where she said, "Hey, this is family,"' Lundvall recalled. 'There was a lot of loyalty on her part.'

On December 22 Barbra attended a lavish party at La Première restaurant in Manhattan, thrown by Columbia to celebrate its new contract with her and a production-talent acquisition deal with Jon Peters. Celebrities ranging from Shirley MacLaine to Bella Abzug attended, and so did dozens of Barbra's relatives. She took it upon herself to make sure the kinfolk were all well fed. 'This is the only way I get to meet my family,' she said as cousins and aunts and nieces lined up to have their pictures taken with the star. She kidded her brother – 'Sheldon thinks he's the star of the family' – and told a group of relatives, 'You wait, I'll be back, okay?' as she moved off with Shirley and Bella for a private tête-à-tête in a corner.

Jon had the flu and couldn't attend, Barbra told the columnist Earl Wilson.

'Is he running a temperature?' Wilson asked.

'You used to ask Jon questions about me,' Barbra said with a laugh. 'Now you ask me questions about him. He must be making out very good.'

He was. Since October Jon had been in New York filming *The Eyes of Laura Mars*, a thriller starring Faye Dunaway and Tommy Lee Jones that he was producing for Columbia. After *A Star Is Born*, which Jon and Barbra had brought in on time and under budget, Peters had become a hot property in Hollywood. And he was determined to prove, both to the public and to her, that he wasn't just Barbra Streisand's boyfriend. 'There is tremendous competition between us,' Jon admitted.

When he had decided to strike out on his own, Jon had met over lunch with Warren Beatty. 'Don't be a schmuck,' Beatty had told him. 'Develop a couple of things at once. Because movies can take a lot of time to get going and you never know when one will be ready to go.'

By 1978 Jon, working seven days a week and sixteen hours a day, had fifteen films in various stages of development, was scouting the country for musical acts for Columbia Records, and was acting as Geraldo Rivera's manager as well as Barbra's. After fifteen years, Marty Erlichman had surrendered to the all-encompassing influence of Jon in Barbra's life and had left the Streisand circle – and he apparently felt some rancor toward Jon. 'Maybe she needed new direction,' Marty said. 'Barbra and I are still close. We speak on the phone once a week. As for Jon Peters? Even before I left, he was calling himself her manager. My thoughts on what he does and how he does it, well, they're not for publication.'

BARBRA'S FIRST ALBUM for Columbia under her new contract was *Songbird*, a disappointing 1978 collection of 'mainly second-rate songs,' Stephen Holden felt, 'that she rides herd over with some of the most shrilly indifferent interpretations of her career.' Still, the album managed to reach number twelve on the charts.

One of the best tracks on *Songbird* was Barbra's rendition of 'You Don't Bring Me Flowers' by Neil Diamond with lyrics by the Bergmans. When Gary Guthrie, a disc jockey in Louisville, Kentucky, heard Diamond's own version of the song and realized that both were in the same key, he used some editing legerdemain to create a duet and played it over the air that night. To the consternation of record-store owners, hundreds of customers started asking for the record, which didn't exist. The phone calls to the station asking Guthrie to play the song again grew so heavy that he added it to his regular Top 40 rotation.

Guthrie sent a copy of the tape to Columbia, and after they slapped a cease-and-desist order on him to keep him from playing what was in fact an illegal tape, Bruce Lundvall persuaded Diamond and Streisand to get together and record a duet for real. When the single was released late in October, it created a sensation across the country. Some 85 percent of radio stations added it to their playlist within the first ten days, an unprecedented acceptance for a Streisand single. A programmer's newsletter said that 'females go berserko and will wait all day to hear this.'

'You Don't Bring Me Flowers' went to number one within six weeks and became Barbra's biggest hit single. The popularity of the song helped propel her next album, *Barbra Streisand's Greatest Hits, Volume II*, to the top of the charts as well when it was included in that package, which sold over four million copies. Under the terms of her new contract, this album, for which she had recorded nothing new, brought Streisand over $6 million in royalties.

'You Don't Bring Me Flowers' was nominated for Grammy Awards as Record of the Year and for Best Pop Vocal Performance by a Duo, Group or Chorus. On February 27, 1980, Barbra and Neil performed the song during the live television broadcast of the Grammy Awards at the Shrine Auditorium in Los Angeles; it was the first time in her career that Barbra had agreed to sing at the Grammy ceremony. She and Diamond appeared suddenly, unannounced, in dramatic pools of light on opposite sides of the stage and walked slowly toward each other as they sang the song, creating near havoc in the audience as they finally met in an embrace at center stage. A wobbly voice betrayed Barbra's nervousness early in the song, but as she moved closer to Neil, she regained control and ended the performance flawlessly. Although their duet didn't win Record of the Year or the performance award, the Streisand-Diamond performance received a prolonged standing ovation and was chosen as one of the highlights of the entire TV season by the producers of a year-end retrospective television special.

W hy am I not working?' Barbra had asked Sydney Pollack early in 1978. 'What am I saving myself for? This is stupid. I should be out there. So every picture won't be great. I just sit and wait and wait – for what? For Chekhov to come along? For Shakespeare?'

The French director François Truffaut had once told Barbra, 'You do your work, and at the end [of your career] you have a body of work. Some of it is good and some of it is not good, but the stuff that's good will override what isn't good – that's what a body of work is. You can't just sit and wait for the perfect thing to come along.' Perhaps Truffaut's words rang in Barbra's ears as she chose a very imperfect vehicle for her return to the screen after two and a half years, a screenplay that was about as far from Shakespeare as it could get.

The Main Event began as an idea of Renee Missel, who became the executive producer of the film with her partner, Howard Rosenman. The story evolved into a script by Gail Parent and Andrew Smith entitled *Knockout*, about Hillary Kramer, the owner of a perfume company whose business manager absconds with all her money. The only asset she has left is Eddie 'Kid Natural' Scanlon, a former boxer and now a driving instructor, whose contract Hillary's business manager had purchased as a tax write-off. By threatening legal action against him, Hillary persuades a reluctant Scanlon to return to the ring and start making her some money. After several skirmishes, romantic as well as pugilistic, they fall in love. Barbra saw the property as a likely candidate for her and Jon to produce in order to fulfill her final commitment to First Artists.

'*The Main Event* was my fault,' Jon admitted. 'I pushed her into that one. It was time to do a movie. I wanted her to do a comedy, and it was material that she really didn't like. It was the last time I think Barbra will be pushed into anything.'

Barbra hoped the script could be fashioned into a contemporary version of the rollicking battle-of-the-sexes romantic comedies that had been a Hollywood staple since the silent era. She also felt the story's premise could allow an exploration of a confusing contemporary issue that fascinated her: the changing societal roles of men and women. How, for instance, would the supermacho boxer react to a female boss?

Typically, she was full of ideas and wasn't shy about passing them on to the screenwriters, who were glad for the input. 'Barbra wasn't just lounging around like some old-time movie star, saying, "Write something clever,"' said Gail Parent. 'She was *there* with us, improvising and suggesting lines.'

Barbra had only one actor in mind to play 'Kid' Scanlon. In an offer she made over the phone she told him, 'Ryan, if you don't want the part, I don't want to make the picture.' Ryan O'Neal, a former amateur boxer, had had a string of disappointing films, had just lost the leads in two other boxing movies, *Flesh and Blood* and a remake of *The Champ*, and had fallen into such a funk that he was close to quitting the business.

Barbra wheedled and cajoled, begged and pleaded with him to come aboard. Finally he replied, 'If you're in it, I'll do it.' No doubt his acquiescence was helped along by Barbra's offer of a $1 million salary.

The showman in Jon Peters agreed that Ryan was the perfect co-star for *The Main Event*; audiences would likely be eager to see the *What's Up, Doc?* co-stars together again. But he was wary of putting Barbra into such close proximity with one of her former lovers. Steve Jaffe was surprised when he heard that Jon had agreed to O'Neal's casting. 'There was a time,' Jaffe said, 'when Jon didn't want to hear Ryan's name mentioned. It was very hard on me because at the time I represented both of them. I'd be in Jon's office, and Ryan would call me and Jon would say, "You're not taking that call *here*." In the maximum sense of machismo, right or wrong, Jon and Ryan were rivals. I could see them flexing. Barbra probably had the last laugh every day on *The Main Event*, because here were two guys who were in love with her, and in her shadow.'

According to Andrew Smith, Ryan enjoyed baiting Jon whenever he had a romantic scene with Barbra. 'Ryan would always put a little extra something in the scene if he knew Jon was watching,' Smith said. 'He'd tweak her ass or bite her earlobe. It drove Jon crazy. He stopped coming around when they did love scenes. He told Ryan that when the movie was over, he was going to get into the ring and beat the hell out of him.'

✫

ONCE THE STAR packaging was completed in early 1978, final contract negotiations with the producers began. 'At the meeting,' Howard Rosenman told the author Shaun Considine, 'Jon Peters began to renege on the deal [that had been] set up with Sue Mengers. He and Barbra decided they would only give us half of what had been originally promised.' When Rosenman heard this, he told his agent to relay a message to Jon: 'You tell Mr Jon Peters to take his new deal and shove it up his ass!'

'I knew I owned the material,' Rosenman said. 'I also knew that Jon had put a million and a half of his own money into the project, signing Ryan and other expenses. He got on the phone. "You self-destructive cocksucker!" he began. "I'm offering you the chance of a lifetime. Your whole career is gonna be made with a Streisand credit. She made Ray Stark; she can do the same for you. You're fucking insane; you belong in Camarillo [a California mental hospital]." And I replied, very calmly, "Jon, when you can pronounce 'Camarillo' I will have a conversation with you . . . Now, here are the *new* terms I'm giving you and your greedy girlfriend." And I added another fifty thousand and another percentage point, and I said, "At the close of business today, if the check isn't in my lawyer's hands, then we will go to Diane Keaton, to Jill Clayburgh, and to Diana Ross, because I own this piece of material and you, Jon, have made it *hot!*"'

Jon swallowed hard and gave the man what he demanded, but Sue Mengers told Rosenman that he was to stay away from the set and do virtually nothing except show up for the premiere. 'And when you see Barbra and she forgets your name, *smile!*'

DURING THE FILM'S preproduction phase, Barbra told the assistant director, Patrick Kehoe, that she might direct the picture. She later decided against it, Kehoe believed, because 'she felt she couldn't prepare as an actress and also as a director in the time that was available.' Still smarting from the debacle with Frank Pierson, Barbra wanted a director who would be willing to accept her as a full-time, hands-on, often pain-in-the-ass collaborator.

After he met with Barbra and Jon, the thirty-six-year-old director Howard Zieff, who had won attention for the quirky *Hearts of the West* in 1975 and *House Calls* in 1978, agreed to the terms and came aboard. One of the conditions of his contract forbade him to write or speak negatively of Barbra and Jon for the rest of his life.

Cast in supporting roles were Patti D'Arbanville as the Kid's sleazy girlfriend, Whitman Mayo as his trainer, and James Gregory as a gruff fight manager. Howard Zieff suggested Allan Miller, Barbra's former acting coach, to play Hillary's ex-husband. But, Miller said, 'I was kept out of the movie because of Barbra.'

It was only after he had read successfully for Zieff that Miller discovered this was a Streisand picture. 'She'll never let me in the movie,' he told Zieff.

'What are you talking about?'

'Well, I won't tell you the whole story,' Miller replied, 'but just by being there I would bring up memories of things she does not want to recall at this point in her life. She might still think of me as a teacher or director, judging her work.'

Zieff laughed off Miller's prediction, but after broaching the idea to Barbra, he admitted to Miller that he had been right. 'Oh, he's a very good actor,' Barbra told Zieff, 'but I can't have him be my husband.' The dourfaced comic actor Paul Sand, who reminded some observers of Elliott Gould, won the role.

With a budget close to $7 million, *The Main Event* went into production for First Artists/Warner Brothers during the first week of October 1978. Barbra and Zieff agreed that the film's energetic comedy would be enhanced by location filming, but boisterous onlookers at every site often made Zieff wish they were on a closed studio set. One brief scene between Barbra and Ryan, set at a sidewalk hot-dog stand on the busy corner of Beverly and La Cienega in West Hollywood, had to be halted when two young women in a passing car shrieked, 'Oh, my *God!* It's *Barbra Streisand!*' Three hours later, after two fender benders at the intersection, the shoot was scrapped. 'You realize what a big star she is,' Howard Zieff said, 'when you go out for a hamburger with her. Fans mob her like they used to mob Valentino or Garbo, she's that popular.'

NEVER FULLY SATISFIED with the finished script, Barbra took suggestions from anyone about how to improve a scene, and she encouraged improvisation. Richard Lawson played the Kid's boxing nemesis, Hector Mantilla, with an amusing accent. For a scene in which Hillary, barely able to keep awake, challenges Mantilla to a winner-take-all match with Scanlon in the midst of a television interview hosted by the sportscaster Brent Musburger, Barbra, Ryan, and Lawson all winged it. 'The lines were basically there,' said Lawson, 'but the imitation Barbra did of my accent was improvisational. The scene took on a life of its own. It was written as a straight interview, but the whole aspect of her falling asleep and Ryan waking her up, and of her calling Musburger "Brett" and "Burt" – all of that was total improvisation.'

Barbra's desire to infuse *The Main Event* with some relevant points about the real-life battle of the sexes was most apparent in a scene she concocted and inserted into the film, against the advice of Zieff and others, after filming had wrapped. Finally giving in to their mutual attraction, Hillary and the Kid make love for the first time during their stay at a training camp. Barbra felt a 'morning after' scene was necessary to further define the two characters and what this new physical relationship might bring. 'I thought it would be [a chance] to see where these two people are coming from [and] how different they are emotionally. [A chance] to say something about men and women and the roles they're supposed to play and yet be funny.' Although unsubtle, the scene allowed for some amusing role reversal as Scanlon expresses his concern that Hillary might not respect him now that she's had her way with him.

IMMEDIATELY AFTER *The Main Event* wrapped production early in 1979, Howard Zieff began to construct his director's print, even though he knew the final cut would be Barbra's. In the meantime, work began on the musical elements of the film. Producer Gary LeMel, who had helped steer Barbra's *Superman* album to the top of the charts, asked longtime Streisand fan Paul Jabara (who had just won a Best Song Oscar for 'Last Dance') to compose a disco-style title number for *The Main Event* to capitalize on the most popular musical genre of the seventies. Written with Bruce Roberts, the song didn't impress Barbra at first because the lyrics didn't reflect the film's boxing theme. Bob Esty, who had produced 'Last Dance' for disco queen Donna Summer, suggested that the song be combined with 'Fight,' a number he and Jabara had developed as a send-up of the camp disco group the Village People. Barbra liked the idea of a medley, but she was timid about venturing into dance-oriented pop for the first time since 'Shake Me, Wake Me' – until twelve-year-old Jason responded strongly to the song. 'He was the one who really sold it,' Esty recalled. 'He loved it and [Barbra] listened to him.'

Warner Brothers opened *The Main Event* in eleven hundred theaters across the country on June 22, 1979. The cornerstone of the promotional campaign was a sexy photograph of Barbra, braless in a tank top and tight satin shorts, and Ryan, bare-chested and in trunks, in a classic nose-to-nose boxing pose. Despite mostly negative reviews, Barbra's popularity and the desire of many moviegoers to see if she and Ryan could re-create the magic of *What's Up, Doc?* brought the film a glittering gross of $66 million, making it Barbra's third most successful picture to that date, behind *A Star Is Born* and *What's Up, Doc?*

A film replete with annoying inconsistencies, *The Main Event* disappointed many Streisand admirers, who had expected Barbra's follow-up to *A Star Is Born* to be something worth waiting almost three years for. She has her amusing moments, but her Hillary Kramer is a bafflingly schizophrenic character. As the head of 'Le Nez' (The Nose) perfumes, she's the picture of competence and business savvy. But in her private quarters, or when confronted with the alien world of professional boxing, she calls to mind Lucy Ricardo at her dizziest. Even as a fish out of water, she is largely an unbelievable character. O'Neal's bumbling, boyish charm is more appealing, but he too is hampered by the silly, sometimes turgid script.

Despite its shortcomings, *The Main Event* showed 'legs' throughout the summer, in part because of the success of the exuberant title song, sung by Barbra, which shot up to number three on the singles chart.

SHORTLY AFTER THE movie's release, several press accounts depicted Howard Zieff as a director who had suffered a meddlesome superstar. A profile in the *Fort Lauderdale News*, headlined 'Wherein an Underrated Director Risks All to Tangle with "La Barbra,"' called Zieff 'a Streisand survivor.'

The piece quoted Zieff, who chose his words carefully so as not to violate the clause in his contract that forbade him to speak ill of Barbra: 'People look at you in amazement when you say you've just directed Streisand. They say, "He can handle movie stars and still bring movies in on time and around budget." . . . Barbra always has final say on her movies.' In another interview he said, 'She just took over the editing and cut the film to her own purpose . . . as producer, she had full control.'

Ryan O'Neal told Rex Reed, 'In *What's Up, Doc?* we did what we were told. Peter Bogdanovich ran the show. This time we tried all kinds of things. [Barbra] played the Bogdanovich role. Howard Zieff was under lots of pressures. I think he held up pretty well.'

Barbra avoided public discussion of her relationship with Zieff, but privately she admitted that the experience was only slightly less painful than her 'collaboration' with Frank Pierson. She considered both men maddeningly unable to make up their minds. To her, 'directing is a good job for someone who has opinions.'

What Barbra didn't know was that she had been urged to hire Zieff as a practical joke. The producer Jennings Lang, in whose home Barbra had sung to raise funds for the Pentagon Papers Defense Fund, recalled that early in 1978 he had attended the farewell performance of Zubin Mehta as the conductor of the Los Angeles Philharmonic. 'Everybody who is anybody is there,' Lang related. '[Walter] Matthau is sitting with his wife, Carol, in one row; Barbra Streisand is with Sue Mengers in the row in front of them. [Walter and I] had just finished a picture called *House Calls*, and we had a lot of problems with Howard Zieff, our director, the man who can't make up his mind. He's a very talented guy, except he changes colors from black to white in ten seconds. He's just not definitive about what he wants to do. He was driving everybody crazy, including Matthau, on the set.'

At intermission, Barbra and Sue Mengers stood up, and Sue noticed Walter Matthau. 'Walter, you know Barbra,' she said. Matthau put his arms around Barbra, kissed her, and burbled to Mengers, 'I've always been in love with her. I always loved her. I miss her so much.'

Barbra quickly cut to the chase. 'Tell me about Howie Zieff.'

'He's the greatest director in the world!' Matthau exclaimed. 'You *can't* use anybody else. He knows every shot he's going to take a week before he's on the set. You won't have to think; he's *marvelous!*'

'GET MY LAWYER on the phone!' Barbra screamed as she threw the magazine across the room. 'I want this off the newsstands!' The offending publication, the November 1979 issue of the sleazy skin rag *High Society*, had blazoned across its cover, along with a photo of Barbra in her modeling outfit from *The Owl and the Pussycat*, not one but two banner headlines: 'Barbra Streisand Nude!' The magazine's editors had gotten ahold of several unfogged frames of Barbra's topless scene in that film and had published them to great fanfare.

Barbra sued for $5 million and demanded that the magazines be recalled. They never were. 'We did agree to send out telegrams to our nearly five hundred wholesalers,' the editor Gloria Leonard said, 'asking that, if they hadn't already distributed the book to newsstands, they tear the pictures out and tape over the word "nude" in connection with Streisand's name on the cover . . . Frankly, I know there will be some distributors who'll just say, "The hell with the wire," and won't go to the bother of following its instructions.'

The photos showed that Barbra had a very appealing bosom, and the issue quickly became a collector's item. Barbra never won any damages from the magazine, but the nude frames, even though the fogging made it impossible to see much, were edited out when *The Owl and the Pussycat* was released on videocassette in 1980.

THE SUCCESS OF 'The Main Event/Fight' led its composers, Paul Jabara and Bruce Roberts, to submit another song to Barbra after they received word that she was planning an album called *Wet*, built around a theme: all the songs had to relate in some way to water. Charles Koppelman, who had left Columbia to form the Entertainment Company and had acted as executive producer for Barbra's recent albums, didn't like 'Enough Is Enough,' a new disco number

Jabara and Roberts had come up with for the album, because the lyrics weren't 'wet.' Undeterred, the team turned it into a medley with another composition of theirs, 'No More Tears.'

When Koppelman still seemed reluctant to suggest the song to Barbra, Jabara took matters into his own hands and approached Streisand directly. He wrangled an invitation to Malibu to pitch 'Enough Is Enough/No More Tears.' He took along Donna Summer, with whom he hoped Barbra would agree to record the song as a duet. 'That would be the ultimate,' Jabara said, 'having the two divas meet and record together.' Through sheer chutzpah, Jabara managed to get Barbra, Donna, and Jason – a big Summer fan – into a small room at the ranch, and while Jon listened outside the door, Jabara 'sang the song to them, performing both parts. Then I got on my knees and begged them to do it together, to try the song just once.'

Barbra agreed to record with Summer in part because of Jason's enthusiasm for the idea. 'My son likes Donna,' Barbra said. 'He never plays my stuff.'

Streisand and Summer, Jabara said, 'were like two high school girls, not like two great artists. When they were home alone rehearsing at the piano, they were wonderful. As soon as there were twenty people around, though, the vibes changed.'

Rumors of tension between the 'dueling divas' were rife, but Donna Summer denied them all. 'It was fun,' she said. 'She's a funny girl. There was a lot of comedy going back and forth between us . . . We were holding the high note of "Enough Is Enough," and I didn't breathe right. I just held the note too long and fell off my stool. Barbra kept holding her note, and then at the end of the note, she said, "Are you all right?" It was hysterical, because by the time she asked me, I was coming to. I hit the floor and it jolted me. She didn't stop holding her note. It was the height of professionalism. She thought I was playing around.'

Still, there couldn't help but be a touch of competition between two superstars, and Jabara admitted that although Streisand and Summer recorded the song face to face, each woman came back into the studio separately to redo some notes. Barbra recognized Donna as the premier disco singer and turned to her for advice. Summer was stunned. 'You're Barbra Streisand,' she replied. 'You're asking *me* how to sing?' John Arrias, Barbra's recording engineer, understood her discomfort. 'She doesn't [ordinarily] sing on the beat,' he said. 'She sings after the downbeat. But for disco you have to be on top of the beat, and that's what Donna was trying to impress upon her.'

'Enough Is Enough/No More Tears' was released in October from Columbia in a standard single format that ran four and a half minutes and from Donna's Casablanca label in an eleven-and-a-half-minute dance-club re-mix in the twelve-inch format. Eagerly anticipated, the driving duet with its wailing vocals hit number one on the singles chart within weeks. Both versions of the song sold over a million copies and topped charts in England, Spain, and Australia.

The album *Wet*, released two weeks after 'Enough Is Enough,' proved only partially successful. The exciting duet with Summer is surrounded by dreamy romantic ballads, while 'Splish Splash' is delivered tongue-in-cheek with Barbra backed by members of the group Toto. Standout cuts include 'Niagara' and 'Kiss Me in the Rain,' two beautifully crafted and powerfully sung new ballads. But overall the water motif provided only a strained cohesion to the package.

Wet climbed to number seven on the album chart, and even critics who didn't care for some of the material Streisand was singing had to admit that she was now a powerful force in pop music, a full decade after *What About Today?* had seemed to indicate that she would never be comfortable with contemporary material. Since 1971 Barbra had not had a studio album – as opposed to a sound-track or a live album – chart at less than number thirteen. Even more remarkably, after failing to sell singles during her meteoric rise to success in the sixties, she had had *four* number one singles in the seventies, the same number as Donna Summer and more than any other Columbia artist.

Nearly twenty years after her start in show business, Barbra Streisand had eclipsed all of her early contemporaries and continued at the peak of success even in the midst of the sea change in popular music represented by the disco craze. It was an unprecedented record of success and longevity. In the wake of 'Enough Is Enough/No More Tears,' *US* magazine voted Streisand and Summer the top female vocalists of the seventies.

�֎

AT HOME AFTER she completed *The Main Event*, Barbra often found herself acting out real, debilitating battles – with Jon. They had always fought with abandon, and early in their relationship they had found the skirmishes emotionally and sexually arousing. 'I don't think we've ever stopped battling,' Barbra said. 'And the more we fight, the closer together we seem to be. We're not phony with each other. We don't lie to each other, and that's something that turns us both on.'

'We fight and war and battle,' Jon confirmed to Jerry Parker of *Newsday*. 'Sometimes she's totally crazy. But Barbra is a very gentle, understanding, giving human being who has helped me through a lot of difficult times . . . Barbra is the first person I ever respected totally – on all levels. In some ways she's almost like a man. She's strong. She's successful. She takes responsibility.'

Jon has said that living with Barbra became difficult because after her initial delight at being in the kitchen for him, she rarely capitulated to his male prerogatives. 'She gives what she feels, as opposed to what's demanded of her. For instance, if I say, "I'm tired, will you rub my head?" she says, "Why don't you rub *my* head? I'm tired, too."'

One method they used to settle these disagreements, Jon said, was to compare notes about their youth. 'We are always arguing about who had the worst life. The one who is the more convincing gets a head massage.'

But as the seventies drew to a close, the battles grew worse and placed a tremendous strain on their relationship. Usually after a particularly bad row, Jon told Rosalie Shann, 'One of us – usually me – will say: "Let's sit down and talk. Do we want to split? Don't we want to be together any more?" That's the bottom line, the worst. We agree we do want to stick together . . . So we sit down and talk.

'The worst fights by far are the quiet ones. Because then I feel sick, really physically sick. We're not communicating and [we're] angry about something, but what we're angry about isn't the real cause. It's something deeper, and we're not getting to it. Those times we go to our therapist and he helps us sort things out.'

The couple went to see 'a truly wonderful psychiatrist' at least once a week at $100 an hour. 'It really does help,' Jon said. 'Our two sons go, too.' Jason had sessions with Dr Stan Ziegler, a renowned expert in adolescent emotional problems.

The therapy couldn't keep Barbra and Jon from the decision to break up. For Barbra, Jon's unpredictable temper was bad enough; she loathed the times he made her fear him, just as she and her mother had feared Louis Kind. But there were also rumors that Jon was seeing other women, and that would have been enough to give Barbra serious second thoughts about staying with him.

What Jon had called 'the bottom line, the worst' happened late in 1979 – he and Barbra split. Jon moved back into a house he still owned in Encino, and after thirteen-year-old Jason's bar mitzvah on January 5, which Jon did not attend, Barbra retreated to Manhattan and her Central Park West penthouse. Within a few days of her arrival the columnist Liz Smith reported that Barbra was in the midst of 'a little away-from-California romance' with a man Smith couldn't identify. 'A male visitor with a handful of flowers went yesterday evening to her twenty-first floor apartment . . . and after more than three hours the superstar and Mr X left together.'

'Mr X' was Arnon Milchan, a forty-something Israeli millionaire who was about to embark on a career as a Hollywood producer that would lead to his producing *Pretty Woman* and *JFK*, among other hits. He escorted Barbra around Manhattan, took her to the theater nearly every night, and kept Liz Smith in a tizzy.

Barbra denied that Milchan was anything more than a friend, and it is likely that her conversations with the man concerned the financing of *Yentl*, a difficult project which she wanted to direct and for which she was having trouble raising money. In any event, Barbra's rendezvous with Milchan ended before very long and resulted in neither romance nor financing.

The news of Barbra's dates with Milchan frightened Jon. He harbored hope that he and Barbra might smooth out their problems, and the thought of her with another man made him face the awful possibility that he might lose Barbra forever. He pleaded with her to take him back, and finally she did. She loved him after all, in spite of their problems, and as Jon had said, on their good days they could still 'fly over the universe.'

In 1976 Barbara Walters asked Barbra and Jon whether they could envision themselves growing old together. 'Yes,' Jon replied quickly.

'No one else would have us,' Barbra added.

O n May 13, 1980, eyebrows shot up around Hollywood with the
announcement from Universal Studios that Barbra would replace
Lisa Eichhorn as Gene Hackman's co-star in the low-profile romantic
comedy *All Night Long*, which was already three weeks into principal photography. Even more surprising were the details: Streisand had agreed to play
an essentially supporting role and had accepted second billing to Hackman
as well.

Word had it that tension between Eichhorn and the film's director,
Jean-Claude Tramont, had led to the actress's dismissal. But cynics doubted
the 'artistic differences' cliché and instead focused on Barbra's longtime
agent-confidante, Sue Mengers, who was married to Tramont. Many sensed
that the powerful Mengers, in a masterfully orchestrated campaign to save her
husband's problem-plagued film, had talked Streisand into doing the picture
as a personal favor. Why else, observers wondered, would a star of her stature
make such a seemingly unfathomable decision?

As details of the arrangement emerged over the next few weeks, the answer
became clearer: Barbra's salary for what was expected to be twenty-four-days'
work would be a stunning $4 million, plus 15 percent of the gross profits.

THE LONG AND troubled saga of *All Night Long* had begun in 1978, when
Jean-Claude Tramont, whose 1977 directorial debut, *Focal Point*, had fizzled
at the box office, approached Alan Ladd Jr at Twentieth Century-Fox about
doing a film based on 'food and immortality.' Given a tentative okay,
Tramont asked the screenwriter W.D. Richter to craft a sophisticated
romantic comedy that explored, in an offbeat way, one man's midlife crisis
and the events that spring from it.

Tramont had Gene Hackman in mind as the film's star from the outset, because he felt Hackman needed to soften his tough-guy image. Hackman, who had taken a three-year hiatus from the screen, liked Richter's quirky script. 'I didn't have to shoot anybody,' he explained. 'I didn't have to get beaten up or beat somebody up. It's just a lighter piece. And it works.'

Hackman was so enthusiastic, in fact, that he offered to lower his usual acting fee for a percentage of the film's profits. But Twentieth Century-Fox executives didn't share the actor's excitement, and the project was dropped from the studio's production schedule. Eventually it was picked up by Universal.

Richter's script told the story of George Dupler, a family man who throws a chair through his insufferable boss's office window and is demoted to the neon-lit lunacy of an all-night drugstore. In the process, he falls in love with Cheryl Gibbons, his muscle-bound son's older girlfriend, who, to further complicate matters, is married to a male chauvinist San Fernando Valley fireman. Cheryl's soft-spoken, sexy, submissive persona seems modeled after Marilyn Monroe, and this ultrafeminine fantasy has visions of country-western singing stardom dancing in her bleached-blond, lavender-kerchiefed head. Eventually, Dupler confronts a series of obstacles, ends his worn-out marriage, quits his job to become an inventor, and winds up with the giddy Gibbons. This 'realistic fairy tale,' as Tramont called it, would depend on strong casting to work, and Sue Mengers thought she had just the right actress to step into Cheryl's suburban slippers: her number one client, Barbra Streisand.

When Barbra read *All Night Long* she reportedly 'laughed her ass off.' Clearly Cheryl Gibbons, a character so unlike anything she had ever attempted on screen, offered her a rare acting challenge. She almost said yes, but she was deeply immersed in preproduction work on *Yentl*, and she wasn't thrilled by Cheryl's subordinate position in the story. Barbra had never been anything but the centerpriece of her films; other actors revolved around her, not she around them. So, with a tinge of regret, she turned the role down, went back to work on *Yentl*, and expected to hear little more about Tramont's film until its release.

After Barbra's pass, Tramont and casting director Anita Dann assembled the company quickly. Lisa Eichhorn, who had co-starred to splendid effect with Richard Gere in *Yanks*, was cast as Cheryl, Diane Ladd as George's put-upon wife, Dennis Quaid as his blockhead son, and Kevin Dobson as Cheryl's unsupportive husband.

The film, budgeted at $7 million, went into production in the San Fernando Valley on April 14. A week later Lisa Eichhorn arrived on the set, reportedly armed with vision, energy, and an attitude. After seven days of filming, Tramont decreed that Eichhorn was unsuitable. According to Tramont, 'The part was too much of a stretch for Lisa,' but he added gallantly, 'It's no reflection on her acting ability.'

Although the *Los Angeles Times* reported that 'observers on the set indicated that tension between the actress and both Hackman and Tramont contributed to her departure,' Hackman refused to join the public fray. '[Lisa's] got enough problems,' he said, 'and I've been fired myself. I know how it hurts.' A source close to the production concurred with the Eichhorn-as-diva scenario, saying she 'was very difficult on the set, objecting to things like camera angles as if she were . . . a star like Streisand.'

According to Eichhorn, 'What happened to me on *All Night Long* came as such a shock. I'd already done three and a half weeks' work on the film when, out of the blue, the director called and said, "I don't think it's working. You're just not funny. We've got someone else."'

That someone else, of course, was Barbra. As soon as Sue Mengers heard that her husband was unhappy with Eichhorn, she approached Barbra again. This time the stakes were much higher. In a flurry of backstage negotiations, Streisand accepted the role after she was offered the $4 million fee, a salary that set a new standard for female stars. The press pounced on the money angle and dubbed Cheryl Gibbons the most expensive supporting role in film history.

Still, Mengers's dollar-drenched deal wasn't the only reason Streisand finally said yes. Still smarting from the criticism of her uneven performance in *The Main Event*, Barbra was eager to prove herself to an increasingly doubtful acting community. *All Night Long*, with its satirical look at life, love, and lust, fascinated her. So did dizzy, daffy, delectable Cheryl, abused and low on self-esteem, in so many ways Barbra's antithesis.

In the days that followed the Streisand casting bombshell, the whispers grew to a crescendo: Hackman couldn't handle the film alone, Tramont's direction was lackluster, the script needed further rewrites, Eichhorn had been a scapegoat, Streisand was valiantly trying to save a friend's sinking ship. But the subject of most of the tongue-wagging wasn't around to hear the latest theories: Barbra had checked into the Ashram in Calabasas, California, a health spa where she dropped fifteen pounds through a rigorous regimen of exercise and Spartan cuisine. To portray Cheryl the temptress, Streisand wanted her figure to look as tempting as possible.

THE ADDITION OF Streisand to *All Night Long* inflated Universal's opinion of the project immediately. 'The sales force loves it,' the screen writer William Goldman observed in his book *Adventures in the Screen Trade*, 'the advertising people are in ecstasy, *fabulous* Barbra Streisand is something very special.'

Robert Brown, the film's unit production manager, was equally excited, even though Streisand's signing had doubled the film's budget from $7 million to $14 million. 'It wasn't all her [salary],' he said. 'It was her entourage, the people that come with her, and the things you have to do to accommodate a star of her stature.' Although Brown had heard the rumors that Eichhorn was pushed out of the film only after Streisand decided she wanted to do it, he remains uncertain about the actual sequence of events.

'I did hear a little bit in the beginning,' Brown recalled, 'that there was a move afoot to replace Lisa Eichhorn, and the next thing I was told was that it had been done, that Barbra Streisand had replaced her, and I needed to come up with a new budget.' The ballooned ledger, Brown recalled, included 'a special motor home [for Streisand] and a driver assigned to her, renting a limousine, and her own makeup, hair, and wardrobe people. Often you end up paying for a personal secretary or assistant of some sort that's with her all the time. There's just a lot of extra care that goes into supporting somebody like her.'

None of this seemed to trouble Gene Hackman. 'Sure, the script is being rewritten for her,' he confided. 'The way the part was written, it wasn't that big and would be a waste of her time and talents. But I'm not afraid she's going to take over the picture. Yes, she can be difficult. So can I. Show me an actor who's not difficult and I'll show you a mediocre actor . . . I'm sure everything will be fine.' Hackman downplayed rumors that Barbra, whether she wanted to or not, would steal the picture from under his nose. 'It's mostly my film. She has five or six good scenes, and that's it . . . it's about my character, not hers.'

✵

THE COSTUME DESIGNER Albert Wolsky was faced with the challenge of creating Cheryl's tacky wardrobe. 'Cheryl's a woman with strawberry blond hair that's always too done, fingernails that are always a little too brightly polished, clothes that are always a little too tight, a little too young,' he said. 'Whether draped in a lavender pantsuit, a peach-colored sweater and slacks, or an all-black funeral ensemble with peekaboo detail work, the look was tacky, tempting and titillating. It was also cheap. The clothes are not expensive, but Barbra doesn't care about that. If she loves it, she doesn't care if it costs two dollars or two thousand.'

Streisand's fame got in the way of her preparation as an actress when she went to a country-western bar in the San Fernando Valley in an attempt to better understand Cheryl. 'I put on a blond wig and ridiculous clothes and many jewels and all this, you know? And as soon as I walked in the door I heard someone say, "Oh, hi, Barbra!" I thought, I don't believe this! Now they think I have this lousy taste!'

AFTER A THREE-WEEK shutdown to prepare for Barbra's assumption of the role, *All Night Long* resumed shooting in South Pasadena amid a barrage of press coverage. With Streisand on board, everyone concerned felt the modest picture's streak of bad luck was finally over. *All Night Long* would certainly be a blockbuster.

'I was dreading working with her because I'd heard stories,' Dennis Quaid admitted. His fears evaporated almost immediately after Barbra's arrival on the set. 'I was really surprised, because she was helpful on the set. She has definite ideas and works very hard. If you can't keep up with her, that's your problem.' Years later Quaid was still enthralled with his brief acting encounter with Streisand. 'She was wonderful. She's very generous and she's real smart. She actually does have this glow about her. A beautiful woman. She's something else.'

Streisand came to work every morning in her studio-rented limousine until, in a clever ploy to make even more money, she decided to use her own Bentley instead. According to Robert Brown, 'Her contract called for us to rent a limousine to bring her to work and to take her home. And she asked me one day if I could rent the Bentley from her instead of [using] the limousine, and I said yeah, I'd be happy to. Might as well give the money to her. We paid her the exact same thing we'd paid the limo service.' Typically, a short time later, Barbra changed her mind. 'She asked us *not* to do that after she'd ridden in it a couple of times,' Brown continued, 'because in the limousine she could stretch out, and she could have her secretary with her so they could conduct business. In the Bentley she really didn't have the room.'

ONE OF BARBRA'S funniest scenes in *All Night Long* has Cheryl at the piano, composing a 'country-Hawaiian' ditty entitled 'Carelessly Tossed.' Robert Brown remembered that for the scene 'her husband in the movie was supposed to get very exasperated with her and tell her to quit fooling around and get the housework done. But when we started to film that scene, she opened her mouth and this incredible voice came out. And everybody on the set just stood there with their mouths open listening to this. Then she stopped because she was supposed to be singing *badly*. She really had to concentrate to sing badly. But it was astounding being in the room with her, and hearing her voice come out. Of course, I'd heard it on recordings many, many times, but being right there with her was a memorable experience.'

Brown observed no temperament from Streisand. 'She treated Tramont with respect. I thought perhaps she might start trying to direct herself, but she didn't. She did have some suggestions at times. Some he followed, some he didn't.' Barbra's only 'demand' during filming had to do with her Ashram-reduced figure. 'There was one shot that was particularly a request of Barbra's,' Brown continued. 'She was very proud that she'd lost all this weight. And in the story, there's a shot of her going up the stairs from below. She definitely wanted that because she thought it really showed off all the weight she'd lost.'

On July 20, just four days before *All Night Long* was scheduled to complete production, a long-threatened actors' strike began. 'Conspicuously hard hit by the strike is Universal's Barbra Streisand starrer,' *Daily Variety* reported. Barbra returned to her work on *Yentl* and waited out a resolution of the labor dispute. *All Night Long*'s bad luck had returned.

WHILE STREISAND THE actress sat at home on strike, Streisand the singer had a new album on release that would become the biggest seller of her career. She had been looking for a new producer, someone who could bring a distinct style and cohesion to a collection of songs. She thought of the Bee Gees – Barry, Robin, and Maurice Gibb – whose bouncy pop sound had produced six number one singles in a row and propelled the 1977 sound track of *Saturday Night Fever* to sales of eleven million copies. 'I really think their music is wonderful,' Barbra said.

In July of 1979 Barbra and Jon had attended a Bee Gees concert at Dodger Stadium in Los Angeles. Sixty thousand people filled the seats, and Barbra said to Jon as they came in, 'Can you imagine filling up this many seats? Sixty thousand people would never come to see me.' As she sat down, Barbra recalled, 'the audience spotted me and started to applaud. And it was like I was in shock. I couldn't believe they would respond to me in that way. It was really thrilling.'

The thought of working with Barbra made Barry Gibb wary. 'I was very nervous at first,' he admitted. 'We all had heard the stories about how tough she is, and she is this *enormous* star. That's got to intimidate anyone. I didn't want to do it at first, but my wife told me to do it or she'd divorce me.' Still unsure, Gibb called Neil Diamond to find out what it was like to work with Streisand. 'He had nothing but glowing reports, so I felt a little less scared.'

Charles Koppelman, working on his fourth straight project for Barbra, sent Barry, the handsome, wavy-haired main composer and lead singer of the group, five songs Barbra wanted to do as one side of the new record. 'My brother Robin and I didn't think any of them had the little extra bit that it takes to make a hit,' Barry said. 'We told her [associates] that, and they asked *us* to write five songs.' Two weeks later Barry played the new tunes for Barbra at the Malibu ranch. 'She loved them,' he recalled. 'It was as easy as that. We hit it off straight away and Barbra asked us to write the other side of the record, too.'

Then matters became a little touchy. In addition to Barry's producing fee, the group's manager, the high-powered Robert Stigwood, demanded three-quarters of the performance royalties for the brothers, on the theory that they were three voices and Barbra was only one. 'But they all sound alike,' Barbra reportedly retorted. 'How much for just one?' A compromise brought the Bee Gees a 50 percent cut of the royalties.

With finances out of the way, 'creative differences' arose and almost killed the collaboration. 'This project could have been a disaster,' Koppelman said. 'You're dealing with a lot of egos here . . . I'm sure Barry was apprehensive at some point that Barbra wouldn't like the music or that she'd want her vocals too far out and the tracks too far back. I'm sure Barbra at certain times was concerned that she didn't want a Bee Gee-esque album.'

'She knew what she wanted,' Barry recalled, 'and I knew what I wanted. We treaded on eggs until we actually got to know one another.' Gibb said he came 'this far away' from quitting, but all went smoothly after he called a summit conference with Barbra 'to work out any differences and come to a mutually acceptable working arrangement. There was never any animosity.' Once Barry had earned Barbra's complete trust, she said to him, 'Just call me when you're ready for me to sing.'

Guilty – named after a song written at the last minute to replace one Barbra didn't think worked – was released in September 1980. By then the first single, 'Woman in Love,' had hit number one, and *Guilty* reached that pinnacle on the album charts as well. With two more singles climbing into the Top 10, the album sold over 10 million copies worldwide and reached number one in twelve countries. It has remained Barbra's most successful album and a state-of-the-art example of 1980s pop.

Clearly Barbra Streisand and the Bee Gees were a match made in heaven. Writing for Streisand had pushed the Gibbs beyond their lightweight pop sensibilities; for this album they produced complex melodies and even more complex – some would say obscure – lyrics. More importantly, the singular Bee Gees sound had brought to the tracks just the cohesion that Barbra had hoped for.

The critics were largely ecstatic. Stephen Holden wrote in *The New York Times* that *Guilty* 'proves to be a sensational blending of talents, since the pair fill in each other's weakness while reinforcing their strengths . . . With less importance placed on rhythm, Mr Gibb concentrates even more on melody, his strongest forte, and serves up an ice cream sundae of pretty tunes . . . Even the angrier love songs have a celestial sweep. For in Miss Streisand's voice the concepts of love, glamour, and stardom are virtually inseparable . . . As a pop confection celebrating the giddiest extremes of the star ethos, *Guilty* is just about perfect.'

THREE MONTHS AFTER it began, the actors' strike was resolved, and Barbra returned from a trip to Paris to resume filming one of *All Night Long*'s final scenes: a jubilant, if secretly terrified, Cheryl slides down a firehouse pole into the arms of George Dupler. Designed as the symbolic ending of Cheryl's marriage to her sexist fireman husband, Cheryl's fall to liberty proved a nerve-racking experience for Barbra, who had gained back fifteen pounds during her hiatus. The moment was captured without incident, though, and *All Night Long* finally wrapped.

Yet just when Jean-Claude Tramont and Sue Mengers thought the long ordeal was over, another more personal controversy arose as the film was being edited: Barbra and Sue Mengers severed their longtime personal and professional relationship. Talk surfaced that Barbra had refused to pay Mengers and ICM their customary 10 percent commission because she had stepped into the film as a favor. Barbra may have felt that way, but of course Mengers was paid. Barbra had a contract with ICM, and all of her salary checks went directly to the agency, which deducted its commission and sent the remainder to Barbra's business managers. A more likely reason for the falling-out was that Mengers did not feel she could get behind Barbra's obsessive drive to make *Yentl*. Whatever the reason, the days of Barbra recording a one-of-a-kind collection of French love songs for Tramont and Mengers as a wedding gift were definitely over.

After a number of disgruntled audience members walked out of several screenings of the picture, Universal took the film away from Tramont and re-edited it to feature Streisand more prominently. The strategy didn't work; *All Night Long* still felt as if it actually did last all night long. Dennis Quaid complained, 'I don't think the film worked on a lot of different levels – in the timing of it, in the relationships. It seemed long to me. It only ran an hour and a half, but it seemed like two hours and ten minutes.'

Worried about the film now, Universal's promotion department decided to tout it as a zany comedy in the vein of *What's Up, Doc?* and *For Pete's Sake*. The ads featured a smarmy sketch of Streisand sliding down a large phallic fire pole, her skirt blowing up à la Marilyn Monroe to reveal her panties, as

Hackman, Quaid, and Dobson leer at her from below. 'She has a way with men,' the copy read, 'and she's getting away with it – *All Night Long.*'

For the film's official opening on March 6, 1981, Barbra, swathed in white mink, attended a private screening party hosted by Tramont and Mengers in New York. Described by *People* magazine as 'cool' to everyone but Hackman and Tramont, Barbra never spoke to Mengers, fueling further rumors that whatever had occurred between them was unlikely to be forgotten anytime soon.

A majority of American critics rebuffed *All Night Long*, although the film did win a small but vociferous group of devotees, including *The New Yorker's* Pauline Kael, who raved over Tramont's 'idiosyncratic fairy-tale comedy about people giving up the phony obligations they have accumulated and trying to find a way to do what they enjoy.' While a number of critics praised Barbra's toned-down performance, Kael found fault with the characterization, saying that 'we don't know who Streisand is. She doesn't use her rapid-fire New York vocal rhythms in this movie, and a subdued Streisand doesn't seem quite Streisand . . . She's a thin-faced, waif-like question mark walking through the movie.'

Unfortunately there was no question about the box office. Despite the ad campaign that promised moviegoers the kind of Streisand comedy they had loved in the past, even the opening weekend receipts were dismal. Eventually the film grossed only $10 million, equalling *Up the Sandbox* as Barbra's least successful film. Among those who had seen the picture, word of mouth was so poor that *The New York Times* wrote an article about it: 'Most pictures that fail commercially do so because of audience indifference. *All Night Long*, a comedy starring Gene Hackman and Barbra Streisand, has joined the select group of movies that audiences actively despise . . . the film is obviously a disappointment to Miss Streisand's fans, and the audience for an askew French-style comedy has never been tempted to sample the movie.'

In 1985 Gene Hackman remembered the failure of *All Night Long* with regret. 'Universal was advertising [the picture] in the theater section of *The New York Times* in a tiny little box . . . obviously they had no faith in the film . . . they didn't know how to sell it. It didn't fall into any kind of particular category that they had any expertise in.'

Barbra's opinion of *All Night Long* can be surmised from a comment she made to Lisa Eichhorn in a telephone conversation shortly after the film opened: 'You were well out of it, kid.'

Barbra tried to hide her nervousness as she walked into Sherry Lansing's office on the Twentieth Century-Fox lot, carrying a reel of super 8 film and an audiocassette. She had just lost financial backing from United Artists for *Yentl*, the project that she had struggled for years to bring to the screen as star, director, co-writer, and producer, the project that had obsessed her, had become her 'life,' her 'passion,' her 'dream.'

Every studio in Hollywood had turned the idea down at least once, including Fox, but Barbra was sure that Lansing, newly installed as the first female president of a major studio, would agree to finance this story of a Jewish woman in 1904 Poland who is forced to masquerade as a man in order to fulfill her dream of pursuing religious and philosophical study forbidden to women. Barbra had shot film of herself walking through the streets of Prague dressed in her masculine guise, and she had made a tape of many of the songs that Michel Legrand and the Bergmans had written for her to sing in the picture.

'It was like being eighteen again and auditioning for a Broadway show,' Barbra recalled. She showed Lansing the film to prove that she could look convincing enough as a man. She played the tape to impress on her that this would be *a Streisand musical.* She excitedly told the story, often playing two or three parts in order to act out a scene.

Lansing listened politely, then turned Barbra down, echoing every other executive in Hollywood as she listed her reasons: 'The story's too ethnic, too esoteric. We just don't see Middle America paying to see this movie. We don't think audiences will buy you as a boy, Barbra. You're fantastic; you're the number one box-office star. Why risk all that? [When] you have an idea for a comedy, we'll talk!'

'I left the office in tears,' Barbra said. 'I couldn't believe that a woman wouldn't understand how universal this story was. I always thought of it as a very contemporary story, a love story that would appeal to people around the world.' Devastated, she went back to Malibu and took to her bed. But not for long. The more rejections she got on this picture, the more firmly resolved she became to prove everyone wrong. 'When you tell Barbra something's not possible,' Marilyn Bergman said, 'all you're doing is firing her up.'

BARBRA'S ONETIME ROOMMATE Elaine Sobel said that she told Streisand about Isaac Bashevis Singer's short story 'Yentl, the Yeshiva Boy' in the early 1960s, but Barbra recalls that she read it for the first time in 1969 when the producer Valentine Sherry sent it to her after her then-agent David Begelman had turned it down without consulting her. 'They were smart enough to send it directly to my house,' Barbra recalled, 'and it was [only] twenty-five pages long and the print was big so I thought, Well, I'll read it in one afternoon.'

When she finished it, she called Begelman and flatly announced, 'I just found my next movie – "Yentl, the Yeshiva Boy."'

'Oh, no,' Begelman replied. 'We just said you weren't interested.'

'What do you mean? I *am* interested.'

'Barbra,' Begelman said, 'for a year you've been telling us that you want to change your image onscreen, that you're tired of playing Jewish girls from Brooklyn. So now you want to play a Jewish *boy?*'

Yes, she did, even though Begelman advised her strongly that the move could damage her burgeoning career. The story had moved her deeply, from its first four words: 'After her father's death . . .' She thought of the piece as 'a poem' to Emanuel Streisand. 'He was a teacher and a scholar just like Yentl's father,' she explained. 'It was my way of saying to my father that I was proud to have him as my papa, that I was proud to bear his name – Streisand.'

She also felt a spiritual kinship with Yentl, the ever-questioning teenager whose make-believe world is turned upside down when she falls in love with a fellow rabbinical student who thinks she's a man. 'I related to this story on many levels,' Barbra said. 'Yentl wants to learn; Barbra always wanted to learn. I was always curious. I wanted to learn Japanese writing when I was sixteen. I read Zen Buddhism and Russian novels. I love knowledge. I was struck by the many similarities between myself and Yentl. And I would have done the same thing she does. I would have dressed up in my father's clothes and gone out as a boy to pursue my dream.'

Barbra optioned the screen rights to the story in 1969, intending only to star in the film, which she saw as a non-musical. Two years later Barbra's company, First Artists, announced that the picture, to be called *Masquerade*, would be produced by Valentine Sherry, directed by the Czechoslovakian

Ivan Passer, and written by Passer and Isaac Singer. The budget, in keeping with First Artists' strict requirements, was set at a mere $2 million. As soon as the announcement was made, the jokes began. *The New York Times* headlined its story, 'A new movie for Barbra: "Funny Boy."'

The package soon fell apart, mainly because Barbra wasn't satisfied with any of the three drafts Passer had produced, first with Singer and then with Jerome Kass. She spoke to another Czech director, Milos Forman, about the movie – clearly she wanted someone who understood Mitteleuropa – but he wasn't interested. Even then, he said, he could tell that Barbra 'was thinking about directing. I don't think anybody could have satisfied her when it came to that project because it was her love affair. It may have been subconscious, but I think she didn't let things happen [to bring the project to fruition at that time] because she had her own vision of it and nobody could even come close.'

She wouldn't let go. During the first weekend they spent together in 1973 Barbra read Jon Peters the short story. After *A Star Is Born*, she decided that in order to make the film exactly as she envisioned it, she would have to direct it. 'I was frightened to direct. I didn't know if I could do it. But I was nearing forty years old and thinking that I must take more risks as an artist and as a person . . . I had this vision of becoming this old lady and talking about this movie I should have made.'

She shopped the idea around to every major studio in Hollywood, but now executives had another reason to turn it down: they didn't feel they could trust a novice director, and a woman at that. Female directors had been few and far between in Hollywood, and the male chauvinist attitude in the industry was that women couldn't be trusted with multimillion-dollar budgets. Warner Brothers, for which Barbra's films had grossed $162 million, said no. Columbia, for which her films had grossed $226 million, said no. Fox, MGM, United Artists, all turned her down. The one hope the bigwigs gave Barbra was that if she turned it into a musical, they *might* be interested. But at this point she didn't see it as anything but a small drama.

She filed the idea away again, but during the spring of 1979, in the midst of doing *The Main Event*, she finally made up her mind to do whatever was necessary to make *Yentl* a reality. Nearly everyone in her inner circle, including Sue Mengers and Jon Peters, had advised her not to pursue the project; and now that Barbra was in her late thirties, the likelihood that she could pull off a masquerade as a rabbinical student in his twenties seemed all the more remote.

Jon recalled that the moment of crystallization for Barbra occurred during a *Main Event* location shoot in the San Bernardino Mountains. 'We were standing there in the snow, and she said, "I *hate* this movie! I'm going to do *Yentl!*" I said, "You're not going to do it!" I had offers for her to go to Vegas, to do shows, for twenty million, thirty million dollars. She turned them all down. I said, "You're not going to ruin your life and mine! You can't play a *boy!* We're gonna do something else together." . . . I was a little domineering, I guess, and I remember her looking at me and saying, "Just because you said that, I'm going to do the movie, *no matter what!*"'

BARBRA AND HER brother, Sheldon, stood by their father's grave at Mount Hebron Cemetery in Queens in the fall of 1979. Barbra had not visited her father's resting place since she was seven, when she had insisted her mother take her there. 'My mother never talked about my father because she said she didn't want me to miss him,' Barbra said. 'I never had a picture of myself with my father. I thought I was born of an immaculate conception, you know, since I never knew him.'

She asked Sheldon to take her picture standing next to her father's headstone, because 'at least that shows that he existed.' Sheldon reminisced for Barbra about the man he remembered, and recollected the sad ritual of his funeral. When she saw the photograph, Barbra noticed that the man buried next to her father was named Anshel. 'I couldn't believe it,' she said. 'That's a very unusual name. I mean, it's not like Irving. And right there next to my father's grave was a man named Anshel, who was Yentl's dead brother whose name she takes when she disguises herself as a boy. To me it was a sign, you know, a sign from my father that I should make this movie.'

Another sign from Emanuel Streisand came later that night, according to Barbra. Sheldon, who was now forty-four and a real estate executive, told his sister that he had gone to see a medium, 'a nice Jewish lady with blond hair' who had been visited by a spirit when she was thirteen years old and had had extrasensory powers ever since. 'I can't tell you the experience I had last night,' Sheldon said. 'I talked to Daddy. We put our hands on this table, and the table moved its legs and started to spell out Daddy's name. Then the table followed me around the room.'

Because this was coming from her brother, a sensible suburban family man, Barbra believed it, and she asked him to bring the psychic to his house. She and Sheldon joined the woman around a table and put their palms on the tabletop. Suddenly the table started to move, and Barbra felt suspicious; she figured that an electrical hookup must be causing the motion. Then 'the table started to spell out letters with its legs.' One tap was *a*, two taps *b*, and so on. 'I started to get very scared. The table was pounding away. Bang, bang, bang! Spelling "M-a-n-n-y," and then "B-a-r-b-r-a." I got so frightened I ran away. Because I could feel the presence of my father in that room! I ran into the bathroom and locked the door.'

When Barbra got up the courage to come back, the medium asked the spirit of Emanuel Streisand, 'What message do you have?' The table tapped out 'S-o-r-r-y.' 'What else do you want to tell her?' 'S-i-n-g p-r-o-u-d' was the answer.

'It sounds crazy,' Barbra admitted, 'but I know it was my father who was telling me to be brave, to have the courage of my convictions, to *sing proud!*'

'THIS HAS TO be a musical!' Marilyn and Alan Bergman exclaimed in unison to Barbra when she showed them a script she had just finished working on. The lyricists had held that opinion for some time, but had kept it to themselves because they were sensitive to the fact that Streisand saw the film as an intimate non-musical drama. But finally they decided they had to try to change her mind. 'We felt it was a wonderful story for a musical . . . because it is [about] a character with a secret,' Marilyn explained. 'Throughout the picture, after her father dies, there is nobody to whom she can talk, to whom she can reveal her essential self. And this rich inner life becomes the [song] score.'

Aware that the studios would be more likely to back the film as a musical, and aware too that its chances of box-office success would be far greater if she sang, Barbra thought seriously about the Bergmans' suggestion. It didn't take her long to come around. Music, she now felt, would 'elevate the piece to something magical, a fairy tale.'

There was never any question that the music should be lush, romantic, and rooted in the European tradition, which made Michel Legrand the clear choice to compose it. 'The kind of music Michel writes is timeless,' Alan Bergman said. 'It could be eighteenth, nineteenth, or twentieth century.'

Marilyn added, 'The challenge was to make the music exotic and colorful, but not so special that it doesn't have universality. And Michel achieved that.'

Once she decided to make *Yentl* a musical, Barbra plunged into the process with her usual gusto. She and Legrand would meet at the Bergmans' house in Beverly Hills and spend the entire day working in the upstairs music room. 'Our housekeeper would bring us food trays and we'd eat up there,' Alan recalled. 'Sometimes we'd go late into the night. It was like there was no outside world . . . The greatest thing about working on the movie, was – where else in the world could you call your director and say, "Come over and sing this song for us"?'

As they worked, Legrand and the Bergmans confronted a realization that made Barbra uncomfortable: if the film's music was meant to represent Yentl's inner thoughts, no one else should sing in the movie. 'That was a decision that was hard to arrive at,' Alan said. 'Barbra was afraid that it might not be perceived properly, but it became more and more inevitable. She is the musical narrator of the piece. Nobody else is part of that inner music.'

According to Marilyn, 'It was almost the same way when Barbra tried to create scenes in which Yentl didn't appear, so she could stay behind the camera wearing only her director's hat. But each time that was tried, we felt that the audience wouldn't know how it was privy to that moment if Yentl wasn't there. The picture is told through her perceptions, seen through her eyes.'

For one of the musical numbers she had conceived with Legrand and the Bergmans, 'Tomorrow Night,' Barbra made a video. 'The four of us were like children playing,' Marilyn said. 'We videotaped the first musical performance in our living room.' Marilyn and Alan played two tailors trying to fit Anshel into a bridegroom outfit. 'We laughed hysterically!' Marilyn recalled. 'What a pair of tailors we made!'

WITH AN IMPRESSIVE original song score to sweeten the project, Barbra once again sought studio backing late in 1979. After several rejections, her dream finally seemed about to come true. Eric Peskow and Mike Medavoy, partners in Orion Pictures, gave her the green light to direct, produce, and star, providing that she could guarantee the film would cost no more than $13 million to make. She hired Rusty Lemorande to help her produce the film, and asked him to come up with separate budget estimates for making the movie in Los Angeles and overseas.

Barbra's biggest concern now was the script, which she felt was far from filmable. Medavoy, having already given her the okay to do practically everything else, suggested she write the movie too. 'You seem to know so well what it is you want,' he told her.

'She wrote out of necessity,' Lemorande recalled. 'I got a tremendous lesson in writing by being at the knee of this process – where she and I would do a draft and then I would find it being critiqued by the likes of Paddy Chayefsky, Elaine May, David Rayfiel, Bo Goldman . . . A lot of people were constantly giving her opinions when she asked for them.'

To make sure she wrote the best possible script, Barbra immersed herself in Judaism, just as Yentl had. She pored over the Torah, attended Bible study classes, went to Hasidic weddings. She became involved in a small Orthodox synagogue in Venice, California, and helped Jason prepare for his bar mitzvah, a ceremony the boy probably would not have participated in had his mother not become so obsessed with Yentl's world. Rabbi Daniel Lapin officiated at the mitzvah, and for months afterward Barbra studied under him. In appreciation, she bestowed a large gift on the rabbi's Jewish day school, which was renamed the Emanuel Streisand School.

The work on the script consumed Barbra. As she wrote, she tried to address every objection she had heard. She raised Yentl's age so that she could more convincingly play her. 'I made her kind of amorphically ageless; I guessed she'd be around twenty-eight. A spinster of the time. A person who wasn't married by that age [in Yentl's time and place] was very, very odd.' She struggled with how to accurately re-create the world of passionate Talmudic scholars without making the movie too ethnic to have broad appeal.

She sought the help of anyone willing to give it. When the novelist and rabbi Chaim Potok told her that *Esquire* magazine wanted him to interview her for a cover story, she replied, 'I don't do interviews.' But she agreed to see him, just to get acquainted. During the meeting, she asked him if he would look over the script of *Yentl*, and Potok sensed an unspoken negotiation: help me with this screenplay and I'll give you an interview. Barbra later admitted as much to him: 'Why am I doing this interview? . . . I want you to help me. I mean, I want to know what you know as a writer and as a rabbi.'

Potok found Barbra's knowledge of the Jewish religion 'confused and rudimentary. Yet she asks questions openly, unselfconsciously, with no hint of embarrassment, and takes notes with the assiduous concentration of one long committed to learning. I have no way of gauging her comprehension. Her mind leaps restlessly, impatiently, from one subject to another: she wishes to know everything, and quickly. At those moments when a good idea comes suddenly from one or another of us, I see on her lips an amazed smile, a near-sensuous delight, and her eyes flash.'

Researching *Yentl* left a strong mark on Barbra. 'I felt more proud to be a Jew,' she said, and she had her eyes opened about a lot of philosophical issues. 'I don't believe God is a chauvinist. When you read the Bible there are two chapters of Genesis that have different interpretations of how woman was created . . . I believe that woman was not created from a rib . . . but was created equally, like it says in one of the chapters: God created Adam and then split him in two so that each side has masculine and feminine qualities. They're different but equal.'

Barbra also discovered that the Talmud does not prohibit women from studying, but says only that women are not *obliged* to study. 'Where is it written that women have to be subservient?' Barbra asked. 'You find that men have interpreted the law to serve themselves and society's needs. In other words, it is *not* written!'

BARBRA WALKED THROUGH the ancient cobblestoned streets of Prague, absorbing the somber ambience of the city, and felt herself transported to Yentl's time and place. It was the fall of 1980, and she and Rusty Lemorande had traveled to Czechoslovakia, where Barbra had decided she must film *Yentl* to ensure authenticity, to scout locations. 'I put on my Yentl costume and walked through the streets. I always wanted to try everything out, see what the black costume looked like against the color of the walls, against the textures, the cobblestones, the light of Czechoslovakia, the air. Every country has its own mists, its own light.'

She wanted the film to look, she said, 'like a Dutch painting . . . I love Rembrandt. When I was sixteen I paid ten dollars for a Rembrandt print of a woman bathing, and I had it hanging in my apartment when I moved away from home.' From Prague she went to Amsterdam, where the director Paul Verhoeven took her to the Rijks Museum. 'I wanted to see the Rembrandts in person, not just in a book because [in reality] the color of the Rembrandt paint is very dark brown, not black, and the edges of the faces are soft, not hard . . . It's very interesting because the light source in the Rembrandt paintings never shows. He had some of the light coming, in a sense, from within.'

A month after their return from Europe, Barbra and Lemorande had prepared a budget that kept within the $13 million limit Orion had placed on them. On the day Barbra submitted the numbers to the studio – November 19, 1980 – Michael Cimino's film *Heaven's Gate* opened in New York. Cimino, the heralded director of the Best Picture Oscar winner of 1978, *The Deer Hunter*, had been given carte blanche by United Artists on this new film, and his costs had ballooned from a projected $7 million to $38 million. Far worse, the picture was savaged by the critics as a plotless mess, an egregious example of self-indulgent auteurism. The studio pulled the three-and-a-half-hour picture from release and slashed seventy minutes from it, but it still flopped miserably and became one of the costliest film failures in history.

The fiasco created shock waves that rocketed through Hollywood – and scuttled Barbra's deal with Orion. *Heaven's Gate*, she said, 'changed the face of the motion picture industry. All of a sudden studios didn't want to hear about any movies over $10 million.' Neither did Orion want to take a risk with a novice director working with esoteric material on foreign locations. They pulled the plug, and *Yentl* was back at square one.

After Barbra suffered a new series of humiliating rejections, including Sherry Lansing's, Jon Peters came to the rescue. Barbra's unflagging determination to make *Yentl* had impressed and touched him, and now that it was to be a musical, he felt it just might work. He had formed PolyGram Pictures with Peter Guber, and the partners gave Barbra another green light. 'Boyfriends sometimes come in handy,' Barbra said with a laugh.

But the marriage with PolyGram wouldn't last. Barbra didn't like many of the ideas Jon and his fellow executives had for the film. 'We found ourselves butting heads,' he said, and that put renewed strain on their relationship.

'For personal reasons,' Barbra explained, 'we decided not to work together on this film. It was a time in my life when I needed to be really independent, both personally and professionally.'

Finally *Yentl* seemed about to settle at United Artists, which was, ironically, the studio that had produced *Heaven's Gate*, but several executive shake-ups left the studio's backing uncertain. 'Every time somebody said they'd make the movie they got fired,' Barbra said. 'You think that means something?' Finally David Begelman, Barbra's former agent, was put in charge of UA.

Despite his joke about Barbra wanting to play a Jewish boy, Begelman threw his support behind the project in June of 1981 – but with a great many conditions.

Before UA would approve a budget of $14 million, Barbra had to agree to take Directors Guild minimum, $80,000, for directing, and $3 million for acting, considerably less than she had received for *All Night Long*. If she went over budget, she would have to give back half her salary and would have to give up almost all her control over the movie. The studio had approval of the script and approval of her co-stars. Most galling to Barbra, the studio executives insisted she give them the right to approve her final cut, and if they didn't like it they could change it in any way they saw fit.

She had no choice but to agree to it all. 'I had to eat shit, put it that way,' she said. 'You want to do it, that's the way you get to do it . . . Nothing mattered to me except getting this movie made.'

MINDFUL OF THE possibility that another studio shake-up might leave her baby an orphan again, Barbra wasted no time putting the elements of *Yentl* together. She polished the script with the British writer Jack Rosenthal, who would share screenplay credit with her, and then turned her attention to one of the film's most vital elements: her co-stars.

To play Avigdor, the handsome, brooding rabbinical student who befriends Anshel (Yentl in disguise) and with whom Yentl falls in love, Barbra had her heart set on Richard Gere, who had made such a strong impact on audiences in *Days of Heaven* and *American Gigolo*. He met with Barbra and told her he was interested, but only if she didn't wear so many hats. 'He said he'd act in it if I didn't direct,' Barbra recalled, 'or he'd let me direct if I didn't act in it.' That was unacceptable to her, of course, as was Gere's reported asking price of $5 million, which she couldn't afford.

She considered a range of actors from Michael Douglas to John Shea to Kevin Kline before choosing Mandy Patinkin, who had played Che Guevara in *Evita* on Broadway and had made an impression in the film *Ragtime*. She liked Patinkin's 'passion,' she said, and was impressed when he told her he didn't think Avigdor as written was serious enough. 'He didn't have enough weight,' Patinkin recalled. 'We went back and forth, but the bottom line is [that Barbra] was absolutely open to whatever feelings I had. Almost every single thing from that initial meeting that I had questions about was satisfactorily changed by the time we shot it. So I was quite taken by how approachable and how caring she was about the piece, and about the material, on every level.'

Barbra had her Avigdor, and soon she would have her Hadass, his beautiful, compliant fiancée. When Barbra's first choice, Carol Kane, proved unavailable, she turned to Amy Irving, the bewitching star of *The Competition*. Barbra had met Amy when her live-in lover, Steven Spielberg, brought her with him to visit Barbra in Malibu in 1979. 'We spent the entire day at the ranch, and [Barbra] pitched *Yentl* to him,' Amy recalled in 1983. She was a little chagrined that day when Barbra couldn't remember her name, but said later, 'Now I realize that was evidence of Barbra's tunnel vision. When she zeroes in on something, she can think of nothing else.'

When Barbra approached her about playing Hadass, Amy was less than thrilled. 'My first reaction to *Yentl* was that it wouldn't be a challenge to me. I just felt like graduating from the young-sweet-thing characters.' Irving sent word to Barbra that she wasn't interested. 'Then everyone was down on me,' she recalled. 'My agent and everyone was saying at least [I should] meet with Barbra Streisand because they loved the project.'

Amy agreed. 'It was a very late-night meeting in her apartment in New York, and we sat and read the script together . . . She described to me things that I didn't read in it – the growing of Hadass's character so that you could see she actually has a mind. Barbra took me through a journey that I eventually did in the film . . . I just [hadn't] read the script very well.'

Barbra then hired the veteran actor Nehemiah Persoff to play her father, a character who did not appear in the short story. 'I have a father now – I created him,' she said with delight. 'Isn't he wonderful?'

WITH HER THREE main co-stars in place and the cinematographer of *Chariots of Fire*, David Watkin, set to photograph her dream, Barbra prepared to leave for London and Prague to begin preproduction. As the day approached, she began to have palpitations. She sensed that if directing *Yentl* represented a crossroad in her career, it was also apt to change her personal life forever. She and Jon, their relationship already shaky, would be separated for almost a year, and Barbra intimated that one of the reasons she had chosen to make the film in Europe was to get away from Jon for a while. 'I had to go away,' she said. 'Obviously there were problems. I had to leave.'

'We reached a point in our lives,' Jon said, 'where we both had to go in separate directions . . . [*Yentl*] was Barbra's statement, and [it offered her the] ability to be completely autonomous and make her own decisions.'

The responsibility weighed heavily on Barbra. 'I was so terrified for years,' she admitted. 'Terrified of failure; I felt I could never do this thing.' But she *could* do it, she told herself again and again, and she *would* do it. 'My mother always told me that my father died because he overworked. So I always felt if you worked too hard, you'd die. So it was like a test, a survival test, making *Yentl*. Could I survive this experience? Emotionally? Physically?'

The first day we were rehearsing *Yentl*,' Barbra said, 'I shook a prop man's hand, and his hand was all sweaty. So I asked him if he was nervous. He said yes, and I said, "Well, feel mine – I'm more nervous than you. And we're all going to make mistakes; me, I'm going to make most of them. So we're in this together."'

She proved she meant that, too. 'I was not afraid to say I didn't know something. I'd say, "This is what I'd like to do, but I don't know if it can be done. Can we try it?" And everybody got behind me and wanted to support me because I never threw my so-called power in their face. I wanted it to feel like a family, like we were all working toward the same goal.' The cast and crew, Barbra said, 'never treated me as a first-time director, or especially a *woman* first-time director.'

Amy Irving had her own opinion about why Barbra had few run-ins with members of the *Yentl* company: 'I think as long as she's directing, she's not taking someone else's job [by making suggestions]. The problem is that when she knows better than the director, it's frustrating for her to keep her mouth shut, so she doesn't, and it can bend people's noses the wrong way. When she's directing and producing her own films, she's a complete joy to work with.'

Barbra confirmed Amy's theory. 'That power was very humbling,' she said. 'I found myself being very soft-spoken, feeling even more feminine than I ever felt, more motherly, more nurturing, more loving. I had patience I never dreamed I would have.'

But to hear the London tabloids tell it, just the opposite was true. The Fleet Street press, who usually lie in wait for visiting American movie stars, jumped on Barbra from day one, criticizing her for arriving with fourteen pieces of luggage. What they didn't say was that the baggage belonged to an entourage of seven. The press continued to beat up on Barbra during the first few months of filming, which began with interiors at Lee International Studios outside London on April 14. Article after article painted the stereotypical portrait of Barbra as a tyrant who was hated by everyone.

Finally one of the crew, Bill Keenan, had had enough. 'Every paper I picked up seemed to be having a pop at her,' he explained, 'and I didn't think it was fair because I knew it wasn't true. Barbra wasn't like that.' Keenan decided to write a letter to the papers. After it had been typed up, he took it around to the rest of the company and asked them to sign it. 'There were over one hundred people on that set, and no one refused.'

'She has completely captivated us all,' the letter said in part. 'Although undoubtedly a perfectionist . . . she has shared jokes, chats and pleasantries each and every day. She appears to have no temperament, her voice is scarcely heard on the set, her smile is seen constantly. We have all worked with directors and stars who are the antithesis of Barbra Streisand, but whose antics don't reach the newspapers.'

Keenan sent the letter to every London newspaper, as well as to *The New York Times*, *Time*, and *Newsweek*. The only publication that printed it was a British movie magazine, *Screen International*.

BEFORE BARBRA DECIDED to hire David Watkin as her cinematographer, she had sat down with him to discuss the look she wanted for the film. Once they agreed that Dutch paintings were a good inspiration, Barbra told Watkin that she wanted to be filmed only from her left side.

'Hold it, Barbra,' Watkin replied. 'I think you're wrong about that. You have to think about the scene and how the scene is going to look. If you go all the way through the movie applying a formula, what have you got? You're walking through the film in a mask, and every scene looks the same. We don't want that. Once we get the right atmosphere for the scene, if you don't look good we'll take a step back and we'll do what we must to make you look good.'

Watkin's ideas pleased Barbra. 'If she hadn't liked my attitude,' Watkin said, 'then she would have used someone else. But because she was intelligent, sensible, and she saw what I was talking about, she took me on.'

Barbra, in fact, went a step further with Watkin's advice: 'I thought, What a perfect opportunity to use the right side of my face for Anshel, for me as a boy – to try to have a more masculine side, kind of a stronger side and a softer side.'

Barbra, Watkin, and his camera operator, Peter MacDonald, worked well together. 'She accepted ninety-eight percent of my suggestions,' Watkin said. 'She had strong ideas but didn't interfere with my work . . . She wanted magic for *Yentl*, and that's what she got.'

'He really can light a whole set,' Barbra said of Watkin, 'and the actors can walk anywhere in it and still everything looks right.' She admitted that he sometimes bristled at her suggestions. 'I would say, "David, why don't we raise the camera, put another light over here, let's add a little smoke, or something like that." And the crew used to say to him, "David, she's trying to get you an Academy Award. Don't fight!"'

One matter the forty-year-old Barbra was particularly sensitive about was her ability to look twenty-eight in the film. According to Watkin, that wasn't much of a problem at all. 'I have had a number of people who have been playing younger than they were, and I had to go to far greater lengths with them than I ever did with Barbra. If you light her carefully and sensibly, there's no problem. She was fine.

'But it was difficult when Barbra was tired or stressed. That's the worst thing. There were a couple of days where she was upset about something or pissed off about something, and it affected her appearance. She saw it in the video monitor, and she said to Peter MacDonald, "What can I do about this?" And he replied, "Get in a better mood." Which, of course, helped get her in a better mood.'

Nehemiah Persoff felt that Watkin was too cavalier about Barbra's appearance in *Yentl*: 'His work was brilliant, but he was insensitive to those needs of Barbra's created by her playing so much younger. That's a problem for anybody because there are lines on the face that have to be camouflaged. And there were times when it was very painful to sit there and see that he was unaware of the problem. She was very much aware of it, and very often she would tell them to move certain lights in order to hide a certain line.'

BARBRA SAT AT Amy Irving's feet, out of camera range, as she directed her in *Yentl*'s wedding-night scene. Eleven years earlier, Barbra had been deeply impressed when she visited Elliott in Sweden while he was making *The Touch* with Ingmar Bergman. 'The camera was on Elliott, and Ingmar was at his feet looking at him, talking to him,' she recalled. 'And I thought, Oh, my God, I'd love [to do] that . . . As an actress sometimes I wanted to give a little hint to the other actor about how it could be better. But I couldn't do that. I had to wait until the director told the actor, and sometimes I would see the director settle for something.

'So here I was having the opportunity to make up for all those moments when I felt frustrated. I wanted Amy to be funny and her instinct is to play a little more serious, but I was at her feet making her laugh, telling her jokes because I wanted certain reactions.'

Amy and Barbra got along beautifully, and the reason surely must have been Amy's attitude toward her position vis-à-vis Barbra. 'I knew this was her film, this was her everything. In order for me to do it, I knew I had to leave my ego in America and go to England and do whatever she wanted. And we got along fine because of that. I think that's what she deserves.'

She knew that her decision to trust Barbra was the right one, Amy said, when she realized how immersed in every aspect of the film Barbra was. 'She has an amazing eye for detail. She had her hand in everything, to the point that I realized, when she picked out the color of my lipstick, that it usually matched whatever fruit was on the set, or the color of the wallpaper. She was just so meticulous about it all . . . I was like a doll to her, and she made certain I looked my best absolutely all the time.'

As the day approached to film the moment when Hadass insists on kissing her husband, Anshel, who has done everything to avoid any physical contact with 'his' bride for weeks into the marriage, Amy noticed that Barbra was nervous. 'We rehearsed for a week before shooting,' Amy said. 'It's funny, during the romantic stuff, she was more nervous than I was. We'd go back to her dressing room to rehearse, but she'd never kiss, and when we finally did, that's when she said it wasn't so bad – it was like kissing an arm. Because it wasn't real passionate or anything. But she cut it off a lot quicker than I would have.'

Streisand's relationship with Mandy Patinkin, who was less inclined to put himself completely in Barbra's hands, proved problematic. Patinkin was disappointed at not being able to sing in the film, and he had difficulty dealing with the many hats Barbra wore. 'If I needed something from the producer,' he recalled, 'I would talk to her in a different way than I would with the director about a scene. Sometimes I'd be talking to the director, but I'd really be talking to the actress. But I didn't want to be talking to the actress, I wanted to talk to the director, and I certainly didn't want the *producer* to hear. Then I'd want the writer in on the discussion, and wait – the writer is here. It was wild.'

Patinkin has never spoken ill of Barbra, probably because of a clause in his contract that forbade it, but a source close to Barbra has confirmed that making *Yentl* was not a pleasant experience for the actor. David Watkin has offered a possible reason why. Although he wouldn't name the actor in question, it seems likely that he was talking about Patinkin, since he is the only member of the cast about whom there has been even a hint of discord with Barbra: 'Somebody wouldn't take direction. And Barbra's behavior, in regard to that person, was exemplary. She was patient. They wouldn't do something she wanted them to do, and I can remember she said very sweetly, "Perhaps if we do enough takes, they'll forget and do what I want."'

IN JULY THE *Yentl* cast and crew packed themselves off to the tiny Czech town of Roztyly, two and a half hours outside Prague, for exterior work. Barbra's mother had begged her not to go behind the Iron Curtain to make the movie. 'There are wars there, and people throw bombs,' Diana pleaded. 'And they don't have any fresh vegetables!'

But nothing mattered for Barbra except the movie. When Jon Peters went over to pay her a visit, he was appalled by the smell of raw sewage in the town. 'Barbra never noticed,' he said. 'There were flies the size of beetles, but they never bothered her. She just swatted them.'

By this time Barbra was close to exhaustion. She would rise at six in the morning, be made up and costumed by ten, film from ten until seven, go back to her hotel, have a quick dinner, and then work on the next day's lines and setups. According to David Watkin, 'Barbra would frequently telephone the camera operator at three-thirty in the morning and talk for an hour about the next day's work. He was awakened practically every night . . . Barbra is a worrier, I suppose is the best way to describe it.'

Never was she more so. 'I don't know how I survived it,' she said as filming came to a close. 'It was so overwhelming I was sick every morning on the way to work, just sick.' What did she worry about? Nearly everything. She fretted that the movie wouldn't turn out well. 'I would think, I'm going to be humiliated. They'll call me a fool, and I'll have to run away and live in China. It's a terrible, terrible fear, the fear that you're not good enough at what you do.' But, she said, 'I knew I had to be strong. I couldn't get sick, couldn't be too tired . . . I couldn't crumble, or everything else around me would crumble.'

BARBRA COMPLETED PRINCIPAL photography on *Yentl* in October 1982. The following April 1, the *Los Angeles Times* ran a headline in its movie section: 'Streisand Ousted as Producer.' The story revealed that a completion bond company that had insured the film for cost overruns had exercised its right to control the picture's editing because Barbra had gone 11 percent over budget, even though that was not so unusual for a foreign-location shoot. The bond had been sprung on Barbra by the studio the day before filming began. 'It was ridiculous,' she said, 'because they paid the company $700,000, which I needed in the movie. They didn't trust me – put it that way, I suppose.'

The bond company demanded that Barbra deliver the picture in its final form in six weeks or they would take it away from her and hire another filmmaker to finish it. Barbra begged them to give her ten weeks. 'I'm going to die from the pressure,' she told them. They refused. Working day and night on the editing and scoring, she did it. 'I did anything to get it done so that they could never take it away from me.'

The last hurdle Barbra faced with *Yentl* was the fact that UA had final cut approval. But 'the studio didn't touch my movie,' she said. 'Not a frame.'

ON NOVEMBER 16, 1983, the day *Yentl* opened in Hollywood, Barbra, trembling with anxiety, went to the theater to check the sound and the picture quality. 'And then I went to the nearest candy store and bought all the candy I could find and all the cookies I could find and a ham-and-cheese croissant and everything fattening and stuffed my face. Just trying to feed that fear that nobody would show up.'

She needn't have worried. The movie opened to tremendous fanfare amid a publicity blitz that put Streisand on the covers of half a dozen national magazines, and most of the reviews were rapturous. Of nine big-city newspapers and nine national magazines, fifteen gave the film strongly positive reviews, one review was mixed, and two, including *The New York Times*, panned it. Even *Time* and *Newsweek*, often antagonistic toward Barbra, raved about *Yentl*.

'It's rare to see such a labor of love, such emotion in almost every frame of a film,' David Ansen said in *Newsweek*. '*Yentl* means a great deal to Barbra Streisand, and she makes you feel this in a movie whose chief excellence is its passionate humanity. Director Streisand has given Star Streisand her best vehicle since *Funny Girl*.'

'The first thing to say about her, now that she's completely in control,' David Denby wrote in *New York*, 'is that the sweetness and even the delicacy of her finest moments as a young performer have returned, taken fresh root, and really flowered. The second thing to say is that Barbra Streisand is a good director.'

Pauline Kael felt that 'Streisand has made a technically admirable movie, with lovely diffuse, poetic lighting and silky-smooth editing. And she brings out the performers' most appealing qualities. It's a movie full of likable people.'

Most exciting of all for Barbra were the film's box-office grosses. The movie made $50 million in the United States – nearly as much as *The Way We Were* – and that much again overseas. The sound-track album sold three million copies worldwide and earned Barbra a huge two-dollar-per-album royalty.

Barbra had proven she could be a responsible producer and a visionary director. But characteristically she was far more hurt by the few potshots directed at the film than she was pleased by the praise. In February Isaac Singer published an 'interview with himself' in which he lambasted Barbra and the movie, saying that his Yentl was never meant to be a feminist, that she didn't sing, and that she wasn't in every scene in his story. 'I must say that Miss Streisand was exceedingly kind to herself [in the film],' Singer said. 'The result is that Miss Streisand is always present, while poor Yentl is absent.'

As much as that hurt, Barbra's worst reaction would come after a *Los Angeles Times* interview with her about the film. Barbra told the reporter an anecdote about showing Steven Spielberg the picture to seek any advice he might have. 'Don't change a frame,' he told her. When the piece ran, Spielberg's reaction was omitted, making it appear that Barbra had needed help with the picture from one of Hollywood's most successful directors. Barbra was devastated. 'That's like saying this woman, this actress, could not make the movie without the help of a man . . . I showed the film to a lot of people.'

Barbra has said that this journalistic betrayal, whether inadvertent or intentional, was the reason she didn't give another interview to the American press for eight years or direct another movie for nearly as long.

BARBRA JUST ABOUT fell out of her chair at the Golden Globe Awards ceremony on January 28 when her name was announced as Best Director. *Yentl* had received five nominations in the Musical or Comedy category, including Best Picture, which it had won, and Best Actress, which Barbra had not. Most observers expected the award in the Best Director category, which includes just five directors from both the dramatic and musical or comedy genres, to go to James L. Brooks, who had directed the quirky Shirley MacLaine-Debra Winger hit *Terms of Endearment*. That morning, Streisand learned she had been overlooked by the Directors Guild of America for their annual award, and thus she was truly stunned when she was named the first female to win a Golden Globe as Best Director.

'Directing for me was a total experience,' she told the crowd at the Beverly Hilton Hotel gala. 'It calls upon everything you've ever seen or felt or known or heard. It was really the highlight of my life. My professional life. This award is very very meaningful to me and I'm very proud, because it also represents, I hope, new opportunities for so many talented women to try to make their dreams realities, as I did.'

Barbra's euphoria didn't last long, however. On February 8 the Academy Award nominations were announced, and *Yentl* was shut out of all the top nominations but one. No Best Picture. No Best Actress. No Best Actor. No Best Director. No Best Cinematography. It got three nominations for its music, however, and one for its art direction, plus a Best Supporting Actress nod for Amy Irving.

Most observers found the snubs outrageous. Gregg Kilday wrote in the *Los Angeles Herald Examiner*, 'One needn't be a rabid fan of *Yentl* or a Streisand fanatic to accuse the Academy of a serious sin of omission in banning *Yentl* from all important award categories . . . Instead, as if it were telling Streisand to stay in her place, the Academy awarded a token nomination to Amy Irving who, tellingly, played a conventional Jewish woman in the movie.'

People magazine ran an article that attempted to explain the slight. Among the theories put forth: Hollywood hated Barbra; Hollywood was jealous of Barbra's success, especially after the project had been ridiculed for so many years; Hollywood was sexist (of the 224 members of the directors' branch of the academy, who did the nominating for Best Director, only 'a couple' were women); and Hollywood just didn't think the movie was good enough.

The movie was clearly good enough; what worked against Barbra was a complex cocktail of feelings and prejudices in Hollywood, some that had to do with her and some that didn't. 'We're still very primitive male chauvinists,' Nehemiah Persoff said. 'If Warren Beatty had done this movie, they would have worshiped him again.'

Only one woman had been nominated as Best Director in the forty-six-year history of the academy, the Italian Lina Wertmuller, so a female would always face an uphill battle being accepted by one of the oldest old-boy networks in America. When that female happened to be Barbra Streisand, with all the ill will many Hollywood insiders still felt toward her, the chances of getting an Oscar nomination would be very slim.

On the evening of the Academy Awards ceremony, a large and noisy protest against the shutout of Streisand, called by the group Principles, Equality and Professionalism in Film, distracted the stars and industry executives as they made their way into the Dorothy Chandler Pavilion. The protesters waved signs that read, 'Oscar at 56 – Is he still a closet chauvinist?' and 'Oscar, Can You Hear Me?' Inside, *Yentl* did manage to win one statuette, for Best Original Film Score.

Whatever the extent of the recognition she received for the movie, Barbra fairly burst with pride that she had made *Yentl* at all, and made it so well.

More than anything else in her professional life, the years she had spent toiling on the film had changed her. 'It was a beautiful experience,' she said. 'It was a feeling where all the parts of myself, the feminine parts, the masculine parts, the part of me that is a mother, that is nurturing, that is loving, is combined with having to become my own father – that was normally the director, you know? I was always trying to please "Papa" [her director], and now I had to please myself. Just like Yentl dressed in the clothes of her father, in a sense I became my father.'

AT THE END of *Yentl*, the following dedication appears: 'To my father . . . and to all our fathers.'

When Diana Kind saw this, she said, 'Why didn't you dedicate the movie to me too?'

'Because you're *alive*, Mama!' Barbra replied. 'You have the gift of *life!*'

When Mrs Kind didn't seem placated, Barbra added, 'Don't worry, Mama. I'll dedicate my next movie to you.'

I'm not thinking of men now,' Barbra had said while she prepared *Yentl* for release. 'There is no one. I'm married to *Yentl*.' During the more than eighteen months that Barbra spent in Europe, her relationship with Jon Peters had unraveled. They had been moving apart for several years, of course, and the prolonged separation destroyed any possibility that they might be able to iron out their problems.

'I don't think she chose between me and the film,' Jon said. 'She chose the film, and then it was time for us to separate.'

While she worked, reports had filtered back to Barbra that Jon was bringing women to the ranch in her absence. He was seen holding hands with the model Lisa Taylor at a New York nightclub. When Barbra returned to Malibu in the fall of 1983 after editing and scoring the picture in London, she and Jon kept very much to their own houses on the property. Then she heard a new rumor: that Jon was involved with a local real estate saleswoman. Barbra was reportedly so angry that when Jon parked his car on her side of the property late one night she had it towed away.

In February 1984, although Jon would still act as Barbra's manager for several more years, he sold all of his Malibu acreage to her, which formalized their breakup. The decision had been Barbra's, and Jon was stunned by the awful finality of it. 'It's a hard one for me to talk about because I love her and feel so close to her,' he said at the time. 'I'm still not exactly sure why we broke up.'

Barbra spoke guardedly about the end of the relationship to European journalists. 'Before, I was afraid to be alone. There was a void inside me. Now I have myself. I feel fulfilled from within. Jon and I are not living together, but we're better friends now. We're less competitive, much more respectful ... We'd been taking each other for granted, the way people do when they live together for a long time. We don't do that anymore.'

Early in her relationship with Jon, Barbra had marveled at how wonderful it was to love someone who was so much like her. Now she seemed to have changed her mind. 'Elliott was sweet and gentle, whereas Jon was aggressive and unpredictable. Maybe I need someone in between . . . Maybe someone has to have a mate with a different personality.'

Barbra wasted little time before looking for a new beau. She cozily chatted with Richard Gere over dinner in an intimate Los Angeles restaurant, then showed up on his arm at a party in Brentwood. An observer breathlessly described them as 'necking up a storm' at the soiree, but that seems unlikely for so publicly circumspect a person as Barbra. What attraction there may have been between the two stars apparently didn't last long; Barbra soon was seen dating Tina Sinatra's ex-husband, the millionaire businessman Richard Cohen, and the Arab playboy-producer Dodi Fayed. She renewed her acquaintance with the producer Arnon Milchan, and Pierre Trudeau escorted her to a reception in her honor in New York thrown by the United Jewish Appeal.

A Christmas party in 1983 provided the setting for Barbra to meet the man who would become her next lover, and very nearly her husband. She couldn't help but notice him. He was very tall – six feet three inches – very good-looking, and solidly built; he had bedroom eyes, a cute smile, and a wild shock of dark curly hair that seemed to extend him into the stratosphere. He seemed like a mensch to Barbra, a sweet guy like Elliott, but he was aggressive enough to approach her toward the end of the evening. 'Most men are so intimidated by me,' Barbra said, 'that if I meet one who has the guts to say hello he's way ahead of the game.'

His name was Richard Baskin, he told her. 'I just wanted to say how much I loved *Yentl*. You should be very proud.'

'Thank you,' Barbra replied. 'Hey, you any relation to Baskin-Robbins ice cream?'

'Yes, as a matter of fact,' Richard replied. 'That's my family.'

'Wow,' Barbra said. 'I love your coffee ice cream!'

Baskin, who stood to inherit part of his family's vast fortune, had forged a career in Hollywood as a musical director on such films as *Buffalo Bill and the Indians*, *Honeysuckle Rose*, and Robert Altman's satire of the world of country music, *Nashville*. He wrote several of the songs in *Nashville* and performed one of them on *Saturday Night Live* in 1975, accompanying himself on guitar.

Barbra began dating Baskin casually in the early spring of 1984, after she returned from a European tour to promote *Yentl*. She loved how protected he made her feel by dint of his sheer size, she enjoyed his sense of humor, and she admired his taste in music. They could speak in musical shorthand, and their sensibilities were finely attuned to each other. By the summer of 1984, they were seriously enough involved that she characteristically made him a part of her latest project, a new pop album entitled *Emotion*. It was her first new studio album since *Guilty* (a 1981 package called *Memories*, containing only two news songs, one of which was her stunning version of 'Memory' from Andrew Lloyd Webber's *Cats*, had sold three million copies), and she wanted to make a sharp departure from the highly traditional music of *Yentl*. Apparently ignoring the lesson offered by the Bee Gees' cohesive production of *Guilty*, Barbra this time put together another mishmash of songs by contemporary songwriters who had been in vogue about two years earlier. The album had *nine* credited producers, including Barbra and Baskin, and eleven arrangers.

Perhaps because Barbra was distracted by Baskin's presence, or perhaps because her heart wasn't in this record, she apparently lost her legendary ear during these recording sessions. Late one evening she, Baskin, and the recording engineer, John Arrias, were trying to choose between two vocals. Arrias would play one, then the other, then the first again. He and Barbra finally agreed they preferred one over the other. They asked Baskin to listen. He agreed with them. Then Arrias, who was curious about some technical aspects of the tapes, played them simultaneously, and then he realized they were both the same vocal. The three of them giggled themselves helpless and decided it was time to go home and get some sleep.

Critics blasted *Emotion* for its uneven quality and lack of cohesion, familiar problems with many of Streisand's pop efforts. The album peaked at number nineteen, Barbra's lowest charting for a studio album since *What About Today?*, but it did manage to sell two million copies. The first single, 'Left in the Dark,' stalled at number fifty, unassisted by Barbra's first music video, a stylish six-minute mini-film noir in black-and-white and color that MTV premiered to great fanfare.

Music Television had revolutionized pop music in the early 1980s with its lightning-paced music videos. Now video images were as important to a song's sales success as its melody and lyrics; looks could make or break a new singer more quickly than ever before. Within a few years MTV would not play any middle-of-the-road material at all, but it aired 'Left in the Dark' for a while along with its more colorful and suitable follow-up, co-directed in London by Barbra and Richard Baskin and featuring Roger Daltry, Mikhail Baryshnikov, and Barbra wearing half a dozen wild outfits while she sang 'Emotion.'

Joel Selvin of the *San Francisco Chronicle* didn't mince words when he reviewed *Emotion*. 'There are people out there who actually respect Streisand as an artist,' he wrote, 'but this could cure them.' John Milward in *USA Today* added, '*Emotion* is Streisand's latest attempt to appear hip, and one must wonder why she bothers. Her talent was nurtured in the world of Broadway and Hollywood. Her art is rooted in a voice whose beauty transcends hip.'

With her next album, Barbra would show that she agreed.

DRESSED IN A rumpled gray sports jacket and skintight jeans tucked into low-heeled black boots, Barbra stood in the recording booth with her arms folded over her chest, swaying absentmindedly. To accommodate the headphones, her hair was pulled back into an untidy knot. Chewing discontentedly on her lower lip, she stared with intense concentration at the floor. Suddenly her face, free of makeup, twisted into a scowl. She shook her head, yanked the headphones off, and moaned, 'I hate it. I *hate* it!'

She had been listening to a playback of 'Can't Help Lovin' That Man,' the classic lament from *Showboat*, that she had just recorded against a bluesy, brass-heavy orchestration. 'I thought the trumpet made it feel a little too jazzy,' Barbra said. 'It didn't feel right.' She recalled seeing the 1951 MGM movie of *Showboat* and being moved by Ava Gardner's languid rendition of the song, and she wanted to re-create 'this magnificent arrangement . . . so simple, the most gorgeous harmonies.'

It was the spring of 1985 and Barbra was recording tracks for a collection of songs from the American musical theater, which she would call *The Broadway Album*. After the disappointment of *Emotion*, Barbra had decided it was time to return to her musical roots and sing show tunes. She had considered this project off and on since the mid-seventies, and it was precisely the kind of recording venture many of Barbra's critics and admirers had suggested she do for years.

'Anybody could have done the songs on *Emotion* as well as or better than I could have done them,' Barbra admitted. 'It was time to do something I truly believed in.' Columbia at first strongly opposed the new album, which they were certain would appeal only to a relatively small audience of Broadway aficionados. As they had with *Classical Barbra*, Streisand's 1976 collection of lieder, Columbia exercised an option in her contract which stated that any album she wanted to record that they considered risky would satisfy her contractual requirements only if it ultimately sold over two and a half million copies. Characteristically, her label's lack of belief in the project only heightened Barbra's determination to prove the naysayers wrong.

For this project, which harked back to her earliest musical efforts, Barbra turned, appropriately, to the man who had arranged and conducted her very first album. Peter Matz hadn't worked with Streisand for over a decade, and he recalled that she attacked this project with typical enthusiasm. 'Barbra had already gone through a tremendous amount of material trying to find the right songs before I came in,' he said. 'There was a stack of records and sheet music a mile high in the [Carolwood] house – all of the music from all of the shows as far back as you could think.' Matz also pulled together a fifty-piece orchestra made up of the most talented studio musicians. Performing amid a full orchestra was a luxury for Barbra, who had become accustomed to singing against a prerecorded orchestral track for the majority of her pop efforts.

Hoping that Columbia would agree to release *The Broadway Album* as a two-disc set, Barbra recorded close to twenty-five songs, including an elaborate medley from *The King and I* that would have taken up an entire side of one disc. (It was later considerably shortened.) Then the project seemed to be shaping up as a tribute to Stephen Sondheim after Barbra decided to include eight of his songs.

Streisand and Sondheim spent hours on the telephone discussing the singular approach Barbra wanted to take with his compositions. Barbra asked the composer if he would rearrange the lyrics to his most famous song, 'Send in the Clowns'; devise a connecting bridge for a medley of the lilting 'Pretty Women' from *Sweeney Todd* and 'The Ladies Who Lunch' from *Company*; and write new lyrics to 'Putting It Together' from *Sunday in the Park with George*, to comment on the never-ending battle between creativity and commerce within the record business rather than in the world of fine art.

Sondheim agreed to most of Streisand's requests and actually enjoyed the fact that Barbra wanted to 'play around' with his melody lines. He did, however, have one condition: he asked her always to retain the original notes in the first chorus so that the melody could be established. Then she could feel free to change notes or embellish the melody.

'It turned into a process that was so exhilarating,' recalled Barbra, who had known Sondheim only casually prior to their collaboration. 'There were moments when I was screaming with joy over the phone.'

In spite of both artists' legendary accomplishments, Sondheim and Streisand acted like teenage fans around each other. Sondheim timidly asked if he could join Barbra in the recording studio. 'To my exultant surprise,' he said, 'she welcomed the prospect of my being present. I was thrilled!'

'Can you imagine?' Barbra marveled. 'He rewrote lyrics for *me!*'

Just prior to the release of the album, Barbra filmed a video of 'Somewhere' at the Apollo Theater in Harlem. Although David Foster's arrangement of the song gave it an eerie space-age setting, the video couldn't have been more traditional: Barbra onstage wearing an ankle-length black dress embellished only with a delicate white lace collar.

The Broadway Album was released as a single disc in November 1985 to ecstatic reviews ('Streisand's back where she belongs!') and record-breaking sales: the package hit number one on the *Billboard* album chart in a matter of weeks. 'Customers are scooping up three and four of these records at a time,' one record store manager exulted. Eager to launch her latest baby successfully, Streisand gave interviews to Stephen Holden of *The New York Times* and to Rod McKuen, who was reviewing the album for *Digital Audio* magazine. Holden's piece centered on Barbra's return to her 'roots' and how youthfully vibrant her voice remained.

The Broadway Album eventually sold three million copies and received three Grammy nominations. Although Barbra lost the Album of the Year award, she received her eighth miniature gramophone for Best Female Pop Vocal. When she accepted the award, Barbra noted that it had been exactly twenty-four years since she won her first Grammy. 'So, with a little luck and your continued support,' she told the cheering audience at the Shrine Auditorium, 'I'll see you in another twenty-four years.'

BY NOW RICHARD Baskin had moved in with Barbra, becoming the third important man in her life after Elliott and Jon. In fact, Peters told friends he fully expected Barbra to marry Baskin; soon after that, Peters wed *his* live-in girlfriend. But as she had with Jon, Barbra seemed content with the romantic status quo. Whenever they went out, Baskin served as Barbra's bodyguard as much as her escort, and occasionally he'd get carried away. While they were in London to shoot the 'Emotion' video, the British press reported that Baskin 'blew his cool as the couple emerged from a restaurant,' tossed a pint of ale at Fleet Street's finest, and 'appeared to offer them a knuckle sandwich.'

Baskin was reacting to Barbra's fear and annoyance, of course; when she was more sanguine, so was he. On her forty-fourth birthday in 1986, he took her to Splash, a restaurant in Malibu. As they left, Bill Moore, an illustrator and fervid Streisand fan, approached her with some sketches he had done of her. 'Richard Baskin rolled his eyes toward heaven when he first saw me, as if to say, "Here we go again,"' Moore recalled, 'and he seemed real protective of her. Barbra was in a good mood, but she was leery of me at first and wanted to know how I knew she was there. I told her a friend had called me. Barbra lightened up and admired my work. She signed both sketches. Once Baskin saw that Barbra wasn't threatened by me, he kind of stood off to the side shyly until she signed the drawings; then he took her arm gently and they left.'

WHILE BARBRA WAS in Aspen over the Christmas holidays in 1985, she learned that Marty Erlichman was also vacationing there. She and Marty had drifted apart since he stopped managing her in 1977, and she felt it was time to rekindle their relationship. A contract she had with Jon had expired, and she wasn't of a mind to renew it. *The Broadway Album* had made her appreciate her musical roots, and no one was more rooted in Barbra's beginnings than Marty Erlichman.

He had become a mini-mogul over the years, producing the successful motion pictures *Coma* and *Breathless*, among others. But his deepest loyalty was to Barbra, and when she broached the idea of his managing her again, he leaped at the chance. 'It's like we were married for sixteen years and then split,' he said. 'When you get back together you kind of know each other. Age has worked well for both of us in the sense that we can talk more shorthand than we used to.'

One of Marty's first suggestions was that Barbra consider a concert tour. She owed it to her fans, he argued; it would help boost her record sales and generate greater interest in the film project she was preparing, *Nuts*. It would be a way to *really* get back to her roots.

Barbra said no. She was too frightened of performing live, and a tour required too much work. Marty kept at her to do *something* – her live appearances over the past decade had been few, brief, and far between.

Barbra singing live was now such a rare event that even her performance of a single song became an event. Her claims of paralyzing stage fright, scoffed at in some quarters, were in fact quite genuine. Rusty Lemorande recalled that she was so nervous backstage at the 1980 Grammy Awards as she waited to go on with Neil Diamond that she almost drew blood when she dug her nails into his hand.

In the nine years since she performed 'Evergreen' at the 1977 Academy Awards, Barbra had performed in public only twice in addition to the televised duet with Diamond. On May 8, 1978, she closed the ABC-TV special *The Stars Salute Israel at 30* by shmoozing with Golda Meir via satellite from Tel Aviv and singing four songs including 'Hativka,' the Israeli national anthem.

On June 1, 1980, the American Civil Liberties Union held a fund-raising concert honoring Marilyn and Alan Bergman at the L.A. Music Center. Barbra sang, to Michel Legrand's accompaniment, an all-Bergman program: 'Summer Me, Winter Me,' 'What Are You Doing the Rest of Your Life,' 'After the Rain,' and 'The Way We Were.' She also included the different version of the last song, discarded in 1973, which she christened 'The Way We Weren't.' Afterward Neil Diamond made a surprise entrance from the audience and joined Streisand for a relaxed version of 'You Don't Bring Me

Flowers.' Barbra admitted later that she'd had a yogi backstage to 'help calm me down.'

At the beginning of one song, a noisy claque of fans in the balcony shouted, 'We love you, Barbra!'

'I love you too,' she replied, 'but I can't hear my intro.'

For many years Barbra had difficulty accepting such public adoration. 'I just don't know what that love means,' she mused. 'I'm tremendously grateful for their support. [But] it's a funny kind of love you get – all that applause. I'd rather be loved by a few people, you know, real love. This other love is a kind of crazy love – the love of a voice, the love of a star.' Following the Bergman tribute, and despite rumors that she would do concert tours to promote *Yentl* and later *The Broadway Album*, Barbra didn't sing a note in a public setting for over six years.

Thus shock and delight were the predominant reactions of many of the top names in the worlds of politics, movies, and music in August 1986 when they received elaborately packaged audiotaped invitations from Barbra to a fund-raising concert at the ranch. 'I could never imagine myself wanting to sing in public again,' she said on the tape. 'But then I could never imagine Star Wars, Contras, apartheid and nuclear winters.' The recipients were urged to 'come join me at my ranch under the stars.' The concert, scheduled for the following month, would be sponsored by the newly formed Hollywood Women's Political Committee to raise money for the campaigns of five Democratic senatorial candidates. As noteworthy as the fact that Barbra would be singing live again was the cost of attendance: $5,000 per couple, with a seating limit of four hundred people for the event.

For many years Barbra had kept her political interests to herself. She had not performed at any fund-raising concerts for Jimmy Carter, who was elected president in the post-Watergate climate of 1976, because she found him too conservative. But neither did she publicly support Ted Kennedy's primary challenge to Carter in 1980 or Walter Mondale's 1984 run against President Ronald Reagan.

But her horror at the disastrous near-meltdown of a reactor core at the nuclear generating plant in Chernobyl in the Russian Ukraine on April 26, 1986, which sent a huge cloud of radioactive material into the atmosphere, shocked a new outspokenness out of her. Her belief that the pro-armament Reagan administration was partly to blame for the proliferation of nuclear plants and warheads around the world pushed Barbra to exploit her most sought-after asset – her fabled voice, live in concert – to raise money to help get as many liberal Democrats as possible elected to the Senate and recapture its control from the Republicans.

On the balmy evening of Saturday, September 6, busloads of celebrities who had parked their cars at the foot of Ramirez Canyon were ushered past no-nonsense security guards to a small amphitheater Streisand had had constructed on her Malibu backyard. Robin Williams delivered a typically wacky opening monologue that poked fun at the price of the tickets. Then, after a short intermission, Barbra appeared from the wings like a vision, dressed in a long white gown with a slit skirt, a sprinkling of rhinestones on each shoulder, singing 'Somewhere.' She was greeted with a standing ovation from an audience that included Whoopi Goldberg, Los Angeles Mayor Tom Bradley, Whitney Houston, Jack Nicholson, Walter Matthau, Bette Midler, Hugh Hefner, Bruce Willis, Jane Fonda, Goldie Hawn, and Kurt Russell. Jason, Chris Peters, and the Bergmans were in the crowd as well.

With just a handful of musicians on electronic instruments behind her, Barbra delivered vocally unchallenging versions of her standards and sang 'Guilty' and 'What Kind of Fool' with Barry Gibb. Because of the relative intimacy of the venue and the lack of a full orchestra behind her, Barbra never reached back to deliver her patented soaring crescendos. Instead, the highlights of the program were exquisitely sung quiet ballads: 'Send in the Clowns,' 'It's a New World,' 'Papa, Can You Hear Me?' and, in a touching tribute to Judy Garland, 'Over the Rainbow.'

Between songs Barbra expressed her pro-environment, pro-peace sentiments: 'We must find new ways to communicate with each other, to understand each other, to be compassionate toward each other. We inhabit this tiny planet together, and if we are to survive, it will be together, or not at all.' Coming as they did from a superstar who had seemed so aloof from the problems of the real world for so many years, Barbra's remarks struck some as naive and others as pretentiously preachy.

But the goal of Barbra's 'One Voice' concert had been accomplished. The event raised $1.5 million – a good deal more, the press pointed out, than a Reagan fund-raiser held the same night in Beverly Hills. Barbra utilized proceeds from the evening to establish the Streisand Foundation, a nonprofit organization to support 'qualified charitable organizations committed to antinuclear activities and the preservation of our environment, civil liberties and human rights.' Four out of the five candidates Barbra supported through the concert were elected in November, which helped turn the Senate back over to the Democrats.

The foundation realized further profits from the event when HBO aired the concert as a television special at the end of the year. Even critics who chided Streisand for her political remarks were lavish in their praise of her performance. 'Streisand's voice is still the best there is,' said the *Los Angeles*

Herald Examiner. 'Her stage presence, her supremely confident air, her hold on an audience, remain a thing of masterful beauty.'

NOW THAT SHE had returned to live singing after six years, Barbra was prepared to return to the screen after four. The project she chose provided her with the grittiest acting challenge she had ever had on film. And it dealt, among other things, with an issue that had gnawed at Barbra since the days of her mother's marriage to Louis Kind: child abuse.

'Don't worry, Mama, I'll dedicate my next film to you,' Barbra had said in 1983. She didn't dedicate *Nuts* to Diana, but she might as well have.

34

B arbra sat beneath the hot lights of the *60 Minutes* set, answering questions from Mike Wallace. The conversation turned to the subject of Barbra's stepfather, and her carefully controlled public mask shattered. She broke down on camera, and a frightened, insecure, and unhappy child emerged. 'You like this . . . that forty million people have to see me do this,' she sniffed to Wallace. For a glaring public moment, Streisand fact and fiction had merged: Barbra looked remarkably like another abused child – Claudia Draper, her character in *Nuts*.

Nuts, an acid-etched portrait of soured family values, would be Barbra's symbolic indictment of the abuse she suffered as a child from Louis Kind. And the angry tone of the film laid bare her lingering bitter feelings toward her mother. 'My stepfather did not physically abuse me,' Barbra said. 'Mentally he did, and my mother allowed it to happen.' (Diana Kind has said that she stayed with Louis only in an effort to hold her family together.)

Tom Topor's caustic play about Claudia Draper and her downward spiral into prostitution, murder, and possible madness centered on dark family secrets, repressed hatred, social hypocrisy, and an important question: what is normal? 'I responded very strongly to the character in this movie,' Barbra said. 'People are not always what they seem to be. Claudia isn't insane; she's just shockingly honest.'

It is clear why Streisand was captivated by the multilayered heroine of Topor's acclaimed play. Claudia is a fascinating mélange of traits: a flawed, heroic, insecure, vain, frightened, and obstreperous high-priced call girl who rejects an insanity plea after murdering a violent client and demands the right to stand trial for the crime. She will not victimize herself further by saying she's 'nuts,' even though her parents have used all their considerable influence to make that happen. She wants her day in court.

Playing Claudia, Barbra later admitted, allowed her to 'let all my rage out ... I don't have to worry [in this movie] about being nice, sweet and polite.'

AS EARLY AS December 1981, word had leaked out that Barbra was already planning a follow-up to *Yentl*. The project that had caught her attention was *Nuts*, which Mark Rydell was preparing to direct. Streisand's interest in playing Claudia Draper intrigued Rydell, but he turned her down. 'She wanted me to delay the project until she finished *Yentl*,' he explained at the time, 'and that won't be for way over a year. I intend to be shooting *Nuts* this summer.'

Rydell, who had directed Bette Midler's stunning film debut in *The Rose* and guided Henry Fonda and Katharine Hepburn to Oscars in *On Golden Pond*, had already decided to cast Debra Winger, whose performance in *Urban Cowboy* had catapulted her into the front ranks of Hollywood's leading ladies.

With Winger, Rydell planned a relatively low-budget production rife with raw language, rough situations, and a battery of highly combustible themes, including Claudia's darkest secret: the incestuous relationship she had been forced into – and paid for – by her stepfather when she was a child. But delays caused by script, budget, and location problems saw to it that Rydell's projected spring 1982 start date was not to be.

'I did draft after draft after draft [of the screenplay],' Tom Topor remembered. 'Next thing I know, I was off the picture. In a way, Mark was right. What I didn't understand viscerally, though I did intellectually, is that it's the director who makes the picture. Mark's emphasis was far more on incest. My emphasis was far more on power (as between the institution and the individual).'

A bogged-down Rydell temporarily left the project to direct *The River* in 1984, and Winger – successful, in demand, and at the time a 'turbulent' woman, as her *Terms of Endearment* co-star Shirley MacLaine said at the 1984 Oscars – bowed out of the film. Determined to save the project, Rydell remembered Barbra's interest and sent the *Nuts* screenplay to her. Streisand was again intrigued, and both felt the next step would be to hire a new writer to fine-tune the script yet again.

By the fall of 1985, Universal had officially placed the beleaguered project in turnaround. 'Someone over there thought it was too hot to handle,' Rydell confessed. 'It's very raw, and I guess they got scared.' Unwilling to relinquish his dream of making *Nuts*, Rydell took the property to Warner Brothers, with whom Barbra had long been associated. Barbra agreed to star, but like so many of her screen projects, *Nuts* would end up waiting for her. Until, and even after, Barbra became firmly involved, the picture would be, as the columnist Army Archerd put it, 'a hard film to crack.'

In his desire to please Streisand, and to entice Warners into buying the property for her, Rydell committed a major faux pas. After asking *Cinderella Liberty* screenwriter Darryl Ponicsan to do a rewrite, he made the same request of Alvin Sargent (*Ordinary People*). After promising both men a deal when he returned, Rydell flew to Hawaii for a vacation. As Rydell basked in the sun, Sargent and Ponicsan, who were friends, compared notes. Understandably angry, they quit the project – but not before Ponicsan dialed Rydell's answering machine and left a message: 'After Hawaii, go directly to hell.'

When Barbra discovered the Rydell-Sargent-Ponicsan imbroglio, she played mediator. She spoke with the two disgruntled writers and suggested that they team up. After Rydell apologized to them, the screenwriters agreed. But the studio felt that their rewrite still wasn't quite acceptable, and after two more writers had come and gone, Streisand herself participated in the script's evolution. According to Barbra, Rydell 'gave me one week to sit down and write out the script as I saw fit.' The end result pleased all concerned, and on September 30, 1985, Warner Brothers gave the green light to *Nuts* for a January 1986 start. Barbra's acting salary would be $5 million. She would also produce through Barwood, for a fee of half a million dollars.

ALTHOUGH WITH RYDELL at the helm *Nuts* appeared to be in good hands, rumors soon began to fly around the Burbank lot that the director was being 'difficult.' Well-placed sources said that he refused to control the ballooning budget, tone down the controversial incest angle, or compromise his overall artistic vision of the film.

Streisand attempted to rectify the situation, but couldn't. In a typically worded puff piece of a press statement, the studio announced on March 18, 1986, 'We greatly regret that a number of factors concerning this picture have come together to create a separation between Warner Brothers and Rydell Productions. We have nothing but respect for Mark's talent and success as a filmmaker. We wish him every success in the future.'

Rydell also played the smiling diplomat. The *Hollywood Reporter* wrote, 'Citing schedule, budgetary, and creative differences, Rydell said: "It is with absolutely no animosity to any of the parties concerned that I take leave of this project. If I have any regrets, it is that I will not be able to work with Barbra Streisand, an immense talent with whom I have enjoyed an excellent working relationship."'

Such genteel diplomacy has always angered Barbra. She felt Rydell's exit reflected badly on her, and she tried once again to reunite the warring forces. 'She tried to become the mediator between Mark and Warner Brothers,' said Marty Erlichman. 'When Barbra found that there was no way she was going to convince Warners to take him back . . . then she said that she would like [another] actor's director. And they selected Marty Ritt.'

But the process, according to studio insiders, wasn't quite as simple as that. After Rydell's departure, a number of names were bandied about. Warners asked Barbra to direct the film herself, but she wasn't prepared to take on that responsibility so soon after *Yentl*, nor did she want to prompt gossip that she had orchestrated Rydell's removal in order to take over the project herself.

Warners approached Alan Pakula about directing without telling Barbra that his customary fee was $2 million, and she was furious. As the producer of *Nuts*, Barbra certainly should have been consulted about this type of offer, and she refused to pay that much for a director. Barbra was further angered when she learned that Warners was keeping a crew on standby at a daily expense of tens of thousands of dollars even though the film was far from ready to go before the cameras.

Stressed, disillusioned, and watching the budget rise precariously, Streisand worried over every aspect of the production, including her role. Was it too confrontational? Too bitter? Too one-dimensional? Until she could find a director she could trust to talk to about these issues, she worried alone. 'I feel so scared and insecure,' she told a friend. 'I want so much to be liked and understood. But I have to be in control, because so much of the world is so stupid!'

At first Barbra thought Martin Ritt might be the kind of director with whom she could feel secure and from whom she could learn. With a string of classic dramas to his credit including *Hud* and *Norma Rae*, Ritt was renowned for his ability to juxtapose intimate personal issues with grand social themes. By April 2, Streisand had spoken with Ritt about the job. Publicly he said he thought Barbra was 'terrific.' Privately he told her he wasn't sure she had the acting ability to play Claudia well. Challenged by Ritt's blunt assessment, Barbra decided she had found her director. 'He got my hair up,' she explained, 'and I said, "Good. You're the one. It's a match."'

Barbra felt she knew Claudia Draper inside and out. 'This is a girl who says exactly what she feels, and I identify with her because ever since I was a little kid, I couldn't learn the rules about conduct,' she said. Then she added a read-between-the-lines comment about her mother: 'You know, I wasn't taught things, like I used to sit at the table with my feet up. I didn't know you're supposed to put a napkin in your lap. My mother ate from a pot standing up at the kitchen stove. We never had set times for dinner, like all the other kids, you know?'

In her quest to uncover every facet of and reason for Claudia's erratic behavior, Streisand interviewed doctors, lawyers, and mental patients, and hired a legal-aid attorney as a consultant for the film. She visited several state hospitals in New York and Los Angeles during the spring. 'I went to see schizophrenics,' she said. 'I felt totally comfortable with them, with their lack of social etiquette, you know, a kind of honesty that was just so engaging, refreshing. I do like to say what I think and you get crucified for that, like [Claudia] does in this picture.'

BARBRA CONSIDERED ACTORS from Richard Gere to Robert Duvall for the important, but substantially smaller, part of Claudia's public defender, Aaron Levinsky. By April 14, she and Ritt had settled on Richard Dreyfuss, whose performance in the Los Angeles stage production of Larry Kramer's *The Normal Heart* had electrified Barbra. Dreyfuss, an Oscar winner for *The Goodbye Girl*, had struggled with substance abuse, but he was now clean and sober and willing to work. A week later, though, he left the contract negotiations to star in *Tin Men* for Barry Levinson. 'We have to start the search for an actor all over again,' said a frustrated Ritt, acknowledging that Dreyfuss's departure would delay the film's start date even further.

Barbra turned to her old friend Dustin Hoffman, who loved the cinematic quality Sargent and Ponicsan had brought to Topor's rather static stage production. According to the columnist Marilyn Beck, 'Hoffman's interest in *Nuts* was strong but not great enough for him to compromise on his financial demands. The deal being negotiated called for him and Streisand to profit equally from the picture, and when push came to shove, Hoffman insisted on so much that Warners decided it would end up with a budget that would be too big a nut to crack.' So, after two months of haggling, Hoffman exited.

Although Paul Newman, Al Pacino, and Marlon Brando reportedly were interested in the role, on June 16 Dreyfuss once again entered the picture. After Ritt and Streisand agreed to delay filming until October, Dreyfuss was cast with a salary of $1.5 million, far below the king's ransom Hoffman had demanded. Dreyfuss, despite rumors to the contrary, was unconcerned about Barbra's penchant for taking over her films. 'No, I never worried about that at all,' he said. 'I knew going in that that was going to be the case. Don't we know this? She knew it. I knew it.'

WHILE SHE STRUGGLED to put *Nuts* together, Streisand had given her *One Voice* concert, and Martin Ritt bitterly questioned the time and attention it took away from *Nuts*. He apparently felt that Streisand the conglomerate was getting in the way of Streisand the serious actress. Later, after *Nuts* began production and Streisand divided her time between the film and her HBO *One Voice* special, the situation between director and star grew even more tense.

With the glittering cast Ritt and Streisand had settled on – Maureen Stapleton and Karl Malden were signed to play Claudia's parents, and Leslie Nielson and Eli Wallach would play secondary roles – the *Nuts* budget mushroomed to nearly $30 million, more money than seven of Barbra's thirteen films had *grossed*. The technical crew was equally impressive: Andrzej Bartkowiak was hired as cinematographer while Jeremy Lubbock would serve as music arranger-conductor. As for the music itself, Streisand decided she would score the film: 'After all, who else would hire me . . . or fire me?'

Barbra flew to New York to begin location work on October 1. After brief exterior scenes of a liberated Claudia walking the streets of New York, the *Nuts* company returned to Los Angeles, where filming continued at the Burbank Studios.

ALMOST FROM THE beginning, sources close to Streisand say she suspected she had erred in hiring Martin Ritt. Although he was a respected Hollywood old-timer, he was set in his ways and unwilling to alter his personal schedule to suit Barbra's chaotic calendar. While many of her other directors had been willing to deal with Barbra's barrage of late-night phone calls, Ritt – sixty-eight and not in the best of health – made it clear to her from the outset that he was not. As filming progressed, and frustration mounted on both sides, Ritt reportedly ended up referring to his star as a 'pain in the ass.'

Still, reports filtered out of the closed set that Barbra was giving a tour-de-force performance as Claudia Draper, that the movie would be a box-office winner, and that Streisand could well garner a Best Actress Oscar nomination. Karl Malden was wildly enthusiastic about the film and its leading lady. 'There has never been a better group of character actors put together to appear in one film than in this one,' he said. 'Every performance, and I mean every performance, could well be called brilliant. Barbra,' he felt, was 'a fascinating, energetic woman, aside from being one of the best singers we've got in the country. She's got an awful lot of vitality.'

Nuts wrapped on February 3, 1987, and then the real work began. After several weeks of relaxation, Ritt began the arduous process of assembling his director's cut for Barbra. He finished the job shortly before May 22, when he screened the film for her. Barbra wanted to make changes and began to edit the film herself on June 1. Ritt was not pleased. As the director explained, 'I don't know what she's doing to the picture. I did my cut; we previewed it, and now she's doing whatever it is she's doing.' Still, Ritt tried to be fair, adding that since he had not been given final cut on the film, Barbra, as producer, 'has the right to come in and do some editing.'

As usual, Barbra remained incommunicado during the postproduction process, but she later claimed that 'some of the arguments that Marty and I had even over the final cut were where I would say: "Take out that close-up of me." But then he would say: "That's a good close-up of you." Nobody would know [about] those arguments. They would think an actress wants close-ups of herself. And it's ridiculous. I have a lot of rage about a lot of things that are misinterpreted,' she said.

While she edited *Nuts*, Barbra was also busy composing the film's score. 'As a courtroom drama, *Nuts* required very little music, so I decided to give it a shot,' she remembered. 'The end title music was written to convey a sense of freedom and personal triumph. Later, Alan and Marilyn Bergman added lyrics to it, and the song became "Two People," [which I] recorded for the *Till I Loved You* album.' In a barroom sequence Streisand also used 'Here We Are at Last,' a song she wrote for *The Main Event* and discarded until it showed up on *Emotion*.

WHEN *NUTS* WAS previewed in the late summer and early fall of 1987, Warner Brothers executives were ecstatic with the audience polling results. Despite Hollywood cynics who felt that Streisand could never get away with portraying a five-hundred-dollar-an-hour hooker, no such protestations of disbelief came from the mesmerized audience members. They realized that most prostitutes do not resemble Elizabeth Taylor in *Butterfield 8*. Tom Topor was pleased. 'I think *Nuts* is a good movie, a *very* good movie. It's not the movie I would have made. It's Barbra Streisand and Marty Ritt's movie.'

Nuts was released to great fanfare on November 20, 1987. After turning down over three hundred interview requests from worldwide media representatives, Barbra agreed to a rare three-part discussion with *Today* movie reviewer Gene Shalit, who raved about the film. Dressed in black, a radiant and relaxed Streisand pulled out all the stops with a flustered Shalit, even offering at the end of the first segment to adjust his famous bow tie. 'Come here,' she teased. The starstruck reviewer looked as if he might faint at any moment.

On the final day, Richard Dreyfuss joined the interview and waxed philosophic about Streisand's much-dissected personality. 'Barbra is a case,' he said. 'She's very specific. I think if there is one thing that you can say is a common denominator to all movie stars, especially female movie stars, from the time of the beginning of the motion picture business, [it's] that they are – as opposed to the other actresses – they are definite. You can see a clear line around Katharine Hepburn's personality and Bette Davis's personality and Joan Crawford and Jean Arthur and Barbra Streisand. That is what sets them apart and makes them compelling for us to watch . . . People might argue with facets of Barbra's personality, but what Barbra is is *definite*.

'And because she's a woman, we take issue with that to a greater degree than if she were a man. If she were a producer, star, director of the male gender, we would accept all of her eccentricities in a much more forgiving, normal, unquestioning way. The fact that she is a woman brings all of those things out in very sharp relief, and that's why we're here in a sense discussing Barbra's personality. That doesn't mean that I forgive her eccentricities, by the way, it just means that's the phenomenon we're discussing, okay?'

Despite the film's positive preview responses, reviews were mixed. Many critics felt Barbra had created a surprisingly hard-edged, gritty character who was light-years away from Yentl, and had finally proved her dramatic mettle. Others accused her of chewing up the scenery, of performing rather than acting. *People* magazine's reviewer wrote, 'Her wicked zest keeps you riveted. Whether she's punching out the family lawyer or shocking the court with her sex-for-sale rates, Streisand shows a robust comic toughness . . . with disarming candor and wit, she has actually made a hymn to herself as a pain in the butt.' Still others felt the film was a pain, period. *Newsweek*'s David Ansen called *Nuts* 'a classic example of A-list liberal Hollywood turning out what it thinks is Important Entertainment.'

Warner Brothers, encouraged by opening-day research figures stating that *Nuts* had a 96 percent chance of being enjoyed, believed that excellent word of mouth could override the critical objections. But a series of problems hurt the film's box-office receipts, beginning with the pulse of the country. In recessionary times, few wanted to see what they perceived to be a depressing story about a crazy prostitute, especially during the holidays. Although the film had a huge opening ten-day take of nearly $12 million on a mere 536 screens, the abysmal ad campaign, featuring a photo of a sour-faced Streisand that called to mind the beast in television's *Beauty and the Beast*, proved to be a turn-off to many potential moviegoers. None of the film's humor, or its ultimate happiness and hope, was explored in the marketing, and *Nuts* suffered because of it.

The box office on *Nuts* dwindled rapidly, and it ended up grossing only $35 million domestically – barely enough to cover its production budget, not to mention the millions spent on promotion. The film was a washout in the year-end New York and Los Angeles Film Critics Awards. It was nominated for Golden Globe Awards in two categories, but it failed to win either Best Picture or Best Actress. The only hope left for its resuscitation revolved around the Oscar nominations. Would the Academy members finally give Streisand some recognition? Most observers agreed that her performance deserved a nomination.

Indeed, for months *Nuts* had been touted by many Hollywood insiders as a front-runner in the Oscar sweepstakes, and some articles even predicted that Streisand would win her third statuette. But when the nominations were announced, *Nuts* was ignored in every category. Cher went on to win the Best Actress Award, for an accomplished but less multilayered performance.

THE CATHARSIS OF *Nuts* brought Barbra only marginally closer to her mother. 'I love her more now than I ever have in my life,' she said. 'I think she also loves me. I understand even her jealousy. Why shouldn't she be jealous? Here's a woman who wanted a career for herself, but she was too frightened, too shy.'

Diana has defended herself against the charge that she never gave Barbra any encouragement as a little girl. Speaking of all three of her children she said, 'Whatever they tried to do, I tried to support, and I was being supportive.' But she admitted, 'They might not have thought I was totally supportive.'

Barbra and her mother are rarely in contact. 'I don't hear from her very often,' Mrs Kind said recently. 'There's no rift, I love my daughter very much, but Barbra's a very busy girl and I'm a busy mother taking care of myself and trying to do the best I can with my life.' On special occasions Barbra will take Diana out to dinner 'if it's convenient,' Mrs Kind said; on Mother's Day and her birthday Barbra's secretary usually sends Diana flowers, but some years she forgets.

But, Diana freely admitted, 'My daughter sure looks after me.' In the early eighties Barbra bought her a $1 million, two-bedroom Beverly Hills condominium, which Diana often shares with Roslyn, who married the producer Randy Stone, then a casting agent, briefly in 1983 but has been single ever since. Barbra also pays all her mother's bills and sends her $1,000 a month, and for a simple woman in her eighties this is virtually the lap of luxury. Her biggest problem, Diana said, is a lack of privacy because of her daughter's fame: 'I never knew that being the mother of someone like this would be such hard work.'

As ever, Diana Kind has little in-depth knowledge of or interest in Barbra's career. After a Streisand fan spent three hours with Diana, he marveled, 'She has no concept of the scope of Barbra's stardom. She could be the mother of Vicki Carr.' Mainly she worries about Barbra's health and happiness and whether she's secure and eating well. She does take pride in Barbra's accomplishments, even if she finds it difficult to tell Barbra that. 'It's for sure she gets her talent from me,' Mrs Kind said.

35

In the ring at the Atlantic City Convention Center in January 1988, world heavyweight champ Mike Tyson was pounding his challenger, Larry Holmes, into mincemeat, but the real show was just north of ringside. As though they were at a Ping-Pong match rather than a prizefight, the spectators kept shifting their gaze between the bloodbath in the ring and a stylishly dressed blond couple sitting knee to knee a few rows back. In a crowd that included Jack Nicholson, Kirk Douglas, Barbara Walters, Bruce Willis, Norman Mailer, Sugar Ray Leonard, and Muhammad Ali, the sight of Barbra Streisand and Don Johnson holding hands riveted everyone in the crowd who could see them. Whispers rippled around the arena as more and more people spotted Barbra with one of America's hottest male sex symbols: 'Isn't that Barbra Streisand with *Don Johnson?* Wow! Are those two a *couple* now?'

Following the brief fight – Tyson knocked Holmes out in the fourth round, just as he had predicted he would – the celebrity guests adjourned to the Imperial Ballroom of the Trump Plaza Hotel for a lavish soiree. 'Don and Barbra walked into the party hand in hand,' recalled one of the guests. 'They mingled, together and separately. Everyone was thrilled to see Barbra there, but to see her with Don Johnson really surprised everyone. They were really cute. Even while talking with other people, they would smile at each other from across the room.'

To a press corps ever salivating for a new superstar pairing, even the hint of a Streisand-Johnson romance proved irresistible. 'It's Barbra & Don & don't say it isn't!' screamed the headline of Liz Smith's column the following Monday. 'They are supposedly giving each other those looks you could pour on waffles,' Smith wrote. In a follow-up report, Smith described a dinner date the two had had at Manhattan's Mayflower Hotel: 'They . . . were seen getting so cozy [in their banquette] that eventually they all but slid down out of sight of the few other diners. [The romance] is something big and electric.'

Within days columnists all over the country were running whatever tidbits they could unearth about 'Hollywood's newest odd couple.' The pair even ended up as the subject of a *Bloom County* comic strip that dubbed Johnson, thirty-eight, 'Streisand's Toy Boy Goy.' Longtime Streisand watchers noted that Barbra, who always professed to crave privacy, had once again chosen to publicly unveil a new lover at a highly ballyhooed prizefight, just as she had done fourteen years earlier with Jon Peters, a man to whom Don Johnson bore several important similarities. Barbra's desire for privacy, it seemed, is less important to her when she wants to show off a new male bauble.

Barbra had met the rakishly handsome star of the flashy, innovative television cop drama *Miami Vice* ten months earlier backstage at the 1987 Grammy Awards in Los Angeles. Johnson and Whoopi Goldberg had announced that year's nominees – including *The Broadway Album* – for the Album of the Year Award. The camera focused on Barbra in the audience as Johnson read the names of the nominees, and when he pronounced her name 'Streizund,' a close-up showed her mouthing the correct pronunciation. Their encounter at the ceremonies was brief; Johnson barely had time to tell Barbra, who was with Richard Baskin, how much he enjoyed her work. She responded with a cheerful thank-you.

Barbra's romance with Richard Baskin had, over the years, cooled to a friendship – one that continues to this day – and thus she spent a 1987 Christmas holiday in Aspen on her own. It was then that she ran into Johnson again, at a party thrown by friends. Johnson had also come alone, and when he noticed Barbra sitting quietly amid a group of chattering guests, he reintroduced himself to her. After a few moments he led her by the hand out to a cozy balcony where the couple talked and laughed intimately in the moonlight for the rest of the evening as the other party guests tried not to be too obvious in their fascination.

A few days later Johnson was a conspicuous guest at a party Barbra threw at her rented chalet in Aspen's exclusive Red Mountain enclave. The couple also dined privately at Johnson's hotel. Because of the demands of his series, Johnson was based in Miami, and after he and Barbra returned to their respective coasts, they spent hours on the phone getting better acquainted. Although well known in the press as a slick womanizer, Johnson was also intelligent, funny, ambitious, and a caring father to his five-year-old son, qualities that drew Barbra to him. That he had recently been chosen 'The Sexiest Man Alive' by *People* magazine couldn't have escaped her notice either.

✳

A SELF-DESCRIBED hell-raiser as a kid in Missouri, who lost his virginity at age twelve to a seventeen-year-old baby-sitter, Don Johnson first came to public attention in the late sixties when the former teen idol Sal Mineo cast him in a Los Angeles stage production of the controversial prison drama, *Fortune and Men's Eyes*. As a pretty-boy rape victim, the teenaged actor received rave reviews and keen interest from the movie industry. But he made only a handful of films in the seventies, including the 1973 cult favorite *The Harrad Experiment*, in which he appeared nude. During filming, Johnson fell in love with Melanie Griffith, the precocious, flaxen-haired fourteen-year-old daughter of his co-star, Tippi Hedren. They married three years later.

It was the twenty-six-year-old Johnson's third attempt at matrimony, and lasted only two years. After the divorce he settled into a long affair with Barbra's *Main Event* co-star Patti D'Arbanville, who became the mother of his son, Jesse, in 1982. By the early eighties, Johnson found himself mired in made-for-television movies such as *Elvis and the Beauty Queen* (in which he played Presley) and *Katie: Portrait of a Centerfold*.

It was well known in Hollywood that Johnson's career problems had for years been exacerbated by drug and alcohol dependency. On any given day, he admitted in one interview, his intake of alcohol 'included a case of beer, a few martinis, several bottles of the best wine, and some good Napoleon brandy after dinner.' In 1982, shortly after Jesse's birth, Johnson joined Alcoholics Anonymous. The following year he was cast as Sonny Crockett in *Miami Vice*.

Set in the Art Deco world of Miami Beach, against a sound track of surging techno-rock, the vividly photographed show became an instant hit for NBC and by its second season had grown into a pop culture phenomenon. With their wardrobe of silk Armani suits and loosely fitted pastel sports jackets worn over snug T-shirts, Johnson and his co-star Philip Michael Thomas became the epitome of hip, unshaven masculine sex appeal. In a matter of months the full-fledged stardom that had eluded Don Johnson for fifteen years was now heaped upon him, and he reveled in it.

Johnson's high-profile celebrity status coincided with the dissolution of his relationship with D'Arbanville, and since maturity had only enhanced his sexual allure, it surprised no one that 'Don Juan-son,' as he was tagged in the fan magazines, reportedly took full advantage of the *Miami Vice* groupies who followed his every move.

Johnson was the most famous, glamorous, and unlikely man Barbra had been linked to romantically for many years, and the tabloid press in particular went into a feeding frenzy over the couple. During the first months of 1988, hardly a week went by without the supermarket rags running some new 'inside' scoop about Barbra and Don.

She had 'dragged him to Brooklyn' to meet her family, the tabloid writers claimed – although none of them still lived there! He had commissioned Gianni Versace to whip up a wedding gown for her. She 'desperately' wanted Don's baby. She insisted Johnson be circumcised prior to their marriage. He had put a down payment on a four-bedroom love nest for her in Aspen. She had lost fifteen pounds because she was too much in love to eat regularly. He had given her an engagement ring of clustered diamonds and emeralds. They planned to buy their own private island off the coast of Mexico. They would co-star in a remake of *The Thin Man*. They intended to record a duet of the Rolling Stones' classic 'Get Off My Cloud' and an album of Christmas songs written by Stevie Wonder and Lionel Richie.

The gossip got sillier and sillier, in part because the couple remained largely mute about their affair. When Barbra and Don did speak about their romance, it was to British reporters, with whom Barbra has always been franker than she is with American journalists. 'I've been with thousands of women,' Johnson told *London Today* magazine, 'but Streisand is supreme, unequaled in all the ways that count. I love her strengths, her direct approach to music, acting, people, and, yes, making love. To me she is beautiful. I know some people make fun of her nose, but let me tell you, she can smell a phony with it a mile away. She makes me laugh, and she makes me think.'

'I like sharing my life with a male counterpart,' Barbra told the *Daily Mail* while she was in London to promote *Nuts*. 'I have found one now, Don Johnson, and it is going very well. Like me, he is often misinterpreted and called a tough guy and difficult – and it is not true. That is one of our common bonds. He is very gentle, sensitive, and nurturing. He has wonderful manners and he can make me laugh. Will it last? How do I know? All I know is this moment. Would I marry again? Yes. But don't ask if I would marry him. I don't know. He makes me happy. I have never been so happy before, so it's something I am learning as if I am a child again. It is a new thing and I have to get used to it.'

To another writer she said, 'When I'm with Don, I can enjoy my celebrity, because I don't have to apologize to the man I'm with for getting all the attention. Don gets as much attention as I do.'

Eager to wring as much 'news' as possible out of the Streisand-Johnson affair, the weekly London tabloid *Chat* ran an interview with Elliott Gould in which he 'warned' Johnson against marrying Barbra and aired his grievances about his ex-wife. 'I don't know why I'm loyal to you,' Elliott claimed to have told Barbra weeks before. 'You're not nice to me. You don't like me. You're mean to me. You don't help me. You're rude to me.'

BACK IN THE States, Barbra was named 'Female Star of the Decade' by the National Association of Theater Owners at the group's annual convention in Las Vegas on February 23, 1988. Scheduled to arrive alone for the luncheon ceremony at Bally's Hotel, Barbra caused 'near pandemonium' when she swept in an hour late – hand in hand with Don. The couple of the moment were 'embraced warmly' at the VIP table by Jon Peters (of all people), and Barbra brought the house down when she quipped, 'Sorry I was a little late. I was auditioning for a part on *Miami Vice*.' Just days later Barbra did indeed tape a wordless walk-on for the show's 'Badge of Dishonor' episode (aired March 18), while she visited Johnson in Florida. Co-stars on the show were hounded by the press for details of what local papers were referring to as 'The Visit,' but they all took a 'no comment' stance. A minor flap erupted when Johnson confiscated a tabloid photographer's film after the man sneaked onto the set. One observer noted that Barbra seemed to turn 'positively giddy' whenever Don drew near.

A few weeks later the venerable show business reporter Hank Grant casually mentioned in his *Hollywood Reporter* column that when Barbra and Don attended a surprise birthday party for Quincy Jones on March 14, they told a few select friends that they were planning a September wedding. This juicy tidbit, coming as it did from a reputable journalist in an industry trade paper, was taken seriously, and press scrutiny of the affair heated up. Asked about the possibility of her daughter marrying Johnson, Diana Kind said, 'I only met him once. I don't know what to think. I'll know when she sends me an invitation.'

At the end of April it was reported that Barbra was devastated when Don failed to attend her forty-sixth birthday party because he couldn't get away from filming a new picture, *Dead-Bang*, in Canada. Gossips insisted, however, that Johnson had avoided Barbra's party because it was thrown by Jon Peters and attended by Don's ex-lover, Patti D'Arbanville, a Malibu neighbor of Barbra's. Don sent flowers and an apology, but Barbra's mood soured again when she heard rumors that Johnson was romancing his pretty young co-star, Penelope Ann Miller.

Perhaps to keep an eye on him, Barbra joined Don in Calgary, Alberta, the first week in May. The visit was idyllic, she told friends; she and Don had held each other all night long and had smooched at a private screening like teenagers on a date. 'It was so warm and loving,' she said. Later in the month the couple returned to Aspen for the final ski weekend of the season, and in July they were spotted with Don's son, Jesse, at an L.A. Dodgers game. (Barbra adored Jesse, who spent several weekends with his father frolicking at the Malibu compound.) A week later they cheered on the L.A. Lakers at the Forum. Clearly, any rift had been patched up. The lovebirds were billing and cooing again.

AS SHE HAD often done with men she loved, Barbra elected to bring Don into her career. For an album she planned that would trace the evolution of a love affair from beginning to end, Barbra decided to include 'Till I Loved You,' a duet from an unproduced pop opera, *Goya . . . A Life*, that Placido Domingo hoped to bring to Broadway. Barbra saw the song as a perfect vehicle for her and Johnson, who was eager to prove that the success of his Top 10 single 'Heartbeat' hadn't been a fluke.

On the day Don was scheduled to visit Barbra at the B&J recording studio in West Hollywood, where she was laying down tracks for the album, Barbra couldn't resist a little showing off. 'Of course, there were a couple of her framed gold records on the walls,' recalled one of the album's recording technicians, who spoke on the condition of anonymity, 'but I heard her tell an assistant to make sure *all* her gold albums were on display as well as some of her most famous magazine covers. It was kind of touching, really, that she felt she had to impress Don Johnson – who couldn't sing his way out of a wet paper bag.'

About the 'Till I Loved You' sessions Barbra said, 'It was a lot of fun singing with Don because he's very musical and has a unique-sounding voice. When he sings, he's an actor – and a really good one – so he knows about being in the moment, which is always new and different and the way I like to work.'

At an early screening of Johnson's latest film, *Sweet Hearts Dance*, a romantic comedy-drama co-starring Susan Sarandon, Barbra couldn't help but suggest a few changes. The picture's director, Robert Greenwald, was unusually receptive. '[She made] some very, very good suggestions,' he said. 'Nothing major. A laugh that seemed inappropriate [or] "This moment here I thought was a little bit ragged" – and she was right.'

As the rumored September nuptial date came and went, more and more column items indicated that Barbra's new romance was in fact fizzling. Johnson was spotted with a nameless blonde in New York and a 'ravishing' brunette in Miami, while Barbra attended a party with Richard Baskin in Hollywood. But Don joined Barbra in New York on September 14 at a concert-party thrown by Stevie Wonder at the Apollo Theater in Harlem. Wonder had performed there for three days before a live audience for his latest music video, and on the last night he was joined onstage by Barbra, Don, Jesse Jackson, Quincy Jones, and Time-Warner head Steve Ross. To the delight of the audience, Barbra joined Stevie in an impromptu duet.

A few days later Don was seen out on the town with the gorgeous eighteen-year-old actress Uma Thurman. Some press reports proclaimed the Streisand-Johnson affair dead, others quoted an 'intimate friend of the couple' to the effect that the wedding had been rescheduled for December. The truth was that the affair was all but over – because, some claimed, Barbra was disturbed by Don's suggestion that they embark on a non-monogamous open marriage.

Still, the duo attended the Hollywood premiere of *Sweet Hearts Dance* on September 18, and their arrival created bedlam. 'The doors of the black limo fling open,' wrote a *Los Angeles Herald Examiner* reporter, 'the paparazzi push forward, knocking over the red velvet ropes but still managing to keep the strobes firing as they trip over each other. Fans scream, bodyguards appear out of thin air, even uniformed LAPD officers are in the human wedge that forms around the arrivees.' Following the screening, Barbra and Don attended a small party where they shared a table with Patti D'Arbanville.

Three weeks later Columbia released a single of the 'Till I Loved You' duet to mixed reviews but heavy radio-audience response. Of Johnson's performance, *Time* said the song had him 'sounding more like a cop than he does on TV.' Many disc jockeys made fun of Johnson's gravelly vocals; one was so unremitting that Johnson called him to complain. 'I don't sing *that* bad!' he pleaded. Although it hit number one on adult contemporary radio formats, the record stopped at number twenty-five on the pop charts, primarily because the public had now learned of Barbra and Don's breakup, which rather spoiled the song's sentiments.

Although her intimates say she was deeply hurt by the collapse of the romance, Barbra kept characteristically mute on the subject. Johnson, however, told *Life* magazine, 'Barbra was more willing to stay [in the relationship]. She's an incredibly bright woman, and she's been through a great deal of therapy. I don't think I'm speaking out of school when I say that. We genuinely tried to make it work. But we'd reached a point where we had to make a commitment or let it go.'

The *Till I Loved You* album was released on October 6, 1988, peaked on the *Billboard* chart at number ten, and went platinum in a matter of weeks. It proved an unsatisfying collection of love songs, and rumors in the record industry claimed that Barbra was so distraught at the collapse of her relationship with Johnson that she couldn't face the rigors of another album of theater songs to follow up *The Broadway Album* and so had decided on this less demanding pop effort. *Till I Loved You* proved yet again Streisand's fallibility when it came to choosing appropriate material from contemporary sources.

ON OCTOBER 16, 1988, Barbra sang at a Los Angeles fund-raiser for Democratic presidential candidate Michael Dukakis. Sponsored by the Hollywood Women's Political Committee and held at the home of Ted and Susie Field in Beverly Hills, the gala attracted politicians from Jesse Jackson to Massachusetts Senator John Kerry and celebrities from Faye Dunaway to Bette Midler.

Hollywood liberals were in an optimistic mood. After eight years of 'benign neglect' of social programs by the Republican administration of Ronald Reagan, Massachusetts Governor Dukakis seemed to have an excellent chance to defeat Reagan's lackluster vice president, George Bush. Barbra threw herself behind the Dukakis campaign, although she did express disappointment that neither he nor Bush had chosen a woman as a running mate, as Walter Mondale had in 1984. 'Either Dukakis or Bush could have buttoned it up right now if they had chosen to run with a woman in November,' she said.

Barbra, of course, was the highlight of the evening as she sang 'Happy Days Are Here Again' and 'America the Beautiful.' The event raised $80,000 for the Dukakis campaign and put a scare into the Bush camp. Ten days later, Bush flew into Los Angeles for a $5,000-per-person reception at Bob Hope's home. An internal campaign memo pointed out that 'the press is allowed in briefly to capture the celebrities and the festivities. This event will impact all of California and offset the post-debate Barbra Streisand reception.'

When the memo was leaked to the press, Mark Goodie, a Bush campaign spokesman, took pains to point out that '"The Way We Were" is a Bush favorite. And actually we were very pleased when Governor Dukakis appeared with Barbra Streisand because we have been trying to remind American voters of the "misty water-colored memories of the way we were" just eight short years ago when the economic ox was in the ditch.'

George Bush won the election after Dukakis proved to be a less than formidable candidate. But Barbra and her fellow Democrats would have their day four years later.

BY THE END of 1988 Don Johnson had rekindled his relationship with Melanie Griffith, following steamy love scenes they played when Melanie appeared on *Miami Vice*. Johnson and Griffith soon announced plans to re-marry, and press reports claimed that Barbra had urged the couple to reconcile even as her own romance with Johnson ebbed. 'It was at the time that Barbra and I were seeing less of each other,' Johnson told the New York *Daily News*. 'During one conversation I told Barbra about the affection I still held for Melanie. Barbra said to me, "Don, in spite of your reputation, you're a family man at heart. You need a base and a family life. It may be that you've never stopped loving Melanie."' Following the couple's remarriage on June 26, 1989, Barbra continued to stay in touch with Johnson. 'She's really sweet,' Griffith told *Life* magazine. 'She sent Alexander [Griffith's son by the actor Steven Bauer] and Jesse the cutest Valentine's Day cards.'

'Barbra is part of the family,' Johnson added.

Perhaps the most enduring legacy of the Streisand-Johnson romance was Barbra's discovery of *The Prince of Tides*. A friend in the music business had first raved to Barbra about Pat Conroy's lyrical story of the deeply buried secrets of a dysfunctional southern family, but it was Johnson who urged her to read the book. Don hoped that he and Barbra might co-star in a film version of the powerfully emotional drama. But after their romance ended and Robert Redford acquired the book's movie rights, Johnson was never seriously in the running to play the lead in what would become Barbra's second directorial effort.

36

T he American South is a land of secrets, a place where laughter masks pain, good manners overrule anger, and appearances matter most. The South is also a region prone to denial – of its past, its present, and its inability to transform its future. Behind its locked wrought-iron gates, its ivy-wreathed walls, and its stately, silent mansions, the South revels in its impenetrable mystery and in the defiant eccentricity of its people. The region provides a perfect setting for *The Prince of Tides*, an epic story about one man's fight to save his future by finally coming to terms with his past.

Barbra, although she is the antithesis of a rural southerner, immediately identified with Pat Conroy's melodramatic novel, for despite its South Carolina low-country setting, *The Prince of Tides* raises a host of universal issues: the damage done to people by their families, the frustration caused by unfulfilled dreams, and the extraordinary freedom and self-discovery one can experience after confronting the psychological demons that lurk within. Like *Yentl* and *Nuts*, *The Prince of Tides* explored the ramifications of familial separation, social injustice, and the transformative power of forgiveness. Unlike the two earlier films, however, *The Prince of Tides* examined these topics from a male perspective. Its message was clear to Barbra – men can be everything: not only can they be 'physical, strong, male . . . [they] also can be nurturing, soft, not afraid to feel,' she said. Whereas Yentl discovered the facets of masculinity that lay within her, Conroy's protagonist, Tom Wingo, is forced to face his own femininity and, ultimately, to appreciate it.

'The southern way' and its 'juxtaposition of appearances,' Barbra later explained, was another theme she wanted to explore. In bringing *The Prince of Tides* to the screen, she worked diligently to reduce the lengthy work to its 'essence . . . its purest, simplest point.' Like most creative odysseys, it was a journey rife with the kind of drama and passion that distinguished the book, a journey that few artists other than the single-minded Streisand would have attempted with as much determination, energy, and vision.

Barbra had listened raptly as Don Johnson read entire passages of the book aloud to her early in their relationship, passages she later memorized in her quest to capture the soul of the novel. 'I was just so intrigued by . . . the poetry of it, the beauty of the writing,' she said, 'so I got the novel and read it and thought, I *have* to make this movie.'

THE PRINCE OF TIDES, published in 1986, tells the story of Henry Wingo, a crusty, often abusive shrimper; his wife, Lila; and their three children: Tom, his twin sister Savannah, and their older brother, Luke. Presented in a series of flashbacks, the children's eccentric, violent, and classically dys-functional southern childhood illuminates Conroy's main narrative: Tom's present-day fight to save the suicidal Savannah, a poet who is living in exile in New York.

At the urging of his insufferably manipulative, social-climber mother, Tom flies to New York to be near Savannah. There he meets and eventually falls in love with his sister's therapist, Dr Susan Lowenstein. Through a series of painful and ever more revealing discussions, Lowenstein attempts to unlock the buried secrets of Tom's past – secrets that hold the key to Savannah's recovery and, as the book makes increasingly clear, Tom's survival as well.

Suffering from a crumbling marriage, a guilt-ridden past, and a less-than-promising future as a football coach, Tom is trapped in a life with little meaning. So too is Lowenstein, whose lacquered, comely exterior masks an unhappy woman who feels alienated from her famous violinist husband and her spoiled son, Bernard. She and Tom learn to help each other in myriad ways; Tom coaches Bernard, helping him to become a decent high-school football player, while Lowenstein helps Tom to admit and accept the horrific truth about his past: as a child he was violently sodomized by one of three escaped convicts while the other two raped Savannah and Lila. With the help of their pet Bengal tiger, Tom and Luke kill the intruders, bury their bodies, and are sworn to secrecy by their devastated mother. As Lila says in the book, 'This didn't happen. Your father would never touch me again if he thought I had sexual intercourse with another man. No fine young man would ever marry Savannah once the word got out that she wasn't a virgin.'

In the denouement, Savannah recovers, Lowenstein and Tom end their passionate relationship, and he returns to his wife and family in the South – the land of marshes and tides, tradition and timelessness, magic and memories, and the place where Tom Wingo's soul resides.

Although *The Prince of Tides* seemed to be a tale that begged to be filmed,

Pat Conroy doubted that his semi-autobiographical labor of love would ever make it to the big screen. 'I don't know how Barbra got the rights to *The Prince of Tides*,' he said. 'But I'm sure fate played some part in it. I listen to music when I write. And Barbra was the performer I listened to while writing *The Prince of Tides*.'

Prior to Streisand's involvement in the film, Robert Redford had been attached to the MGM/UA-based project. With Andrew Karsch, a business associate of Conroy's, set to produce the film, Redford hoped to step into the multi-textured role of Tom Wingo as his follow-up to the disappointing *Legal Eagles*, released in 1986. But the script needed work.

By the fall of 1988, as rumors circulated that Streisand and Redford had met with Sydney Pollack to discuss a sequel to *The Way We Were*, Barbra had become actively involved in *The Prince of Tides*. When it became clear to Redford that she was passionate about making the film, only one question remained: would Redford agree to star in a film that Streisand wanted to direct?

On April 9, 1989, it was official: Streisand would not only direct *The Prince of Tides* for MGM/UA but would also star as Susan Lowenstein. 'I couldn't have gotten the picture made if I wasn't in it,' she later revealed. 'I certainly wouldn't have gotten to direct.' Andrew Karsch would produce along with Streisand, and principal photography was tentatively scheduled to commence in the late summer of 1989. But Robert Redford would no longer play Tom Wingo. Apparently unwilling to be directed by Barbra, he had chosen to star instead in Sydney Pollack's *Havana*, which turned out to be a major career miscalculation.

BARBRA COULDN'T GET Pat Conroy to return her calls. 'I had heard rumors,' Conroy explained, 'that Barbra Streisand [would direct the film], but I did not know for sure. I started getting telephone messages to call her, but I thought that was just a joke. Friends had played similar tricks on me. So I just didn't return her calls.'

Barbra was not amused. 'I wasn't ever offended, but I was disturbed, hurt,' she admitted. 'I thought, What? Why isn't he returning my calls?' Her passion for the project grew with each passing day, and she longed to talk to Conroy about the novel. 'When I read the book I saw the movie. I felt the movie. I felt what would be the important themes: how everyone's relationship has changed through compassion and through love.'

Undeterred by Conroy's seeming snub, Barbra sat down with the screen-writer Becky Johnson during the summer and rewrote the script in a furious rush of creative energy. 'The first draft of the screenplay only took three weeks,' Barbra said, 'but then there was six months of discussing things with therapists and doctors, and another two and a half months of discussing another version of the script. Then the roof fell in. The studio [ran] out of money.'

The news that MGM/UA had dropped *The Prince of Tides* due to its own financial difficulties crushed Barbra. She instructed her agents to shop the floundering project around even as she continued to work on the script. Just as she had with *Yentl*, she refused to give up.

BARBRA'S SEARCH FOR her perfect 'prince' began the moment Redford bowed out. Very few actors, she realized, would be capable of fully realizing the multifaceted depth of Tom Wingo, and casting that role became her top priority. (Despite protests from purist fans of the book who felt Streisand wasn't beautiful enough to portray the lioness Lowenstein, Barbra felt no trepidation. 'When I first read the book, I thought, Jesus, I'm perfect for this part. I identify with this woman completely, even to a line in the book that says she is in the middle of aging extraordinarily well,' she said with a laugh.)

After fruitless discussions with Tom Berenger, Dennis Quaid, and Kevin Costner, Barbra began to narrow down an already slim list of possibilities. Jeff Bridges and his father, Lloyd, were asked to play Tom and his father, an interesting casting concept. Jeff said no – a mistake Lloyd has never let him forget. Finally, after asking to see a videocassette of the *Rich Man, Poor Man* television miniseries, Streisand knew she had found her man: Nick Nolte.

Nolte had caused a sensation in 1976 playing blond bad boy Tom Jordache in producer Jon Epstein's groundbreaking television production. The press dubbed him the new Redford, but Nolte, never comfortable with that matinee idol label, spent the rest of his checkered career trying to prove them wrong. Moving from one character role to another, he obscured his handsome features in a portfolio of guises, most of them far less dashing than his star-making turn in *Rich Man, Poor Man*. After Nolte played a filthy bum in *Down and Out in Beverly Hills*, the director Paul Mazursky noted that 'Nick's got a whole thing going on underneath and inside that he's not going to say to you.' Streisand recognized this rare quality as well, and she wanted to bring out that duality for the first time onscreen.

Like Streisand, the forty-nine-year-old Nolte believed in fate. 'Unlike the common perception, the material doesn't come to you from studios; it comes to you from other people, and usually by happenstance, circumstances, and usually by luck.' Luck did enter into the scenario, with a secret push from Barbra. While Nolte was filming *Q & A* for Sidney Lumet, the film's producer, Burt Harris, gave him *The Prince of Tides* to read.

Nolte found it 'wonderful' but was puzzled when Harris told him that Barbra wanted to meet with him about playing Tom. 'It was peculiar,' he recalled, '[because] at that time I was playing a character in *Q & A* and I weighed maybe 250 pounds. I had a mustache that came over both lips, and black hair. So I don't know what possessed her to think I could play that character.'

When she met Nolte, Barbra immediately knew her instincts had served her well. 'I saw a lot of pain in his work, in his eyes,' she remembered. 'And then, in talking to him, he was at a vulnerable place, ready to explore feelings – romantic feelings, sexual feelings, and deep, secretive feelings.'

Nolte concurred. 'I'd wanted to work with a female director for maybe five years. I knew you'd get a different kind of insight,' he said. 'With a male director, there's always an agreement about how far a conversation about emotions can go. It's analytical. You lay out the emotions a character would feel, and the two men sit there and say, "Yeah, that's it. Fine." With a female, it's never "it."'

Barbra and Nick began extensive discussions about how best to illuminate the bruised and battered boy hidden within the adult Tom Wingo. 'Barbra was the perfect person to bring this story to the screen,' Nolte said later. 'There are the obvious reasons [such as] the wonderful Jewishness that she shares with the character of Lowenstein . . . But once we got to talking we realized we both knew a lot about dysfunctional families and co-dependency . . . [and] that's a lot of what this film is about.'

Nick and Barbra's conversations often lasted for hours. 'One thing about Barbra, there is not going to be a leaf unturned,' he said. 'We spent many days before we shot discussing masculinity, femininity, women, men, relationships, love, mothers, fathers. That's the process I wanted to get into. I wanted to follow it through and see what the female aspect of it was, because that's what Tom Wingo's problem is. He's trying to figure out the women in his life.'

Although Tom Wingo is a man trying to understand femininity, Streisand wanted Nolte to play him partly because she found the actor to be so utterly masculine on the exterior. As she learned about Nolte's years of hard drinking and hard living, and a childhood filled with pain, Barbra increasingly felt that Nick's reality dovetailed with Tom's fictional story in many ways.

She also felt that he needed a touch of romance. 'I looked at all his films,' Barbra said, 'and the love scenes were always truncated. There's never a bedroom scene. He's much more comfortable in character roles . . . I know he's a man, a physical man, a sensual man, so why not incorporate that in the part?'

Streisand knew, too, that Nolte had the inner strength to get back into shape for the film quickly; he had done it several times before, beginning with *Rich Man, Poor Man*. Nolte eventually lost over thirty pounds for *The Prince of Tides* and, through sheer will, transformed himself into a golden lion once again.

BARBRA HAD A sickening feeling of déjà vu. As had happened with *Yentl*, she couldn't persuade anyone to finance *The Prince of Tides*. After Warner Brothers became the latest studio to turn the picture down, Barbra turned once again to Jon Peters, who was now the co-chairman of Columbia Pictures Entertainment. Jon came through and offered to back the film, but the studio balked at Barbra's asking price of $7 million for starring, directing, and producing. They offered her $6 million. Barbra refused.

'They wanted me to [accept] almost a million dollars [less] for [*The Prince of Tides*],' she recalled. 'I thought that was too much, and I'd [accept] half a million dollars [less]. If they didn't take that [compromise] I wouldn't have done the movie.' Again as she had with *Yentl*, Barbra soon got a sign from another sphere. 'I went to bed, where I have a painting of a beautiful lady in pink. There's a light over the painting. In the middle of the night I was awakened by a click. The light goes on over the painting. I sit up in bed and what came to me was, "Light up your art." Totally visual and *totally* real. I was cynical anyway, so I turned off the light and went to bed, and a few hours later the light went on again and it was like, "You didn't *believe* me?" The next morning [Columbia] called back and said I only had to [take] half a million dollars [less]. Who knows? I took it as a sign.'

JON PETERS MADE sure that Barbra was treated with the respect she deserved at Columbia. Because she had helped Jon to become a producer and studio executive – he was now one of the most powerful in the business – cynics dubbed Streisand's jump to Columbia 'payback time for Peters.' Barbra ignored the negative whispers and joked again about the benefits of her relationship with Jon, this time saying that '*ex*-boyfriends come in handy.'

Barbra resumed her efforts to get Pat Conroy on the phone, still without success. 'Finally,' Conroy said, 'she caught up to me at a hotel in Los Angeles and asked me why I hadn't called. It did seem rude on my part. And so after that I agreed to go to New York to work with her for a two-week polish on the script.'

Although much of Conroy's book concerned Luke Wingo – Luke, not Tom, is 'the Prince of Tides' – Barbra felt the drama should revolve around Tom's inner journey, and each new version reflected that attempt to capture the essence of the story. She also wanted to accentuate the love affair between Tom and Susan Lowenstein because she saw the film as a romance.

By focusing primarily on Tom's present-day problems, Streisand felt justified in making the Lowenstein role more central to the story. After all, it is Dr Lowenstein who becomes the savior of the entire Wingo family. It is Lowenstein who changes Tom's life and saves Savannah's; it is Lowenstein's name that Tom speaks in the final lines of the book, and it is his memories of Lowenstein that will sustain him in the years ahead. But none of Streisand's several *Prince of Tides* scripts ever deviated from placing the overall emphasis on Tom. 'The story is not about me,' Streisand said.

THE FIRST MEETING between Barbra and Pat Conroy took place at her Carolwood home in the spring of 1990, and it was a memorable experience for both of them. 'When I first met Barbra, she asked me if she looked like the doctor, and I said no. So she said, "Does this look like Lowenstein?" and she flipped this button and this huge image of her came up on her screen. She had not tested for the part, of course, but she dressed for it and she was in character in the scene. I told her "Yeah, that's Lowenstein."'

Because Conroy realized that 'her determination is the reason this movie is getting made,' he felt an obligation to please Barbra. 'She would give me homework, five or six scenes to look at a night,' he said. 'I was afraid not to have it done the next day. I couldn't imagine coming in and saying, "Barbra, I didn't do it. I couldn't. It didn't come to me.'

'My favorite part of the whole thing was when we would sit there and she would read the part of the psychiatrist and I would read the part of the coach. I was her co-star for a couple of weeks. How many writers get to live a fantasy life like this?'

Streisand characteristically questioned Conroy incessantly. 'The first day I was with her, she asked me question after question about the book. I remember she asked me about this reference to the Carolina shag. I said, "Well, that's how we used to dance in South Carolina when I was a kid." So she asked me to teach it to her. I said, "Barbra, I feel like a bit of an idiot." She said, "Just go ahead."' A videotape of the couple doing the shag to a classic Carolina beach tune shows the student Streisand executing the intricate arm-twisting, body-spinning dance better than her teacher. 'You see,' Conroy continued, 'what I did not know about her was that she has an incredible sense of fun. Like everyone else, I had read stuff about her. I thought, Holy God, I am going to be working with the Bride of Frankenstein. I thought she would yell at me, hurt my feelings, slap me around. I was completely stunned to find out that she was a delight.'

After working together for two weeks, Streisand and Conroy were pleased with the results. 'I've never seen anyone go through a total immersion in a project like she does,' he said. 'It completely obsesses her and takes over her life. I mean, here is how much input I had on the script: I think Barbra actually wrote it. She certainly wrote more of it than I did. She whipped that thing into shape the way she liked it, and I just helped with the polish. She should have taken a screenwriting credit on it. I think she even tried for one, but the Writers Guild works in Byzantine ways, which I don't understand. She certainly deserved it.'

While Streisand worked with Conroy, she also discussed her final casting choices for the film, budgeted at $25 million and now set to go before the cameras in June 1990. Earlier in the year she had scouted locations throughout the southern Atlantic seaboard, and had settled on Beaufort, South Carolina, the town Conroy had lived in as a teen and the real-life counterpart of Colleton, the fictional town where the Wingo children were raised. Set among the marshlands and inlets off the coast of South Carolina, Beaufort's rural beauty is a bewitching blend of Spanish moss-draped trees, soft, sandy soil, and atmospheric, weather-beaten homes. Streisand considered it the perfect place to bring Conroy's novel to life.

In addition to Nolte, Barbra surrounded herself with the finest actors, beginning with Blythe Danner as Tom's wife, Sallie. According to Streisand, Danner exuded a 'warm and homey' aura and was 'easy to talk to, easy to like.' And these soothing qualities defined Sallie's character as well.

Barbra originally considered Kate Nelligan to play Sallie, but after she spoke to the forty-year-old Canadian-born actress she changed her mind. She found Nelligan so beautiful and charismatic she immediately saw her as the young Lila Wingo. After Nelligan's reading, Barbra changed her mind again: now she wanted Nelligan to play both the young and the older Lila in the kind of tour-de-force acting challenge Nelligan loved. 'She's the only one who could pull it off, really,' Barbra said with admiration.

For the role of Herbert Woodruff, Lowenstein's tyrannical husband, Streisand chose Jeroen Krabbé, whose work in *Crossing Delancey* caused Streisand to shout 'That's the guy!' In the small but important role of Savannah, Barbra chose Melinda Dillon, and she finally picked the comedian George Carlin to play Savannah's gay Greenwich Village neighbor, Eddie.

Barbra has always said and done exactly as she felt, of course, and the casting of Bernard, Lowenstein's hostile teenage son, is an example. The mother-son dynamic in *The Prince of Tides*, so evident in Lila and Tom's volatile relationship, is also explored in the subplot involving Susan and Bernard. Angry, disillusioned, and lonely, Bernard feels trapped by the well-mapped plan his parents have laid out for his life. His father expects him to play the violin, but Bernard wants to play varsity football as well. With Tom as his coach, he accomplishes his goal – and in the process breaks free from his parents' smothering concern.

When Jason Gould read the script, he very much wanted to play Bernard. He had already made tentative forays into acting, totally independent of his mother, and had appeared in small roles in several films and television shows. Now he did something he had never done before: he asked Barbra to give him the part. At first, fearful of being criticized for nepotism, she said no: 'I resisted hiring him, even though he read the [part] at a reading we had the first time we finished the script, and he was absolutely brilliant. But I thought he was too old for the part [Jason was twenty-four, Bernard seventeen]. And I was concerned about the complexities of mother-son direction and so forth.'

Those complexities, indeed, were the main reason Barbra was initially so reticent about casting Jason. Although she has admitted that she and Jason share many similarities, including a love of privacy and a disdain for 'the glamorous side of show business,' there are also many differences between them. Barbra is ambitious; Jason far less so. According to Barbra, this particular difference began at birth, when he was delivered by cesarean section. 'Even though I went through labor for eight hours, he didn't have to struggle through the birth canal . . . I find that's connected somehow. In a way, something was too easy for him. Everything he does, he's very gifted; he'll sit down and play you something, having never taken a lesson, make a film, draw, write a screenplay. But he's not driven like I am.'

Barbra decided to cast Chris O'Donnell, who would soon make a strong impression with Al Pacino in *Scent of a Woman*, as Bernard. But fate, in the form of Pat Conroy, intervened on Jason's behalf. 'Barbra showed me this kid that she had cast for the role of her son, a very handsome blond kid,' Conroy said. 'Of course, everyone looks wonderful in Hollywood, but I said, "That ain't the kid." So she said, "I already hired him." I said, "That still ain't him." And she said, "Look, he's a good athlete." I said, "This kid [Bernard] is *not* a good athlete; that's the point." So she sort of flipped me through other kids she'd auditioned. She finally came to this one kid. I didn't know it was her son. But he showed a snarling, wonderful teenage quality. I said, "That's the kid right there."'

Barbra was stunned. Then she realized that Jason fit Conroy's description of Bernard almost exactly. 'He's described in the book just as Jason looks: dark curly hair, dark eyes, long legs, prominent nose and full lips like his mother,' Barbra said. Still, she wavered. 'I thought he was too thin. He's my son, I never think he eats enough, you know? And I said, "He's too thin," and Pat said, "He's thin in the book. I wrote [that] he weighs a hundred forty pounds." I said, "No, I think Jason weighs one twenty-five." So I called Jason, and I asked how much he weighed and he said, "A hundred forty pounds. Why?" And I thought, This was meant to be.'

So O'Donnell was out and Jason was in, but Barbra still fretted about directing her son. 'In real life he never wanted me to criticize him or tell him how to wear his hair. I told him as the director of the movie, you're gonna have to accept that from me.' She also warned him how cruel Hollywood and the ever-cynical press could be. 'Be willing to accept getting attacked [for this movie] because you're my son,' she told him. 'You have to be prepared for all that.' Jason assured her he could handle it.

Something Jason didn't expect to have to handle popped up in the May 15, 1990, issue of the *Star*, a supermarket tabloid. Across the top of the front page blazed the headline, 'Barbra Streisand heartsick – her only son hangs out at gay bars.' Jason, needless to say, hated this intrusion into his personal life, and Barbra was furious. 'I've just about gotten used to the garbage they've been writing about me for years,' she said, 'but this is a new low in rag journalism.'

It got lower. In July 1991 another tabloid, the *Globe*, ran a story, 'Barbra Weeps over Gay Son's Wedding,' which alleged that Jason had 'married' the male model David Knight in an elaborate ceremony in his West Hollywood home. The report of the wedding was nonsense of course, but Jason was indeed involved with the exceptionally handsome young man, who had been featured on the cover of the *International Male* catalog and with whom Jason worked out at the Sports Connection, a West Hollywood health club. Barbra was angrier than ever about her son's loss of privacy.

Jason's 'outing' and the pain it caused brought him and Barbra closer together. It also opened her eyes to many of the problems faced by homosexuals in today's society. As would any mother, Barbra worried about Jason's happiness and about his health in the midst of the AIDS epidemic. But she never condemned him for his sexuality; she told him she loved him and accepted him no matter what.

As for the tabloid's assertion that Barbra was devastated by Jason's homosexuality and had 'refused to attend the wedding,' she retorted, 'I don't care if my son marries a chimpanzee; I would be at the wedding.'

Elliott was less accepting at first, although he did come around. 'That's [Jason's] preference, his business,' he told Corinna Horan in the *Courier-Mail*. 'It's something that's new to me, and it's an acutely delicate subject. But I'm more than just empathetic. Whether it has been a problem for Barbra, I don't know. It's really important not to be prejudiced, and both of us are devoted to him.'

✳

PRINCIPAL PHOTOGRAPHY ON *The Prince of Tides* was scheduled to begin in Beaufort in June. Months before, Barbra's production crew had begun constructing the lavishly detailed interior sets that would capture Conroy's evocative locales. Under the supervision of the Oscar-winning production designer Paul Sylbert, who would later complain bitterly about Streisand's perfectionism, the interior of the Wingo family home was constructed in a local gymnasium; a dusty county warehouse became Lowenstein's chic high-rise New York apartment, and the National Guard armory housed both Lowenstein's wood-paneled office and Savannah's Greenwich Village flat.

Everything was soon in place for the arrival of La Streisand. Soon the sleepy town of Beaufort, South Carolina, would be awakened from its antebellum slumber with a high-tech Hollywood jolt. As the *News-Press* in the neighboring town of Savannah put it, 'Beaufort is going bonkers for Barbra.'

37

Barbra's staff scurried around Beaufort faster than a duck on a June bug, as they say in the South, in anticipation of the star's imminent arrival. Everything had to be perfect. The white wood three-story antebellum mansion rented by Streisand for the duration of the shoot had been fitted with a white canvas backyard security screen to keep the gawkers at bay. Her Oyster Cove production office staff solicited local résumés for extra work, manned a slew of perpetually ringing phones, and orchestrated the endless details, from food to flowers, that Barbra's film required.

For starters, no environmentally incorrect plastic plates were to be used by the caterers; long-stemmed gardenias, out of season in the South, had to be flown in from South America; fresh-cut flowers were to fill Barbra's house daily; her rented Ford Crown Victoria station wagon and silver Cadillac Coupe De Ville needed to be kept clean; and an enclosed air-conditioned walkway that would lead from her Winnebago to the set had to be constructed. Bystanders later complained that this peculiar structure proved that Streisand didn't want to be seen, but crew members knew the real reason: it was hot that summer in Beaufort, and Barbra didn't want her makeup to melt.

The gossip about Barbra mushroomed as her arrival grew near. When she had flown to Beaufort in February to scout locations, the town had been charmed by her. She had dined at Plums on Bay Street, fallen in love with their 'Diet Center Maintenance' turkey sandwich, then gone off the diet wagon with a scoop of Oreo coffee ice cream for dessert. She had worn little makeup, dressed unassumingly, appeared to be 'shy but sweet,' and spent lots of money in antique shops throughout the county. Perhaps, the townspeople of Beaufort thought, she wasn't as inaccessible as they had been led to believe.

When filming began on June 18, however, a very different Barbra emerged, and the message was clear: she had come to work, not socialize. The distant diva persona returned, and her popularity suffered. Streisand was unconcerned; she had a movie to direct, produce, and star in. Nick Nolte, on the other hand, quickly ingratiated himself with the people of Beaufort via his daily jogging and good ol' boy dinners at local restaurants, but his schedule was far less demanding than Barbra's. She simply didn't have the time to stop and talk to hordes of tourists; the pressure on her to finish *The Prince of Tides* on schedule and within budget was intense. After all, Hollywood was watching.

CHIEF AMONG THE problems Barbra faced while making *The Prince of Tides* was her strained relationship with the film's production designer, Paul Sylbert. His professional association with Barbra was respectful at best, argumentative and threatening at worst. Disagreements between these two strongly opinionated artists began soon after Streisand arrived in South Carolina. After inspecting his black-and-white set for Dr Lowenstein's New York apartment, Streisand reportedly told him to change it. Sylbert, who argued that Lowenstein's home should reflect a sophisticated European coldness, refused. Tempers flared. Sylbert allegedly threatened to walk off the picture and take his art department with him. Streisand stewed, and finally compromised.

Later, Barbra admitted that Sylbert had been right, but she didn't like him any better for it. Their relationship would end with Sylbert accusing Barbra of bad-mouthing him all over Hollywood. Barbra has never commented on the feud specifically, although she later told journalist Michael Shnayerson, 'They said I fire people and it hasn't been true. But they're going to say that about you anyway because you're at the top of the heap, so you might as well do what you have to do. The craft takes so much out of you that it's very important for the soul, the spirit, the body, to be surrounded by a loving support system. I didn't have that on *Prince of Tides*. The grips, the prop people, the gaffers, were wonderfully supportive, but there was a handful of "boy's-clubbers" who were not, and it made my job extra difficult. I want to work with people who say, "Yes, it can be done." And I won't be afraid to fire people who constantly say "It can't."'

DESPITE THE LOCAL griping about Barbra's aloofness, the filming was a boon to Beaufort's economy. 'Although exact figures are not yet available,' wrote Kay Graves in the Savannah *News-Press*, 'Beaufort conservatively expects to take in from $2 million to $4 million by the time the filmmakers leave town August 13.' The money that poured into the Beaufort coffers represented every expenditure imaginable: office supplies, hotel room rentals, groceries, restaurant meals, flowers, department store purchases.

One story that made the locals see red ran in the Savannah *News-Press*: 'According to at least one source, Madame Director telephoned the nearby Marine Corps Air Station and asked that the field's jet-flight pattern be changed to accommodate her "quiet on the set" requirements. No dice, said the Marines.' The Who-does-she-think-she-is? sniping grew stronger every day.

Perhaps the final insult came from Beaufort police officer B. R. Anderson, who was hired to patrol the sets daily. 'Barbra's rude,' he said in blunt southern-macho fashion. 'I think she owes her fans more than she gives them.' As for Barbra's fashion sense while directing – she usually wore comfortable but frumpy *shmattehs* – Anderson said, 'She reminds me of that Carol Burnett character, the cleaning lady.'

BARBRA HAD FAR more serious issues to deal with. Her mother, now eighty-two, underwent heart bypass surgery in Los Angeles three weeks after the filming began, and Barbra was suddenly faced with the sobering issue of her mother's mortality. 'When I was faced with the potential loss of my mother, the movie became much easier,' she said. 'It lost its importance. It took the proper place – it's much more secondary to life. That's what *The Prince of Tides* is about in a way – learning to appreciate your mother.'

Although Streisand felt that *The Prince of Tides* explored the damaging emotional ramifications of being 'programmed as children by our parents,' she came to realize that as far as her own mother was concerned, 'I saw she did the best she could, you know? It's just another generation. And she obviously caused me to be who I am today. Because I was only trying to prove to my mother that I was something. That I could make it.'

After Diana recovered, Barbra said, 'I remember feeling, once my mother survived her operation, that this was all such a gift. I mean, the movie was only a movie, but how lucky I was to have this opportunity to have my mother still alive, that that was the important thing – *life*.' In fact, according to Streisand, her mother played a pivotal role in her desire to become a director. 'Being a director is probably the best job for me because I was a kid who always told her mother what to do. It's the way I was brought up; my mother gave me so much power.'

THE ACTORS IN *The Prince of Tides* found Barbra to be a sensitive, calm, and brilliantly observant director. Throughout the entire production, she placed the other actors first; her own performance became nearly an afterthought. 'You see,' she explained, 'when I direct and produce a movie, the actress comes last . . . in other words, I serve the film first. So for this one, I filmed all my scenes last . . . I don't ever cater to the actress.'

Nick Nolte felt that Streisand's musical sense helped make her a better director. 'Having been an actress, she knows the problems of the actor. She also thinks in rhythms, musically, because of the music, so she's very tuned in to sound, and that translates into scenes, how they rhythmically should play.'

Barbra often felt awkward during her love scenes with Nolte. 'When we were doing the love scenes at first,' he remembered, 'they would just get hot, just start to really work, and she'd cut! The actress would jump and say, "Wait, wait, wait," and the actress would order the director to cut. And I would say, "Barbra, why are you cutting it? It's just getting good." And she'd say, "Well . . ." and get flustered. Then she saw the dailies, and she said, "If I cut the camera any time when it's really going good, don't let me do that.' Nolte was pleased to comply with her request.

'I'm not an exhibitionist in any way,' Barbra explained. 'I do not like scenes like that.' She also refused to allow nudity in the film because of her belief that it distracts the audience from the story. In Tom and Susan's first love scene, she decided to 'leave our clothes on and do it against the wall.' In a later amorous moment in bed, she didn't remove her nightgown, but her sheer top ended up showing more than she expected of her breasts. 'I showed [that scene] in a preview,' she said. 'I got a feeling that it took people out of the scene. It was like, all of a sudden, there's Barbra Streisand's breasts, instead of the emotion of the scene. So I cut it differently. I made it into a two-shot in close-ups.'

BARBRA'S LEGENDARY ATTENTION to detail is evident throughout *The Prince of Tides*, beginning with her own onscreen wardrobe and hairstyles. Streisand wanted Lowenstein to slowly blossom after meeting Tom; her wardrobe, which mirrored that personal renewal, grows less somber and studied as the relationship grows more romantic. We initially see Lowenstein in dark severely tailored suits, sleek, straight hair and perfectly applied makeup. But as she emerges from her shell, we see her in white, pink, and floral-patterned ensembles, with curly windswept hair and minimal cosmetics.

In Tom and Lila's emotional confrontation scene, Streisand commissioned a portrait of Lila to hang behind Tom, so that when he turned away from her in the heat of their argument, he would still be confronted with her stern, omnipresent face. For the spectacularly beautiful underwater sequence that opens the film, shot in a huge water tank at MGM, Barbra spent two weeks getting the color of the water exactly right, and had real seaweed and ocean grasses sent in for authenticity.

Barbra carefully designed the film's emotional climax – the crucial catharsis scene that follows Tom's childhood rape revelation to Lowenstein – for maximum effect. Streisand made certain that this very difficult scene, heightened by dramatic close-ups and tension-filled dialogue, was the final one Nolte shot. To prepare the actor fully for the intensely vulnerable moment, she also showed him the full sequence of Tom's rape.

Tom's breakdown in Lowenstein's arms, of course, proved a particularly demanding moment for Nolte, and for Streisand. An enormous amount of trust and understanding were involved, especially on Nolte's part. With a lesser director, the scene could have been an embarrassment. But Nolte's inner emotions were summoned to the surface so brilliantly by Streisand's patient direction that many critics felt this was the moment in which he was guaranteed an Oscar nomination.

The scene struck a deep chord in Barbra. 'That happened to me in therapy,' she recalled. 'My therapist touched my hand and I just broke down. I thought at the time, This must be what it feels like to be held by your mother.'

ON AUGUST 13, with most of *The Prince of Tides* in the can, Barbra said good-bye to hot, humid Beaufort and flew to New York to film outdoor location scenes. She was in a far less anxious state than she had been three months earlier. Although she was still consumed with work, the initial terror she had felt after not having directed a film in eight years had lessened. When she arrived in Manhattan, she acted as though she had fallen in love with the city and its singular electricity all over again.

She stopped traffic while filming scenes in Central Park; hundreds of fans stood and watched Barbra direct Jason and Nick in the football-coaching sequences. A fan's videotape of the Central Park shoot shows Barbra playing delightedly with Nolte's toddler son, lying on her back and balancing him in the air on the bottoms of her feet. The video camera also caught her sitting in her director's chair, watching the action. When she notices the fan's camera, her expression turns sour and she points at someone to make him stop.

Streisand wasn't above using her enormous fame when a Greenwich Village shot needed more background traffic: she simply approached unsuspecting motorists and requested that they appear in the scene. 'So I walk down the street – which is great because as Barbra Streisand the actress I would've been so shy, but now as Barbra Streisand the director I can *use* being known as an actress – and I walk over to some guy's car and go, "Hi, I'm Barbra Streisand; I'm directing a movie here. Would you mind being in the shot?"' Most motorists complied with delight.

The complexities of the personal and professional relationship between Barbra and her son became clear during one scene between Jason and Nick. Barbra was unsatisfied with a certain line reading Jason gave, and she later admitted, 'Jason got mad. He said, "What's wrong, you don't like it?" I said, "Jason, you have to separate here. I'm saying everything you're doing is wonderful, but I don't believe this particular line reading, and I can't lie to you, so let's work on it, and don't be mad at me as your goddamned mother."'

Despite that moment of tension, mother and son usually worked together very effectively, most notably during a two-day shoot of one of the film's most difficult scenes, Bernard's violin solo in the midst of bustling Grand Central Station. Streisand, instead of being nervous, relished the pressure. 'Those were the hottest days, the most spontaneous,' she said. 'It was so much fun. It was so alive.'

Jason saw things differently. 'Oh, God, that was the worst part of it. When you have hundreds of people watching you, it's terrifying,' he said. 'Actually, practically all my scenes were outside in parks and public places where there were crowds of people.'

The company went to upstate New York to film the love montage that details the growing romantic relationship between Tom and Susan. Detractors later scoffed that the footage resembled a 'soft-focus coffee ad.' Streisand disagreed, and explained that the gauzy, ultra-romantic outdoor moments were a technical accident: mist had formed on the camera lens, creating a 'pastoral, impressionistic' look.

AFTER *THE PRINCE OF TIDES* wrapped in September 1990, Barbra went to work on editing and scoring the picture as well as planning the marketing for its release a year later. For John Barry, initially hired to compose the score, the experience proved traumatic. Barry and Streisand locked horns from day one; his unwillingness to incorporate her ideas into his score was a nightmare for both of them. He left the project in a storm of bitter recriminations.

'She is the worst person I have *ever* had to work with,' he told a reporter in the spring of 1991. 'Everyone told me I must be crazy working with her, but I thought it would probably work out. But she had to be involved with everything that I and everyone else on the film was doing. She would never leave you alone. She was a complete control freak, very bossy and into the superstar bit.'

Barry's replacement, thirty-nine-year-old James Newton Howard, was far more open to Barbra's all-encompassing involvement in the scoring process. So receptive was he, in fact, that they became romantically involved shortly after the 1990 holiday season, and their relationship made the papers after he escorted her to a star-studded January 13 tribute to Quincy Jones at the Century Plaza Hotel in Los Angeles.

Howard had in fact known Barbra for years; a former keyboard player for Elton John, he had worked on *Songbird* and *Emotion* with Streisand prior to getting reacquainted with her late in 1990. Tall, good looking, and talented, the ex-husband of Rosanna Arquette, he had scored *Pretty Woman* and *Flatliners*, but working with Barbra was a career highlight for him. 'Barbra is a sweetheart,' he said, 'but she can be quite blunt. If you're not thick-skinned, then she's not easy to take. I happen to think she's a genius. The process of working with her is a difficult one because her perfectionism is unequaled. She's incredibly demanding, but I can truthfully say that working with her has elevated my own work.'

In addition to the score, Howard also composed 'Places That Belong to You,' the film's love theme, with lyrics by Alan and Marilyn Bergman. Barbra recorded the song as a possible end-credit vocal, but she wavered on whether or not to include it in the film, mainly because she didn't want to take the emphasis away from Tom's character at the end of the picture. More importantly, Barbra felt she would be taken more seriously as a director without it. Although 86 percent of the film's preview audiences wanted the song to be included in the final version, Streisand, calling its presence 'just wrong,' said no.

When Columbia first previewed *The Prince of Tides* in June 1991, Barbra was overjoyed with the positive audience reaction, and the studio was so pleased that they pushed back the film's previously announced September launch date to December so that *Tides* could be its major holiday release. Barbra objected. After years of work on the project, she said, 'I would rather it be released earlier. The angst is awful, you know? It's like, get this thing out already!'

As happens so often to Barbra, a pall was cast over *The Prince of Tides* even before its release when Caryn James of *The New York Times*, in a preview of fall films, compared *The Prince of Tides* to the ignominious Bruce Willis bomb *Hudson Hawk* and called it 'a vanity production.' Two weeks later the paper published a letter from Columbia Pictures Chairman Frank Yablans, taking issue: 'No Hollywood studio screens a movie four months before opening unless it knows one thing: the picture is outstanding . . . We were particularly incensed to see this film labeled a vanity production. It is not unusual for talented people – among them Woody Allen, Kevin Costner and Warren Beatty – to direct and star in pictures. Why is Barbra Streisand, when she chooses to do the same, singled out for such criticism?'

The *Los Angeles Times* said that 'about the only negative to report is that the movie has what's described as numerous glamour shots of Streisand's body parts filmed through what looks like a Vaseline-coated lens.' This prompted the film's cinematographer, Stephen Goldblatt, to send his own letter of protest. 'Your spies must be myopic,' he wrote, 'because there are no such shots in the movie and we have never had to use a "Vaselined" lens to photograph Streisand. She is fortunate enough not to need that kind of help.'

THE PRINCE OF TIDES premiered in rain-soaked New York on December 9. Back in Los Angeles, Streisand heard the resoundingly positive news: her labor of love was an audience-pleasing triumph. According to Liz Smith, 'Not a single person I spoke to after this premiere had anything but raves for the Nick Nolte-Streisand film . . . [and] nothing could dampen the evening's "high" over the romance of *The Prince of Tides*. It's too bad Streisand wasn't on hand to enjoy her triumph.'

Escorted by Jon Peters, Barbra did attend a gala Los Angeles premiere on December 11, and no one in the wildly enthusiastic crowd complained about the length of her nails, the shots of her legs, or mist-covered camera lenses. After the disappointment of *Nuts* and the esoteric quality of *Yentl*, the consensus was that *The Prince of Tides* had the potential to be the biggest Streisand film since *A Star Is Born*. When the film went into wide release on December 25, audiences and the majority of critics around the country embraced it with huge box office, rave reviews, and gold-plated Oscar predictions.

Most reviews praised the film's extraordinarily strong performances, especially Nolte's best-of-career turn, and Barbra's sure-handed, fluid direction. The film grossed $90 million domestically to make it Barbra's second most successful film after *A Star Is Born*. Since Hollywood loves nothing so much as a winner, it appeared that Streisand finally was on her way to a Best Director Oscar nomination. Many fearless Hollywood insiders went further than that. Ray Stark, for one, felt Barbra would probably win the award.

Things started out well. In January Barbra became only the third woman nominated as Best Director by the prestigious Directors Guild of America when she was cited along with Jonathan Demme for *The Silence of the Lambs*, Barry Levinson for *Bugsy*, Ridley Scott for *Thelma and Louise*, and Oliver

Stone for *JFK*. *Daily Variety* felt that Barbra's DGA nomination 'now gives her a strong likelihood of becoming the first American woman ever nominated for a directing Oscar.'

Liz Smith, who felt Barbra deserved to win the Academy Award, wondered: 'Will [Barbra Streisand] win the Oscar for directing *The Prince of Tides*, which most people seem to feel is an amazing and wonderful movie of great quality, brilliantly directed? . . . The answer seems to come back: "No, no, a thousands times no!" Comment: "Hollywood won't give Barbra another Oscar. They hate her. The movie community thinks she is selfish and impossible."'

On February 19 the Motion Picture Academy honored *The Prince of Tides* with seven Oscar nominations, including Best Picture, Best Actor, and Best Supporting Actress (Kate Nelligan). Barbra's name was not among the directing nominees; in addition to the men cited by the DGA, the Academy instead nominated John Singleton for *Boyz N the Hood*, not a Best Picture nominee.

The National Organization for Women protested Barbra's snub, calling it 'an obvious exhibition of sexism.' From London, where she had attended the royal premiere of the film and met Princess Diana, Barbra told the press that she was 'thrilled' by the seven nominations but 'disappointed' to be overlooked among the Best Director nominees. 'I can't blame anybody,' she added. 'Blame keeps you a victim and I'm not a victim.'

ON FEBRUARY 22 *Saturday Night Live* featured a hilarious 'Coffee Talk' segment starring Mike Myers in drag as the obsessed Streisand fan and cable talk-show hostess Linda Richman, guest star Roseanne, and an uncredited Madonna. As usual on the skit, Barbra was deified in delightful fashion: her legs were 'like buttah,' Linda Richman proclaimed. *The Prince of Tides* was 'like buttah,' too. Everything about Streisand was 'like buttah.'

'Wait,' Myers-as-Linda said, choking with emotion about how 'like buttah' Barbra was, 'I'm getting a little *farklempt*. I need a moment. Talk amongst yourselves . . . I've got *shpilkes* in my *genecktegezoink*.' Then, to the genuine astonishment of everyone, including Myers, Roseanne, and Madonna, Barbra strode out in a black outfit and an oversized black hat and proclaimed, 'All this talk about food is making me hungry, girls!' Roseanne fell out of her chair and the audience cheered and stomped as Barbra swept off stage left. Even Streisand's sharpest critics thought it was the hippest thing she had done in years.

IN MARCH BARBRA appeared at a Directors Guild symposium, 'Meet the Nominees: A Forum on the Art of Filmmaking,' along with Oliver Stone and Barry Levinson. She arrived at the event escorted by Stone, but onstage he and Levinson subjected Streisand to a rude example of old-boyism at its worst.

Throughout the evening the two men looked to each other for help in explaining a concept or giving an example, but they never looked to Streisand. Several times Stone leaned in front of Barbra to ask Levinson a question, as though she weren't even there.

When an audience member asked Barbra to talk about the writing of her film's script, she said that getting it right was so difficult she had moved the scenarist Becky Johnston into her house for months. Then another question came Streisand's way: 'What about the score?' Barbra started to reply that it had been written by James Newton Howard, but she was interrupted by Stone.

'And what about him?' Stone sniggered. 'Did you move *him* into your house too?'

'Shut up, you son of a bitch!' Barbra shot back as the audience tittered nervously.

NICK NOLTE WON the Golden Globe award as Best Actor in a Drama, and he was considered a near shoo-in for the Oscar. All five *Los Angeles Times* film critics polled for the newspaper's Oscar predictions issue chose Nolte to win the award. But in a sweep of all five top awards by *The Silence of the Lambs*, Anthony Hopkins was chosen as Best Actor for his powerful performance as the cannibalistic killer Hannibal Lecter. *The Prince of Tides* won no Oscars.

PERHAPS THE MOST gratifying legacy of *The Prince of Tides* for Barbra was her newfound closeness with her son, who had given a natural, believable performance as Bernard Woodruff. By the end of the filming, Jason would look at his mother in an entirely new light. 'The nice thing about the experience is not only did I gain confidence and grow as an actor,' he said, 'but my relationship with my mother grew too – it went beyond the trust we have as a mother and son to that of actor and director.'

Barbra agreed. 'I went through a hard time with Jason when he was a teenager, when he was belligerent and angry,' she admitted. Working on the film 'deepened our relationship because we had to deal as mother-son, director-actor, and it was pretty intense. When he came to a screening, he leaned over and said "I'm very proud of you, Mom." It was a thrill because he had never said that to me.'

RECALLING THE TIME he spent with Barbra Streisand, Pat Conroy, in his patented poetic fashion, defined her special brand of personal and professional charisma: 'When Barbra enters a room, the whole atmosphere changes. Stars appear in the east. Magi begin moving toward the room like camels. Women will follow her to the rest room. Besides, since Barbra has come into my life I can name-drop in a way I never could before. And people just love listening to it. I can say, "And Barbra said . . ." and, like an E. F. Hutton ad, I can feel them all lean in.'

For Barbra, the most meaningful accolade she won for her direction of *The Prince of Tides* arrived after Pat Conroy saw the film. He sent her a copy of his book with this inscription:

To Barbra Streisand: You're many things, Barbra, but you're also a great teacher . . . one of the greatest to come into my life. I honor the great teachers and they live in my work and dance invisibly in the margins of my prose. You've made me a better writer, you rescued my sweet book, and you've honored me by taking it with such seriousness and love. Great love and great thanks and I'll never forget that you gave *The Prince of Tides* back to me, as a gift. Pat Conroy.

PART 6

Diva

'There seems to be a need for

this Diva thing.'

—*Barbra in 1991*

38

On Saturday, April 25, 1992, three hundred high-powered guests and one hundred of their children streamed into Jon Peters's twelve-acre Beverly Hills estate for a lavish party to celebrate Barbra's fiftieth birthday, which had fallen on the day before. Frank Sinatra was there, and so were Nick Nolte, Meryl Streep, Tom Hanks, and Warren Beatty and Annette Bening with their new baby, among many others. Mrs Kind, Roslyn, Jason, Elliott, and Richard Baskin attended, as of course did the Bergmans and Cis and Harvey Corman.

At an expense of $200,000, Jon had transformed his property into 'Barbra's Magic Castle.' Clowns, jugglers, fortune-tellers, and stilt-walkers roamed the grounds while magicians and fire-eaters performed their tricks. Thrilled children posed for photographs with Beauty and the Beast, stroked a pony and other small animals in the petting zoo, and marveled at the circus elephant. Other kids romped inside a giant inflatable structure and donned Velcro pantsuits to climb a Velcro wall.

Barbra, dressed in an off-white off-the-shoulder peasant dress, spent most of her time inside a huge tent, where she ate from a sumptuous spread of food and watched marionettes and a magic show with her three-and-a-half-year-old godchild, Caleigh, Jon's adopted daughter.

She was surrounded by children, by friends, by love. And at fifty, Barbra stood astride the pinnacle of her career after three decades of unprecedentedly diverse success. Her fifty albums had sold over one hundred million copies worldwide. Her fifteen movies had grossed over one billion dollars worldwide. She had won Oscars for acting and songwriting; Emmys for her television shows; a Tony as Star of the Decade; ten Golden Globes for acting, directing, producing, songwriting and as World Film Favorite; and eight Grammys for singing. She had been awarded more gold, platinum, and multi-platinum albums than any other artist. And, of course, her most recent directing effort had been nominated for seven Academy Awards, including Best Picture.

Hers was a career unparalleled in show business history, and in February the Academy of Recording Arts and Sciences had named her the recipient of its Grammy Legend Award. In September 1991 she had released a four-disc retrospective of her musical career, *Just for the Record*, which contained ninety-five tracks, sixty-seven of them previously unreleased, beginning with the acetate recording of 'You'll Never Know' that she had made at thirteen in the Nola Recording Studio. The collection, although priced around sixty dollars on sale, sold over a million copies.

The retrospective served as the centerpiece of Stephen Sondheim's tribute to Barbra when he introduced her at the Grammy Awards ceremony. 'The lady we're honoring tonight recently released a remarkable recording. It covered in one extraordinary musical package a career that might well be the envy of any performer who ever stood in front of a microphone and made music . . . She's the delight of every writer who hopes for a performance of his song better than what he heard in his head . . . She's as good as they come.'

'I don't feel like a legend,' Barbra said as she accepted the trophy. 'I feel like a work in progress.'

IN MANY WAYS she was very much a work in progress, especially when it came to politics and the world's social problems. She had always been concerned with various issues as a private citizen, and occasionally she would speak out to raise money for the causes she believed in. But in 1992 Barbra truly came into her own as a social and political activist. What more was there for her to prove as an entertainer? Only that she had the courage – and retained the drawing power – to stage a successful concert tour. That would come.

But now she felt she must speak out against discrimination of all stripes, and the neglect of so many social problems by the presidential administrations of Ronald Reagan and George Bush. Her first opportunity came when she was inducted into the Hall of Fame of the Women in Film organization in June 1992. Her feminist speech was hard-hitting but not devoid of humor:

> We've come a long way. Not too long ago we were referred to as dolls, tomatoes, chicks, babes, broads. We've graduated to being called tough cookies, foxes, bitches, and witches. I guess that's progress. Language gives us an insight into the way women are viewed in a male-dominated society . . . A man is commanding – a woman is demanding. A man is forceful – a woman is pushy. A man is uncompromising – a woman

is a ball breaker. A man is a perfectionist – a woman's a pain in the ass . . .

I'm angry about the way they treated Anita Hill. I'm angry about what happened to Rodney King. I'm angry that the right of a woman to control her own body is even being questioned . . . I look forward to a society that is color- and gender-blind, that judges us by the value of our work, not the length of our legs. That accepts the fact that a woman can be many, many things: strong *and* vulnerable, intelligent *and* sexy, opinionated *and* flexible, angry *and* forgiving . . . Of course, all this applies to men as well.

On *Larry King Live* in February, Barbra had said that she hadn't yet made up her mind whom to support for the Democratic presidential nomination. 'Maybe Harkin,' she said, naming the most liberal of the candidates, Senator Tom Harkin of Iowa. Her first choice had been the liberal lion Mario Cuomo, the governor of New York. But he had declined to run, just as he had several times in the past.

By June, after Harkin faltered in the Democratic primaries, Barbra had decided to back, as she put it, 'the only viable candidate' – Governor Bill Clinton of Arkansas. On September 16, 1992, she headlined a $1.5 million Beverly Hills fund-raiser for Clinton, now the party's nominee, and his running mate, Tennessee Senator Al Gore. The two Democratic women running for the U.S. Senate from California, Dianne Feinstein and Barbara Boxer, also benefited from the money raised.

Attended by twelve hundred people and broadcast via satellite to fund-raisers in New York City, Washington, D.C., Atlantic City, and San Francisco, the event featured performances by Dionne Warwick, Tammy Wynette, and the reunited comedy team of Mike Nichols and Elaine May. Then Barbra, dressed in black and appearing relaxed, came onstage to the strains of 'People' for a twenty-four-minute song set that included 'People,' 'On a Clear Day,' 'Come Rain or Come Shine,' 'It's a New World,' 'Children Will Listen,' 'It Had to Be You,' 'Happy Days Are Here Again,' and 'God Bless America.'

Between songs, she bantered. 'I used to be a director and now I've become a backyard singer,' she quipped. 'Did you notice? . . . The last time I sang live was six years ago to help elect a Democratic Senate. What motivated me was the disaster at Chernobyl. And what motivates me now is another kind of disaster: the possibility of four more years of George Bush and Dan Quayle.'

In a fascinating three-way race on November 3, the country agreed: William Jefferson Clinton was elected president with 43 percent of the vote. President Bush received 38 percent, and the independent candidate Ross Perot garnered 19 percent. And as icing on the cake for Barbra and her fellow liberals, both Dianne Feinstein and Barbra Boxer won their races, making California the first state in history to send two female senators to Washington at the same time.

HAVING HELPED ELECT a Democratic president for the first time in sixteen years, Barbra wasted no time resting on her laurels. On November 18 she accepted the AIDS Project Los Angeles Commitment to Life Award as a co-honoree with the recording mogul David Geffen. In many ways it was her own coming-out to the AIDS crisis. She had been criticized for not doing nearly as much to fight the disease that had afflicted mostly gay men in America since 1981 as had Bette Midler, Madonna, and especially Elizabeth Taylor.

In the September 1991 issue of *Vanity Fair*, Barbra had addressed that criticism. 'That's their opinion,' she said of those who faulted her lack of fervent AIDS activism. 'I give loads of money. I've given a lot to pediatric AIDS ... and all the proceeds from the single "Somewhere" from my Broadway album went to AmFAR [the American Foundation for AIDS Research]. I don't give public appearances; Madonna and Bette Midler like to perform. Elizabeth Taylor has this as her *one* cause.'

But within a year Barbra had jumped into the battle to find a cure for AIDS. She quietly joined the board of directors of Hollywood Supports, an organization founded by industry bigwigs Barry Diller and Sid Sheinberg, and contributed $350,000 to various AIDS causes.

But it was at AIDS Project L.A.'s Commitment to Life Awards ceremony at the Universal Amphitheater that she went public on the issue in a big way. After a show built around a *West Side Story* theme that featured performances of the Bernstein-Sondheim score by Natalie Cole, Patti LaBelle, Sheila E., Wynonna Judd, Kenny Loggins, and Elton John offering a campy 'I Feel Pretty' while wearing pearls and fluttering a fan, Barbra provided an electric finale as she joined Johnny Mathis for a duet medley of 'One Hand, One Heart' and 'I Have a Love.' Then Streisand really grabbed the audience. After Warren Beatty introduced her with a warm, personal, and effusive tribute, she delivered a fiery oration that had the audience cheering 'Barbra for President!'

Few of us have responded with enough urgency to meet this crisis of catastrophic proportions ... And a disease that has infected far more heterosexuals than homosexuals throughout the world was dismissed as a gay disease with that official, homophobic wink – implying that those deaths didn't really matter.

I will never forgive my fellow actor Ronald Reagan for the genocidal denial of the illness's existence; for his refusal to even utter the word 'AIDS' for seven years, and for his blocking funding for research and education which could have saved hundreds of thousands of lives . . . When Pat Buchanan thundered [at the 1992 Republican convention], 'We stand with George Bush against the amoral idea that gay and lesbian couples should have the same standing in law as married men and women,' I wondered: Who is Pat Buchanan to pronounce anybody's love invalid? How can he deny the profound love felt by one human being for another, a love that all too often takes them to the bitter end, holding each other in hospices and hospitals all over this nation?

I feel that we are now entering a time of healing. We are grateful that our new president is committed to life . . . But lest we be lulled into a false sense of security, the struggle goes on: just look at the vote for hate in Colorado where voters rescinded any protection for gays in employment or housing. There are plenty of us who love the mountains and rivers of that truly beautiful state, but we must say clearly that the moral climate there is no longer acceptable, and if we're asked to, we must refuse to play where they discriminate.

Barbra topped off the evening with a stirring performance of 'Somewhere,' a richly appropriate song for the occasion with its subtext that seemed both to offer hope for tolerance of homosexuality in our society and, with its otherworldly arrangement, hope for a peaceful and loving eternity for those whom AIDS had claimed and would claim. Her performance drew tears and brought the house down.

BARBRA'S IMPLIED SUPPORT for a proposed boycott of Colorado in her speech created a firestorm of praise and criticism. Boycott organizers exulted in the publicity Streisand's comments received around the country. Other gay leaders felt a boycott wasn't the way to go, especially since the city that stood to lose the most, Aspen, had voted three to one against Amendment Two, which rescinded gay rights laws that had been in effect in Colorado since 1977.

But the strongest criticism of Streisand's stand came from Hollywood, where hundreds of stars, directors, producers, and moguls were poised to make their annual Christmas vacation migration to Aspen. On December 2 *The New York Times* ran an article from Hollywood that began: 'This town is engulfed in a virtual civil war. The rich are in turmoil ... What's a politically correct entertainment personage to do? Go to Aspen over Christmas or not?'

The article by Bernard Weintraub quoted 'one studio executive' as saying, 'This flap proves the axiom that people in Hollywood are perfectly willing to speak out on issues so long as it doesn't affect them or inconvenience them.' Weintraub claimed that Barbra had 'backed off' from her support for a boycott, and he theorized that Hollywood's anger at her stemmed from the fact that 'she broke one of the town's cardinal rules, which is that the issues that Hollywood speaks about should remain as remote as possible, like apartheid in South Africa ... The farther away the better.'

On December 11, as she addressed a gathering of the American Civil Liberties Union, which had presented her with its Bill of Rights Award, Barbra thundered, 'I did not *ever* back off, back down, or back away from my original statement, as some of the press reported. So let me clearly state my position tonight: it appears that a boycott is under way in Colorado, and I will personally honor it and find some other state to vacation in.'

The boycott lost Colorado millions of tourist dollars before the state's supreme court struck down Amendment Two. But the specter of a renewed boycott arose on February 21, 1995, when the U.S. Supreme Court agreed to decide the following October whether the state court had acted properly in overturning the gay rights ban.

BARBRA USED TO be controversial because of her emotional singing, her idiosyncratic acting, her bluntness, her perfectionism, her occasional rudeness, and her choice of lovers. Now she was controversial because of her political beliefs, and the controversies that surrounded her mushroomed now that she was an F.O.B. – a Friend of Bill, one of the new president's extended circle of intimates and advisers. (*People* magazine called the president 'the First F.O.B. – Friend of Barbra.')

The new controversy began with her performance at the inaugural gala at the USAir Arena in Landover, Maryland, on January 19, 1993. After a rehearsal the night before that was open to anyone who brought a bagful of groceries for the hungry and homeless, Barbra strode out confidently as the evening's final act (Michael Jackson had relinquished the star spot in deference to her), dressed in a sleek dark gray pin-striped Donna Karan suit with a daring slit up the side of its floor-length skirt. Despite a sore throat that had almost forced her to cancel, she sang a lovely 'Evergreen,' the president-elect's favorite Streisand song; 'Children Will Listen'; and 'God Bless America.' After 'Children Will Listen' she told the crowd and the new president, 'We cannot abuse children, either by word or deed. What is done to them, they will do to society.'

When Barbra concluded her smooth-as-silk fifteen-minute performance, Clinton bounded onstage and embraced her. It had been a glamorous, star-studded, nationally televised evening, and Barbra Streisand had been its centerpiece. The next day Bill Clinton and Al Gore were sworn in amid the highest hopes of millions of Americans.

A week later the *New York Post* ran a blazing headline: 'Senator Yentl.' The story claimed that Barbra was mulling over a bid to gain a seat in Congress, possibly running in a primary against New York's Democratic Senator Daniel Patrick Moynihan. The report, of course, was absurd. Those who know her were highly amused by the idea of Barbra, who could be reduced to terror when approached by a lone autograph seeker, wading into crowds and glad-handing voters. Barbra put the kibosh on the story quickly. 'Running for the Senate is out of the question,' she said. 'There should be no confusion between someone with political passion and someone with political ambition.'

Two days later *The New York Times* ran an op-ed column by Anne Taylor Fleming, blasting Barbra for the sexy outfit she wore to the inaugural. Barbra's 'getup,' Fleming wrote, 'sent the wrong message' that strong independent women also have to be 'femmes fatales.'

The in-your-face feminist commentator Camille Paglia, however, saw things differently. In a lengthy essay-profile of Barbra entitled 'America's Second Lady,' published in the London *Sunday Times*, Paglia wrote that 'one of the supreme moments in recent popular entertainment was when Barbra Streisand sang "Evergreen" for Bill Clinton at his inaugural . . . She looked spectacular, wearing a business suit with big padded shoulders and a long skirt slit up the thigh. I was delirious. She was all man and all woman.'

Barbra enjoyed a lull in the controversies surrounding her until May, when they exploded once again after she made a whirlwind trip to Washington at the invitation of the president. On her first night in town, Saturday, May 1, she attended the White House Press Correspondents Dinner, where she had sung for JFK in 1963, and hobnobbed with General Colin Powell, chairman of the Joint Chiefs of Staff.

People magazine, in a cover story, described the excitement generated by Streisand's arrival at the dinner: 'And then *she* entered. Wearing an off-the-shoulder white satin gown and exuding that slightly cross-eyed charisma, she calmly navigated a moving sea of videocam lights and popping flashbulbs. Bringing conversations to a halt. Making forks drop and heads turn . . . it seemed that everyone – politicians, magazine editors and New York City celebs alike – wanted desperately to get a glimpse, a touch, even (oh, God!) a few words with the fifty-one-year-old woman from Brooklyn with the *looong* fingernails and no college degree. Ladies and Gentlemen and Leaders of the Free World ... Barbra Streisand!'

The next day, Sunday, Barbra dined with Attorney General Janet Reno. On Monday she met with a group of congresswomen, attended Senate hearings on gays in the military, and took a personal tour of the C-SPAN television studios. On Tuesday she went to dinner with Labor Secretary Robert Reich and Democratic senators Bob Kerrey of Nebraska, Christopher Dodd of Connecticut, and William S. Cohen of Maine. On Wednesday she visited Thomas Jefferson's home at Monticello, which inspired her to redecorate her Central Park West apartment in the Early American style, and on Thursday she wound up her Washington week at a party in honor of the new ambassador to France, Pamela Harriman, at the home of the *Washington Post* publisher Katharine Graham.

It didn't take long for conservative knees to jerk in response to Streisand's apparent influence with the Washington power brokers, especially when it came to light that she had quietly spent several nights in the White House in March. Rush Limbaugh ridiculed her on his radio program. Nasty members of the opposition hinted that she and the president were having an affair; nastier members of the opposition suggested that she and the first lady were having an affair.

Serious criticism followed, and it cut at Barbra badly. *The Wall Street Journal* ran a front-page article in which Timothy Smith said that Streisand 'finds herself cast as the presumptive leader of a sort of flying wedge of glamorous nitwits, jetting in from the Coast to have their political credentials validated ... She never did have time to go to college, and she takes her education about public affairs where she finds it.'

The *New Republic* said of Barbra and other Hollywood celebrities, 'The idea that these insulated and bubbleheaded people should help make policy is ridiculous. Hollywood actors are even more out of touch than elected politicians.'

The lowest blow came from Jonathan Yardley of the *Washington Post*, who wrote a column entitled 'Miss Marmelstein Goes to Washington.' After describing Barbra's first Broadway triumph, Yardley wrote, 'The mousy Miss Marmelstein has metamorphosed into a conglomerate capable of terrorizing any persons unfortunate enough to find themselves in her path. At the moment, those in this vulnerable position range from the chairman of the Joint Chiefs of Staff to the president of the United States; the possibility that any or all of them will be blown away by Hurricane Barbra must be taken very seriously ... It is all well and good to wring one's hands over nuclear annihilation and AIDS research and other matters with which La

Barbra has chosen to become involved, but it is another thing to think them through clinically and objectively . . .

'So here they come, traipsing down the Yellow Brick Road: La Barbra and her legions. Not since Coxey's Army has so bizarre an invading power launched so quixotic an assault on Washington.'

Yardley's column, reprinted in a number of newspapers across the country, touched off a storm of criticism. A letter to the editor in the *Los Angeles Times* stated, 'What Yardley's "perspective" most sings of is sour grapes: the Democrats are in power and Hollywood's heavyweights helped put them there. But could there be a more sinister motive in his singling out of Streisand? It's telling that he chose to resurrect a relatively unknown stage character Barbra created thirty-two years ago as the centerpiece for his essay. Could the reason be that the name Marmelstein is so resoundingly Jewish? I'd like to think not.'

In an interview with Robert Scheer published in the *Los Angeles Times* on May 23, Barbra fought back. 'This is so unfair,' she said. 'And it's smearing the main industry in our community. It's saying there isn't a brain around. Did the entertainment industry create the national debt? How come nobody attacked the Republican White House for their involvement with Arnold Schwarzenegger, Charlton Heston, and Bruce Willis? Remember when actor John Gavin was appointed ambassador to Mexico? I understand why the conservatives attack us – they deem us a very dangerous crowd, especially because of the kind of money some of us can raise for the Democrats.'

THE FOLLOWING MONTH, publicity of a different kind swirled around Barbra's comely shoulders when she went to England to attend the Wimbledon tennis championships. She wasn't there as a tennis fan; she had come to cheer on the defending champion Andre Agassi, the sport's latest long-haired pinup boy. Agassi, the London press breathlessly reported, was Barbra's 'special friend.'

Her relationship with the twenty-three-year-old athlete had come to light the previous September when she rooted for him from the stands at the U.S. Open match. They had met shortly after Agassi saw *The Prince of Tides*, when he telephoned Barbra to tell her how much the film had moved him. They talked for two hours, and not long afterward they went on a dinner date.

At the U.S. Open, television cameras spent nearly as much time on Streisand as they did on the match. One commentator noted that Barbra seemed to look at the handsome Agassi as though he were 'an ice cream cone with a cherry on the top.' To reporters who asked about the friendship, Barbra said that Agassi 'is very intelligent, very, very sensitive, very evolved –

more than his linear years. And he's an extraordinary human being. He plays like a Zen master. It's very in the moment.'

The 'Zen master' comment prompted widespread ridicule, as did the twenty-eight-year age difference between the two. Barbra attended another match of Andre's in Los Angeles, and he reportedly gave her several private tennis lessons.

At Wimbledon in June 1993, the Fleet Street press went into a frenzy at Barbra's presence. Pictures of her biting her nails with worry or waving her arms and cheering Agassi along as he battled his challenger, Pete Sampras, made the front page of nearly every paper in the country. Wearing a sailor cap and a navy-and-white sailor jacket, which she removed to reveal a white tank top, Barbra jumped up and down and called out Agassi's name. When he lost the match, the *Daily Mirror* headlined its front-page photo of a crestfallen Streisand, 'Barbra Cry-Sand.' The *Sun* chose a picture of Barbra biting her nails for its front page, with the headline 'Chew Love! Barbra bites nails as her friend Agassi is beaten.'

Even *The New York Times* jumped into the act, reporting at length on the excitement created by Barbra's presence at the match. 'Not since Chris Evert dated Burt Reynolds in the mid-seventies,' Maureen Dowd wrote, 'has there been such a closely watched duet of tennis and Hollywood royalty . . . Asked whether the relationship was platonic, Agassi replied in a valley-girl, handkerchief-dropping manner: "You know? To say we are, like, just friends, you know, I know what everybody's definition of friend is. They use it so loosely. So I like to say she's my version of a friend."'

To *London Today* he sounded more Zen-like: 'I've been learning about the sweet mysteries of life, and this is one of them. I'm not sure I can fully explain. Maybe she can't either. But it doesn't matter. We came from completely different worlds, and we collided, and we knew we wanted to be in each other's company right then.'

Judging from Agassi's apparent history with women, it is unlikely that his friendship with Barbra ever moved beyond the platonic. His longtime girlfriend Wendi Stewart was reportedly angry enough at his attentions to Barbra to throw some Streisand CDs out of Agassi's limousine window and cry, 'That woman is old enough to be your mother!' But the London *Sunday Mirror* reported that Andre and Wendi had never had sex during their years-long 'romance' because of 'their strong Christian religious convictions,' and that the couple slept in separate bedrooms when she traveled with him.

In 1987 Wendi apparently stood by the sidelines as Andre conducted another 'friendship,' this one with Amy Moss, a courtesy driver at an American tennis tournament. Moss told the *Mirror*, 'If you want to know about Andre's sex life, go by the Bible. Having sex is wrong in the Bible, and that is what he follows.'

Whatever the extent of Barbra's relationship with Andre Agassi, it didn't last very long, perhaps because this 'very intelligent, very, very sensitive, very evolved' young man turned out to be a homophobe. The *Village Voice* reported that after he won a match in 1991, Agassi had told reporters, 'I'm as happy as a faggot in a submarine.' And the New York *Daily News* ran an item reporting that after Pete Sampras received a good-luck bouquet from Elton John prior to a match, Agassi told him, 'You can't go around getting flowers from a fag like that.'

So much for Zen masterhood.

ON JUNE 29, 1993, Columbia Records released Barbra's fiftieth album, *Back to Broadway*. The prior December she had signed a new contract with Sony Corporation, Columbia's parent company, and the details of the deal made front-page news. Since March 1991 the recording industry had offered the hottest musical stars a series of contracts that staggered the imagination: $40 million to Janet Jackson, $60 million to Michael Jackson, $60 million apiece to Madonna and Prince.

In the 1960s Marty Erlichman had always demanded more money for Barbra than the highest-paid artist was getting at the time, even if the difference amounted to only one dollar. In 1992 he wasn't about to let Barbra settle for less than the other top artists of the day were getting. On December 14, the *Los Angeles Times* reported that Barbra's new contract, covering both records and films, was worth $60 million.

The *Times* report added that the deal guaranteed Barbra a $4 million advance against 10 percent of gross revenues for every movie in which she acted; $3 million in advance against an undetermined percentage of the gross for every movie she directed; and a $5 million advance for every album, against a top-of-the-line royalty rate of 42 percent of the wholesale price – nearly $3.00 per CD sold. It was an extraordinary pact for any entertainer, but for a fifty-one-year-old woman who had made her first album thirty years earlier, made her film debut twenty-five years earlier, and had directed only two movies, it moved into the realm of fantasy.

Back to Broadway, Barbra's first effort under the new pact, proved that Sony's faith in her was well placed. The disc, propelled by strong public interest after the success of *The Broadway Album*, *debuted* at number one on the *Billboard* chart, the first Streisand album ever to achieve that rare status.

Reviews were mixed, however. Stephen Holden of *The New York Times* felt that, 'While the record includes some of the most thrilling singing of Ms

Streisand's career, it also has some of the most overbearing.' David Patrick Stearns in *USA Today* criticized Barbra's voice on the disc: 'Though Streisand again proves that she sings Broadway music better than just about anyone, the vocal decline hinted at on *One Voice* five years ago is now undeniable. Her high notes are thin, her vibrato nervous, and her voice doesn't bloom as much at high volume.'

Ultimately *Back to Broadway* didn't have the staying power of its predecessor; it sold only one-third as many copies as *The Broadway Album*. But its position at the top of the charts made Barbra the only singer in history to have a number one album in four consecutive decades.

A few months later, Barbra returned to the recording studio to work on an unusual project: a duet of 'I've Got a Crush on You' with Frank Sinatra, to be included on his latest album, *Duets*, in which he would also sing with Bono, Liza Minnelli, Kenny G, and Gloria Estefan, among others. What was singular about the Sinatra album was that the seventy-eight-year-old crooner refused to record in person with any of his partners. Instead he laid down his tracks alone, and the other artists were expected to record theirs at another time and place.

Amazingly, Barbra agreed to this bizarre arrangement, and even more surprisingly, she brought such warmth and intimacy to the duet that no one would have guessed the two singers had never been in a recording studio together. She is in fine voice on the song (better than for most of *Back to Broadway*), which helps make Sinatra's tentative and scratchy vocal more palatable.

In her patented way, Barbra improvised a little by using Sinatra's name in the song; he responded by overdubbing a new line at the last minute: ''Cause I have got a crush, my Barbra, on you.' Although the album received mixed reviews and garnered criticism for the poor quality of Sinatra's vocals and the impersonal dual recordings, its novelty and big star names propelled it to debut at number two on the *Billboard* chart.

'BARRY, I NEED money. I'm broke.' Incredibly, this is what Barbra told her old friend Barry Dennen – the man who had helped create her musical style in 1960 – during the spring of 1993. She had telephoned Dennen, and during a long catching-up conversation she dropped the bombshell that despite all her success was having cash-flow problems. 'All my money's tied up in investments and real estate,' she said.

Many of those investments had apparently turned sour, a serious problem because Barbra had tremendous overheads. Her agent and manager each took 10 percent of her income. She paid full staffs at the Carolwood house, at the

Barwood offices in Hollywood and New York, at the Malibu ranch, and at her Central Park West apartment. (Just watering the Malibu grounds cost Streisand $22,000 a year.) She supported her mother and frequently helped her sister and son financially. She often donated between five hundred thousand and one million dollars a year to various charities through her Streisand Foundation. And her taxes, of course, were huge. She turned over an estimated 30 percent of her income to Uncle Sam after deductions, and the property taxes at Ramirez Canyon were close to $200,000 a year.

For years she had tried to sell the Malibu compound. First, in 1987, she asked $16 million; when she found no buyer she hiked the price to $19 million. By 1992 she had lowered the price to $11.9 million, but the property remained unsold despite reported interest from Michael Jackson. Finally, unable to afford to keep up the sprawling twenty-two-acre spread, she decided to donate it to the Santa Monica Mountains Conservancy, a California state agency, and take a $15 million tax write-off for it.

'How can I raise some money quickly?' Barbra asked Dennen.

'Why don't you concertize?' Dennen replied. 'Do a ten-city, twenty-city tour. You'll make a fortune.'

'But what about security?'

'What *about* security? You'll make sure you have whatever security you need.'

There was a long silence on the other end of the phone. Then Barbra said, 'Well . . . *maybe*.'

The curtains parted, and Barbra stepped tentatively out onto the balcony of her elegant white tearoom set in front of fifteen thousand standing, screaming fans in the MGM Grand Garden in Las Vegas. At the long stair rail in front of her she hesitated and drew in a deep breath. The crowd quieted to utter silence, and with one hand clutching the rail so tightly her knuckles visibly whitened, Barbra began to sing 'As If We Never Said Goodbye' from *Sunset Boulevard* in a tremulous, unsure voice: 'I don't know why I'm frightened . . . I know my way around here.'

The audience roared anew, cheering Barbra's acknowledgment of her fear of performing before such a large audience for the first time in twenty-two years. She seemed to gain confidence as she ambled down the staircase, her full-length black off-the-shoulder gown flowing behind her. By the time she finished her next number, a personalized reworking of Stephen Sondheim's 'I'm Still Here' ('I kept my nose to spite my face'), everyone in that cavernous hall had relaxed into the certainty that Barbra Streisand's long-awaited return to the concert stage would be, just as they had anticipated, an unforgettable event.

STREISAND FANS HAD begun to surge into Las Vegas early in the morning of December 31, 1993, clutching their oversized green photo tickets to that night's performance, the next night's, or both. They came from all fifty states and from Canada, England, France, Holland, Japan, Argentina, and other countries. They streamed through the eighty-eight-foot-high stucco lion's head entrance to the brand-new $1 billion MGM Grand Hotel. They stood in long lines to have their pictures taken beside a huge poster advertising the Streisand shows, with Barbra's image smiling coyly out at them. They rushed to the merchandise stands to buy $20 posters, $25 programs, $25 photo T-shirts, $75 sweatshirts, $100 gold key rings, $75 commemorative Streisand postage stamps issued by St Vincent, West Indies, $85 champagne glasses, and $400 suede-and-wool jackets. Ruth Davidson, a fan from England, spent nearly $5,000 on the concert tickets, airfare to America, and every conceivable piece of Barbra memorabilia. 'I would have paid practically *anything* to come,' she said. 'What if Barbra decides she doesn't like it and never performs live again?'

The same thought propelled thousands of fans to spend more than they could afford to attend the concert. 'There hasn't been an event with this type of demand in years, including the championship fights,' said Thomas Willer, vice president of marketing for the Las Vegas Hilton, where Streisand had last performed for pay early in 1972.

Tickets went on sale at eight in the morning of November 7 at prices ranging from $100 to $1,000. Within twenty-four hours over a million calls had been logged by the telephone company. Only a fraction got through; most fans had to call repeatedly for hours. 'My phone was literally hot from pressing redial,' one said. Another 'carried the portable phone with me everywhere – even the bathtub.'

When the dust settled, the Streisand concerts had grossed over $13 million in ticket sales – double the previous record box-office take for two shows. Streisand's net personal earnings, minus production costs, were estimated at nearly $8 million, with another $5 million to $10 million possible from concession sales and projected television, record, and video revenues.

EARLIER IN THE year the entrepreneur Kirk Kerkorian had worked feverishly to open his MGM Grand Hotel, the largest in the world, by December 18. He knew he needed a blockbuster attraction to draw worldwide publicity to the hotel and enough patrons to fill its 5,005 rooms and its 15,000-seat Grand Garden. He never seriously considered anyone but Streisand, who had opened his International Hotel (now the Las Vegas Hilton) in 1969. But would she do it? He knew that she had turned down millions of dollars in offers for live performing for two decades, but he had also heard rumors that she was considering a concert tour. He thought he could convince her; he would just have to make it worth her while.

He did. First he informed her, without mentioning that he wanted her to perform at the hotel, that his Lincy Foundation would make a $3 million donation to the charities of her choice. 'There were no strings attached,' recalled Marty Erlichman, 'but Kirk's generosity made us look very carefully at the MGM Grand proposal when it came in.' (Barbra asked that $2 million of the money be earmarked for various AIDS causes.)

Then the money Kerkorian offered her – 90 percent of a take he estimated would be $10 million – took Barbra's breath away. 'Really?' she gasped. 'You'd pay me that much?' It seemed folly at first to pay any performer that kind of money for two nights' work, but Kerkorian knew that the publicity and prestige a Streisand appearance would bring the new hotel would be priceless and would guarantee not only full room bookings but millions of dollars in gambling income as well.

Kerkorian's largesse, so timely in light of Barbra's cash flow problems, was only part of the reason she accepted the offer to sing at the MGM Grand. She had vowed never again to perform in a Vegas showroom, where she'd had to fight everything from cigar smoke to clattering cutlery. But the Grand Garden was an arena, not a glorified lounge. Even more important was her desire to fight the demons of fear that had kept her off the concert stage except for sporadic charity and political events.

One step along the way was a birthday party a friend, the clothing designer Donna Karan, threw for her in 1991. 'Liza Minnelli got up to sing,' Barbra recalled, 'and I'm sitting there thinking, How does she do this? How does anyone get up in front of people and sing? I could never get myself to sing at parties . . . with people looking at me. I can sing onstage because it is a black curtain out there. I can see just a few people and even that disturbs me . . . I didn't like accepting that fright. I am frightened by a lot of things, but what I hope is good about me is that I go through the fear.'

She had been working at that for twenty-five years, undergoing intensive therapy in an attempt to understand herself and grow as a person and as a performer. She had made great strides in a number of areas. She had tackled her fear of directing, become less suspicious of her fans, grown less rigid in her opinions. The major hurdle remained her overwhelming anxiety at facing a crowd. Kerkorian's offer – to sing in front of 30,000 people over two days – offered her an unprecedented and lucrative opportunity to get over it.

Still, she remained unsure to the very last minute. The day before the MGM Grand staff needed to make the announcement in order to have the necessary time to work out all the logistics, Barbra still hadn't signed the contract. When a copy with her signature finally came by fax machine, 'There were high fives and hugs all over the place,' said Thomas A. Bruny, the hotel's director of advertising and public relations.

Once she had made the commitment, Streisand flew into action. She asked an assistant to compile a list of every song she had ever sung, over five hundred of them. Characteristically, she relied on her friends to put the show together with her. She designed two outfits in collaboration with Donna Karan. She asked production designers Marc Brickman and David George to re-create the tearoom from Thomas Jefferson's magnificent Monticello home, which had so impressed her during her visit to Washington and Virginia earlier in the year. She brought together a sixty-four-piece orchestra to back her up and asked Marvin Hamlisch, the composer of 'The Way We Were,' to arrange and conduct.

For three weeks she rehearsed in New York, choosing this song, discarding that one. Marilyn and Alan Bergman wrote the show as a meander through Barbra's life, weaving her signature songs into a tapestry that included her childhood, her years of therapy, her love affairs, her family, and her political activism.

In the middle of December, rehearsals moved to Los Angeles, at Soundstage 24 of the Sony Studios on the former MGM lot. A few days before she left for Las Vegas, Barbra invited two hundred people to hear her perform Act One. Robert Osborne, in the next day's *Hollywood Reporter*, proclaimed the show 'nothing short of spectacular.'

But a few days later, on the plane to Las Vegas, Barbra's nerve started to give out. What have I done? she asked herself. What am I doing?

JULIE EDLER, A forty-one-year-old army production assistant from Salt Lake City, arrived at the Grand Garden at three in the afternoon on New Year's Eve for that night's eight-o'clock show. As she had hoped, she stood first in line. 'Never in my whole life did I think I'd ever see her live,' she said. 'I *had* to be here.'

Six hours later, an hour after the show's scheduled start time, hordes of fans were still piling past nine metal detectors set up outside the main doors by hotel security. These extraordinary measures were augmented by a crack Israeli unit trained in counterterrorism and by explosive-sniffing dogs supplied by Streisand's own security force. Reportedly, concession stands were forbidden to provide straws (they might be used to launch projectiles), and a uniformed guard escorting President Clinton's mother, Virginia Kelley, was denied admission.

Inside, the impatient crowd burst into rhythmic clapping several times, and amused themselves by gawking at and cheering for the Who's Who of celebrities filing into front-row seats over the two nights: Michael Jackson, Kim Basinger and Alec Baldwin, Gregory Peck, Coretta Scott King, Prince, Michael Crawford, Mel Gibson, Richard Gere and Cindy Crawford, Jay Leno, Steven Spielberg, Kathie Lee Gifford, Michael Douglas, Andre Agassi, Jon Peters, and Elliott Gould, among others.

As the overture began to swell, the crowd roared and the excitement peaked. It was finally about to happen – Barbra Streisand live in concert! For the vast majority of the people in the audience, this was the first time – and, they knew, probably the last time – they would see Streisand perform in person.

The first thing the audience noticed as Barbra emerged from the wings was how lovely she looked. Slim, glowing, her blond hair falling softly about her shoulders, she looked closer to thirty-five than fifty-one.

As her breathy nervousness gave way to growing confidence, Streisand's voice grew stronger. By the second act she was in voice nearly as pure and as powerful as she had ever been. Ten times, the audience leaped to their feet for standing ovations. At one point during a prolonged ovation fans in the back rows began to stomp their feet, rock-concert style. As the rest of the audience picked up the cue, a palpable wave of noise and reverberation swept from the periphery of the arena down to the stage. The cacophony startled Barbra. 'Wow! You're incredible!' she called out above the din.

Although she adhered faithfully to the script – all of the lines, including 'ad-libs' and most of her reactions, were flashed on TelePrompTers in front of her – Barbra the actress left her audience convinced that each word had just sprung to mind and popped out. And the autobiographical elements of the show were tailor-made to appeal to Streisand fans, many of whom cared about her every triumph and trial nearly as much as their own.

Pictures of Barbra as a baby and as a young girl flashed on a huge screen above the set as she spoke of her early dreams of acting. Seeing *The Diary of Anne Frank* on Broadway, she said, changed her life. She had adored Ava Gardner in *Show Boat*, the first movie musical she had ever seen. And when, at thirteen, she saw Marlon Brando in *Guys and Dolls*, she fell in love. 'This man was beautiful! I imagined myself up there on the screen with him.' At that a clip from the film of Brando singing 'I'll Know' appeared on the screen – and Barbra sang a 'duet' with him. When the scene widened to include Jean Simmons, a photo of the teenage Barbra was superimposed over Brando's co-star. 'What a mieskeit!' Barbra said of her young self. The audience laughed, cheered, applauded. Now, unquestionably, Barbra had them.

No matter how successful, rich, and powerful she has become, Barbra has always had a genius for casting herself in the role of underdog. During the show she reminded the audience of her early struggle for success despite her narrow-minded mother and an unremitting procession of naysayers, and she sang spirited renditions of 'Everybody Says Don't' and 'Don't Rain on My Parade.' Then she moved on to wistful early love ('Will He Like Me?' and 'He Touched Me') and, later, lost romance ('The Way We Were,' 'You Don't Bring Me Flowers').

After clips from two films in which she played a psychiatric patient (*On a Clear Day You Can See Forever* and *Nuts)* and one in which she played a therapist *(The Prince of Tides)*, Barbra telescoped her own three decades of psychoanalysis into a running exchange with two doctors, both of whom mispronounced her name 'Streizund.' 'It's Strei*sand!*' Barbra wailed. 'Like sand on a beach!' (One of her pet peeves, the frequent mispronunciation of her name has led Barbra to exclaim, 'How famous do you have to be!')

After all this therapy, Barbra announced, she finally felt she could sing 'On a Clear Day' with authority. And she did, her voice every bit as strong as it was in the 1970 movie, to end Act One on a rousing high note.

For the second act, Barbra changed into a white suit top with a long skirt slit up the side, a variation on the outfit she had worn at Clinton's inaugural gala. She reminded the audience of the criticism the outfit had elicited from Anne Taylor Fleming. As Streisand began to sputter her disagreement, a voice rose from the audience. 'Don't listen to that woman, Barbra! You look sensational! You're like *buttah!*'

The comedian Mike Myers, dressed as Linda Richman, ran up to the stage. 'I can't believe I'm here with *Barbra!*' Myers-as-Richman exclaimed. 'I'm *fahrklempt.*'

'*You're fahrklempt?* I've got *shpilkes* in my *genecktegezoink*,' Barbra responded, continuing to mimic Myers's regular *Saturday Night Live* shtick as she turned to the audience: 'I need a moment. Talk amongst yourselves. I'll give you a topic: *The Prince of Tides* was neither about tides nor princes. Discuss.'

The audience loved it.

As the concert wound to a close, Barbra drew close the cloak of family and friends. She dedicated a medley of Disney songs to her five-year-old goddaughter, Caleigh, who was sitting on the lap of her father, Jon Peters. As she began to sing 'Evergreen' she looked down at Peters and asked, 'Remember, Jon?' Then she added, 'And there's Elliott, sitting right behind him!' When she returned to the song, she repeated the first verse rather than picking up the second. 'I forgot the words to my own song!' she exclaimed. She recovered immediately, but it was the fear of precisely that kind of miscue that had most worried her about performing live. To the audience it was a touching slip-up amid seemingly superhuman perfection, and it brought them closer to her. Finally she dedicated a rendition of 'Not While I'm Around' to Jason.

Before she sang 'Happy Days Are Here Again,' the final song of the second act, she introduced Martin Luther King's widow, Coretta Scott King, and President Clinton's mother, Virginia Kelley. The second night, she also introduced her own mother. As Mrs Kind, eighty-four and sitting in a wheelchair, rose in response to the crowd's cheers, Barbra told her, 'I love you, Mama.' It was the most intimate moment of the two evenings.

To introduce 'Happy Days,' images of the Great Depression flashed across the video screen, followed by a review of President Clinton's successes in his first year in office. Barbra sang the song not as a dirge, as she had for thirty years, but in the more traditional up-tempo version: for the first time since Lyndon Johnson in 1965, there was a Democrat in the White House whom Barbra could support.

Standing, stomping ovations brought Barbra back for two encores, a thrilling 'My Man' and a touching 'For All We Know.' As she drank in the crowd's adulation, the most exciting concert comeback since Judy Garland's 1961 triumph at Carnegie Hall behind her, she turned to Marvin Hamlisch and exclaimed, 'I did it! I did it! I did it!'

The fans chattered with excitement and awe as they left the Grand Garden. For them the evening had lived up to the most inflated hype and expectations. But would the critics agree? Robert Hilburn, the rock reviewer for the *Los Angeles Times* who had dogged Barbra with testy reviews for a quarter of a century, was won over. 'Streisand combined in these two hours all that she has learned as an artist,' Hilburn wrote. 'Drawing upon her experience in movies and music, Streisand injected the production with a director's sense of atmosphere and occasion, an actress's feel for character and intimacy, and a singer's vocal beauty and command.'

Streisand's New Year's concerts crystallized her long metamorphosis from gawky Brooklyn urchin through kooky nightclub act to international trendsetter and movie superstar, through comedienne to sex symbol to controversial auteur, from traditional balladeer to disco queen and back again, from the butt of journalistic jokes to Hollywood powerhouse and White House intimate.

Now she was more than ever the diva. A pop diva, a movie diva, even a political diva. Now only one question remained: would she keep her act together and take it on the road?

ON JANUARY 17, 1994 the early-morning calm of Greater Los Angeles was shattered by a 6.7 earthquake. The tremor, which killed fifty-seven people, injured 8,700, and caused $2.8 billion in damage, 'freaked Barbra out,' an associate recalled. Her first thought after the deafening rumble and terrifying shaking had subsided was for the new puppy she had purchased two days earlier. She rushed down to the Carolwood kitchen, carrying a flashlight because the electricity had gone out, and found the puppy unhurt.

When the sun rose, the full extent of the damage to Barbra's house became clear. Three of her chimneys had collapsed, and large surface cracks ran through the ceilings and walls. There was no major structural damage, but one of her Grammys and many of her treasured tchotchkes had shattered, including ten rare pottery jugs that smashed to the floor when a mirror above them came crashing down.

Within weeks of the earthquake a memorabilia shop in Hollywood was offering for sale small plastic bags full of Barbra's rubble that they had collected from her trash. Bits of plaster sold for $10, while an 1870s tintype photograph scratched by its broken glass commanded $500. Business in the items was apparently brisk.

STREISAND'S UNDAMAGED COLLECTIBLES moved even more briskly at Christie's New York auction house in March, when she put up for sale 535 magnificent artworks, furniture pieces, cars, clothing items, and tchotchkes. Among the treasures were Tiffany lamps, Gustav Stickley sideboards, a Jacques Lipchitz sculpture, leaded glass casement windows by Frank Lloyd Wright, and Lalique crystal pieces. 'It's so hard to let go of these beautiful things that I have loved for so many years,' she said, 'but I want to simplify my life . . . Sometimes when it's been hard to relate to people, I could relate to inanimate objects. They didn't give me an argument, they didn't think I was crazy. And therefore we had a good relationship . . . The earthquake put things in proper perspective . . . while I love to be surrounded by beautiful things, they're still things.'

Prior to the March 3–4 auction, three previews were held, in Tokyo, Paris, and West Hollywood. On February 17, Barbra appeared at the Art Deco-inspired St James's Club on Sunset Boulevard, where twenty-five of the choicest items were on display for anyone willing to spend $250 to see them. (The event doubled as a fund-raiser for the UCLA Breast Cancer Center.)

Streisand seemed uncomfortable at the event. 'All this for my furniture?' she said with a laugh when she arrived with Richard Baskin to see three hundred people craning their necks to study everything on display in an anteroom off the club's dining room. But as she entered the main room to introduce Dr Susan Love of UCLA, Barbra stared straight ahead, unsmiling, and acknowledged no one in the crowd. Atop a few steps that led from the dining room to the lounge, she read a brief tribute to Dr Love and her work entirely from cue cards, never once raising her gaze to make eye contact with the people watching her. In contrast, Dr Love spoke entirely off the cuff, exuding a sincerity that Barbra must have felt but did not convey.

As she left, a fan asked her for an autograph. She reluctantly obliged, never looked at the young man, and signed her name without breaking her stride as she moved toward a waiting limousine. Many of the people at the event shook their heads in amazement that Barbra Streisand, after more than thirty years of stardom, still found it so difficult to be gracious to strangers.

THE AUCTION PROVED a sensational success. Barbra's 'furniture' brought $5.3 million, including a record price of $2 million for the Tamara de Lempicka painting *Adam and Eve*, which had been featured along with Streisand on the cover of *Architectural Digest* in December of 1993 and had been expected to bring a high bid of $800,000. (The anonymous buyer was Madonna.) Another bidder paid a record $717,500 for a Tiffany cobweb lamp that Barbra had bought in the sixties for $55,000.

Barbra listened to the auction by phone from Carolwood, saying that she was 'thrilled,' especially since all these items had been saved from damage only because she had shipped them to Christie's before the earthquake. A few days later, Marty Erlichman brought her a surprise. She had expressed regret at letting an Art Nouveau music stand go, so Marty bid $6,900 for it and returned it to her as a gift.

Three months later, A. N. Abell's Auction Company in Commerce, California, conducted a bargain-basement version of the Christie's auction. Hundreds of Streisand fans attended the event and bought dozens of practical items like Barbra's toaster ($90), her waffle iron ($35), her hot-fudge warmer ($99), and her chrome-and-wood coffee set ($100). Tom Colwell bought the coffee set and waffle iron. 'I figured,' Colwell explained, 'that now when I make breakfast, I will think of her.'

The phone lines were jammed at TicketMaster offices across the country on Sunday, March 27, 1994. Barbra had announced her first concert tour in twenty-eight years, with performances in Washington D.C., Detroit, San Jose, Anaheim, and New York City, and her fans were in a frenzy. Despite top ticket prices of $350, *five million* calls were logged by telephone companies across the country during the first morning of ticket sales. Many die-hard fans redialed the TicketMaster number a hundred times an hour for two days, desperately trying to be one of three hundred thousand Streisand admirers lucky enough to get a seat.

Many of those who couldn't get through paid scalpers up to $5,000 a ticket. For them, any amount of money was justifiable to hear the woman who was generally acknowledged as the greatest pop voice of the century in what would likely be the last large-scale concert appearances of her career.

EVEN BEFORE THE full extent of the financial and critical success of the Las Vegas concerts could be measured, speculation had run high that Barbra would embark on a full-scale concert tour. The prior January 27 *Daily Variety* ran a front-page story headlined 'Streisand Eyes April for Tour,' in which Marty Erlichman admitted, 'We have lots of [venues on hold], lots of different dates.' But he also insisted that 'no decision' to tour had been made. A week later a company based in Glasgow, Scotland, ran ads in eight British newspapers in which they offered tickets for Streisand concerts to be held in November in Glasgow and Manchester – at a top price of $80. British fans went into a tizzy, but it soon became clear that the promotion was a fraud. Just days later Marty Erlichman officially announced that Barbra had decided on a 'three-month tour of the United States and Europe' that might commence 'as early as April.'

Her concerts in Las Vegas were 'such a lovely experience,' Streisand said in a statement that accompanied the announcement, that she decided to do a limited tour 'to express my appreciation for the love and support I have received for such a long time.'

Marty revealed no specific dates or cities on the schedule and cited the bogus British promotion and other rampant speculation as his reason for making such an early and incomplete announcement. On Valentine's Day, Streisand's publicist, Dick Guttman, revealed that Barbra would begin her tour at London's Wembley Arena with concerts on April 20 and 27. Guttman added that although Marty Erlichman was still in talks with promoters in Paris, Canada, and Tokyo, the London concerts would most likely be the only dates Streisand would play outside the United States.

Barbra hadn't performed live in England since she closed in *Funny Girl* twenty-eight years earlier, and thousands of her loyal British fans scooped up tickets (at a top price equivalent to almost $400) so furiously that two more dates (April 25 and April 29) were added and sold out in less than an hour.

From the outset, many in the media jumped on the financial aspects of the tour as the easiest to exploit in the controversy that apparently must accompany every Streisand endeavor. Why had Barbra, an advocate of inclusionary multiculturalism, and recently the most vocal Democrat not in politics, charged rates for her concerts that even many well-heeled Republicans would find steep? And why were her ticket prices higher than those for upcoming, much-anticipated tours of the Rolling Stones, Pink Floyd, and the reunited Eagles?

Streisand defenders pointed out that Barbra's show had tremendous overheads. She had to lug an enormous complicated set, an expensively produced video presentation, a huge security staff, and over sixty musicians with her from city to city – to say nothing of the princely salary Marvin Hamlisch commanded as her musical director and conductor. (Barbra later admitted that the two shows in Las Vegas had cost her $4 million to produce.) Had she thrown together a simple presentation to play mid-range auditoriums in dozens of cities, Barbra might have been able to keep the prices down. But her fans understood that this was a once-in-a-lifetime event, and they didn't seem to care much about having to pay stratospheric ticket prices to see it.

Even the charitable elements of Barbra's tour drew fire as some observers grumbled about the way tickets had been turned over to various charities by the Streisand camp. The tickets were sold at face value to organizations ranging from a Michigan homeless shelter to an alliance for children's rights, and the charities then offered them for sale at inflated prices. Many felt the tickets should have been donated outright rather than sold. The press reported that the charity tickets, priced as high as $1,000, were not selling out, but what wasn't well known was that Barbra bought back any unsold tickets and turned them over to the box office for general sale.

The sniping did little to lessen the huge excitement created by Barbra's decision to tour. 'She is one of the biggest, if not *the* biggest act in the world,' said promoter John Scher of Metropolitan Concerts. 'Her limits – ticket price, dates, venue size – are all whatever she wants them to be. She could get any price she wants.' Another Midwest promoter offered, 'She could play for years and still not be able to perform for every fan that wants to hear her.'

WITH THE NEWS that the editors of the *Guinness Book of World Records* might include in their next edition the speed with which Barbra's Wembley concerts sold out, the Fleet Street press – as hostile as the British fans were supportive – lay in wait for Streisand's arrival in London on Saturday, April 16. Amid rumors that she would perform behind huge sheets of bulletproof glass and that the ground floor at Wembley would be carpeted to keep her from catching drafts (the rug actually created better acoustics), Barbra took over an entire floor at the Dorchester Hotel and spent three days organizing and rehearsing her show, set to open the following Wednesday.

That evening, before a crowd that included Elton John, Sean Connery, George Michael, Shirley Bassey, and Michael Caine, Barbra offered a show that varied only slightly from her Vegas concerts. 'People have been asking me why I decided to perform in Europe after all this time,' she told the audience. 'I live in Los Angeles, and if you'd been through earthquakes, riots, and fires, believe me, you'd hit the road too!' Although the huge crowd leaped to its feet eight times for standing ovations during the course of the show, Barbra's reviews from the often catty British critics were mixed. The *Daily Telegraph* raved, 'Great, a true star. She is the supreme communicator.' But the *Guardian* sniffed, 'Stilted and hesitant, the Streisand phenomenon defies logic.' *The Times* felt Barbra had provided 'a bravura performance for her fans, magic, a diva who delights.'

A frequent complaint of reviewers was that Barbra's show was overly scripted and that she had relied too heavily on TelePrompTers. Barbra took the issue by the horns the next night: 'I went out and said to the people . . . "Look, I use TelePrompTers! I could never *be* here if I couldn't use [them]. I have a fear of forgetting the words." . . . When I was self-conscious about the [prompters], [the press] mentioned them. When I wasn't, they didn't.'

On April 24, Streisand celebrated her fifty-second birthday with pasta and champagne at Mimmo d'Ischia restaurant in the company of Steven

Spielberg, Carrie Fisher, Elton John, and Michael Caine and his wife. Elliott Gould was also in London but didn't make Barbra's guest list. He complained to the *Sunday Express* that his former wife lived like 'an empress who wants to be treated as somebody whose intentions and work are perfect.' Then he added, 'Do I still love her? She is the mother of my son, so I have no choice.' The *Express* noted that despite Elliott's 'bitchiness,' he had sent Barbra a telegram: 'Happy birthday today and every day. You are not only a success, you are a shining and guiding light.'

For the next evening's concert, Barbra turned over two hundred tickets to be sold to benefit Prince Charles's charitable foundation. As a salute to the prince, who was in the audience surrounded by Holly Hunter, Priscilla Presley, and Joan Collins, Barbra sang 'Some Day My Prince Will Come' and showed a film clip of a brief public encounter she had had with him in 1974 when he visited the Burbank Studios while she was recording the sound track for *Funny Lady*. (She mistakenly identified the meeting as having taken place during a *What's Up, Doc?* recording session.)

Recalling that she was distracted by her work and ungracious to the prince that day, she joked to the audience, 'Who knows? If I had been nicer to him, I might have been the first *real* Jewish princess!' Following the concert, Charles broke protocol by going backstage to see Barbra, and as she stepped out of her dressing room to greet him in her low-cut velvet gown, he smiled appreciatively and said, 'You look pretty good after all these years.' Barbra laughed and replied, 'You look pretty good yourself.' Just days later word leaked out about a soon-to-be-published biography, *The Prince of Wales*, in which Charles admitted that over the years, Streisand had been 'My only pinup . . . she is devastatingly attractive and with a great deal of sex appeal.'

Fleet Street journalists, hungry for any new angle on the romantically dysfunctional royal family, yearned for a relationship to unfurl between 'Hollywood's Queen and England's future King,' but before the tabloids could drum anything up, Barbra had completed her concerts and flown to the Tuscany region of Italy for a rest before returning to the States on May 4 to prepare for her first American concert date a week later in Washington.

Barbra's concert commitments forced her to decline an invitation to attend the inauguration in Pretoria of Nelson Mandela as the president of South Africa. The former New York mayor David Dinkins hand-delivered a message from Barbra to Mandela: 'Your election stands as one of the great moments in our lifetime, the fulfillment of Martin Luther King's dream . . . I cherish our friendship and look forward to greeting you soon as Mr President.'

ON MAY 10, Barbra launched her American tour at the USAir Arena in Washington, D.C., where she had sung for Clinton's inaugural a year earlier. The president and Mrs Clinton were there again, along with hundreds of other Washington power brokers from both parties. Barbra reminded the crowd that her first trip to Washington had been in 1963 when she sang for John F. Kennedy, and she couldn't resist complaining about her recent treatment by the press. She got a big laugh when she told the audience, 'I once confessed in an article that I used to steal bubble gum when I was a kid from this candy store. So I could never run for office . . . even if I wanted to, which I don't – get this right guys, I *don't!* – [because] I know this would come out. I can just see the headlines now, "Bubblegate!"'

Always tinkering with the song format of her show, Barbra now included a show-stopping medley of songs from *Yentl* and added a rousing 'Somewhere' for her last encore, replacing the more downbeat 'For All We Know.' Reviews for the concerts were uniformly excellent. *Newsweek* said, 'For two hours of video recollections, thirty songs, and a liberal dose of liberal politicking, the First Voice ruled a senate's worth of congressmen, cabinet members, and judges.'

THE STREISAND CARAVAN moved on to Michigan, where Barbra played three dates at the Palace in the Detroit suburb of Auburn Hills. She won over the locals when she announced early in her first concert on May 15 that her decision to perform in Detroit was 'a sentimental journey' because her engagement at the Caucus Club in 1961 had been her first nightclub gig outside New York. 'I remember all the friends I made here,' she said, 'and how nice everyone was to me. I remember my friends who used to come to every show and take me into their homes and feed me . . . and I *never* forget people who feed me.' As she recalled the old days, Barbra mentioned from the stage that she was trying to locate her Caucus Club pianist, 'Mike Matthews.' Columnist Mitch Albom reported the next day that 'some guys in Streisand's orchestra' had dined after the show at a restaurant where they ran into Matt Michaels and told him that Barbra wanted to give him a couple of tickets to the show.

Streisand's staff left tickets for him at the box office for the next evening. This time Streisand got his name right when she introduced him from the audience, and she greeted him warmly backstage. 'She hugged me,' Michaels said. 'She said it was good to see me and that she still uses some of my arrangements.'

In Detroit, the physical challenge of performing live for two-plus hours every other night got to Barbra. 'I thought, I don't know how I'm going to get through the next fifteen shows,' she later admitted. 'It's a lot of breathing; you have to be in pretty good shape. And I don't work out vocally, I don't practice. It's the most boring thing you can imagine, doing scales. So I just said, "Fuck it, I can't." I'm just too tired the next day after a concert.'

Finally the rigors of the tour affected her health. Although it wasn't apparent to her audience, Barbra performed her final Detroit concert with a 102-degree fever. After her doctor diagnosed her ailment as viral laryngitis, she announced the postponement of the first four of the six dates of her next stand, in Anaheim, scheduled for May 25–31. 'She feels lousy,' a spokesman for Barbra, Ken Sunshine, said. 'She's been ordered not to talk at all. Barbra feels terrible about any inconvenience this has caused fans. People have flown in from all over the world.' As Barbra lay bedridden at Carolwood, communicating by scribbling on a notepad, the four canceled shows were rescheduled for July 18–24.

Less than two weeks later, although she wasn't completely recovered, Barbra opened at Anaheim's Arrowhead Pond to rapturous fan reaction and rave reviews. 'In a dazzling multimedia tour de force, La Streisand showed the opening-night audience why she is so worthy of all the hoopla,' said the *Orange County Register*. 'In this realm,' wrote the *Hollywood Reporter*, 'no one can touch Barbra Streisand.' During the concert, to jokingly confront rumors that she hadn't really been ill but just wanted to take a break, Barbra borrowed a comedy staple of David Letterman's and read a Top Ten List of the *real* reasons she had interrupted her tour. The list, which garnered big laughs and reams of publicity the next day, included these items: 'Number eight, I didn't know it would take a whole week to dust all this furniture. Number seven, I was at home waiting for the cable guy. Number five, I wanted to get Barbra Streisand tongue depressors into the boutiques. Number three, I thought my concert tour needed more publicity. Number two, it took me three days to read Dan Quayle's new book – and four days to correct the spelling. And number one, there was a shoe sale at Nordstrom's.'

ON THE NEXT stop of the tour, San Jose, Barbra stayed in nearby San Francisco at the Fairmont Hotel on Nob Hill. She leased an entire floor, rented all of the rooms on the floor below for security reasons, and had the hotel lay white carpeting over the gray rugs in her rooms at a cost to her of $50,000. Apparently because of a sudden (and short-lived) fear of flying, Barbra motored from Los Angeles to San Francisco in a Winnebago. The concerts at the San Jose Arena went typically well, in spite of a truly scathing review from the conservative *San Francisco Chronicle*, a longtime Streisand nemesis.

FOLLOWING A JUNE 13 state dinner at the White House, to which she was escorted amid tremendous publicity (and romance rumors) by the television news anchorman Peter Jennings, Barbra moved on to New York, where she opened at Madison Square Garden on June 20 for four dates. Although the Anaheim makeup concerts in July had spoiled her plan to conclude the tour in her hometown, she approached the Manhattan dates as the highlight of the tour, and they proved to be just that. Her opening night brought out the usual coterie of celebrities, including Liza Minnelli, Barbra Walters, and Peter Jennings, and most notably the frail eighty-eight-year-old Jule Styne, in his last public appearance before his death three months to the day after the concert. Styne, teary-eyed, received an ovation when Barbra dedicated 'People' to him. 'This is beyond excitement,' he told *USA Today*. 'I have no doubt she's the greatest singer ever in my lifetime.'

Although she had savored nightly doses of adoration since the start of the tour, Barbra was overwhelmed by the reaction of the New York fans. 'I knew she would probably be very nervous,' said Ellen Silver, who was in charge of VIP seating for Madison Square Garden, 'and she was. But she was so happy when she was so well received. The audience went berserk and there was just such an outpouring of love that she was *fahrklempt* at one point herself! You could see she was close to crying. It was that overwhelming.'

Liz Smith called the concert 'Sublime and utter perfection . . . Age has, if anything, improved Barbra's astonishing voice. As [she] hit the final soul-searching notes of the evening's last song, I thought the top of my head – and the roof of the Garden – would come off! All about her were hysterical, but Barbra was in total, brilliant control – the calm glittering eye of her own self-created hurricane.'

Under a tongue-in-cheek headline – 'Local Girl Makes Good, Sings' – *The New York Times* noted that 'The concert wasn't exactly a song recital. It was kind of a state visit with a woman who has proved herself as singer, actress, director and producer, who is now returning in triumph to her most uncontroversial calling: the Tin Pan Alley songbird.' The most derisive notice Barbra received in New York came from Rex Reed, who spent most of his review complaining that Streisand wasn't Judy Garland. 'Great singing comes from the soul,' Reed proclaimed, 'but she'd rather have her press-on nails (read talons) ripped off than reveal her inner self. This is why I prefer Judy on a bad day to Barbra in peak form. Babs puts up a wall. Judy kicked it down so the audience could touch her, and they jumped out of balconies to do it.' (Apparently Reed would have preferred Barbra to forget lyrics, ramble incoherently in the middle of songs, perform with barely a voice to call on, and pass out onstage the way Judy did on some of her bad days.)

During Barbra's stay in New York, which was extended to accommodate two more shows 'for fans only,' the local press covered her every move. *New York* magazine featured a pull-out illustrated map that pinpointed the various addresses in Barbra's Brooklyn and Manhattan history; the *Daily News* ran a series of biographical articles; and the *Post* held a daily 'Barbra Watch,' with reporters and photographers camped outside her Central Park West building for weeks to catch her, which they finally did toward the end of the stand. Streisand hadn't received so much newspaper space in New York since the fevered first days of *Funny Girl* on Broadway.

On July 12 Barbra paid a surprise walk-on visit to the David Letterman show. The scarcity of Streisand tickets had been a running gag on the show for weeks, and when Barbra strode out of the wings to the strains of 'People' – and to wild applause from the audience – she handed two tickets to Letterman and told him to 'stop kvetching, already.'

For her last concert in New York, Barbra decided to give 'a gift' to the city and have her last encore, 'Somewhere,' beamed on the giant video screen above Times Square. Tens of thousands of people crowded onto Forty-second Street in a scene reminiscent of New Year's Eve and cheered when Barbra cried, 'Hello, Times Square!'

Billboard magazine proclaimed Barbra's Madison Square Garden concerts 'The largest grossing engagement in American music history.' The promoters of the event, Delsener/Slater Enterprises, estimated that the seven shows had grossed over $60 million.

BACK AT ANAHEIM'S Arrowhead Pond for the tour's new finale, Barbra taped the last two shows for HBO and CBS television specials. The final concert on July 24 was one of the most exciting of the tour. Relaxed and radiant, Barbra was in strong, pure voice, and the audience responded with seven prolonged standing ovations in the first act alone. 'Wow!' Streisand exclaimed from the stage. 'I've got a great closing-night audience!' At one point she told a pregnant Annette Bening that she might hurt herself if she didn't stop popping up and down in her seat.

No one in the audience budged at the concert's conclusion when Barbra asked if they wanted to stay and watch her sing a couple of songs again for the television cameras. She did a handful of repeat performances, including 'Somewhere,' 'You Don't Bring Me Flowers,' and 'Evergreen.' Then she sang, for the first time during the tour, a moving version of

'What Are You Doing the Rest of Your Life?' to be included in the CBS special.

WHEN IT WAS all over, Streisand fans filed out of the Arrowhead Pond beaming with the knowledge that they had been part of a very special night on a very special tour that Barbra had said she will never repeat. 'You have to put makeup on and wear high heels,' she complained by way of explanation. 'My feet get cramps.' More to the point, she had proven something to herself and to the world. 'It all worked out; it was right. It was right for me to gain this confidence, to feel absolutely at ease onstage, to feel I belonged there and deserved to be there, that I could give and receive the love of those audiences. I really *am* grateful to those people.'

THE MOST STARTLING moment of the entire tour – one that was edited out of the television presentations of the concert – took place during Barbra's last performance at the Arrowhead Pond. Three hundred thousand people had cheered themselves hoarse for her over the past four months; she was at the peak of her extraordinary powers; she had proven herself as one of the most beloved entertainers of her generation.

This night her audience, perhaps because they knew this was the last time they would see Streisand perform live, burst into a stomping, cheering, ear-splitting standing ovation the minute she took the stage. For minute after long minute the wave of cacophonous adulation wouldn't let up. But none of that mattered to Barbra as much as the reaction of one frail woman sitting in the second row. As the cheers of fifteen thousand people reverberated around her, Barbra Streisand looked down at the lady being helped up from a wheelchair and said quietly, 'Are you proud of me now, Mama?'

The Artist as Citizen

'I have opinions.

Nobody has to agree.'

—*Barbra at Harvard, 1995*

THE FORUM
INSTITUTE OF POLITICS

S he wanted the man to get on with it. As Harvard University's interim president, Albert Carnesale, sang her praises in a lengthy introduction to the seven hundred students jammed into the cafeteria of the John F. Kennedy School of Government, Streisand fidgeted, took deep breaths, rolled her eyes skyward, and at one point nearly jumped out of her seat to make him stop. When Carnesale turned to see what all this commotion was about, Barbra said to him, 'You've heard of *shpilkes?*'

She was nervous, more nervous than anyone could remember seeing her, at the prospect of delivering a speech entitled 'The Artist as Citizen' to the students of one of the finest political science colleges in the world, a talk that would be taped for broadcast on the C-SPAN network. She had been asked a year earlier to speak at the school – which had hosted Secretary of State Warren Christopher, Russian President Mikhail S. Gorbachev, Newt Gingrich, Al Gore, and scores of other world leaders – and she had worked on her speech with her usual obsessiveness. She wrote and rewrote; she sought help from friends and from political writers like Robert Scheer of the *Los Angeles Times*.

Streisand's impending arrival had created an inordinate amount of excitement in Cambridge. So many students wanted to hear her that a lottery system was instituted, and the same security system used to protect visiting heads of state was put into place for her.

She flew into Boston by private jet on Wednesday, February 1, 1995, two days before the speech, and took up residence in the $1,500-a-night presidential suite at the ritzy Charles Hotel in Harvard Square. 'A few days before Barbra checked in,' the Boston *Herald* reported, 'there was a frantic search for a mandatory requirement for the diva's suite – a full-size Hollywood vanity mirror. They found it.' Fans inundated her rooms with flowers until, the newspaper said, 'it was wall-to-wall roses, tulips, calla lilies, French lilacs, and daffodils up there.'

On Thursday John F. Kennedy Jr. escorted Barbra around the Harvard campus. They toured the university's libraries and museums, then lunched at the Kennedy School with Sharon Pratt Kelly, the former mayor of Washington, D.C., the former Tennessee senator Jim Sasser, and a select group of students that included Chris Garcia, a Republican with whom Streisand got into a spirited debate that she later said she enjoyed immensely.

WHEN ALBERT CARNESALE completed his introduction, Barbra stood at the lectern looking crisply professional in a dark gray pin-striped Donna Karan suit and a single strand of pearls. 'I've stood up and performed before thousands of people, but this is much more frightening,' Barbra said to explain her obvious jitters. 'Maybe it's because this is the John F. Kennedy School of Government at Harvard. And I'm neither a politician nor a professor. I like to think of myself as a perpetual student.'

Barbra reminded the audience of the subject of her talk and said, 'This is an important moment to deal with this subject because so much of what the artist needs to flourish and survive is at risk now. When I was asked to speak here a year ago, I was much more optimistic [because] we had a president who judged our ethnic, cultural, and artistic diversity as a kind of strength rather than a weakness. And then came the election of 1994, and suddenly the progress of the recent past seemed threatened by those who hungered for "the good old days" when women and minorities knew their place. In this resurgent, reactionary mood, artists are derided as "the cultural elite" and are convenient objects of scorn. And those institutions that have given Americans access to artistic works such as the National Endowment for the Arts and the Corporation for Public Broadcasting are in danger of being abolished.

'All great civilizations have supported the arts. However, the new speaker of the house, citing the need to balance the budget, insists that the art programs be the first to go. But the government's contribution to the NEA and PBS is really quite meager. To put it in perspective, the entire budget of the NEA is equal to one F-22 fighter jet, a plane some experts say may not even be necessary. And the Pentagon is planning to build 442 of them. One less plane, and we've got the whole arts budget! . . . So maybe it's not about balancing the budget. Maybe it's about shutting the minds and mouths of artists who might have something thought-provoking to say.'

She found it difficult to contain her anger at the name-calling she had been subjected to by conservative commentators. 'In Victorian times,' she said, 'there were signs requiring actors and dogs to eat in the kitchen. And as recently as last year artists who have spoken out politically have been derided as airheads, bubbleheads, and nitwits . . .

'Imagine having this kind of contempt for an industry that is second only to aerospace in export earnings abroad. According to *Business Week*, Americans spent $340 billion on entertainment in 1993. Maybe policymakers could learn something from an industry that makes billions while the government owes trillions! . . .

'I know that I can speak more eloquently through my work than through any speech I might give. Speeches make me very nervous, as you can see. So as an artist, I've chosen to make films about subjects and social issues that I care about, whether it's dealing with the inequality of women in *Yentl* or producing a film about Grethe Cammermeyer, who was discharged from the army for telling the truth about her sexuality.'

INDEED, BARBRA HAD been a driving force behind *Serving in Silence: The Margarethe Cammermeyer Story*, which aired over NBC on February 6, 1995 and garnered mixed reviews and good ratings. When Barbra read news accounts of how Colonel Cammermeyer, after years of exemplary service as a nurse in the army and the National Guard, was drummed out of the Guard when she admitted that she was a lesbian, Barbra exclaimed to her producing partner, Cis Corman, 'We have to do something about this. We have to tell this story.' To Barbra, Cammermeyer's dismissal represented 'discrimination, fear, prejudice, and narrow-mindedness, and I don't think there is a place for that in a just society . . . If we can help change some people's opinions, make them less frightened of something they don't understand; if they can look at this story and feel compassion and perhaps even anger at the military for this injustice, then it will be worthwhile.'

Streisand put together the package, which included Glenn Close, a movie star who rarely does television, as Colonel Cammermeyer. 'Thank God for Barbra and Glenn,' said Craig Zadan, one of the film's six producers, along with Streisand and Close. 'We hear so much about the bad aspects of star power, but getting this movie made is a perfect example of how star power can be a force for good.'

STILL TAKING FREQUENT deep breaths and fidgeting almost constantly, Barbra continued her speech: 'I'm also very proud to be a liberal. Why is that so terrible these days? [The audience cheered.] The liberals were liberating. They fought slavery, fought for women to have the right to vote . . . fought to end segregation, fought to end apartheid. Thanks to liberals, we have Social Security, public education, consumer and environmental protection, Medicare, Medicaid, the minimum-wage law, unemployment compensation. Liberals put an end to child labor. They even gave us the five-day work week. What's to be ashamed of? . . .

'I have opinions, nobody has to agree – I just like being involved, and after many years of self-scrutiny, I've realized that the most satisfying feelings come from things outside myself . . .

'So until women are treated equally with men, until gays and minorities are not discriminated against, until children have their full rights, artists must continue to speak out, and I will be one of them. Sorry, Rush, Newt, Jesse – the artist as citizen is here to stay.'

The students cheered as Carnesale led Barbra off the podium, and a few moments later he escorted her back to answer questions. 'Whaddaya wanna know?' she called to the audience. 'Whaddaya wanna know?' As she replied to nearly a dozen queries, Barbra spoke as eloquently as she had from her prepared text, and promptly acknowledged that she didn't know much about complicated policy issues. When one young woman asked what citizens could do to make sure such programs as Medicaid and Medicare stay in place, Barbra replied, 'Vote for the Democrats next time.'

One student, Stacey Woolf, heaped praise on Barbra. 'I know you've told us that you're very nervous, but we've all witnessed here tonight that you're an outstanding public speaker. Since you're such a passionate and engaging public speaker, you're wealthy, you're intelligent, you're enormously popular—'

Barbra interrupted her: 'You got a guy for me?'

WEALTHY, INTELLIGENT, ENORMOUSLY popular – but still no guy. Barbra has had three great loves in her life – Elliott Gould, Jon Peters, and Richard Baskin – but none has lasted except in friendship, and she faces middle age alone. Over the last few years she had been linked with Peter Jennings, the Australian actor Peter Weller, Liam Neeson, and most recently Jon Voight, but these 'romances' were usually created by the tabloids out of one or two dinner dates. 'What I find is that the media destroys relationships before they can even begin,' Barbra said. 'They write terrible things, they assume things. Because I go to see Andre Agassi play at Wimbledon, they write that I'm his girlfriend. Then they say he "left" me for Brooke Shields. It's ridiculous.'

Years earlier Barbra had admitted, 'I'm probably in the worst position for finding a man,' and today that is truer than ever. Her work and her friends and Jason and her godchildren fulfill her, of course, but there is a void at the middle of Barbra Streisand's life, one that so many legendary Hollywood ladies from Joan Crawford and Bette Davis to Ava Gardner and Lana Turner have felt: the lack of a man to share the rest of her life with.

'She makes her own happiness,' her mother said in 1994. 'She has a lot of friends. If somebody nice comes along and they really get on together, maybe things will be different. But at this stage it's really sad that she has to make her own life without a husband.'

'WOULD YOU PLEASE consider running for public office?' a student asked her to much applause.

'No, no, no,' Barbra replied. 'I'm passionate about certain issues, but I think I can be much more effective doing what I do. You know, making films about Colonel Cammermeyer, or making a film about everybody's right to love in *The Normal Heart*.'

IN 1986 STREISAND had optioned *The Normal Heart*, Larry Kramer's searing off-Broadway play about the AIDS epidemic and the government's shocking indifference to it. Nine years later, after a series of delays and difficulties, she appeared ready to produce, direct, and co-star in the film. 'I have written twenty drafts of a screenplay over the years,' Kramer said, 'five for her. I told her I wanted it to be perfect, and she said there is no such thing . . . [then she added], "I'm trying not to do that to myself anymore."'

Barbra spent hours with Kramer, himself ill with AIDS, both at Carolwood and in his Greenwich Village apartment, working on the script. 'I'm loving it,' Kramer said. 'It's keeping me going . . . She'll challenge you on every word; she'll act out the words . . . She'll recall draft four when you've forgotten every previous draft.'

A disagreement between Barbra and Kramer arose out of a line in the play when the gay protagonist tells his straight brother, 'I'm the same as you. Just say it!'

Barbra didn't believe that the two brothers were the same. As she put it during her concert tour, 'Just imagine how boring life would be if we were all the same. My idea of a perfect world is one in which we really appreciate each other's differences – short, tall, Democrat, Republican, black, white, gay, straight. A world in which all of us are equal, but definitely not the same!'

Kramer tried to change Barbra's mind, but he found her intractable. 'I can't put that in my movie,' she said, 'because I don't believe it.'

Barbra appeared ready to begin production on *The Normal Heart* in the spring of 1995, but she has had difficulty raising 'enough money' to make it, she said, and the actor she wanted for the film's lead, Ralph Fiennes, proved unavailable due to a commitment to play Hamlet on the London and New York stages. As of this writing, Barbra has decided to put *The Normal Heart* off once again and instead direct *The Mirror Has Two Faces*, a drama about a dowdy professor who undergoes a total makeover in order to bring some passion into her platonic marriage. Barbra will play the professor and Jeff Bridges will play her husband. Filming was set to begin in October 1995.

'I think I'm always drawn to films about the mystery of appearances,' Barbra said. '*The Mirror Has Two Faces* is a really charming love story. But it has serious overtones about vanity and beauty, the external versus the internal.'

AFTER QUESTIONS FROM the Harvard students about AIDS, about how Barbra can be so mainstream and yet fight against the mainstream mentality ('I don't think of myself as mainstream'), about what international problems she's interested in ('I don't know that much about Bosnia'), and about how her religion informs her work, the question and answer session came to a close. Albert Carnesale, acknowledging the success of Barbra's talk amid the lusty cheers of the students, joked that since she wasn't interested in running for the Senate, she should accept the open job of Dean of the Kennedy Center.

As Barbra laughed and waved good-bye to the cheering crowd, two students stood up and held aloft a banner that read: 'Babs in '96.'

IN MAY 1995 Barbra received an honorary doctorate of humane letters from Brandeis University. As she accepted the degree, Barbra told the cheering graduating class, 'My father would be very proud.' Indeed, Emanuel Streisand's daughter had become one of the most accomplished, one of the wealthiest and most charitable, and one of the most influential women of her day, a close friend of the president of the United States, a performer who brings joy to millions and who stands up defiantly to the sniping of others who recite a litany of complaints against her. 'She's a Streisand,' Manny might have boasted.

On June 6, Barbra sat for an hour-long television interview with Larry King. The CNN talk show host had been after her for nearly a year to appear on his program, but she resisted until he assured her that most of the hour would be devoted to her views on social and political issues.

Dressed all in white, Barbra frequently donned eyeglasses in order to refer to notes she had made for the appearance. A few days later, King revealed in his *USA Today* column several things Barbra had written in her notes but hadn't had time to say on the air. About Senator Bob Dole's criticism that Hollywood executives had 'sold [their] souls ... for the sake of corporate profits,' Barbra planned to ask him, 'Isn't the Republican Congress selling its soul for corporate profits when it comes to the tobacco industry, the chemical companies, and corporate polluters?'

Barbra also planned to say, 'Rap music may make your flesh crawl, but the message of hopelessness should not be ignored.'

The hour was most enlightening when it came to Barbra's personal life, about which she spoke frankly. Of her lack of a romantic relationship, she said, 'I have had love and passion. I want a partner. I want the masculine to my feminine and the feminine to my masculine ... I'm also a little girl, a weak child. I'm many things. If somebody wants many women in his life, then I'm the person.'

King asked Streisand what her remaining goals are. 'To be a better person,' she replied. 'After many years of therapy, I still don't understand myself in many areas ... I wish I could have more peace in my life. I wish I could get less angry. I wish I could transcend certain feelings.'

AT TWO AND a half, she climbed atop her mother's dresser, smeared lipstick on her face, and nearly fell off as she admired her handiwork in the mirror. Fifty years later little has changed. Barbra is still going where many tell her not to; she is still eager to transform herself, and still willing to risk falling off the edge in order to fulfill her artistic desires.

For thirty years she has surprised, delighted, angered, polarized, and riveted the public. Barbra Streisand has always been creatively restless, personally seeking, artistically challenging to herself and others. She will continue to fascinate millions of people the world over because she remains, as she would proudly say, a work in progress.

SOURCE NOTES

Over two hundred people contributed their recollections of Barbra Streisand to this book. Most have been quoted in the text; the others were extremely helpful in providing background and insight. Half a dozen people spoke only on the condition of anonymity, and they are thus not listed here. Interviews were conducted by the author of this book and by Chris Nickens and Mike Szymanski between 1992 and 1995:

Charlie Abruzzo, Joe Albertson, Walter Alford, Irvin Arthur, Annabelle Atkins, Tom Atkins, Jonathon Axelrod, Alan Bagenski, Lansing Bailey, Kevin Bannon, Joseph Battaglia, Adrienne Behr, Ron Bergey, Charles Biasiny-Rivera, Gerry Blumenfeld, Abba Bogin, Laura Borenstein, Gary Bornstein, Irving Borokow, Ronnie Brahms, Carolyn Bernstein Brostoff, Robert Brown, Shawn Burns, Artie Butler, Albert Callin Jr, Howard Cates, Cliff Chappell, Emily Cobb, Anita Cohen, Cee Cee Cohen, Ron Coleman, Shanna Coleman, Trude Coleman, Frank Comstock, Anita Miller Cooper, Gordon Cornish, William Corride, John Cotter, Alexander Courage, Wilma Curley, Bill Dager, Joe Darconte, Chico Day, Mrs Roger De Koven, Jim Dickson.

Bradford Dillman, Bob DiNardi, Marion Disanto, Mark Discowitz, Phyllis Dorroshow, Michael Druxman, Maurice Tei Dunn, Maxine Eddleson, Minnie Eddleson, Fred Farber, Walter Finley, Iris Fisher, Ed Fishman, Connie Forslund, Anne Francis, David Frankel, Larry Fuller, Myer Galpern, Sam Galpern, Dick Gautier, George Gaynes, James Geller, Linda Gerard, Stefan Gierasch, Ron Girsch, Richard Gordon, Stewart Gorelick, Billy Gorson, Nancy Grashow, Peter Greenleaf, Eva Greenstein, Michael Greer, Paul Grein, Simon Gribben, Joyce Hannes, Maureen Harmon, Jim Hauser, Marta Heflin, Richard Heinrich, Milt Hinton, Arno Hirsch, Diane Hirschfeld, Gerald Hockberg, Alice Blacksin Horevitz, Ben Indick, Jan Ippolito, Ed Isseks, Debbie Iwrey, Steve Jaffe, Judi James, Mike Johnson, Roberta Johnson, Marcia Mae Jones.

Dave Kapralik, Lainie Kazan, Herb Kessner, Guratma Khlasa, Merwyn Saul Kind, Raya King, Robert Klein, Bill Kling, Sylvia Kling, Howard Koch, Leonard

Kohn, Ed Kramer, Bernie Kukoff, Don Lamond, Jay Landesman, Marie Lawrence, Phil Leeds, Ernest Lehman, Terry Leong, Jacqueline Goldstein Levine, Natalie Turner Levy, Richard Lewine, Viveca Lindfors, Anna Lopatton, Mike Lubell, Moss Mabry, Ceil Mack, Mary Manford, Jack Manning, Bob McDonald, Loya McDonald, Michael McGarry, Allyn Ann McLerie, Matt Michaels, Allan Miller, Carol Morgan, Harry Myers, David Newman, Victor Nikaido, Henya Novick, Richard O'Brien, Barbara Sgroi Oishi, David Parker, Debbie Parrish, Austin Pendleton, Bob Perry, Jerry Pomerantz, Dr Peter Reddick, George Reeder, Eli Rill, Dennis Ritz.

Joan Rivers, Jack Roe, Eleanor Rosenbaum, Stan Rosenberg, Robert Rosenthal, Cynthia Roth, Helen Rothstein, Ted Rozar, Mary Ryan, Nick Salerno, Bob Samuels, Ralph Sandler, Rich Sandler, Arnold Scaasi, Hal Schaefer, Jerry Schatzberg, Robert Scheerer, Norm Schimmel, Ed Schreyer, Bob Schulenberg, Mike Schuman, Bob Scott, Roy Scott, Joseph Seley, Harriet Gellin Selverstone, Howard Senor, Bob Sherman, David Shire, Scott Siegel, Stanley Simmonds, Joy Simmons, Ron Simone, Whitey Snyder, Elaine Sobel, Jane Soifer, Warren Spencer, Judith Jacobsen Sperling, Arnold Stark, Marvin Stein, Adele Lowinson Stern, Emily Schottenfeld Stoper, Harry Stradling Jr.

Beth Streisand, Molly Streisand, Anita Sussman, Todd Sussman, Rochelle Taboh, Linda Mantel Teischer, Gene Telpner, Jerry Vale, Terry Silver Vogel, Ingrid Meighan Waldron, Trudy Wallace, Glenn Walter, Ken Wannberg, Henry Warshaw, David Watkin, Esther Waxman, Ruth White, Harvey Wielstein, Les Wielstein, Vance Wilson, Neil Wolfe, James Wright.

MANY OF THE quotes from Barbra, Jon Peters, and Elliott Gould in this book have been culled from numerous interviews they have done over the years with Canadian, British, and European newspaper and television journalists. All three are much franker when talking to reporters in foreign countries, and the material is a treasure trove never utilized by a Streisand biographer before. The interviews are specified in the notes that follow.

PART 1

Major interviews conducted for this section, in order of their quotes, were with Barbra's aunts Molly Streisand Parker and Beth Streisand, Irving Borokow, Louis Kind's son Merwyn Saul Kind, Barbra's Brooklyn neighbors and classmates Maxine Eddleson, Carolyn Bernstein, Diane Hirschfeld, Trudy Wallace, Anita Sussman, Esther Waxman, Marvin Stein, and Cee Cee Cohen; Emily Cobb, Allan Miller, Anita Miller Cooper, Roy Scott, Maurice Tei Dunn, Eli Rill,

Bob Schulenberg, Michael Greer, Ted Rozar, Matt Michaels, Elaine Sobel, and Abba Bogin.

Details of life in Isaac Streisand's hometown in Galicia came from two articles, one in the July-December 1899 issue of *Menorah* entitled 'What Can Be Done for the Galician Jews?' and the other in vol. 104 of the *Fortnightly Review*, 1915, 'Life in Eastern Galicia.' The New York City Municipal Archives provided birth and marriage certificates for Barbra's parents and grandparents. Peter Carucci of the State of New York Department of Health provided specifics of the date and time of Emanuel Streisand's death. The 1910 and 1920 census records of the Department of Commerce were helpful in tracing the births, immigration dates, ages, and addresses of Barbra's forebears, as were the ship manifests held in the New York Public Library.

The biographical listing for Emanuel Streisand in the 1941 directory *Leaders in Education* provided information on his schooling, degrees, and professional achievements.

The separation papers of Diana Kind and Louis Kind, including depositions from both parties, were obtained from the archives of the Supreme Court of the State of New York in Brooklyn. Some of the quotes from Diana Kind in this section are from an interview with Rebecca Hardy published in the London *Daily Mail*. Barbra revealed her thoughts as a teenager about losing her father to Geraldo Rivera in an interview televised on November 17, 1983.

Some of the quotes from people who knew Barbra in Detroit are contained in an article in the March 27, 1966, *Detroit Free Press* entitled 'Looking Back at the Compleat Detroit Streisand,' and in an article in the October 24, 1968, *Detroit News*, 'Barbra, when.'

Karen Swenson's five-part article 'One More Look at the First Decade' in the British fan magazine *All About Barbra* provided information about Barbra's early years and about her career through 1972.

Jeff Harris's quotes are from a 1980 interview with the author of this book.

PART 2

Major interviews for this section were conducted with Wilma Curley, Elaine Sobel, Dave Kapralik, Marvin Stein, Lainie Kazan, Allan Miller, George Reeder, Larry Fuller, and Linda Gerard.

Most of the quotes from Arthur Laurents about *I Can Get It for You Wholesale* and from Garson Kanin about *Funny Girl* are from 1980 interviews with the author of this book. Jerome Weidman wrote his reminiscences of Barbra in the November 1963 issue of *Holiday*. Milton Rosenstock shared his recollections at a symposium conducted by the New York Sheet Music Society on September 8, 1990.

Some of Barbra's quotes about her life during this period came from an article in the October 1963 issue of *Men's Digest*. Elliott Gould's quotes were gleaned from a number of interviews he has given over the years in the United States and in Great Britain. Among them are interviews by Diana Lurie, published in the *Ladies' Home Journal* in August 1969; Judith Michaelson, the *New York Post*, May 23, 1970; Trudi Pacter, the London *Sunday Mirror*, January 22, 1984; Jack Hicks, *TV Guide*, December 1, 1984; Corinna Horan, the *Courier Mail*, October 1, 1994; and *Playboy*, November 1970.

Rafe Chase's article, 'Barbra Streisand at the hungry i,' in *All About Barbra* provided information about that stop on Barbra's 1963 tour.

Major articles published around this time that contributed information and/or quotes include those in *Time* on April 10, 1964; the New York *Daily News* on April 26, 1964; *Life* on May 22, 1964; and *The New York Times Magazine* on July 4, 1965.

Karen Swenson's article 'Her Special Charms' in the fan magazine *Barbra Quarterly* provided information about Barbra's television specials. Marty Erlichman reminisced with the author of this book for a special *Billboard* issue, 'The Legend of Barbra Streisand,' published on December 10, 1983.

Some of Barbra's quotes about her pregnancy and Jason's birth are from *Ladies' Home Journal*, August 1966; *Cameo Baby Magazine*, January-February 1967; and *Look*, July 25, 1967.

Michel Legrand's quotes are from the book *Barbra Streisand: Une Femme Libre* by Guy Abitan. They were translated by Michel Parenteau.

Rex Reed's article 'Color Barbra Very Bright' was published in *The New York Times* on March 27, 1966. Some details of the taping of *Color Me Barbra* were gleaned from an article in *Look*, March 18, 1966.

PART 3

Major interviews contributing to this section were with Jack Roe, David Shire, Robert Scheerer, Anne Francis, Harry Stradling Jr., Ernest Lehman, Arnold Scaasi, Howard Koch, Don Lamond, Milt Hinton, Robert Klein, and Ed Schreyer.

Some of the details of the production of *The Belle of 14th Street* were gleaned from the October 1967 issue of *Monsanto* magazine and the May 20, 1967, issue of *Business Week*.

Martha Weinman Lear's observations of the preparations for 'A Happening in Central Park' were published in *Redbook*, January 1968. Karen Swenson's article 'The Making of Funny Girl' in *Barbra Quarterly* provided information. Joyce Haber's article, 'Barbra's Directing Her First Movie,' appeared in *New York* magazine on April 15, 1968. Some of Barbra's quotes in this section are from 'The Kosher Kid from Brooklyn,' published in the London *Sunday Times Magazine*, January 12, 1969.

Several of Walter Matthau's quotes are contained in the article 'Matthau in Full Flower' published in the December 1968 issue of *Esquire*. Herb Ross's observations were shared with the author of this book for *Billboard*, December 10, 1983.

PART 4

Major interviews conducted for this section were with Steve Jaffe, Austin Pendleton, Stefan Gierasch, Jerry Schatzberg, Howard Koch Jr., Moss Mabry, Harry Stradling Jr., Bradford Dillman, Viveca Lindfors, and Jack Roe.

The quotes from Richard Perry, Buck Henry, Irvin Kershner, and Peter Yates are from 1980 interviews with the author of this book, as are some of Arthur Laurents's. Some of the quotes from Robert Redford and Sydney Pollack are from 1976 interviews with the author of this book. Other quotes from Pollack and Laurents are from the Donald Zec and Anthony Fowles biography *Barbra*.

Background about the making of *Barbra Streisand . . . and Other Musical Instruments* was obtained from Jerry Parker's *Newsday* article, 'She'd Rather Stay Home,' published October 28, 1973, and from Peter Genower's profile published in the London *Sunday Times* on December 16, 1973.

Many of Jon Peters's quotes are from interviews by Julia Orange published in Australia in 1974, Rosalie Shann published in Great Britain in 1975, and Jerry Parker published in *Newsday* in 1976. Some of Barbra's quotes are from *McCall's*, April 1975.

Gary Klein's quotes about *ButterFly* were published in *Billboard*'s special Streisand issue published December 10, 1983.

PART 5 AND PART 6

Major interviews for these sections were with Jerry Schatzberg, Jonathan Axelrod, Steve Jaffe, Marta Heflin, Ralph Sandler, Joe Kern, Trudy Coleman, Ruth White, Leonard Kohn, Richard Gordon, Robert Brown, and David Watkin.

Details of the various court actions against Jon Peters are preserved in the Los Angeles court system's public archives.

Marie Brenner's article 'A Star Is Shorn' was published in the January 24, 1975, issue of *New Times*. Frank Pierson's article 'My Battles with Barbra and Jon' was published in *New West* and *New York* magazines on November 15, 1976. Barbra's *Playboy* interview appeared in the October 1977 issue.

Some of the quotes from Barbra and Jon about *A Star Is Born* were given to a UCLA symposium conducted in December 1976.

The quotes from Barry Gibb were contained in the December 10, 1983, *Billboard* issue devoted to Streisand and in an interview with Mikki Dorsey published in the *Toronto Star* on October 20, 1980. A number of the quotes from Marilyn and Alan Bergman were also culled from the *Billboard* Streisand issue.

Barbra's observations about *Yentl* were gleaned from interviews during the fall of 1983 and the spring of 1984 with Gene Shalit on the TV show *Today*; Dale Pollack of the *Los Angeles Times*; Chaim Potok in *Esquire*; Geraldo Rivera on *20/20*; Brian Linehan on *City Lights* in Canada; Ian Johnston on the BBC in London; with the French television show *A la Une*; and with the Dutch television show *Coupe de Weijden*.

Barbra's quotes about Don Johnson are contained in an interview with David Lewin published in the London *Daily Mail*. Don's observations about Barbra were shared with Terry Willows and published in *London Today*.

The observations by Barbra, Nick Nolte, Pat Conroy, and Jason Gould about *The Prince of Tides* were gleaned from various sources, including the Criterion laser disc edition of the film and interviews in the *Los Angeles Times*, *Vanity Fair*, *Cosmopolitan*, *Ladies' Home Journal*, *Empire* magazine, *US* magazine, and television interviews aired in London and Amsterdam during the spring of 1992.

The quotes from Amy Moss about her relationship with Andre Agassi were published by the London *Sunday Mirror* on June 27, 1993. Agassi's 'faggot' remarks were reported in the November 16, 1993, issue of *The Advocate*.

Some of Barbra's quotes about the Las Vegas concerts and her tour are from *Vanity Fair*, November 1994.

Jonathan Yardley's column 'Miss Marmelstein Goes to Washington' appeared in the *Washington Post*, the *Los Angeles Times*, and other newspapers in May 1993. Robert Scheer's interview with Barbra in the *Los Angeles Times* was published on May 23, 1993.

People magazine's cover story 'A Star Is Reborn' ran in the May 31, 1993, issue.

FILMOGRAPHY

Funny Girl (Columbia Pictures, 1968). Directed by William Wyler; produced by Ray Stark; screenplay by Isobel Lennart; musical numbers directed by Herbert Ross; original music by Jule Styne; lyrics by Bob Merrill; photographed by Harry Stradling. Starring Barbra Streisand as Fanny Brice; Omar Sharif as Nick Arnstein; Kay Medford as Rose Brice; Anne Francis as Georgia James; Lee Allen as Eddie Ryan; Walter Pidgeon as Florenz Ziegfeld.

Hello, Dolly! (Twentieth Century-Fox, 1969). Directed by Gene Kelly; written for the screen and produced by Ernest Lehman; associate producer Roger Edens; music and lyrics by Jerry Herman; photographed by Harry Stradling. Starring Barbra Streisand as Dolly Levi; Walter Matthau as Horace Vandergelder; Michael Crawford as Cornelius Hackl; Marianne McAndrew as Irene Molloy; E.J. Peaker as Minnie Fay; Danny Lockin as Barnaby Tucker.

On a Clear Day You Can See Forever (Paramount Pictures, 1970). Directed by Vincente Minnelli; produced by Howard W. Koch; screenplay and lyrics by Alan Jay Lerner; music by Burton Lane; photographed by Harry Stradling. Starring Barbra Streisand as Daisy Gamble/Melinda Tentrees; Yves Montand as Dr Marc Chabot; Jack Nicholson as Tad Pringle; Larry Blyden as Warren Pratt; Bob Newhart as Dr Mason Hume; John Richardson as Robert Tentrees.

The Owl and the Pussycat (Columbia Pictures, 1970). Directed by Herbert Ross; produced by Ray Stark; screenplay by Buck Henry based on the play by Bill Manhoff; music by Richard Halligan performed by Blood, Sweat & Tears; photographed by Harry Stradling and Andrew Laszlo. Starring Barbra Streisand as Doris Wilgus; George Segal as Felix Sherman; Robert Klein as Barney; Roz Kelly as Eleanor; Allen Garfield as Dress Shop Proprietor.

What's Up, Doc? (Warner Brothers, 1972). Directed and produced by Peter Bogdanovich; screenplay by Buck Henry and David Newman & Robert Benton from a story by Peter Bogdanovich; photographed by Laszlo Kovacs. Starring

Barbra Streisand as Judy Maxwell; Ryan O'Neal as Howard Bannister; Madeline Kahn as Eunice Burns; Austin Pendleton as Frederick Larrabee; Kenneth Mars as Hugh Simon; Mabel Albertson as Mrs Van Hoskins.

Up the Sandbox (First Artists, 1972). Directed by Irvin Kershner; produced by Irwin Winkler and Robert Chartoff; screenplay by Paul Zindel based on the novel by Anne Richardson Roiphe; photographed by Gordon Willis. Starring Barbra Streisand as Margaret Reynolds; David Selby as Paul Reynolds; Ariane Heller as Elizabeth; Terry and Garry Smith as Peter; Paul Benedict as Dr Beineke; Jane Hoffman as Mrs Yussim.

The Way We Were (Columbia Pictures, 1973). Directed by Sydney Pollack; produced by Ray Stark; screenplay by Arthur Laurents based on his novel; music by Marvin Hamlisch; photographed by Harry Stradling Jr. Starring Barbra Streisand as Katie Morosky; Robert Redford as Hubbell Gardiner; Bradford Dillman as J.J. Jones; Patrick O'Neal as George Bissinger; Lois Chiles as Carol Ann; Viveca Lindfors as Paula Reisner.

For Pete's Sake (Columbia Pictures, 1974). Directed by Peter Yates; produced by Martin Erlichman and Stanley Shapiro; screenplay by Stanley Shapiro and Maurice Richlin; photographed by Laszlo Kovacs. Starring Barbra Streisand as Henrietta Robbins; Michael Sarrazin as Pete Robbins; Estelle Parsons as Helen Robbins; William Redfield as Fred Robbins; Molly Picon as Mrs Cherry; Vivian Bonnell as Loretta.

Funny Lady (Columbia Pictures, 1975). Directed by Herbert Ross; produced by Ray Stark; screenplay by Jay Presson Allen and Arnold Schulman; original music by John Kander and Fred Ebb; photographed by James Wong Howe. Starring Barbra Streisand as Fanny Brice; James Caan as Billy Rose; Omar Sharif as Nick Arnstein; Roddy McDowall as Bobby; Ben Vereen as Bert Robbins.

A Star Is Born (Warner Brothers, 1976). Directed by Frank Pierson; produced by Jon Peters; screenplay by John Gregory Dunne & Joan Didion and Frank Pierson; based on a story by William Wellman and Robert Carson; music supervision by Paul Williams; photographed by Robert Surtees. Starring Barbra Streisand as Esther Hoffman; Kris Kristofferson as John Norman Howard; Paul Mazursky as Brian Wexler; Gary Busey as Bobby Ritchie; Joanne Linville as Freddie Lowenstein; M. G. Kelly as Bebe Jesus.

The Main Event (Warner Brothers, 1979). Directed by Howard Zieff; produced by Jon Peters and Barbra Streisand; screenplay by Gail Parent and Andrew Smith; photographed by Mario Tosi. Starring Barbra Streisand as Hillary Kramer; Ryan O'Neal as Eddie 'Kid Natural' Scanlon; Paul Sand as David; Whitman Mayo as Percy; Patti D'Arbanville as Donna Rochester; James Gregory as Leo Gough.

All Night Long (Universal Pictures, 1981). Directed by Jean-Claude Tramont; produced by Leonard Goldberg and Jerry Weintraub; screenplay by W. D. Richter; photographed by Phillip Lathrop. Starring Gene Hackman as George Dupler; Barbra Streisand as Cheryl Gibbons; Dennis Quaid as Freddie; Kevin Dobson as Bobby Gibbons; Diane Ladd as Helen Dupler.

Yentl (MGM/UA, 1983). Produced and directed by Barbra Streisand; screenplay by Jack Rosenthal and Barbra Streisand based on the short story by Isaac Bashevis Singer; music by Michel Legrand; lyrics by Marilyn and Alan Bergman; photographed by David Watkin. Starring Barbra Streisand as Yentl/Anshel; Mandy Patinkin as Avigdor; Amy Irving as Hadass; Nehemiah Persoff as Papa; Steven Hill as Reb Alter Vishkower; Alan Corduner as Shimmele.

Nuts (Warner Brothers, 1987). Directed by Martin Ritt; produced by Barbra Streisand; screenplay by Tom Topor and Darryl Ponicsan and Alvin Sargent based on the play by Tom Topor; music by Barbra Streisand; photographed by Andrzej Bartkowiak. Starring Barbra Streisand as Claudia Draper; Richard Dreyfuss as Aaron Levinsky; Karl Malden as Arthur Kirk; Maureen Stapleton as Rose Kirk; James Whitmore as Judge Stanley Murdoch; Eli Wallach as Dr Herbert Morrison.

The Prince of Tides (Columbia Pictures, 1991). Directed by Barbra Streisand; produced by Barbra Streisand and Andrew Karsch; screenplay by Pat Conroy and Becky Johnston based on the novel by Pat Conroy; music by James Newton Howard; photographed by Stephen Goldblatt. Starring Nick Nolte as Tom Wingo; Barbra Streisand as Dr Susan Lowenstein; Kate Nelligan as Lila Wingo Newbury; Blythe Danner as Sallie Wingo; Jason Gould as Bernard Woodruff; Jeroen Krabbé as Herbert Woodruff; Melinda Dillon as Savannah Wingo; George Carlin as Eddie Detreville.

ANNOTATED DISCOGRAPHY

I Can Get It for You Wholesale. Broadway cast (Columbia. Released April 1962). Produced by Goddard Lieberson. Barbra is heard on four songs: I'm Not a Well Man; Ballad of the Garment Trade; Miss Marmelstein; and What Are They Doing to Us Now?

Highest sales chart position: 125.

Pins and Needles. Twenty-fifth anniversary recording of the musical revue (Columbia. Released May 1962). Produced by Elizabeth Lauer and Charles Burr. Barbra is heard on six songs: Doing the Reactionary; Nobody Makes a Pass at Me; Not Cricket to Picket; Status Quo; Four Little Angels of Peace; and What Good Is Love?

This album did not make the Top 200 albums chart.

The Barbra Streisand Album (Columbia. Released February 1963). Produced by Mike Berniker. Songs: Cry Me a River; My Honey's Loving Arms; I'll Tell the Man in the Street; A Taste of Honey; Who's Afraid of the Big, Bad Wolf?; Soon It's Gonna Rain; Happy Days Are Here Again; Keepin' Out of Mischief Now; Much More; Come to the Supermarket (in Old Peking); A Sleepin' Bee.

Highest chart position: 8. Certified gold. Grammy Awards: Album of the Year; Best Female Vocal Performance; Best Album Cover. Grammy nominations: Record of the Year (Happy Days Are Here Again).

The Second Barbra Streisand Album (Columbia. Released August 1963). Produced by Mike Berniker. Songs: Any Place I Hang My Hat Is Home; Right as the Rain; Down with Love; Who Will Buy?; When the Sun Comes Out; Gotta Move; My Coloring Book; I Don't Care Much; Lover Come Back to Me; I Stayed Too Long at the Fair; Like a Straw in the Wind.

Highest chart position: 2. Certified gold.

Barbra Streisand/The Third Album (Columbia. Released February 1964). Produced by Mike Berniker. Songs: My Melancholy Baby; Just in Time; Taking a Chance on Love; Bewitched (Bothered and Bewildered); Never Will I Marry; As Time Goes By; Draw Me a Circle; It Had to Be You; Make Believe; I Had Myself a True Love.

Highest chart position: 5. Certified gold.

Funny Girl. Broadway cast (Capitol. Released April 1964). Produced by Dick Jones. Songs: If a Girl Isn't Pretty; I'm the Greatest Star; Cornet Man; Who Taught Her Everything?; His Love Makes Me Beautiful; I Want to Be Seen with You Tonight; Henry Street; People; You Are Woman; Don't Rain on My Parade; Sadie, Sadie; Find Yourself a Man; Rat-tat-tat-tat; Who Are You Now?; The Music That Makes Me Dance; Don't Rain on My Parade (reprise).

Highest chart position: 2. Certified gold. Grammy nomination: Best Broadway Cast Album.

People (Columbia. Released September 1964). Produced by Robert Mersey. Songs: Absent Minded Me; When in Rome; Fine and Dandy; Supper Time; Will He Like Me?; How Does the Wine Taste?; I'm All Smiles; Autumn; My Lord and Master; Love Is a Bore; Don't Like Goodbyes; People.

Highest chart position: 1. Certified gold. Grammy Awards: Best Female Vocal Performance; Best Album Cover. Grammy nominations: Album of the Year; Record and Song of the Year (People).

My Name Is Barbra (Columbia. Released May 1965). Produced by Robert Mersey. Songs: My Name Is Barbra; A Kid Again/I'm Five; Jenny Rebecca; My Pa; Sweet Zoo; Where Is the Wonder?; I Can See It; Someone to Watch over Me; I've Got No Strings; If You Were the Only Boy in the World; Why Did I Choose You?; My Man.

Highest chart position: 2. Certified gold. Grammy Awards: Best Female Vocal Performance. Grammy nominations: Album of the Year; Best Album Cover.

My Name Is Barbra, Two (Columbia. Released October 1965). Produced by Robert Mersey. Songs: He Touched Me; The Shadow of Your Smile; Quiet Night; I Got Plenty of Nothin'; How Much of the Dream Comes True?; Second Hand Rose; The Kind of Man a Woman Needs; All That I Want; Where's That Rainbow?; No More Songs for Me; Medley: Second Hand Rose, Give Me the Simple Life, I Got Plenty of Nothin', Brother Can You Spare a Dime?, Nobody Knows You When You're Down and Out, Second Hand Rose, and The Best Things in Life Are Free.

Highest chart position: 2. Certified platinum.

Color Me Barbra (Columbia. Released March 1966). Produced by Robert Mersey. Songs: Yesterdays; One Kiss; The Minute Waltz; Gotta Move; Non C'est Rien; Where or When; Medley: Animal Crackers in My Soup, Funny Face, That Face, They Didn't Believe Me, Were Thine That Special Face, I've Grown Accustomed to Her Face, Let's Face the Music and Dance, Sam, You

Made the Pants Too Long, What's New Pussycat?, Small World, I Love You, I Stayed Too Long at the Fair, and Look at That Face; C'est Si Bon; Where Am I Going?; Starting Here, Starting Now.

Highest chart position: 3. Certified gold. Grammy nominations: Album of the Year; Best Female Vocal Performance; Best Album Cover.

Harold Sings Arlen (with Friend) (Columbia. Released March 1966). Produced by Thomas Z. Shepard. The composer sings his own compositions. Barbra joins him in a duet of Ding-Dong, the Witch Is Dead and sings one solo: House of Flowers.

This album did not make the Top 200 albums chart.

Je m'Appelle Barbra (Columbia. Released October 1966). Produced by Ettore Stratta. Songs: Free Again; Autumn Leaves; What Now, My Love?; Ma Première Chanson; Clopin Clopant; Le Mur; I Wish You Love; Speak to Me of Love; Love and Learn; Once upon a Summertime; Martina; I've Been Here.

Highest chart position: 5.

Simply Streisand (Columbia. Released October 1967). Produced by Jack Gold and Howard A. Roberts. Songs: My Funny Valentine; The Nearness of You; When Sunny Gets Blue; Make the Man Love Me; Lover Man; More Than You Know; I'll Know; All the Things You Are; The Boy Next Door; Stouthearted Men.

Highest chart position: 12.

A Christmas Album (Columbia. Released October 1967). Produced by Jack Gold. Songs: Jingle Bells?; Have Yourself a Merry Little Christmas; The Christmas Song; White Christmas; My Favorite Things; The Best Gift; Sleep in Heavenly Peace (Silent Night); Gounod's Ave Maria; O Little Town of Bethlehem; I Wonder as I Wander; The Lord's Prayer.

Highest chart position: 1 (on seasonal album chart). Certified triple platinum.

A Happening in Central Park (Columbia. Released September 1968). Produced by Jack Gold. Songs: I Can See It; A New Love Is like a Newborn Child; Folk Monologue/Value; Cry Me a River; People; He Touched Me; Marty the Martian; Natural Sounds; Second Hand Rose; Sleep in Heavenly Peace; Happy Days Are Here Again.

Highest chart position: 30. Certified gold.

Funny Girl. Motion picture sound track (Columbia. Released July 1968). Produced by Jack Gold. Songs: I'm the Greatest Star; If a Girl Isn't Pretty; Roller Skate Rag; I'd Rather Be Blue; His Love Makes Me Beautiful; People; You Are Woman, I Am Man; Don't Rain on My Parade; Sadie, Sadie; The Swan; Funny Girl; My Man; Finale.

Highest chart position: 12. Certified platinum. Grammy nomination: Best Female Contemporary Pop Vocal Performance.

What About Today? (Columbia. Released July 1969). Produced by Wally Gold. Songs: What About Today?; Ask Yourself Why; Honey Pie; Punky's Dilemma; Until It's Time for You to Go; That's a Fine Kind of Freedom; Little Tin Soldier; With a Little Help from My Friends; Alfie; The Morning After; Goodnight.
Highest chart position: 31.

Hello, Dolly! Motion picture sound track (Twentieth Century-Fox Records. Released December 1969). Produced by Lennie Hayton and Lionel Newman. Songs: Just Leave Everything to Me; It Takes a Woman; It Takes a Woman (reprise); Put on Your Sunday Clothes; Ribbons Down My Back; Dancing; Before the Parade Passes By; Elegance; Love Is Only Love; Hello, Dolly!; It Only Takes a Moment; So Long, Dearie; Finale.
Highest chart position: 49.

Barbra Streisand's Greatest Hits (Columbia. Released December 1969). Various producers. Songs: People; Second Hand Rose; Why Did I Choose You?; He Touched Me; Free Again; Don't Rain on My Parade; My Coloring Book; Sam, You Made the Pants Too Long; My Man; Gotta Move; Happy Days Are Here Again.
Highest chart position: 32. Certified double platinum.

On a Clear Day You Can See Forever. Motion picture sound track (Columbia. Released July 1970). Produced by Wally Gold. Songs: Hurry! It's Lovely Up Here!; Main Title – On a Clear Day (chorus); Love with All the Trimmings; Melinda; Go to Sleep; He Isn't You; What Did I Have That I Don't Have?; Come Back to Me; On a Clear Day (Montand); On a Clear Day (Streisand).
Highest chart position: 108.

The Owl and the Pussycat. Dialogue and incidental music from the motion picture (Columbia. Released December 1970). Produced by Thomas Z. Shepard. Performed by Blood, Sweat & Tears.
Highest chart position: 186.

Stoney End (Columbia. Released February 1971). Produced by Richard Perry. Songs: I Don't Know Where I Stand; Hands Off the Man (Film Flam Man); If You Could Read My Mind; Just a Little Lovin'; Let Me Go; Stoney End; No Easy Way Down; Time and Love; Maybe; Free the People; I'll Be Home.
Highest chart position: 10. Certified platinum.

Barbra Joan Streisand (Columbia. Released August 1971). Produced by Richard Perry. Songs: Beautiful; Love; Where You Lead; I Never Meant to Hurt You; One Less Bell to Answer/A House Is Not a Home; Space Captain;

Since I Fell for You; Mother; The Summer Knows; I Mean to Shine; You've Got a Friend.

Highest chart position: 11. Certified gold.

Live Concert at the Forum (Columbia. Released October 1972). Produced by Richard Perry. Songs: Sing/Make Your Own Kind of Music; Starting Here, Starting Now; Don't Rain on My Parade; Monologue; On a Clear Day; Sweet Inspiration/Where You Lead; Didn't We; My Man; Stoney End; Sing/Happy Days Are Here Again; People.

Highest chart position: 19. Certified platinum. Grammy nomination: Best Female Pop Vocal Performance for Sweet Inspiration/Where You Lead.

Barbra Streisand . . . and Other Musical Instruments (Columbia. Released October 1973). Produced by Martin Erlichman. Songs: Piano Practicing; I Got Rhythm; Johnny One Note/One Note Samba; Glad to Be Unhappy; Medley: People, Second Hand Rose, and Don't Rain on My Parade; Don't Ever Leave Me; Monologue, By Myself; Come Back to Me; I Never Has Seen Snow; Auf dem Wasser zu Singen; The World Is a Concerto/Make Your Own Kind of Music; The Sweetest Sounds.

Highest chart position: 64.

Barbra Streisand featuring 'The Way We Were' and 'All in Love Is Fair' (Columbia. Released January 1974). Produced by Tommy LiPuma. Songs: Being at War with Each Other; Something So Right; The Best Thing You've Ever Done; The Way We Were; All in Love Is Fair; What Are You Doing the Rest of Your Life?; Summer Me, Winter Me; Pieces of Dreams; I've Never Been a Woman Before; Medley: My Buddy and How about Me?

Highest chart position: 1. Grammy Award: Song of the Year (The Way We Were). Certified platinum.

The Way We Were. Motion picture sound track (Columbia. Released January 1974). Produced by Fred Salem. Incidental music from the film. Barbra sings two versions of the title song.

Highest chart position: 20. Certified gold. Grammy Awards: Song of the Year; Best Original Motion Picture Score.

ButterFly (Columbia. Released October 1974). Produced by Jon Peters. Songs: Love in the Afternoon; Guava Jelly; Grandma's Hands; I Won't Last a Day Without You; Jubilation; Simple Man; Life on Mars; Since I Don't Have You; Crying Time; Let the Good Times Roll.

Highest chart position: 13. Certified gold.

Funny Lady. Motion picture sound track (Arista. Released March 1975). Produced by Peter Matz. Songs: How Lucky Can You Get?; So Long, Honey Lamb; I Found a Million Dollar Baby in a Five and Ten Cent Store; Isn't This

Better?; Me and My Shadow; If I Love Again; I Got a Code in My Doze; Great Day; Blind Date; Am I Blue; It's Only a Paper Moon/I Like Him/Her; More Than You Know; Clap Hands, Here Comes Charley; Let's Hear It for Me.

Highest chart position: 6. Certified gold.

Lazy Afternoon (Columbia. Released October 1975). Produced by Rupert Holmes and Jeffrey Lesser. Songs: Lazy Afternoon; My Father's Song; By the Way; Shake Me, Wake Me; I Never Had It So Good; Letters That Cross in the Mail; You and I; Moanin' Low; A Child Is Born; Widescreen.

Highest chart position: 12. Certified gold.

Classical Barbra (Columbia. Released February 1976). Produced by Claus Ogerman. Songs: Beau Soir; Brezairola; Verschwiegene Liebe; Pavane; Après un Rêve; In Trutina; Laschia ch'io pianga; Mondnacht; Dank sie Dir, Herr; I Loved You.

Highest chart position: 46. Grammy nomination: Best Classical Vocal Soloist Performance.

A Star Is Born. Motion picture sound track (Columbia. Released November 1976). Produced by Barbra Streisand and Phil Ramone. Songs: Watch Closely Now; Queen Bee; Everything; Lost Inside of You; Hellacious Acres; Evergreen; Woman in the Moon; I Believe in Love; Crippled Crow; With One More Look at You/Watch Closely Now; Evergreen (reprise).

Highest chart position: 1. Certified quadruple platinum. Grammy Awards: Song of the Year and Best Female Pop Vocal (Evergreen). Grammy nominations: Record of the Year (Evergreen); Best Original Film Score.

Streisand Superman (Columbia. Released June 1977). Produced by Gary Klein. Songs: Superman; Don't Believe What You Read; Baby Me, Baby; I Found You Love; Answer Me; My Heart Belongs to Me; Cabin Fever; Love Comes from Unexpected Places; New York State of Mind; Lullaby for Myself.

Highest chart position: 3. Certified platinum.

Songbird (Columbia. Released May 1978). Produced by Gary Klein. Songs: Tomorrow; A Man I Loved; I Don't Break Easily; Love Breakdown; You Don't Bring Me Flowers (solo); Honey, Can I Put on Your Clothes?; One More Night; Deep in the Night; Songbird.

Highest chart position: 12. Certified platinum. Grammy nominations: Best Female Pop Vocal Performance; Song of the Year (You Don't Bring Me Flowers).

Eyes of Laura Mars. Motion picture sound track (Columbia. Released July 1978). Various producers. Includes songs by Odyssey; KC and the Sunshine Band; Michael Zager Band; Michalksy & Oosterveen. Barbra sings one song: Prisoner.

Highest chart position: 125.

Barbra Streisand's Greatest Hits Vol. 2 (Columbia. Released November 1978). Various producers. Songs: Evergreen; Prisoner; My Heart Belongs to Me; Songbird; You Don't Bring Me Flowers (duet with Neil Diamond); The Way We Were; Sweet Inspiration/Where You Lead; All in Love Is Fair; Superman; Stoney End.

Highest chart position: 1. Certified quadruple platinum. Grammy nominations: Record of the Year; Best Pop Vocal Performance by a Duo or Group (You Don't Bring Me Flowers).

The Main Event. Motion picture sound track (Columbia. Released June 1979). Various producers. Includes songs by Frankie Valli and the Four Seasons; Loggins & Messina. Barbra sings the title song in the short (45 rpm) version, in a longer dance remix, and as a ballad.

Highest chart position: 20. Certified gold.

Wet (Columbia. Released October 1979). Produced by Gary Klein. Songs: Wet; Come Rain or Come Shine; Splish Splash; On Rainy Afternoons; After the Rain; No More Tears/Enough Is Enough (duet with Donna Summer); Niagara; I Ain't Gonna' Cry Tonight; Kiss Me in the Rain.

Highest chart position: 7. Certified platinum.

Guilty (Columbia. Released September 1980). Produced by Barry Gibb, Albhy Galuten, and Karl Richardson. Songs: Guilty (duet with Barry Gibb); Woman in Love; Run Wild; Promises; The Love Inside; What Kind of Fool (duet with Barry Gibb); Life Story; Never Give Up; Make It Like a Memory.

Highest chart position: 1. Certified quintuple platinum. Grammy Award: Best Pop Vocal by Duo or Group (with Barry Gibb). Grammy nominations: Album of the Year; Record and Song of the Year (Woman in Love); Best Female Pop Vocal Performance (Woman in Love).

Memories (Columbia. Released November 1981). Various producers. Songs: Memory; You Don't Bring Me Flowers (duet with Neil Diamond); My Heart Belongs to Me; New York State of Mind; No More Tears/Enough Is Enough (duet with Donna Summer); Comin' In and Out of Your Life; Evergreen; Lost Inside of You; The Love Inside; The Way We Were.

Highest chart position: 6. Certified quadruple platinum.

Yentl. Motion picture sound track (Columbia. Released November 1983). Produced by Barbra Streisand and Marilyn and Alan Bergman. Songs: Where Is It Written?; Papa, Can You Hear Me?; This Is One of Those Moments; No Wonder; The Way He Makes Me Feel; No Wonder (reprise); Tomorrow Night; Will Someone Ever Look at Me That Way?; No Matter What Happens; No Wonder (reprise); A Piece of Sky; The Way He Makes Me Feel (studio version); No Matter What Happens (studio version).

Highest chart position: 9. Certified platinum. Grammy nominations: Best Original Score for a Motion Picture.

Emotion (Columbia. Released October 1984). Various producers. Songs: Emotion; Make No Mistake, He's Mine (duet with Kim Carnes); Time Machine; Best I Could; Left in the Dark; Heart Don't Change My Mind; When I Dream; You're a Step in the Right Direction; Clear Sailing; Here We Are at Last.

Highest chart position: 19. Certified platinum.

The Broadway Album (Columbia. Released November 1985). Various producers. Songs: Putting It Together; If I Loved You; Something's Coming; Not While I'm Around; Being Alive; I Have Dreamed/We Kiss in a Shadow/Something Wonderful; Adelaide's Lament; Send in the Clowns; Pretty Women/The Ladies Who Lunch; Can't Help Lovin' That Man; I Loves You Porgy/Bess You Is My Woman; Somewhere.

Highest chart position: 1. Certified triple platinum. Grammy Awards: Best Female Pop Vocal; Best Arrangement Accompanying Vocal. Grammy nomination: Album of the Year.

One Voice (Columbia. Released April 1987). Produced by Richard Baskin. Songs: Somewhere; Evergreen; Something's Coming; People; Send in the Clowns; Over the Rainbow; Guilty (duet with Barry Gibb); What Kind of Fool (duet with Barry Gibb); Papa, Can You Hear Me?; The Way We Were; It's a New World; Happy Days Are Here Again; America the Beautiful.

Highest chart position: 9. Certified platinum. Grammy nominations: Best Pop Vocal Performance, Female; Best Instrumental Arrangement Accompanying Vocal; Best Performance, Music Video.

Till I Loved You (Columbia. Released November 1988). Various producers. Songs: The Places You Find Love; On My Way to You; Till I Loved You (duet with Don Johnson); Love Light; All I Ask of You; You and Me for Always; Why Let It Go?; Two People; What Were We Thinking Of?; Some Good Things Never Last; One More Time Around.

Highest chart position: 10. Certified platinum.

A Collection . . . Greatest Hits and More (Columbia. Released October 1989). Various producers. Songs: We're Not Makin' Love Anymore; Woman in Love; All I Ask of You; Comin' In and Out of Your Life; What Kind of Fool (duet with Barry Gibb); The Main Event/Fight; Someone That I Used to Love; By the Way; Guilty (duet with Barry Gibb); Memory; The Way He Makes Me Feel; Somewhere.

Highest chart position: 26. Certified platinum.

Just for the Record. Four-disc boxed set (Columbia. Released September 1991). Produced by Barbra Streisand and Martin Erlichman. Songs: over sixty-five tracks covering Barbra's singing career from 1955 to 1988, including duets with Judy Garland, Ray Charles, Harold Arlen, Neil Diamond, Barry Gibb, Burt Bacharach, and Louis Armstrong.

Highest chart position: 38. Certified platinum. Grammy nominations: Best Traditional Pop Vocal Performance (Warm All Over); Best Package Design.

The Prince of Tides. Motion picture sound track (Columbia. Released December 1991). Produced by Barbra Streisand and James Newton Howard. Barbra sings two songs: For All We Know and Places That Belong to You.

Highest chart position: 84.

Back to Broadway (Columbia. Released July 1993). Various producers. Songs: Some Enchanted Evening; Everybody Says Don't; The Music of the Night (duet with Michael Crawford); Speak Low; As If We Never Said Goodbye; Children Will Listen; I Have a Love/One Hand, One Heart (duet with Johnny Mathis); I've Never Been in Love Before; Luck, Be a Lady; With One Look; The Man I Love; Move On.

Highest chart position: 1. Certified double platinum. Grammy nominations: Best Traditional Pop Vocal Performance; Best Pop Performance by a Duo or Group (Music of the Night, with Michael Crawford); Best Arrangement Accompanying a Vocal (Luck, Be a Lady; Some Enchanted Evening).

Barbra: The Concert (Columbia. Released September 1994). Two discs. Produced by Barbra Streisand and Jay Landers. Songs: As If We Never Said Goodbye; I'm Still Here/Everybody Says Don't/Don't Rain on My Parade; Can't Help Lovin' that Man; I'll Know; People; Lover Man; Will He Like Me?; He Touched Me; Evergreen; The Man That Got Away; On a Clear Day; The Way We Were; You Don't Bring Me Flowers; Lazy Afternoon; Disney Medley: Once Upon a Dream, When You Wish Upon a Star, and Someday My Prince Will Come; Not While I'm Around; Ordinary Miracles; *Yentl* medley: Where Is It Written?, Papa, Can You Hear Me?, Will Someone Ever Look at Me That Way?, and A Piece of Sky; Happy Days Are Here Again; My Man; For All We Know; Somewhere.

Highest chart position: 10. Certified platinum. Grammy nominations: Best Female Pop Vocal Performance (Ordinary Miracles); Best Traditional Pop Vocal Performance (for the album). Special honor: Lifetime Achievement Award to Streisand.

ALL BARBRA STREISAND albums have been released on compact disc except *The Owl and the Pussycat* and *Eyes of Laura Mars*.

BIBLIOGRAPHY

Bach, Steven. *Final Cut: Dreams and Disaster in the Making of Heaven's Gate.* New York: William Morrow, 1985.

Bacon, James. *Hollywood Is a Four Letter Town.* New York: Avon, 1977.

Bruck, Connie. *Master of the Game.* New York: Simon & Schuster, 1994.

Carrick, Peter. *Barbra Streisand: A Biography.* London: Robert Hale, 1991.

Cattell McKeen, J. *Leaders in Education.* 2d ed. New York: Science Press, 1941.

Chevalier, Maurice. *I Remember It Well.* Boston: G.K. Hall, 1972.

Conroy, Pat. *The Prince of Tides.* Boston: Houghton Mifflin, 1986.

Considine, Shaun. *Barbra Streisand: The Woman, the Myth, the Music.* New York: Delacorte, 1985.

Crist, Judith. *Take 22: Moviemakers on Moviemaking.* New York: Viking, 1984.

Davis, Clive, with James Willwerth. *Clive.* New York: Ballantine, 1977.

Dunne, John Gregory. *Studio.* New York: Simon & Schuster, 1968.

Engel, Lehman. *This Bright Day.* New York: Macmillan, 1974.

Gavin, James. *Intimate Nights: The Golden Age of New York Cabaret.* New York: Grove Weidenfeld, 1991.

Goldman, Albert. *Elvis Presley.* New York: McGraw-Hill, 1981.

———.*The Lives of John Lennon.* New York: William Morrow, 1988.

Graham, Sheilah. *Confessions of a Hollywood Columnist.* New York: William Morrow, 1969.

Griffin, Merv, and Peter Barsocchini. *Merv.* New York: Simon & Schuster, 1980.

Harvey, Stephen. *Directed by Vincente Minnelli.* New York: Harper & Row, 1989.

Hirschorn, Clive. *Gene Kelly.* London: W.J. Allen, 1974.

Holt, Georgia, and Phyllis Quinn, with Sue Russell. *Star Mothers.* New York: Simon & Schuster, 1988.

Jordan, René. *The Greatest Star.* New York: Putnam, 1975.

Katz, Ephraim. *The Film Encyclopedia.* New York: Harper Collins, 1994.

Kimbrell, James. *Barbra: An Actress Who Sings*. Boston: Branden, 1989.

——.*Barbra: An Actress Who Sings, Volume II*. Edited by Cheri Kimbrell. Boston: Branden, 1992.

Liberace. *Liberace: An Autobiography*. New York: Putnam, 1973.

Madsen, Axel. *William Wyler*. New York: Crowell, 1973.

McCullough, David. *Brooklyn . . . And How It Got That Way*. New York: Dial Press, 1983.

Miller, Allan. *A Passion for Acting*. New York: Backstage Books, 1992.

Preminger, Otto. *Preminger, An Autobiography*. New York: Doubleday, 1977.

Reed, Rex. *Do You Sleep in the Nude?* New York: New American Library, 1968.

Reise, Randall. *Her Name Is Barbra*. New York: Birch Lane Press, 1993.

Rivera, Geraldo, with Daniel Paisner. *Exposing Myself*. New York: Bantam, 1991.

Rivers, Joan. *Enter Talking*. New York: Delacorte, 1986.

Sanders, Coyne Steven. *Rainbow's End: The Judy Garland Show*. New York: William Morrow, 1990.

Sharif, Omar. *The Eternal Male*. New York: Doubleday, 1976.

Spada, James, with Christopher Nickens. *Streisand: The Woman and the Legend*. New York: Doubleday, 1981.

Suskin, Steven. *Opening Night on Broadway*. New York: Schirmer Books/ Macmillan, 1990.

Swenson, Karen. *Barbra – The Second Decade*. Secaucus, N.J.: Citadel Press, 1986.

Teti, Frank, and Karen Moline. *Streisand through the Lens*. New York: Delilah, 1983.

Tormé, Mel. *Judy Garland: The Other Side of the Rainbow*. New York: William Morrow, 1970.

Waldman, Allison J. *The Barbra Streisand Scrapbook*. Secaucus, N.J.: Citadel Press, 1994.

Wilson, Earl. *The Show Business Nobody Knows*. Chicago: Cowles, 1971.

Zec, Donald, and Anthony Fowles. *Barbra*. New York: St Martin's Press, 1981.

ACKNOWLEDGMENTS

N o biography can be written without the help of many people, and
I am very grateful to all those who assisted me with this one. I'm
particularly indebted to my friend and associate Chris Nickens,
who brought his encyclopedic knowledge of Barbra Streisand's career and of
Hollywood history to the project. He did much research, conducted many of the
interviews, and reviewed the manuscript at every phase. This book is inestimably
better because of his contributions.

Mike Szymanski worked his usual wonders as researcher, scouring vital
records, court records, property rolls, tax rolls, and business records in Los
Angeles, Las Vegas, and New York for information about Barbra. He also
located and interviewed some of the people quoted in this book.

I am most thankful to the late Larry Rowland, whose impressive collection
of Streisand audiotapes enriched this book. Larry obsessively taped Barbra's
earliest television appearances and many of her live performances, beginning
in 1961. I will always be grateful for his willingness to let me listen to them.

Bill Doty, Carol Salvo, Patricia McNamee, Richard Gelbke, and Helen Boyden
of the National Archives were very helpful in my efforts to trace Barbra's genealogy,
as was the staff of the New York Public Library genealogy division. Staff members
at the Academy of Motion Picture Arts and Sciences, the University of Southern
California library, the Brooklyn Public Library, the Columbia University Archives,
and the Los Angeles Public Library, were also helpful.

Theresa Frank of the Erasmus Hall Alumni Association helped me trace
dozens of Barbra's high school classmates. And I am grateful to Ernest Lehman
for allowing me access to his papers, which are housed at the University of Texas
at Austin.

My editor Betty Prashker, whose idea this book was, contributed a keen
editorial eye to these pages, as did David Groff, my original editor. Ken
Sansone, Julie Lovrinic, Phyllis Fleiss, Andrew Martin, Jo Fagan, Mark

McCauslin, Lauren Dong, Nancy Maynes, and Heather Kilpatrick of Crown provided many professional courtesies.

Kathy Robbins, my agent, provided invaluable advice and guidance, as always. Elizabeth Mackey, Steve Bromage, Larry Platt, Bill Clegg, and Meghan Sercombe of the Robbins Office were always cheerfully helpful.

Others whose help is greatly appreciated are J. B. Annegan, Brad Aul, Trevor Bandera, Joellen Bard, Jim Bloor, Gary Bornstein, Richard Branson, Kevin Burns, Anthony Caldera, Rick Carl, Harvey Caspari, Rafe Chase, Emily Cobb, George Coleman, Maurice Tei Dunn, Ronnie Durrence, Joni Evans, Lydia Encinas, Mrs Phyllis Farrand, Cindy Koren Gerstl, Richard Giammanco, Tom Gilbert, Phil Graham, Paul Grein, Cathy Griffin, Stacie Guy, Susan Kamil, George Maharis, Rick Miller, Michel Parenteau, Arlene Patlevic, Vernon Patterson, Lynne Pounder, Gregory Rice, Randall Riese, Eli Rill, John Sala, Patricia Scarborough, Dave Scheer, Bob Scott, Anne Sheehan of the *Chatham Courier*, Elaine Sobel, Lyle Spielman, Karen Swenson, Sam Teischer, Jan van Willigen, Guy Vespoint, Allison Waldman, Faye Wallace, Lois Weinsaft, and George Zeno.

Finally, love and thanks to my family and friends, whose support means so much to me: my father, Joe Spada; my brothers, Richard and Lewis; and my treasured friends Glen Sookiazian, Laura Van Wormer, Dan Conlon, Mark Meltzer, John Figg, Michael Koegel, Kevin Scullin, and Mark Lemeier.

INDEX